Thirteenth Edition

News Reporting & Writing

The Missouri Group

Brian S. Brooks
Beverly J. Horvit
Daryl R. Moen

School of Journalism
University of Missouri

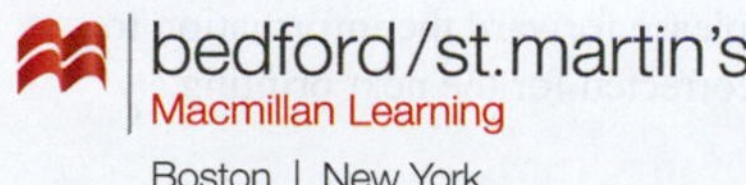

bedford/st.martin's
Macmillan Learning
Boston | New York

For Bedford/St. Martin's
Vice President, Editorial, Macmillan Learning Humanities: Edwin Hill
Senior Program Director for Communication: Erika Gutierrez
Marketing Manager: Amy Haines
Director of Content Development, Humanities: Jane Knetzger
Associate Editor: Kimberly Roberts
Senior Content Project Manager: Peter Jacoby
Senior Workflow Project Supervisor: Susan Wein
Production Supervisor: Robert Cherry
Media Project Manager: Sarah O'Connor
Senior Media Editor: Tom Kane
Project Management: Lumina Datamatics, Inc.
Composition: Lumina Datamatics, Inc.
Text Permissions Manager: Kalina Ingham
Text Permissions Researcher: Mark Schaefer, Lumina Datamatics, Inc.
Photo Permissions Editor: Angie Boehler
Photo Researcher: Richard Fox, Lumina Datamatics, Inc.
Director of Design, Content Management: Diana Blume
Text Design: Rick Korab
Cover Design: William Boardman
Printing and Binding: LSC Communications

Manufactured in the United States of America.

1 2 3 4 5 6 24 23 22 21 20 19

For information, write: Bedford/St. Martin's, 75 Arlington Street, Boston, MA 02116

ISBN 978-1-319-20816-5

Acknowledgments
Text acknowledgments and copyrights appear at the back of the book on pages 488–489, which constitute an extension of the copyright page. Art acknowledgments and copyrights appear on the same page as the art selections they cover.

At the time of publication, all internet URLs published in this text were found to link accurately to their intended website. If you find a broken link, please forward the information to kimberly.roberts@macmillan.com so that it can be corrected for the next printing.

NEW EMPHASIS ON KEY AREAS AND CRITICAL ISSUES

PUBLIC RELATIONS

In a new age of public relations writing, the new edition has revamped its PR chapter to show the new and creative ways persuasive writing is being used.

MEDIA LAW

Understanding the protections and limitations of media law is critically important for every journalist and media professional. This edition's media law chapter has been deeply revised and reframed to provide a clear understanding of the first amendment.

Where Students Learn

launchpadworks.com

LAUNCHPAD SOLO FOR JOURNALISM 2.0

The thirteenth edition of *News Reporting & Writing* can be packaged with *LaunchPad Solo for Journalism* to take advantage of extensive writing tools specific to media writing and reporting courses. This digital learning space has been remodeled to make accessing student resources easier than ever. *LaunchPad Solo for Journalism 2.0* features:

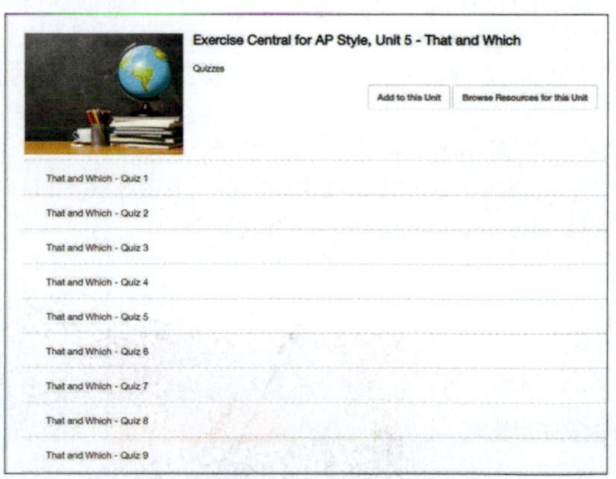

Photo by wragg / Getty Images

- Thousands of exercises in Exercise Central for AP Style that directly address the most common writing, grammatical and style issues journalism students face;
- *News Reporting & Writing*'s complete and newly revised student workbook;
- Videos to facilitate discussion and broaden understanding of how concepts throughout the book can be applied. Topics range from convergence and media literacy, to Facebook journalism and the ethics involved in journalism;
- Instructor resources for *News Reporting & Writing*.

Turn to the inside back cover for more information on how to access *LaunchPad Solo for Journalism* along with a full list of available videos.

Preface

Many students are asking why they should go into journalism these days. The constant partisan attacks on the press at the national level roll like an avalanche down to the smallest news outlet. Trust in the media has suffered from the toxic atmosphere. Journalists are subjected to verbal and sometimes physical abuse.

So why become a journalist?

Now, perhaps more than ever, the country needs young people who are willing to ask questions of those in power. Who are willing to spend hours at meetings and hours poring over documents to reveal what public officials are doing. Who are willing to support democracy by doing the hard work of being watchdogs.

Fortunately, enrollment at many journalism schools is rising again. As some news organizations shrink and even disappear, others spring anew. All across the country, there are efforts to provide the coverage that people need to evaluate their public officials and report effectively and clearly about the state of their town, county or country.

This edition reports on journalism's problems, but also its possibilities. The thirteenth edition has been completely reframed, meeting students in the current state of the news industry, an ever-evolving landscape of media and reporting. The book is full of examples of the work journalists do — from covering meetings to covering California wildfires; from covering politics in Washington to covering the city council in your hometown.

Students schooled in journalism do all that and more. They work for the news media, they work at advertising agencies and they work in public relations. Some take their skills to hundreds of other websites. Some use journalistic writing to support their careers in law and court proceedings. This edition of the book recognizes that the skills and knowledge taught in journalism classes are transferable to countless other careers. That's why we have expanded our efforts to show and teach the central role that social media plays in the communication chain.

More than ever, the staff of today's converged newsrooms can agree that editors want journalists who report fully and write clearly, whether for an online news outlet, a professional blog, a cable news show or a print newspaper. When it comes to integrated media, we practice what we preach: The new edition of *News Reporting & Writing* combines print and digital media into a single accessible package. Callouts in the book's margins link to videos on ***LaunchPad Solo for Journalism*** that offer insider perspectives on issues of modern journalism, including the legal rights of bloggers, journalistic ethics, the common ground between real news and fake news and the power of images. Our integrated media program takes *News Reporting & Writing* beyond the limits of the printed page.

Even as we expand further into the digital realm, we continue to stress the essential reporting and writing skills that are the foundations for both journalism and public relations, no matter the medium. We've also updated our current examples and issues, while still modeling in these examples — and in our own writing — the clear and descriptive writing that journalism students must learn. Our emphasis on these topics in the textbook, combined with robust online support and practice opportunities, ensures that students will have more opportunities than ever before to practice and refine their skills.

New to This Edition

We welcome to this edition our first new co-author since the first edition, published in 1980. Beverly J. Horvit is an experienced journalist who for six years has taught and served as coordinator of our basic news-writing class at the University of Missouri. After having used the book for even longer, she was able to make invaluable contributions to this edition with a fresh, diverse perspective.

She replaces retired colleagues George Kennedy and Don Ranly. Much of their work remains in this edition. We are grateful for their outstanding contributions through the first 12 editions and wish them well in retirement.

Revisions to the thirteenth edition of *News Reporting & Writing* address changes to the journalism landscape and provide additional opportunities for students to refine their reporting and writing skills in today's world. Specifically, this new edition offers the following features:

- Chapter 2, **The State of the News Industry previously (The Future of Journalism)**, takes an unvarnished look at the declining profitability of print media and the ways media companies are attempting to solve the problem. The renaming and reframing of this chapter is centered around the understanding that students are writing and reporting in a media- and social media-heavy world. The chapter also examines the problem of news credibility and updates the outlook for jobs for those seeking to enter the news industry.
- Chapter 11, **Writing for Digital Media**, has been updated with examples of how news sites used new techniques to report the confirmation of a Supreme Court justice. The section on how writing for the web differs from writing for other media is expanded and upgraded. Techniques for driving traffic to your website through social media are explored.
- ***LaunchPad Solo for Journalism* 2.0**, an updated and reorganized version of the previous edition, includes the downloadable student workbook, videos with discussion questions, thousands of Exercise Central for AP Style quizzes, and downloadable instructor resources including lecture outlines and recommended in-class activities. The videos get students thinking critically about news media by giving them an insider's look at journalism from a variety of provocative angles while the Exercise Central for AP Style quizzes give them further opportunity to hone in on skills that will improve their writing at its core.
- New material in the law chapter includes tips on gaining access to public records, as well as a section on prior restraint.
- **Two new annotated models**, "Using Quotes Effectively" (Chapter 5) and "Analyzing a Speech Story" (Chapter 13), deconstruct stories, to show students how all the pieces of a story fit together.
- **Ten new "On the Job" boxes** that prepare students for contemporary careers and provide a more diverse set of subjects and jobs for students to explore. In every chapter, a working journalist illustrates how the skills students learn in class have prepared them for careers across the media and in public relations in today's challenging and evolving job market. Many of the newest boxes focus on new job opportunities and challenges created by a field in transition. They discuss how a journalist's role can change and expand unexpectedly because of technology, and they suggest ways journalists and public relations professionals can embrace that change and stay engaged with their work.

- Our new chapter on public relations reflects the growing role of public relation activities in a range of applications including the evolving role of social media. By showing how PR fits into the broader strategic communications field, we broaden the number of career possibilities for students.
- A reorganization of Chapters 3-5 (Gathering and Verifying Information, Interviewing and Quotations and Attributions), allows students to more easily build upon skills as they make their way through the text, creating a more seamless flow of content.

Enduring Features of the Text

Users of *News Reporting & Writing* have come to expect that every new edition of our textbook will be readable and current as well as deeply focused on journalistic essentials. We are proud to continue to offer the following features:

- **Comprehensive coverage of all aspects of reporting and writing the news.** *News Reporting & Writing* teaches students the elements of good reporting and writing and also provides the basic tools they need to become journalists across various media platforms. We include advice on how to conduct interviews and research and how to employ multimedia to enrich their reporting and create rich and well-crafted stories for the basic beats.
- **A focus on storytelling.** From life stories to world-news reports, local meetings to national press conferences, good journalism means good writing. We use real-life examples, up-to-the-minute news story samples and a consistent focus on writing essentials to show students how to craft rich and interesting stories. In addition, Chapter 9, Writing to Be Read, helps students master coherence, effective language and other techniques central to captivating an audience.
- **Thorough coverage of media convergence and online journalism.** *News Reporting & Writing* ensures that students learn how to prepare stories effectively for multiple forms of media. Reflecting changes to the journalism landscape, this book covers the rising role of technology, the emergence of integrated newsrooms, the challenges to legacy media.
- **Unparalleled discussion of legal and ethical issues.** The law chapter has been thoroughly revised and updated. In addition, throughout the book, we offer students a framework for critically assessing the ethical questions they will face as journalists. In addition, we dedicate Chapters 19 and 20 to legal and ethical matters.
- **A chapter on math for journalists.** *News Reporting & Writing* includes a chapter on "Reporting with Numbers" (Chapter 7), which stresses the importance of using and understanding data—a vital skill for political and business news writers in particular.
- **Coverage of common grammar issues, Associated Press style, and proofreading and copy editing symbols—in print and with the best online tools.** The appendices provide helpful information students need to turn in polished, professionally edited copy and an easy-to-find reference for proofreading and copy editing symbols is located at the end of the book. In addition, thousands of accompanying online exercises offer students additional opportunities to improve their grammar and AP style knowledge (**launchpadworks.com**).
- **New digital formats.** The PDF e-book for *News Reporting & Writing* includes the same content as the print book, offering an affordable option for students. Learn more about PDF e-books at **macmillanlearning.com/ebooks**.

Resources for Students and Instructors

As before, *News Reporting & Writing* is supported by a range of effective resources for students and instructors. For more information, please visit the online catalog at **macmillanhighered.com/newsreporting13e/catalog**. The following ancillaries are available with this edition:

- ***LaunchPad Solo for Journalism 2.0.*** This new online course platform includes the downloadable student workbook, videos with discussion questions, the huge Exercise Central for AP Style question bank, and downloadable instructor resources including lecture outlines and recommended in-class activities. ***LaunchPad Solo for Journalism*** can be purchased separately or packaged together with *News Reporting & Writing,* 13th Edition. To order the student edition of this book packaged with ***LaunchPad Solo for Journalism***, please use ISBN 978-1-319-27874-8.
- **Online student *Workbook for News Reporting & Writing*, 13th Edition.** Supplementing the exercises at the end of each text chapter, the revised workbook gives students extra practice mastering the principles of journalism. The workbook is a resource in ***LaunchPad Solo for Journalism***.
- **Online *Instructor's Manual for News Reporting & Writing*, 13th Edition.** This revised and updated manual contains a sample syllabus; additional teaching resources; and chapter-specific overviews, teaching tips, lecture outlines, classroom activities and discussion questions, as well as answers to the end-of-chapter exercises from the main text and answers to the workbook exercises. The instructor's manual is available for immediate download at **macmillanhighered.com/newsreporting13e/catalog**. The manual is also downloadable in modules from ***LaunchPad Solo for Journalism***.

Acknowledgments

Our colleagues and students at the University of Missouri have given us invaluable feedback on the book, for which we are grateful.

We especially appreciate the contributions of our faculty colleagues who revised these chapters: Margaret Duffy, public relations; David Herzog, investigative reporting; Brett Johnson, law; Marty Steffens, business; Scott Swafford, beats; and Stacey Woelfel, radio and television. In addition, our colleages Jeanne Abbott, Ruby Baily, Elizabeth Brixey, Annie Hammock, Holly Higgenbotham, Jeimmie Nevalga, Amy Simons, Elizabeth Conner Stephens and Ryan Thomas provided their expertise.

We are also grateful to our former student, Karl Grubaugh of American River College and Granite Bay High School, for his superb work on the student workbook and instructor's manual for this edition. Thanks are also due to Sandy Davidson for her thorough data and research used in the Media Law chapter, as well as Dorothy Carner for her invaluable help in reviewing the thirteenth edition.

We thank all of the instructors who thoughtfully reviewed the 13th edition text: Jon Bekken, Albright College; Raymond Blanton, University of the Incarnate Word; Michael Friedman, Farmingdale State College; Aileen Gallagher, Syracuse University; Kerry Jarvis, Trident Technical College; Donna Krache, Georgia State University; Maria McClure,

Austin Peay State University; Candi Meriwether, Columbia College Chicago; Selene Phillips, University of Louisville; Janita Poe, Georgia State University; Ladonia Randle, Texas Southern University; Gary Shaffer, Ocean County College; and David Shanks, Louisiana State University.

We also thank those who reviewed previous editions: Jill Adair, Arizona State University; Betsy B. Alderman, University of Tennessee at Chattanooga; Anne Becker, Oakland University; Mark Berkey-Gerard, Rowan University; Annie-Laurie Blair, Miami University; Debra Brenegan, Westminster College; JoAnne C. Broadwater, Towson University; Mary Elizabeth Carey, University of Massachusetts; Justin Catanoso, Wake Forest University; Betty S. Clapp, Cleveland State University; Jan Barry Crumb, Rutgers University; Helene DeGross, Lake Forest College; Dee Drummond, University of Toledo; Bettina Durant, Georgia State University; Rory Faust, Northern Arizona University; Sandra Fish, University of Colorado; Jennifer Follis, University of Illinois; Gwen R. Fowler, Coastal Carolina University; Peter Friederici, Northern Arizona University; Eddye Gallagher, Tarrant County College; Mark Grabowski, Adelphi University; Tim Hanson, Francis Marion University; Patrick Harwood, College of Charleston; Ron Hollander, Montclair State University; Amani Ismail, California State University, Northridge; Elena Jarvis, Daytona State College; Kevin R. Kemper, University of Arizona; Alec Klein, Northwestern University; Laura Krantz, Tyler Junior College; Anup Kumar, Cleveland State University; Andrew Levy, Borough of Manhattan Community College–City University of New York; Linda Loomis, State University of New York, Oswego; Therese Lueck, University of Akron; Kimberley Mangun, The University of Utah; Suzanne McBride, Columbia College Chicago; Carole McNall, St. Bonaventure University; Kristi Nies, Peru State College; Jean Reid Norman, University of Nevada, Las Vegas; Carolyn Olson, Maryville University; Debra Patterson, Motlow State Community College; Deidre Pike, Humboldt State University; Richard Puffer, Coker College; Leland "Buck" Ryan, University of Kentucky; Cathy Stablein, College of DuPage; Scott A. Strain, Laney College; Margaret Tebo, Columbia College Chicago; Cynthia Thomas, Grand Valley State University; Hai Tran, DePaul University; Mike Trice, Florida Southern College; Maureen Tuthill, Westminster College; Tsitsi Wakhisi, University of Miami; Tracy Warner, Indiana-Purdue, Fort Wayne; Thomas E. Winski, Emporia State University; and Vallorie Wood, Kennesaw State University.

We have worked with editors at Bedford/St. Martin's for more than 30 years now. With each edition, they have challenged us to improve, and we appreciate their efforts. We would like to acknowledge the expert work of associate editor, Kimberly Roberts who kept this revision smooth and on schedule. Thanks are also due to Catherine Burgess, Erika Gutierrez, Susan McLaughlin, Tom Kane and Audrey Webster. We are equally grateful to the production team, which includes Peter Jacoby and Gunjan Chandola well as our photo researcher, Richard Fox and text researcher, Mark Schaefer. We'd like to extend further thanks to our marketing team, led by Amy Haines.

As always, we value your comments. You can reach us via email at BrooksBS@missouri.edu; HorvitB@missouriedu; and MoenD@missouri.edu.

Brian S. Brooks
Beverly Horvit
Daryl R. Moen

Brief Contents

Contents

PART THREE STORYTELLING

News Reporting & Writing

CHAPTER 1 THE NATURE OF NEWS

Photo credit: Chip Somodevilla/Getty Images News/Getty Images

In this chapter, you will learn:

1. What journalism and the news are, including the presentation of news in different media and the rise of citizen journalism.
2. What roles journalism plays in a democracy, including contemporary challenges and journalists' responsibilities.
3. How to distinguish between hard news, soft news and commentary.
4. What the elements of a good news story are.
5. How convergence and the forces of technology are reshaping journalism.
6. How to apply principles of accuracy and fairness and how to avoid bias.
7. How to think about the issue of objectivity.
8. How to distinguish news from content that is *not* news.

Let's begin with the basics. This book is intended to help you learn about journalism. So we'll first answer two fundamental questions: What is news? And what is journalism? Neither answer is as simple as you might expect.

To illustrate, take a look at four newspaper websites on the same day:

- The *Star Tribune* in Minneapolis led with a story about a Minnesota officer who had been charged with sexually abusing two girls.
- *The Dallas Morning News* led with a story about an area doctor and two nurses who had been convicted of fraudulently billing Medicare $13 million.
- In Walla Walla, Washington, the lead story in the *Union-Bulletin* reported that the local Elks Club building was for sale.
- And in Newark, New Jersey, the *Star-Ledger* was reporting on budget debates in the state capital.

None of these stories appeared in more than one of these papers, but they have one thing in common: They are important to a local audience. No national news outlet would have led with those stories because they aren't relevant to people nationwide. Big picture news, however, such as reporters interviewing United States Press Secretary Hogan Gidley about U.S. relations with North Korea, are applicable to people across the country. As you'll learn later in this chapter, relevance to readers is a key ingredient in news judgment, whether you are writing for residents of your city or smartphone users nationwide.

Journalism and the News

To put it simply, news is what's new. It's what happened today — or what happened earlier and was just discovered today — in your neighborhood, your city, your country, your world. News can be a speech by the president, a tornado touching down, an assault on campus. It can be a car accident or an earthquake, a 75th wedding anniversary or a terrorist attack.

The people whose job it is to report, analyze and present the news are journalists. Of course, not everyone who writes or talks about events or personalities is a journalist, and not every celebrity Instagram post or tweet is journalism.

Journalism has characteristics that set it apart from gossip, rumor or propaganda, and many pieces of information that interest you as a private individual aren't necessarily relevant or interesting to the broad public.

No one has described journalism and the news journalists report better than Bill Kovach and Tom Rosenstiel in their book *The Elements of Journalism: What Newspeople Should Know and the Public Should Expect.* The authors state that "the purpose of journalism is to provide people with the information they need to be free and self-governing." They offer 10 principles that define journalism and distinguish it from other forms of communication:

1. Journalism's first obligation is to the truth.
2. Its first loyalty is to citizens.
3. Its essence is a discipline of verification.
4. Its practitioners must maintain independence from those they cover.
5. Journalism must serve as an independent monitor of power.
6. It must provide a forum for public criticism and compromise.
7. It must strive to make the significant interesting and relevant.
8. It must keep the news comprehensive and proportional.
9. Its practitioners must be allowed to exercise their personal conscience.
10. Citizens, too, have rights and responsibilities when it comes to the news.

In these principles, you can hear echoes of the Journalist's Creed, written nearly a century earlier by Walter Williams, founding dean of the world's first journalism school at the University of Missouri. Dean Williams wrote that "the public journal is a public trust… (and) acceptance of a lesser service than the public service is a violation of this trust."

The Role of Journalism

To understand the 10 principles defining journalism and the Journalist's Creed, the role of journalism in American society needs to be understood. The First Amendment to the U.S. Constitution protects the five freedoms that the nation's founders considered essential to a democracy: freedom of speech, religion, the press, petition and assembly. In the 1830s, French aristocrat Alexis de Tocqueville came to study the U.S. and wrote his classic *Democracy in America*. He was struck by the central role played by the only journalism available then: newspapers. "We should underrate their importance if we thought they just guaranteed liberty; they maintain civilization," he wrote.

> **"If you have any message at all, in any form, that you want to convey to the world, you now have a platform to do so. . . . Your fans and supporters are never more than a click or two away, and they're ready to help you make history—or change it."**
>
> ■ **David Mathison, *Be the Media: How to Create and Accelerate Your Message . . . Your Way***

Challenges to American Journalism

More than 200 years after they were guaranteed in the Constitution, the First Amendment freedoms are still essential and still under threat. After the terrorist attacks of Sept. 11, 2001, a new emphasis on national and personal security tempted government officials and citizens alike to question just how much freedom is compatible with safety. The role of journalism in guaranteeing liberty and maintaining civilization is challenged by those who make news and those who need it.

American journalism is also under threat from growing public skepticism about how well today's journalists are fulfilling their historic roles. On the one hand, national surveys by the

Pew Research Center for the People and the Press show, for example, that more than half the public sees bias in the news. About half say that journalists' reports are often inaccurate. Fewer than half say that journalism protects democracy, and about one-third say that journalism is hurting democracy. Views of the press increasingly vary with political affiliation. Republicans are much more critical than Democrats. And those who get their news online rate the major information sources—such as Facebook and Google—even lower than the traditional media.

On the other hand, the same surveys show that credibility has improved, at least a little, from historic lows. Comfortable majorities say that thcy believe all or most of what they read in newspapers and see on television news. Most people give higher ratings to the particular newspaper or TV station they use than to the news media in general. And two-thirds rate journalists as highly professional. (For regular samplings of public opinion about journalism, visit www.journalism.org, the website of the Pew Research Center.)

Journalists' Responsibilities in a Democracy

People who are making efforts to reform or restore journalism recognize these vital functions of journalists in a free society:

- **Journalists report the news.** News reporting, the first and most obvious function of journalists, is the foundation of the rest. Reporters cover the U.S. Congress and local council meetings, describe accidents and disasters, and show the horrors of war and the highlights of football games. This reporting takes many forms: tweets, live television, online bulletins, next-day newspaper analyses and long-form magazine narratives.

- **Journalists monitor power.** The power that Americans most often are concerned about is the power of government. Lately, private power has become more of a worry and more of a source of news. *The Kansas City Star* was nominated for a Pulitzer Prize for its investigation of the Kansas government's lack of transparency in such matters as law enforcement and child welfare. Monitoring is required even if power is used legitimately—when governments raise taxes or take us to war, for example, or when businesses close plants or cut health care benefits for employees. When the power is used illegally or immorally, another important function comes into play.

- **Journalists uncover injustice.** Each year's journalism awards highlight the work of reporters in all media who reveal abuses. *The Washington Post*, for example, won a Pulitzer for revealing sexual harassment allegations against Roy Moore, then a candidate for the U.S. Senate in Alabama. The organization Investigative Reporters and Editors also honors this type of journalistic work, but these types of local stories appear almost daily in newspapers and on television.

- **Journalists tell compelling stories that dismay us and that delight us.** Stories abounded when President Donald Trump ordered the U.S. Border Patrol to separate children from parents who were seeking asylum in the U.S. To most

Americans, these were upsetting stories. But the media also reported that grassroots fundraising efforts to help these families reached millions of dollars. Volunteers flocked to the border to help.

- **Journalists sustain communities.** These communities may be small towns, cities or even virtual communities of people connected only by the internet. *The Cincinnati Enquirer* won a Pulitzer Prize for a series of articles on the city's heroin epidemic, but many other newspapers across the country also reported in depth on the problem in their areas. Whether the story is about the condition of the streets, the quality of the drinking water or racism, journalists produce work that informs and sustains their communities.
- **Journalists fact-check politicians and other public figures.** Because so many politicians consistently misrepresent the facts, journalists have added fact-checking to their daily duties. *The Washington Post* has a database of falsehoods. *The Post* reported that in President Trump's first 497 days in office, he made 3,251 "false or misleading claims." Fact-checking is a natural extension of the work that reporters do on their own stories and that copy editors do after them.

The Cincinnati Enquirer *won a Pulitzer Prize for its series "Seven Days of Heroin." Community-based reporting keeps citizens informed about the issues that impact their lives.*

It's a little after sunrise on the first day of another week, and Cincinnati is waking up again with a heroin problem. So is Covington. And Middletown. And Norwood. And Hamilton. And West Chester Township. And countless other cities and towns across Ohio and Kentucky.

This particular week, July 10 through 16, will turn out to be unexceptional by the dreary standards of what has become the region's greatest health crisis.

18 DEATHS	AT LEAST 180 OVERDOSES
MORE THAN 200 HEROIN USERS IN JAIL	15 BABIES BORN WITH HEROIN RELATED MEDICAL PROBLEMS

This is normal now, a week like any other. But a terrible week is no less terrible because it is typical. When heroin and synthetic opiates kill one American every 16 minutes, there is little comfort in the routine.

There is only the struggle to endure and survive.

The rise of stories that are deliberately misleading or made up has also forced journalists to monitor social media carefully. As of midyear 2018, Facebook had 25 fact-checking organizations in 14 countries trying to weed out false memes and misrepresentations. The Associated Press compiles a report at least weekly of stories that have circulated in social media but are not true. For instance, the AP rebutted a story making the rounds on Facebook that a volcano in Hawaii was spewing out gemstones.

Some fact-checking is automated, and more automation is being developed. Facebook is using machine learning to locate articles that already have been identified as fake. Facebook also has automated programs that detect manipulated photos and videos. The Duke Reporters' Lab has a computer program that monitors CNN broadcasts, Twitter and NBC News' *Meet the Press*. From this, the research institute provides statements to PolitiFact, FactCheck.org and *The Washington Post* to check.

Now that we've discussed the role of journalism in society and the challenges facing journalists today, let's move on to the types of news and the elements that make for good storytelling.

Kinds of Stories

When Dean Williams wrote the Journalist's Creed, journalism was produced in newspapers and magazines. Those still exist, but the multiplication of media today would startle and amaze anyone who hasn't been a news consumer in the past 10 years. Just think of how you keep up with the news.

Chances are good that you got some news today from an Instagram post, a Twitter feed or another social media source. The chances also are good that the news report you read or watched originated with a newspaper or broadcast source, which put it on a website, where it was grabbed by an aggregator. A friend of yours may have spotted it on her Apple News app and posted it on Facebook. However, although social media and news aggregators multiply our sources of news and other information, the content of journalism remains more important than the medium through which it reaches us. That content can include hard news, soft news and commentary.

Hard news is the straightforward reporting of a news event. It is usually delivered as clearly and simply as circumstances permit. Hard news is probably what most of us think of as journalism, but it is often only the beginning of the public conversation.

A close cousin is analysis, or **explanatory journalism**, which can come immediately or later. To see how the two differ, consider this: All major media—print, broadcast and digital—reported the U.S. Supreme Court's decision that allows states to collect sales taxes on all internet sales. That's hard news. CNBC.com quickly followed with an analysis of the decision under the headline "Here's what the Supreme Court's sales tax decision means to you." That's explanatory. Analysis journalism is intended to explain what the hard news means to those who read, watch or listen to it.

News is usually about people. So another important part of journalism's public conversation is the reporting that introduces or helps us understand the people who are part of the news. We often call this **soft news**, or **features**. In the wake of the Court's sales tax ruling, the spotlight might have fallen on Ruth Bader Ginsburg, a liberal justice who in this case voted with the conservatives in the 5-4 decision.

There's more. Journalism also includes **commentary**, or opinion. There's certainly room in the public conversation for opinions from all sides, as long as those opinions are identified as commentary and not confused with either hard or soft news. After the sales tax ruling, you may have read or heard commentary that supported the Supreme Court's ruling or disagreed with it.

Understanding the differences between these types of news will help as you start pitching stories of your own. Let's now move on what to makes a good news story.

Elements of a Good News Story

We've discussed what news is and what the various types of news are. Now let's consider the criteria that professional reporters and editors use to decide what's important enough to share. The standards that journalists use to evaluate news can be summarized in three words:

- Relevance
- Usefulness
- Interest

Relevance, usefulness and interest for a specific audience are the broad guidelines for judging the news value of any event, issue or personality. These criteria apply generally, but journalists use them in a specific context that gives them particular meaning. That context is supplied by the audience—the reader, listener or viewer. As we saw with the varying leads from newspaper websites in the beginning of this chapter, journalists always determine newsworthiness with a particular audience in mind.

Within the broad news standards of relevance, usefulness and interest, journalists look for more specific elements in each potential story. The most important elements are these:

- **Impact.** The potential impact of a story is another way of measuring its relevance and usefulness. How many people are affected by an event or idea? How seriously does it affect them? The wider and heavier the impact, the better the story. Sometimes impact isn't immediately obvious. Sometimes it isn't very exciting. The challenge for good journalism is making such dull but important stories lively and interesting. That may require relying on the next three elements.
- **Conflict.** Conflict is a recurring theme in all storytelling, whether the stories told are journalism, literature or drama. Struggles between people, among nations or with natural forces make fascinating reading and viewing. Conflict is such a basic element of life that journalists must resist the temptation to overdramatize or oversimplify it.
- **Novelty.** Novelty is another element that is common to journalism and other kinds of stories. People or events may be interesting and therefore newsworthy just because they are unusual or bizarre.
- **Prominence.** Names make news. The bigger the name, the bigger the news. Ordinary people have always been intrigued by the doings of the powerful, rich and famous. Both prominence and novelty can be, and often are, exaggerated to produce "news" that lacks real relevance and usefulness. As stated earlier, however, journalists can use these elements productively to engage readers with stories that seem dull but are nonetheless relevant and useful.

Elements of a Good News Story

- Impact
- Conflict
- Novelty
- Prominence
- Proximity
- Timeliness
- Engagement
- Solutions

- **Proximity.** Generally, people are more interested in and concerned about what happens close to home. When they read or listen to national or international news, they often want to know how it relates to their own community. Some news organizations are turning to hyperlocal coverage as they seek to reconnect with readers; they report at the neighborhood level, sometimes by soliciting story contributions from residents. Independent websites devoted to this kind of extremely local coverage are springing up across the country. Increasingly, however, journalists and scholars are recognizing that communities organized around a particular interest — a sport, a hobby or an issue — are at least as important as geographic communities.

What's the grammar error in this sentence?

The U.S., the U.K., Germany, China, Russia and France all agreed to the historic Iran nuclear deal.

See Appendix 1, Rule 1.

- **Timeliness.** News is supposed to be new. With the internet, cable and smartphones, *new* means "instantaneous." Events are reported as they happen, prompting "breaking news" banners on TVs and notifications on smartphones. This poses a challenge for journalists. Speed conflicts with thoughtfulness and thoroughness. Opportunities for error multiply. Perspective and context are needed today more than ever, but both are more difficult to supply with little time for thinking. Despite the drawbacks of 24/7 news coverage, it's clear that for news to be relevant and useful, it must be timely. For example, it is much more useful to write about an issue facing the city council before the issue is decided than afterward. Timely reporting can give people a chance to be participants in public affairs rather than remain mere spectators.

The digital age — with its often confusing multitude of sources, splintering of audiences and growing complaints about negative news — has inspired most journalists to add two new criteria for assessing the value of stories:

- **Engagement.** When news was only printed on paper or broadcast, the flow of information was one way — from journalists to audiences. No more. Today, a news report is often just the beginning of the conversation. Audience members online respond to, correct and criticize the journalism. Many reporters and commentators maintain blogs and invite responses on social media to encourage such involvement. Both individual journalists and news organizations aim to engage the public with the news and with the news provider. When news happens, journalists send a short summary, about the length of a headline, on social media. Some of that news comes from politicians or celebrities who use social media to release information about themselves.

- **Solutions.** Scholars and audiences alike complain that journalists too often report problems and controversies without offering solutions. Political scientist Thomas Patterson has even argued that the negative tone of much coverage of politics and government

Now that news apps can send breaking news alerts directly to your smartphone, journalists are pressured to publish their stories faster than ever. Because speed can increase opportunities for error, however, journalists need to practice extra vigilance in their reporting.

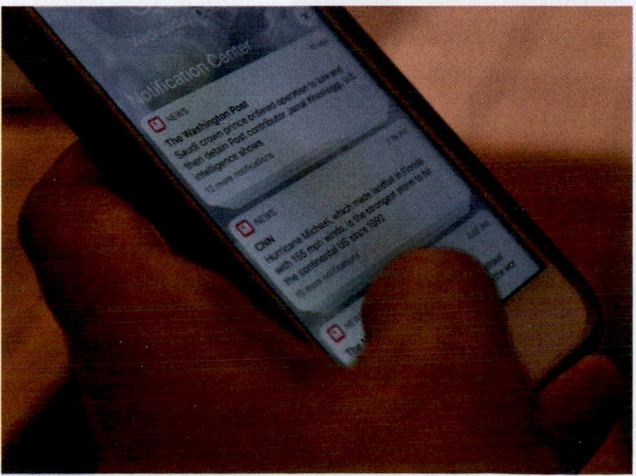

Catherine Burgess

has the effect of increasing cynicism and decreasing participation in the most basic activities of citizenship, such as voting. More and more journalists are seeking out expert sources and inviting audience members not only to explain complex problems but also to suggest solutions.

Convergence in Journalism

Convergence is the term that describes efforts to use the different strengths of different media to reach broader audiences and tell the world's stories in new ways. Convergence forces journalists to be flexible. They need to be able to work with words, sound and video. Reporters who like to write longer stories find themselves summarizing their stories into a television camera and tweeting with video while an event unfolds before them. Videographers find themselves selecting images to be published in the partner newspaper. Both print and broadcast journalists look for web links to connect their stories to the worldwide audience and nearly infinite capacity of the internet. Smartphones also provide new outlets and require new storytelling techniques.

The technological revolution also has exploded traditional definitions of just who is a journalist. Millions of people across the world have launched blogs, podcasts or video channels. Although one estimate is that only 5 percent of those sites include original reporting and although most have tiny audiences, many have become influential voices in the public conversation. In an effort to add personality and encourage interactivity with audience members, traditional news organizations are encouraging staff members to write blogs or create other content.

launchpadworks.com
WATCH: **"Murky Waters: Debating the Role of Citizen Journalism"**

- What is the value of citizen journalism?
- What kinds of news stories might inspire you to seek out a citizen journalist for information?

Increasingly, members of the public are being invited to respond to stories that are published or broadcast. Citizens are even being enlisted as amateur reporters. **Crowdsourcing**, as it is called, has become a reporting tool at news organizations from North Dakota to Florida. Readers and viewers are invited to submit their own stories, photographs and video. When they do, they are often called **citizen journalists**. Some are also asked to lend their expertise to help solve community problems.

The Public Insight Network takes crowdsourcing to the next logical step. Pioneered by public radio, the Public Insight Network is, as the name suggests, a network of citizens who agree to share their knowledge and their insights with professional reporters. National Public Radio and *The New York Times* have teamed up in a Public Insight Network. So have the investigative nonprofit ProPublica and local news organizations. Network members may be experts in any field of public interest. Some have professional credentials; others have valuable life experience. They join the network as volunteers. Their pay is the satisfaction they derive from enriching the content and improving the accuracy of journalism.

Even the fundamentals of journalism are evolving as technology speeds up the communication process, provides new sources for both reporters and audiences, and reshapes journalism from a one-way flow of information to a give-and-take with audiences and competitors.

As technology evolves, journalists must also consider how different news media give different weights to the criteria for assessing the value of news stories and require different approaches to telling those stories. For example, newspapers and magazines are better than television or radio for explaining the impact of an issue or the causes of a conflict. Scholars have learned that although most people say they get most of their news from television, few can remember very much of what they've seen or heard on a newscast. But print can't compete with television in speed or emotional power.

The differing strengths and limitations of each medium make it more likely that you'll find a lengthy explanatory story in a newspaper or magazine and learn of an event from television, radio or the internet. A newspaper lets you read the details of a budget or a box score, but television shows you the worker whose job was cut or the player scoring the winning basket.

The unique power of online journalism is that it brings together the immediacy of television and the comprehensive authority of print, with endless opportunities for users to pursue their interests through the web. Social media create new communities of interest and allow audience members to join the public conversation. As you begin your own reporting, you'll need to consider the strengths and weaknesses of each medium and decide which platform is best for telling your story.

Despite the revolution in technology, the basic skills required of every journalist haven't changed. Whatever the medium, the skills of news gathering and storytelling are essential to good journalism.

The importance of accuracy and fairness hasn't changed, either. The essential role of journalism in a democratic society remains the one assigned to it by James Madison in 1822: "A popular government without popular information or the means of acquiring it is but a prologue to a farce or a tragedy, or perhaps both."

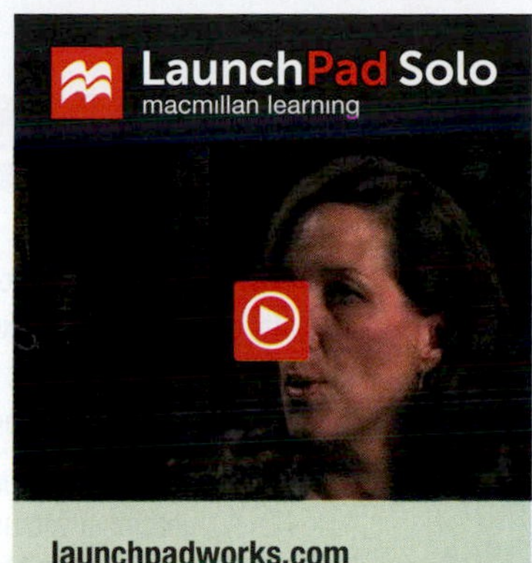

launchpadworks.com
WATCH: **"Convergence and Essential Skills"**

- What impact does convergence have on journalistic quality?
- What situations call for a specialist, such as a photojournalist?

Accuracy, Fairness and Bias

The goal toward which most journalists strive has seldom been expressed better than in a phrase used years ago by Bob Woodward, then an editor at *The Washington Post*. Woodward was defending in court an investigative story published by *The Post*. The story, he said, was "the best obtainable version of the truth."

A grander-sounding goal would be "the truth," unmodified. But Woodward's phrase, while paying homage to the ideal, recognizes the realities of life and the limitations of journalism. Despite centuries of argument, philosophers and theologians are still unable to agree on what truth is. Even if there were agreement on that basic question, how likely is it that the Roman Catholic Church and Planned Parenthood would agree on the "truth" about abortion or that a president and an opposition presidential candidate would agree on the "truth" about the state of the U.S. economy?

In American daily journalism, that kind of dispute is left to be argued among the partisans on all sides, on the editorial pages and in commentaries. The reporter's usual role is simply to find and write the facts. The trouble is that the task rarely turns out to be simple.

ON THE JOB Career Crosses Media Lines

Courtesy of Damon Dahlen/ The Huffington Post

Sara Bondioli, after working at daily newspapers and a specialty publication, is now an editor at *HuffPost*, an online news organization that didn't exist when she graduated from journalism school. Here's her description of today's newsroom:

> One of the major differences I see working at a newer, online-only publication versus other places I've worked is that people really are jacks of all trades. Reporters and editors will help out journalists on another beat. Social media editors will step in to help out on a section of the website. Reporters will cut and edit video for their stories. Video editors will report and write a story that interests them.
>
> The newsroom is very collaborative, and journalists have the opportunity to learn new skills and try new things on a regular basis. I've seen situations such as when a page editor shadowed the video team for a week simply because she wanted to learn more about what they do. With that in mind, journalists interested in working in a digital newsroom like this should aim to be well-rounded with a large skill set and enthusiastic to learn new skills regularly.
>
> The competition to post breaking news quickly is fierce in the digital media world, and we want to have our story up and our email and mobile push alert sent first. However, we also have a process to help ensure that what we post is accurate. On the flip side, the lack of a print deadline often allows journalists to devote the time needed to do longer stories without the pressure of filling a daily newshole.
>
> Social media and search engine optimization are bigger focuses here than at other places I've worked. We also have pushed the use of user-generated content, which we often curate via social media.
>
> The advantage of starting in the media world now is that young journalists fresh out of college are in tune with new digital technologies that are influencing newsrooms. That digital knowledge can translate into big opportunities for young journalists who can apply it to newsrooms looking for new ideas and energy.

Sometimes it's hard to get the facts. The committee searching for a new university president announces that the field of candidates has been narrowed to five people but doesn't release the five names. Committee members are sworn to secrecy. What can you do to find the names? Should you try?

Sometimes it's hard to tell what the facts mean. The state supreme court refuses to hear a case in which legislators are questioning the constitutionality of a state spending limit. The court says only that there is no "justiciable controversy." What does that mean? Who won? Is the ruling good news or bad news, and for whom?

Sometimes it's even hard to tell what is a fact. Pew Research Center studied Americans' ability to tell fact from opinion. Of five factual statements and five opinion statements, most people got three correct in each category. However, that result is about the same as if they randomly guessed. A quarter of the people got them all wrong. Among the opinion statements in the test were "Democracy is the greatest form of government" and "Government is almost always wasteful and inefficient." Among the factual statements were "Spending on Social Security, Medicare and Medicaid make up the largest portion of the federal budget" and "Immigrants who are in the U.S. illegally have some rights under the Constitution."

Respondents were told that a factual statement was one that could be proved based on objective evidence.

Daily journalism presents still more complications. As a reporter, you usually have only a few hours — or at most a few days — to try to learn as many facts about an event as possible. Even in such a limited time, you may accumulate enough information for a story of 2,000 words, only to be told that there is space or time enough for just 1,000 words or fewer. Online platforms offer more space but no more time for reporting. When you take into account all these realities and limitations, you can see that reaching the best obtainable version of the truth is challenge enough for any journalist.

How can you tell when that goal has been reached? Seldom, if ever, is there a definitive answer. But every responsible journalist should ask two questions about every story before being satisfied: Is it accurate? Is it fair?

"The new media tools and techniques are wonderful ways to generate information much, much faster. They don't so much take away from the actual reporting as they allow the reporter to know so much more."

■ **Karen Dillon, reporter, *The Kansas City Star***

Accuracy and Fairness

Accuracy is the most important characteristic of any story, great or small, long or short. Every name must be spelled correctly; every quote must be only what was said; every set of numbers must add up. And that still isn't good enough.

You can get the details right and still mislead unless you are accurate with context, too. The same statement may have widely different meanings depending on the circumstances in which it was uttered and the tone in which it was spoken. Circumstances and intent affect the meaning of actions as well.

You will never have the best obtainable version of the truth unless your version is built on accurate reporting of detail and context. The best at their job of being accurate, according to a Gallup/Knight Foundation study, are PBS News, NPR, *The New York Times*, the AP, *The Washington Post* and *The Wall Street Journal*. All were considered very or extremely accurate by at least 42 percent of the respondents.

Accuracy and fairness are related, but they are not the same. Being fair requires asking yourself if you have done enough to uncover all the relevant facts and have delivered those facts in an impartial manner, without favoring one side or another in a story. The relationship between accuracy and fairness — and the differences between them — can be seen in the following analogy from the world of sports.

The referee in a basketball game is similar, in some ways, to a reporter. Each is supposed to be an impartial observer who calls developments as he or she sees them. (The referee's job is to describe and make judgments on those developments, whereas the reporter's job is only to describe them. Rendering judgment is the role of columnists, bloggers and other opinion writers.)

Television has brought to sports the instant replay, in which a key play — for example, one in which a player may have been fouled while taking a shot — can be examined again and again, often from an angle different from the referee's line of sight. Sometimes the replay shows an apparent outcome different from the one the official called. Perhaps the players didn't actually make contact. Perhaps what looked like an attempted shot was really a pass.

	News Stories	Commentaries
Accuracy	• Make sure facts (events, names, dates, statistics, places, quotes) are correct. • Verify facts with multiple sources. • Use reliable sources for statistics. • Use facts as the substance of the story. • Discover and include all necessary facts.	• Make sure facts (events, names, dates, statistics, places, quotes) are correct. • Include all the facts needed to prove a point of view. • Possibly leave out facts that don't support the argument, but ideally provide context or ideas that explain the facts.
Fairness	• Provide context for facts. • Give all relevant sides of a story. • Strive for balance.	• Provide context for facts. • Use facts and reason to persuade the audience of a point of view. • Appeal to emotion but not by distorting the facts.
Bias	• Leave personal bias out of the story. • Use neutral language.	• Support personal bias with facts and reasoning. • Acknowledge and rebut other points of view. • Use civil language, not highly charged language or personal attacks.

FIGURE 1.1

Accuracy, fairness and lack of bias are essential in news stories. Writers of commentaries (editorials, blogs, written and spoken essays, reviews and letters to the editor) must also be accurate and fair in order to be credible.

The difference may be due to human error on the official's part, or it may be due to differences in angle and in viewpoint. Referees recognize this problem. They try to deal with it by obtaining the best possible view of every play and by conferring with their colleagues on some close calls.

Still, every official knows that an occasional mistake will be made. That is unavoidable. What can and must be avoided is unfairness. Referees must be fair, and both players and fans must believe they are fair. Otherwise, their judgments will not be accepted. They will not be trusted.

With news, too, every event or issue can be observed from different viewpoints, and each viewpoint may yield a different understanding of what is occurring and of what it means. In journalism as in sports, there also is the possibility of human error, even by the most careful reporters.

Fairness requires reporters to try to find every viewpoint on a story. Rarely will there be only one; often there are more than two. Fairness requires that you allow ample opportunity for response to anyone who is being attacked or whose integrity is being questioned in a story. Fairness requires, above all, that you make every effort to avoid following your own biases in your reporting and in your writing (Figure 1.1). However, neither fairness nor objectivity requires that every viewpoint receive the same amount of time or space.

Dealing with Bias

Bias — real or perceived — is all around us. Gallup and the Knight Foundation surveyed 1,440 respondents in a 2018 survey about bias. They reported that Americans think 62 percent of the news in newspapers, on television or on radio is biased. They think 80 percent of the news on social media is biased. Republicans and independents see more bias than Democrats. The least biased sources, according to this survey, are, in order: PBS News, the Associated Press, NPR, *The Wall Street Journal, USA Today*, CBS News and ABC News.

A chorus of critics claims that journalists lean to the left. A smaller chorus complains of a rightward tilt. Books and cable television talk shows add heat, if not light, to the criticism. How valid is it?

One answer is that American journalism has many biases built into it. For example, journalists are biased toward conflict. War is a better story than peace. Journalists are biased toward novelty. Airplanes that don't crash are seldom reported. Journalists are biased toward celebrity. The lives and deaths of celebrities are chronicled in detail on the network news as well as in fan magazines.

There's a less obvious but even more important bias that probably accounts for much of the criticism. It is hidden in the job description of journalism. What do journalists say they do? What makes them proudest? What do they honor?

Journalists describe themselves as the outside agitators, the afflicters of the comfortable and the comforters of the afflicted. They see their job as being the watchdog against the powerful, the voice of the voiceless, the surrogate for the ordinary citizen, the protector of the abused and downtrodden. Journalists expect themselves to be forever skeptical, consistently open-minded, respectful of differences, sensitive to what sociologists call "the other." Neither patriotism nor religion should be exempt from their critical examination.

Does that job description seem more "liberal" or more "conservative"?

Consider that conservatives generally are respectful of authority and supportive of the status quo. Is it any surprise, then, that the overwhelming majority of conservatives and many liberals see a liberal bias in journalism—at least on the surface? Notice that this bias has little or nothing to do with partisan politics.

Now suppose we had a journalism that wasn't questioning, disrespectful of authority, open to new ideas, dogging the powerful and speaking for the weak. Who would benefit, and who would suffer? Would society and democracy be better or worse off?

At a deeper level, however, mainstream American journalism is profoundly conservative. Journalists seldom examine critically the foundation stones on which the American way of life is based. Among these are capitalism, the two-party system, and the concepts of the ethnic melting pot and of social mobility. When was the last time that you saw any of these ideas questioned seriously in the mainstream press?

One conclusion suggested by this analysis is that in societies that aren't free—such as America before independence from Great Britain—a free press is a revolutionary instrument. In a society such as 21st-century America, which considers itself free and is overall self-satisfied, the free press becomes, at a fundamental level, conservative.

The Issue of Objectivity

The rules that mainstream journalists follow in attempting to arrive at the best obtainable version of the truth—to report accurately, fairly and without bias—are commonly summarized in the concept of **objectivity**. Objectivity has been and still

FIGURE 1.2

The Media Bias Chart

A media bias chart can give you a broad understanding of the leanings of different organizations' reporting. The amount of bias tends to exist on a spectrum.

Source: Vanessa Otero, Ad Fontes Media, Inc.

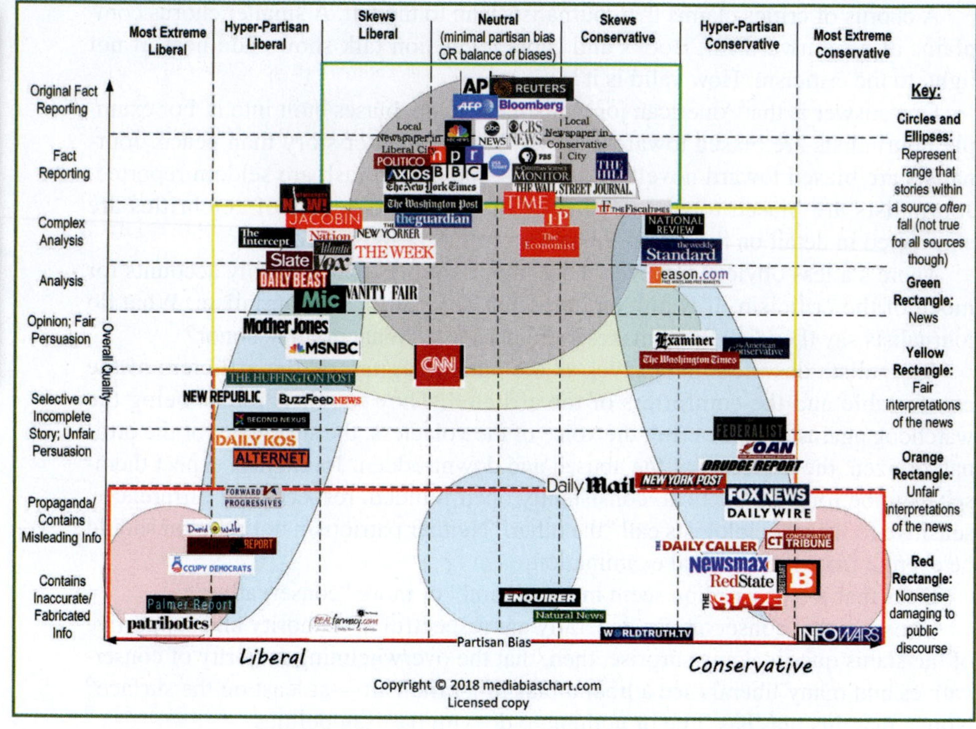

FIGURE 1.3

Gallup Survey Chart

The amount of bias that news consumers perceive within a news organization's reporting tends to be influenced by political leanings. Where do some of your preferred news outlets fall on the political spectrum? Do you agree with the level of bias that the chart shows?

Source: Republished with permission of Gallup, Inc. "Perceived Accuracy and Bias in the News Media," Survey on Trust, Media and Democracy, 2018, Permission conveyed through Copyright Clearance Center, Inc.

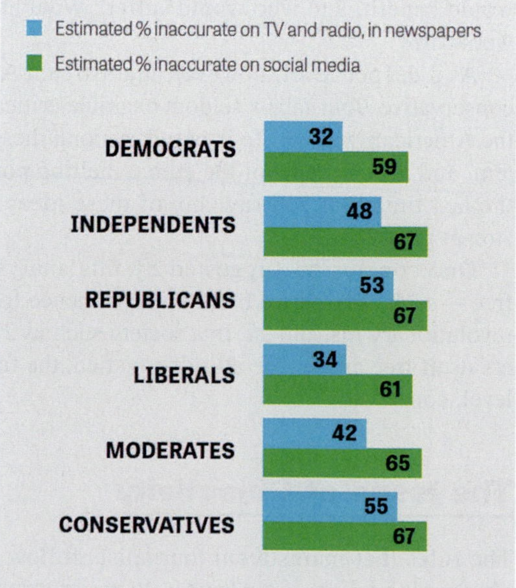

is accepted as a working credo by most American journalists, as well as by students and teachers of journalism. It has been exalted by leaders of the profession as an essential, if unattainable, ideal. Its critics, by contrast, have attacked objectivity as, in the phrase of sociologist Gaye Tuchman, a "strategic ritual" that conceals a multitude of professional sins while producing superficial and often misleading coverage.

In his classic *Discovering the News: A Social History of American Newspapers*, Michael Schudson traces the rise of objectivity to the post–World War I period. During this time, scholars and journalists alike turned to the methods and the language of science in an attempt to make sense of a world that was being turned upside down by the influence of Sigmund Freud in psychology and Karl Marx in politics, by the emergence of new economic forces and by the erosion of traditional values. Objectivity was a reliance on observable facts, but it was also a methodology for freeing factual reporting from the biases and values of source, writer or reader. It was itself a value, an ideal. Schudson writes, "Journalists came to believe in objectivity, to the extent that they did, because they wanted to, needed to, were forced by ordinary human aspiration to seek escape from their own deep convictions of doubt and drift."

Objectivity, then, was a way of applying to the art of journalism the methods of science. Those methods emphasized reliance on observable fact. They also included the use of a variety of transparent techniques for pursuing truth and verifying facts. In science, transparency means that the researchers explain their objectives, their methods, their findings and their limitations. In journalism, only part of that methodology is usually followed. Journalists seldom describe their methods or discuss the limits of their findings. If they did, at least some members of the public might be less suspicious and less critical.

In *The Elements of Journalism*, Kovach and Rosenstiel worry that a kind of phony objectivity has replaced the original concept. The objectivity of science does not require neutrality or the artificial balance of two sides in a dispute. Scientists are free and expected to state their conclusions, as long as they report how they reached those conclusions. However, as usually practiced today, journalistic objectivity employs both neutrality and balance, sometimes instead of the kind of openness that is essential in science. This misunderstanding or misapplication of the real principles of objectivity has opened the way for critics to call for its abandonment. Journalists would be more honest, these critics argue, if they were open about their biases. In much of Europe, for example, journalists practice openly biased reporting, which their audiences expect.

The problem with that approach is easy to see in European journalism or, closer to home, in the opinionated journalism of partisan publications, cable television or many blogs. One-sided reports appeal to audiences that share the reporter's bias, but they repel those that don't. Fairness and accuracy too often are casualties in what Kovach and Rosenstiel call journalism of assertion, rather than of verification.

Properly understood, objectivity provides the journalistic method most likely to yield the best obtainable version of the truth. True objectivity, Kovach and

Rosenstiel argue, would add scientific rigor to journalistic art. Without that, journalists and audiences alike can be misled.

What Is *Not* News

Although there's debate about how objective a reporter can possibly be, journalists and scholars all agree about one thing: Reporting the news is not the same as expressing an opinion. The primary goal of a news story is to inform. Whether using words, audio or video, a reporter's job is to communicate pertinent facts and enough background information to help the audience understand those facts. Accuracy and fairness are paramount. By contrast, the primary goal of opinion writers and speakers is to persuade. Accuracy and fairness are still important—though they sometimes get lost in argument. A commentator is expressing a point of view rather than reporting the views of others.

To see for yourself the differences in style and substance, watch *NBC Nightly News*. Then, later in the evening, switch to MSNBC, a sister network. Now move to Fox News. The events of the day haven't changed, but their context and meaning sound very different from the viewpoints of the political left (MSNBC) and right (Fox News). For another clear example of the differences between reporting and commentary, compare a story on *The New York Times* homepage with an editorial on the same subject on the opinion page. The former is seeking to inform you; the latter, to persuade you.

Because the aims are different, news stories and commentary approach accuracy, fairness and bias differently.

In 1947, the Hutchins Commission on freedom of the press concluded that what a free society needs from journalists is "a truthful, comprehensive and intelligent account of the day's events in a context which gives them meaning." The goal of this chapter is to show you how the journalists of today and tomorrow understand that need, how they are trying to meet it, and how complex the task is. The rest of the book helps you develop the skills you'll need to take up the challenge. There are few challenges as important or as rewarding.

CHAPTER RESOURCES

SUGGESTED READINGS

The *Columbia Journalism Review* reports and analyzes the most important issues of contemporary journalism in every issue and on every publishing day on its website.

Gallup/Knight Foundation Study. "Perceived Accuracy and Bias in the News Media." 2018. www.knightfoundation.org.

Kovach, Bill, and Tom Rosenstiel. *The Elements of Journalism: What Newspeople Should Know and the Public Should Expect*. Rev. and updated 3rd ed. New York: Three Rivers Press, 2014. This little book, packed with practical advice and inspiration, offers a kind of applied ethics for journalists in any medium.

Schudson, Michael. *Discovering the News: A Social History of American Newspapers*. New York: Basic Books, 1978. This well-written study traces the development of objectivity in American journalism.

SUGGESTED WEBSITES

LaunchPad Solo

launchpadworks.com

When you visit LaunchPad Solo for Journalism, you will find research links, exercises and LearningCurve adaptive quizzing to help you improve your grammar and AP style usage. In addition, the site's video collection hosts the videos highlighted in this and other chapters as well as additional clips of leading professionals discussing important media trends.

cjr.org

Columbia Journalism Review is the oldest of the magazines devoted to the critical analysis of journalists' performance. You'll find critiques of major stories, essays on ethics, book reviews and trade news.

www.journalism.org

The site of the Pew Research Center for Journalism & Media contains relevant research and articles on the current state of journalism. See especially the "State of the News Media" reports for the most comprehensive look at the current performance of all the major news media.

journalistsresource.com

Operated by the Shorenstein Center on Media, Politics and Public Policy, this site is full of research journalists can use to pursue stories. It also has tip sheets full of questions that journalists should ask on topical subjects.

www.politifact.com

This site is one of the best fact-checking sites. It is operated by the *Tampa Bay Times* in Florida and staffed by professional journalists. Its analyses usually provide not only fact but context.

www.poynter.org

This site is an excellent starting point for journalism students. The Poynter Institute is the leading center of continuing professional education for journalists. On this site, you'll find not only a guide to the services and resources of the institute itself but also links to the sites of every major professional organization and a variety of other useful resources.

EXERCISES

1. With a classmate, compare your sources of news. Do either of you read a newspaper in print or on the web, watch the nightly news on television or rely on social media? How do you assess the accuracy of the news items that you receive from these sources? Where does the news on social media originate?
2. Choose a news event of some importance. Then compare the coverage of the event in at least three different news media — for example, on television, in the print edition of a newspaper and in an online news source accessed through your smartphone. How does each medium cover the story? What is each medium's unique contribution? Do the media complement each other? Or does getting the news from one source render the other sources unnecessary?
3. Go to the Pew Research Center for Journalism & Media (www.journalism.org), and click on "State of the Media" to read the most recent "State of the News Media." What strikes you as most important? How do the research findings compare with your own experience as a news consumer?
4. In this chapter, you saw a ranking of news organizations from least biased to most biased. Look at the NPR website, from the top of the rankings, and compare it to Breitbart News, from the bottom. What are the differences in the way they approach stories?
5. Get copies or visit the websites of your local newspaper, a paper from a city at least 50 miles away and a paper of national circulation, such as *USA Today* or *The Wall Street Journal*. Analyze the front page or homepage according to the criteria discussed in this chapter, and answer the following questions:
   a. What does the selection of stories on the front page or homepage tell you about the editors' understanding of each paper's audience?
   b. If you find stories on the same topic on the front page or homepage of two or more newspapers, determine whether the stories were written differently for different audiences.
   c. On the basis of what you've learned in this chapter, do you agree or disagree with the editors' news judgments? Why?
6. **Your journalism blog.** Create your own blog for the class (www.blogger.com is a good place to start). For your first post, write about your goals for the blog. Email the blog's name and link to your classmates and instructor. Use your blog throughout the term to discuss the issues raised in this and other chapters, especially the tricky ones such as objectivity and fairness.

CHAPTER 2 THE STATE OF THE NEWS INDUSTRY

Robert Rivard's early career was all about newspapers. He began that career in 1976 and eventually rose through the ranks to serve as editor and executive vice president of the *San Antonio Express-News*. In 2011, he resigned when the *Express-News* cut the newsroom staff from more than 300 at its peak to less than 200. It's now down to about 100.

"I just didn't see much hope for newspapers in cities the size of San Antonio," he says. So he set out to create something different—a not-for-profit news website that could produce quality local news. He launched the Rivard Report in 2012, and he hasn't looked back: "There are now more than 165 city and state nonprofit news organizations that belong to the Institute for Nonprofit News. The concept has grown rapidly."

Those members have different business models, but Rivard insists that's fine. The objective is to provide a source of high-quality local news:

> **Our mission is very different than that of a corporate-owned, for-profit newspaper, where the bottom line comes first, community an increasingly distant second.... We want our journalism to inform and connect the city's most engaged citizens, the people who vote, buy homes, and support local schools and neighborhoods. We want our journalism to contribute to all the other efforts underway to make the city a better, more equitable, more sustainable and more livable place for everyone who calls San Antonio home.**

The shrinking newsroom staff of the *Express-News* is not an aberration. You've probably heard similar stories about other newspapers around the country. According to the Pew Research Center, the number of employees in U.S. newspaper newsrooms declined from about 70,000 in 2008 to about 40,000 in 2018. That's a sharp decline, and with it comes a decreasing ability to cover the news. Consider the local newspaper where you live now or where you grew up: What would happen if it could no longer cover what's important to you or your community?

What troubles many about the decline of newspapers is that historically they have been the primary source of news creation. One recent study estimated that, even now, 85 percent of all news consumed daily in the U.S. originates at newspapers, regardless of where people read or view it.

Even if you "get your news" from platforms like Apple News, Google News, Facebook or Twitter, these organizations don't—for the most part—report news. They redistribute it, and as a result they are **content aggregators** that rely on algorithms and human editors to select the news you see. Even local radio and television stations, with their relatively small reporting staffs, often depend on newspapers to let them know what's going on in town today.

For more than two centuries, newspaper staffs constituted the largest and best news-gathering force in every U.S. city. Even when there was only one newspaper in town, it typically employed more journalists than all the broadcast stations combined. That's still true in some cases, but the severe job cuts at newspapers have nonetheless greatly diminished their news-gathering capability.

In this chapter, you will learn:

1. How new ways of financing the news are being created.
2. How changing technology has affected journalism.
3. Why the media have a credibility problem.
4. What fake news is and why it's disturbing.
5. How journalists can better engage with audiences.
6. How changes in journalism require new job skills.

One reason for newspapers' decline is that they were slow to adapt to the internet. Most paid little attention when the World Wide Web arrived in the mid-1990s, which they regret today. They are playing catchup to a bevy of new competitors. Only a handful—most notably *The New York Times, The Washington Post* and *The Wall Street Journal* with their national audiences—have managed to build profitable businesses on the internet.

Those three are likely to be around for a long time to come, but if other newspapers continue their downward spiral, which is likely, who will gather the news, particularly at the local level? Rivard, for one, thinks that nonprofit news-gathering staffs might well be the answer, and he's not alone. Consider these examples, all members of the Institute for Nonprofit News that depend mostly on donations to survive:

- **Austin Bulldog.** This online site describes itself as being engaged in investigative reporting in the public interest: "Our focus is almost entirely on what's happening in our hometown, the city of Austin, Texas, although we will occasionally cover important stories on the outskirts. We will investigate matters involving government, media, politics and anything else warranting close scrutiny that's within our resources." Sites similar to this are popping up in cities throughout the U.S.
- **Ensia.** This entity describes itself as an independent, nonprofit, web-based magazine that presents new perspectives on environmental challenges and solutions to a global audience.
- **Women's eNews.** This award-winning nonprofit news service covers issues of particular concern to women and provides women's perspectives on public policy. With writers and readers around the globe, its audience stretches from New York City to New Delhi and all points between. It now produces a site in Arabic.

Although nonprofit news sites are a realistic possibility for protecting the country's news-gathering capability, that's not the only approach. All sorts of financing schemes are being tried to protect top-notch journalism. For the better part of two centuries, printing newspapers in the U.S. was a license to print money. It was not at all uncommon for a newspaper to earn 40 cents in profit for each dollar that came through the door. That, in turn, financed the best news-gathering apparatus the world has ever seen. Slowly but surely, that advantage has eroded.

Today, even *The Times*, *The Post* and *The Journal*, which operate profitable websites, earn less than half of their revenues on the web. Print advertising, although shrinking, still drives those companies' bottom lines. The real problem is this: How do we best finance news gathering in a society where the vast majority of media operations are for-profit corporations? And how do we do this when profits are shrinking?

A discussion of financial stability is so important that we focus on it in this chapter. We'll also explore several other problems that confront journalists and journalism and that you may face as you enter the news industry. When possible, we'll suggest solutions to help solve those problems.

The Problem of Financing the News

As newspapers and other traditional media companies struggle to find new revenue and as nonprofits try to carve a place for themselves in journalism, some are experimenting with other business models. They seek financing through various means, hoping to turn a profit or at least break even. Several models for these new forms of mostly online-only journalism are emerging:

- **Financed by foundations.** Some organizations are launched or supported by funding from large foundations. The Sandler Foundation, for example, made a major, multiyear commitment to launch ProPublica, which — thanks to the Sandler Foundation and more than 40 others — spends more than 85 cents of each revenue dollar on news. That's almost the exact opposite of traditional print news organizations, which spend about 15 percent of revenues on news. The model is working. Since it began publishing in 2008, ProPublica has won four Pulitzer Prizes, three Peabody Awards, two Emmy Awards, five George Polk Awards, three Online Journalism Awards for General Excellence, a National Magazine Award and many others. One ProPublica Pulitzer was for a series on Wall Street bankers who enrich themselves at the expense of their clients and sometimes even their own companies. One of the Peabody Awards, the highest honor in broadcast journalism, was for a story about a mass murder in Guatemala and a prosecutor who helped bring the perpetrators to justice. ProPublica typically offers its stories to traditional media operations, which we refer to as **legacy media**. It offers those stories free of charge for publication or broadcast, and the local outlet often helps with the reporting. After a period of exclusivity for the partner organization, the story on the ProPublica website. ProPublica also carries ads on its website.

  The Chicago-based John D. and Catherine T. MacArthur Foundation also provides substantial funding to startup news organizations. It has been a significant supporter of ProPublica and now supports three major nonprofit news operations in Chicago. These include the following:

  - City Bureau, a small operation on the South Side whose mission is to diversify news coverage in the city.
  - Free Spirit Media, an experimental learning newsroom on Chicago's West and South sides.
  - Chicago Public Media, which operates WBEZ and will expand reporting and interaction with Vocalo, the station's urban alternative music platform.

- **Financed by venture capital.** Some sites, like HuffPost.com and Newsy.com, received startup financing from private investors and became nationally popular, attracting significant amounts of advertising. Some also charge for subscriptions to premium content or feed news to companies for a fee.

- **Financed as an old media/new media hybrid.** The website Politico was created by former *Washington Post* journalists with capital provided by Robert

Allbritton, owner and founder of *Capitol Hill*, a political newspaper in Washington. It has been enormously successful, expanding to include Politico Playbook, an email newsletter; Politico Pro, a firewall-protected online newsletter covering a dozen targeted areas at an annual cost of more than $1,000 per topic area; *Politico* magazine, published online and bimonthly in print; state political sites covering New York, New Jersey and Florida; and a European edition based in Brussels.

- **Financed with other hybrid models.** Some nonprofit sites, like MinnPost, are hybrids funded by advertisers, corporate sponsors and individual donors. This early example of a nonprofit news site seeks to provide high-quality journalism in Minnesota. It publishes online Monday through Friday with a limited edition on Saturday. Most of its journalists have decades of experience in the Twin Cities media. St. Louis Beacon, a startup website staffed largely by veterans of the *St. Louis Post-Dispatch*, merged with St. Louis Public Radio in 2013 to form one multimedia news organization dedicated to covering important news in St. Louis. It concentrates on politics, race, education, economic innovation, science, health and the arts. The funding model, which teams public radio stations with other news organizations, is basically that of public radio.
- **Financed by individual entrepreneurs.** Other sites, like WestSeattleBlog.com, were established with spare change and hope to attract enough advertising to survive.

Some of the founders of these sites don't even think of themselves as journalists. They're merely filling a perceived void in news coverage in their communities. Others, like the founders of MinnPost, are displaced journalists with formal training and significant experience in news gathering.

News organizations employ different models for funding their reporting. City Bureau, for example, relies on support from the MacArthur Foundation and ensures diverse news coverage in Chicago's South Side.

For the most part, private citizens, families or publicly traded companies own the legacy media operations in the U.S. As a result, these companies continue to exist only if they earn a profit. Traditionally, most revenue has come from advertising, with some additional revenue from newsstand sales, subscriptions and event sponsorships. Many new journalism sites aim to follow the same model by supporting themselves through advertising or subscriptions. Nonprofit sites, however, seek only to support their operations—to pay staff and other costs—and not to make a profit for owners or investors.

The Problem of Technology-Driven Change

Through all this, one thing is clear: The news industry is having to reinvent itself, and as in other industries, disruptive technologies are a primary cause of its problems. The ride-sharing companies Uber and Lyft, for example, have caused major difficulties for the taxicab industry. Thanks to mobile phone technology, it's often easier to summon an Uber or Lyft driver than it is to call a taxi. And often Uber and Lyft are significantly less expensive for what is frequently better service. The same ideas apply to Amazon and the retail industry, AirBnB and the hotel industry, and Netflix and the entertainment industry.

> **"I think Twitter primarily is a news system. Early on we didn't necessarily know what it was. We thought social networks."**
>
> ■ **Evan Williams, co-founder of Twitter**

Similarly, legacy media have been hurt by the arrival of the internet. The Pew Research Center produces reports each year that attempt to track changes in how people consume news. It's fairly easy to summarize those results: Those age 70 and older still prefer newspapers, which they grew up with, read throughout their working careers and continue to read.

Younger people, however, prefer to get their news from television, and even younger people prefer to get news through their smartphone, tablet or computer (See Figure 2.1). According to Pew, fully 95 percent of teenagers have access to a smartphone, and 45 percent report being online "almost constantly." They aren't consuming news that often, but when they do, they usually find out about a news story on YouTube, Instagram, Twitter or Snapchat. Facebook usage is fading among this group, perhaps because many of their parents are there.

As older newspaper readers continue to die, they simply are not being replaced by younger readers. That, in a nutshell, is the problem that newspapers face, along with the fact that most of a newspaper's revenue still comes from print advertising. Without revenue, legacy media cannot keep up with the ever-changing technological trends that engage young news consumers.

It should be noted that newspapers are not the only news gatherers that are affected by changing technologies. Television local and network news audiences have shrunk markedly since the arrival of cable television news channels, including MSNBC, CNN and Fox News Channel.

Magazines, too, face many of the same problems as newspapers; they are old-style manufactured products that are costly to produce and distribute. Nevertheless,

FIGURE 2.1

Platforms like Apple News, Snapchat Discover and Facebook Instant Articles make it possible for organizations like *The New York Times* to distribute their stories more widely and attempt to earn more revenue from them.

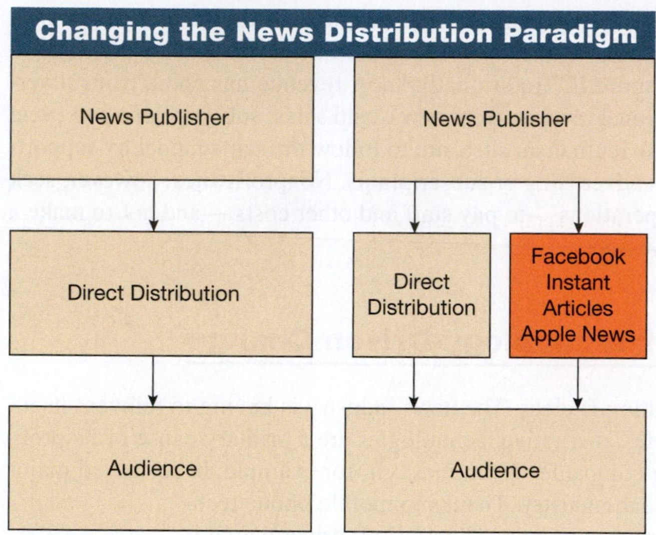

the problems of magazines are not nearly as severe as those of newspapers. The majority of magazines appeal to niche audiences, which general-circulation newspapers cannot. Examples range from *Twins and Tantrums* to *Potato Review* to *Brass Band World*. Advertisers covet those niche audiences—in this case, parents with twins, potato growers and people who play in brass bands—because they can target product advertising more directly to those who are likely to be most interested.

As we go about creating a new business model for the news media that can weather technological change, what we must save is not specific newspapers and television programs and not necessarily the companies that own them, but the high-quality reporting they produce. True, replacing **spot news**—breaking news that occurred today—might not be tough. After all, if a plane crashes, some blogger or citizen, if no one else, is bound to report it. So are the cable television networks, which thrive on wars, accidents, fires and disasters. Why? Those kinds of stories make for good video and audio—unlike important stories like city council meetings, court hearings and the actions of state legislatures. And as is discussed in the last chapter, these stories are frequently the ones that need to be reported because they may have the greatest impact on the public.

Even more problematic is the potential loss of in-depth **investigative journalism**—what journalist Alex S. Jones calls establishing in the public a new understanding of an issue derived from intensive journalistic investigation. Jones is the former director of the Joan Shorenstein Center on the Press, Politics and Public Policy at Harvard University. In his book *Losing the News: The Future of the News That Feeds Democracy*, he praises the technological changes that are altering the journalism landscape, but he fears the loss of the "iron core of news that serves as a watchdog over government, holds the powerful accountable and gives citizens what they need." He's hopeful and optimistic that the "iron core" can be saved. Doing just that is what the startup ventures mentioned earlier are all about.

Despite threatening the "iron core" of journalism, technological changes open up many new job opportunities at all types of news organizations. We discuss these later in the chapter.

ON THE JOB The Lure of New Media

Courtesy of Adam Falk

Adam Falk graduated with a degree in magazine journalism, but he knew that he wouldn't be entering the magazine world right away. There was too much more he wanted to try. At the University of Missouri, he focused on building a new-media skill set to tell stories in innovative ways. Just after graduation, he took a web design internship with the Media Policy Center, a nonprofit film company in Santa Monica, California.

Eventually, he found his way to the startup world. He moved to Newsy, a video news company headquartered in Columbia, Missouri, where he had worked while attending college. Then he went back to Los Angeles to start a small Newsy studio there:

> The best thing about working for a startup is that your presence makes an impact and your work gets seen. Chances are, I wouldn't have the same opportunities working an entry-level job at a larger media company.

Then *The Wall Street Journal* came calling. Falk now lives in New York and works as assistant mobile news editor for the *Journal*:

> I work on What's News, the *Journal*'s first-ever, mobile-first product. It is an app that takes its name from a column of news briefs in the paper, and, like the column, it is designed to catch up mobile readers on the need-to-know news quickly. Specifically, I edit copy from *Journal* stories for the app and create motion-graphic explainers to give those stories more context.

The Credibility Problem

Changing technology is causing financial difficulty for the news industry, but that's far from the industry's only problem. In a 2018 Reuters-Ipsos poll, only 48 percent of Americans surveyed expressed "a great deal" or "some" trust in the news media. Mark Oppenheimer, a contributing writer to the *Los Angeles Times*, noted wryly: "People trust reporters at about the same rate they trust vaccines (only 51 percent believe they're safe) or believe in haunted houses (which 47 percent believe exist)." Polls show that among major job categories only lawyers and business executives are more despised by the public than journalists. Clearly, a significant number of Americans simply don't trust the press.

The Poynter Institute got similar results in a national poll it conducted in late 2017. Only 12 percent of the public expressed a "great deal" of confidence in the news media, and 37 percent a "fair amount" of confidence. Thirteen percent had "no confidence at all," and 39 percent had "not very much" confidence. As recently as the mid-1970s, about 73 percent of the public expressed a positive level of confidence in the news media.

Oppenheimer compares these results to similar polls on the popularity of Congress. In those, most express contempt for Congress but give high marks to their own representative. Similarly, press credibility for local newsgatherers is almost always rated higher than for the national press. A 2016 Pew Research survey found that 82 percent of U.S. citizens have "some" or "a lot" of confidence in their local news organizations.

Perhaps it's not surprising that the press is reviled more than ever. Reporters are frequently booed and threatened. They receive death threats on Twitter, and in 2018 five reporters at the *Capital Gazette* were murdered in their offices in Annapolis, Maryland. President Donald Trump often describes the press as "the enemy of the American people."

Indeed, contempt for the press tends to be divided along party lines. In a 2017 Pew Research Center poll, 70 percent of Americans supported the media's role as watchdog over government officials as provided for in the First Amendment to the Constitution, but Democrats were 47 percent more likely than Republicans to support this role. The gap, Pew noted, was the widest ever since the question was first asked in 1985. Although President Trump plays to his base of supporters when he criticizes the press, it's likely that his criticism has had a negative impact on perception of the media that has widened the split between Democrats and Republicans on the issue. As Democrats have moved ever more resolutely toward the left and Republicans have embraced the right wing of the party, that split is clearer than ever.

Much of the Republican distrust of the press comes from both Trump and those on the political right who have a longstanding perception that the media have a left-leaning bias. Studies have shown that their perception is at least partially true: Most journalists lean to the left. Why? As is discussed in Chapter 1, the people who are attracted to journalism also tend to be naturally attracted to liberal values. Many news journalists have a desire to make the world a better place through their work. Journalists are out on the streets every day and see all of society's warts—poverty, inequality and hopelessness imposed by a system that neglects the invisible.

As a result, they tend to believe in a social safety net represented by Social Security, Medicare, Medicaid and food stamps. They believe that young people should have a chance to lift themselves out of poverty and that states and the federal government should help them do so by making college more affordable. Those are positions that many Democrats support, so perhaps it's not surprising that many journalists lean leftward.

But rarely do journalists intentionally produce biased journalism. More often, they allow personal biases to creep into their stories without recognizing it.

Journalists need to be aware of their biases and do everything possible to keep those biases out of the news columns. As is noted in Chapter 1, in their important work *The Elements of Journalism*, longtime journalists Bill Kovach and Tom Rosenstiel reject the traditional concept of journalistic objectivity. As practiced by journalists throughout most of the 20th century, they write, it was seriously flawed. Every effort was made to balance an expert opinion—or a political argument—with an opposing view to achieve "fairness and balance." A much better form of objectivity, Kovach and Rosenstiel argue, is to duplicate the scientific method: Create a hypothesis, and then use a variety of techniques to pursue truth and verify facts.

That's a great way for journalists to approach the news, but there's a potential trap. Most people, including journalists, confuse the "truth" with what they already believe and rationalize their own prejudices as telling the truth. You can prevent that by following the process that scientists follow. First, state your opinion as a hypothesis. Second, try honestly to *disprove* it. Third, view all the evidence on both sides fairly, unwedded to your initial bias. Finally, make a conclusion as a juror does, disregarding any previous ideas you may have had.

The truth must be seen as not what you initially thought but what you honestly, impartially decided after a skeptical but open-minded process. Fighting the perception of bias is difficult, but journalists should make their best possible effort to do so by pursuing what we'll call **skeptical open-mindedness**. They also should make sure that opinion and commentary are clearly labeled as such. Neither should be allowed to creep into the news columns.

The Fake News Problem: What's Fake and What's Not?

You've probably heard the phrase "fake news" many times in recent years from politicians, government officials, family, friends and professors. It's been used to describe both the false news stories that are intentionally written to deceive the public, as well as the traditional news stories that are politicized by those who don't agree with the news reported.

"Fake news" is now a catchall term that has proliferated discourse since the 2016 presidential election, when then-candidate Trump used the phrase to play into his constituents' dislike of what they perceive to be the liberal press.

But just because news is called "fake" doesn't make it so. President Trump has used the phrase when referring to news in *The New York Times* and *The Washington Post*, but he seldom hurls such criticism at *The Wall Street Journal*. The reality is that, despite Trump's pronouncements, those are three of the most respected newspapers in the world. They would not intentionally print information they knew was false.

And don't confuse those publications' news columns with their editorial positions. Although the editorial pages of *The Times* and *The Post* tilt heavily leftward, those of *The Journal* lean just as far to the right. So when Trump rails away at *The Times* and *The Post*, it's usually because he doesn't agree with the news they have printed. Again, that doesn't make it false.

It's not at all unusual for U.S. presidents to criticize or mistrust the press. Trump's predecessor, Barack Obama, held far fewer press conferences than most former presidents and had numerous harsh words for Fox News Channel, which tilts heavily to the right. But a president's use of the term "fake news" to describe content in the mainstream media is unprecedented.

Fake news — stories that undeniably alter the truth with intention — does exist, and a common theme is to try to fool readers into believing that material comes from a legitimate news source. The following are a few examples of impostor websites:

- ABCnews.com.co. The real ABC site is ABCnews.go.com, a Disney company.
- Breaking-CNN.com. This impostor site published numerous death hoaxes while hoping that readers would confuse it with the real site, CNN.com.

launchpadworks.com
WATCH: **"Is Facebook the Future of Journalism"**

- How might Facebook's collection of user data affect the news to which you're exposed?
- What are some effects of having news integrated into a Facebook social media experience?

- DrudgeReport.com.co. This site has appropriated the name of the right-leaning Drudge Report, which can be found at DrudgeReport.com.
- WashingtonPost.com.co. This site masqueraded as the real site, WashingtonPost.com.

An internet arbitration panel ruled in 2015 that the last one's "fake news content misleads readers and serves as 'click bait' to drive readers to other sites, or to share the fake news content with others on social networking websites, to generate advertising revenue." Wikipedia contains a great list of fake news sites as well as reports of fake news around the globe, showing that this issue extends far beyond the U.S.

Perhaps even more problematic than fake news, which most intelligent people can easily recognize, are those sites that lean to the far right or far left politically. Although these sometimes carry news that is defensible and has some basis in fact, they do not attempt to be fair or balanced in any way, as mainstream journalists strive to do. They publish news that is deliberately distorted to appeal to readers who already share their biases. Examples on the left are the Palmer Report, Occupy Democrats, Patribiotics and Bipartisan Report. Equivalents on the right are Breitbart, the Conservative Tribune, Red State, Newsmax, the Blaze and InfoWars.

Independent arbiters often cite these as the most inflammatory sites on the internet. They have been condemned for producing nonsense that damages public discourse, and they have the most bias to the left or right. Readers often send the reports from these sites to their friends or post them on other social media sites, where they are widely distributed. When they do that, they often leave out the source of the report.

Also of concern are sites that independent arbiters say contain unfair representations of the news. These include Daily Kos, Alternet, BuzzFeed news, the *New Republic* and HuffPost on the left, and Fox News, the *New York Post*, the *Daily Mail*, the Drudge Report and The Federalist on the right.

MSNBC and CNN, while often targets of the right, are viewed by most independent arbiters as providing fair representations of the news. MSNBC is considered liberal, and CNN, despite the criticism it gets from Trump and his allies, ranks very close to neutral with a slight lean to the left in most independent assessments. By comparison, Fox News is ranked as leaning as far to the right as MSNBC leans to the left while scoring much lower in accuracy. Some Fox anchors, including Shepard Smith, have criticized the network when it has leaned too far to the right while ignoring accuracy.

Where can people go for accurate news that is fairly presented and with minimal bias? The Associated Press, the British news service Reuters, the French news agency Agence France-Presse, Bloomberg, the three major television networks (ABC, CBS and NBC), *The New York Times, The Washington Post, The Wall Street Journal* and *Time* magazine rank at the top of the list. Such ratings aren't perfect and are subject to question, but they are reasonably accurate, despite their subjectivity. A Pew Research Center review of the ratings of these independent arbiters confirmed their accuracy.

We don't mean to suggest that errors never occur in the best of the mainstream media. They do. But when those occur, they are corrected, and most often the errors are made while reporting and are not intentionally conveyed untruths. The mainstream media simply do not trade in false news.

BoCfips

launchpadworks.com
WATCH: **"Student Reporting Lab: Media Literacy"**

- What is the role of the audience in combating fake news and misinformation?
- What does the audience need to learn when consuming news online?

A Solution: Engaging Readers, Listeners and Viewers

One way to help solve the credibility problem and the perception that journalists create fake news is to do a better job of engaging readers, listeners and viewers. For years, newspapers, radio and television covered their communities with little or no engagement from their audiences. They operated as one-to-many operations that served as gatekeepers, deciding what readers would read about and setting the public agenda. There was some feedback, of course—letters to the editor, the occasional radio caller, the compliment or complaint delivered by mail or telephone. But for the most part, the public had few opportunities to react to the journalist's product.

Joy Mayer, a leading expert in the community engagement movement, says the reason for that disconnect was simple: "To enhance their ability to fairly report the news, journalists (thought that they) needed to stand apart from their community rather than be participants." Journalists also moved from job to job and often ended up with no roots, history or context in their communities.

Mayer argues that journalists still prefer to "celebrate otherness more than they do connection." Writing for *Nieman Reports*, she says, "Ever mindful of conflicts of interest—actual or perceived—they hold themselves apart from influence and are wary of being swayed by sources or vocal readers."

Yet in conversations with her, journalists often say the following:

- They want community members to feel invested in and connected to the news product.
- They want as much information as they can get about what their readers want and need to know.

Mayer points out that most journalists subscribe to a host of journalistic values—obligation to the truth, loyalty to citizens, monitoring people in power and serving as a forum for public discussion. Says Mayer:

> **I would argue that today's media landscape now requires an additional element—a new principle to keep us in tune with our digital times: Journalists have an obligation to identify and attempt to connect with the people who most want and need their content.**
>
> **Adhering to this obligation is good for journalism's challenging bottom line. It mimics marketing, in a way—find the customer, meet the need, bring eyeballs to the product and build brand loyalty. It's customer service, too—anticipating needs, inviting feedback, being responsive to input and acting like a human being. It also is the right thing to do for our communities.**

Toward this end, Mayer created a community involvement team at the *Columbia Missourian*, one of the first such efforts nationwide. In effect, it extended marketing into the newsroom, where that concept once was viewed with disdain. Now she serves as director of the Trusting News project at the Poynter Institute.

The concept Mayer advocates allows readers and reporters to interact on the website and also at forums where they can interact face-to-face. She calls it a "take-the-party-to-the-people" philosophy: "Let's not ignore the value that comes from those person-to-person interactions that inform coverage, encourage content sharing and foster brand loyalty."

What's the grammar error in this sentence?

Scientists report that if greenhouse gas emissions continue at their current rates many areas of the world will feel the effects by 2040.

See Appendix 1, Rule 6.

If this means inviting the public to an open forum, do it. The St. Louis Beacon, the online site mentioned earlier that evolved into a partnership with St. Louis Public Radio, did just that with a series of open breakfast forums it called "Beacon and Eggs." At those sessions, readers and Beacon staffers discussed issues important to the community. Today, the original concept has evolved into a rich agenda of community events where staff members can interact with the public.

Another approach is to allow readers to write their own stories and take their own photographs. Newspapers print them and run them online. Those things, Mayer argues, build reader loyalty to the publication, to the website or to the broadcast station.

"Editors ought to require that story pitches and budget lines include an engagement component reflecting community conversation, collaboration and outreach," she says. "In many cases, conversations about stories need to include these questions: Who is going to benefit most from this information? And how will reporters, editors and producers be sure those people find it?"

A Solution: Embracing, Not Fighting, Citizen Journalism

The best media companies are embracing the public's involvement in the news-gathering process and allowing readers and viewers to contribute to stories for print, broadcast and online products. Citizen journalists increasingly provide photos and videos, especially when they were on the scene of an event and professional journalists were not. The old "one provider to many consumers" model is becoming a thing of the past, and audience participation in the process of presenting the news is now considered desirable by most journalists.

Citizen journalism — which is introduced in the previous chapter — is increasingly popular on websites around the world, much of it on the sites of established media companies. For example, when the BBC asked users around the world to snap photos of scheduled antiwar protests and send them in, hundreds of photos were submitted. When an F-15 fighter crashed, a citizen in Virginia shot photos that she sent to a local television station. The photo taken immediately following the impact was used in the newscast along with video footage taken later.

Citizen journalists can be an asset to legacy media, particularly those with decreasing staff sizes. When terrorists planted bombs on a London subway, the first images of the disaster came from survivors who used their mobile phones to take photos and transmit them to the outside world from below ground. When an airplane struck birds during takeoff and was forced to land, nearly miraculously, on New York's Hudson River, some of the first images came from nearby apartment dwellers who took photos and video from their windows. During the ongoing war in Syria, citizen reporting through social media sometimes is often the only source of news as repressive governments ban reporters from the scenes. Social media allow citizens to provide eyewitness accounts, which are picked up and distributed by mainstream media.

Although many mainstream media outlets are allowing citizens to participate, they are moderating what goes onto their sites. As a result, back in the newsroom, journalists often find that their roles have changed. Not only do they perform their traditional roles, but they also edit stories, photos and videos shot by readers and viewers; moderate discussion forums; write blogs; and post breaking news on Twitter, Facebook and other social media sites. As a result, newsrooms have begun to look different from those of the past. Journalists are being trained in digital audio and video editing, and some even find themselves in front of cameras or microphones to create mini-newscasts or podcasts that appear on the organization's website or mobile app.

Much of the video and still footage taken by people who happen to be on the scene finds its way to blogs and social media, but when it finds its way onto the sites of mainstream media, as the examples above show, citizen journalists effectively serve as an extension of the media outlet's traditional reporting staff.

The Washington Post/Getty Images

Amateur photographer Devin Allen, featured here with one of his photographs at the Reginald Lewis Museum, documented the protests occurring in Baltimore after the death of Freddie Gray. Embracing citizen journalism, Time *ran one of his photos on the cover of the magazine.*

When Citizen Journalism Fails

Citizen journalism often works, but occasionally it goes awry, just like professional journalism. Many citizen journalists have little or no training in the profession, which means that they have little sense of journalistic standards. Some journalists continue to dismiss the idea of citizen journalism, citing the likelihood of inaccuracies.

But it may be telling that nearly 20 years after the advent of citizen journalism, relatively few instances of major errors have been found in national media. One significant error was a false report posted in 2008 on CNN's iReport that Apple CEO Steve Jobs had suffered a heart attack. The erroneous story, which rattled investors, led to a $12 decline in Apple's stock price before the company debunked it three hours later. Jobs died in 2011, but in 2008 he was very much alive.

Forms of Citizen Journalism

Although some citizen journalism finds its way onto the sites of legacy media, today's web publishing environment makes it easy for citizens to create their own videos, podcasts or websites and sidestep the legacy media entirely. Anyone, it seems, can become a publisher. In an article in Online Journalism Review, J. D. Lasica sorted the media forms used in citizen journalism into six types:

- **Audience participation** (user comments attached to news stories, personal blogs, photos or video footage captured from mobile phone cameras, local news written by members of the community). Mainstream media outlets such as MSNBC.com give readers the chance to post comments and other items on their sites.
- **Independent news or information websites** (such as the Drudge Report). These sites are published by those not normally associated with traditional media and often have a political bent.
- **Participatory news sites** (Northwest Voice). Here, readers get to write, take photos and publish their work, perhaps even in newspaper format, with the assistance of professional editors.
- **Collaborative and contributory news sites** (Slashdot.org). These sites, often featuring a specific subject-matter area, are based on reader comments and contributions.
- **Thin media** (mailing lists, email newsletters). Through thin media, targeted news content is directed to those with narrowly defined interests.
- **Personal broadcasting sites**. On these sites, the operators provide news-based subject matter in a specific area of interest, such as technology. The result is downloadable audio or video.

There are more sources of information than ever before, and the public is embracing those alternatives. Many websites target specific groups of readers with great precision. Interested in knowing more about the conflict in the Middle East? There are multiple websites for that. Interested in a nontraditional take on local politics? There may well be a blog for that. All of these new alternatives are eroding the strength of legacy media.

launchpadworks.com
WATCH: **"Newspapers Now: Balancing Citizen Journalism and Investigative Reporting"**

- What are some strengths and weaknesses of citizen journalism?
- When are citizen journalists useful?
- Will citizen journalism ever replace traditional journalism?

A Solution: New Skills for Jobs in Journalism

If you're reading this book to prepare for a career in journalism, all this may be a bit daunting—and depressing. Remember, though, that while changing technology has reshaped the journalism industry, only certain sectors of the industry—most notably newspapers—are affected adversely. Newspapers are employing far fewer journalists than they did only a few years ago, but those losses have been more than offset by job gains in growth sectors of the larger media industry. There are far more cable television channels than there were 20 years ago, and employment at websites is booming. The net result is that despite a major shift in where jobs can be found, there are still plenty of jobs for graduating journalism majors.

Consider what happened to Jenifer Langosch. When she went to college, she was intent on covering sports journalism, probably for a newspaper. Thirteen years into her career, she's writing about sports, but her destination changed when she was offered a job with MLB.com, first covering the Pittsburgh Pirates and now the St. Louis Cardinals.

"It's hard to narrow down the things I like about this job," Langosch says. "The fact that I get to do so many different types of writing appeals to me. Writing a game story is quite different from writing an in-depth feature story, which is quite different from writing a hard news article. On a weekly basis, I typically have to do all of these."

Langosch urges journalists in training to immerse themselves in all forms of the craft: "Even if you're a writer, learn how to use a camera and camcorder. Find a way to allow social networking to help you better reach out and interact with readers."

What Langosch found when she entered the job market was that newspaper sportswriting jobs were tough to find. But she also quickly learned that emerging media outlets on the web and elsewhere presented a host of new possibilities.

Working at MLB.com allowed her to combine her passion for writing with newly learned skills in audio and video editing. In her first few years with the company, she found herself covering baseball's All-Star Game as well as the World Series.

"Working at an online company has put me in a position to better weather the storm that the journalism industry finds itself in right now," she says.

As Langosch learned, the good news is that for graduates who can write, edit or design, there is no shortage of job possibilities in journalism. Today, journalism jobs are found in a wide range of organizations, many of which did not exist 20 years ago, like those discussed in the beginning of the chapter.

For every newspaper job that was lost in the last decade, another has been created in another sector of the industry. Yes, it's tougher than ever to find a job as a sportswriter at a daily newspaper. Instead, as Langosch did, try MLB.com, the site of Major League Baseball, which has hired writers in every city where a team is located.

Can't get a job at *Time* magazine? Try landing one at the magazine published for the employees of one of your local companies. There are literally thousands of such publications.

Are local television reporting jobs tough to find? Try one of the many cable networks that did not exist 20 years ago. Or try any website. Video and audio editing skills are in demand at websites of all sorts — news as well as non-news sites.

More and more competitors are entering the news industry, and they are hiring journalists to staff their operations. In particular, they are hiring young journalists who grew up feeling comfortable with computers, social media and the web. There is more demand than ever for news and journalism. There are also more competitors. There was no BuzzFeed or Facebook or HuffPost 20 years ago. New digital channels offer consumers a dazzling array of options, all of which compete for time and attention.

There also are thousands of niche websites, some that are designed to appeal to users with common interests. Passionate college football fans, for example, can follow their teams' recruiting on sites like Rivals.com, 247sports.com and ESPN.com. Then there are the magazine-like sites that have no print equivalent, including Slate.com. All of these offer jobs to young journalists.

And yes, there are still thousands of jobs to be had at legacy media companies, even at newspapers. More than 1,200 daily newspapers employ thousands of journalists, beginners among them. Local television is here to stay, and nobody can count just how many magazines are out there. They're found in almost every city of any size and are published by national media organizations and also by governments, companies, nonprofits and others. Young people right out of school who are armed with knowledge of the web and mobile communication are prime candidates for all those jobs.

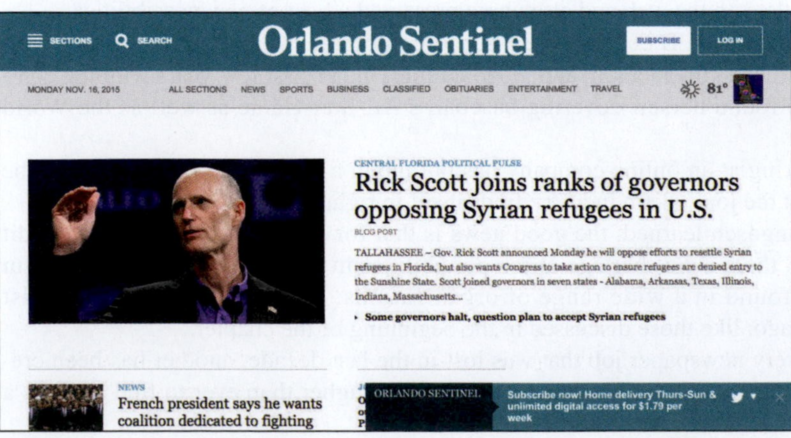
SECTIONS SEARCH Orlando Sentinel SUBSCRIBE LOG IN

MONDAY NOV. 16, 2015 ALL SECTIONS NEWS SPORTS BUSINESS CLASSIFIED OBITUARIES ENTERTAINMENT TRAVEL 81°

CENTRAL FLORIDA POLITICAL PULSE

Rick Scott joins ranks of governors opposing Syrian refugees in U.S.

BLOG POST

TALLAHASSEE – Gov. Rick Scott announced Monday he will oppose efforts to resettle Syrian refugees in Florida, but also wants Congress to take action to ensure refugees are denied entry to the Sunshine State. Scott joined governors in seven states - Alabama, Arkansas, Texas, Illinois, Indiana, Massachusetts...

- **Some governors halt, question plan to accept Syrian refugees**

NEWS

French president says he wants coalition dedicated to fighting

ORLANDO SENTINEL

Subscribe now! Home delivery Thurs-Sun & unlimited digital access for $1.79 per week

The Orlando Sentinel *is among the large-market print newspapers still doing well, yet its online version is steadily growing.*

The changing media environment poses a challenge to journalism schools and departments and to their students. No longer is it adequate for students to focus tightly on preparation for becoming a newspaper reporter, a magazine designer or a print photojournalist. Today, all those jobs — indeed, all jobs in journalism — also require the following:

- A thorough working knowledge of the web as both a source of information and as a platform for extending your company's reach.
- A knowledge of the differences between web and print content.
- Video skills, both shooting and editing.
- Audio skills, both capturing audio and editing it.
- Familiarity with mobile devices and the ways that the public uses them.
- An understanding of audiences and the ways that you can connect with them.
- Basic familiarity with web analytics and other means of determining what users are consuming and how they are doing so.

Seek out opportunities on or off campus to develop these skills. Your school's student newspaper, alumni magazine or other college publications are always looking for help. Campus websites or radio and television stations also can provide good experience to hone these skills. The good news is that students who possess these skills will have no trouble finding jobs.

Many of those jobs are vastly different from those of 20 years ago. They sometimes have different names:

- **Digital producer:** One responsible for creating the content of a website.
- **Digital designer:** One responsible for the design of a website.
- **Analytics specialist:** One who analyzes users of a website.
- **Audience development specialist:** One who finds ways to expand the audience of a website or mobile services.
- **Engagement editor:** One responsible for coordinating efforts of a media outlet to connect with the public.

Dozens of similar titles simply did not exist in newsrooms 20 years ago.

The changes extend to related fields, too. Many schools and departments of journalism have majors in **strategic communication**, a combination of advertising and public relations that increasingly is in demand. These majors need many of the same skills today that journalists need — the ability to write and edit, the ability to produce websites, the ability to understand and analyze audiences, and the ability to edit audio and video. Why? Because even in advertising agencies, graduates find themselves working for clients who need them to produce news articles, audio, video and websites targeted to specific audiences.

Multimedia Requirements for Today's Journalists

- Know how to use the internet as an information source.
- Understand how the internet can benefit your organization.
- Understand how online, mobile and print content differ.
- Know how to shoot and edit video.
- Know how to capture and edit audio.
- Be familiar with mobile devices and the ways that the public uses them.
- Understand how to connect with audiences.
- Have a basic familiarity with analytics.

These requirements have forced schools and departments of journalism to buy large amounts of audio and video equipment to provide practical training for all students in audio and video editing. The changes in the media industry also have necessitated a complete revision of journalism curricula. For the student new to a job, at a minimum the skillset needed almost invariably encompasses writing for print, writing for the web and mobile, audio and video editing, and basic web production.

Newspapers may show signs of continuing their decline, but journalism as a whole does not. Indeed, it is an essential ingredient in our information age society. Young people who can produce news and other types of information in this environment will continue to be in demand at companies of all sorts. For journalism, if not for some newspapers, the future is bright.

CHAPTER RESOURCES

SUGGESTED READINGS

Barclay, Donald A. *Fake News, Propaganda, and Plain Old Lies: How to Find Trustworthy Information in the Digital Age.* Lanham, Md.: Roman and Littlefield, 2018. This book gives guidance on how to determine whether news is trustworthy.

Bartlett, Bruce. *The Truth Matters: A Citizen's Guide to Separating Facts from Lies and Stopping Fake News in Its Tracks.* New York: Ten Speed Press, 2017. More on separating fact from fiction in the news.

Briggs, Mark. *Journalism Next: A Practical Guide to Digital Reporting and Publishing.* Thousand Oaks, Calif.: Sage, 2015. This is a good reference for publishing online.

Brock, George. *Out of Print: Newspapers, Journalism and the Business of News in the Digital Age.* Philadelphia: Kogan Page, 2013. An excellent treatise on the status of the newspaper business and the ways technology has changed it.

Chaney, Paul. *The Digital Handshake: Seven Proven Strategies to Grow Your Business Using Social Media.* Hoboken, N.J.: John Wiley, 2009. This excellent book discusses the importance of social media in spreading the word about new websites.

Jones, Alex S. *Losing the News: The Future of the News That Feeds Democracy.* New York: Oxford Univ. Press, 2009. This is a superb review of why legacy media are so critical to democracy.

Marsden, Paul. *Entrepreneurial Journalism: How to Go It Alone and Launch Your Dream Digital Project.* New York: Routledge, 2017. Anyone can become a publisher, and this book describes how to do it.

Meyer, Philip. *The Vanishing Newspaper: Saving Journalism in the Information Age.* 2nd ed. Columbia: Univ. of Missouri Press, 2009. In this excellent book, Meyer discusses the importance of newspapers in the news-gathering process.

Wollan, Robert, Nick Smith and Catherine Zhou. *The Social Media Management Handbook: Everything You Need to Know to Get Social Media Working in Your Business.* Hoboken, N.J.: John Wiley, 2011. This is a good primer on incorporating social media into a business model.

SUGGESTED WEBSITES

LaunchPad Solo
launchpadworks.com
When you visit LaunchPad Solo for Journalism, you will find research links, exercises and LearningCurve adaptive quizzing to help you improve your grammar and AP style usage. In addition, the site's video collection hosts the videos highlighted in this and other chapters as well as additional clips of leading professionals discussing important media trends.

www.huffingtonpost.com
HuffPost is one of the premier news sites on the web. It was founded with venture capital and designed to be free of the weight of legacy media. It is now owned by AOL.

https://inn.org/
The Institute for Nonprofit News is a trade organization for news sites that operate in the public without expectation of financial gain. Most of its members seek merely to break even.

www.journalists.org
The Online News Association was organized in 1999.

www.magazine.org
The Association of Magazine Media is the professional organization for magazine journalists.

www.nab.org
The National Association of Broadcasters is the primary trade organization of the broadcast industry.

www.newsmediaalliance.org
The News Media Alliance accepts members in all areas of news content.

www.people-press.org
The Pew Research Center for U.S. Politics & Policy is an excellent source that tracks the changing attitudes of the American people toward the press. Pew's research can be found here.

www.politico.com
Politico is an excellent example of a new politically oriented media site that is supported by advertising. It has a companion newspaper that is traditional in nature.

www.propublica.org
This excellent foundation-supported site brings together some of the nation's top journalists to pursue investigative reporting.

www.rtdna.org
The Radio Television Digital News Association, a leading trade group for broadcast journalists, tracks trends in that field.

EXERCISES

1. Interview two college students to determine their top three sources of news. Then do the same with two people age 40 or older. Write a one-page report on the differences that you found in media consumption patterns.

2. Go to www.politico.com. Choose a political story from that site, and contrast how the same story is covered on www.washingtonpost.com.

3. Research two legacy media companies — one that is primarily print-oriented and one that is broadcast-oriented. Using publicly available reports, describe any differences you find in the commitment of those companies to online news.

4. Set up a Twitter account if you don't already have one. Choose at least three news sites to follow on Twitter. Analyze the tweets that you receive over a three-day period. How similar (and different) are the tweets and links from the different sites? If Twitter were your main source of news, how well-informed would you be?

5. Search online to find five job openings that might appeal to you after you become a professional journalist or a strategic communication professional. Based on the descriptions of those jobs, list the skills that you would need to land each of the five.

6. **Your journalism blog.** Find a blog or website that tries to cover local news with intensity. Interview the editor about the nature of the site. Does it make money? Does he or she care? Why? Post your findings on your own journalism blog and invite comments from your classmates.

CHAPTER 3 GATHERING AND VERIFYING INFORMATION

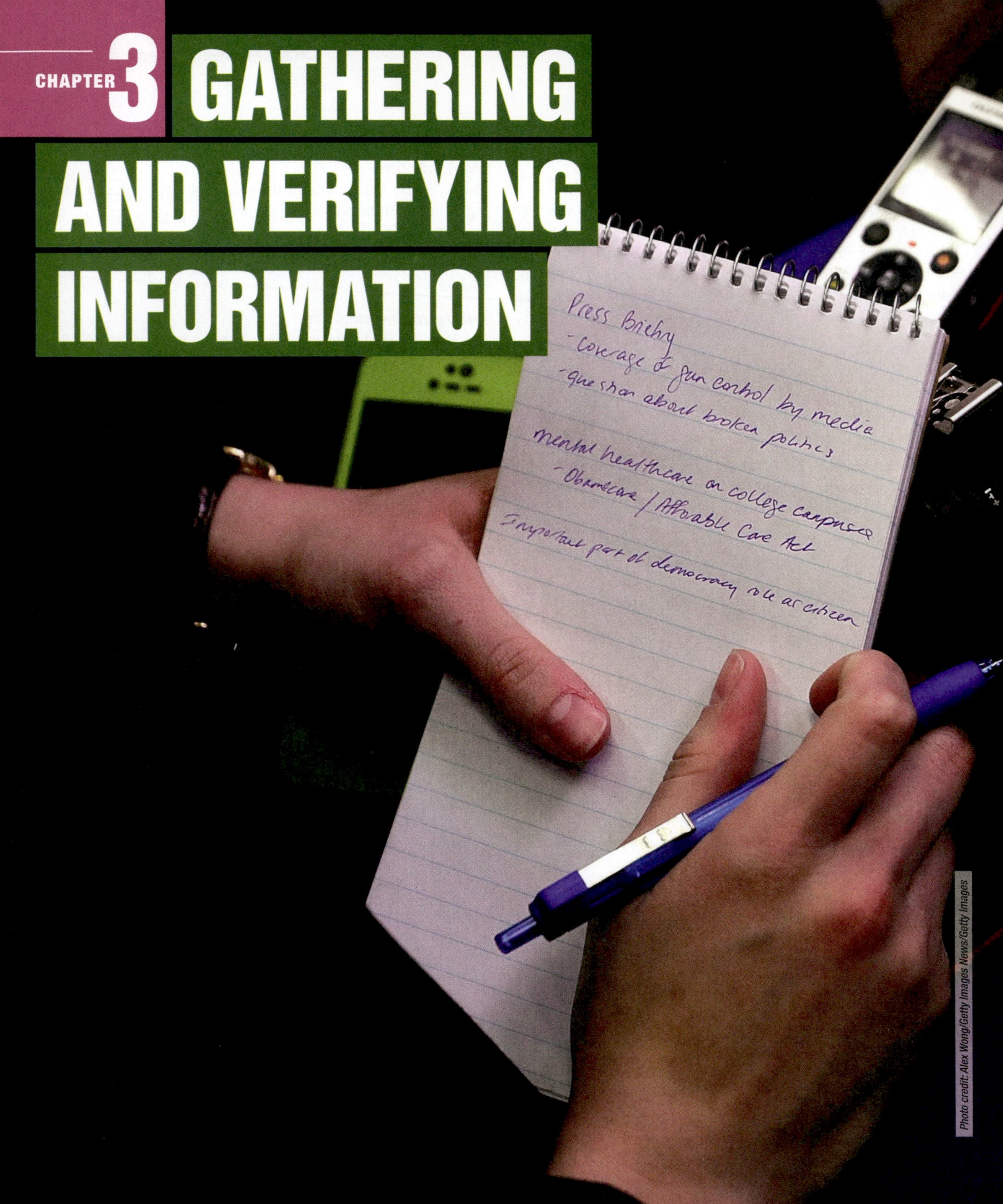

Photo credit: Alex Wong/Getty Images News/Getty Images

For the people of Raqqa, Syria, life under ISIS control was more inhumane than the almost 30 years of abuses under former President Hafez al-Assad's regime and the almost 20 years under current President Bashar al-Assad. When the terrorist organization took control of Raqqa in early 2014, it almost immediately began closing Christian churches and Shia mosques. A public execution followed, and the group began committing countless human rights violations. ISIS also hunted down protestors.

Those resisting ISIS control soon started "Raqqa Is Being Slaughtered Silently," a social media network designed to inform the world of what was happening in the city that ISIS had chosen as the capital of its caliphate. The situation soon became intolerable and sometimes deadly for those who dared to protest and report the news through RBSS. Many citizen journalists were imprisoned or slaughtered. Others escaped to Turkey. Some eventually made their way to Germany and finally the U.S.

One of those who reached New York, Abdalaziz Alhamza, was a leader of the group and continued to work with RBSS journalists who were still in the country. Finally, intense air strikes by U.S. and allied warplanes reduced 90 percent of the city to rubble and ended the ISIS occupation in October 2017.

"This is a liberation in the media. Not in Raqqa," Alhamza told David Remnick of *The New Yorker*. Alhamza and everyone he knew had lost relatives or friends—some as a result of ISIS atrocities, some as a result of the bombing. There was no euphoria.

Even today, much of what the outside world knows about Raqqa is a result of the reporting done by RBSS. Neither the Assad regime nor ISIS wanted mainstream media reporters to report on the atrocities committed there. Citizen journalists filled the gap courageously.

Raqqa still is not a safe place to go, and there's little left standing if you manage to get there. It wasn't always that way.

"Life in Raqqa before the war was as normal as any city in the world," Alhamza told Remnick. "We had schools, universities, parks, bars and cafes."

That's the Raqqa indelibly etched in the mind of Lamis Aljasem, a Syrian exile now studying in Paris. She took with her an amazing collection of videos and photos of Raqqa, her hometown. Now she's sharing those on social media so the world does not forget what once was. Most of the sites she photographed, including her own home, are now nothing but rubble.

Persistent social media coverage of a difficult-to-reach crisis area by people like Alhamza and Aljasem plays an important role in reporting the news of today. It's a development that most journalists welcome. It's particularly important in places like Syria, where war and unfriendly combatants make it almost impossible for mainstream journalists to go.

Fortunately, not all the news is this difficult or dangerous to report. And although social media are useful and often report the news first, they depend almost solely on personal observation. Professional journalists must do much

In this chapter, you will learn:

1 How to ensure accuracy in information gathering through the disciplines of multiple sources and verification.

2 How to find and evaluate information from online sources.

3 How to use traditional sources of information to check facts.

more. They must sort through a mass of information from various sources, verify it and make sense of an event or issue. It's their job to separate fact from fiction, the good information from the bad. Call this "curating" if you wish. Most journalists simply call it good journalism.

In this chapter, we'll explore the process of not only finding information on the web, on social media and elsewhere but also getting it right.

Accurate Information: The Basis of a Good Story

Ask any editor whether a reporter can be a good writer without being good at information gathering, and you're likely to hear a resounding "No!" That's because good writing depends on good reporting. To be thorough and accurate, journalists employ two main techniques—the discipline of multiple sources and the discipline of verification.

The Discipline of Multiple Sources

Good writing is important, as we explore in other chapters, but the quality of writing depends in large part on good fact gathering. It's impossible to write a great story without first doing a great job of reporting. Gathering information requires skilled interviewing, as we'll discuss in Chapter 4. It also requires knowing how to use the many sources of information readily available—and there are hundreds of places to find information.

Good reporters know that the worst kind of news story is one with a single source. Rarely is such a story worth publishing. Even a personality profile should be based on more than just an interview with the subject. To get a fuller perspective, the journalist also needs to talk with individuals who know the subject. Gathering information from several sources is one of the keys to good writing and good communication. It's also the best way to ensure accuracy. When several sources are used, information is more likely to be verified. Checking additional sources improves the chances that a story will be accurate.

Imagine how many sources the reporters for the *Milwaukee Journal Sentinel* used in their award-winning series about how the federal government allowed chemical manufacturers to influence the approval of potentially harmful substances in everyday products. Even in the short excerpt from the multipart series that is shown in the annotated model "Integrating Multiple Sources into a Story," it's evident that the reporters used dozens of sources, including peer-reviewed research journals that most reporters seldom touch.

Such reporting requires analyzing thousands of pages of data, poring over online and paper records, interviewing dozens of people, and checking, cross-checking and rechecking. Such reporting is both time-consuming and tedious, but work of this sort is exactly what journalists must do as they act as watchdogs over the actions of government agencies and others. Getting it right is of paramount importance. And as we'll discuss in Chapter 19, this vigilant reporting is what defends news organizations against claims of defamation and libel.

ANNOTATED MODEL Integrating Multiple Sources into a Story

Using summaries, bulleted lists and quotes, the writers integrated research from a range of sources seamlessly into the story.

Chemical Fallout: Bisphenol A Is in You

By Susanne Rust, Cary Spivak and Meg Kissinger
Milwaukee Journal Sentinel

For more than a decade, the federal government and chemical-makers have assured the public that a hormone-mimicking compound found in baby bottles, aluminum cans and hundreds of other household products is safe. But a *Journal Sentinel* investigation found that these promises are based on outdated, incomplete government studies and research heavily funded by the chemical industry.

The lead hints at the many sources the journalists consulted to counter safety claims.

In the first analysis of its kind by a newspaper, the *Journal Sentinel* reviewed 258 scientific studies of the chemical bisphenol A, a compound detected in the urine of 93 percent of Americans recently tested. An overwhelming majority of these studies show that the chemical is harmful—causing breast cancer, testicular cancer, diabetes, hyperactivity, obesity, low sperm counts, miscarriage and a host of other reproductive failures in laboratory animals.

Here the article gets specific about the wide scope of the newspaper's research.

The article summarizes the main findings regarding health hazards.

Studies paid for by the chemical industry are much less likely to find damaging effects or disease.

U.S. regulators so far have sided with industry by minimizing concern about the compound's safety.

Last week, a panel commissioned by the National Toxicology Program released a report finding bisphenol A to be of some concern for fetuses and small children. It found that adults have almost nothing to worry about.

The report outlines the most recent finding of toxicity in the chemical compound.

Its recommendations could be used by the U.S. Environmental Protection Agency and other regulators to assess federal policies on how much bisphenol A is safe and may have huge ramifications for the multibillion-dollar chemical industry.

The story hints at a possible government change of position and its impact on the chemical industry.

The panel said it considered more than 700 studies by university scientists, government researchers and industry-funded chemists. It picked the work it felt was best and threw out the rest.

The *Journal Sentinel* found that panel members gave more weight to industry-funded studies and more leeway to industry-funded researchers.

The newspaper's investigation finds fault with previous claims of safety.

- The panel rejected academic studies that found harm—citing inadequate methods. But the panel accepted industry-funded studies using the same methods that concluded the chemical does not pose risks.

Faulty methodology in government studies is reported.

(continued)

ANNOTATED MODEL Integrating Multiple Sources into a Story *(continued)*

More reliable university research differs with federal conclusions.

• The panel missed dozens of studies publicly available that the *Journal Sentinel* found online using a medical research internet search engine. The studies the panel considered were chosen, in part, by a consultant with links to firms that made bisphenol A.

• The panel accepted a Korean study translated by the chemical industry's trade group that found bisphenol A to be safe. It also accepted two studies that were not subjected to any peer review — the gold standard of scientific credibility. Both studies were funded by General Electric Co., which made bisphenol A until it sold its plastics division earlier this year.

An expert finds fault with the government position.

"This undermines the government's authority," said David Rosner, professor of history and public health at Columbia University. "It makes you think twice about accepting their conclusions."

Panel chairman Robert Chapin, a toxicologist who works for Pfizer Inc., the pharmaceutical giant, defended his group's work.

"We didn't flippin' care who does the study," said Chapin, who worked as a government scientist for 18 years before joining Pfizer.

The chairman of the government panel defends his group's work.

If the studies followed good laboratory practices and were backed with strong data, they were accepted, Chapin said. . . .

The Discipline of Verification

In addition to finding and analyzing multiple sources, journalists need to verify the information that they obtain from those sources. To do this, journalists follow the same investigative system employed by scientists. They develop a hypothesis and then seek facts to support or reject it.

As Philip Meyer of the University of North Carolina suggests to journalists Bill Kovach and Tom Rosenstiel in their classic book *The Elements of Journalism*: "I think (the) connection between journalism and science ought to emphasize objectivity of method. That's what scientific method is — our humanity, our subjective impulses . . . directed toward deciding what to investigate by objective means."

As we've discussed in previous chapters, this concept of objectivity — developed by journalists in the 20th century — was an elusive idea that was often misinterpreted. What objectivity isn't, Kovach and Rosenstiel argue, is blind loyalty to the concepts of fairness and balance, as some amateur journalists might believe. Fairness, they argue, can be misunderstood if it is seen as a goal unto itself. Fairness should mean that a journalist is fair to the facts and to the public's understanding of them. It should not mean, "Am I being fair to my sources, so that none of them will be unhappy?" or "Does my story seem fair?" Those are subjective judgments that lead the journalist away from the task of independent verification.

Similarly, balance should not mean that it's necessary to get an equal number of scientists speaking on each side of the global-warming debate, for example, if an overwhelming number of scientists believe that global warming is a reality.

Kovach and Rosenstiel argue that sharpening the meaning of verification and resisting the temptation to simplify it are essential to improving the credibility of what journalists write. Although citizen journalists may rush to post information quickly on Twitter and Facebook without much regard for accuracy, professional journalists seek to get it right — while also producing news as quickly as possible.

The journalistic process of layered editing helps get facts right. At a good newspaper, magazine, radio or television station, or website, after the reporter writes a story, it may be subjected to extensive review by several editors. Each may find facts to correct or language to clarify in the quest for a story that is as compelling — and accurate — as possible. Thus, as a story flows through the editorial process (Figure 3.1), the goal is to make it as nearly perfect as possible.

Editors talk about the need to look at a story on both the micro and macro levels. *Microediting* is the process of paying attention to detail:

- Are the facts correct?
- Are the names spelled correctly?
- Is the grammar sound?

Macroediting, on the other hand, looks at the big picture:

- Will readers understand this?
- Are there any ambiguities?
- Are there unanswered questions or inconsistencies in the story?
- Does this agree with what I know from previous stories on the subject?

All of this, and much more, goes into the editorial process of verification. In the end, the goal is to get the story right.

As they strive to get it right, journalists use many types of sources, including interviews, source documents and a variety of other sources ranging from the obvious (such as a Google search) to online sites, computer databases and traditional sources (like printed almanacs and encyclopedias). Good reporters make frequent use of all these sources.

launchpadworks.com
WATCH: **"The Objectivity Myth"**

- Is objectivity a myth?
- Why is it in such great demand?
- What effect does the goal of being objective have on journalists?

FIGURE 3.1

Editing and producing a newspaper is a fast-paced and complex process in which editors at different levels review stories. Shown here is a typical copy-flow pattern for a daily news operation.

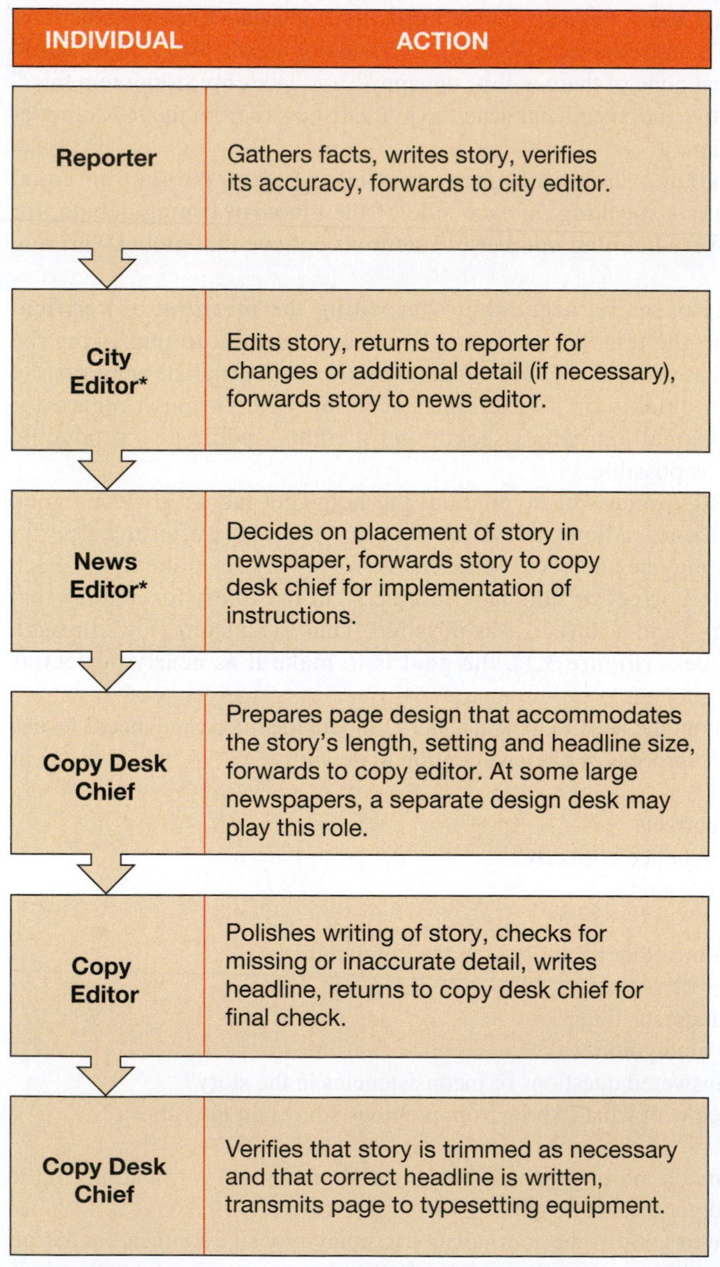

INDIVIDUAL
ACTION
Reporter
Gathers facts, writes story, verifies its accuracy, forwards to city editor.
City Editor*
Edits story, returns to reporter for changes or additional detail (if necessary), forwards story to news editor.
News Editor*
Decides on placement of story in newspaper, forwards story to copy desk chief for implementation of instructions.
Copy Desk Chief
Prepares page design that accommodates the story's length, setting and headline size, forwards to copy editor. At some large newspapers, a separate design desk may play this role.
Copy Editor
Polishes writing of story, checks for missing or inaccurate detail, writes headline, returns to copy desk chief for final check.
Copy Desk Chief
Verifies that story is trimmed as necessary and that correct headline is written, transmits page to typesetting equipment.

* Or assistant

Note: At any point in the process, a story may be returned to an earlier editor for clarification, amplification or rewriting.

Online Sources of Information

Reporters and editors today have a wealth of information available at their fingertips. From the news library in your local office to national databases of published newspaper, magazine, radio and television stories, the amount of online information is staggering. Primary sources of online information include the following:

- **The news archive, or morgue,** maintained digitally by your own publication, radio or television station or website. When you're hired, one of the first things you must do is learn to use your organization's archive. The background material you find there will help you provide context for the stories you cover. You may even link to some of these stories within your article, if appropriate.
- **Search engines** (such as Google, Bing, Yahoo, Dogpile, DuckDuckGo and others). Anyone can use Google, right? Well, learning to use search engines wisely is important to a journalist. Some of the tools that we use to search the web have as their main purpose selling advertising. Page-rank algorithms and filters that personalize search results can yield misleading material. In Google, Bing and Yahoo, for example, search results are ranked based not on quality but on several factors related to audience targeting. These three search engines filter information and rank their results accordingly. One of the other search engines, DuckDuckGo, does not filter or personalize results.
- **Wikipedia.** The online encyclopedia's content at its best is well-documented with footnotes showing where the information originated. Wikipedia is especially valuable for gaining an overview of a topic. But because anyone can post a change to an article there, be careful before using material from it. It's good practice to verify Wikipedia information with another source.
- **News sites, social media and content aggregators** (such as USAToday.com, NYTimes.com, msnbc.com, CNN.com, Yahoo News, Google News and others).
- **Other sites on the web.** Millions of organizations maintain websites with useful information. Learning to evaluate their accuracy is important, and later in this chapter we'll give some tips to assist you in doing that.
- **Mobile apps.** News apps are available for *The New York Times*, the Associated Press, NPR, CNN, Reuters and Newsy as well as for most other prominent media outlets.
- **Commercial database services** (such as Factiva, LexisNexis, NewsBank, ProQuest and others).
- **Government databases** (city, county, state and federal).
- **Special-interest databases** (those created by organizations with a cause).
- **Custom databases and spreadsheets.**

Let's explore the usefulness of some of these.

News Archives: The Place to Start

Digital archives are a marvel that good reporters and editors cherish. Before they were available, doing research for a story was a laborious process that involved trips to the newspaper, magazine or television station library to sift through hundreds or even thousands of tattered, yellowed clippings, old scripts, videotape or even microfilm or microfiche. Too often, clippings and scripts disappeared, were misfiled or were misplaced, which made such research a hit-or-miss proposition. Despite those shortcomings, the library was considered a valuable asset. Reporters were routinely admonished to check there first.

Ten Sources of Story Ideas

- Other people
- Other publications
- News releases
- A social services directory
- Government reports
- Stories in your own newspaper
- Advertisements
- Wire copy
- Local news briefs
- You

You still hear that advice in newsrooms today, but most of today's news libraries are online or are in the process of being digitized. This almost ensures that an item will not disappear and will be easy to locate. Typically, you can do a check of the archive from your own computer, sometimes even from a remote location. This makes it easier than ever to do good background work on a story. Your ability to search online databases is limited only by your skill with search techniques and your access to the databases you need.

Digital news archives are full-text databases. All words in the database have been indexed and are searchable. Such capability gives you great flexibility in structuring searches using Boolean search commands. Boolean operators such as AND, OR and NOT allow you to structure a search to find the material most closely related to the subject being researched. For example, if you are interested in finding articles in Factiva, a Dow Jones database, on German Chancellor Angela Merkel's visits to the U.S., you might issue this command on the search line:

Merkel AND U.S.

This search command pulls all articles in which both "Merkel" and "U.S." appear, generating almost 30,000 hits. That's too many, though, so you need to narrow your search. Try this:

Merkel SAME U.S.

This search generates more than 6,000 articles in which both terms appear in the same paragraph. You can then narrow further:

Merkel w/3 U.S.

This command asks for the Merkel-U.S. combination that occurs within three words of one another. This yields more than 300 articles, which is closer to a manageable number. The next step is to narrow by date, region or source to find what you really need.

There are limitations. Some digital archives do not allow you to see photos or articles as they appeared in the newspaper or magazine. PressReader.com, however, provides PDF files of thousands of newspapers from about 100 countries. (A **PDF file** preserves the formatting of the original document.) Some radio and television stations, including NPR and PBS, have podcasts or vodcasts—downloadable audio or video files — stored on their websites. Factiva also contains audio and video interviews and news clips along with transcripts.

Search Engines and Wikipedia

Google is the first stop for many journalists. Indeed, Google and other search engines (such as Yahoo, Bing, Dogpile and DuckDuckGo) can be helpful journalistic tools. The key to using them successfully is recognizing whether the information contained on the website that the search takes you to is accurate and therefore usable.

Journalists also need to be aware that many search engines (like Google, Yahoo and Bing) filter information, personalizing it based on information that they have gathered about the user's previous searches and online purchase history. Good journalists supplement these well-known search engines with others that do not filter, like DuckDuckGo.

Information from well-known sites may be reliable, but information from websites advocating a cause may not be. If you're visiting such a site, be sure to review the "About" page to learn the mission or history of the organization so that you can properly evaluate the information you find there.

Additionally, be wary of Wikipedia, a user-written and user-edited social encyclopedia. Although much of the information on Wikipedia is excellent, anyone can publish erroneous information on it. Errors or misrepresentations are usually corrected quickly by others, but beware of depending on information from only that source. We discuss how to evaluate such information later in this chapter.

BoClips

launchpadworks.com

WATCH: **"A New Generation of War Crimes Investigators Turn to High-Tech Methods"**

- How do new advances in technology enhance journalists' ability to gather and verify information?
- What new types of information can they access?
- How else might journalists use these technologies to their benefit?

News Sites, Social Media and Content Aggregators

Some might consider it strange to think that news websites, social media and content aggregators can be useful sources of information for reporters. Don't tell that to the reporters who use them. Such sites are accessible to anyone with a computer and an internet connection. News sites are those published by established media outlets such as *The New York Times*, *The Wall Street Journal* and CNN.

Although mainstream media offer blogs, those found on blog sites such as Google's Blogger or WordPress are usually classified as social media. In part, they are different because their writers answer only to themselves, not to editors. Social media also include Twitter, Instagram, Facebook, Snapchat and other "friending" sites. Twitter has become so important to journalists that it now has its own journalism and news manager. Many journalists now "tweet their beat." They tweet events live and seek to increase followers for their company's website. Twitter is just one of the social media tools that journalists use to increase engagement with their audience.

Not only do journalists often learn about breaking news (such as airplane crashes, fires and shootings) from tweets, but they also communicate with readers through social media. They post links to their stories on Facebook, and they ask Twitter readers to suggest story ideas and sources.

The most popular content aggregators include Yahoo News, Google News, Feedly, Flipboard and Newsy. These aggregators summarize stories and link to the originating media for the full report. Newsy does so with the additional benefit of video.

Commercial Database Services

Commercial databases make it easy to see what has been written about a subject in other newspapers and magazines. But there are potential problems with using excerpts from those stories:

- **Copyright laws must be obeyed.** Take care not to use too much material without obtaining permission. Courts have ruled that small amounts of text can be incorporated into your story under *fair-use* provisions, but exactly what constitutes a small amount is not clear. As a result, be cautious, and credit anything you use to its source.
- **Not all articles that appeared in a newspaper can be found in a database.** Wire-service and market reports, death notices, box scores, social announcements and items written by freelancers often are excluded.
- **Publication doesn't ensure accuracy.** History is littered with incidents of newspapers quoting each other's inaccuracies.
- **The reporter might not be credible.** The reporter who wrote the story may not have any real knowledge of the subject matter. Using information from that reporter may introduce an inaccuracy into your story.
- **Databases aren't infallible.** The information is entered by humans, who are susceptible to mistakes. Also, databases are occasionally doctored in an attempt to prove a position or promote a cause.

On many topics, searching your own digital archive will not be sufficient. If U.S. Rep. Steve Cohen is making his first appearance in your community, your archive probably won't help; little will have been written about him in your city. It probably will be much more useful to search the web or commercial databases for articles published both in Tennessee, where he resides, and nationally. This research will arm you with questions to ask about recent events. In such situations, the national commercial databases are invaluable.

The three leading commercial database services are Factiva (see Figure 3.2), NewsBank and ProQuest Newsstand, all of which provide full-text access. If your employer does not subscribe to any of these, see if your local library does. While you are a student, you have access to many databases through your school's library.

Government Databases

For years, government agencies have maintained large databases of information as a means of managing the public's business. These databases cover almost every conceivable service that government offers, from airplane registration and maintenance records to census data to local court records. They are maintained by the federal and state governments and also by the smallest city and county agencies.

Today, any reporter with a computer and training can find stories in numbers. Among those taking advantage of them is Penny Loeb, who now writes books after

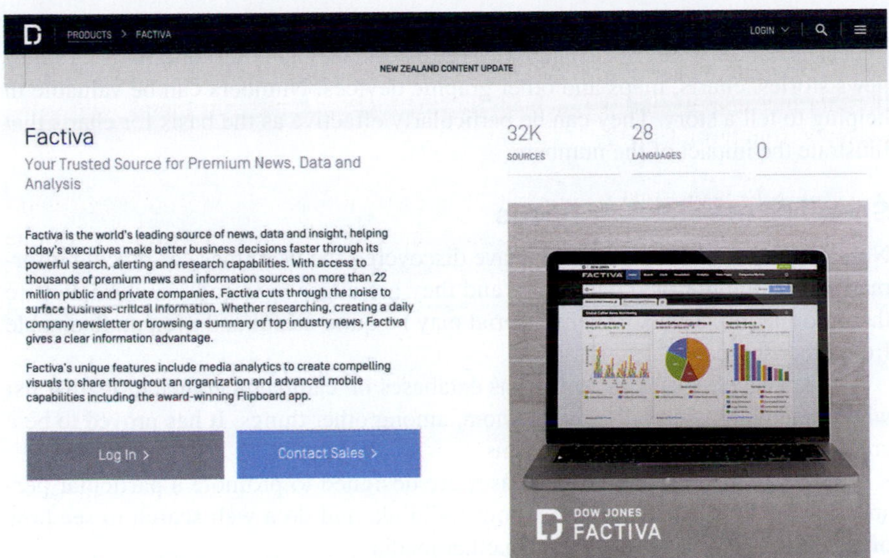

FIGURE 3.2

Factiva is owned by Dow Jones & Co., the parent company of *The Wall Street Journal*, and allows subscribers to perform in-depth research on "more than 35,000 global news and information sources from 200 countries in 28 languages," according to www.dowjones.com.

a 30-year reporting career. When she worked for *New York Newsday*, she used a computer analysis of tax and property records to reveal an astounding story: New York City owed $275 million to taxpayers as a result of overpayments on real estate, water and sewer taxes. To get that story, Loeb had to analyze millions of computer records. Doing that by hand would have consumed many lifetimes, but with the assistance of a computer, she accomplished the task in a matter of weeks. Still, Loeb cautions against expecting instant stories.

Analyses of this type usually are done with relational database programs. **Relational database programs**, unlike simpler **flat-file databases**, permit you to compare one set of data to another. A classic example would be to compare a database of a state's licensed school-bus drivers to another database of the state's drunken-driving convictions. The result would be a list of school-bus drivers who had been found guilty of such offenses.

After the introduction of this technology, investigative reporters were among the first to use it, but reporters can use database programs in their day-to-day work just as easily. For example, you might want to analyze federal records on airplane maintenance to produce a story on the safety record of a particular airline. If the records are maintained in an easily accessible format, the next time that an airplane crashes it will be possible to call up the complete maintenance record of the aircraft merely by entering its registration number. Such information can be extremely useful, even in a deadline situation.

Another common use of computers has been to compare bank records on home mortgages to census data. By tracking how many mortgages are issued to homeowners in predominantly black or Hispanic areas, reporters have been able to document the practice of *redlining*, through which banks make it difficult or impossible for minorities to obtain loans.

Again, such records are useful even after the investigation is complete. Access to census data, bank records and other forms of data can be used daily to produce news stories, charts, maps and other graphic devices. Numbers can be valuable in helping to tell a story. They can be particularly effective as the basis for charts that illustrate the impact of the numbers.

Special-interest Databases

Numerous special-interest groups have discovered the usefulness of placing information in computerized databases, and they are eager to introduce journalists to that information. Some of their material may be quite useful and even unobtainable from other sources.

For instance, OpenSecrets.org has databases on campaign contributors that list who is spending what to lobby to whom, among other things. It has proved to be a credible source for news organizations.

But other special-interest databases are designed to promote a particular perspective on a topic. Check the "About Us" link, and do a web search to see how often the group's material appears in other media.

Custom Databases

Journalists Tracy Weber, Charles Ornstein and Maloy Moore had reason to believe that the California Board of Registered Nursing was failing in its duty to ensure that nurses are competent, sober and law-abiding. To find out for sure, they had to build their own analysis tool.

Using a database manager, they entered and analyzed all the accusations that were filed and all the disciplinary actions that the board took over a six-year period. The printouts involved more than 2,000 nurses.

The team, representing the online news organization ProPublica and the *Los Angeles Times*, described the task as an enormous amount of work. But in the end, the database enabled the reporters to flag the best cases to use as examples and also to highlight a number of weaknesses in the board's oversight. Among the problems they uncovered were nurses who were involved in multiple disciplinary cases and those with multiple criminal convictions.

The project had an immediate impact. The day after their first story appeared, California's governor replaced a majority of the nursing board's members. A day later, the board's longtime executive director resigned.

Evaluating Digital News Sources

Journalists must differentiate carefully between fact and fiction on the web. Lately, journalists have assumed the task of curating citizen contributions, particularly when citizens are the first to break the news. When two bombs exploded at the Boston Marathon on April 15, 2013, the first reports came on Twitter from people who were at the scene. It took another 10 minutes before CNN and NPR reported the blasts. The Associated Press and other cable news networks were next.

This shows just how important Twitter has become in breaking news stories, but it's important for journalists to verify such information before sending it out to the world. In Twitter Best Practices, produced by Twitter itself, Jennifer Preston, a writer for The Lede blog at *The New York Times*, suggested a cautious approach:

> **I consider most posts on Twitter a "tip," not a fact. We seek to apply the same good judgment and reporting practices to information on Twitter as we would anywhere else. It's not difficult to find official sources and/or whether user-generated content has been actually produced by an eyewitness.**

Evaluating digital media sources is not a guessing game. You won't always be correct in your assessment of a report's credibility, but you can dramatically improve your chances.

Journalists have developed methods of gathering and editing news that help ensure accuracy, although they don't guarantee it. Those methods are described in several other chapters in this book. The web presents its own problems and solutions. How do you differentiate between a credible website and one that has a hidden agenda? Wikipedia is more popular than reputable print encyclopedias, but is it as credible? How do you know if a tweet or a Facebook posting is true? The answer lies in the discipline of verification.

A traditional method of verification relies on the journalistic process of layered editing. At most print and digital news media, after the reporter writes a story, it is subject to extensive review by one or more editors. Each may find reporting inadequacies, such as facts to correct or language to clarify. Individual bloggers and those who post on social media outlets aren't edited. That's why curating and editing news posted on social media have become important new functions in newsrooms.

The web is a great resource for reporters, but determining the credibility of online information can be problematic. If the source is a respected media organization such as *The New York Times* or *The Washington Post*, the information is probably solid. But if the information was published by an organization promoting a cause, there is ample reason to be wary.

Stan Ketterer, a journalist and journalism professor at Oklahoma State University, tells reporters to evaluate information on the web by following the same standard journalistic practices they would use for assessing the credibility and accuracy of any other type of information:

- **Before using information from a website in a story, verify it with a source.** There are exceptions to this rule, including taking information from a highly credible government site like the U.S. Census Bureau. Sometimes you can't contact the source on a breaking story because of time constraints. An editor must clear all exceptions.

Authoritative Websites

- www.factcheck.org
- www.infoplease.com
- www.people-press.org
- www.politifact.com
- www.snopes.com
- www.usa.gov
- www.webmd.com

- **In most cases, information taken directly from the web and used in a story must be attributed.** If you have verified the information on a website with a source, you can use the organization in the attribution, for example, "According to the EPA" or "EPA figures show." If you cannot verify the information after trying repeatedly, attribute unverified information to the website—for example, "According to the Voice of America website." Consult your editor before using unverified information.
- **If you have doubts about the accuracy of the information and you cannot reach the source, get it from another source, such as a book or another person.** When in doubt, omit the information.
- **Check the extension on the site's web address to get clues as to the nature of the organization and the likely slant of the information.** The most common extensions used in the U.S. are *.gov* (government), *.edu* (education), *.com* (commercial), *.mil* (military), *.org* (not-for-profit organization) and *.net* (internet administration). Most government and military sites have credible and accurate information. In many cases, you can take the information directly from the site and attribute it to the organization. But consult your editor until you get to know these sites.
- **Treat the sites of colleges and universities as you would other sites.** If college and university sites have source documents, such as the U.S. Constitution, attribute the information to the source document. But beware. Personal homepages can have .edu extensions, and the information on them is not always credible.
- **In almost all cases, do not use information directly from the websites of commercial and not-for-profit organizations without verification.**
- **Check the date when the site was last updated.** The date generally appears at the top or bottom of the first page of the site. Although a recent date does not ensure that the information is current, it does indicate that the organization is paying close attention to the site. If no date appears, if the site has not been updated for a while or if it was created some time ago, do not use the information unless you verify it with a source.
- **Check to see whether the website is what it appears to be.** The www.martinlutherking.org website was registered in 1999, but if you search its domain registration (whois.net), you'll find it is registered to a white supremacy organization, not the King family. The site ranks high in search results based on its longevity on the web, its domain name (which includes Martin Luther King's name) and external links to the site. It has not been endorsed by the King family, and in fact, family members have tried many times to have the site removed. However, the domain was registered legitimately, and copyright doesn't protect website domain names. This is an excellent example of poor-quality or fraudulent sites ranking high in search results.

ON THE JOB Use All Available Tools

Courtesy of Laken McDonald

Right after graduation, **Eric Dundon** decided to jump at the chance to become a top-ranking editor at a small newspaper rather than becoming a reporter at a large one. He's enjoying his experience as managing editor of the *Hannibal (Mo.) Courier-Post.*

At the local level, he says, engagement with the community can often lead to stories. "Key in to social media—particularly Facebook and Twitter—to discover possible issues that pose problems to people in the community," Dundon says. "These tools are particularly beneficial because ideas found here can often impact a wide circle of people and elicit strong feedback. Participation in and knowledge of social, civic and charity organizations can also provide an endless array of story ideas."

But whether you're working at a large paper or a small one, Dundon says, verification of information is essential.

> In a small-town environment, a boots-on-the-ground mentality is the strongest way to effectively verify information. The community is your newsroom. Don't assume that all information can be verified from behind a reporter's desk. A reporter must rely on the power of observation, which means seeing a situation in person, talking to a witness or neighbor at the scene, or going to the site of an event. Writing will improve from having firsthand experiences.

Dundon believes that some of the most underused tools for a journalist in a small-town setting are Sunshine Laws, or open meetings and records laws:

> Because municipalities with smaller populations generally have fewer media outlets to serve as a watchdog, the Sunshine Law can illuminate and verify information like few other tools. The Sunshine Law, in brief, allows anyone to request public documents from government agencies or sit in on a public meeting.

Already in his career, Dundon has used Sunshine Law requests to get the following:

- Emails between county commissioners discussing a highly controversial construction project.
- Full police reports detailing an officer-involved shooting.
- Closed-session minutes from a school board meeting where a well-liked principal was placed on leave.

"Knowing and using your state's Sunshine Law can help you get information that will best serve and inform the public," Dundon says.

Traditional Sources of Information

Accessing information through computerized sources is quick and easy, but more traditional reference sources also are valuable. In some cases, the sources listed in this section cannot be found on computers.

The Traditional Newsroom Library

Every working reporter gets this advice from an editor early in his or her career: Check the morgue. The morgue, or newsroom library, is often more than a digital archive. At most publications and some broadcast stations, it's also a physical place with a real librarian. We list it here because many such libraries house bound volumes of old printed editions and clippings of news stories that predate

What's the grammar error in this sentence?

Donald Trump the real estate magnate says he hopes to become "the greatest jobs president that God ever created."

See Appendix 1, Rule 4.

the publication's digital archive. The digital archive is usually the first stop for a reporter on any kind of assignment, but the traditional library also may be of great help, particularly when a reporter needs to understand the historical background of a story.

Covering a speech? Look up background information on the speaker. Covering a sports event? What are the teams' records? Who are the coaches? What's the history of the rivalry? Reporters answer questions like these, and many others, by checking both the digital and analog sources in the library.

One other note on the print or broadcast archive: Here you can find photos of a speaker or coach you haven't met. You'll also find historic photos. A contemporary photo might help you recognize that person for a possible one-on-one interview before the speech or game begins. An old photo may show readers a sports hero who set a record decades ago.

Other Traditional Sources

Traditional sources of information — such as reference books, dictionaries and encyclopedias — still play an important role in the production of the daily news product. Good reporters and editors make a habit of checking every verifiable fact. Here is a list of commonly used references. An increasing number of these are now available online, as noted below, but some are still available only in print form.

- **City directories.** You can find these directories, not to be confused with telephone books, in many cities. They provide the same information as a telephone book but also may include information on the occupations of citizens and the owners or managers of businesses. Useful street indexes provide information on the names of neighbors. City directories usually are found in print form only. However, most public libraries have access to Reference USA, a database of business and residential information, which includes phone numbers, addresses and demographic information. Because much government information is now online, one of the best ways to locate people is through their property tax assessment records. Each county has a database that will provide information about each property owner as well as surrounding neighbors.
- **Local and area telephone directories.** Use telephone books for verifying the spelling of names and addresses. They usually are reliable, but they are not infallible. Remember that people move and have similar names. Almost all landline telephone numbers in North America are now listed on various web-based services, including Switchboard.com and Smartpages.com.
- **Maps of the city, county, state, nation and world.** Local maps usually are posted in the newsroom. MapQuest.com, Google Maps and Google Street View can help direct you around town. GoogleMyMaps allows you to import data and customize your maps.
- **State manuals.** Many state governments publish directories that provide useful information on various government agencies. These directories, most of which are online, sometimes list the salaries of state employees.

- ***Bartlett's Familiar Quotations*** (Pantianos Classics). The 18th edition (2012) of this writing resource by author John Bartlett has been edited and updated by Geoffrey O'Brien. The 10th edition (1919) is now available for free at Bartleby.com.
- ***The Cambridge Dictionary of American Biography*** (Cambridge University Press). There are several such biography sources, and this one lists famous deceased people up through 1995. There is no comparable online source for biographies of living people. LexisNexis has a "research people" function that provides biographies from newspapers, magazines and biographical directories.
- ***Congressional Directory*** (Government Printing Office). The directory provides profiles of members of Congress. It's available electronically at www.congress.gov/members.
- ***Congressional Record*** (Government Printing Office). The complete proceedings of the U.S. House and Senate are published in the *Congressional Record*. The *Record* is available at www.congress.gov/congressional-record.
- ***Guinness World Records*** (Guinness Superlatives). World records in countless categories are listed here. From 1955 to 2000, its UK title was *The Guinness Book of Records*, and its U.S. title was *The Guinness Book of World Records*. These records are also available online at www.guinnessworldrecords.com.
- **InfoPlease Almanac.** This online resource includes an encyclopedia, biographies, almanac information and an atlas. It is available at Infoplease.com.
- **Journalist's Resource** (journalistsresource.org). This site provides research background for current topics.
- **Readers' Guide to Periodical Literature** (EBSCO). This index to magazine articles on a host of subjects is available online for a fee.
- ***Webster's Biographical Dictionary*** (Merriam-Webster). This dictionary is a good resource for historical biographical information.
- ***Webster's New World College Dictionary***, 5th edition (Houghton Mifflin Harcourt). This is the primary reference dictionary recommended by both the Associated Press and United Press International.
- ***Webster's Third New International Dictionary*** (Merriam-Webster). The AP and UPI recommend this edition of the unabridged dictionary as a backup to *Webster's New World College Dictionary.*
- ***Who's Who*** (Various publishers). Several companies produce biographical information on prominent people, generally organized by geographic region or topic. There is also a Who's Who Online at www.whoswho.com.
- **Wolfram Alpha** (www.wolframalpha.com). A massive online computational knowledge base where all information is gathered from quality sources. It includes statistics, weather and sports information.
- ***The World Almanac and Book of Facts*** (Simon & Schuster). This almanac is published annually.

These useful publications and websites, and many others like them, enable reporters to verify data and to avoid the embarrassment caused by errors in print or online. Traditional printed sources of information include government records, business documents, pamphlets published by government and nongovernment agencies, books, newspapers and magazines.

Be careful when using material from a source with which you are not familiar. Some publications come from biased sources that are promoting a cause. It's the reporter's job to determine whether the information is unbiased and reliable. A good way to do this is to balance information from one source with information from another source with an opposing viewpoint. It may not always be possible for you to determine who's correct. Ensuring balance between two viewpoints is the next best thing.

CHAPTER RESOURCES

SUGGESTED READINGS

Associated Press Stylebook and Briefing on Media Law. New York: Associated Press, 2019. This definitive work on stylistic matters in journalistic writing is published annually. It is also available as an online subscription.

Brooks, Brian S., James L. Pinson and Jean Gaddy Wilson. *Working with Words: A Handbook for Media Writers and Editors*. 10th ed. New York: Bedford/St. Martin's, 2019. This handbook is a comprehensive work on the correct use of language in journalistic writing and editing.

Callahan, Christopher, and Leslie-Jean Thornton. *A Journalist's Guide to the Internet: The Net as a Reporting Tool*. Boston: Allyn & Bacon, 2007. Journalists will find this a useful guide to using the internet as a reporting resource.

IRE Journal. This quarterly magazine is available from Investigative Reporters and Editors in Columbia, Missouri. It's a great source of information for those interested in investigative reporting.

SUGGESTED WEBSITES

LaunchPad Solo

launchpadworks.com

When you visit LaunchPad Solo for Journalism, you will find research links, exercises and LearningCurve adaptive quizzing to help you improve your grammar and AP style usage. In addition, the site's video collection hosts the videos highlighted in this and other chapters as well as additional clips of leading professionals discussing important media trends.

www.ire.org

Investigative Reporters and Editors maintains an excellent website for anyone interested in investigative reporting.

www.journalism.org

Research reports of the Pew Research Center for Journalism & Media may be found here.

EXERCISES

1. Do an internet search on material in a story from your local newspaper. Write a 500-word explanation of how the story could be improved by using online sources. List all your sources, or use links.
2. If you needed to determine where Apple Inc. is located and the name of its chief financial officer, where would you look? What other sources of information about the company are available?
3. **Your journalism blog.** On your blog, post a one-page biographical sketch of your congressional representative based on information from your library or a database. Send a tweet or a short email to your classmates highlighting a recent important action by the representative.
4. Using the internet, find the following information:
   - The census of Rhode Island (or your home state) in 2010.
   - The size of Rwanda in land area.
   - The latest grant awards by the U.S. Department of Education.
   - The name of a website that contains the complete works of Shakespeare.
   - The name of a website that contains federal campaign contribution data.
5. Go to Google News, and attempt to determine where the top three stories originated. Are any of them from the wire services or newspapers?

CHAPTER 4

INTERVIEWING

Photo credit: Alex Wong/Getty Images News/Getty Images

Journalists get much of their information by asking people questions. This can be seen in simple situations, like Washington Times reporter Emma Ayers interviewing U.S. Representative Eleanor Holmes Norton at Norton's 20th annual job fair in Washington, D.C. There are also more sensitive cases, however. When Jack Healy of *The New York Times* was sent to Parkland, Florida, to cover the devastating mass shooting at Marjory Stoneman Douglas High School in February 2018, his editors wanted a story that captured the essence of Parkland and the experience of living through the shootings. He needed people to tell him about one of the worst days of their lives and the days that followed. To bring the story home to readers, he focused on 14-year-old Brooke Harrison:

> **She had watched gunfire explode through her Honors English class that Feb. 14 afternoon as she and her classmates worked on an essay about hardship and education. Three students from her class alone were killed. She had heard their last breaths, crawled through glass and put pressure on a wounded student's torso before escaping through the school parking lot and running as fast as she could to reach her home in a subdivision lined by coconut palms.**

How did Healy find Brooke and get her—and her parents—to cooperate for the story? How did he capture details about events he did not witness? He earned the Harrisons' trust and engaged in extended, purposeful conversations.

Healy met the family on the day that school officials reopened the campus so students could retrieve belongings they left behind the day they fled the shooter. He approached the parents first and explained who he was and what type of stories he had in mind. He then chatted with Brooke. When he followed up later in the day, the Harrisons were willing to be interviewed. "They had already met me," Healy said. "Seeing that you're a real person helps establish a baseline of trust." The Harrisons even arranged to have other Stoneman Douglas students come to their house that evening.

For Brooke's first day back to class, he got permission to arrive at her house before she awoke. He asked countless questions to establish what was routine and what was not.

For his stories, he also used one of his favorite interviewing techniques: a road trip. "Road trips, even if they're requested by you as the reporter to get someone talking, are an incredible way to get people conversant about the place where they live and how it ties them to things that have happened to them," he said. During some of the biggest moments in people's lives, they often have to drive from point A to point B: "Literally walk through that and re-create that with them because they'll remember things," Healy said, "and they can sort of describe what happened to them then, and it will jog in their memory certain details." Brooke's mother drove him to Stoneman Douglas and recounted her experience. Brooke opened up, as well. When Brooke and two of her friends were safely at Brooke's home, Healy wrote that the day of the shooting, they:

> **sat at her house and feverishly tried to confirm which of their friends was safe. They sent group text messages asking who was missing and who had been found. They posted photos on social media. They knew, before any names were officially released or parents were notified, which of their friends were not coming home.**

In this chapter, you will learn:

1. How to prepare for an interview for a news story, profile or investigative piece.
2. How to conduct an audio or a video interview.
3. How to evaluate the pros and cons of doing interviews by telephone, email, instant messaging or Skype.
4. How to set up an interview.
5. How to prepare your questions.
6. How to establish rapport with a source.
7. How to ensure accuracy and fairness.
8. How to end an interview.

Healy was able to re-create the scene thanks to his ability to win the Harrisons' trust and to skillfully interview.

You may not be doing the type of in-depth interview Healy was doing, but **interviewing** — having conversations with sources — is the key to most stories you will write. Your ability to make people feel comfortable with you is often the difference between mediocre reporting and good reporting. Although communicating online or through text messages is ubiquitous in today's digital environment, a face-to-face interview is always preferable to a telephone interview, which in turn is preferable to having a source answer questions by email. Face-to-face interviews allow you to develop a rapport with a source. Developing that kind of rapport is difficult, if not impossible, to achieve over the telephone or by email or instant messaging. If you meet sources in their offices, you might find photos or objects that give you a way to break the ice with a nonthreatening conversation.

When a deadline looms on a breaking news story, however, you may be forced to settle for a telephone interview. This also may be necessary if you and the source are not in the same city or area. Least desirable of all is the email interview, which does not allow any sort of rapport to be established. You'll often get dry, overly polished and uninformative answers to questions posed by email, and you won't have an opportunity to ask the follow-up questions you might ask during a face-to-face interview.

Information is a journalist's raw material. Although some of it is gathered from records and some from observation, most is gathered in one-on-one conversations. You try first to talk to **primary sources**, those who witnessed the event or have authority over documents. If you can't get to a primary source, you may be forced to go to a **secondary source**, someone who talked to a witness, such as a public safety official, a lawyer or a neighbor.

Even when you are doing a **profile**, a feature story about a person, determine how your source knows your profile subject. Does your source work with the subject? If so, he's probably not much of an authority on the subject's after-hours activities. Does she play poker with the subject? If so, she probably doesn't know the subject in the workplace. After you know how your source knows what he or she knows, then you can start the conversation. If you're interviewing for a video or an audio piece to be broadcast or posted online, your goals and techniques may be different from those of a print reporter, but the basics are the same.

Preparing for the Interview

How you prepare for an interview depends in part on what kind of story you intend to write. (Figure 4.1 shows a checklist you can use in doing interviews.) You may be doing a news story, a personality profile or an investigative piece. In each case, you check your news organization's archives and search online databases, talk to other reporters and, if there's enough time, read magazine articles and books. Social media sites offer you information on some people you might not otherwise be able to contact. Don't use information from these sites without verification. Healy also recommends using internet archiving sites

Figure 4.1 Interviewing Checklist

Before the Interview

1. Know the topic.
   - Seek specific information.
   - Research the topic.
   - List the questions.
2. Know the person.
   - Find biographical information.
   - Understand the person's expertise regarding the topic.
3. Set up the interview.
   - Set the time.
     - Schedule at the interviewee's convenience, but suggest a time.
     - Estimate the length of time needed.
     - Ask about possible return visits or follow-up phone calls.
   - Set the place.
     - Choose the interviewee's turf or neutral turf.
4. Discuss arrangements.
   - Will you record the interview?*
   - Will you bring a photographer or a videographer?*
   - Will you let the interviewee check the accuracy of quotes?

During the Interview

1. When you arrive:
   - If possible, control the seating arrangement.
   - Place your digital recorder at the optimum spot.
   - Warm up the person briefly with small talk.
   - Set the ground rules: For example, you might assert that everything is on the record after the recorder is turned on.
2. During the interview itself:
   - Use good interviewing techniques.
     - Ask open-ended questions, which require the source to elaborate rather than give simple yes or no answers.
     - Allow the person to think and to speak; pause.
     - Don't be threatening in voice or manner.
     - Control the conversational flow, but be flexible.
   - Take good notes.
     - Be unobtrusive.
     - Be thorough.
   - Use a digital recorder or smartphone to record.
     - Make sure it's on and working, but take notes, too.
     - Note the number on the digital counter at important parts in the interview so you can find quotes easily.
3. Before you leave:
   - Ask if there's anything else the interviewee wants to say.
   - Check facts: spellings, dates, statistics and quotes.
   - Set a time for rechecking facts and quotes.
   - Discuss when and where the interview might appear.
   - For a print publication, ask if the interviewee wants extra copies.

After the Interview

1. Organize your notes immediately.
2. Craft a proper lead.
3. Write a coherent story.
4. Check facts for accuracy with the interviewee.

*Some sources may feel uncomfortable being recorded, videotaped or photographed.

such as the Wayback Machine (archive.org/web) to double-check someone's history.

Interviews are best used to solicit reactions and interpretations, not to gather facts. Good reporters gather their facts *before* an interview. To prepare for a news story, you pay more attention to clips about the subject of the story than those about the personality of the interviewee. To prepare for a profile, you look for personality quirks and information about the subject's interests, family, friends, travels and habits. To prepare for an investigative piece, you want to know both your subject matter and the person you are interviewing. No matter what type of story, also ask people in your newsroom for their insights about the person or subject. Let's look more closely at each of these types of common stories.

Interviewing for the News Story

Reporters usually don't have much time to prepare to cover a breaking news story. You'll be lucky if you have a few minutes to dig into your newsroom's digital archive for background on the event or the issue. With a few more minutes, you can go online to see what other reporters have written on similar topics. Those hurried searches will provide background and perhaps some context. Assuming that you're not driving yourself, you may be able to use a smartphone or tablet to check more online sources en route to the interview or just before it.

There are three important mental steps you can take as you chase the news. First, review in your head what you've turned up in your quick background research. If you're off to meet a political candidate, a public official or a celebrity, when was the person last in the news? For what? What will your audience (or your supervisor) most likely want to know now? If you're headed for a crime scene or a disaster, what do you know about the neighborhood? Has anything like this happened lately? With what results?

Second, plan your approach. Whom will you seek out at the scene? Who's likely to be in charge? What do you know about that person and her or his attitude toward reporters? Are you alone on this assignment and expected to capture audio or video? If so, double-check your equipment. Will you be reporting live on camera? If so, double-check your appearance. ESPN's Tisha Thompson recommends wearing something dark that looks both professional and nondescript. She says you don't want your appearance to distract people from the information you're reporting.

Finally, plan out your first few questions. Sometimes, those are obvious. If the news involves a crime or disaster, you'll want to know what happened. Was anybody hurt? What's the damage? If the story is focused on an issue or a person, you'll have some choices to make. Ideally, your background research has gotten you past the most basic "Who are you?" and "Why are you here?" questions. So you may want to start with something like "What are you hoping to accomplish here?" or "Why do you think this issue is so important?"

Most news interviews aren't adversarial, but if you have tough questions, save them for the end of the conversation. That way, they won't keep you from getting most of what you need. In addition, the more time you have to develop rapport with a source, the more candid the source might be.

From there, follow your instincts and your training to find the story.

Interviewing for the Profile

Sometimes, the hardest part is convincing a source to talk with you. When Texas high schooler Mack Beggs was seeking his second state championship, local and national media were competing for exclusive interviews. Beggs, a transgender male, had wanted to enter in the boys' division. State athletic officials said no. Amid controversy and national attention, he had to compete with the girls. The then-18-year-old's parents said they would not allow any interviews until after the competition.

Tisha Thompson, an investigative reporter for ESPN's Enterprise Unit, produces stories for multiple platforms like *Outside the Lines*, *E:60*, *SportsCenter* and *ESPN*

The Magazine. An interviewing pro, she did her homework on Beggs and his situation. She talked to experts in the LGBTQ community about the transition process for transgender individuals. She was told that for someone who has made the transition, the former self—the self with the other gender—is dead.

She knew how to show sensitivity, instead of ignorance. She was also patient.

On the first day of the tournament, she and her producer asked Beggs' parents if she could sit with them as they watched. They said yes. She spent the day watching high school wrestling. "The whole time his mom was really interviewing me," Thompson said. The parents needed to feel that the whole family could trust Thompson.

Beggs and his mother agreed to the interview the next day, and he shared with Thompson (and a national television audience) information about some of his darkest hours, including when he wanted to take his own life in the seventh grade. He hadn't yet told his family this secret, but he told Thompson. "I made him comfortable," Thompson said. "I listened, and I made sure he knew I cared."

Like Thompson, you need to research the subject and the person you'll be profiling. For most profiles, you will be talking not only to your subject but also to his or her friends, family and co-workers. In many cases, you will get their names from your subject. Ask how your subject knows them: co-worker, social acquaintance, recent or lifelong friend. Then ask the co-worker or friend how he or she knows your profile subject. With this information, you won't ask inappropriate questions. You don't want to ask about your subject's love for tennis, for example, if the interviewee knows the person only from work.

ON THE JOB Getting the Tough Interview

Courtesy of Derek Kravitz

Derek Kravitz, the director of research at ProPublica, has also worked as a reporter for *The Washington Post* and The Associated Press. But a story that he did years ago while on his first job at the *Columbia* (Missouri) Daily Tribune is a strong reminder of how important it is to be persistent to get people to open up and talk. He explains:

> Alan Farha was wanted by Columbia police for scamming area churches, so he was on the move. I found a phone number for his father in Georgetown, Texas, and left a voicemail. Later that night, I got a call from Farha on my cellphone. We spent the next hour discussing why I not only shouldn't interview him (he said he had nothing to say and his case was unimportant) but why we shouldn't focus resources on a larger story on his case (it could affect his fragile sobriety, he said, and he could fall into a deeper hole with his drug addictions).
>
> I told him that many people, not just in Columbia, but across many states and in countless churches, thought he was a con man. He said he wasn't. I gave him the opportunity to tell his story, and after laying out the Police Department's case against him, he described his addictions and how he had resorted to asking people for money to get by. That didn't make him a con man, he said. That made him a beggar. And a Columbia police detective I spoke to agreed.
>
> We ran the story. Farha left Columbia and since has been charged with (but not arrested for) scamming churches . . . in Indiana, Texas and New Hampshire.
>
> The *Tribune* story seems to follow him because every time he hits a new town, I'll get an email or a link from a local newspaper asking about him. He hasn't stopped, but his story is now well-known, mainly thanks to Google.
>
> Oddly enough, I also got a "friend request" from Farha on LinkedIn recently. His profile says he's still struggling with his addictions.

Interviewing for the Investigative Story

The casual conversations that you want to have for profile interviews are not always possible for the investigative reporter. An adversarial relationship determines both the preparation required for an investigative piece and the atmosphere of the interview itself. **Investigative reporting** is the pursuit of information that has been concealed, such as evidence of wrongdoing. An investigative reporter is like an attorney in a courtroom. Wise attorneys know in advance what the answers to their questions will be. Investigative reporters often do, too, but they also are open-minded enough to switch gears if sources convince them they are on the wrong track. Regardless, preparation is essential.

Lowell Bergman, a veteran investigative reporter who worked in both print and television, advises, "Learn as much about the subject before you get there, regardless of whether you play dumb because you want them to explain it to you, or whether you just want them to know that you're not going to waste their time."

Gathering information

In the early stages of the investigation, you conduct some fishing-expedition interviews. Because you don't know how much the source knows, you cast around. Start with people on the fringes. Gather as much as you can from them. Study the records. Only after you have most of the evidence should you confront your central character. You start with a large circle and gradually make it smaller.

Requesting an interview

Investigative reporters frequently have problems getting an interview because the information they seek is often damaging to the person. Sources who believe you are working on a story that will be critical of them or their friends often try to avoid you. Steve Weinberg, author of an unauthorized biography of industrialist Armand Hammer, had to overcome the suspicion of many former Hammer associates. Their former boss had told them not to talk to Weinberg. Instead of calling, Weinberg approached them by mail. "I sent letters, examples of my previous work, explained what I wanted to cover and why I was doing it without Hammer's blessing," Weinberg says.

Weinberg recommends that you use a letter or an email to share some of what you know about the story that might surprise or impress the source. For instance, a reference such as "And last week, when I was checking all the land records . . ." indicates the depth of your research.

In his letter to former Hammer associates, Weinberg talked about how Hammer was one of the most important people in the history of business. The letters opened doors to all seven of Hammer's former executive assistants whom Weinberg contacted.

Weinberg also offers to show the sources relevant portions of his manuscript as an accuracy check. An **accuracy check** just verifies the facts; it does not give the source the option of choosing what goes in and what stays out of a story. Weinberg makes it clear in writing that he maintains control of the content.

Requesting an interview in writing can allow you to make your best case for getting it. And an offer to allow your sources to review the story assures them that you are serious about accuracy. Email makes both the request and the offer simpler and faster.

Doing an Audio or a Video Interview

When you're interviewing someone in front of a camera or microphone, thc basic rules of preparation and interviewing don't change. For instance, Bob Schieffer, who retired after hosting *Face the Nation* on CBS for 24 years, says the most important preparation before every interview is to know as much about the story as possible.

Some of your objectives and techniques, however, do change. Audio and video journalists are also performers. Sure, they have to report and write, but they also have to be able to tell their stories with both words and voice (and if you're on camera, body language, too) to people who are watching and listening—not reading. An important part of the reporter's performance is the interview. You must ask questions and respond to answers smoothly. And if the camera is on you, you don't want to be seen fumbling through your notes. For that reason, ESPN's Thompson recommends carefully thinking through your questions and practicing them.

Reporters often interview to develop information that can be used in further reporting, but audio and video interviews usually have a different goal. This goal is the **sound bite**, the few seconds of words (sometimes with accompanying video) that convey both information and emotion. The best interviews reveal how a situation feels to the participants or witnesses. When Thompson interviewed Beggs, she and her producer had already decided what the story was: How did Beggs and his family feel and experience his situation? What detractors said about the young wrestler was already well-known.

Al Tompkins, the Poynter Institute's group leader for broadcast and online journalism, says that great stories depend on sound bites that connect emotionally with viewers. In his book *Aim for the Heart: Write, Shoot, Report and Produce for TV and Multimedia*, he says that subjective questions lead to emotional responses. Here are some tips that show both the similarities and differences between print and television interviewing:

- **Ask both objective and subjective questions.** To gather facts, ask objective questions: "When?" "Where?" "How much?" But subjective questions usually produce the best sound bites: "Why?" "Tell me more about . . ." "Can you explain . . . ?" "How did you feel about . . . ?"
- **Focus on one issue at a time.** Vague, complicated questions produce vague, complicated, hard-to-follow answers. Remember that readers can reread until they understand, but viewers often can't. And even if an interview is posted online, viewers might not think (or want) to rewind or replay it. Help

launchpadworks.com
WATCH: **"Radio: Yesterday, Today and Tomorrow"**

- Will the internet (and online music sources) be the end of radio, or will radio stations still be around decades from now?
- What example from the video supports your view?

viewers follow the story by taking your interviewee through it one step at a time. Additionally, Thompson says that if a source gives her a complicated answer, she might ask, "If you were explaining this to a sixth-grader, what would you say?"

- **Ask open-ended questions.** For print, you occasionally want a simple yes or no. That kind of answer can stop a television interview. Open-ended questions encourage conversation, and conversation makes for a good interview. (For more on this, see the section "Open-Ended Questions" later in this chapter.)
- **Keep questions short.** Make the interviewee do the talking. (That's good advice for print reporters, too.) Tompkins points out that short questions are more likely to produce focused responses. They also keep the viewer's attention on the person being interviewed and on the things that she or he says.
- **Build to the point.** The best interviews are like the best stories: They don't give away the punch line in the first few words. Ask soft, easy questions to encourage the interviewee to relax and trust you. Then move to the heart of the issue.
- **Be honest.** Although it is as true for television as for print and online, the importance of honesty is too often overlooked by rookie reporters. You do neither your source nor yourself a favor if you lead the source to expect an interview about softball when you have an indictment in mind. Tell the source ahead of time that you'll want to ask some tough questions. Say that you want to get the whole story to be fair — and mean it. Then politely but firmly dig in. As Tompkins notes, honesty has the added benefit of helping you defend yourself against any later accusations of malice.

Using the Telephone, Email, Instant Messaging or Skype for Interviews

Interviews, as noted earlier, are more successful if conducted in person. But when you have to interview by phone, there are at least three points to remember — especially if you're working on a feature story or an investigative piece.

First, if this is the first time that you've spoken to the source, attempt to establish rapport, just as you do in a face-to-face interview. Don't immediately start firing questions. Express your appreciation for the person's time. Explain why you are calling and how important the interviewee is to the story. If you have talked to others who know and like this person, mention that to help your source relax.

Second, depending on how much time is available and how important this interview is, you may want to record it. You should seek the permission of the person you are interviewing: "Is it OK to record this conversation? I want to make sure I get it accurately, and this way, I can concentrate more fully on the content." For your protection, put the request on the recording.

The Associated Press states that federal law and most states allow **one-party consent**, meaning that one person involved in the phone call knows the call is being recorded. However, in some states, everyone involved must agree. Be sure to know the rules where you live, and make sure you follow your news organization's policies.

In addition, take notes even if you are recording. If the recorder malfunctions or there's interference on the phone line, you'll still have material for your story. To guard against technical problems, test your equipment beforehand.

Third, just as in any other interview, try to have a conversation rather than a Q&A session. (A Q&A — **question-and-answer** — story is more or less a verbatim transcript of an interview. The interview material isn't digested and reworked into a story.) React to what is said with affirmations. Laugh when appropriate. Admit when you don't understand, and ask for more explanation.

The phone can be a friend, but it can never replace personal contact. Neither can email, but reporters are using email more frequently as they face more deadline pressures. Also, sometimes sources will only agree to an email interview, perhaps because they are busy and often because they hope to control their message.

Email interviews have many weaknesses. They don't permit you to establish rapport. And you need to be certain that the person with whom you are corresponding is the person you think he or she is. The classic *New Yorker* cartoon shown below explains the risk.

"On the Internet, nobody knows you're a dog."

You can't be sure who's on the other end of an email message or if other people are helping the interviewee respond to your questions.

On the other hand, email is quick and convenient as a follow-up to personal or phone interviews. Email can also be effective for a Q&A story. The email captures the original questions and preserves the responses. After you've made contact and established identity, an email interview can be useful and even surprisingly revealing. Some people will say things at a keyboard they wouldn't say face to face. Some get carried away by the power of their own prose. Some are cryptic and not forthcoming.

Instant messaging and text messaging have the same strengths and weaknesses as email, but they are potentially much faster. You can best use IM for follow-up questions, clarifications and checking information to ensure accuracy.

Don't forget that email and IM are permanent. Don't ask or say anything you wouldn't want to see forwarded to others. Make your questions clear and grammatically correct. The permanence works *for* you, too. The answers are equally permanent. They can't be taken back or denied later. And it's difficult to misquote an email.

Online videoconferencing through Skype, Google Hangout, FaceTime, Zoom or Facebook Messenger offers the advantages of email and eliminates one major drawback: You're communicating in real time with someone you can see. And you're talking as opposed to typing. This means that you know you have the right person on the other end of the link, and you can add the visual information that's missing from an email or phone interview. Soldiers deployed overseas use videoconferencing to stay in touch with their families. Reporters can use the same technology to interview sources they might never see in the flesh.

Setting Up the Interview

All this homework is important, but something as trifling as your appearance may determine whether you will have a successful interview. You would hardly wear cutoff shorts into a university president's suite, and you wouldn't wear a three-piece suit to talk to underground revolutionaries.

Most interviews are conducted in the source's office. If the story is a profile or a feature, however, it is often better to also get the source away from his or her work. If you are doing a story about a rabbi's hobby of collecting butterflies, seek a setting that is appropriate to the topic. Suggest meeting where the rabbi keeps the collection.

In some interviews, it is to your advantage to get the source on neutral territory. If you have questions for the provost or a public official, suggest meeting in a coffee shop at a quiet time. A person has more power in his or her official surroundings.

Let the source know how much time you need and whether you expect to return for further information. And if you don't already know how the source might react to a recording device, ask when making the appointment.

Preparing Questions

Funcrunch Photo/Alamy Stock Photo

This reporter dresses to fit in with the marchers he is interviewing and gains their confidence by being friendly and attentive.

You've now done the appropriate homework. You're dressed for the occasion. You've made an appointment and told the source how much time you need. Before you leave to meet your source, write down your questions. (Pro tip: Have those questions ready when you first call to request the interview—just in case that is the only time the source is available.)

Your questions will guide you through the interview and prevent you from missing important topics altogether. You'll also be more relaxed. Having questions prepared relieves you of the need to be mentally searching for the next question while the source is answering the last one. If you are trying to think of the next question, you can't pay close attention to what is being said, and you might miss the most important part of the interview. Being prepared helps you engage in a more spontaneous conversation.

Researching Questions

Preparing the questions for an interview is hard work, even for veterans. If you're writing for your campus newspaper, seek suggestions from other staff members. You'll find ideas in the newspaper's electronic database. If you anticipate a troublesome interview with the chancellor, you might want to seek advice from faculty members, too. What questions would they ask if they were you? Often, they have more background knowledge or have heard faculty talk around campus. Staff members also are valuable sources of information.

Although you may ask all of your prepared questions in some interviews, in most you probably will use only some of them. Still, you will have benefited from preparing the questions in two important ways. First, even when you don't use all of them, the work you do thinking about the questions helps prepare you for the interview. Second, sources who see that you have a prepared list often are impressed with your seriousness.

On the basis of the information you have gathered already, you know what you want to ask. Now you must be careful about how you phrase the questions.

Phrasing Questions

A young monk asked his superior if he could smoke while he prayed and was rebuked sharply. A friend advised him to rephrase the question. "Ask him if you can pray while you smoke," he said. The young monk was discovering that how questions are structured often determines the answer. Journalists face the same challenge. Reporters have missed many stories because they didn't know how to ask their questions. Quantitative researchers have shown that only a slight wording change affects the results of a survey. If you want to know whether citizens favor a city plan to beautify the downtown area, you can ask the question in several ways:

- Do you favor the City Council's plan to beautify the downtown area?
- The City Council plans to spend $3 million beautifying the downtown area. Are you in favor of this?
- Do you think that downtown needs physical changes?
- Which of the following actions do you favor?
  - Prohibiting all automobile traffic in an area bounded by Providence Road, Ash Street, College Avenue and Elm Street.
  - Remodeling all the downtown storefronts in a uniform style and putting in brick sidewalks, shrubbery and benches.
  - None of the above.

How you structure this type of question may affect the survey results by several percentage points. Similarly, how you ask questions in an interview may affect the response.

Many reporters signal the response they expect or the prejudices they have with the way they phrase the question. A reporter who says, "Don't you think that the City Council should allocate more money to the Parks and Recreation Department?" is not only asking a question but also influencing the source or betraying a bias. Another common way of asking a leading question is this: "Are you going to vote against this amendment like the other City Council members I've talked to?" A neutral phrasing would be, "Do you think the City Council should allocate more money to the Parks and Recreation Department?" To avoid leading or even irritating your source, ask neutral questions.

Also ask the interviewee one question at a time. Listen to journalists at news conferences. Because they occasionally jump up and ask two or three questions at a time, sources can choose the one they wish to answer and ignore the rest. Sometimes the results are comical. After Barack Obama's first 100 days in office, a *New York Times* reporter asked, "What has surprised you the most about this office, enchanted you the most about serving in this office, humbled you the most and troubled you the most?" "Let me write this down," Obama responded. After he and the press corps shared a laugh, the president didn't bother answering the question about what had troubled him the most. This can happen in one-on-one interviews, too.

In situations where you have to ask embarrassing or awkward questions, Thompson recommends being upfront. She often warns sources when she has tough questions, but she also tells them that she thinks it's important for their side to be told and that she is just doing her job: It's nothing personal.

Sometimes the reporter's phrasing of a question unwittingly blocks a response. A reporter who was investigating possible job discrimination against women conducted several interviews before telling her city editor that the women she talked with didn't seem to be responding frankly. "When I ask them if they have ever been discriminated against, they always tell me no. But three times now during the course of the interviews, they have said things that indicate they have been. How do I get them to tell me about it?" she asked.

"Perhaps it's the way you are asking the question," the city editor replied. "When you ask the women whether they have ever been discriminated against, you are forcing them to answer yes or no. Don't be so blunt. Ask them if others with the same qualifications at work have advanced faster than they have. Ask if they are paid the same amount as men for the same work. Ask them what they think they would be doing today if they were male. Ask them if they know of any qualified women who were denied jobs."

The city editor was giving the reporter examples of both closed- and open-ended questions. Each has its specific strengths.

Open-ended questions

Open-ended questions allow the respondent some flexibility. People may not respond frankly when asked whether they have ever been discriminated against. The question calls for a yes or no response. But an open-ended question such as "What would you be doing at work today if you were a man?" is not as personal. It does not sound as threatening. In response to an open-ended question, the source often reveals more than he or she realizes or intends to.

A sportswriter who was interviewing a pro scout at a college football game wanted to know whom the scout was there to see. When the scout diplomatically declined to say, the reporter tried another approach. He asked a series of questions:

- "What kinds of qualities does a pro scout look for in an athlete?"
- "Do you think any of the players here today have those talents?"
- "Who would you put into that category?"

The reporter worked from the general to the specific until he had the information he wanted. Open-ended questions are less direct and less threatening. They are more exploratory and more flexible.

However, if you want to know a person's biographical data, don't ask, "Can you tell me about yourself?" That question is too general. Phrase your questions to get information about specific times and places. (As discussed earlier, before interviewing someone, you should already know some biographical data. It's better to confirm information than to show ignorance and lack of preparation.)

Closed-ended questions

Eventually, you need to pin down details and get the respondent to be specific. **Closed-ended questions** are designed to elicit specific responses.

Instead of asking the mayor, "What did you think of the conference in Washington, D.C.?" you ask, "Which sessions did you attend?" Instead of asking the university official how much debate went into a policy change, ask her, "How many stakeholders did you consult?" and "Which stakeholders?" Instead of asking a previous employee to appraise the chancellor-designate's managerial abilities, you ask, "Do the people who work for her have specific job duties? Does she explain her decisions?"

A vague question invites a vague answer. By asking a specific question, you're more likely to receive a specific answer. You're also communicating to your source that you have done your homework and that you are looking for precise details.

Knowing exactly when to ask a closed-ended question or when to be less specific is not necessarily something you can plan. The type of information you are seeking and the chemistry between you and the source are the determining factors. You must make on-the-spot decisions. The important thing is to keep rephrasing the question until the source answers it adequately. Sportswriter Gary Smith wrote in Walt Harrington's *Intimate Journalism: The Art and Craft of Reporting Everyday Life*, "A lot of my reporting comes from asking a question three different ways. Sometimes the third go at it is what produces the nugget, but even if the answers aren't wonderful or the quotes usable, they can still confirm or correct my impressions."

Every good reporter also seeks anecdotes. When the source talks in generalities, ask a follow-up question to get to specifics. "You say Mary is a practical joker. Can you think of an example of a practical joke she played?" The answers to these types of questions yield the anecdotal nuggets that make your story readable.

Closed-Ended Questions	Open-Ended Questions
Do you like the proposal?	What are the strengths of the proposal? What are the weaknesses?
Did you have trouble coping when your child was in the car accident?	How did you cope after your child was in the car accident? Why did you attend counseling sessions?
Did you keep your promises to exercise today?	What was your exercise routine today?
Did you give the theater teacher permission to stage that play?	What did you tell the theater teacher when she asked if her group could perform the play?
Do you use Gmail chat in your work?	How do you use Gmail chat in your work?

Establishing Rapport

The most basic requirement of any successful interview is a reasonable degree of trust between reporter and source. Reporters usually have to earn that trust.

ESPN reporter Wright Thompson recalls a time when he worked for *The Kansas City Star* and wanted to do a story about a former college football player named Ernest Blackwell. Blackwell had gone on a rampage in his neighborhood, shot a child and almost kicked another to death. He'd collapsed on a police gurney afterward and died en route to the hospital. No one could figure out what had happened. Media outlet after media outlet approached the family for an interview. All were turned down. Thompson tried a unique approach:

> **When I called, I had a line. I told them I was going to talk to the cops and was going to do a story about Ernest. The police, I told them, would give me more than enough detail about the last five minutes of Ernest's life. Then I said, "I think there's a lot more to his life than the last five minutes. I think he deserves to be remembered for how he lived and not just how he died."**

Thompson's reasoning won him the interview. His conclusion: "Have a plan. You must give someone a reason why it's better if they talk to you than if they don't."

Because he earned the trust of the family, he was able to develop the insights that allowed him to write this:

> **Those who knew him wonder how Blackwell arrived on that day with so much rage in his heart, so much bad intent. Truth is, none of them could peer into the man's soul and see the hate that grew until it reached the breaking point.**
>
> **On Aug. 11, 2004, Blackwell could take no more.**
>
> **"Lord, why didn't I see the signs?" says his aunt Joyce Strong, who mostly raised Blackwell. "Why didn't I see he was reaching out for help? He must have been a ticking time bomb waiting to go off."**

That's the payoff on the investment in building trust.

You probably won't have many assignments as difficult as Thompson's. It always helps, though, to have a plan. It also helps to have the honesty and empathy that lead strangers to be honest with you. Act like a human being.

Rapport — a harmonious relationship between the reporter and the source — can be crucial to the success of the interview. It helps a reporter get better story information. The type of relationship that you try to establish with your source is determined by the kind of story you are doing. Several approaches are possible.

Interview Approaches

For most news stories and personality profiles, the reporter can put the subject at ease by starting with small talk. Ask about a trophy, the plants or an engraved pen. Bring up something humorous you found during your research. Ask about something that you know the source will want to talk about. If you think the subject might be skeptical about your knowledge of the field, open with a question that demonstrates your knowledge.

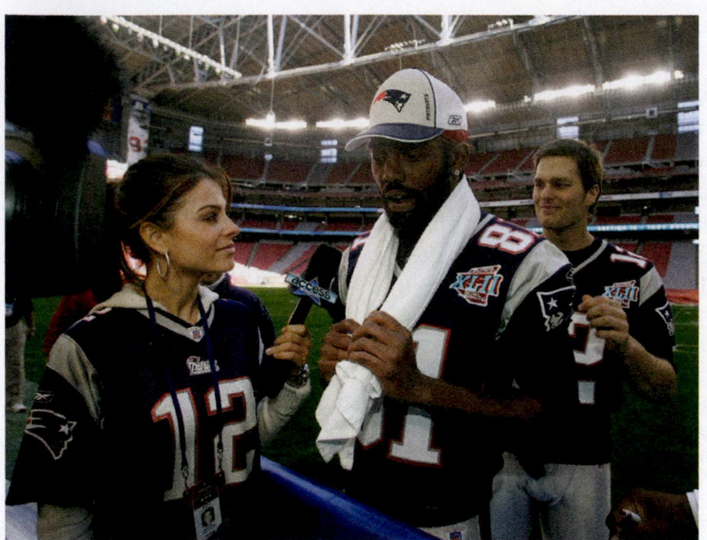

Francis Specker/MCT/Newscom

Establishing rapport with interview subjects helps a reporter get better story information.

Rapport also depends on where you conduct the interview. Many people, especially those who are unaccustomed to being interviewed, feel more comfortable in their workplace. Go to them. Talk to the businessperson in the office, to the athlete in the locker room, to the conductor in the concert hall.

A source's comfort level may depend on the story. If you're interviewing people about their supervisors, you might not receive candid responses at the workplace. If your topic is unrelated to someone's work, he or she might not feel comfortable taking time away from work for an interview. A different setting, outside of work hours, might be better.

Similarly, if the source cannot relax at the workplace or is frequently interrupted, you may get a better interview elsewhere. Reporters have talked to politicians during car rides between campaign appearances. They've gone sailing with businesspeople and hunting with athletes. One student reporter who was doing a feature on a police chief spent a weekend with the chief as he painted his home.

To do a profile, which requires more than one interview, vary the location. New surroundings can make a difference.

However, there are times when the reporter would rather keep the source on edge. When you are doing an investigation, you may want the key characters to feel uneasy. You may suggest you know more than you actually do. You want them to know that the material you have is substantive and serious. Seymour Hersh, a Pulitzer Prize–winning investigative reporter, used this tactic. *Time* magazine once quoted a government official commenting on Hersh: "He wheedles, cajoles, pleads, threatens, asks a leading question, uses little tidbits as if he knew the whole story. When he finishes you feel like a wet rag."

In some cases, however, it is better to take a low-key approach. Let the source relax. Talk around the subject, but gradually bring the discussion to the key issues. The surprise element may work in your favor.

So may the sympathetic approach. When the source is speaking, you may nod or punctuate the source's responses with comments such as "That's interesting." Sources who think you are sympathetic are more likely to volunteer information. Researchers have found, for instance, that a simple "mm-hmmm" affects the length of the answer interviewers get.

> **"I need to create what I call accelerated intimacy. We can't write the beautiful narrative stories that we all dream of unless we can get some things from the mouths of our sources. They must be comfortable enough to tell us *anything*. In journalism school, no one called the interactions between journalists and sources *relationships*, but that's what they are."**
>
> ■ **Isabel Wilkerson, winner of the Pulitzer Prize for journalism**

Other Practical Considerations

Where you sit in relation to the person you are interviewing can be important. Unless you are deliberately trying to make interviewees feel uncomfortable, do not sit directly in front of them. Permit your sources to establish eye contact if and when they wish.

A digital recorder ensures accuracy of quotes, but it can make many speakers self-conscious or nervous. If you have permission to use a recorder, place it in an inconspicuous spot and ignore it except to make sure it is working properly. Writing notes longhand may interfere with your ability to digest what is being said. But not taking any notes at all is risky. Only a few reporters can leave an interview and accurately write down what was said. Certainly no one can do it and reproduce direct quotes verbatim. You should learn shorthand or develop a note-taking system of your own.

Be sure that you address the people you are interviewing correctly. If you are unsure how they should be addressed—*Mrs.*, *Miss*, *Ms.*, *Dr.*, *Professor*—ask them.

If you are interviewing someone from a culture or race different from your own, recognize and avoid your own stereotypes. Perhaps you are uncomfortable in the presence of an Islamic woman wearing a veil when she attends school in the U.S. Instead of letting your feelings influence your actions, respect her beliefs. As a reporter, take pride in your ability to move among people from all cultures. This requires that you read about cultural differences. It might help you to know that in Chinese society, people are generally uncomfortable with too much eye contact. Many Arabs consider it improper for a man to look into a woman's eyes. No one knows everything about every culture, but you can prepare for some situations, and you can also recognize what you don't know. These days, it is easy enough to do a quick internet search about possible cultural differences before you conduct an interview.

Ensuring Accuracy and Fairness

Accuracy is a major problem in all interviews. Both the question and the answer may be ambiguous. You may not understand what is said. You may write it down incorrectly. You may not remember the context of the remarks. Your biases may interfere with the message.

Personal Pronouns for Transgender People

The Associated Press Stylebook recommends using the pronoun (*he*, *she*, *they*) that the person prefers. If you don't know the person's preference, ask. If an individual prefers to be referred to with the plural pronouns *they*, *them* and *their* and the use of a pronoun is essential, "explain in the text that the person prefers a gender-neutral pronoun," the stylebook states.

Using a Recorder

The only way to be sure that you capture the content of any interview with word-perfect accuracy is to record it. Careful listening is important, and taking good notes is essential. But using a recorder is the only way that you can be certain you've got exactly what was said, both by the source and by you. That's important journalistically. As sources and audiences become increasingly skeptical, absolute accuracy adds to credibility and protects against complaints and even lawsuits. It's also increasingly common for sophisticated sources to use their own recorders as a form of self-protection from reporters they may not trust.

Today's digital recorders are so small and powerful that it's often possible to use them while they're in your pocket, purse or briefcase. However, there's seldom a need to be secretive. Moreover, you may get a clearer recording by putting the device in full view on a nearby desk or table or even on the floor in front of you. Putting the device on a stable surface helps eliminate the transient rustling noises you might make when you move in your chair. (If you're using your smartphone to record, you can get special equipment to serve as a tripod or shoulderpod.)

Taking Notes

Here are some helpful guidelines for taking notes during an interview:

- Write the date, the place and the interviewee's name at the top of the page.
- Develop a consistent shorthand. For example, always use "w/" to mean "with."
- Use a narrow spiral-bound notebook with pages that are easy to turn and that lie flat. Narrow is better because your hands can move more quickly across the page.
- Make sure you have several working pens or sharpened pencils.
- Leave a wide margin so that you can annotate your writing later on.
- Look up at the interviewee frequently as you write.
- Ask for the spellings of names.
- Always take notes, even if you are recording.

When you're doing a phone interview, you may be able to download an app for your smartphone that will make it easy to record the call. However, if your interviewee is in a different state, you will have to adhere to the consent laws of that state, as well as those of your own. Whichever method you choose, be sure to practice with your device prior to the interview to ensure you can manage it smoothly.

Taking Notes

Knowing the background of your sources, having a comfortable relationship with them and keeping good notes are three important elements of accuracy. But they were missing when a journalism student, two weeks into an internship at a major daily, interviewed the public information officer for a sheriff's department about criminal activity in and around a shelter for battered women.

The reporter had never met the source. She took notes on her phone interview with the deputy and others in whatever notebook happened to be nearby. She didn't record the time, date or even the source. There were no notes showing context, just fragments of quotes that were scrawled in nearly illegible handwriting.

After the story was published, the developer of the shelter sued. Questioned by attorneys, the deputy swore that the reporter misunderstood him and used some of his comments out of context. In several cases, he contended, she completed her fragmentary notes by putting her own words in his mouth. He testified that most reporters come to see him to get acquainted. Many call back to check his quotes on sensitive or complex stories. She did neither.

When the court ordered the reporter to produce and explain her notes, she had trouble reconstructing them. She had to admit on several occasions that she wasn't sure what the fragments meant.

The accuracy of your story is only as good as your notes. David Finkel, whose story on a family's TV-watching habits became a Pulitzer Prize finalist, took extra steps to be certain his material was accurate. Observing what his subjects were watching, he obtained transcripts of the shows so that he could quote accurately from them. If he knew transcripts would not be available, he set his recorder near the TV to record the program.

Verifying Information

Reporters should do research after an interview to determine specific figures when a source provides an estimate. For example, if a restaurant owner says that she runs one of 20 pizza parlors in town, check with the city business-license office to get the exact number.

When you finish your interview, review the key points in your notes to confirm them with the interviewee. Read back quotes to be sure that you have them right. Realize, too, that you will need to confirm some of the information with perhaps more authoritative sources. And if your interview produces allegations against other people or organizations, you will need to talk to those named and work to avoid **libel**, the defamation of someone's character (libel and other legal concerns are addressed in Chapter 19).

Some possibilities for making errors or introducing bias are unavoidable, but others are not. To ensure the most accurate and complete reporting possible, you should use all the techniques available to obtain a good interview, including observing and asking follow-up questions. Let's examine these and other techniques.

What's the grammar error in this sentence?

South Korean President Park Geun-hye was impeached and she was later sentenced to 24 years in prison for corruption.

See Appendix 1, Rule 8.

Observing

Some reporters look but do not see. The details they miss may be the difference between a routine story and one that is a delight to read. Your powers of observation may enable you to discover a story beyond your source's words. Is the subject nervous? What kinds of questions are striking home? The mayor may deny that he is going to fire the police chief, but if you notice the chief's personnel file sitting on an adjacent worktable, you may have reason to continue the investigation.

Wright Thompson says, "It's all about the scenes. Don't just ask questions. Be an observer." Like any good writer, he offers an example to show what he means:

> I was doing a story about former Heisman Trophy winner Eric Crouch. It was almost exactly one year since he'd won the trophy, and that year had been tough for him. He'd quit pro football and had been forced to ask some hard questions about his life.
>
> As we sat in an Omaha (Nebraska) bar, a clip of him running the football came on the television. One of the women at the table said, "You're on TV, Eric." I remember he looked up at the screen and spat, "That's not me, man." Then he took a shot of liquor. No amount of interviewing could breathe life into the idea that he had changed like that scene.

Asking Follow-Up Questions

If you understand what the source is saying, you can ask meaningful follow-up questions. There's nothing worse than briefing your city editor on the interview and having the editor ask you, "Well, did you ask . . . ?" Having to say no is embarrassing.

Even if you go into an interview armed with a list of questions, the most important questions will probably be the ones that you ask in response to an answer. A reporter who was doing a story on bidding procedures was interviewing the mayor. The reporter asked how bid specifications were written. In the course of his reply, the mayor mentioned that the president of a construction firm had assured him that the last bid specifications were adequate.

The alert reporter picked up on the statement:

> "When did you talk to him?"
> "About three weeks ago," the mayor said.
> "That's before the specifications were published, wasn't it?"
> "Yes, we asked him to look them over for us."
> "Did he find anything wrong with the way they were written?"
> "Oh, he changed a few minor things. Nothing important."
> "Did officials of any other construction firms see the bid specifications before they were advertised?"
> "No, he was the only one."

Gradually, thanks to one offhand comment by the mayor, the reporter was able to piece together a solid story on the questionable relationship between the city and the construction firm.

Three questions are always useful. One is "What did you mean by that?" That simple follow-up can elicit details and clearer explanations for your audience. The second is "How do you know that?" This question helps you judge the credibility of the information and perhaps points you to additional sources. And the third is "Is there anything I haven't asked that I should?" That question might result in additional and even better story ideas.

Using Other Techniques

Although most questions are designed to get information, some are asked as a delaying tactic. A reporter who is taking notes may fall behind. One good trick for catching up is to say, "Hold on a second. Let me get that" or "Say that again, please." Other questions are intended to encourage a longer response. "Go on with that" or "Tell me more about that" encourages the speaker to add more details.

You don't have to be stalling for time to say that you don't understand. Don't be embarrassed to admit when you haven't grasped something. It's better to admit to one person that you don't understand something than to advertise your ignorance worldwide online, in print or on the air.

Another technique for making the source elaborate is not a question at all; it is a pause. You are signaling to the source that you expect more. But the lack of a response from you is much more ambiguous than "Tell me more about that." It may indicate that you were skeptical of what was just said, that you didn't understand, that the answer was inadequate or several other possibilities. The source will be forced to react. Try not to be the one who breaks the silence first.

Ending the Interview

There are two things you should always do when you finish your questions. First, check key facts, figures and quotes. Then put away your pen or recorder, but keep your ears open. Depending on the ground rules that you've set, you're not breaching any ethical rule if you continue to ask questions after you have put away your pen or turned off the recorder. Many dull interviews become interesting after they end. That's when some sources loosen up.

> **"Today one has the impression that the interviewer is not listening to what you say, nor does he think it important, because he believes that the tape recorder hears everything. But he's wrong; it doesn't hear the beating of the heart, which is the most important part of the interview."**
>
> ■ **Gabriel García Márquez, Colombian writer and Nobel laureate**

Quickly review your notes and check facts, especially dates, numbers, quotes, spellings and titles. Besides helping you get it right, this review shows the source that you are careful. If necessary, arrange a time when you can call to check other parts of the story or clear up questions you may have when you are writing. Researchers have found that more than half of direct quotations are inaccurate, even when the interview is recorded. That reflects an unacceptable sloppiness. Make sure you are the exception.

As a matter of courtesy, tell the source when the story might appear. You may even offer to send along a link to the article when it's completed. And always thank the source for granting the interview in the first place.

CHAPTER RESOURCES

SUGGESTED READINGS

Chimera, Paul. *Nuts, Bolts and Anecdotes*. Amherst, N.Y.: Chimera Communications, 2015. Designed as a practical guide for journalists, this book covers interviewing, among other topics.

Kramer, Mark, and Wendy Call, eds. *Telling True Stories*. New York: Plume, 2007. This book contains excellent advice, including how to prepare for and conduct interviews.

Lee-Potter, Emma. *Interviewing for Journalists*. 3rd ed. New York: Routledge, 2017. Lee-Potter offers a useful description of interviewing techniques for journalists.

Sedorkin, Gail. *Interviewing: A Guide for Journalists and Writers*. 2nd ed. Crows Nest, New South Wales, Australia: Allen and Unwin, 2011. This book is an excellent guide to interviewing skills for reporters and writers.

Tompkins, Al. "The Art of the Interview." In *Aim for the Heart: Write, Shoot, Report and Produce for TV and Multimedia*, 3rd ed. Thousand Oaks, Calif.: CQ Press, 2018. Tompkins is the lead broadcast and online trainer for the Poynter Institute for Media Studies.

SUGGESTED WEBSITES

LaunchPad Solo

launchpadworks.com

When you visit LaunchPad Solo for Journalism, you will find research links, exercises and LearningCurve adaptive quizzing to help you improve your grammar and AP style usage. In addition, the site's video collection hosts the videos highlighted in this and other chapters as well as additional clips of leading professionals discussing important media trends.

cjr.org

Excellent advice on interviewing from Ann Friedman appears on the site of the Columbia Journalism Review at www.cjr.org/realtalk/the_art_of_the_interview.php

IRE.org

Investigative Reporters and Editors offers its members thousands of tipsheets, including many on interviewing and other investigative techniques. College students can become members for $25 annually.

JulianSher.com

Julian Sher is a renowned Canadian investigative and documentary journalist who conducts training worldwide. His website includes a presentation on how to do interviews for investigative reports.

Poynter.org

The Poynter Institute for Media Studies specializes in training journalists on such topics as ethics and fact-checking. Search for "interviewing" to find helpful articles by Chip Scanlan and Jacqui Banaszynski.

RTDNA.org

The Radio Television Digital News Association provides advocacy and training for broadcast and digital journalists. Search this online resource for numerous guides, including one specifically on interviewing juveniles (https://rtdna.org/content/interviewing_juveniles).

youtube.com/user/TheBBCAcademy/videos

The BBC Academy channel includes a helpful video with interviewing tips produced by journalists at the British Broadcasting Corp.

EXERCISES

1. Learn to gather background on your sources by writing a memo of one or two pages about your state's senior U.S. senator. Concentrate on details that allow you to focus on how the senator views health care issues or another major issue. Indicate the sources of your information.
2. List five open-ended questions that you would ask the senator you researched for exercise 1. Then list five closed-ended questions you would ask.
3. Interview a classmate about his or her hobbies. Then switch roles and do the interview again. Write a brief summary of what you learned, and list three additional questions you would ask if you had more time.
4. **Your journalism blog.** In your blog, describe your experience completing exercise 3. What did you learn about interviewing? Comment on the blog post of the classmate you interviewed. What can you add to each other's assessments of the exercise?
5. Interview three strangers, and ask them about their school or work. Try to get an email address or telephone number for each. Then write a one-page summary of what you experienced and what you learned.
6. Discuss with a classmate the advantages, if any, of knowing how to conduct a good interview if you are pursuing a career in public relations or marketing.

CHAPTER 5

QUOTATIONS AND ATTRIBUTIONS

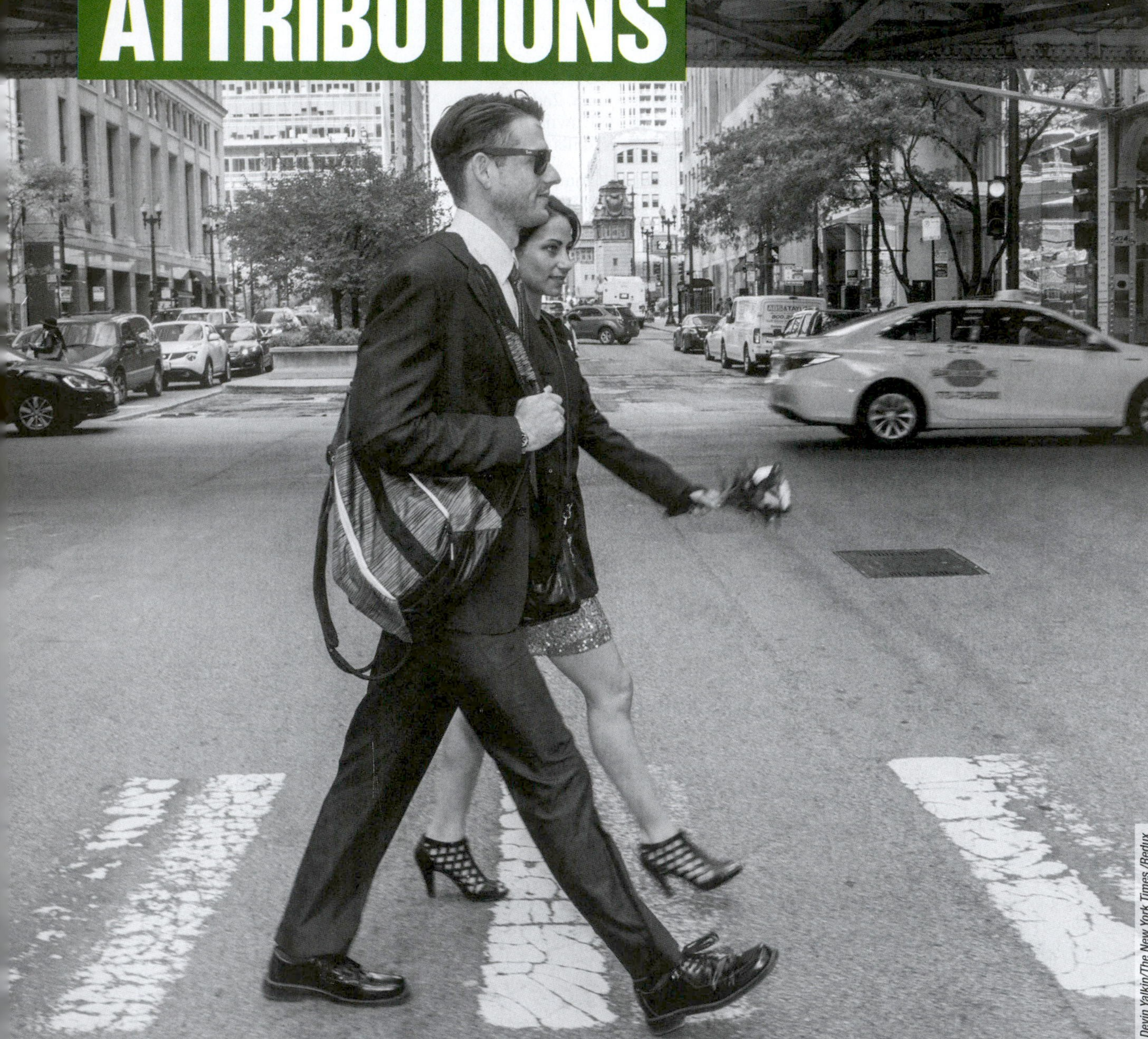

Photo credit: Devin Yalkin/The New York Times /Redux

In 2017, C.J. Chivers won the Pulitzer Prize for feature writing for a *New York Times* piece about Samuel J. Siatta, a U.S. Marine fighting to overcome post-traumatic stress disorder. Later that year, Chivers wrote about Siatta again, this time chronicling his engagement and wedding to Ashley Volk, "his off-again, on-again girlfriend since the sixth grade." Chivers' beautiful writing provides the setup:

> **Let it be known that Ashley Volk had loved Sam Siatta since elementary school, the age of True Love Always in sidewalk chalk. She loved him before he joined the Marines and went to war, before he descended into depression and alcoholism upon his return, beforc he was convicted on a felony charge for a crime he did not remember through a blackout fog.**

But Chivers' quote selections capture the essence of the people. Here he recounts the words of the judge who married Volk and Siatta (shown on the previous page after their wedding):

> **Calling her a "tiny, giant-of-a-woman who stands before us today," he declared that "Ashley is not a quitter."**
>
> **"When Sam was not all that communicative while in battle in Afghanistan, she didn't give up," he said. "When he came back and was a more distant and remote kind of guy, she didn't give up."**
>
> **"When he was convicted and imprisoned, she didn't give up. She kept on fighting, for him and for them."**

You can't blame a reader for tearing up. Direct quotes, good ones, have that kind of power.

Direct quotes—the exact words that a source says or writes—add color and credibility to your story. By using a direct quote, you put your readers in touch with the speaker in your story. Like a handwritten letter, direct quotes are personal. Quotation marks, which usually enclose a direct quote, signal to the reader that something special is coming. Direct quotes provide a story with a change of pace, a breath of fresh air.

As Paula LaRocque, former writing coach and assistant managing editor of *The Dallas Morning News*, says, "The right quotes, carefully selected and presented, enliven and humanize a story and help make it clear, credible, immediate and dramatic. Yet many quotations in journalism are dull, repetitive, ill-phrased, ungrammatical, nonsensical, self-serving or just plain dumb."

Now that's a quotation worth quoting!

Not everything that people say is worth quoting. You need to learn what to quote directly, when to use partial quotes and when to paraphrase. You also must learn how and how often to attribute quotations and other information. **Attribution** simply means giving credit to the source who gave you the information. Remember, though, that attributing a remark or some information does not excuse you from a possible libel suit. A libelous statement is a false report that damages a person's reputation.

Finally, you want to be fair. Being fair is difficult, especially when sources do not want to be quoted. You must learn how to deal with off-the-record quotes and background information.

In this chapter, you will learn:

1. How to determine what is worth quoting directly.
2. How to ensure accuracy and fairness in quotations.
3. Whether, when and how to alter quotations.
4. When and how to attribute direct and indirect quotes.
5. How to handle both on- and off-the-record information.

What to Quote Directly

Crisp, succinct, meaningful **quotes** spice up any story. But you can overdo a good thing. Inexperienced writers, whether they are working for news organizations or public relations firms, often tend to use too many direct quotations.

You need direct quotes in your stories, but you also need to develop your skill in recognizing what is worth quoting directly. Let's look at the basic guidelines.

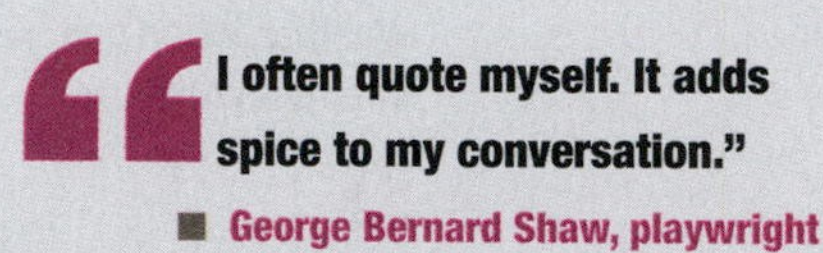

I often quote myself. It adds spice to my conversation."
George Bernard Shaw, playwright

Unique Material

A source sometimes tells you information you would not get in any other way. When you can say, "Ah, I've never heard *that* before," you can be sure your readers would like to know exactly what the speaker said. Sometimes it is something surprising, something neither you nor your readers would have expected that person to say.

When singer Dolly Parton was asked how she felt about dumb-blonde jokes, she replied: "I'm not offended by all the dumb blonde jokes because I know I'm not dumb—and I also know that I'm not blond."

Use good judgment in selecting quotes

Striking statements like Parton's should be quoted, but not always. The *Arizona Daily Star* did a profile of a chef who writes a weekly column. Describing his food philosophy, the chef said, "I have a food philosophy, but it's a kind of an angry one. I'd eat a baby if you cooked it right. Yeah, that's pretty much it."

The *Star*'s reader advocate wrote that at least a half dozen readers objected. Said one, "Shame on the chef for saying it, and shame on the *Star* for printing it."

Don't use direct quotes for straight facts

There is no reason to place simple, factual material inside quotation marks. Here is an excerpt from a story about similarities in the careers of a father and son that needed no quotes at all:

> **"My son was born on campus," says the elder Denney.**
>
> **"In fact, he was born in the same hospital that I met my wife," he says. Since that time, his son has earned his bachelor's degree "technically in agriculture with a major in biological science and conservation."**

Although the quoted material is informative, it contains nothing particularly interesting, surprising, disturbing, new or even different. As a writer, you can and should provide the same information more concisely in a paraphrase.

Avoid quotes that provide statistics. You can usually make a clearer, more succinct presentation by paraphrasing and attributing the information to your source. In a video or television broadcast, statistics are more understandable in a slide display. Save quotes (or soundbites) for reaction and interpretation.

Use quotes that move the story forward

A direct quotation should say something significant, and it should not simply repeat what has been said indirectly. It should move the story forward. Here's a passage from a story in the *Columbia* (Missouri) *Daily Tribune* about a falconer. First, the reporter sets up the quote:

> **Duffee-Yates does not fly her birds during programs at parks but describes how they are used for hunting.**

The story goes on to discuss this topic with this introduction:

> **"It's all about food motivation, all weight control," Duffee-Yates said. "You get the bird down to the weight where it is hungry enough to want to eat and then reward the bird for good behavior."**

The quotation is not just thrown in. It moves the story forward and serves as an introduction to the ways that Duffee-Yates hunts with her birds.

Redundant quotes do not move a story forward. They waste the audience's time. Here's an example:

> **The police chief said she knows citizens are worried about crime. "We're well aware that our citizens are concerned about crime," she said.**

Avoid the temptation to repeat yourself. Space and time are precious commodities.

When to Use Direct Quotes

- Someone says something unique.
- Someone says something uniquely.
- Someone important says something important.

Consider using dialogue to tell part of the story

Sometimes spoken material is unique not because individual remarks are surprising or new but because extended dialogue can tell the story more effectively than writers can in their own words. Dialogue is not the same as a quotation. A quotation comes from a source speaking to the reporter. **Dialogue** occurs when two or more sources are speaking to one another.

Here's an example from Chivers' "Vows" story of how dialogue can move the story along and "show" rather than "tell." Chivers could have written that Siatta picked Halloween to be the couple's wedding date. Instead, he provides the scene:

> **In September he and Ms. Volk were on a date to see the movie *It* and stopped for a meal at Noodles & Company. They were waiting for their food when he revisited the question.**
>
> **"You know what, I think we should get married on Halloween," he said. "We can get dressed up. We love Halloween. It will be fun."**
>
> **Ms. Volk was confused. "You mean next Halloween?"**
>
> **"No," he said. "This Halloween. In a few weeks."**
>
> **She started screaming, there in the restaurant, jumping up and down, kissing him.**

The use of dialogue puts the reader in the moment and captures the emotion.

The Unique Expression

Be on the lookout for the clever, the colorful, the colloquial. For example, an elderly man talking about his organic garden said, "It's hard to tell people to watch what they eat. You eat health, you know."

A professor lecturing on graphic design said, "When you think it looks like a mistake, it is." The same professor once explained that elements in a design should not call attention to themselves: "You don't walk up to a beautiful painting in someone's home and say, 'That's a beautiful frame!'"

Now and then, even a commencement address can yield a great quote or two, especially if the speaker is the renowned historian and film documentarian Ken Burns. At Washington University in St. Louis in 2015, for example, he said this:

> **But the isolation of those two mighty oceans has also helped to incubate habits and patterns less beneficial to us: our devotion to money and guns; our certainty—about everything; our stubborn insistence on our own exceptionalism, blinding us to that which needs repair, our preoccupation with always making the other wrong, at an individual as well as global level.**

> **"Read. The book is still the greatest manmade machine of all—not the car, not the TV, not the computer or the smartphone."**
>
> ■ Ken Burns, film documentarian

You might want to keep a book of classical quotations handy. Sometimes a quote from the classics fits the mood of your piece perfectly, even as a lead.

Here Charles Lane quotes Jonathan Swift in his lead about a story on the harm that reporters do when they mislead the public or rush to a story without all the facts:

> **"Falsehood flies, and truth comes limping after it," wrote Jonathan Swift, "so that when men come to be undeceived, it is too late; the jest is over, and the tale hath had its effect."**

In *The Editorial Eye*, Jane T. Harrigan suggests that writers allow themselves only two quote leads in their lifetimes. (For further information on leads, see Chapter 8.) The Swift quote is so elegant and appropriate to the content that it might merit using half of Harrigan's recommended quota.

Sometimes something said uniquely is a colloquialism. A person from Louisiana might say, "I was just fixing to leave when the phone rang." In parts of the South, you're apt to hear, "I might could do that." A person from near Lancaster, Pennsylvania, might "make the light out" when turning off the lights. In some parts of the U.S., people "redd up" the dishes after a meal, meaning that they wash them and put them away. Colloquialisms and regional usages can add color and life to your copy, but as we'll discuss later in the chapter, it's important to be mindful of how you are characterizing your subjects with the colloquialisms you choose.

Important Quotes by Important People

If citizen Joe Smith says, "Something must be done about this teachers' strike," you might or might not consider it worth quoting. But if the mayor says the same words, you are likely to include the quote. Generally, reporters quote public officials or known personalities in their news stories (although not everything they say is worth quoting). Remember, prominence is an important property of news.

Quoting sources whom readers are likely to know lends authority, credibility and interest to your story. Presumably, a meteorologist knows something about the weather, a doctor about health, a chemistry professor about chemicals. However, it is unlikely that a television star knows a great deal about cameras even if he or she makes commercials about cameras. Important, knowledgeable people are good sources for quotes even if what they say is not unique or said uniquely.

ANNOTATED MODEL Using Quotes Effectively

Alabama College Student Walks Almost 20 Miles Overnight to First Day of Work; CEO Gives Him His Car*

By N'dea Yancey-Bragg
USA Today, July 17, 2018

What started as every employee's worst nightmare had a pretty happy ending for Walter Carr, 20, a college student from Alabama.

The night before Carr's first day on the job, his 2003 Nissan Altima broke down.

He called his friends and his girlfriend to try to get a ride, but nothing worked out. He checked his GPS and saw that without a car it would take him about 7 hours to get from his house in Homewood, Alabama, to the town of Pelham for his first day at Bellhops moving company.

He decided to walk.

Carr started his 20-mile trek sometime around midnight.

The quote moves the story forward by showing Carr's motivations.

"I wanted to be there before 8," he said. "I wanted to beat the crew members there to let the company know how dedicated I am."

He made it about 14 miles to Pelham when police officers stopped him on the side of the road around 4 a.m.

"He was like, 'Where are you going?' and I was like, 'It's hard to believe, it's going to sound real crazy, but I'm actually headed to work,'" Carr said.

Notice that the reporter has not edited out all the "likes." Instead, she is capturing how the source talks.

When they heard his story, the officers decided to take him to breakfast at Whataburger and made sure he got something for lunch, too.

This and the next paragraph provide some basic chronology. There's no need for a direct quote because the reporter can write it more concisely.

Carr said the officers debated for a little while where they could safely drop him off and eventually landed on First Methodist Church. The officers said they would send someone to check on him.

Pelham Police Dept
@PelhamPoliceAL
Follow

Proud to have encountered this young man. He certainly made an impact on us!

#PelhamPD #belikewalter

4:40 PM - 16 Jul 2018

The online version of the story included screenshots from the Pelham Police Department's Twitter account.

(continued)

ANNOTATED MODEL Using Quotes Effectively *(continued)*

Carr rested for a while before he started walking again. He had less than 4 miles to go when another officer pulled up to check on him.

The dialogue in this quote from Carr captures some of the emotion of the day. Note, also, how the quote is punctuated. The quote within a quote uses single quotation marks.

"He said, 'Are you Walter Carr?' and he was like, 'Get in the car, I got you,'" Carr said.

The officer dropped him off at the home of Jenny Hayden Lamey, who Carr was scheduled to help move that day. Carr said once the officer told Lamey and her husband Chris his story, they insisted he rest for a while.

"They were overwhelmed," he said. "We argued about five minutes about me resting."

After the moving job was done, Lamey, impressed by Carr's determination, shared his story on Facebook.

The writer introduces another source, who helps verify the story and provides more background on Carr to move the story along.

She said while waiting for the rest of the crew to arrive, they started to chat, and Lamey learned that Carr is enlisted to become a Marine. She said he and his mother moved to Birmingham after losing their home in New Orleans during Katrina.

"I just can't tell you how touched I was by Walter and his journey," she wrote [in a Facebook post]. "He is humble and kind and cheerful and he had big dreams!"

The newspaper provided a hyperlink to Lamey's Facebook post about Carr, which, as of July 19, 2018, had been liked 8,400 times.

Lamey's post went viral and caught the attention of Luke Marklin, the Bellhops CEO, on Sunday morning. Marklin said he started getting texts about Carr's story and got his team together to figure how they could thank him.

"Just sitting there reading it, I was just blown away," Marklin said. "The more we learned, the more we realized Walter was just a special person."

. . .

Marklin met Carr on Monday to thank him and decided to gift him his personal Ford Escape. Carr was surprised, to say the least.

"I think he was pretty happy," Marklin said, laughing. "His resolve to get through challenges is just something that legends are made of, really." . . .

*The story was trimmed for space reasons.

Accuracy and Fairness in Direct Quotations

The first obligation of any reporter is to be accurate. You must learn how to get the exact words of the source.

It's not easy.

Scribbled notes from interviews, news conferences and meetings are often difficult to decipher and interpret. A study by Adrienne Lehrer, now professor emeritus of linguistics at the University of Arizona, found that only 13 of 98 quotations taken from Arizona newspapers proved to be verbatim when compared to recordings. Only twice, however, were the meanings of the nonverbatim quotes considered inaccurate.

Be sure to check the policy of your employer. Some news organizations might accept minor changes to a direct quotation to correct a grammatical slip, but some, including The Associated Press, will not. The quotation marks are meant to signify that the words within the quotation marks are being captured verbatim. But no one expects reporters to insert every "huh" or "ya know," and there is almost never cause to embarrass anyone with limited English skills.

Whatever the platform, quotes also need to be presented with adequate context. Similarly, a soundbite out of context distorts the meaning of what the source has said and is also unethical.

> **"I think of quotes as spices. Spices in themselves have no nutritional value. They make nutritious things taste better, but, like spices, quotes should be used sparingly."**
>
> ■ Isabel Wilkerson, Pulitzer Prize–winning reporter at *The Washington Post*, quoted in Jack Hart, *A Writer's Coach: The Complete Guide to Writing Strategies That Work* (2006)

Verification

When someone important says something important but perhaps false, putting the material in quotes does not relieve you of the responsibility for the inaccuracies. Citizens, officials and candidates for office often say things that may be partially true or altogether untrue and perhaps even libelous. Quotations need verification, like any other information you gather.

In the interest of balance, fairness and objectivity, many news organizations leave out, correct or point out the errors and inconsistencies in quotations. They do this in the article itself or in an accompanying story.

If Candidate A says that his opponent, Candidate B, is a member of the Ku Klux Klan, you should check before you print the charge. Good reporters don't stop looking and checking just because someone gives them some information. Look for yourself. Your story will not be complete unless you talk to all sides.

Quoting from Email, Social Media, the Internet and Chat Rooms

When you quote from an email you have received personally, you can usually be sure the sender has written those words. If you have doubts, be sure to check with your correspondent. It's also a good idea to let readers know that you obtained the quote through email and did not speak with the source in person. That could be important context for the quote: Was it carefully crafted and polished, or was it dashed off quickly? The reader will be able to evaluate the quote more critically.

If you find a quote on the web, you need to be much more careful. Try to verify the quote with the source, but if you can't do that, at least be sure to tell readers that the quote comes from the web, and then cite the URL.

Reading what people are saying in chat rooms, blogs and tweets can be useful to reporters. However, quoting what people write in these forums is unwise because some statements might be unverifiable and even libelous. Verification is important because you don't want to give your audience the wrong impression.

Don't be the young television reporter who shared someone else's Facebook post with her audience and suggested gang violence caused a young man's death because she didn't understand one of the references. The community was outraged, and police said the death was an accident.

However, if you have verified the information, identified the person who is saying it, and specifically state where you obtained the information, you might on occasion use a quote from social media. Identifying the person might be impossible, though, because some people use screen names, aliases or pseudonyms.

Many publications include a screenshot of the tweet. That's not verification, though. Anyone can masquerade as another person. Journalists have to track down the source.

The Associated Press provides this guidance as a starting point:

> **You must never simply lift quotes, photos or video from social networking sites and attribute them to the name on the profile or feed where you found the material. Most social media sites offer a way to send a message to a user; use this to establish direct contact, over email or by phone, so you can get more detailed information about the source.**

Using Someone Else's Direct Quotations

If you use a direct quotation that you did not personally get from a source, always indicate your source for the quote. Jessica Heslam wrote on BostonHerald.com that a *Boston Herald* review of WBZ-TV political analyst Jon Keller's book

A reporter's quotations must be accurate. Always review your notes to make sure you have the quote exactly as it was said. If you aren't sure, go back to your source during prepublication review. You'll protect your news organization against libel and boost your credibility.

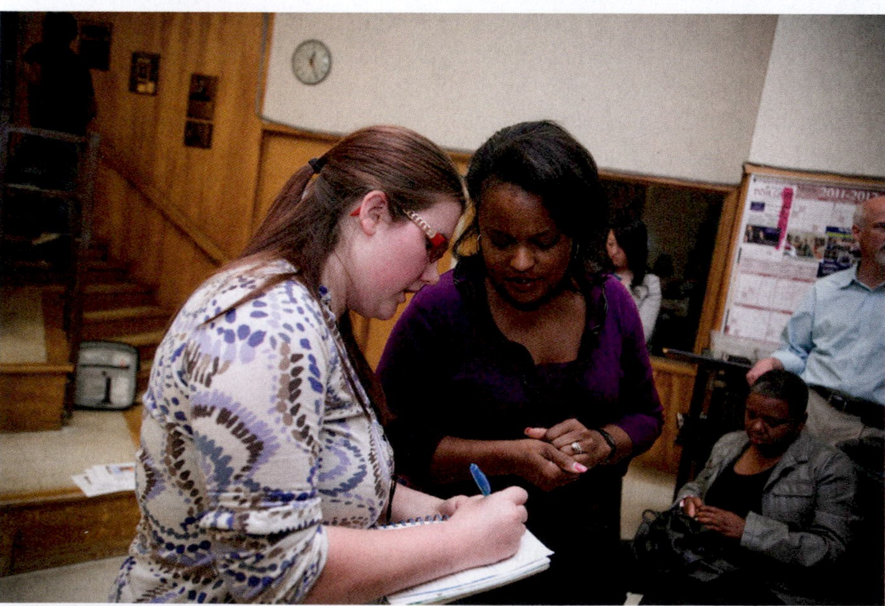

Lynn Donaldson/WireImage/Getty Images

The Bluest State: How Massachusetts Created the Massachusetts Blueprint for American Political Disaster revealed "almost three dozen instances of direct quotes and other material lifted from numerous newspaper articles without any attribution." Keller received some bad press. Other journalists have faced suspensions and firings. (See Chapter 20 for a thorough discussion of plagiarism and ways to avoid it.)

The Public Relations Society of America doesn't mind if you use material from a news release without attribution. Gerard Corbett, past chair and CEO of PRSA, says doing so is not plagiarism, but he does recommend attribution when reporters use direct quotes, facts or figures from releases.

For transparency, your attribution should tell readers the quote came from a news release. For example, you wouldn't just write this:

> **"I'm excited to work for such a great institution," the new athletic director said.**

This quote would make it appear that you interviewed the new employee or heard the quote directly. Instead, write something like this:

> **"I'm excited to work for such a great institution," the new athletic director said in a news release.**

In any case, it's best to get your own direct quotes and to avoid the direct quotes you find in news releases. Including the news release's carefully crafted quote doesn't typically achieve one of the aims of using a direct quote: adding life, color and emotion to your story. In addition, direct quotes in a news release might have been written by the public relations person and not come directly from the person quoted.

Practicing Prepublication Review

Decades ago, you would not have had an editor tell you to check the accuracy of your direct quotations with your source before publication. Today, it is standard practice for many news organizations. Steve Weinberg, a former Missouri School of Journalism professor and former head of Investigative Reporters and Editors, calls it PPR—prepublication review.

Weinberg states candidly that sensitivity to the feelings of his sources is not what motivates him to use PPR. Rather, he finds that prepublication review loosens the tongues of tight-lipped sources and gets their statements on the record.

Prepublication review also extends to checking the facts. Most professional journalists insist that it does not make them surrender control over their stories or feel compromised.

Another reason for prepublication review is that it serves as a defense against libel. Jurors are less likely to find "reckless disregard for the truth" in an article that was reviewed by the source of the quote.

> **"When you see yourself quoted in print and you're sorry you said it, it suddenly becomes a misquotation."**
>
> ■ Laurence J. Peter, author of *Peter's Quotations: Ideas for Our Times* and *The Peter Principle: Why Things Always Go Wrong*

Getting good quotes in a television interview takes skill and practice.

The White House/Sipa USA/Newscom

But what happens when sources want to change a quote? Weinberg says to make it clear that the source should check only for accuracy. The reporter can consider comments about interpretation, phrasing or tone but retains the right to change or not change the quotes.

And what happens if someone denies saying part of his or her direct quote? That possibility is why you need to have good notes, Weinberg says, even if they are in shorthand. Having the interview recorded is even better.

On occasion, journalists have gone overboard in allowing sources to review quotations. When news broke in 2012 that major publications, including *The New York Times*, had agreed to let politicians and campaigns approve quotations before the quotes appeared in print, media critics were dismayed. Just two months later, then–*New York Times* Executive Editor Jill Abramson wrote a memo to her staff that said this:

> **So starting now (Sept. 20, 2012), we want to draw a clear line on this. Citing *Times* policy, reporters should say no if a source demands, as a condition of an interview, that quotes be submitted afterwards to the source or a press aide to review, approve or edit.**

Note the words "review, approve or edit." What could be wrong with checking the accuracy of a quote? Does "edit" mean change the wording or change the meaning? You certainly need to check the accuracy of the facts in your story. Doesn't it make sense to check the accuracy of the quotations? What if you misunderstood the context? What if you misheard the quote? A simple reading of the quotes, direct and indirect, and surrounding material to the source could help ensure accurate information is conveyed.

If you have evidence that you quoted your source correctly but your source misspoke, perhaps it is time to paraphrase your source and not use a direct quotation. On the other hand, if your source is a high-ranking government official or political candidate, you and your editors may feel you have an obligation to hold the source accountable for a false statement.

In any case, as a journalist you have the freedom to decide what's news and what should and should not be included in your stories. Consult your editors, but don't abdicate that responsibility to your sources.

ON THE JOB Reinventing a Career

Courtesy of Rachel Reese

When **Diana Reese** was a journalism student, she never imagined she would someday write for *The Washington Post*.

"Back then, I was not interested in writing news," she said, "so I was in the magazine sequence."

Her first career goal was editor of a regional publication such as *Missouri Life*—a job she had by the age of 23. She later worked in Knoxville, Tennessee, and New York City as an editor for Whittle Communications, a company founded by the young entrepreneurs who bought *Esquire* magazine.

Reese fulfilled her second career goal when she moved to Kansas City to freelance, specializing in articles on health for national consumer magazines. She soon discovered that getting and using good direct quotations were key to getting her articles accepted and read.

After taking a break to raise her children, she returned to freelancing, only to discover a different world. "Most of the magazines I'd written for were out of business," she said.

She wrote for a variety of websites until a personal article she did about unemployment among the middle class in middle America landed her a spot as a regular contributor to *The Washington Post* women's blog "She the People."

She discovered she liked "the adrenaline rush" of covering or commenting on breaking news and seeing it online almost immediately.

Her Midwest location was often an advantage. The race between then-Sen. Claire McCaskill, D-Mo., and challenger Todd Akin (he of "legitimate rape" fame) took place in neighboring Missouri. Reese's take on Sarah Palin's campaign speech in a you-pick blueberry patch just outside of Kansas City trended as the most-read article on the *Post* website.

Reese did more than 200 articles for "She the People" until it was discontinued in January 2015. She continues to freelance and is putting together a collection of her favorite "She the People" pieces for an e-book so she can learn how self-publishing works.

She has mixed feelings about the term *blog*. "I did a lot of reporting and a lot of digging for 'She the People,'" she said. "Lively quotes always made for more interesting stories."

She offers these tips for getting great quotations:

- **Let sources talk.** Wait to ask the next question: People want to fill the silence. "I think I asked actress Mariska Hargitay one question," Reese said. "Her comment about being a 'badass' at age 50 was a great ending for the story."
- **Be ready.** "No one expected Mindy Corporon—whose son and father were killed in the shooting at the Jewish Community Center in Kansas—to show up at a vigil afterwards," Reese said. "Her comment, 'I know they're in heaven together,' was beautiful and heart-breaking."
- **Ask hard questions, but stay human.** "I'm working on an article about a 20-year-old who committed suicide, and I had to say to the parents, 'Tell me about the day your son died.'"
- **Don't let physicians (or other professionals) get away with jargon.** Ask for an explanation in nonmedical terms.
- **Check quotes for accuracy, if you need to, by calling sources and reading their words back to them.** Don't be tempted—or bullied—into sending a copy of the entire story.
- **Avoid email interviews.** Sources usually sound too formal in emails.

Finally, don't forget about pulling a catchy quote to use on Twitter and other social media when promoting a story.

We all need to remember that we write for our readers.

We also need to remember that we are human and sometimes make mistakes. Craig Silverman, an award-winning journalist and author, has reported for the Poynter Institute on mangled direct quotations from the past and the present. No paper is immune, and neither is history.

He writes that while doing research for his book *Regret the Error: How Media Mistakes Pollute the Press and Imperil Free Speech*, he found that William Randolph Hearst did not say, "You furnish the pictures; I'll furnish the war"; President Lyndon B. Johnson did not say, "If I've lost Cronkite, I've lost Middle America"; and Vice President Al Gore "sure as hell" never claimed to have invented the internet.

If you Google "misquotations," you will find a list of about 100 quotations under "Misquoted or Misattributed" and "Unsourced, Unverified or Other Best Guesses." You will also find a list of people who are most commonly misquoted. The name on top of the list? Yogi Berra. However, according to *The New York Times,* the American baseball legend did indeed say, "It ain't over 'til it's over."

Altering Quotations

By now you realize that although you should use direct quotations, they present many challenges. For starters, is the social media post really from the stated author? Is the information in the direct quotation you obtained accurate? Who, if anybody, really said that famous quote you think you remember? Now, assuming all the information in the direct quotations you have is accurate, how and when should you use those quotes? And should you ever edit them?

TIPS

Getting Accurate Quotes

- Use a digital recorder or smartphone to record interviews, and be sure the interviewee knows you are using it.
- Develop a consistent shorthand method for note taking so you can reliably read your own notes.
- Check your written quotes against any available video or audio of the situation.
- Call the source to verify the exact wording of any quote you're unsure of.

Paraphrasing Quotes

Although there is no set number of quotations you should strive to include, a story with no quotes often lacks life and substance. Including lengthy quotes indiscriminately, however, is a sign that you haven't really digested the material for your audience. Instead of quoting someone at length, look for the effective kernel within a long quotation. **Paraphrase** — or put in your own words — the remainder of the information you want to use. A paraphrase is an **indirect quotation**.

Some quotations need verification; others need clarification. Do not quote someone unless you are sure what that person means. It is usually better to skip a quotation altogether than to confuse the reader. However, if a country's president, for example, posts a tweet or makes a public comment that needs clarification or even correction, one option might be to use a direct quote from the president, seek clarification from his or her aides and other experts, and include their responses in your story.

In general, the best way to avoid confusing or wordy quotes is to paraphrase. As a reporter, you must have confidence that you will sometimes be able to convey the speaker's meaning in fewer words, in better language and more clearly than the source did. The task of digesting, condensing and clarifying quotes takes more effort than simply repeating them word for word.

Here is a quote that should be cut drastically:

> **"When I first started singing lessons, I assumed I would be a public school teacher and maybe, if I was good enough, a voice teacher," he said. "When I graduated from the university, I still thought I would be a teacher, and I wanted to teach voice."**

A paraphrase conveys the meaning more succinctly:

> **When he first started singing lessons and even after he graduated from college, he said, he wanted to be a voice teacher.**

Using Partial Quotes

It is much better to paraphrase or to use full quotes than to use fragmentary or partial quotes. Partial quotes often make for choppy, interrupted sentences. Some editors would have you avoid these "orphan quotes" almost altogether.

Here is an example of the overuse of partial quotes:

> **The mayor said citizens should "turn off" unnecessary lights and "turn down" thermostats "to 65 degrees."**

Because the quoted words are so mundane and uncontroversial, the sentence would be better with no quotation marks at all.

Taking out the quotation marks would turn this sentence into an indirect quotation. In an indirect quotation, the reporter includes attribution but doesn't use quotation marks. Indirect quotations need to meet the same test for accuracy that direct quotations require.

If a particular phrase has special significance or meaning, a partial quote may be justifiable. Sometimes you might want to put a word or phrase in quotation marks to indicate that this was precisely what the speaker said. Look at this use of a one-word quote in a story about genetic engineering in *The Atlantic*:

> **By all but eliminating agricultural erosion and runoff—so Brian Noyes, the local conservation-district manager, told me—continuous no-till could "revolutionize" the area's water quality.**

The writer thought it important that readers know that "revolutionize" was not his word but the word of his source. And he was right; "revolutionize" is a strong word.

When you do use partial quotes, do not put quotation marks around something the speaker could not have said. Suppose a speaker told a student audience at a university, "I am pleased and thrilled with your attendance here tonight." It would be incorrect to write the following:

> **The speaker said she was "pleased and thrilled with the students' attendance."**

The correct version is this:

> **The speaker said she was "pleased and thrilled" with the students' attendance.**

Better yet, just use a shorter, indirect quote:

> **The speaker said she was thrilled by the students' attendance.**

What's the grammar error in this sentence?

In May 2018, Prince Harry and Meghan Markle were married in St. George's Chapel that King Edward IV began building at Windsor Castle in 1475.

See Appendix 1, Rule 5.

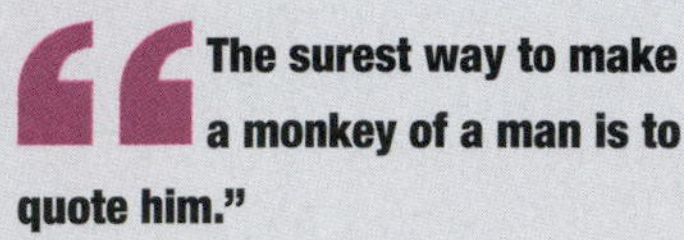

The surest way to make a monkey of a man is to quote him."

■ **Robert Benchley, humorist**

"Thrilled" isn't a very thrilling word. There's no harm in using it, but there's also no need for quotation marks.

Partial quotes often contain an ellipsis (three periods) to tell the reader that some of the words of the quote are missing. For example:

> **"I have come here tonight . . . and I have crossed state lines . . . to conspire against the government."**

When using ellipses, you should not keep the reader guessing about what is missing. Sometimes the speaker's actual meaning is distorted when certain words are dropped. If a critic writes about a three-act play, "A great hit—except for the first three acts," an ad that picks up only the first part of that quote is guilty of misrepresentation. A journalist who uses the technique to distort the message is no less guilty.

Capturing Dialect or Accent

Using colorful or colloquial expressions helps the writer capture a person in a particular environment. The same can be true when you write the way that people talk:

> **"Are you gonna go?" he asked.**
> **"No, I'm not goin'," she replied.**

In everyday speech, hardly anyone enunciates perfectly. But when conversation is written down in newspaper reporting, readers expect correct, full spellings. Not only is correct spelling easier to read, but it is also less difficult to write.

Capturing dialect consistently is difficult, as these passages from a newspaper story about a Hollywood actor illustrate:

> **"Boy, it's hot out theah," she started. "I could sure use a nice cold beer. How about it, uh? Wanta go get a couple beers?"**

If she said "theah," wouldn't she also say "beeah"? Perhaps she said, "How 'bout it, uh?" And if she said "wanta," maybe she also said "geta."

In another passage, the writer has the actor speaking "straight" English:

> **"Would you believe I used to dress like that all the time? Dates didn't want to be seen with me. I was always being asked to change clothes before going out."**

It is unlikely that a person would be that inconsistent in her speech.

The writer of this story tried to show us something of the actor's character. If he wanted to convey her speech patterns, he should have either been consistent or simply reported that she talked the same off the set as on it.

Be cautious about transcribing regional and other cultural speech idiosyncrasies. Sometimes when a newspaper attempts to quote someone saying something uniquely, it betrays a bias. A Southern politician is more likely to have his quote spelled phonetically than an Eastern politician who says "idee-er" (for "idea") and "yahd" (for "yard").

Still, you should not make everyone's speech the same. Barbara King Lord, former director of editorial training for The Associated Press, laments "our frequent inability to write other than insipid speech" and "our tendency to homogenize the day-to-day speech patterns of the heterogeneous people we write about." She acknowledges that writers worry about exposing to ridicule the immigrant's halting or perhaps unconventional speech, while the stockbroker's speech appears flawless.

Lord calls the argument specious. People should not be exposed to ridicule through their speech. "The point here," she says, "is simply that when the writer's intention in writing dialects, quaint expressions, nonconventional grammar, flowery or showy speech, or the Queen's English is to make a person human, that intention is not only acceptable, it's desirable."

The only way you can make people human is to listen to them. Lord says reporters and writers usually hear but rarely listen. She advises reporters to "listen for expressions, turns of phrase, idiosyncratic talk" and to work these into their stories.

J. R. Moehringer of the *Los Angeles Times* did this in his Pulitzer Prize–winning article:

> **"No white man gonna tell me not to march," Lucy says, jutting her chin. "Only make me march harder."**

Here the actual speech makes the speaker's determination and passion all the more evident.

But be especially careful when quoting people for whom English is a second language. Nearly any attempt to quote nonfluent speakers exactly will be looked at as making fun of their English. Instead, paraphrase their comments, or, as some would advise, slightly edit the quotations — so slightly that even the speakers don't notice. However, if you have audio from baseball star Albert Pujols on your website, for example, and have the same quotes in perfect, fluent English in the written text, many would see the discrepancy as a serious problem. Others would say that you are hurting the uniqueness and character of the great slugger, who was born in the Dominican Republic. These problems are as old as radio and television, but convergence of the media has increased their frequency.

Mixing and Matching Questions and Answers

Writers often agonize over whether they must use quotations in the exact order in which the speaker said them. The primary questions you must ask yourself are these: Why am I changing the order? Am I being fair? Am I distorting the meaning? Am I putting quotes together that change what the speaker intended to say?

Here are two versions of statements made by the police chief in Columbia, Missouri, in response to shooting incidents in the summer of 2018:

> **"I want to reinforce that this is not a dangerous place," [Chief Ken] Burton said. "We've had a couple incidents that occurred and it's very high visibility and people get the impression that it's all-the-time shoot em' ups in downtown. It's just not that way. We have no problem with people coming down and enjoying each other.**
>
> **"Even the tailgating is not a problem until you get one knucklehead that wants to act out. We want downtown to be welcoming to everyone. And to that regard, we are going to provide the resources we think are necessary to maintain peace and tranquility down there."**

Here's another version of Burton's statement:

> **"People get the impression that there are all the time shoot-em-ups, and it's just not that way. Even the 'tailgating' is not a problem until you get one knucklehead that decides to act out."**

The second, shorter version was posted online about two and half hours earlier than the longer version. Should that reporter have spent more time ensuring that the direct quotation used was complete? Without listening to a tape, the reader has no idea whose version, if either, is more accurate, but a reader who compares the stories might question why a writer left out some of Burton's statement.

Correcting Grammar in Quotes

Perhaps the most perplexing problem tied to the proper handling of direct quotations is this: When should you correct grammatical errors in a direct quotation? Should you expect people in news conferences or during informal interviews to speak perfect English?

The case for correcting grammar

It is accepted practice at many newspapers to correct mistakes in grammar and to convey a person's remarks in complete sentences. None of us regularly speaks in perfect, grammatical sentences. But if we were writing down our remarks, presumably we would write in grammatically correct English.

Reporters are expected to use standard American written English:

- **Standard.** News audiences expect to read or hear the most widely and generally accepted English.
- **American.** Some words have different spellings and meanings in England, Australia and other English-speaking countries.
- **Written.** Admittedly, people often use words and expressions when speaking that they do not use when writing.

The case against correcting grammar

Most news organizations do not have a written policy on correcting grammatical errors in direct quotations. Because so many variables are involved, these matters are handled on a case-by-case basis. Some argue that you should sacrifice a bit of accuracy in the interest of promoting proper English—except in the speech of elected officials and public figures.

On the subject of correcting grammar in direct quotations, read what *The Associated Press Stylebook* says under the entry "quotations in the news":

> **Never alter quotations even to correct minor grammatical errors or word usage. Casual minor tongue slips may be removed by using ellipses but even that should be done with extreme caution. . . . If there is a question about a quote, either don't use it or ask the speaker to clarify.**

In this age of convergence, a writer or another journalist (or citizen journalist) might also have shot video or recorded audio. The quotation you're tempted to edit might be heard by millions of people on radio or television or online. Changing the quote even slightly might make viewers and listeners question the credibility of your written report. Readers might also ask why writers feel the need to act as press agents who strive to make their subjects look good.

This caution applies to celebrities of all kinds (such as actors and sports figures), but it might also apply to political candidates and elected officials. At least, some argue, news agencies should have some consistency. If a reporter quotes a farmer using incorrect grammar, then shouldn't the same be done for a mayor or for a college professor?

The age of social media, particularly Twitter, raises more issues. Most politicians, news organizations, public figures, celebrities and the like use Twitter for a variety of reasons. And with some people having dozens of millions of followers, grammatical mistakes are are bound to happen and be seen. What to do? Here's what The Associated Press recommends:

> **Use *sic*, the Latin word meaning *thus* or *so*, to show that quoted material or person's words include a misspelling, incorrect grammar or peculiar usage. Place (*sic*) in the text directly after the problem to show that the passage is precisely reproduced.**

Although using *sic* shows the error is not yours as a writer, using *sic* also runs the risk of causing readers to think you are making fun of the source. Fortunately, if your story is appearing online, on a mobile platform or on television, you can easily include screenshots of the tweets to let readers see the tweets for themselves.

Removing Redundancies

Another question reporters deal with is whether to remove redundancies and other irrelevant material by using ellipses. Again, there is no agreement in the industry. For most reporters and editors, the answer to the problem of correcting quotes is to take out the quotation marks and to paraphrase. However, when you do that, you can lose a lot. The value of quotes often lies in their richness and uniqueness.

When the *Columbia Missourian* quoted University of Missouri basketball star Keon Lawrence after a winning game, it dropped a sentence:

> **"That felt good," Keon Lawrence said. "I look forward to doing that again."**

The *Columbia Daily Tribune* wrote it this way:

> **"Oh, that felt good," Lawrence said a few minutes after the game that hardly anyone thought the Tigers could win. "I didn't never do that. I look forward to doing that again."**

Which version do you like better? Which version would you have written?

Deleting Obscenity, Profanity and Vulgarity

Many news organizations never allow some words that people say to be printed or broadcast—even if they are said uniquely. You won't even find direct examples in this chapter. Some language offends readers or listeners, and editors and producers know better than to print or broadcast it without good reason. The trouble is that few people have the same labels for these words:

- **Obscenities:** Language that is in some way lewd, lascivious or indecent.
- **Profanities:** Words that are used irreverently to refer to a deity or to beings, places or objects that people regard as divine or sacred; cursing.
- **Vulgarities:** Words that primarily refer to excretory matters; coarse, crude.

There are legitimate reasons to use proper sex-related terms in health stories and in some crime stories, including child molestation stories. News stories about sexual assaults or accusations sometimes contain words such as these, especially if the people involved are celebrities or politicians.

Additionally, the rules are different for what some call "swear" words in a direct quotation. Some papers follow *The Associated Press Stylebook* rule:

> **Do not use them (obscenities, profanities, and vulgarities) in stories unless they are part of direct quotations and there is a compelling reason for them. . . . If the obscenity involved is particularly offensive but the story requires making clear what the word was, replace the letters of the offensive word with hyphens, using only an initial letter: *f---*, *s---*.**

News is likely to reflect the sensibilities of its audience. Like it or not, language that was once considered vulgar in polite society is now tolerated more widely. Indeed, some high-ranking officials have drawn headlines in recent years for their vocabulary choices.

In 2013, *The New York Times* eased up a bit on its strict policy against printing vulgarities and obscenities. Philip Corbett, the associate managing editor for standards, told news aggregator site *The Wire* in an email, "The new version allows for a wider range of exceptions in cases where an offensive term is central to a news story." Here's what the updated *New York Times* style guide says:

> **If the precise nature of an obscenity, vulgarity or other offensive expression is essential to the readers' understanding of a newsworthy event — not merely to convey color or emotion — editors should consider using the term or a close paraphrase.**

At times, you might wish to use vulgarities to show the intensity of someone's anger, terror, frustration or bitterness. Few inside the news media condone the casual, gratuitous use of vulgarities, however. And neither do most readers and listeners.

But what if you are reporting on an individual who is running for or already holds a high public office? Would reporting on that individual's use of a vulgarity give voters insight into that person's character or beliefs?

In 2016, Donald Trump was heard on an old *Access Hollywood* tape using a vulgarity to refer to part of the female anatomy. The tape attracted countless headlines. Some news organizations, including *The Wall Street Journal*, wrote exactly what the president said; some were more oblique. NBC News, for example, bleeped out the word.

Nearly two years later, journalists faced another challenge. When now-President Trump discussed immigration with lawmakers, he referred to some countries as "s*hole" countries. Major news outlets reported the president's comments, and *The New York Times* also reported on how national organizations handled the expletive, which ranged from using the exact quote to blanking it out:

> **"It would be futile to mask the word when the language itself, in reference to Haiti and African countries, was so extraordinary," said the AP's vice president for standards, John Daniszewski.**
>
> **Phil Corbett, the associate managing editor for standards at *The New York Times*, said in an email: "It seemed pretty clear to all of us that we should quote the language directly, not paraphrase it. We wanted to be sure readers would fully understand what the story was about."**
>
> ***The Times*, unlike some papers, omitted the obscenity from its headline and push alert, using the term "vulgar language" instead. "We are still inclined to be somewhat restrained — for instance, by avoiding the actual vulgarities in headlines," Mr. Corbett said.**

What do you think of the news outlets' decisions? How might today's 24-hour news cycle affect journalists' decisions? What difference does it make, if any, that Trump was the president of the United States as opposed to a star athlete?

With someone else, a journalist might choose to have a little fun. When he was a sportswriter for the *Columbia* (Missouri) *Daily Tribune*, Joe Walljasper offered this wry observation when Cincinnati Reds manager Bryan Price unburdened himself for five minutes and 34 seconds to some reporters early in the 2015 season. Walljasper kept track: "Final tally: 971 words, 77 of which were the F-bombs, a 7.9 percent rate." He wrote: "That was enough to put him in elite company."

He then went on to compare Price's performance to those of Royals manager Hal McRae and Cubs manager Lee Elia—using the same method of measurement. He concluded: "Price has achieved notoriety that will last a lifetime, although, if the managerial history of McRae and Elia is a guide, it will be the only reason he is remembered."

Avoiding Made-Up Quotes

Fabricating a direct quote, even from general things that a source has said or from what the source might say if given the chance, is never acceptable. Even seasoned reporters are sometimes tempted to put quotation marks around words that their sources "meant to say" or to clarify or simplify a quote. They reason that it's more important to have a clear and concise quote for the reader than to be a slave to the verbose and unclear words of the source. That's bad reasoning. It's better to paraphrase.

Even worse is fabricating a quote that makes a source look bad or that is perhaps even libelous. Doing so can result in a lawsuit. In 1991, in *Masson v. Malcolm*, the U.S. Supreme Court ruled that suits regarding quotations can proceed to trial if the altered quote "results in a material change in the meaning conveyed by the statement."

Libel or no libel, your credibility as a reporter demands that you be scrupulously exact when you place people's words inside quotation marks. When in doubt, paraphrase.

Attributing Direct and Indirect Quotes

Now that you've learned some of the complexities of using quotations, let's take a look at when and how to attribute them to a source.

When to Attribute

Attribution involves giving the name of (and sometimes other identifying information about) the source of a direct quotation, an indirect quotation or other paraphrased material. You should almost always attribute direct quotes—with some exceptions. You would not, for example, attribute a quotation to a 7-year-old who witnessed a gang shooting. You might not wish to attribute a quote to someone who saw a homicide suspect with the victim. To do so in either case could put the source in danger.

You need a good reason to allow an entire paragraph of direct quotations to stand without an attribution. However, if you are quoting from a speech, an interview or a news conference and only the speaker is mentioned in the story, it might be excessive to put an attribution in every paragraph.

ANNOTATED MODEL Using Attributions

More Details Emerge About Shark Theft as San Antonio Man Makes Bond*

By Brian Contreras, Staff Writer
San Antonio Express-News, Updated 11:16 am CDT, Wednesday, August 1, 2018

When Leon Valley police got a call over the weekend that someone had stolen a shark from the San Antonio Aquarium, they initially thought it was a hoax. After all, it was Shark Week.

"You'd never think (of) something like that," Leon Valley Police Chief Joseph Salvaggio said.

The quotation provides support for the lead without restating it. The attribution "said" is in the past tense. Because the source's title is relatively short, the writer put the source's name and title before the "said."

But the theft was no joke. Now, a man accused of stealing the shark is facing a state felony theft charge and possibly federal charges.

Although there is no attribution in this paragraph, the police chief explains the possible charges later in the story.

Salvaggio said Antone Shannon, 38, has admitted taking Miss Helen, a small gray horn shark. Shannon was released on bond Tuesday afternoon.

The attribution is simple and direct. There is no need to repeat the source's title.

There is no need to attribute this information as long as the reporter confirmed it with jail records.

Police said Shannon, working with a woman and another man, snatched Miss Helen out of her tank, wrapped her in a blanket and pushed her out of the aquarium in a baby carriage. In the process, Salvaggio said, Shannon dumped a bucket of a bleach solution into a water filtration system and used the bucket to help move the shark.

Because the whole story accuses Shannon of a crime, attribution is essential. In addition, the newspaper also posted a video from the aquarium's security footage that showed the incident. https://www.mysanantonio.com/news/local/article/More-details-emerge-about-shark-theft-as-San-13121537.php.

"Our marine husbandry team was able to counter that in time for it to not do any damage to the other exhibits," said Jenny Spellman, general manager of the aquarium.

The quote introduces an additional source. Spellman's title is slightly longer, so the writer has put the verb of attribution "said" before the source's name. There's no need for a second comma because of the period.

As the thieves started to leave the aquarium, Salvaggio said staff noticed water dripping from the carriage, prompting them to follow the trio.

In the parking lot, Shannon brushed off requests to look inside the carriage, saying "they were heading out to get their baby medication (because) it was sick," said Spellman, one of the staffers who went after the thieves.

By putting "said" before the source's name, the writer is able to weave in more background information about the source. A broadcast story would have introduced Spellman first: Spellman was one of the staffers who went after the thieves.

After the three left, she said staff reviewed security footage and confirmed a theft had occurred before calling the police.

Salvaggio said the other man and the woman have been identified and admitted their roles, but charges haven't been filed yet. The trio consists of a married couple and a neighbor, Salvaggio said.

. . .

According to online court records, Shannon has a lengthy criminal history in Bexar County. He's been convicted of at least six charges, including vehicle theft, drug possession and evading arrest.

The reporter has done some digging to provide more background information on the suspect. Because the reporter is referring to records and not the words of someone he interviewed, "according to" is the appropriate form of attribution.

The second sentence does not need to be attributed because it's clear that this information also came from the online court records.

*The story was trimmed for space reasons.

Ordinarily, you also should attribute indirect quotations. You should usually have a source for the information you write, and when you do, attribute the information to that source. The source can be a person or a written document. However, there are exceptions.

If you are a witness to damage or injuries, do not name yourself as a source in the story. If possible, attribute this information to the police or to other authorities.

But you do not have to attribute the totally obvious. If you are on the scene of an accident and can see that three people were involved, you do not have to write, "'Three people were involved in the accident,' Officer Osbord said." If you are unsure of the information or if there are conclusions or generalities involved, your editor probably will want you to attribute the information to an official or a witness. Avoid, however, attributing factual statements to "officials," "authorities" or "sources." "Such constructions," writes journalist Jack Hart, "suggest that we are controlled by form and that we have forgotten about function."

If you are quoting from an interview conducted by someone other than yourself, be sure to note that. Do not imply that you obtained the quote yourself by writing, "In an interview, Smith said . . ." This makes it seem as though you conducted the interview. Instead, write: "In an interview with the XYZ news organization, Smith said . . ." By doing so, you are being transparent with your audience and the sources you've quoted.

Hart pleads for common sense regarding attributions. "Let's save them for direct quotations or paraphrased quotes laced with opinion," he writes. "Or for assertions likely to be especially sensitive. Or controversial." He says we should attribute only "if it matters."

This is good advice for the veteran. Nevertheless, although it is possible to attribute too often and although you do not always need to attribute, when you have doubts, include an attribution. In other words, it's better to attribute too much than not enough.

This goes for attributing information to anonymous sources, too. You should seldom use them, but when you do, you must include some attribution. Try to preserve your credibility by giving as much information as you can about the sources without revealing their identities. For example, you might report "a source close to the chancellor said." For the second reference to the same source, use "the anonymous source said."

Whether or not we like them, anonymous sources are common, even at the best of news organizations.

Sometimes, as in stories about crime victims, you might have to change someone's name and follow the pseudonym with "not her real name" in parentheses to protect the source's privacy or to avoid endangering the source's life or family.

TIPS

Attribution Not Needed

You need not attribute information to a source if you are a witness or if the information:

- Is a matter of public record.
- Is generally known.
- Is available from several sources.
- Is easily verifiable.
- Makes no assumptions.
- Contains no opinions.
- Is noncontroversial.

How to Attribute

In composition and creative writing classes, you may have been told to avoid repeating the same word. You probably picked up your thesaurus to look for a synonym for "to say," a colorless verb. Without much research, you may have found 100 or more substitutes. None of them is necessarily wrong. Indeed, writers might search long for the exact word they need to convey a particular nuance of meaning. For example:

The presidential candidate *announced* the choice of a running mate.
The arrested man *divulged* the names of his accomplices.
The judge *pronounced* her sentence.

At other times, in the interest of precise and lively writing, you might write:

"I'll get you for that," she whispered.
"I object!" he shouted.

Nevertheless, reporters and editors prefer forms of "to say" in most instances, even if these are repeated throughout a story. And there are good reasons for this word choice. "Said" is unobtrusive. Rather than appearing tiresome and repetitious, it hides in the text and calls no attention to itself. "Said" is also neutral. It has no connotations. To use the word "said" is to be objective.

Some of the synonyms for "said" sound innocent enough, but be careful. If you report that a city official "claimed" or "maintained" or "contended," you are implying that you do not quite believe what the official said. The word "said" is the solution to your problem.

In some reports about labor negotiations, company officials always "ask" and labor leaders always "demand." "Demanding" sounds harsh and unreasonable, but "asking" sounds calm and reasonable. A reporter who uses these words in this context is taking an editorial stand—consciously or unconsciously.

Other words that you may be tempted to use as a substitute for "said" are simply unacceptable because they represent improper usage. For example:

"You don't really mean that," he winked.
"Of course I do," she grinned.
"But what if someone heard you say that?" he frowned.
"Oh, you are a fool," she laughed.

You cannot "wink" a word. Similarly, it is impossible to "grin," "frown" or "laugh" words. But you might want to say this:

"Not again," he said, moaning.
"I'm afraid so," she said with a grin.

This usage is correct. Words like "moaning" or phrases like "with a grin" sometimes are needed to convey the speaker's meaning, but often they are not necessary or even helpful.

Learning the correct words for attribution is the first step. Here are some other guidelines to follow when attributing quotations:

- **If a direct quote is more than one sentence long, place the attribution at the end of the first sentence.** This placement makes the copy flow better and doesn't keep the reader in the dark about the attribution for too long. For example:

  "The car overturned at least three times," the police officer said. "None of the four passengers was hurt. Luckily, the car did not explode into flames."

That one attribution is adequate. It would be redundant (and a waste of space) to write the following:

"The car overturned at least three times," the police officer said. "None of the four passengers was hurt," he added. "Luckily, the car did not explode into flames," he continued.

Nor should you write this:

"The car overturned at least three times. None of the four passengers was hurt. Luckily, the car did not explode into flames," the police officer said.

Although you should not keep the reader wondering who is being quoted, in most cases, you should avoid placing the attribution at the beginning of a quote. Do not write the following:

The police officer said: "The car overturned at least three times. None of the four passengers was hurt. Luckily, the car did not explode into flames."

- **However, if direct quotes from two different speakers follow one another, start the second with its attribution.** This placement avoids confusion for the reader:

  "The driver must not have seen the curve," an eyewitness said. "Once the car left the road, all I saw was a cloud of dust."

  The police officer said: "The car overturned at least three times. None of the four passengers was hurt. Luckily, the car did not explode into flames."

  Notice that when an attribution precedes a direct quotation that is more than one sentence long, wire service style requires that a colon follow the attribution.

- **Separate partial quotes and complete quotes.** Avoid constructions like this one:

  The mayor said the time had come "to turn off some lights. We all must do something to conserve electricity."

  The correct form is to separate partial quotes and complete quotes:

  The time has come "to turn off some lights," the mayor said. "We all must do something to conserve electricity."

- **The first time that you attribute a direct or an indirect quote, identify the speaker fully by first and last names.**

- **Attribute direct quotes to only one person.** For example, don't do the following:

  "Flames were shooting out everywhere," witnesses said.

  If witnesses made statements like this, you should eliminate the quotation marks to turn this into an indirect quotation. For example:

  Several witnesses said that flames were shooting out everywhere.

- **Do not make up a source. Never attribute a statement to "a witness" unless your source is indeed that witness.** At times you might ask a witness to confirm what you have seen, but never invent quotes for anonymous witnesses. Inventing witnesses and making up quotes is dishonest, inaccurate and inexcusable. If you witnessed or experienced something, make that clear to your audience.

"Here's what we saw," a *New York Times* reporter said in a video dispatch about Zimbabwe's 2018 presidential election. A similar first-person construction could also work in print and online.

In another example, a *New York Times* reporter included this line in a feature story about the busy post office atop Japan's Mount Fuji: "To experience firsthand what's involved in delivering mail from the summit, I climbed aboard the tractor last month for the bone clattering four-hour round trip up and down the mountain."

- **In stories covering past news events, use the past tense in attributions, and use past tense throughout the story.** However, features and other stories that do not report on news events might be more effective with attributions in the present tense. In a feature story like a personality profile—when it is safe to assume that if a person said something in the past, he or she would say the same thing today—you might use the present tense. For example, when you write, "'I like being mayor,' she says," you are indicating that the mayor still enjoys her job.
- **Ordinarily, place the noun or pronoun before the verb in attributions:**

  "Everything is under control," the sheriff said.
  "Everything is under control," Sheriff Dwayne Carey said.

  However, if you must identify a person by including a long title, it is less cumbersome to begin the attribution with the verb:

  "I enjoy the challenge," says Janet Berry, associate dean for graduate studies and research.

A Conversation About Punctuation: How to Handle Direct Quotations

"Always put the comma inside quotation marks," she said. Then she added, "The same goes for the period."

"Does the same rule apply for the question mark?" he asked.

"Only if the entire statement is a question," she replied, "and never add a comma after a question mark. Also, be sure to lowercase the first word of a continuing quote that follows an attribution and a comma.

"However, you must capitalize the first word of a new sentence after an attribution," she continued. "Do not forget to open and close the sentence with quotation marks."

"Why are there no quotation marks after the word 'comma' at the end of the third paragraph?" he asked.

"Because the same person is speaking at the beginning of the next paragraph," she said. "Notice that the new paragraph does open with quotation marks. Note, too, that a quote inside a quotation needs single quotation marks, as around the word 'comma' in the paragraph above."

Attributing Written Sources

Do not use the word "says" when quoting from written sources. "States" or "stated" is better. You might be general at times and write, "As *Time* magazine reported last week . . ." or "According to *Time* magazine . . ."

When you know the author of the piece, you might wish to include it: "As Katha Pollitt wrote in the June 8, 2015, issue of *The Nation* . . ."

For a report, survey or study cited in a news story, it's usually enough to identify the authors, the date of publication and the name of the journal or the issuing agency. (For guidance on avoiding unintentional plagiarism, see Chapter 20.)

Handling On- and Off-the-Record Information

Your job would be easy if all of your sources wished to be "on the record." Some sources do not want to be named for sound reasons. You must learn to use professional judgment in handling the material they give you. If you agree to accept their information, you must honor their request to remain off the record.

Be careful. If you try to confirm the information they give you with other sources and only a limited number of people have that information, your original source might be identifiable. Breaching that confidence destroys trust and credibility. Doing so also might get you in trouble with the law.

Emma McIntyre/VF18/Getty Images

New Yorker reporter Ronan Farrow, who has published exclusive coverage of sexual harassment and assault claims against Harvey Weinstein, Eric Schneiderman and others, needed his sources to speak on the record in order for the articles to be fit for publication.

Problems with Anonymous Sources

Be thoughtful before granting anonymity to sources. Whether journalists should use such sources is fiercely debated, a debate that was rekindled when the opinion editor of *The New York Times* ran a piece in September 2018 from a senior Trump administration official without disclosing the writer's name. (The controversy over that opinion piece, "I Am Part of the Resistance Inside the Trump Administration," will be examined in Chapter 20 on ethics.) As the Society of Professional Journalists' Ethics Code states, journalists should "be cautious when making promises, but keep the promises they make."

Not naming sources is dangerous for three important reasons. First, such information carries less credibility and makes the reporter and the newspaper suspect. Why should readers believe writers who won't cite the sources of their information? Who is to say that the writers didn't simply make things up to suit their stories?

Second, the source might be lying. He or she might be out to discredit someone or have other ulterior motives. The source also might be floating a trial balloon—that is, testing public reaction on some issue or event. Skilled diplomats and politicians know how to use reporters to take the temperature of public opinion. If the public reacts negatively, the sources will not proceed with whatever plans they leaked to the press. In such cases, the press has been used—and it has become less credible.

Finally, after you have promised anonymity to a source, you cannot change your mind without risking a breach-of-contract suit. In 1991, the U.S. Supreme Court ruled 5–4 in *Cohen v. Cowles Media Co.* that the First Amendment does not prevent news sources from suing the press for breach of contract when the press makes confidential sources public. That's why at many news organizations, only a senior editor has authority to commit the organization to a pledge of confidentiality.

Disagreement About Terminology

Some reporters make these distinctions regarding sources and attribution:

- **Off the record.** You may not use the information.
- **Not for attribution.** You may use the information but with no reference to its source.
- **Background.** You may use it with a general title for a source (for example, "a White House aide said").
- **Deep background.** You may use the information, but you may not indicate any source.

By no means is there agreement on these terms — not among journalists or sources. It's important for you and your sources to agree. For most people, "off the record" means not for attribution. For some, it means that you cannot use the information in any way. Some find no difference between "background" and "deep background." Journalists are vague about the meaning of the terms, and so are sources. Your obligation is to make sure you and your sources understand each other. Set the ground rules ahead of time. Clarify your terms. Make sure you agree on them.

Be careful not to allow a speaker to suddenly claim something is off the record. Sometimes in the middle of an interview, a source will see you taking notes and try to change the rules: "Oh, I meant to tell you, that last example was off the record." With all the tact you can muster, try, without losing the source altogether, to change the person's mind. At the least, tell the person to try to avoid doing that for the rest of the interview. The more experience a source has dealing with journalists, the more comfortable you should feel about asserting that your questions — and the source's answers — were on the record unless the source said the material was off the record *before* answering the question.

TIPS

Three Reasons to Avoid Anonymous Sources

- You damage your credibility.
- Your source may be lying or floating a trial balloon.
- You may be sued if you later reveal your source.

Background Interviews

If a city manager or police chief wishes to have a background session with you, you should not refuse (unless it is against your news organization's policy). Often these officials are trying to be as open as they can under certain circumstances. These sessions can help you prepare to cover complex issues intelligently.

But be aware that you are hearing only one point of view and that the information might be self-serving. For this reason, you might ask later that some information be attributed to the source. Better yet: If the topic is certain to be hotly debated — think tax increases or pay raises — then you might insist the session be on the record.

Some sources make a habit of saying everything is off the record and of giving commonplace information in background sessions. Although you should not quote a source who asks to remain off the record, you might use the information if one or more of the following is true:

- The information is a matter of public record.
- It is generally known.

- It is available from several sources, and you can attribute the information to those sources.
- You are a witness.

So as not to lose credibility with your source, it's a good idea to make it clear that you plan to use the information for one or more of the preceding reasons.

Remember these two important points:

- When possible, set the ground rules with your sources ahead of time.
- Know your news organization's policy regarding these matters.

Knowing when and how to attribute background information is an art you should continue to develop as a reporter.

CHAPTER RESOURCES

SUGGESTED READINGS

Brooks, Brian S., James L. Pinson and Jean Gaddy Wilson. *Working with Words: A Handbook for Media Writers and Editors.* 9th ed. New York: Bedford/St. Martin's, 2017. The section on quotations is informative and follows Associated Press style.

King, Barbara. "There's Real Power in Common Speech." *Ottaway News Extra*, no. 137 (Winter 1989): 8, 16. The author presents an excellent discussion on using real quotes from real people.

Marcus, Jon. "The Ethics of Leaks: The Increasing Use of Anonymous Sources and Leaks Has Intensified the Debate over How to Vet Information and Sources." *Nieman Reports* 71, no. 3 (Summer 2017): 14–23. This article provides a thorough discussion of recent leak cases, including The Panama Papers and stories related to WikiLeaks.

Pjesivac, Ivanka, and Rui, Rachel. "Anonymous Sources Hurt Credibility of News Stories Across Cultures: A Comparative Experiment in America and China." *International Communication Gazette* 76, no. 8 (December 2014): 641–660. This study demonstrates why using anonymous sources is problematic, and it also shows how scholars' research can be relevant to journalists.

Stein, M. L. "Ninth Circuit: It's OK to Make Up Quotes." *Editor & Publisher*, Aug. 12, 1989, 16, 30. This article reports reactions from the press and lawyers to the court decision allowing quotes that are not verbatim.

Stimson, William. "Two Schools on Quoting Confuse the Reader." *Journalism Educator* 49, no. 4 (Winter 1995): 69–73. Strong arguments against cleaning up quotes are presented in this article.

Stoltzfus, Duane. "Partial Pre-publication Review Gaining Favor at Newspapers." *Newspaper Research Journal* 27, no. 4 (Fall 2006): 23–37. A practice that was long thought unconscionable among journalists gains acceptance.

Stovall, James Glen. *Writing for the Mass Media*. 9th ed. Knoxville: Univ. of Tennessee Press, 2014. Originally published in 1984, this practical text was among the first that introduced students to writing for all the mass media.

Weinberg, Steve. "Thou Shalt Not Concoct Thy Quote." *Fineline* (July–August 1991): 3–4. In this article, Weinberg presents reasons for allowing sources to review quotations before publication.

SUGGESTED WEBSITES

LaunchPad Solo
launchpadworks.com
When you visit LaunchPad Solo for Journalism, you will find research links, exercises and LearningCurve adaptive quizzing to help you improve your grammar and AP style usage. In addition, the site's video collection hosts the videos highlighted in this and other chapters as well as additional clips of leading professionals discussing important media trends.

owl.purdue.edu
The Purdue Online Writing Lab offers numerous resources related to writing, including citation styles and guidance in using quotation marks.

nytimes.com/series/understanding-the-times
The New York Times staff is using this series to explain the news organization's practices to readers. Topics include such issues as the use of anonymous sources, the use of leaked classified information and the rules for off-the-record interviews.

quill.spjnetwork.org/
The Society of Professional Journalists' digital publication, The Quill, addresses ethical issues journalists face on the job, including whether and how to use anonymous sources. The website features numerous blogs to help journalists think more critically about their work, and the quarterly print publication is included with SPJ membership.

www.apstylebook.com
The Associated Press provides its stylebook in several formats, including as a traditional printed book, an online subscription and a mobile device (smartphone or tablet) application.

EXERCISES

1. **Your journalism blog.** Interview three different news reporters or editors working in online media, print, radio or television about their policies for handling sources regarding the following types of information:

   a. Off the record
   b. Not for attribution
   c. Background
   d. Deep background

   Write a blog post on your findings, and state which of the policies you think are the best—clearest, easiest to follow, most ethical.

2. Rewrite the following story. Pay special attention to the use of quotations and attribution. Note the sensitive nature of some of the quotations. Delete or paraphrase when you think it's necessary.

   Christopher O'Reilly is a remarkably happy young man, despite a bout with meningitis eight years ago that has left him paralyzed and brain-damaged.

   "I am happy," O'Reilly commented, as he puffed a cigarette. He has much to be happy about. Physical therapy has hastened his recovery since the day he awoke from a 10-week-long coma. He has lived to celebrate his 26th birthday.

   "I had a helluva birthday," he said. "I seen several friends. I had big cake," he added slowly.

   He lives in a house with his mother and stepfather in the rolling, green countryside near Springfield.

   O'Reilly's withered legs are curled beneath him now, and his right arm is mostly paralyzed, but he can do pull-ups with his left arm. He can see and hear.

   "When he came back, he wasn't worth a damn," his mother said. "The hack doctors told me he would be a vegetable all his life," she claimed.

   "He couldn't talk; he could only blink. And he drooled a lot," she smiled.

   Now, Chris is able to respond in incomplete sentences to questions and can carry on slow communication. "He don't talk good, but he talks," his mother commented.

   It all began when he stole a neighbor's Rototiller. His probation was revoked, and he found himself in the medium-security prison in Springfield. Then came "inadequate medical treatment" in the prison system. O'Reilly's family argued that he received punishment beyond what the Eighth Amendment of the U.S. Constitution calls "cruel and unusual."

   "Those prison officials were vicious," they said.

   As a result, he was awarded $250,000 from the state, the largest legal settlement in federal court in 10 years. "That sounds like a lot of money. But it really isn't, you know, when you consider what happened and when you consider the worth of a human life, and the way they treated him and all, we thought we should get at least a million," his mother remarked.

   O'Reilly contracted the infection of the brain after sleeping "on the concrete floor" of a confinement cell, his mother maintained. He had been placed in solitary confinement because he would not clean his cell. The disease went undiagnosed for eight days, leaving him paralyzed and brain-damaged, she said.

   Now O'Reilly likes watching television. "I like TV," he grinned. "And smoking."

   His mother said she "never gives up hope" that "one day" her son will "come out of it."

3. Attend a meeting, a news conference or a speech, and record it. While there, write down the quotes you would use if you were writing the story for your local newspaper. Then listen to the recording, and check the accuracy of your written quotations.

4. Pair up with a classmate, and interview one another about your lives. Use your smartphones to record the interview. Referring only to your notes and not the recording, write a story based on the interview. Use as many direct quotes as you think are fitting. Then check the accuracy of the story with your classmate, and check the accuracy of the direct quotations against your recording. How did you do?

5. Using Factiva or some other database, go to presswire.com, and read a handful of news releases about your favorite company. How would you rate the writers' use of direct quotations? Are they used effectively to convey color, life or emotion? Do they seem overly polished?

CHAPTER 6

USING NEWS RELEASES AS SOURCES

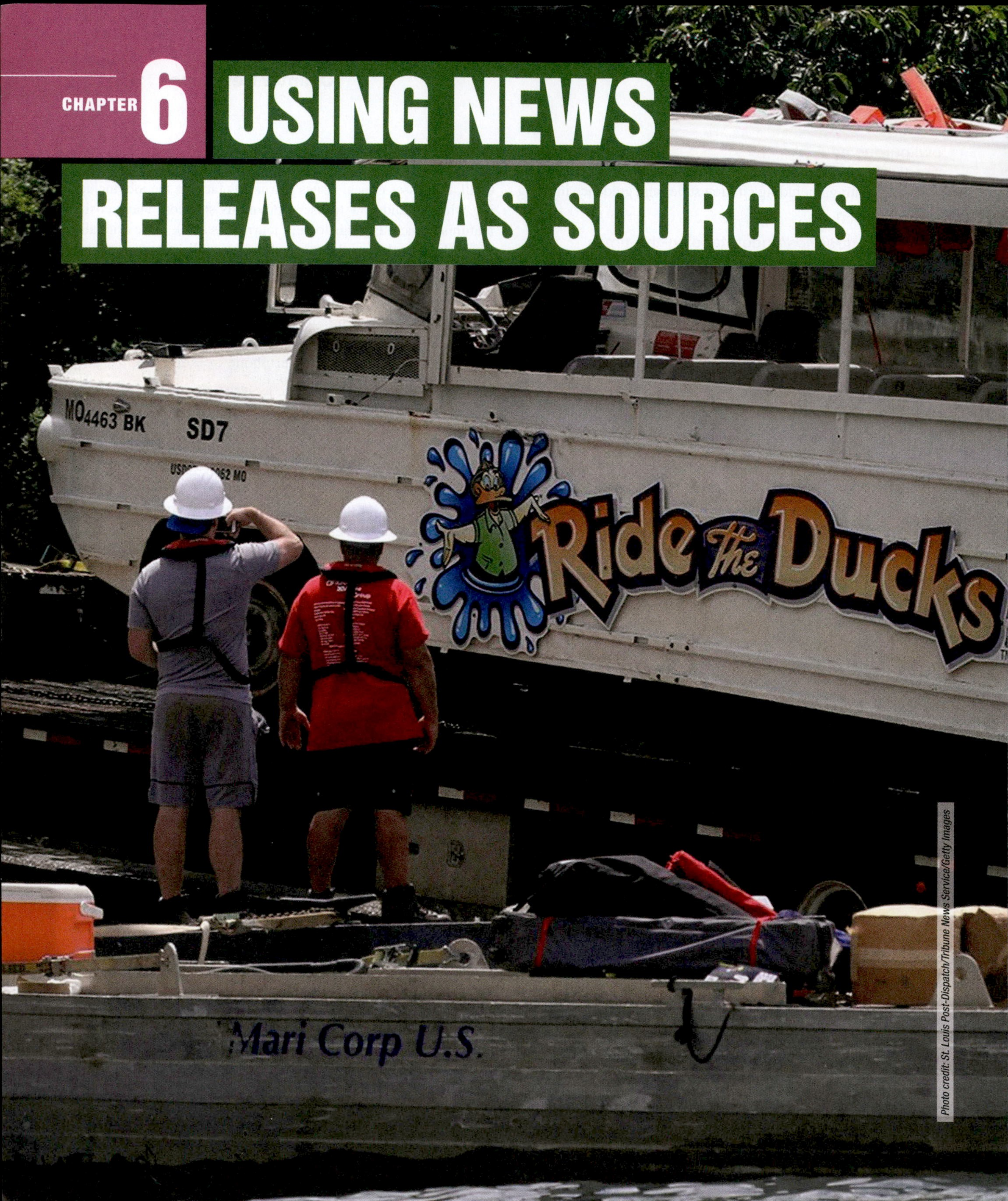

Photo credit: St. Louis Post-Dispatch/Tribune News Service/Getty Images

In this chapter, you will learn:

1 How to understand the importance of news releases.

2 How to recognize the types of news releases.

3 How to use a news release as a starting point for a story.

Family vacations quickly turned into nightmares when a boat capsized during a storm on a popular lake in southern Missouri one summer. Seventeen people, including nine people from the same Indianapolis family, perished in the July 2018 accident.

Federal and state authorities immediately started investigating what went wrong in the duck boat tragedy at Table Rock Lake. It wasn't the first deadly accident involving the amphibious vehicles, which can move across water and land, but it was among the deadliest.

"Critics," *The New York Times* reported, "say duck boats have avoided tougher safety requirements, in part because oversight for them is divided among various entities, including the Coast Guard, the National Highway Traffic Safety Administration, and the various state and city governments where the boats operate."

The story made headlines for weeks in Missouri and across the nation as journalists followed up with news stories on investigations and with human interest stories about those who died.

Six weeks later, the story made headlines again. Missouri's attorney general, Josh Hawley, issued a news release announcing that he was suing the owner of the tourist attraction to try to keep duck boats from ever operating in Missouri again.

For those journalists who might not have thought to check court filings in Taney County, Missouri, every day, the news release was a gift: a major update about an important story that the journalists didn't need to work hard to find.

Here is Hawley's release, which appeared in the email inboxes of journalists throughout Missouri and included a hyperlink to Hawley's court motion.

FOR IMMEDIATE RELEASE
August 31, 2018
Contact: Mary Compton, Communications Director
Office: 573-751-3321
AG Hawley Files Lawsuit Against Branson Duck Vehicles and Ripley Entertainment

Jefferson City, Mo.—Missouri Attorney General Josh Hawley today filed a petition in the Circuit Court of Taney County urging the court to enjoin Branson Duck Vehicles, LLC and Ripley Entertainment, Inc. from operating duck boats in Missouri. The Attorney General's Office alleges violations of the Missouri Merchandising Practices Act, Missouri's principal consumer-protection statute.

On July 19, seventeen people drowned while on a tour of Table Rock Lake when their duck boat sank during severe weather. The petition cites safety violations that are alleged to have occurred that day—including ignoring life jacket requirements and weather warnings.

The suit alleges the defendants have "been on notice for decades of ongoing safety hazards that posed a present and deadly danger to every person who boarded a duck boat. Defendants kept that information from passengers and made false promises, fraudulent statements, and misrepresentations to consumers that safety was a top priority when in actuality it was their own profits."

> **"This tragedy should not have happened," Hawley said. "As Missouri's top law enforcement officer, I am charged with protecting Missouri consumers. My hope is that this lawsuit will ensure that unsafe duck boats and companies who put profits ahead of safety will not continue to operate. Consumers have a reasonable expectation of safety and that was not met on July 19."**

The release provides some basic facts about the accident but does not provide details about "decades of ongoing safety hazards." Nor does the release explain how often—and how successfully—the Missouri Merchandising Practices Act has been used to help consumers. A journalist might not have time to dig for those answers on a daily story, but she could do more reporting later.

Note that the news release includes four sentences of direct quotes attributed to Hawley. One, which essentially defines an attorney general, is relatively self-serving: "As Missouri's top law enforcement officer, I am charged with protecting Missouri consumers." What the news release does not say is that while Hawley was reminding readers about his duties, he also was campaigning for a U.S. Senate seat. What should news organizations do with this quote?

The *St. Louis Post-Dispatch* and *Columbia Missourian* both used an Associated Press story about the suit, and their stories did not include that direct quotation. Neither did the *Springfield (Missouri) News-Leader.* The Springfield paper chose to cite specifics from the suit itself. Although *The Kansas City Star* used the full quote, the *Star* made it clear the quote was obtained from a "statement."

For none of the news organizations was the news release the sole source of information. All added additional context. That's a good practice.

The Importance of News Releases

Reporters do not always generate their own story ideas. Many ideas come to them via news releases that are emailed, mailed, telephoned, posted on Twitter or another social networking service, faxed or hand-delivered by people who want to get something in "the news."

They come from people or offices with different titles: communication directors, press agents, press secretaries, public affairs officers, media relations departments, public relations departments, public information offices, community relations bureaus and publicity offices. The people who write these news releases also sometimes call them press releases or handouts.

Estimates vary on how much journalists depend on news releases. As the number of traditional newsroom jobs has declined over the past decade, some critics lament what they disparagingly call "churnalism," a practice in which journalists publish information supplied via news release rather than produce their own material. One recent study found that about one in 10 newspaper articles originated with a news release, and other estimates are much higher. When researchers looked at stories about new products, for example, they found that information from a news release comprised about half of the average story.

Whatever the statistics, journalists and strategic communicators need each other. The overworked, understaffed journalists save time and energy when story ideas, or even complete stories, are handed to them. And if journalists see the news releases as newsworthy, the people writing them gain an expanded audience for their clients' messages. When journalists publish information from the news release, they also add another level of legitimacy to that information. It becomes not just PR but news.

However, don't expect all these entities' communication efforts will come directly to you, the journalist. These days, organizations can bypass the media and publish news for the public on their own websites and social media accounts whenever they wish. The media are no longer the gatekeepers. Indeed, Michelle Baumstark, director of community relations for Columbia Public Schools in Missouri, says she tends to use social media to reach parents and other stakeholders quickly and writes news releases primarily when she has detailed, complicated information to share.

As a journalist, you need to know the value and limitations of news releases for news organizations. Depending on your career goals, though, you might want to be among the people who write news releases or handle social media accounts for universities, corporations and organizations of all kinds. If that's your goal, studying news releases, social media posts and how news organizations handle them will help you be successful in public relations. Knowing how reporters are taught to deal with news releases will help you write better releases and do a better job of anticipating journalists' questions.

Skilled public relations practitioners know how to write news stories, and they apply all the principles of good news writing in their news releases. A good news release meets the criteria for a good news story: It's newsworthy, clear, accurate and concise.

Nevertheless, news releases are not intended to take the place of reporters. In *On Deadline: Managing Media Relations*, Carole Howard, formerly with *Reader's Digest*, and Wilma Mathews, formerly with AT&T and Arizona State University, write that news releases simply acquaint an editor with the basic facts of potential stories. Those who write news releases accept that reporters will check the facts and rewrite some of those carefully crafted sentences.

As a reporter, you must recognize that news releases can be both a help and a hindrance. They are a help because without them, news organizations would need many more reporters. They can be a hindrance because they sometimes contain incomplete or even incorrect information. Because they are intended to promote the interests and favorable reputation of the individuals and organizations that disseminate them, news releases, by their very nature, also tend to present one point of view or interpretation of the facts.

Regardless, wise journalists do not discard news releases without reading them. And editors regularly give them to reporters, often the newest ones, as starting points for stories.

What's the grammar error in this sentence?

Ballot selfies, which may reveal who a person voted for, could prompt the return of vote-buying, according to a prominent elections expert.

See Appendix 1, Rule 13.

Types of News Releases

After you have read a number of news releases, you will notice that generally they fall into three categories:

- Announcements of coming events or of personnel matters, such as new hires, promotions, retirements and the like.
- Information about a cause.
- Information that is meant to build someone's or some organization's image.

launchpadworks.com
WATCH: **"Filling the News Hole: Video News Releases"**

- How might a video news release interview differ from an interview conducted by a journalist?
- Would you want to see video news releases on televised news broadcasts? What rules should television news stations follow when airing a video news release?

Recognizing the types and purposes of news releases (and recognizing that some serve more than one purpose) will help you determine how to rewrite them and build on them.

Announcement Releases

Organizations use the news media to tell their members and the public about coming events. For example:

> **The Camera Club will have a special meeting at Wyatt's Cafeteria at 7 p.m. Wednesday, March 20. Marvin Miller will present a slide program on "Yellowstone in Winter." All interested persons are invited.**

Although the release promotes the Camera Club, it also serves as a public service announcement.

Community newspapers and websites that offer such announcements are serving their readers. They might choose to present the information in a calendar of coming events. Depending on the topic, they might also want to assign a reporter. Here is another example:

> **The first reception of the new season of the Springfield Art League will be Sunday, Sept. 8, 3 to 5 p.m. in the Fine Arts Building.**
>
> **Included in the exhibition will be paintings, serigraphs, sculpture, batiks, weaving, pottery and jewelry, all created by Art League members who, throughout the summer, have been preparing works for this opening exhibit of the season.**
>
> **The event also will feature local member-artists' state fair entries, thus giving all who could not get to the fair the opportunity to see these works.**
>
> **The exhibition continues to Friday, Sept. 13. All gallery events and exhibitions are free.**

As an aside, note that the previous two examples do not follow Associated Press style on the dates of the events. AP says to use either the day of the week or the date depending on whether the time element is within a week of publication. Because strategic communicators do not necessarily know when a news organization will publish an announcement, using both the date and day of the week makes sense.

Other news releases concern appointments, promotions, new hires and retirements. The announcement of an appointment might read like this:

> **James McAlester, internationally known rural sociologist at Springfield University, has been appointed to the board of directors of Bread for the World, according to William Coburn, executive director of the humanitarian organization.**
>
> **McAlester attended his first board meeting Jan. 22 in New York City. He has been on the university faculty for 10 years. Prior to that, he served as the Ford Foundation representative in India for 17 years.**
>
> **The 19,000-member Bread for the World organization is a "broad-based interdenominational movement of Christian citizens who advocate government policies that address the basic cause of hunger in the world," says Coburn.**

The occasion is the appointment of McAlester, but the release also describes the purpose of the Bread for the World organization. By educating readers about the organization's purpose, the writer hopes to publicize its cause.

Companies often send releases when an employee has been promoted. For example:

> **James B. Withers Jr. was named senior vice president in charge of sales of the J.B. Withers Co., it was announced Tuesday.**
>
> **Withers, who has been with the company in the sales division for two years, will head a sales force of 23 people.**
>
> **"We are sure Jim can do the job," James B. Withers Sr., company president, said. "He brings intelligence and enthusiasm to the job. We're pleased he has decided to stay with the company."**
>
> **Founded in 1936, the J.B. Withers Co. is the country's second-largest manufacturer of dog and cat collars.**

A release like this one is an attempt by the company to get its name before the public and to create employee goodwill. Whether the effort succeeds depends on how newsworthy journalists believe the announcement is.

ON THE JOB Reading News Releases: Sweat the Small Print

Courtesy of Doug Mills/The New York Times/Redux

Lara Jakes is the foreign policy editor in the Washington bureau of *The New York Times*. She was previously managing editor for news at the bimonthly magazine *Foreign Policy* and its daily website ForeignPolicy.com. Jakes began covering politics and national security in Washington at The Associated Press in 2002. From 2006 to the end of 2008, she covered the Justice Department. She later covered the Pentagon and State Department for AP and also worked as an AP correspondent and bureau chief in Baghdad.

She has covered fighting in Iraq, Afghanistan, Israel, the West Bank and Northern Ireland. Her reporting has won a number of awards, including a homeland security fellowship at the Knight Center for Specialized Journalism at the University of Maryland's Philip Merrill College of Journalism.

Once on a quiet day in her Justice Department pressroom office, Jakes went back to a release handed out weeks earlier about new penalties for fraud, waste and abuse in government contracts. Attached to the release was the language of regulations outlining the kinds of abuses that would be prosecuted. And buried within that language was a multibillion-dollar loophole that specifically exempted penalties for overseas government work by private companies — despite U.S. contracts in Iraq and Afghanistan that had cost taxpayers more than $102 billion over five years.

None of the other Justice Department reporters who had gotten the release had written about the exemption, and at first Jakes assumed she had misread or misunderstood the small print in the rules' language:

> So I called the prosecutor who was in charge of the program. He somewhat sheepishly agreed there was a major loophole in the regulations and blamed the White House (under President George W. Bush) for the wording of the new rules.

Her stories caught the attention of Congress, sparking House of Representatives hearings and an investigation into how the loophole was quietly slipped into rules that were supposed to punish abusive contractors. One congressman called it an "egregious and flagrant disregard of taxpayer rights." Five months later, Congress passed a law to close the loophole and force stricter oversight of overseas contracts.

Justice Department prosecutors later jokingly referred to the rules that closed the loophole as "L.J.'s law." Jakes says it was one of those stories that just seemed too good to be true — especially since it was initially handed over in a press release.

"I would have never found it if I'd not read the text of the regulations," she says. The prosecutor who confirmed that the loophole was in the rules seemed surprised only that she'd found it — not that it was there. "It was almost like they were daring us to not read the release or pay attention to what was going on," Jakes says.

The moral: Sweat the fine print — even in news releases.

Cause-Promoting Releases

As the classification implies, news releases in this category seek to further a cause. Some of these releases come from organizations that need funds or volunteers. The letter reprinted here is from a county chairman of the American Heart Association to the editor of a newspaper. It is not written as a news release, but its effect is meant to be the same:

> **The alumnae and collegiate members of the Alpha Phi Sorority have just completed their annual Alpha Phi "Helping Hearts" lollipop sale. This year Valerie Knight, project chairwoman, led sorority members to achieve record-breaking sales. The lollipop sale is a national project of the Alpha Phi Sorority.**
>
> **Sunday, March 5, Valerie Knight presented a check for $1,800 to the American Heart Association, Shelby County Unit. The contribution was presented during a reception at the Alpha Phi house. This contribution is an important part of the annual fundraising campaign of the American Heart Association.**

Any release, notice or letter that an organization can get reported by the media for free leaves more money for the group's cause.

Image-Building Releases

Another kind of news release serves to build up the image of a person or organization. The Mayo Clinic release below is an example. This news release seeks to enhance the images of the medical facility and two local NBA teams and also to serve to announce a new partnership:

Courtesy of Mayo Clinic News Network

Courtesy of Mayo Clinic News Network

> **NEWS RELEASE**
>
> **Celebrating Grand Opening Today for Mayo Clinic Square: Mayo Clinic, Minnesota Timberwolves, Minnesota Lynx**
>
> **MINNEAPOLIS — Dignitaries from the worlds of medicine, sports, business and politics hit the court today, Wednesday, June 17, to dedicate Mayo Clinic Square in downtown Minneapolis.**
>
> **The event was the first in a series of grand-opening events marking the strategic collaboration of Mayo Clinic, the Minnesota Timberwolves and Minnesota Lynx.**
>
> **"At Mayo Clinic we pride ourselves in teamwork," said John Noseworthy, M.D., president and CEO of Mayo Clinic. "We are proud to be part of the team that made this day possible."**
>
> **Mayo Clinic Square is home to Mayo Clinic Sports Medicine and the new headquarters of the Minnesota Timberwolves and Minnesota Lynx. Mayo Clinic Sports Medicine provides medical services to the teams and is located just across from their training facility and practice court.**
>
> **"I've never seen anything like this," said Adam Silver, commissioner of the NBA. "It's the gold standard."**
>
> **"I couldn't be prouder to be a partner of the Mayo Clinic," said Laurel Richie, president of the WNBA.**
>
> **Guests at Wednesday's dedication ceremony got a behind-the-scenes look at Mayo Clinic Sports Medicine, a 22,000-square-foot facility that opened in October 2014. It serves players and the public alike.**
>
> **MEDIA CONTACT: Rhoda Madson, Mayo Clinic**

What happens at the Mayo Clinic is often news, and professional basketball's involvement enhances the value of the story. All the quotes in the release are upbeat and promote a positive image, but they are short on specifics. If you pursue the people involved, you might be able to get better quotes and details. For instance, the release is vague about how Mayo Clinic Sports Medicine serves "players and the public alike." You could search for some examples. You might discover a compelling feature story about a recreational athlete who overcame injury thanks to the clinic.

Organizations and government agencies at all levels often try to build their public image. Many of them persuade local mayors to proclaim a day or a week of recognition for their group, as in the following:

> **Mayor Juanita Williams has proclaimed Saturday, May 11, as Fire Service Recognition Day. The Springfield Fire Department in conjunction with the University Fire Service Training Division is sponsoring a demonstration of the fire apparatus and equipment at the Springfield Fire Training Center. The displays are from 10 a.m. to 5 p.m. at 700 Bear Blvd. All citizens are urged to attend the display or visit their neighborhood fire station on May 11.**
>
> **Our PRODUCT is your SAFETY.**

An editor who hands you a release like this has probably decided that you should find a story here.You can start by finding the names of the people in charge or at least their public information people. Just what will the "demonstration" involve? What kinds of equipment will be there? Will visitors be allowed to climb onto or into the equipment? You should be able to get some good quotes from the city and university fire chiefs.

You need to know, too, if this is the first such Recognition Day and if this will be an annual event. See if you can get a photographer to accompany you. You should be able to get a good story and, if not that, then a brief to publicize the event.

Handling News Releases

Regardless of the type of news release, be sure to read the information that appears at the top (see the news release in Figure 6.1). It might be useful to you. Even so, many news releases leave unanswered questions. You will probably want to contact people other than the director of information or even the contact person. But for routine accuracy checks, the people listed on the release can do the job. They might lead you to other helpful sources, too. Sometimes you might have sources of your own. And sometimes you might uncover a better story from people who are neither connected to nor recommended by the director of information.

As for the release date, you might have to consult your editor. Most news media honor release dates. However, sometimes waiting would render the information useless. Also, after a release is public knowledge, editors feel justified in releasing whatever information it contains, even before the suggested release date. A release date is broken for all when it is broken by one.

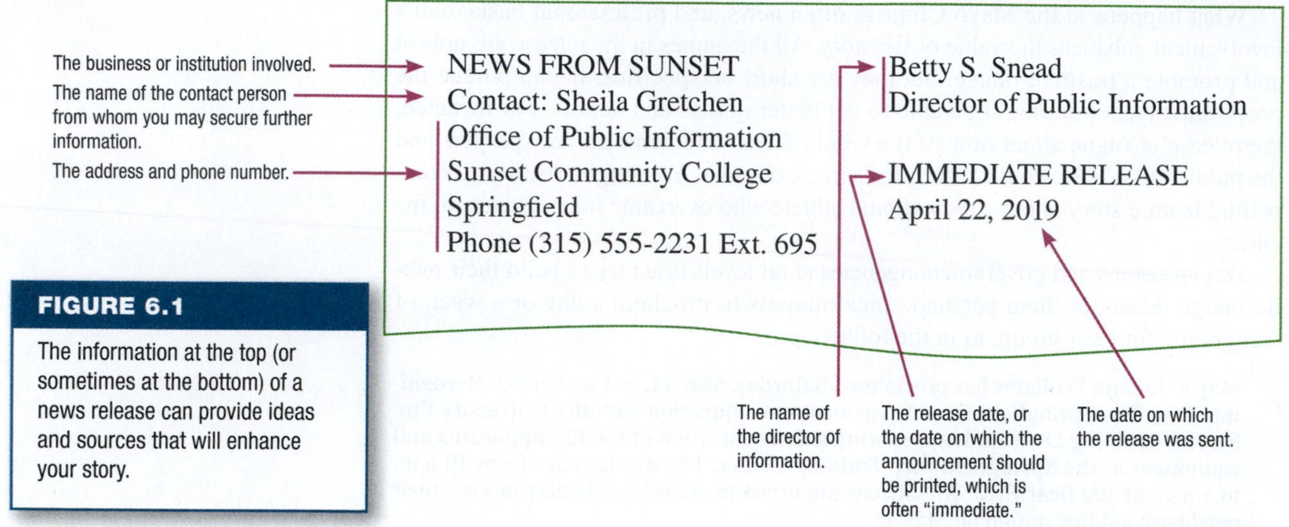

The business or institution involved.
The name of the contact person from whom you may secure further information.
The address and phone number.
NEWS FROM SUNSET
Contact: Sheila Gretchen
Office of Public Information
Sunset Community College
Springfield
Phone (315) 555-2231 Ext. 695
Betty S. Snead
Director of Public Information
IMMEDIATE RELEASE
April 22, 2019
The name of the director of information.
The release date, or the date on which the announcement should be printed, which is often "immediate."
The date on which the release was sent.

FIGURE 6.1

The information at the top (or sometimes at the bottom) of a news release can provide ideas and sources that will enhance your story.

Using an Announcement Release

Sometimes directors of information want nothing more than a listing on the record or calendar page of a newspaper or news site. Here is an example of an announcement release:

> **FOR THE CALENDAR**
>
> **Elisabeth Bertke, quiltmaker and designer from Salem, Massachusetts, will discuss her work at 7:00 o'clock P.M. Tues., February 7, in Charters Auditorium, Hampton College. Two quilts designed and constructed by Bertke are included in the exhibit "The New American Quilt," currently on display at the Smith Art Gallery.**
>
> **"This is an exciting display," Betty Martin, president of the Smith Art Gallery board of directors, said. "You simply can't afford to miss it."**

This simple release might go directly to the news desk or to a special calendar editor.

If you receive it, rewrite it. Some news organizations insist that you rewrite every news release to avoid the embarrassment of running the same story as a competing news outlet. For some, it is a matter of integrity and professionalism.

After reading through the release, check all the facts. Confirm the spelling of Bertke's name, and see if there is an apostrophe in "Charters Auditorium." The Smith Gallery might or might not be on the Hampton campus.

Next, if time allows, do some additional reporting. Call the gallery to ask how long the exhibit will be there. Have local residents made quilts in the exhibit? Perhaps your questions will lead to a feature story on local quilting.

Then do your rewrite. Drop Martin's quotation: It is too promotional. But you might call Martin, Bertke or someone else connected to the event to try for a better quote that explains what's special about Bertke's work. Reread your story to make sure the lead works and the writing is tight and clear.

Finally, correct any violations of AP style. In the preceding example:

- A hyphen should be inserted in "quilt-maker," or you could replace the two words with "quilter."
- "7:00 o'clock P.M." should be "7 p.m."
- "Tues." should be spelled out "Tuesday."
- "February" should be abbreviated "Feb."

Don't assume that a copy editor will clean up your copy. Take responsibility for your own work. The copy editors may be too busy or, depending on the size of the news organization, not even exist. That's also true for those of you pursuing a career in strategic communication. You will be the one to write the news releases.

Here is another example of an announcement release:

> **Mr. Richard G. Hernandez has been selected as the Outstanding Biology Teacher of the Year by the National Association of Biology Teachers. He was previously selected as Nevada Science Educator of the Year.**
>
> **As an outstanding representative of good high-school biology teaching Hernandez will receive a certificate and a series 50 binocular microscope with an engraved citation. Hernandez has been teaching at Hickman High School for 20 years.**

In large markets, this kind of release might not get much **play**—that is, it might not be prominently displayed. Smaller markets, however, will use it and perhaps enlarge on it.

A first reading of the release tells you that it is wordy and leaves many questions unanswered. Hernandez might be an interesting fellow, but the release tells us little about him. You should approach this release in the same way you approach any news release: Finish the reporting, and then rewrite it. News style demands a new lead to the release:

> **A Hickman High School science teacher has been named Outstanding Biology Teacher of the Year by the National Association of Biology Teachers.**
>
> **Richard G. Hernandez, a Hickman teacher since 2001, will receive a certificate and a series 50 binocular microscope with an engraved citation.**
>
> **Previously selected as Nevada Science Educator of the Year, Hernandez . . .**

There the story runs out of information. You need to ask the following questions:

- Age?
- Degrees from where?
- Local address?
- Annual award? One teacher selected from each state?
- Any previous Hickman winners? Any from other local high schools?
- Year he received Nevada Science Educator award?
- Nominated for the award by whom?
- Date and place of bestowal? Public ceremony?
- Value of a series 50 binocular microscope?

Then call Hernandez, and find out how he feels about the award. Talk to the principal, to fellow teachers and to some of Hernandez's students. Better yet: Get permission to attend one of Hernandez's classes. Good quotations and observations will spice up your story. The length of the story will ultimately depend on how much space your editor wishes to give it. That might depend on how interesting your reporting is.

Using a Cause-Promoting Release

News media generally cooperate with causes that are community-oriented. News releases like the following get attention, and well they should. This one comes from the American Association of Poison Control Centers:

> **FOR IMMEDIATE RELEASE**
> **January 16, 2018**
> **ALERT: American Association of Poison Control Centers Warn About Potential Poison Exposure to Single-Load Laundry Packets**
>
> **Alexandria, VA—The American Association of Poison Control Centers (AAPCC) strongly warns individuals about the dangers of using single-load laundry packets other than as intended. Proper storage is advised to reduce the chances of potential harmful exposure to these products.**
>
> **During the past five years, poison control centers have received well over 50,000 calls relating to liquid laundry packet exposures. While unintentional misuse by children five and under accounted for the majority of these calls, a recent trend among teenagers ingesting the packets—and uploading videos to various internet platforms including video-sharing websites, social media, and vlogging platforms—has caused significant concern among poison control centers.**
>
> **According to AAPCC data, in 2016 and 2017, poison control centers handled thirty-nine and fifty-three cases of intentional exposures, respectively, among thirteen to nineteen year olds. In the first fifteen days of 2018 alone, centers have already handled thirty-nine such intentional cases among the same age demographic. Ingestion accounted for ninety-one percent of these reported exposures.**
>
> **"The 'laundry packet challenge' is neither funny nor without serious health implications," said Stephen Kaminski, JD, AAPCC's CEO and Executive Director. "The intentional misuse of these products poses a real threat to the health of individuals. We have seen a large spike in single-load laundry packet exposures among teenagers since these videos have been uploaded."**
>
> **The resulting health implications from misuse can be serious. Known potential effects include seizures, pulmonary edema, respiratory arrest, coma, and even death.**
>
> **"Everyone needs to be aware of the dangers of swallowing the contents of a single-load laundry packet. Only use the packets for their intended use and be sure to store them up and away," said Kaminski. "If you or a loved one misuses a liquid laundry packet or has a question about the risk of an exposure to one, a poison control expert can be reached 24/7 at 1-800-222-1222."**

The cause promoted in this news release is public safety. As a consumer of social media, you might have seen videos that show young people encouraging each other to take the Tide pod challenge. The news release doesn't mention Tide pods by name, but it does alert the media that these challenges are not just viral videos that entertain: They are videos that encourage dangerous actions.

The news release gives you hard data from an expert source—the American Association of Poison Control Centers—as well as concrete details about the health implications.

Although not written according to strict Associated Press style, the news release does something extremely important: It tells you, the journalist, that there is *new* news. The release reminds journalists that thousands of young children have accidentally ingested the pods and also notes that calls related to teenagers have spiked, especially in the first two weeks of 2018. That's the *new* news.

You could argue that the news release buries the lead, but if you read it carefully, the news is clearly there.

What to do? If you happen to have not noticed the "laundry packet challenge" in your social media feeds, the news release gives you a clue: a "recent trend among teenagers ingesting the packets — and uploading videos to various internet platforms including video-sharing websites, social media. . . ."

Video-sharing websites? Sounds like YouTube. Social media? Perhaps Twitter, Facebook or Instagram? Do a quick search to see one for yourself.

You'll notice right away that a particular brand has the misfortune of being most associated with the "challenge": Tide. Who makes Tide? Is the company doing anything in response?

Again, do more research. You'll find that 2018 was not the first time that Procter & Gamble made headlines because of its laundry detergent pods. *Consumer Reports* warned about problems in May 2012. What's happened in the years since? You can use Factiva or another commercial database to build a chronology that provides more context for the new issue.

By examining Procter & Gamble's website, you'll find that the company has created child-resistant packaging, and added a bitter taste to the outer layer of its Tide, Gain and Ariel pods. It also has posted a safety guide online. As you search the site, you'll find a link to sign up for email alerts and a link to the Tide product line's Twitter account. Procter & Gamble also has enlisted Gronk — football star Rob Gronkowski of the New England Patriots — to post a public service video announcement on Twitter about what Tide pods are for: "DOING LAUNDRY. Nothing else."

With all this background, you are ready for some local reporting. Have teenagers in the community participated in the challenge and suffered ill effects? A check on the local hospitals and clinics would be a good first step. What are pediatricians and parents saying about these experiences?

In addition, the American Association of Poison Control Centers provides links to all the centers in the United States. You could call the closest poison center and ask if there have been any local cases of pod-soap poisoning.

Other soap companies make pods, too. Which are they? You could try calling one or two and asking the public information person whether the company has had any lawsuits or serious complaints about the small packets.

Now you can develop a major story from a news release. Whatever kind of news organization you work for, odds are your news organization has social media accounts and a website. Use those to your advantage.

Like Lindsey Bever of *The Washington Post*, you can embed hyperlinks in your story that take readers to supplementary content, such as the original news releases issued by the poison control association, previous reporting on the dangerous stuff teenagers dare each other to do, warnings posted by the U.S. Consumer Product Safety Commission, a YouTube video titled "Don't Eat the Laundry Pods. (Seriously. They're Poison.)" and Gronk's PSA.

Tide pods became the center of a dangerous trend among teenagers in 2018.

Daniel Acker/Bloomberg/Getty Images

The Post also created its own video—a compilation based on other videos with explanations, warnings and examples. By August 2018, the "Don't Eat the Laundry Pods" video had been viewed more than 4 million times, and Gronk's PSA, which Tide released on Twitter, had been viewed more than 10 million times and retweeted nearly 93,000 times. Why not be part of that conversation and help shed light on public safety?

Using an Image-Building News Feature

Sometimes an organization will write profiles or biographies about their employees in an effort to show consumers that the organization is not an anonymous entity but a group of engaging, highly qualified people. NASA published the biography below (only the first half is shown), which is typical of image-building news features:

Roscosmos/NASA

Serena M. Auñón-Chancellor (M.D.) NASA Astronaut

Summary:

Dr. Serena M. Auñón-Chancellor began working with NASA as a Flight Surgeon in 2006. In 2009, she was selected as a NASA astronaut. During her NASA career, Dr. Auñón-Chancellor spent more than nine months in Russia supporting medical operations for International Space Station crew members in Star City. She also served as Deputy Crew Surgeon for STS-127 and is board certified in both Internal and Aerospace Medicine. Serena most recently served as served as Flight Engineer on the International Space Station for Expedition 56 and 57.

Personal Data:

Dr. Auñón-Chancellor came to Johnson Space Center in August 2006, employed as a Flight Surgeon under the UTMB/Wyle Bioastronautics contract. She spent more than nine months in Russia supporting medical operations for International

Space Station crew members in Star City, including water survival training in the Ukraine. Dr. Auñón-Chancellor served as the Deputy Crew Surgeon for STS-127. She also held the role of Deputy Lead for Orion-Medical Operations.

Education:

Graduated from Poudre High School, Fort Collins, Colorado in 1993. Received a Bachelor of Science in Electrical Engineering from The George Washington University, Washington, D.C., in 1997 and a Doctorate of Medicine from The University of Texas-Health Science Center at Houston in 2001. Completed a three-year residency in internal medicine at The University of Texas Medical Branch (UTMB) in Galveston, Texas, in 2004, and then completed an additional year as Chief Resident in the Internal Medicine Department in 2005. She also completed an aerospace medicine residency at UTMB as well as a Master of Public Health in 2007. She is board certified in Internal and Aerospace Medicine.

Experience:

Dr. Auñón-Chancellor came to Johnson Space Center in August 2006, employed as a Flight Surgeon under the UTMB/Wyle Bioastronautics contract. She spent more than nine months in Russia supporting medical operations for International Space Station crew members in Star City, including water survival training in the Ukraine. Dr. Auñón-Chancellor served as the Deputy Crew Surgeon for STS-127. She also held the role of Deputy Lead for Orion-Medical Operations.

This biographical sketch from the NASA website fulfills two purposes: First, it introduces us to one of NASA's brilliant veteran astronauts, and by telling us what she has done, tells a lot about the aims, purposes and work of the NASA. Second, in building the surgeon's image, it also substantiates NASA's image.

Nevertheless, the sketch is vague and somewhat repetitive. If you keep reading, however, you'll see that Auñón-Chancellor completed a mission to the International Space Station in December 2018. How cool is that?

Auñón-Chancellor sounds like a good person for a story. How does her surgical expertise come in handy on the International Space Station? What kind of procedures has she had to do? How is practicing medicine different in space? What was it like to work with Russian crew members? What sorts of medical issues arise during emergency water landings? You could ask her those questions and also find out more about her as a person: When did she first fall in love with medicine or space? Which mission made her the proudest? What does a typical day look like? What does she do in her free time?

What If You're the One Writing the News Release?

To increase the odds that your news release will be used by the media, follow these tips:

- Get the *new* news in the lead — your first paragraph.
- Think like a journalist. What will make your pitch news — prominence, novelty, impact, proximity, conflict or timeliness? Focus on the most relevant news value in your release.
- Show, don't tell. For example, don't say that your product or cause is amazing. Instead, provide concrete details or statistics that provide evidence.
- If you're writing an announcement release, answer as many of the five Ws and the H as you can while still meeting your organization's needs.
- Try to anticipate journalists' questions.
- Make sure everything in the news release is accurate. Are the names spelled correctly, for example?

TIPS

How to Rewrite a News Release

- Carefully read the news release, including the information at the top of the release form.
- Check for accuracy and fairness. Question missing information. Verify any spellings or information you have doubts about.
- Fill in missing information with your own reporting — research and interviews.
- Call the news release contact person, and find additional sources.
- Write the story. Make sure your lead is strong, tighten the copy and check for AP style.
- Look for other possible news stories — local angles, reactions and the like — triggered by the release.

Using a News Release as a Starting Point: An Example

Sometimes a news release can lead to an interesting story that has broad implications for the community, even if the actual release is self-serving — or misleading. Suppose you receive the following news release:

NEWS RELEASE
Springfield Community Teachers Association
Lillian A. Briggs, President
Contact: Tom Monnin, SCTA Salary Committee Chairman
Phone: 555-555-6794 (Central High School),
555-555-2975 (home)

For Immediate Release

SPRINGFIELD — Police officers and firefighters in Springfield earn a greater starting salary than Springfield teachers, as discovered in a recent survey by the Springfield Community Teachers Association. According to their research, a new teacher in the Springfield public school system makes $40,000, while a firefighter starts at $40,725, $725 more than a new teacher. "This is a shameful situation for an educational community," said Tom Monnin, SCTA Salary Committee chairman.

The statistics gathered by the SCTA Salary Committee indicate that police officers with a bachelor's degree make $42,758. A dogcatcher with no college education earns just $6,536 less a year than a beginning teacher. Following is a comparison of starting salaries of some Springfield city employees and of public school teachers for the school year:

Occupation	***Starting Salary***
Police officer with bachelor's degree	$42,758
Firefighter with bachelor's degree	$40,725
Meter reader	$32,402
Animal control officer	$33,464
Bus operator	$32,402
Teacher with bachelor's degree	$40,000

"Springfield teachers do not think that city employees are overpaid but that teachers are underpaid," Monnin said.

Even though teachers work under a 9 1/4-month contract, the workweek is not 40 hours. When the hours for preparing and grading, attending sports events, musical concerts, dances, other after-school activities and PTA meetings are considered, a teacher's workweek is much longer than 40 hours. Summer break is used by many teachers for advanced preparation at the university, at their own expense.

The SCTA Salary Committee will present the salary proposal at the next meeting of the Springfield Board of Education.

The SCTA represents approximately 523 members in the public school system.

Read the News Release Carefully

Your first task is to read the release, including the information at the top of the form, closely a couple of times, making notes in the margin about items that stand out for you. For example, the second paragraph cleverly suggests that dogcatchers make nearly as much money as teachers do, but you notice that it speaks only of starting salaries.

The more you read the release, the more uncomfortable you start to feel with it. No one can blame teachers for wanting more money, but there are other factors to consider.

Check for Accuracy and Fairness

You should ask yourself what information is missing and what other viewpoints you should consider. For example, you might wonder, What about working conditions? Teachers in Springfield's schools don't have to put their lives on the line the way police officers and firefighters do. And most people do not want to spend their lives chasing stray dogs.

Take special care when news releases cite studies, polls or surveys. Check the source of the figures for accuracy and possible bias. If you can't confirm the figures and their reliability, don't use them.

The fact that teachers work for a little more than nine months a year is down in the fourth paragraph. The release fails to mention a two-week winter break and a week off in the spring semester. Most police officers and firefighters get two weeks off per year when they are hired.

Is the release trying to suggest that because teachers actually spend more than 40 hours a week working, they should not have to work more than 9 1/4 months? Not all teachers spend their summers going to school. You probably know several who have summer jobs or who take long vacations.

Do Additional Research and Interviews

Before you turn in a rewrite of this release, you have a lot of checking to do. But you also decide to go beyond checking to do some of your own reporting.

First, you go to the city of Springfield's website and gather all of the salary information you need. But you still have some questions. You call the personnel office. When asked about the $40,725 starting salary of a firefighter, the official replies: "You wouldn't begin at that salary. Everyone is hired at $39,225 for a trial period of at least six months. If you work out OK, you might jump up to $40,725. Again, there are a lot of considerations besides the college degree."

Now you know you are on to something. Comparing starting salaries is one thing. But how much can a person eventually earn in a position?

You then ask about the starting salary for a police officer. "Yes," the director of personnel says, "$42,758 is the beginning salary for a police officer with a B.S. degree."

You then ask whether anyone with a B.S. degree can get hired at that salary.

"Most people wouldn't stand a chance of being hired," he says. "We have more than 100 applicants for every position, so we can be quite choosy. Unless a person has had some real experience as a police officer, I don't think he or she would make it."

Further questioning reveals that a top salary for a police officer is $54,712 after six years of service.

You also find the website of the Springfield public school system and check its salary schedule for teachers. Then you call a high school teacher. You ask her if she has to put in more than 40 hours a week at her job.

"Oh, yes," she says. "I teach a section of English composition, and I have a lot of papers to grade. I used to spend a lot of evenings preparing for classes, but once you've taught a course, it gets easier. And then I have to go to all those football games and basketball games."

You discover that she is indeed required to attend the games, but only because she is in charge of the cheerleaders. When you express sympathy, the teacher replies, "No, I really don't mind. After all, I get $3,500 a year extra for being in charge of the cheerleaders."

You then learn from someone at the Springfield schools' personnel office that quite a few teachers receive compensation for after-school activities — coaching, directing plays and musical activities, advising the staffs of the school newspaper and senior yearbook, and chaperoning dances. Teachers sponsoring class and club activities can earn from $1,000 to $4,000 a year; a sponsor of the pep squad can earn up to $2,300. The top teacher's salary without any of these extras is $67,214.

You note that top pay for a city dogcatcher is $37,626, so you think it might be interesting to interview one. You find Mike Jones, an animal control officer. It doesn't take much prodding to get Jones to talk. "I sure wish I got summers off like those teachers," he says. "I've got nothing against teachers. But most of them make more money than I'll ever make. . . . Besides, students don't bite many teachers."

Get Back to the News Release Contact with Questions

Now you are ready to call Tom Monnin, the man whose name is on the release, for additional information. Here's how your interview might go:

Q: Is it fair to compare a new teacher's salary with a new police officer's salary when the top pay for a police officer is $54,712 and the top teacher's salary is $67,214?

A: Well, it takes 17 years for a teacher with a master's degree plus 75 hours of continuing education classes to reach that top salary. A teacher with a bachelor's degree can make $54,219 after 11 years of teaching.

ANNOTATED MODEL Integrating News Release Information

Journalists can do their own research to build a story prompted by a news release.

The Springfield Community Teachers Association said Tuesday that new police officers can earn over $2,000 more than new teachers. ← Lead gives SCTA claim.

What the teachers did not say was that a teacher eventually can earn $12,502 more a year than a police officer can. ← Info from research adds a differing point of view.

Incorrect info about firefighters' starting salary is omitted. → The SCTA statement was included with a survey that lists starting teachers' salaries at $40,000. Other figures listed as starting salaries are these: police officer with a bachelor's degree, $42,758; animal control officer, $33,464; meter reader, $32,402; bus operator, $32,402.

"This is a shameful situation for an educational community," said Tom Monnin, the SCTA Salary Committee chairman. "Springfield teachers do not think city employees are overpaid but that teachers are underpaid." ← Quotes from news release give teachers' point of view.

Info from the release is paraphrased and attributed to association officers. → The association officers said that even though teachers work under a nine-month contract, extracurricular activities extend the workweek beyond 40 hours. Summer break, they said, is used for advanced study at the teachers' own expense.

"I figure I work a 60-hour week," Monnin said in an interview. "That means I work 51 weeks of 40 hours each a year." ← Source of quote from interview is included.

Common knowledge is confirmed by two sources. → Some extracurricular activities, such as coaching, directing plays and supervising cheerleaders, earn extra compensation.

Teachers are not compelled to attend after-school functions, but "we do feel the responsibility to attend," Monnin said. ← Quote clarifies info in earlier paragraphs.

Facts verified by government sources are common knowledge. → Teachers also feel compelled to continue their education. Top pay for a teacher with only a bachelor's degree is $54,219 after 11 years of teaching. A teacher with a master's degree plus 75 hours of classes can earn $67,214 after 17 years of teaching.

A police officer with a bachelor's degree can reach a top salary of $54,712 after six years of police work. But a person with a bachelor's degree and no police work experience is not likely to be hired, said Phil James, the Springfield director of personnel. James also said all firefighters are hired at $39,225. If a person has a bachelor's degree and stays on, he or she could make $40,725 after a six-month trial period. ← Paraphrased opinion is attributed to source.

Quote adds color to the story. → Top pay for a dogcatcher is $37,626. "I sure wish I got summers off like those teachers," said Mike Jones, an animal control officer. "I've got nothing against teachers. But most of them make more money than I'll ever make. . . . Besides, students don't bite many teachers."

The SCTA Salary Committee will present its salary proposal at the next meeting of the Springfield Board of Education. ← The "so what" appears at the end.

Q: What about summers off and other vacations?
A: I figure I work a 60-hour week. That means I work 51 weeks of 40 hours each year.

Q: Aren't teachers paid extra for after-school activities?
A: Many are paid. But not all of them are, and there are many activities we do feel the responsibility to attend.

Q: Teachers don't have to put their lives on the line the way police and fire officials and even dogcatchers do. Isn't that a factor?
A: It's debatable who has to put their lives on the line. We're not as bad off as some schools, but we often have to restrain students physically. We read about school shootings all of the time, and we can't help but wonder whether that could happen here.

Write the Story

You've checked for accuracy, found out the important facts, and taken all the viewpoints into account. Now you are ready to write the story. Write a lead that communicates the news, make sure your writing is tight, and check for AP style.

The annotated model, "Integrating News Release Information," shows one possible story that could result from the news release. This story does with a news release what you should do with many of them.

You should not be satisfied with the way a news release is written or its information. By asking some important questions, you can often put together an informative and more accurate story.

Without saying that the news release was dishonest or misleading, a good reporter can correct or clarify some of the information it contains. Here, the plight of the teacher is told clearly and objectively, but it is placed in a much fuller context than in the news release.

Like many news releases, this one was the basis for a story the news outlet otherwise would not have had. That is why editors pay attention to news releases and why reporters look for the real story.

CHAPTER RESOURCES

SUGGESTED READINGS

Bivins, Thomas H. *Public Relations Writing: The Essentials of Style and Format.* 8th ed. Lincolnwood, Ill.: NTC/Contemporary Publishing Group, 2013. This book explains how public relations professionals approach a wide variety of writing tasks.

Howard, Carole, and Wilma Mathews. *On Deadline: Managing Media Relations.* 5th ed. Prospect Heights, Ill.: Waveland Press, 2013. This practical book offers suggestions on how organizations should deal with the news media.

Jackson, Daniel, and Kevin Moloney. "Inside Churnalism: PR, Journalism and Power Relationships in Flux." *Journalism Studies* 17, no. 6 (2016): 763–780. Jackson and Moloney trace the rise of churnalism and interview strategic communicators about their perceptions of their relationships with journalists. The article is valuable reading for both those who want to do journalism and those who want to work in public relations.

Wilcox, Dennis L., and Lawrence W. Nolte. *Public Relations Writing and Media Techniques*. 7th ed. New York: HarperCollins, 2013. The authors cover the writing, production and distribution of a variety of public relations materials. The book has real-world examples and tells how to distribute these materials through traditional and social media.

SUGGESTED WEBSITES

LaunchPad Solo

launchpadworks.com

When you visit LaunchPad Solo for Journalism, you will find research links, exercises and LearningCurve adaptive quizzing to help you improve your grammar and AP style usage. In addition, the site's video collection hosts the videos highlighted in this and other chapters as well as additional clips of leading professionals discussing important media trends.

www.odwyerpr.com

This is the website of the hard-hitting O'Dwyer's online newsletter. It does a thorough job doing what it says it does—getting "Inside News of Public Relations and Marketing Communications."

www.pressflash.com/resources_anatomy.php

On this website for a news release distribution service, you will find a terse description of a good news release.

prssa.prsa.org/

The Public Relations Student Society of America offers students networking opportunities and other resources to help them become professional communicators. The society provides guidance on ethics, diversity, trademarks and other topics pertinent to public relations specialists.

prwatch.org

The nonprofit Center for Media and Democracy runs this website. According to the website, the center "is a national watchdog group that conducts in-depth investigations into corruption and the undue influence of corporation on media and democracy."

EXERCISES

1. Read the following release. Then interview people in three households, and ask these questions:

   a. When did you last change the batteries in your smoke alarms and carbon monoxide detectors?
   b. Do you test your alarms on the same day each year?
   c. Do you replace them every 10 years?
   d. Do you and those you live with have an evacuation plan in case of a fire?

   Finally, write your story.

   SPRINGFIELD FIRE DEPARTMENT
   News Release
   For Immediate Release
   Reminder: Change Smoke Alarm Batteries and Clocks

   The Springfield Fire Department is reminding residents to change the batteries in their smoke alarms and carbon monoxide detectors when they turn their clocks back this weekend.

   Working smoke alarms cut in half the risk of dying in a home fire, yet Springfield Fire Department data shows less than half of Springfield homes have a working smoke alarm. Worn or missing batteries are the most common cause of a smoke alarm or carbon monoxide detector malfunction. Changing the batteries is one of the simplest, most effective ways to prevent tragic deaths and injuries.

   In addition to changing the batteries, smoke alarms should be tested monthly and replaced at least every 10 years.

   This weekend also serves as an ideal time for families to review their home evacuation plans. All family members should plan two ways to escape from each room and practice escape routes with the entire family at least twice a year.

   For information on how you can receive a free smoke alarm, call the Springfield Fire Department at 555-1500.

   Media only: For more information, contact: Fire and Life Safety Educator Cara Restelli Erwin.

2. Read each of the following news releases. First, indicate the type of news release it is. Second, list questions that you would have if you were to rewrite it, including the facts you would check and the sources you would turn to for the answers. Third, suggest ideas for visuals or videos that would accompany a web story. Finally, correct all departures from Associated Press style rules.

a. **NEWS RELEASE**
For further information, contact:
Humane Society of Missouri Media Center
314-802-5712

Humane Society of Missouri Confirms: Guilty Pleas Entered in Federal Court to Charges from Largest Dog Fighting Raid and Rescue in U.S. History

Photos and Video of Dogs at Rescue Sites and Emergency Shelter Now Available

ST. LOUIS, Mo., September 14, 2015—The Humane Society of Missouri today confirms guilty pleas have been entered in connection to the July 8, 2015 multistate federal dog fighting raid that resulted in the rescue of more than 500 fighting dogs. Federal agents made 26 arrests and dogs were rescued in 8 states.

This rescue operation is the largest dog fighting raid in U.S. history. The Humane Society of Missouri participated in the 18-month investigation and led the subsequent rescue and shelter operations, working in partnership with the Federal Bureau of Investigation, the Missouri State Highway Patrol, the United States Department of Agriculture's Office of the Inspector General, the U.S. Marshals Service and the United States Attorney.

Four eastern Missouri men—Robert Hackman of Foley, Teddy Kiriakidis of Leasburg, Ronald Creech of Leslie and Michael Morgan of Hannibal—pled guilty today in U.S. District Court in St.Louis to charges connected to the dog fighting raid. Another man arrested in connection with the dog fighting raid, Jack Ruppel of Eldon, pled guilty to charges on September 4 in federal court in Jefferson City.

"We can confirm that five of the individuals charged with this gruesome form of animal abuse are being brought to justice," said Kathy Warnick, president of the Humane Society of Missouri. "Today's guilty pleas raise awareness that dog fighting is unacceptable, inhumane and illegal and will not be tolerated. The unprecedented scale of this investigation and rescue operation should alert the entire nation to what a horrible crime dog fighting is and what a dangerous and serious affect it can have on animals and communities.

Warnick continued, "We sincerely hope these guilty pleas will result in sentencing that sends the message that this form of animal abuse will no longer be tolerated. Humane Society of Missouri staff and our many partners have selflessly sacrificed much of their personal lives in the pursuit of this investigation and the care of these dogs. We fervently desire that this historic effort marks the beginning of the end to dog fighting in the United States."

"This was the largest dog fighting raid in U.S. history, but it will not be the last," warned Michael Kaste, Assistant Special Agent in Charge of the FBI in St.Louis. "This case sets precedents for the FBI along with our local, state and federal partners to aggressively root out underground dog fighting rings where people have absolutely no qualms about torturing man's best friend for money and entertainment."

b. **NEWS RELEASE**

Goodyear Innovation Challenge Invites U.S. Graduate Students to Submit Entries

By The Goodyear Tire & Rubber Company on Aug. 24, 2018

AKRON, Ohio, Aug. 24, 2018 /PRNewswire—The Goodyear Tire & Rubber Company (NASDAQ: GT), in collaboration with the Weatherhead School of Management at Case Western Reserve University, in Cleveland, Ohio, is sponsoring a hackathon-style competition to identify innovative ideas related to future transportation.

The Goodyear Innovation Challenge invites graduate business and design students from across the U.S. to submit a business case by Oct. 12 in response to the challenge, "How does Goodyear make a play beyond tires?" for the chance to compete in a two-day event at the university's Larry Sears and Sally Zlotnick Sears think[box], a world-class center for innovation and entrepreneurship.

Recognizing the fast-changing world of mobility, especially in urban areas, Goodyear already has focused on "beyond tires," with engineers, business designers and data scientists at its innovation labs in San Francisco, Akron, Luxembourg and Shanghai working on many possibilities. Building on this, the upcoming competition challenges some of the best young minds to mirror that kind of future-state thinking.

Five team proposals will be selected to participate in the Nov. 8–9 hackathon in Cleveland, where students will be asked to bring their ideas to life with both physical prototypes and "back of the envelope" business model calculations.

A jury of Goodyear leaders and digital innovation scholars will select the first-, second- and third-place winners for awards of $5,000, $3,000 and $2,000, respectively.

For more information, including rules and how to submit a team proposal, visit https://design.case.edu/.

3. Assume that you are a reporter for the Springfield paper. Rewrite the following release as a news story. Your instructor will be your news source for any questions you have.

   NEWS RELEASE
   Nearly 11,000 seat belt violation warnings were issued to motorists by the State Highway Patrol during the first month the new seat belt law was in effect.

   Colonel Howard J. Hoffman, Superintendent of the State Highway Patrol, reported today that 10,908 warnings were issued to motorists in passenger vehicles for not wearing their seat belts as required by State Law.

   Colonel Hoffman also noted that during this same reporting period, 50 persons were killed in traffic accidents investigated by the Highway Patrol. Only two of the persons killed in these mishaps were found to be wearing seat belts.

   "The value of wearing a seat belt cannot be overemphasized," Hoffman said. "We don't know how many of these investigated traffic deaths could have been avoided by the use of seat belts. It is known, however, that seat belts have saved lives and prevented serious injuries to others. We will continue to vigorously enforce the State seat belt law and hopefully more and more motorists will make it a habit to buckle their seat belts."

4. Assume that you are the editor of a news website. Write an email to the staff explaining why you read every news release.

5. **Your journalism blog.** Explain in a blog to a nonjournalism student the clear difference between a news story and a news release. Send a tweet to your classmates asking them to read your blog post.

CHAPTER 7

REPORTING WITH NUMBERS

Photo credit: Tetra Images/AGE Fotostock

Whatever the story and whatever the subject, you probably can use numbers to clarify issues for readers and viewers. All too often, however, numbers are used in ways that muddy the water. Many journalists have some trepidation about working with numbers, and they create confusion unwittingly when they work with the volatile mixture of numbers and words.

Jennifer LaFleur, featured in the "On the Job" box in this chapter, says she has seen numerous reports from government agencies with math errors that a quick double-check by a reporter would have found. "Reporters background-check sources. They verify anecdotes with documents. But seldom do we double-check numbers," she reminds us.

One website that does check numbers regularly is PolitiFact.com. It examines and, if necessary, corrects statements by office holders and challengers, often by providing numbers to establish the fact. A common problem that shows up almost weekly is the reporting of the size of audiences that watch the cable news and network news programs.

Sometimes, journalists encourage misunderstandings by describing large increases in percentage terms. For example, when gasoline prices increased from about $2 to nearly $4 a gallon, some in the media reported, accurately, that the price had doubled. Others, however, incorrectly called it a 200 percent increase instead of a 100 percent increase: $\$2 + (100\% \times \$2) = \$4$.

Another trouble spot for mixing numbers and words occurs when reporters calculate how much larger or more expensive something is. For example, a class that grew from 20 students to 100 students is five times bigger than it was ($5 \times 20 = 100$), but it has four times as many students as it had before: $(4 \times 20) + 20 = 100$.

The lesson to be learned from these examples is not to avoid numbers but rather to use great care to ensure accuracy. Picking the right numbers to use and using them wisely will help your news stories have the biggest impact. Here are two examples of important stories built on numbers.

In one example, ProPublica, the nonprofit investigative reporting newsroom discussed in Chapter 2, teamed with *Fortune* magazine and found that investors were using a tax law loophole that was designed to protect the environment. These investors were buying land, inflating its value and creating a tax deduction for themselves. ProPublica found that one group of investors bought an unused golf course, set its value at eight times higher than what they paid, and then took a $4 tax deduction for every $1 they had spent. Experts calculated that the tax loophole was costing the government between $1.2 billion and $2.1 billion a year.

In another example of using numbers, reporters from ProPublica and WBEZ radio in Chicago analyzed the impact of increasing the fee for the city's vehicle stickers from $120 to $200. The city projected revenue would increase by $16 million a year. Four years later, reporters found that the new stickers were bringing in only a few million dollars more but that people who

In this chapter, you will learn:

1 How to put numbers in context by using proportion.

2 How to report on simple and compound interest.

3 How to report on inflation.

4 How to figure and report on taxes.

5 How to read and report on budgets.

6 How to translate financial reports.

7 How to use and report on public opinion polls.

were ticketed owed the city $275 million. The report concluded that a disproportionate number of those owing money were from the city's poorest neighborhoods.

Numbers were the foundation for these two stories and can be for many other stories that journalists gather. This chapter covers the basics that will help you deal with numbers correctly in daily stories. First, we'll discuss some of the mathematical skills you'll need, focusing on how to calculate proportions, interest, and taxes. Then, we'll cover where and how you can apply these skills in your reporting.

Proportion

One of the most important services journalists perform for their readers is to give **proportion** to numbers in the news—by explaining things relative to the size or the magnitude of the whole. A municipal budget that is going up by $500,000 would be a windfall for a small town in New Hampshire but a minor adjustment for a metropolis such as New York, Chicago or Minneapolis. In one recent example, Florida had to deal with a $1.6 billion deficit in 2018.

Other figures might mean a lot or a little, depending on the context. If you know little or nothing about baseball, you might think that Babe Ruth's career batting average of .342—which means that he had 34.2 hits for every 100 times at bat—indicates that Ruth wasn't a good hitter. After all, he failed almost two out of three times at bat. But when you look at the context—other players' averages—you realize that Ruth was exceptional. For instance, more than halfway through the 2018 season, only one player had a higher average *for the year* than Ruth had for his career.

Percentages and Percentage Change

Percentages are basic building blocks used to explain proportion. Batting averages explain the number of hits compared with the number of times at bat. The political strength of a public official is partly reflected in the percentage of votes won at the polls. Stories about budgets, taxes, wages, retail sales, schools, health care and the environment all are explained with percentages.

To calculate a percentage, take the portion that you want to measure, divide it by the whole and then move the decimal two places to the right. For example, suppose you want to know what portion of the city's budget is allocated to police services. Divide the police budget by the city budget, move the decimal point two places to the right, and you get the percentage of the budget that pays for police services.

TIPS

To Calculate a Percentage

- Divide the portion by the whole: Portion ÷ Whole = .xxx.
- Move the decimal point two places to the right: .xxx = xx.x percent.

To calculate a percentage:

Step 1. Divide the portion by the whole:
Portion (police budget) ÷ Whole (city budget) = .xxx.
$30,000,000 ÷ $120,000,000 = .25

Step 2. Move the decimal point two places to the right: 25%.

Precision in the use of numbers requires that you ask some basic questions. Reporters need to be careful of percentages that might mislead or tell only part of a story.

Populations, Samples and Margins of Error

If someone is giving you percentages, you must ask on what **population** the figures are based. For instance, suppose that a juvenile officer tells you 70 percent of the juvenile offenders do not have to return to his program. Your first question should be, "What population was used to figure the percentage?" Was it all the juveniles in the program during the last calendar year? If so, perhaps the success rate is high because the period being measured isn't long enough to take less successful years into account. And how has your source counted juveniles who are old enough now to be certified as adults? How does he account for juveniles who may have committed a crime in another jurisdiction?

The officer might explain that the figure is based on a sample of people who were in the program over a particular 10-year period. A **sample** is a small number of people who are picked at random to represent the population as a whole. Using common statistical tables, researchers draw a sample of the names of all juveniles who were in the program over a particular 10-year period and contact them. From those contacts, they can determine the success rate of the program.

If the figure is based on a scientific sampling like the one just described, there will also be a **margin of error**, which is expressed as "plus or minus *x* points." If the margin of error for this sample is 4 percentage points, the success rate for the juvenile offender program is between 66 and 74 percent.

The base on which a percentage is calculated is significant. If you make $30,000 and a colleague makes $40,000, those are your base salaries. At performance time, your employer gives out raises—a 5 percent increase to you and a 4 percent increase to your colleague. Before you begin feeling too good about your raise, however, consider that your raise is $1,500 and your colleague's raise is $1,600. Your colleague received a bigger raise, and the gap between your two salaries has grown. But you have to know the base to understand the significance of the numbers.

In one investigative report, the *St. Louis Post-Dispatch* recognized that it had percentages with different bases, and it handled them correctly. The newspaper examined repeat drunken-driving offenders in seven jurisdictions in its circulation area. In Missouri, drivers convicted two times of driving while intoxicated are supposed to be charged with a felony on the third offense. In reporting on the results, the reporters carefully gave the percentages and the base for each jurisdiction. That was important because the base ranged from seven cases in the city of St. Louis to 120 in St. Louis County. The percentages of cases handled correctly ranged from 29 to 51 percent. When the numbers are small, the percentages are less meaningful.

What's the grammar error in this sentence?

The Alaskan peak known as Mount McKinley was officially restored to it's original Koyukon name, Denali.

See Appendix 1, Rule 12.

Percentage Change and Percentage Points

Confusion often occurs when people talk about the difference between two percentage figures. For example, say the mayor won the election with 55 percent of

To Calculate Percentage Change

- Subtract the old number from the new number: New number – Old number = Change.
- Divide the change by the old number: Change ÷ Old number = .xxx.
- Move the decimal point two places to right: .xxx = xx.x percent.
- The percentage change can be a positive or a negative number.

the vote and had only one opponent, who received 45 percent. The mayor won by a margin of 10 **percentage points**. The percentage points, in this case, equal the difference between 55 and 45.

However, the mayor won 22 percent more votes (10 divided by 45 equals .22, or 22 percent). Because the 55 and 45 percentages are based on the same whole number—in this case, the total number of votes cast—the percentages can be compared. But if you compare the percentage of a city budget devoted to law enforcement in consecutive years, you will need to include the actual dollar amounts with the percentages because total spending probably changed from one year to the next.

Another important aspect of percentages is the concept of **percentage change**. This number explains how much something has gone up or down. For example, take a look at the city budget summary shown in Figure 7.1 (page 147). If you look at "Revised Fiscal Year 2018" under "Appropriations," you'll see that total spending in 2018 was $18,654,563. The proposed budget for 2019 ("Adopted Fiscal Year 2019") is $19,570,518. What is the percentage increase? You find a percentage change by dividing the increase or decrease by the old budget.

To calculate a percentage change:

Step 1. Find the change: $19,570,518 – $18,654,563 = $915,955 (increase).

Step 2. Divide the change by the base amount: Change ÷ Base amount = .xxx.
$915,955 ÷ $18,654,563 = .049

Step 3. Move the decimal point two places to the right: 4.9 percent.

Rounded off, this is a 5 percent increase in spending. If the 2016 budget is increased 4.9 percent again in the following year, that will be a $958,955 increase, or $43,000 larger increase than the year before, because of the bigger base.

When changes are large, sometimes it is better to translate the numbers into plain words rather than using a percentage figure. That $1.6 billion deficit in Florida amounted to $344 for every person living there.

Averages and Medians

Averages and medians are numbers that can be used to describe a general trend. For any given set of numbers, the average and the median might be quite close or quite different. Depending on what you are trying to explain, it might be important to use one instead of the other or to use both.

The **average**—more technically called the *arithmetic mean*—is the number that is obtained when you add a list of figures and then divide the total by the number of figures in the list. The **median** is the midpoint of the list: Half the figures fall above it, and half the figures fall below it.

To calculate an average:

Step 1. Add the figures.

Step 2. Divide the total by the number of figures: Total ÷ Number of figures = Average.

To find the median:

Step 1. Arrange the figures in rank order.

Step 2. Identify the figure midway between the highest and lowest numbers. That figure is the median.

When you have an even number of figures, the median is the average of the two middle figures.

As a general rule, you are safe using averages when there are no large gaps among the numbers. If you have seven numbers that range from 1 to 104 and the numbers are distributed evenly within that range, then the average would be an accurate reading. If your seven numbers are 1, 4, 12, 22, 31, 89 and 104, however, the average is 37.6. This average distorts the numbers because the average is higher than five of the seven numbers. The median, or midpoint, is 22, which might be a more accurate way to handle these seven numbers.

"Average" Can Mean Different Things to Different People

Although most people understand the word *average* to refer to "arithmetic mean," the word is sometimes used for other types of statistical results, including median and mode.

In reporting statistics, be certain you know which average is involved. All of the following are averages:

- **Mean.** The mean is the arithmetic average, which is found by adding all the figures in a set of data and dividing by the number of figures. The mean of 2, 4 and 9 is 5: 2 + 4 + 9 = 15; 15 ÷ 3 = 5.
- **Median.** The median is the middle value in a set of figures. If there is no middle value because there is an even number of figures, average the two middle numbers. The median of 2, 4 and 9 is 4. The medians of 5, 7, 9 and 11 and of 3, 7, 9 and 15 both are 8: 7 + 9 = 16; 16 ÷ 2 = 8.
- **Mode.** The mode is the most frequent value in a set of figures. The mode of 2, 5, 5, 5, 15 and 23 is 5.

When Averages Distort

A class of 15 students took a final exam, and the students scored 95, 94, 92, 86, 85, 84, 75, 75, 65, 64, 63, 62, 62, 62 and 62 on the exam. In this case, both the average (that is, the arithmetic mean) and the median are 75.

The picture can look quite different when the figures bunch at one end of the scale. Consider this example from professional baseball. In 2017, the New York Yankees had a payroll of about $172 million. With a range of salaries from $551,000 to $25 million, the median salary was $1.3 million. However, the average, or mean, was $6 million ($172 divided by 28 players). Much of the payroll went to a few players at the high end of the pay scale.

Rates

A **rate** is used to make fair comparisons among different populations. One example of a rate comparison is per capita ("for each person") spending. Per capita calculations can be useful in crime reporting, too. A team of reporters at the *Tampa*

Bay Times created a spreadsheet to record all marijuana arrests in its two primary counties. They translated the main finding this way: "Black people in Pinellas and Hillsborough counties are at least six times as likely to be arrested for marijuana possession as white people on a per capita basis."

The counties do not have equal populations, so by using a per capita calculation, they were able to compare the numbers correctly.

TIPS

To Calculate Per Capita Spending

Divide the budget by the number of people: Budget ÷ Population = Per capita spending.

When it comes to spending, even though a big-city school budget looks large to someone in a small community, the money has to stretch over more students than it would in a small district. As a result, spending per capita provides a better comparison between districts with different enrollments.

Suppose that your school district (district A) has 1,000 students and spends $2 million each year. You want to compare spending in your district with spending in district B, which has 1,500 students and an annual budget of $3 million. You would use the following formula to calculate per capita spending:

To calculate per capita spending: Divide the budget by the number of people.

Budget in dollars ÷ Number of people = Dollar amount per capita
District A: $2,000,000 ÷ 1,000 = $2,000 per capita
District B: $3,000,000 ÷ 1,500 = $2,000 per capita

In this case, school district B spends $1 million more a year than district A, but both districts spend the same amount per pupil.

To compare crime incidents or spending amounts among municipalities with varying populations, use per capita figures.

TIPS

To Calculate Simple Interest and Total Amount Owed

- Express the interest rate as a decimal by moving the decimal point two places to the left.
- Multiply the principal by the interest rate: $1,000 × .05 = $50.
- Add the principal to the interest owed: $1,000 + $50 = $1,050.

The same result can be obtained another way.

- Multiply the principal by 1 plus the interest rate expressed as a decimal: $1,000 × 1.05 = $1,050.

Interest and Compounding

Interest is a financial factor in just about everyone's life. Consumers pay interest on home mortgages, car loans and credit card balances. Individuals and businesses earn interest when they deposit money in a financial institution or make a loan. Federal regulations require the interest rates charged by or paid by most institutions be expressed as an **annual percentage rate (APR)** so that interest rates are comparable from one institution to another.

There are two types of interest: simple and compound. **Simple interest** is interest that is paid on the **principal**, the amount borrowed. It is calculated by multiplying the amount of the loan by the annual percentage rate.

Suppose that a student borrows $1,000 from her grandfather at a 5 percent annual rate to help cover college expenses. She needs only a one-year loan, so the cost is figured as simple interest:

To calculate simple interest:

Multiply the principal by the interest rate: $1,000 × .05 = $50.

To find the amount the student will repay her grandfather at the end of the year, add the principal to the interest: \$1,000 + \$50 = \$1,050. The student will owe \$1,050.

If the loan is made over a period longer than a year, the borrower pays **compound interest**. Compound interest is interest paid on both the total of the principal and also the interest that already has accrued.

Suppose that the student borrows \$1,000 at an annual percentage rate of 5 percent and pays her grandfather back four years later, after graduation. She owes 5 percent annual interest for each year of the loan. But because she has the loan for four years, each year she owes not only simple interest on the principal but also interest on the interest that accrues each year.

At the end of year one, she owes \$1,050. To see how much she will owe at the end of year 2, she has to calculate 5 percent interest on \$1,050: \$1,050 × .05 = \$52.50.

Here is how to calculate the interest for all four years. (Note that 1.05 is used instead of .05 to produce a running total: principal and interest. If you multiply 1,000 by 1.05, you get 1,050; if instead you multiply 1,000 by .05, you get 50, which you then have to add to 1,000 to get the principal and interest.)

$$\$1{,}000 \times 1.05 \times 1.05 \times 1.05 \times 1.05 = \$1{,}215.5062, \text{ rounded up to } \$1{,}215.51$$

Because most consumers pay off student loans, car loans, mortgages and credit card debt over a period of time and because interest is compounded more often than once a year, calculations usually are far more complicated than those in the example. Many financial websites and computer programs offer calculators for computing interest that are easy to find and use.

Student loans that are taken out through federal programs administered by banks, credit unions and universities are a prime example of more complicated transactions. Suppose that a student has a \$5,000 guaranteed student loan with an interest rate of 8 percent per year. After finishing school, the student has 10 years to repay the loan, and each year she pays 8 percent interest on the amount of the original principal that is left unpaid. If the student makes the minimum payment of \$65 on time each month for the 10-year life of the loan, she will pay the bank a total of \$7,800. She pays \$2,800 in interest on top of the original principal of \$5,000. If she does not pay the balance down each month, the interest she owes will be even higher.

The same effect can work for the benefit of consumers. When consumers put money in interest-bearing accounts, their interest compounds. When people make good investments in the stock market, their earnings are compounded when they are reinvested.

To Calculate Compound Interest

- Add 1 to the interest rate expressed as a decimal: 1 + .05 = 1.05.
- Using a calculator, multiply the principal by $(1.05)^n$. The superscript *n* represents the number of years of the loan.
- The result is the total amount owed.

Reporting with numbers may seem daunting, but mastering a few simple equations will open new possibilities for unique coverage in your stories.

wutzkohphoto/Shutterstock.com

Inflation

Inflation is an increase in the cost of living over time. Because prices rise over time, wages and budgets also have to increase just to keep up with inflation. A worker who receives a 2 percent pay increase each year will continue to have the same buying power each year if inflation also rises at 2 percent. Because of inflation, reporters must use a few simple computations to make fair comparisons between dollar amounts from different years.

Let's say the teachers in your local school district are negotiating for a new contract. They claim that their pay is not keeping pace with inflation. You know that the starting salary for a teacher was $50,000 in 2014 and was $55,000 in 2017. To determine whether the teachers' claim is true, you convert 2014 dollars to 2017 dollars. You will find that the starting salary in 2017 would have been $54,900 if the district had been keeping up with inflation. In other words, in constant dollars, the school district was staying slightly ahead of the rate inflation with its pay increases. (Numbers that are adjusted for inflation are called *constant*, or *real*, *dollars*. Numbers that are not adjusted for inflation are called *nominal*, or *current*, *dollars*.)

The most common tool used to adjust for inflation is the Consumer Price Index, which is reported each month by the U.S. Bureau of Labor Statistics, an agency of the Labor Department. You can get current CPI numbers on the web at www.bls.gov/cpi.

Taxes

To Calculate Sales Tax

- Multiply the price of the item by the sales tax rate.
- To obtain the total cost, add the result to the price of the item.

Reporters not only pay taxes but also have to report on them. Governments collect taxes in a variety of ways, but the three major categories are sales taxes, income taxes and property taxes. Tax rates are expressed as percentages.

Sales Taxes

State, county and municipal governments can levy sales taxes on various goods and services. Sales taxes — also known as *excise taxes* — are the simplest to figure out.

To figure a sales tax, multiply the price of an item by the sales tax rate. Add the result to the original price to obtain the total cost.

Take the example of a student who buys a computer for $1,800 before beginning school at the University of Virginia. If he shops in his home state of Delaware, he will pay no state sales tax. If he buys the computer after arriving in Virginia, where the state sales tax is 6 percent, he will pay a state sales tax of $108 and another $13.50 in county sales tax, for a total of $1,921.50.

Sales taxes are an excellent way for you to track sales in your city, county or state. The appropriate government unit — a finance or comptroller's office, for instance — will have sales tax revenues, which are a direct reflection of sales. They therefore are an excellent resource for reporting on the economy in your area.

Income Taxes

Governments tax your income to support such services as building roads, running schools, registering people to vote and encouraging businesses to grow. Income taxes are paid to the federal government, to most state governments and to some municipalities.

Calculating income taxes can be tricky because many factors affect the amount of income that is subject to the tax. For that reason, the only way to figure a person's income tax is to consult the actual numbers and follow tables published by the Internal Revenue Service (www.irs.gov) or the state department of taxation.

Governments use tax incentives to encourage people to undertake certain types of economic activities, such as buying a home, saving for retirement and investing in business ventures. By giving people and businesses tax deductions, the government reduces the amount of income that is taxable.

A tax deduction is worth the tax rate times the amount of the tax deduction. The most common tax deduction is for the interest that people pay on their home loans. Tax deductions are worth more to people with higher incomes.

Take the example of two families who own homes. Both pay $2,500 in interest on their home mortgage in a year, the cost of which is deductible for people who itemize deductions on their income tax forms. The lower-income family is in the lowest federal income tax bracket, where the tax rate is 10 percent. So this family saves $250 on its tax bill ($2,500 × .10 = $250).

The higher-income family, which is in the federal income tax bracket of 35 percent, saves $825 on its tax bill ($2,500 × .35 = $875). Realistically, the family in the 35 percent tax bracket probably owns a more expensive home and probably pays much more than $2,500 in mortgage interest a year. The impact is that the family saves even more on its income tax.

Income tax rates are based on your *adjusted gross income*. In 2018, for example, if you were single and made less than $9,525 after deductions, you paid $838, or 10 percent. If you made more than $9,525 but less than $38,700 after deductions, your rate was 12 percent of your income over $9,526.

Property Taxes

City and county governments collect property taxes. When people talk about property taxes, they usually mean taxes on the value of houses, buildings and land. In some places, people also are taxed each year on the value of their cars, boats and other personal property.

The two key factors in property taxes are the assessed value and the millage rate. The **assessed value** is the amount that a government appraiser determines a piece of property is worth. The **millage rate**—the rate per thousand dollars—is the tax rate determined by the government.

To calculate property taxes:

Step 1. Divide the assessed value by 1,000: $140,000 ÷ 1,000 = 140.

Step 2. Multiply the result by the millage rate: 140 × 2.25 = $315 in taxes.

ON THE JOB Working with Numbers

From city budgets to election results to economic meltdowns, today's important stories frequently involve numbers. Unfortunately, reporters too often avoid them or leave their interpretation to officials.

But understanding how to interpret and present numbers in a news story can make a big difference. As a data editor for newspapers and nonprofit newsrooms, **Jennifer LaFleur** saw that reporters who had these skills were able to break important stories.

For instance, at *The Dallas Morning News*, math skills led education reporters to uncover millions of dollars in misspending in the Dallas Independent School District. At the nonprofit investigative newsroom ProPublica, many of LaFleur's first stories involved the nation's economic crisis of 2008 to 2009 and the nearly $800 billion federal stimulus package. At the Reveal website at the Center for Investigative Reporting, where she was a senior editor, data and math help reporters dig into environmental and public safety issues.

LaFleur is now data journalist in residence at American University, where she hopes to train future journalists to use numbers correctly in their journalism. Over the years, LaFleur has noticed these common problems:

- Love for the superlative leads some reporters to use phrases such as "Texas has the most hunting accidents" or "California has the most cars" without putting the numbers in perspective. Big states have lots of everything, so the numbers should be adjusted for the population.
- Things cost more today than they did in the past, but too often reporters fail to adjust the figures for inflation. A dollar in 1950 was worth a lot more than it is today.
- In striving for precision, some reporters give readers a false message. A poll of only 400 people can't be precise, so we shouldn't report that 43.25 percent of those respondents said something.

"In a time when every reporter is asked to do more, no reporters should be without the basic skills to interpret the numbers they run across every day," LaFleur says. "They should know how to compute a percentage change, percent of total and per capita and know what all those things mean."

Photo by Rachel de Leon, The Center for Investigative Reporting

TIPS

To Calculate Property Tax

- Divide the assessed value by 1,000: $140,000 ÷ 1,000 = 140.
- Multiply that result by the millage rate: 140 × 2.25 = $315.

Counties and cities hire professional appraisers to assess the values of land and buildings in their jurisdiction, and typically their assessments have been far lower than the actual market value of the property. Because of abuses and public confusion, most states in recent years have ordered revaluations to bring assessments into line with market values, and they have adjusted tax rates accordingly, though assessments can vary widely from appraiser to appraiser.

Appraisals are based on complicated formulas that take into account the size, location and condition of the property. Still, the government might say your house is worth $160,000, even if you know you could sell it for $180,000.

When you are reporting tax rate changes, you should find out how they affect houses in different value brackets to help explain the impact. By talking to the assessor or tax collector, you should be able to report, for instance, that the taxes for a house valued at $140,000 would be $315 and that taxes for a house valued at $250,000 would be $562.50.

Now that we've discussed some of the basic mathematical calculations you'll need in your reporting, let's move on to where you can use them: budgets, financial reports and public opinion polls.

Budgets

The budget is the blueprint that guides the operation of any organization, and a reporter must learn to read a budget just as a carpenter must learn to read a set of blueprints. It's not as difficult as might appear at first glance.

In many cases today, you'll be able to get the budget (and other financial information) for your city or school district in an electronic file. You might also be able to view it on a local website, but you probably cannot download that file into a spreadsheet database.

After you have the budget in an electronic file, you can create your own spreadsheet and perform analyses that not long ago only the institution's budget director could perform. This is one of many ways the computer has become an essential newsroom tool. However, with a computer or without, first you need to know the basics of budgeting.

Budget Basics

Every budget, whether it's your personal budget or the budget of the U.S. government, has two basic parts—*revenues* (income) and *expenditures* (outgo). Commercial enterprises earn their income primarily from sales; not-for-profit organizations depend heavily on contributions from public funding and private donors. Government revenues come from sources such as taxes, fees and service charges, and payments from other agencies (such as state aid to schools). The budget usually shows, in dollar amounts and percentages, the sources of the organization's money.

Expenditures go for such items as staff salaries, supplies, utility bills, construction and maintenance of facilities, and insurance. Expenditures usually are listed either by line or by program. The difference is this: A **line-item budget** shows a separate line for each expenditure, such as "Salary of police chief—$150,000." A **program budget** provides less detail but shows more clearly what each activity of the agency costs—for example, "Burglary prevention program—$250,000."

Common Budget Story Concerns

- Changes
- Trends
- Comparisons

Finding Stories in Budget Changes, Trends and Comparisons

Now let's see what kinds of stories budgets might yield and where to look for those stories. Take a minute to scan Figure 7.1 on page 147, a summary page from the annual budget of a small city. The summary shows two sections—revenues

Some Guidelines for Reporting Numbers

- Cite sources for all statistics.
- Use numbers judiciously for maximum impact.
- Long lists of figures are difficult to read in paragraph form. Put them in charts and graphs when appropriate.
- Graphs sometimes include estimates. If you use figures from a graph, make sure they are precise.
- Round off large numbers in most cases. For example, use $1.5 million rather than $1,489,789.
- Always double-check your math, and verify any statistics a source gives you.
- Be especially careful with handwritten numbers. It is easy to drop or transpose figures in your notes. Write neatly so that when you read your notes, you can tell a 1 from a 7.
- If you don't understand the figures, get an explanation.

("Appropriations") and expenditures ("Department Expenditures"). You can apply the skills of reading a city's annual budget to similar accounting documents on other beats — for example, annual reports of businesses and not-for-profit organizations.

The most important budget stories usually deal with changes, trends and comparisons. Budget figures change every year. Generally, as costs increase, so do budgets.

But look under "Department Expenditures" in our sample budget at the line for the parks and recreation department. There's a decrease between revised fiscal year 2018 and adopted fiscal year 2019. Why? The summary page doesn't tell you, so you'll have to look further.

Sometimes this information will be in the detail pages; other times, you'll have to ask the department director. You might discover, for example, that the drop resulted from a proposal by the city staff to halt funding of a summer employment program for teenagers. That's a story.

Another change that may be newsworthy is the increase in the police department budget. In 2018, spending totaled $4,139,085, and the budget adopted for 2019 is $4,375,336. In this case, it turned out that most of the increase was going to pay for an administrative reorganization that would add new positions at the top of the department. The patrol division was actually being reduced. Another story.

Look again at the police department line. In two years, the expenditures for police increased by nearly one-third, from $3.3 million actually spent in 2017 to nearly $4.4 million budgeted for 2019. That's an interesting trend. The same pattern holds true for the fire department. More checking is in order.

With copies of previous budgets, you can see how far back a growth trend runs. You can also get statistics on crimes and fires from the individual departments. Are the budget-makers responding to a demonstrated need for more protection, or is something else at work?

More generally, you can trace patterns in the growth of city services and city taxes, and you can compare those with changes in population. Are the rates of change comparable? Is population growth outstripping growth in services? Are residents paying more per capita for city services than they paid five or 10 years ago? More good story possibilities.

Another kind of comparison can be useful to your readers. How does your city government compare in cost and services with the governments of comparable cities? Some professional organizations have recommended levels of service — such as the number of police officers or firefighters per 1,000 inhabitants — that can help you help your readers assess how well they're being governed.

The same guidelines can be applied to the analysis of any budget. The numbers will be different, as will the department names, but the structures will be much the same. Whether you're covering the school board or the statehouse, look for changes, trends and comparisons.

FIGURE 7.1

Summary Page of a Typical City Budget

General Fund Summary

PURPOSE

The General Fund is used to finance and account for a large portion of the current operation expenditures and capital outlays of city government. The General Fund is one of the largest and most important of the city's funds because most governmental programs (police, fire, public works, parks and recreation, and so on) are generally financed wholly or partially from it. The General Fund has a greater number and variety of revenue sources than any other fund, and its resources normally finance a wider range of activities.

APPROPRIATIONS

	Actual Fiscal Year 2017	Budget Fiscal Year 2018	Revised Fiscal Year 2018	Adopted Fiscal Year 2019
Personnel services	$9,500,353	$11,306,619	$11,245,394	$12,212,336
Materials and supplies	1,490,573	1,787,220	1,794,362	1,986,551
Training and schools	93,942	150,517	170,475	219,455
Utilities	606,125	649,606	652,094	722,785
Services	1,618,525	1,865,283	1,933,300	2,254,983
Insurance and miscellaneous	1,792,366	1,556,911	1,783,700	1,614,265
Total operating	15,101,884	17,316,156	17,579,325	19,010,375
Capital additions	561,145	1,123,543	875,238	460,143
Total operating and capital	15,663,029	18,439,699	18,454,563	19,470,518
Contingency	—	200,000	200,000	100,000
Total	**$15,663,029**	**$18,639,699**	**$18,654,563**	**$19,570,518**

DEPARTMENT EXPENDITURES

	Actual Fiscal Year 2017	Budget Fiscal Year 2018	Revised Fiscal Year 2018	Adopted Fiscal Year 2019
City Council	$75,144	$105,207	$90,457	$84,235
City Clerk	61,281	70,778	74,444	91,867
City Manager	155,992	181,219	179,125	192,900
Municipal Court	164,631	196,389	175,019	181,462
Personnel	143,366	197,844	186,247	203,020
Law Department	198,296	266,819	248,170	288,550
Planning and Community Development	295,509	377,126	360,272	405,870
Finance Department	893,344	940,450	983,342	1,212,234

(continued)

Figure 7.1 *(Continued)*

DEPARTMENT EXPENDITURES

	Actual Fiscal Year 2017	Budget Fiscal Year 2018	Revised Fiscal Year 2018	Adopted Fiscal Year 2019
Fire Department	2,837,744	3,421,112	3,257,356	3,694,333
Police Department	3,300,472	4,007,593	4,139,085	4,375,336
Health	1,033,188	1,179,243	1,157,607	1,293,362
Community Services	50,882	74,952	74,758	78,673
Energy Management	—	—	54,925	66,191
Public Works	2,838,605	3,374,152	3,381,044	3,509,979
Parks and Recreation	1,218,221	1,367,143	1,400,334	1,337,682
Communications and Information Services	532,153	730,129	742,835	715,324
City General	1,864,200	1,949,543	1,949,543	1,739,500
Total Department Expenditures	15,663,028	18,439,699	18,454,563	19,470,518
Contingency	—	200,000	200,000	100,000
Total	**$15,663,028**	**$18,639,699**	**$18,654,563**	**$19,570,518**

> **"Ninety-nine percent of all statistics only tell 49 percent of the story."**
>
> ■ **Ron DeLegge II, author**

Financial Reports

Another document that is vital to understanding the finances of local government or of any organization is the annual financial report. This report explains the organization's financial status at the end of a fiscal year, which often is not the same as it is at the end of the calendar year. (For example, a fiscal year might end on June 30.)

In the report, you will find an accounting of all the income the organization received during the year from taxes, fees, state and federal grants, and other sources. You'll also find status reports on all the organization's operating funds, such as its capital improvement fund, its debt-service fund and its general fund.

Making sense of a financial report, like understanding a budget, isn't as hard as it may look at first. For one thing, the financial officer usually includes a narrative that highlights the most important points, at least from his or her viewpoint.

But you should dig beyond the narrative and examine the numbers for yourself. The most important section of the report is the statement of revenues, expenditures and changes, which provides important measures of the organization's financial health. Depending on the comprehensiveness of the statement, you may have to refer to the budget document as well. You can check the following:

- Actual revenue received compared with budgeted revenue.
- Actual spending compared with budgeted spending.
- Actual spending compared with actual revenue.
- Changes in balances available for spending in years to come.

Lies, Damned Lies and Statistics

Here are some of the ways that statistics can deceive:

- **Social factors can influence the credibility of a survey.** For example, a national survey on sexual behavior indicated that 1 percent of 3,321 men questioned said they were gay, compared with the 10 percent commonly accepted as constituting the gay population. When reporting the survey results, *Time* magazine pointed out that people might be reluctant to discuss their sexual orientation with a "clipboard-bearing stranger."
- **One year does not a trend make.** A large increase in the number of rapes merits a story, but it might represent a fluctuation rather than a trend. Depending on the subject matter, you need to study at least five to 10 years of data to determine whether there is a significant shift.
- **Different organizations compile figures differently, which can distort comparisons.** The Scripps Howard investigation of sudden infant deaths, for example, found what one expert called a "deeply muddled approach." There were wide variations in reporting from one state to the next, which distorted real results and made accurate comparisons impossible. Jurisdictions with inadequately trained medical examiners reported many times as many "unexplained" deaths as did jurisdictions with more rigorous standards. Inadequately trained journalists unknowingly spread misinformation.
- **Conclusions that sound credible might not hold up under the scrutiny of cause and effect.** Advocacy groups that call for less violence on television say studies show TV violence causes violence in children. They cite research done at Yale University showing that prolonged viewing of violent programs is associated with aggressive behavior among children. But the association could be that children who tend to be aggressive watch more violent programming, not the other way around.

The guidelines offered here should help you shape your questions and understand the answers. With financial statements, as with budgets, look for changes, trends and comparisons, and ask for explanations.

Public Opinion Polls

Surveying is a powerful journalistic tool. It is also a tool that is often misused. In every election, many commentators and some candidates misread poll results and many media misreport them. Despite the problems, many journalists, politicians, businesses and scholars today are using poll results because they show more reliably than anecdotes or ordinary interviews what the public thinks about important issues.

Many news organizations now go beyond reporting the findings of national polling firms such as Gallup and Harris Interactive and conduct or commission their own surveys.

Some pollsters are described as "Democratic" or "Republican." That's really a shorthand way of saying they usually work for candidates of one or the other party. It doesn't mean the polls' results are slanted. An accurate sense of the public mood is at least as important to politicians as to journalists. If you report the results of one of these one-party pollsters, though, make sure you explain the connection.

Every day, new poll results illustrate what people think about various topics in the news. And just about every day, journalists confuse readers when they try to interpret the results.

The Margin of Error

The most important thing to keep in mind about polls and surveys is that they are based on samples of a population. Because a survey reflects the responses of a small number of people within a population, every survey has a *margin of error*—the difference between what you would find for the entire population compared to what you would find in a random sample. The results must be presented with the understanding that scientific sampling is not a perfect predictor for the entire population.

Suppose that your news organization buys polling services that show that Candidate Hernandez has support from 58 percent of the people surveyed, Candidate Jones has support from 32 percent and 10 percent are undecided. The polling service indicates that the margin of error of the poll is plus or minus 3 percentage points. The margins separating the candidates are well beyond the margin of error, so you can safely write that Hernandez is leading in the poll:

Candidate	Percentage of Support	Percentage of Support Adjusted for Margin of Error (+/− 3%)
Hernandez	58%	55–61%
Jones	32%	29–35%
Undecided	10%	7–13%

Now suppose that Hernandez has 52 percent support and Jones has 48 percent. The difference between them is within the margin of error, less than plus or minus 3 percentage points. That margin of error means that Hernandez could have as little as 49 percent and Jones could have as much as 51 percent. Seldom would results vary that much, but caution is the best guide. In this case, report that the results are too close to call.

Candidate	Percentage of Support	Percentage of Support Adjusted for Margin of Error (+/− 3%)
Hernandez	52%	49–55%
Jones	48%	45–51%

When polls are conducted properly and reported carefully, they can tell us something we could not know otherwise and perhaps even lead to wiser public policies. But when they are badly done or sloppily reported, polls can be bad news for journalists and readers alike.

The chances are good that sometime in your reporting career you will want to conduct an opinion poll or at least help with one that your employer is conducting. The Suggested Readings listed at the end of the chapter will tell you much of what you need to know for that. Even if you never work a poll, you almost certainly will be called on to write about polling results. What follows will help you understand what you are given and will help you make sure your readers understand it, too.

Public Opinion Polls and the 2016 Presidential Election

Many journalists and political observers expressed shock on election night 2016. Nearly all national opinion polls predicted an easy victory for Democratic presidential nominee Hillary Clinton, but through the night and into the next morning it became clear that the insurgent Republican candidate Donald Trump would receive a substantial majority of votes in the Electoral College and win the presidency. How could the polls have been wrong?

Political scientist James Endersby, an associate professor at the University of Missouri, specializes in American political behavior, such as voting and elections. He's an expert on polling and explains what happened:

> It is important to note that public opinion polls in 2016 were accurate by historical and statistical standards. Pre-election estimates in 2016 were consistent with margins from previous elections. On average, national polls predicted a Clinton lead of about 3 percentage points. Clinton won the popular vote by more than 2 percentage points. For most polls, the election outcome fit well within the margin of error.
>
> Contemporary election polls suffer from several difficulties. The response rate has fallen dramatically in recent years. This decline is because of several factors: increased cellphone use, the regulation of calls to cellphones, technological innovations such as caller ID and voicemail, and a growing reluctance of many citizens to respond to political surveys. Researchers face continuing challenges to create a representative sample. Pollsters also have difficulty distinguishing likely voters from nonvoters. In addition, a particular poll's definition of a likely voter is often proprietary, creating inconsistency and confusion with interpretation. Turnout also increased in 2016, perhaps underestimating Trump support among former nonvoters.
>
> In 2016, the presidential contest was decided in a few states, particularly in the upper Midwest, where polls indicated a very narrow Clinton lead. In a close presidential election, commentators should focus on state data rather than on national trends. Yet state polls typically have smaller sample sizes and uneven quality control compared to national samples.
>
> Most surveys use post-sample weighting to reflect a representative sample because, for example, college graduates are more likely to respond to pollsters than those with lower levels of education. (Post-sample weighting means adjusting a particular demographic group's responses so that its proportion of the sample matches its proportion in the overall population.) However, a study by the American Association for Public Opinion Research found that many 2016 polls did not adjust results for education, thus underestimating respondents with lower levels of education, precisely those more likely to support Trump. Finally, general public dissatisfaction with both 2016 nominees may have led many voters to make last-minute decisions. Survey evidence suggests that these late deciders, especially in the upper Midwest, broke disproportionately for Trump.
>
> The prominence of internet sites offering poll averaging or aggregating — sites such as FiveThirtyEight, RealClearPolitics and HuffPost — as well as pollsters' natural reliance on sample weighting that encourages cautious reporting of results in sync with other surveys, constructed a herd mentality. The sheer number of national polls predicting a slim lead produced a false expectation of Clinton's invincibility in the 2016 presidential election. A more careful interpretation of polls suggests the race was too close to call. That's what journalists should have reported.

Poll Information to Share

The Associated Press Media Editors has a checklist of the information you should share with your audience about any poll on which you are reporting. Several of the checklist's points require some explanation:

- **Identity of the sponsor.** The identity of the survey's sponsor is important to you and your readers because it hints at possible bias. Most people would put more trust in a Gallup or Harris poll's report that, for instance, Hernandez is far ahead of Jones in the presidential campaign than they would in a poll sponsored by the Hernandez for President organization.
- **Wording of the questions.** The wording of the questions is important because the answers received often depend at least in part on how the questions were asked. (See Chapter 4 on interviewing for more detail.) The answer might well be different, for example, if a pollster asks, "Whom do you favor for president, Jones or Hernandez?" rather than "Wouldn't Jones make a better president than Hernandez?"
- **Population sampled.** In science, the *population* is the total number of people (or documents or milkweed plants or giraffes) in the group that is being studied. For an opinion survey, the population might be, for example, registered voters in the state, black males under 25 or female cigarette smokers. To understand the meaning of a poll's results, you must know what population was studied. The word *sampled* refers to the procedure in which a small number—or sample—of people is picked at random so as to be representative of the population. In a scientific poll, every member of the population has an equal chance of being selected as part of the sample.
- **Sample size and response rate.** The sample size is important because—all other things being equal—the larger the sample, the more reliable the survey results should be. The response rate is especially important in surveys conducted by mail, in which a low rate of response may invalidate the poll.
- **Margin of error.** The margin of error, or sampling error, of any survey is the allowance that must be made for the possibility that the opinion of the sample might not be exactly the same as the opinion of the whole population. For large populations, such as the people who are involved in an election, the margin of error depends mainly on the size of the sample. For instance, all other things being equal, a sample of 384 would have a margin of error of 5 percentage points, and a sample of 1,065 would have a margin of error of 3 percentage points.

  As was seen earlier, if a poll with a margin of error of 3 percentage points has Hernandez with 58 percent of the votes and Jones with 32 percent, you can be confident that Hernandez actually has between 55 and 61 percent and Jones actually has between 29 and 35 percent. The laws of probability say that the chances are 19 to 1 that the actual percentages fall within that range. Those odds make the information good enough to publish.

- **Results that are based on part of the sample.** The problem of sampling error helps explain why it is important to know which results may be based on only part of the sample. The smaller that part is, the greater the margin of error. In political polls, it is always important to know whether the results include responses from all eligible voters or only from individuals who are *likely* to vote. The opinions of the likely voters are more important than the opinions of others.
- **Date that the interviews were collected.** The date that the interviews were collected may be of critical importance in interpreting a poll. During campaigns, for example, the candidates themselves and other events may cause voters' preferences to change significantly within a few days. Think of presidential primaries. As candidates join or drop out of the race, support for each of the other candidates changes. A week-old poll may be meaningless if something dramatic happens after it was taken. Candidates have been known to use outdated results to make themselves appear to be doing better than they really are or make their opponents seem to be doing worse. Be on guard.

Polling voters is an excellent way to forecast election results. Random digit dialing includes cellphones, but cellphone users are less likely than landline owners to take a call from an unknown number. In the general population, about 25 percent of people who own cellphones do not own a landline. Pollsters must be careful to get a proper proportion of cellphone users.

Poll Information to Share with Your Audience

- The identity of the poll's sponsor.
- The exact wording of the questions asked.
- A definition of the population sampled.
- The sample size and response rate.
- The margin of error.
- Which results are based on only part of the sample (for example, probable voters).
- When the interviews were conducted.
- How the interviews were conducted — in person, by mail, and so on.

— Associated Press Media Editors

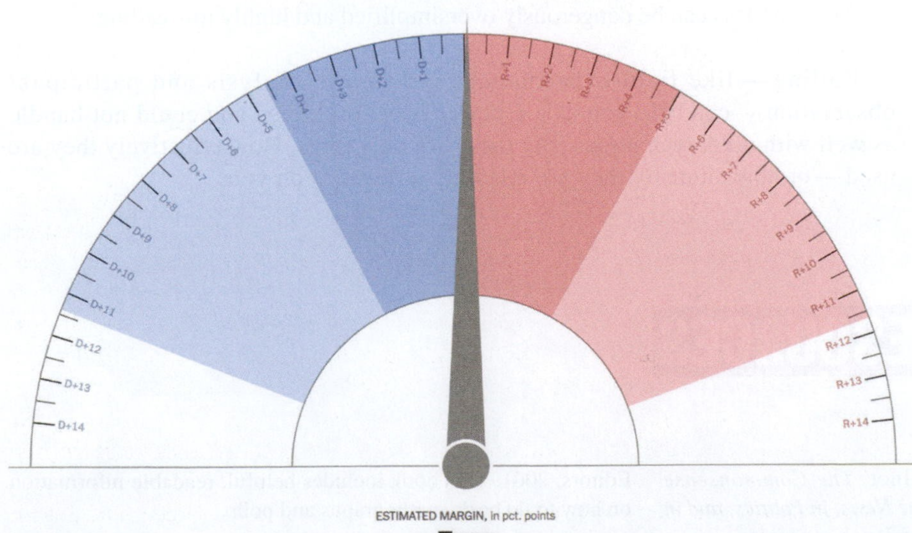

The New York Times election needle shows a way to measure live election results and measure for uncounted votes. During the 2016 presidential election, the needle captured the attention of many as it tried to predict the outcome.

Caution in Interpreting Polls

Whether you are helping conduct a survey or reporting on one produced by someone else, you must exercise caution. Be on guard for the following potential problems:

- **The people interviewed must be selected in a truly random fashion if you want to generalize from their responses to the whole population.** If the selection wasn't randomized, you have no assurance that the interview subjects are really representative. For this reason, the old-fashioned people-in-the-street interview is practically worthless as an indicator of public opinion. The man or woman in the street probably differs in important ways from all those men and women who are not in the street when the questioner is.

  Also invalid are the questionnaires that members of Congress mail to their constituents. Only strongly opinionated — and therefore unrepresentative — people are likely to return them.

  For the same reason, the "question-of-the-day" feature that some newspapers and broadcast stations ask listeners to respond to online tells you nothing about the opinions of the great mass of people who do not respond.

  Even worse are the TV polls that require respondents to call or send a text message to a number to register their opinions. Because there is a charge for such calls, these pseudopolls produce not only misleading results but profits that encourage their use.

- **Beware of polls that claim to measure opinion on sensitive, complicated issues.** Many questions of morality or social issues such as race relations do not lend themselves to simple answers. Opinions on such matters can be measured but only by highly skilled researchers who use carefully designed questions. Anything less can be dangerously oversimplified and highly misleading.

Cautions About Using Poll Data

- The people interviewed must be selected in a truly random fashion if you want to generalize from their responses to the whole population. Random means that any person in the population has as much chance as any other of being selected.
- Beware of polls that claim to measure opinion on sensitive, complicated issues.

Polling — like field experiments, systematic analysis and participant observation — can help you as a reporter solve problems you could not handle as well with other techniques. But these are only tools. How effectively they are used — or how clumsily they are misused — depends on you.

CHAPTER RESOURCES

SUGGESTED READINGS

Blastland, Michael, and Andrew Dilnot. *The Commonsense Guide to Understanding Numbers in the News, in Politics, and in Life*. New York: Penguin, 2009. You can laugh as you learn more about handling numbers.

Cohen, Sarah. *Numbers in the Newsroom: Using Math and Statistics in News*. Columbia, Mo.: Investigative Reporters and Editors, 2001. This book includes helpful, readable information on how to do basic math, graphs and polls.

Cuzzort, R.P., and James S. Vrettos. *The Elementary Forms of Statistical Reason*. New York: St. Martin's Press, 1996. Nonmathematicians in the humanities and social sciences who must work with statistics will appreciate this basic guide.

Paulos, John Allen. *A Mathematician Reads the Newspaper*. New York: Anchor Books, 1997. Structured like the morning paper, this book investigates the mathematical angles of stories in the news and offers novel perspectives, questions and ideas.

Silver, Nate. *The Signal and the Noise*. New York: Penguin Press, 2012. The creator of the FiveThirtyEight blog explains how to evaluate predictions in fields ranging from politics to the weather.

SUGGESTED WEBSITES

LaunchPad Solo
launchpadworks.com
When you visit LaunchPad Solo for Journalism, you will find research links, exercises and LearningCurve adaptive quizzing to help you improve your grammar and AP style usage. In addition, the site's video collection hosts the videos highlighted in this and other chapters as well as additional clips of leading professionals discussing important media trends.

www.bankrate.com
Bankrate offers calculators to figure everything from interest rates to currency conversions.

www.bls.gov/data/inflation_calculator.htm
The Bureau of Labor Statistics has a calculator that enables you to adjust dollar amounts for inflation. In addition, the website provides Consumer Price Index information for the entire nation, broken down by region and type of spending.

www.math.temple.edu/~paulos
John Allen Paulos, a professor at Temple University, is the author of *Innumeracy: Mathematical Illiteracy and Its Consequences*. At this site, you can read more from the master of numbers.

www.minneapolisfed.org
The Federal Reserve Bank of Minneapolis maintains a great website that helps you calculate inflation. It also has clear and simple explanations of how inflation is calculated and how to use the Consumer Price Index.

www.robertniles.com/stats
Robert Niles, who has worked at newspaper internet sites in Denver and Los Angeles, is a self-described "math and computer geek." His explanations of statistics are simple and clear.

EXERCISES

1. Go to PolitiFact.org and select an item the site checked involving numbers. Write a succinct report on the statement and the findings.

2. Your local school board sets the tax rate at $3.33 per thousand valuation, up from $3.21. Explain to readers the impact on a typical home.

3. Find a national survey released by any of the national media or by one of the major polling firms, such as Gallup or the Pew Research Center. Report the margin of error, and determine whether the main results are within that margin or exceed it.

4. The federal minimum wage began in 1938 at 25 cents an hour. In 1968, it was $1.60. Calculate how much $1.60 in 1968 is worth today. Compare those numbers with the present minimum wage in the state where you attend school. Determine the percent your state is above or below the federal minimum wage of $7.25. Suggest a story idea based on the result. (Consult www.dol.gov/whd/minimumwage.htm for the current federal minimum wage and www.dol.gov/whd/minwage/america.htm for the current state minimum wages.)

5. If a poll says that one candidate will get 48 percent of the vote and another will get 52 percent, what else do you need to know to accurately report the poll results?

6. Search for the payrolls by player of all the teams in the National Football League. Choose three teams, and calculate their average salary and their median salary. Which is the fairest comparison for each of the teams?

7. If a city budgets $186,247 for personnel one year and $203,020 the next, what is the percentage increase?

8. A city of 219,000 had 103 murders last year. Another city of 88,812 in the same state had 48 murders. How many murders were there per 1,000 residents in each city?

9. **Your journalism blog.** Find out how much your college charged for tuition in 1997, 2007 and 2017. Adjust those numbers for inflation so they can be compared. (Use an inflation calculator like the one at www.minneapolisfed.org.) Write a blog post about the cost of going to college, and use figures adjusted for inflation. Remember to keep your readers in mind. Are you writing for students? Parents? University officials? All of these?

CHAPTER 8 THE INVERTED PYRAMID

Photo credit: Aretha Franklin Mural painted by Sintex; photo by Timothy A. Clary/AFP/Getty Images

In this chapter, you will learn:

1. Why the inverted pyramid story is important.
2. How to translate news values into leads.
3. How to create variations on the inverted pyramid lead.
4. How to organize a story using the inverted pyramid.
5. How to use the inverted pyramid across media platforms.
6. How to improve your accuracy.

The **inverted pyramid** — a news story structure that places all the important information in the first paragraph or two — has been used to write the "first draft of history" in the U.S. for generations. The first paragraph is called the **lead**. Here is The Associated Press lead on the first use of the atomic bomb in 1945:

> **An atomic bomb, hailed as the most destructive force in history and as the greatest achievement of organized science, has been loosed upon Japan.**

Twenty-four years later, here is how the AP started its story of the first moon landing in 1969:

> **Man came to the moon and walked its dead surface Sunday.**

These days, news providers such as AP use the inverted pyramid technique lead to distribute breaking news. When Aretha Franklin died in 2018, the news flashed across mobiles. Using the inverted pyramid lead, AP reported:

> **Publicist for Aretha Franklin says the Queen of Soul died Thursday at her home in Detroit.**

This news alert, written more like a headline than a traditional sentence, conveys the most important information quickly. The same format would work well for a short post on social media such as Twitter. In fact, citizens who are suddenly thrust into reporting what's happening around them are tweeting in inverted pyramid style. The brevity of a tweet neatly reflects the goal of the traditional inverted pyramid news lead: Report the most important news succinctly.

With this goal, citizen journalists have joined the mainstream press and specialized financial news services such as Bloomberg News, which relies on the inverted pyramid. So do newspapers, despite many editors' encouragement of new writing forms. So do radio, television, the internet and newsletters. Businesspeople often use the inverted pyramid in company memos so their bosses don't have to read to the end to find the main point. Public relations professionals use it in news releases to gain the attention of news editors. Strategic communications professionals also use it for in-house and client communication.

The Importance of the Inverted Pyramid Story

Frequently misdiagnosed as dying, the inverted pyramid has more lives than a cat — perhaps because the more people try to speed up the dissemination of information, the more valuable the inverted pyramid becomes. In the inverted pyramid, information is arranged from most important to least important. The King of Hearts in *Alice's Adventures in Wonderland* would

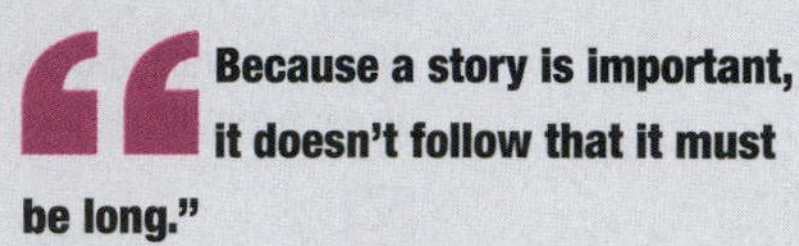

never succeed in the electronic news service business. When asked where to start a story, he replies, "Begin at the beginning . . . and go on till you come to the end: then stop." Reporters, however, often begin a story at its end.

Subscribers to financial services such as Reuters, Dow Jones' Factiva and Bloomberg, for instance, react instantly to news about the financial markets to gain an edge over other investors. They don't want narration; they want news. This is a typical Reuters inverted pyramid lead:

> **LONDON (Reuters)—Britain on Thursday told companies trading with the European Union they would face a tangle of red tape, possible border delays and more costly credit card payments if the government fails to negotiate an exit deal before Britain leaves the bloc.**

On average, newspaper readers spend about 15 minutes a day reading the paper. Online readers, who skip around sites as if they were walking barefoot on a hot stove, spend even less time. Both prefer very short stories with the news on top. If a reporter were to write an account of a car accident by starting when the driver left the house, many readers would never read far enough to learn that the driver and a passenger had been killed. Instead, such a story starts with its climax:

> **Two people died Thursday when a backhoe fell off a truck's flatbed and sliced off the top of an oncoming vehicle near Fairchild Air Force Base.**

In the inverted pyramid, the lead sits atop other paragraphs arranged in descending order of importance. These paragraphs explain and provide evidence to support the lead. That's why print editors can quickly shorten a story by cutting from the bottom; the paragraphs at the end are the least important. On the internet, space is not a consideration, but readers' time is. That's why the same inverted pyramid used in newspapers is the most common story structure found on such news websites as CNN.com, MSNBC.com, CBSNews.com and ABCNews.com. For instance, MSNBC.com used the inverted pyramid to report this breaking news:

> **DNA from at least one of the two escaped New York prisoners was found at a burglarized cabin in a rural town about 20 miles from the prison, sources told NBC News on Monday.**

The inverted pyramid has yet another attribute that endears itself to websites. Because the keywords are in the first couple of paragraphs, you increase your chances of showing up high in an internet search.

The inverted pyramid does have some shortcomings. Although it delivers the most important news first, it does not encourage people to read the entire story. Stories stop; they don't end. There is no suspense. In a Poynter Institute study, researchers found that half of the 25 percent of readers who started a story dropped out midway through. Interest in an inverted pyramid story diminishes as the story progresses. But the way people use it attests to its value as a quick form of information delivery. Readers can leave a story whenever their needs are met, not when the writer finishes the story. In an age when time is golden, the inverted pyramid still offers value.

The day when the inverted pyramid is relegated to journalism history is not yet here and probably never will be. Perhaps 80 percent of the stories in today's newspapers and almost 100 percent of the stories on news services for target audiences such as the financial community are written in the inverted pyramid form. As long as news organizations compete to be first with breaking news, the inverted pyramid and its variations will have a role.

There are many other ways to structure a news story. However, before you explore the alternatives, you should master the inverted pyramid. As you do, you will master the art of making news judgments. The inverted pyramid requires you to identify and rank the most newsworthy elements in each story. This is important work. No matter what kinds of stories you write — whether obituaries, accidents, speeches, news conferences, fires or meetings — you will be required to use the skills you learn here.

The Inverted Pyramid

- Requires the writer to rank the importance of information.
- Puts the most important information first.
- Arranges the paragraphs in descending order of importance.

Finding the Lead

To determine a lead — a simple, clear statement consisting of the first paragraph or two of a news story — you must first recognize what goes into one. As you read in Chapter 1, you begin by determining the story's relevance, usefulness and interest for readers. One way to measure these standards is to ask "So what?" or "Who cares?" So what if there's a car accident downtown? If it's one of hundreds a month, it may not be news. Any holdup in a community of 5,000 may be news because the "so what" is that holdups are uncommon and some residents probably know the victim.

It's unlikely newspapers, radio or television stations would report the holdup in a metropolitan area where holdups are common. But if the holdup appears to be part of a pattern or if someone is killed, the story becomes more significant. One holdup may not be news, but a holdup that authorities believe is one of many committed by the same person may be news. The "so what" is that if the police catch this robber, they stop a crime spree.

To determine the "so what," you have to answer six basic questions: who, what, where, when, why and how. The information from every event you witness and every story you hear can be reduced to answers to these six questions. If the answers add up to a significant "so what," you have a story. Consider this example of an incoming call at fire headquarters.

> **"Fire Department," the dispatcher answers.**
>
> **"Hello. At about 10 o'clock, I was lying on my bed watching TV and smoking," the voice says. "I must have fallen asleep about 10:30 because that's when the football game was over. Anyway, I woke up just now, and my bedroom is on fire."**

This dialogue isn't informative or convincing. It is more likely that this sleepy television viewer woke up in a smoke-filled room, grabbed his cellphone and punched in 9-1-1. The conversation with the dispatcher probably went like this:

"9-1-1 call center."
"FIRE!" a voice at the other end yells.
"Where?" the dispatcher asks.
"At 1705 West Haven Street."

When fire is licking at their heels, even nonjournalists know how to present the lead. How the fire started is not important to the dispatcher; she needs to know what's happening (a house is burning) and where it's happening (the location of the house).

The journalist must go through essentially the same process to determine the lead. Just as the caller served himself and the Fire Department, reporters must serve their readers. What is most important to them?

After the fire is over, there is much information a reporter must gather. Among the questions you would routinely ask are these:

- When did it start?
- When was it reported?
- Who reported it?
- How was it reported?
- How long did it take the Fire Department to respond?
- How long did it take to extinguish the fire?
- How many fires this year have been attributed to smoking in bed?
- How does that number compare with figures from previous years?
- Were there any injuries or deaths?
- What was the damage?
- Who owned the house?
- Did the occupant or owner have insurance on the house?
- Will charges be filed against the smoker?
- Was there anything unusual about this case?
- Who cares?

TIPS

The Six Basic Questions

1. Who?
2. What?
3. Where?
4. When?
5. Why?
6. How?

More questions:

- So what?
- What's next?

With this information in hand, you can begin to write the story.

Writing the Inverted Pyramid Lead

Start by looking over your notes:

Who? The owner, a smoker, Henry Smith, 29. The age is important. Along with other personal information, such as address and occupation, the age differentiates the subject from other Henry Smiths in the readership area.

What? A fire caused damage estimated by the fire chief at $2,500.

Where? 1705 W. Haven St.

When? The call was received at 10:55 p.m. Tuesday. Firefighters from Station 19 arrived at the scene at 11:04. The fire was extinguished by 11:30. Those times are important to gather even if you don't use them. They show whether the Fire Department responded quickly.

Why? The fire was started by carelessness on the part of Smith, according to Fire Chief Bill Malone.

How? Smith told fire officials that he fell asleep in bed while he was smoking a cigarette.

If you had asked other questions, you might have learned more from the Fire Department:

- This was the eighth fire this year caused by smoking in bed.
- All last year there were four such fires.
- Smith said he had insurance.
- The Fire Chief said no charges would be filed against Smith.
- It was the first fire at this house.
- Smith was not injured.

Have you figured out the "so what"?

Assume your city editor has suggested you hold the story to about six paragraphs. Your first step is to rank the information in descending order of importance. There are lots of fires in this town, but eight this year have been caused by smoking in bed. Perhaps that's the most important thing about this story. You begin to type:

> **A fire started by a careless smoker caused an estimated $2,500 in damage to a home Tuesday.**

Only 17 words and 91 characters. That's even shorter than a tweet. You should try to hold every lead to fewer than 25 words unless you use more than one sentence.

Maybe this is too brief, though. Have you left out anything? Maybe you should include the time element to give the story a sense of immediacy. Readers will also want to know where the fire occurred. Is it near their house? Is it someone they know? You rewrite:

> **A Tuesday night fire started by a careless smoker caused an estimated $2,500 in damage to a home at 1705 W. Haven St.**

Just then the city editor walks by and glances over your shoulder. "Who said it was a careless smoker?" she asks. "Stay out of the story."

You realize you have committed a basic error in news writing: You have allowed an unattributed opinion to slip into the story. You have two choices. You can attribute the "careless smoker" information to the fire chief in the lead, or you can omit it.

You choose to rewrite by attributing the opinion. You also revise your sentence to emphasize the cause instead of the damage. You write:

> **A fire that caused an estimated $2,500 in damage to a home at 1705 W. Haven St. on Tuesday was caused by smoking in bed, Fire Chief Bill Malone said.**

Now 30 words and only 149 characters have answered the questions "what" (a fire), "where" (1705 W. Haven St.), "when" (Tuesday) and "how" (smoking in bed). And the opinion is attributed.

But you have not answered "who" and "why." You continue, still ranking the information in descending order of importance:

> **The owner of the home, Henry Smith, 29, said he fell asleep in bed while smoking a cigarette. When he awoke about 30 minutes later, smoke had filled the room.**
>
> **Firefighters arrived nine minutes after receiving the call. It took them about 26 minutes to extinguish the fire, which was confined to the bedroom of the one-story house.**
>
> **Malone said careless smokers have caused eight fires this year. Smith, who was not injured, said the house was insured.**

You take the story to the city editor, who reads through the copy quickly. As you watch, she changes the lead to emphasize the "so what." The lead now reads:

> **A smoker who fell asleep in bed ignited a fire that caused minor damage to his home on West Haven Street on Tuesday, Fire Chief Bill Malone said. It was the city's eighth fire caused by smokers, twice as many as occurred all last year.**

The lead is 45 words, but it is broken into two sentences, which makes it more readable. The importance of the "so what" changes the direction of the story. The fire was minor; there were no injuries. However, the increase in the number of fires caused by smokers may force the Fire Department to start a public safety campaign against careless smoking. The city editor continues:

> **The owner of the home, Henry Smith, 29, of 1705 W. Haven St., said he fell asleep in bed while smoking a cigarette. When he awoke about 30 minutes later, smoke had filled the room.**

Too many numbers bog down a lead. Focus on the impact of the figures in the lead, and provide details later in the story.

When the editor checks the telephone listings and the city directory, she uncovers a serious problem. A check of the house address on the internet and in the city directory lists the man who lives at 1705 W. Haven St. as Henry

What's the grammar error in this sentence?

The growth of gambling in New York, Pennsylvania, Maryland and Delaware have cut into casino revenue in Atlantic City, New Jersey.

See Appendix 1, Rule 16.

When Writing the Lead, Remember

- Always check names.
- Keep the lead to fewer than 25 words.
- Attribute opinion.
- Find out the who, what, where, when, why and how.
- Tell readers what the news means to them.
- Gather basic information even if it's routine.

Smyth: S-m-y-t-h. Such listings can be wrong, but at least they can alert you to possible errors. Confirm spellings by going to the original source, in this case, Mr. Smyth.

Never put a name in a story without checking the spelling, even when the source tells you his name is Smith.

Look at the annotated model "A Sample Inverted Pyramid Story" later in this chapter to see the completed fire story. There are several lessons you can learn from this example:

- Always check names.
- Keep the lead short, usually fewer than 25 words, unless you use two sentences.
- Attribute opinion. (Smoking in bed is a fact. That it was careless is an opinion.)
- Find out the who, what, where, when, why and how. However, if any of these elements have no bearing on the story, they may be omitted.
- Write a sentence or paragraph telling readers what the news means to them.
- Gather information basic to the story even if it is routine. Not everything you learn is important enough to be reported, but you'll never know unless you gather the information.

When you are learning to write an inverted pyramid story, the process is deliberate. You'll check your notes to be certain you have the six basic questions answered. Eventually, though, you will mentally check off those questions quickly, even though you will not always be able to find answers immediately to "how" and "why." Sometimes, experts need time to analyze accidents, crimes, fires and so on.

After you've checked your notes, ask yourself, "What else do readers need to know?" Using the news values of relevance, usefulness and interest and figuring out the "so what," decide which answers are the most important so you can put them in the lead. The rest go in the second and third paragraphs. In the Annotated Model "A Sample Inverted Pyramid Story," the news values and "so what" are these:

Relevance Eight similar fires are more relevant than one minor fire.

Usefulness Highlighting the number of fires also establishes usefulness by pointing out the bigger problem. The story also serves as a warning for smokers and those who live with them.

Interest Multiple fires attract more interest than one minor one.

The "so what" One minor fire lacks impact, but the fact that eight fires this year were caused by smoking suggests a public safety problem.

> **"Writing is easy; all you do is sit staring at a blank sheet of paper until the drops of blood form on your forehead."**
>
> ■ Gene Fowler, author

In what order are the key questions answered in the fire story? What does that order say about news values?

Emphasizing Different News Values

In the lead reporting the house fire, the "what" (fire) is of secondary importance to the "how" (how the fire started). A slightly different set of facts would affect the news value of the elements and, consequently, your lead. For instance, if Smyth turned out to have been a convicted arsonist, you would probably emphasize that bizarre twist to the story:

> **A convicted arsonist awoke Tuesday to find that his bedroom was filled with smoke. He escaped and later said that he had fallen asleep while smoking.**
>
> **Henry Smyth, 29, who served a three-year term for . . .**

This lead emphasizes the news value of novelty.

If Smyth were the mayor, you would emphasize prominence:

> **Mayor Henry Smyth escaped injury Tuesday when he awoke to find his bedroom filled with smoke. Smyth said he had fallen asleep while smoking in bed.**

What, So What and What's Next

You know that the answer to "what" is often the lead. The preceding example also illustrates the "so what" factor in news. A $2,500 fire is not news to many people in large communities where there are dozens of fires daily. Even if you crafted a tightly written story about it, your editor probably would not want to print or broadcast it. In small communities, the story would have more impact because there are fewer fires and because a larger proportion of the community is likely to know the victim.

The "so what" factor grows more important as you add other information. If the fire occurs during a fire-safety campaign, the "so what" would be the need for fire safety even in a community where awareness of the problem is already heightened. If the fire involves a convicted arsonist or the mayor, the "so what" would be stronger. Oddity or well-known people increase the value of a story. If someone is injured or if the damage is $1.2 million instead of $2,500, the "so what" factor might even push the story into the metropolitan press. As discussed, after you answer all six of the basic questions, you need to ask yourself what the answers mean to the reader. That answer is your "so what" factor.

In many stories, it is also important to answer the question "What's next?" The City Council had its first reading of its budget bill. What's next? "Members will

ANNOTATED MODEL A Sample Inverted Pyramid Story

The inverted pyramid structure dictates that the most important information goes in the beginning lead paragraphs. It is the job of the writer and the editor to decide what that information is.

A smoker who fell asleep in bed ignited a fire that caused minor damage to his home on West Haven Street Tuesday, Fire Chief Bill Malone said. It was the city's eighth fire caused by smokers, twice as many as occurred all last year.

The identification of "who" is delayed until the next paragraph because the person is not someone readers would recognize and because his name would make the lead unnecessarily long. Also in the lead are the "what," "when," "how" and, most significantly here, the "so what." The lead also identifies the source of the information.

The owner of the home, Henry Smyth, 29, of 1705 W. Haven St., said he fell asleep in bed while smoking a cigarette. When he awoke about 30 minutes later, smoke had filled the room.

The "who" is identified. More details on the "how" are given.

The Fire Department, which received the call at 10:55 p.m., had the fire out by 11:30.

The performance of the Fire Department is monitored.

Malone said the damage, estimated at $2,500, was confined to the bedroom. The house was insured.

Careless smokers caused only four fires last year in the city. Malone said that he is considering a public awareness campaign to try to alert smokers to the hazards. Those four fires caused total damages of $43,000. This year, fires started by careless smoking have caused total damages of $102,500, Malone said.

Details on the "so what" are given. The impact question is answered with the possible campaign.

No charges will be filed against Smyth because no one other than the smoker was endangered, Malone said.

Least important: If someone else had been endangered and charges had been filed, this information would move higher in the story.

vote on it next month." Jones was arrested Monday on suspicion of passing bad checks. What's next? "The prosecuting attorney will decide whether there is enough evidence to file charges."

Kip Hill (see "On the Job" later in this chapter) wrote about defendants in a marijuana case. One of his subheads asked "What's next?" Then he answered:

> **The sentencing hearing for Firestack-Harvey and the Greggs is scheduled for June 10. No defendants are in custody.**
>
> **Telfeyan has asked for more time to review the trial transcript before that hearing takes place, and the government hasn't objected, meaning the hearing could be pushed back.**
>
> **Zucker, who pleaded guilty to growing more than 100 marijuana plants, faces a potential prison sentence of 63 months to 78 months. He is scheduled to be sentenced July 24.**

A reader in a focus group once told researchers that she just wants to be told "what," "so what" and "what's next." That's a good guideline for all journalists to remember.

Variations on the Inverted Pyramid Lead

Journalists don't rely on formulas to write inverted pyramid leads, but you may find it useful, especially in the beginning, to learn some typical types of leads. The labels in the following sections are arbitrary, but the approaches are not.

The "You" Lead

Regardless of which of these leads journalists use, they are trying to emphasize the relevance of the news to the audience. One good way to highlight the relevance is to speak directly to readers by using "you." This informal, second-person lead—the **"you" lead**—allows the writer to tell readers why they should care. For instance:

You will find the lowest rates in two years if you are buying a home.

Most Springfield banks yesterday lowered the 15-year loan rate to 2.85 percent Tuesday, down from 3.9 percent a year ago.

Readers want to know what's in it for them. The traditional approach is less direct:

The real estate mortgage rate hit a two-year low Tuesday.

As with any kind of lead, you can overdo the "you" lead. Rather than writing, "You have another choice in the student president's race," just tell readers who will be running. However, you may use those words in writing for radio or television news as a setup for the story to come. And in tweets and on Facebook, where you are talking to readers one-on-one, the more conversational approach is usually appropriate.

The Immediate-Identification Lead

In the **immediate-identification lead**, one of the most important facts is "who," or the prominence of the key actor. Reporters often use this approach when someone important or well-known is making news. Consider the following example:

Scarlett Johansson has been named as the world's highest-paid female actor after earning $40.5m (£31.2m) in the year to June 2018.

Names make news. Remember the AP alert about Aretha Franklin? The AP did not report "Legendary soul singer dies." It included her name first because it is widely known.

When writing for your campus or local newspaper, you would use names in the lead that are known locally but not necessarily nationally. The name of your student body president, the chancellor, the mayor or an entertainer who has a local following would logically appear in the lead. None of these names would be used in the lead in a newspaper 50 miles away.

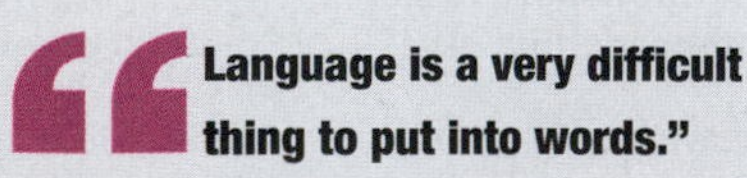

"Language is a very difficult thing to put into words."

■ Voltaire, philosopher

In small communities, names almost always make news. The "who" involved in an accident is usually in the lead. In larger communities, names are not as recognizable. As a rule, if the person's name or position is well-known, it should appear in the lead.

The Delayed-Identification Lead

Usually a reporter uses a **delayed-identification lead** when the person or organization involved has little name recognition among readers. Thus, in fairly large cities, an accident is usually reported like this:

> **MADISON, Wis. — A 39-year-old carpenter was killed today in a two-car collision two blocks from his home.**
>
> **William Domonske of 205 W. Oak St. died at the scene. Mary Craig, 21, of 204 Maple Ave., and Rebecca Roets, 12, of 207 Maple Ave., were taken to Mercy Hospital with injuries.**

However, in a smaller community, names almost always make news. Unless a name is nationally recognized, it often appears in the second paragraph:

> **ALFRED, Maine (AP)—A man accused of beating his grandmother with a golf club, stabbing her dozens of times and setting fire to the house they shared has been convicted of murder in Maine.**
>
> **A jury returned the verdict Friday in the trial of Derek Poulin, of Old Orchard Beach.**

The name Derek Poulin was not widely known except in his local area, so his identification was delayed until the second paragraph.

The Summary Lead

Reporters dealing with several important elements may choose to sum up what happened in a **summary lead** rather than highlighting a specific action. This is one of the few times when a general statement is preferable to specifics.

The Associated Press chose a summary lead to give the overall view of the weather in Arizona:

> **PHOENIX (AP)—Arizona is in the midst of a prolonged heat wave that has produced record-high temperatures in Phoenix, prompted dozens of daily calls to the Humane Society about overheated pets, and sparked triple-digit temperatures in typically cooler mountain locations.**

Likewise, if a city council rewrites city ordinances, unless one of the changes is of overriding importance, most reporters will use a summary lead:

> **MOLINE, Ill.—The City Council replaced the city's 75-year-old municipal code with a revised version Tuesday night.**

Summary leads do not appear only in reports of board meetings. A Spokane, Washington, reporter used a summary lead to report a neighborhood dispute:

> **An Idaho farmer's fence apparently was cut last week. It set off a chain of events Friday night that landed three people in the hospital, killed a cow and totaled a vehicle in the eastern Spokane Valley.**

The basic question you must answer is whether the whole of the action is more important than any of its parts. If the answer is yes, use a summary lead.

The Multiple-Element Lead

In some stories, choosing one theme for the lead is too restrictive. In such cases, you can choose a **multiple-element lead** to work more information into the first paragraph. But you should write the lead within the confines of a clear, simple sentence or sentences. Consider this example:

> **PORTLAND, Ore.—The City Council on Tuesday ordered three department heads fired, established an administrative review board and said it would begin to monitor the work habits of administrators.**

Notice that the actions are parallel, as is the construction of the verb phrases within the sentence. Parallel structures also characterize the following news extract, which presents a visual picture of the scene of a tragedy:

> **BAY CITY, Mich.—A flash fire that swept through a landmark downtown hotel Saturday killed at least 12 persons, injured 60 more and forced scores of residents to leap from windows and the roof in near-zero cold.**

ON THE JOB Advice to a Beginning Journalist

Courtesy of Colin Mulvaney

Kip Hill graduated with a master's degree in journalism in May 2013. Since that time, he's worked at *The Spokesman-Review* newspaper in Spokane, Washington, covering congressional politics, wildfires, the budding marijuana industry and a murder-for-hire federal case. Here is his advice to a beginning journalist:

If you were at a bar (or coffee shop), how would you start a story to your friends?

All journalists writing for the web should ask themselves that question. You're vying for the attention of readers whose attention span can be measured in 140 characters. That's how long you have to hook readers glancing at your story before they're off to another picture of kittens or the latest GIF du jour.

With breaking news, this is often an easy proposition. Prominently place the subject, then the verb, then the most important detail. You can worry about filling in the details in a later version of the story or put them lower in the story. If your readers don't immediately connect to what you're telling them, they're already reading someone else.

But what if the story is about government, where the verb can be elusive? "The City Council discussed Tuesday the possibility of testing sewage in town for remnants of marijuana." This could have been the lead of a story I wrote for *The Spokesman-Review* in Spokane. But the first four words are all wrong. While there's a subject and verb prominent, it's a vague subject and a weak verb. There's the nugget of a great story here, but the fact that some elected officials are jawing isn't how you'd introduce it at a bar.

You'd make a joke, right?

So here's the lead sentence that I ran with: "The most important numbers to Spokane city officials looking for accurate data about residents' marijuana use may be one and two."

Remember that your first sentence isn't the only thing that draws readers into a story. They've clicked the headline; they know you're going to write about sewage and marijuana. So why not have a little bit of fun with it? You would if you were talking to friends. And isn't that the relationship you should have with your readers?

We are told what happened, where it happened and how many were killed and injured.

Some multiple-element leads consist of two paragraphs. This occurs when the reporter decides that several elements need prominent display. For example:

> **The Board of Education Tuesday night voted to lower the tax rate 12 cents per $100 valuation. Members then approved a budget $150,000 less than last year's and instructed the superintendent to decrease the staff by 25 people.**
>
> **The board also approved a set of student-conduct rules, which includes a provision that students with three or more unexcused absences a year will be suspended for a week.**

This story, too, could emphasize the "so what" while retaining the multiple elements:

> **The Board of Education lowered your real estate taxes Tuesday. Members also approved a budget $150,000 less than last year's and instructed the superintendent to decrease the staff by 25 people.**

Simpler leads are preferable. But a multiple-element lead is one of your options. Use it sparingly.

Many newspapers are using graphic devices to take the place of multiple-element leads. They use summary boxes to list other actions. Because the box appears under the headline in type larger than the text, it serves as a graphic summary for the reader who is scanning the page. The box frees the writer from trying to jam too many details into the first few paragraphs. On the web, such methods are even more common. When news breaks, organizations like CNN often post stories with multiple elements like videos and highlights lists. (See Figure 8.1 for an example of this approach.)

Another approach is to break the coverage of a single event into a main story and a shorter story called a **sidebar**. This approach offers the advantage of presenting the information in short, palatable bites. It also allows the writer to elevate more actions into lead positions.

Researchers have found that breaking stories into small segments increases readers' comprehension and retention. For instance, in the Board of Education lead above, the angle about the superintendent's having to decrease staff could be spun off into a short sidebar:

In digital editions, there is an additional advantage. The more stories you have with separate headlines, the better chance you have to increase the number of **page views**, the measurement of how many people open the stories. In Figure 8.1, the Sessions item includes a video, and the opinion item is a separate column.

> **"The lead should be a promise of great things to come, and the promise should be fulfilled."**
>
> ■ Stanley Walker, City Editor

FIGURE 8.1

A list, such as CNN's "What we're covering here" on the left, highlights parts of the story that allows the writer to simplify the lead.

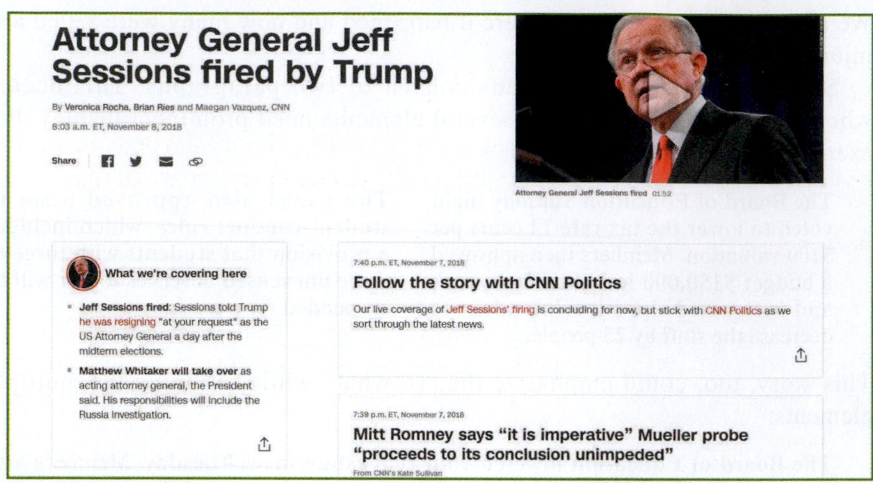
Attorney General Jeff Sessions fired by Trump

By Veronica Rocha, Brian Ries and Maegan Vazquez, CNN

8:03 a.m. ET, November 8, 2018

Danger Signals

Here are some leads that understandably raise red flags to editors:

- **Question leads.** Readers don't know the subject, don't know why they are being asked a question and probably couldn't care less. So the next time you are writing a weather story and are tempted to begin with "So how hot was it yesterday?" lie down until the temptation passes. Either tell readers the temperature, or open with an anecdote of a specific roofer sweating on the job. That's showing how hot it is.
- **Leads that say what might happen or what might have happened.** News organizations try to report what happened. Stay away from leads like this: "Springfield residents might be looking forward to warmer weather." Or they might not. Talk to people. Don't speculate.
- **Leads that overreach.** Report what you know. You might think it's harmless to write, "Springfield residents warmly greeted spring yesterday," but you don't know that all Springfield residents were happy about it. Maybe the guy who runs a snow-removal business would rather see winter last longer.

Leads with Flair

Although the inverted pyramid tells readers the news first and fast, not all stories begin with the most important statement. When the news value you want to emphasize is novelty, often the lead is unusual.

> **CASTLE SHANNON, Pa. (AP)—This deer wasn't caught in the headlights. It was called on the carpet.**
>
> **A Pittsburgh-area carpeting store has been cleaning up after the wild animal smashed into the store and ran amok Tuesday.**

A less imaginative writer might have written:

> A deer ran through the window of a Pittsburgh-area carpeting store Tuesday.

The second approach is like slapping a generic label on a Mercedes-Benz. The inverted pyramid approach is not so rigid that it doesn't permit fun and flair.

Story Organization

Like a theater marquee, the lead is an attention-getter. And just as some movies don't fulfill the promises of the marquee, some stories don't fulfill the promises of the lead. In either case, the customer is dissatisfied.

The inverted pyramid helps you put information in logical order. It forces you to rank, in order of importance, the information you will present.

The One-Subject Story

As we have seen in this chapter, constructing an inverted pyramid news story involves making a series of judgments based on classic news values and the specific news outlet. A fire or an accident in a small community is bigger news than a fire or an accident in another, larger area. Earlier events will also influence how you write a story.

The annotated model "A Single-Subject Inverted Pyramid Story" later in this chapter shows a story about the arrest of a suspect in an assault case. Police say drugs were involved. If there had been a string of assaults or a pattern of drug-related violence, the writer probably would have emphasized different aspects of the story. For instance, the writer could have emphasized the suspect's criminal record with this lead:

> **A Columbia man who was convicted of assault three times was arrested again Thursday night for an attack on his girlfriend.**

The Memo-Structure Story

The memo structure (as illustrated in the annotated model "A Memo-Structure Story" later in this chapter) is one of many hybrid forms journalists are experimenting with online. In this structure, journalists use subheads to organize information that has no narrative and few voices. You can use it to write an **advance** about upcoming meetings and to update developing stories. The categories can follow the standard who, what, where, when, why, how and so what, or you can create your own subject categories. Reporters can write memo-structure stories quickly, and readers can scan them quickly — a convenient feature for readers using a small-screen device such as a smartphone.

Axios, a media company whose goal is to deliver news in "the most efficient, illuminating and shareable ways possible," uses the format often. In a story about the people who detect the internet trolls who spread disinformation, the writer begins like this:

> **A surge of nefarious activity online has created new businesses, research disciplines and newsroom beats focused on studying and combating internet propaganda.**

The story continues with subheads that include one or two paragraphs: "Why it matters," "The big picture," "Nonprofits," "For-profits," "Journalists," and "Academics and big tech." It concludes:

> **The bottom line: Even though the global threat of misinformation is getting bigger as bad actors become more sophisticated, there's a much higher level of awareness and attention towards the issue than ever before.**

The Multiple-Element Story

Multiple-element stories are most commonly used in reporting on the proceedings of councils, boards, commissions, legislatures and courts. These bodies act on numerous subjects in one sitting. Frequently, their actions are unrelated, and more than one action is often important enough to merit attention in the story. You have four options:

- **You can write more than one story.** This would require permission from your editor.
- **You can write a story highlights list.** The list would be displayed along with the story either in print or online. In it, you would list the council's major actions or the court's decisions.
- **You can write a multiple-element lead and story.** Your lead would list all the major actions at the board meeting. The remainder of the story would provide more details about each action.
- **You can write a single-element lead and cover the other elements further on in the story.** Your lead would focus on the element that you believe readers would find most interesting, relevant and useful.

Let's go back to a multiple-element lead we saw earlier:

> **The Board of Education voted Tuesday night to lower the tax rate 12 cents per $100 valuation. Members then approved a budget $150,000 less than last year's and instructed the superintendent to decrease the staff by 25 people.**
>
> **The board also approved a set of student-conduct rules, which include a provision that students with three or more unexcused absences a year will be suspended for a week.**

ANNOTATED MODEL A Single-Subject Inverted Pyramid Story

This typical one-subject story written in the inverted pyramid form features a delayed-identification lead.

Man Arrested in Attack, Charged with Child Endangerment

By Elizabeth Phillips
Columbia Missourian

The arrest, not the assault, is the latest development, so it is emphasized.

Police arrested a Columbia man in connection with an attack on his girlfriend Thursday night.

The lead gives "who," "what" and "when."

Details of the charges are in the second paragraph because the list is too long to put in the lead. The name is not in the lead because most readers would not recognize it.

Darrell Vanness Johnson, 37, was arrested on suspicion of second-degree domestic assault, unlawful use of a weapon, felony possession of a controlled substance, misdemeanor possession of a controlled substance and endangering the welfare of a child at about 9 p.m. Thursday in the 1500 block of Greensboro Drive.

The writer adds details, attributed to the police, on how the assault occurred. This information includes the "why." "Where" is identified. "When" is made more specific than in the lead.

Johnson and his girlfriend began arguing over drugs Thursday evening, Columbia Police Sgt. Ken Hammond said. Johnson choked her and held a revolver to her head before she was able to escape and call 911 from a neighbor's house, Hammond said. Three children, two 9-year-olds and a 4-year-old, were in the home during the attack, Hammond said.

Information about the children is pertinent because it adds to the "so what"—the children were also endangered.

This paragraph continues the chronology of the assault and capture.

When Columbia police arrived, Johnson was driving away from the Greensboro Drive home with the three children in the car, Hammond said. When police arrested Johnson, they found marijuana and cocaine, Hammond said.

The victim was taken to an area hospital by ambulance for treatment of bruises and scratches to the hands, neck and back, Hammond said. Her injuries were not life threatening.

The writer offers evidence of the injuries and attributes this information.

Now that the basic facts are established, the writer adds background on the suspect, attributed to a public safety website.

According to MissouriCase.net, Johnson has pleaded guilty to third-degree domestic assault three times in the past four years in Boone County Circuit Court, serving close to seven months in jail for those charges. He has also pleaded guilty to theft, first-degree trespass and second-degree property damage in Boone County Circuit Court, serving 75 days in Boone County Jail for the theft charge and receiving two years of unsupervised probation for the trespass and property damage charges.

Johnson violated his probation on the trespass and property damage charges and was scheduled to appear in Boone County Circuit Court for a probation violation hearing in December. He was charged with theft last October in Boone County Circuit Court.

He faces up to 40 years in prison and up to a year in jail in connection with the attack.

The writer gives the "what's next."

ANNOTATED MODEL A Memo-Structure Story

In a memo-structure story, subheads can reflect the answers to essential questions.

Parks and Recreation, City Council Discuss Plans for Parks Tax

By Asif Lakhani
Columbia Missourian

The multiple-element lead gives basic facts — the "who," "what" and "when."

COLUMBIA — Earlier this month, Columbia voters approved the extension of the park sales tax. On Monday night, the Columbia City Council and the Parks and Recreation Department attended a work session where they discussed where the tax revenue would go.

Subheadings introduce the paragraphs.

What happened: Mike Hood, director of parks and recreation, presented a proposed five-year plan to council members.

Subsequent paragraphs organize information by categories, not necessarily by importance.

The writer has chosen categories that are relevant to the reader.

Cost: During the next five years, the one-eighth-cent sales tax is expected to garner about $12 million for Columbia's parks.

Timetable: The proposed plan divides projects into four categories: land acquisition and annual park funding, new facility and park development, improvements to existing parks, and trails and greenbelts. . . .

Projects: The five-year plan would be front-loaded with construction projects over a four-year fiscal period, which would leave more room for land acquisition later on, Hood said. Most of the construction projects are listed under new facility and park development and improvements to existing parks. . . .

Comments: First Ward Councilman Paul Sturtz and Sixth Ward Councilwoman Barbara Hoppe voiced concern about front-loading the plan with construction. Both said land acquisition is more important because its value could increase over the next five years. . . .

The last paragraph wraps up the story.

What's next: The proposed plan now goes to the Parks and Recreation Commission. After, it will go to the City Council for consideration. The council plans to discuss the suggested land acquisition at an upcoming council meeting.

Four newsworthy actions are mentioned in those two paragraphs: changing the tax rate, approving a budget, cutting staff and adopting student-conduct rules. In stories that deal with several important elements, the writer usually highlights the most important. When this is the case, it is important to summarize the other, lesser actions after the lead.

If you and your editor judge that changing the tax rate was more important than anything else that happened at the school board meeting, you would approach the story like this:

Lead	The Board of Education voted Tuesday night to lower the tax rate 12 cents per $100 valuation.
Support for lead	The new rate is $1.18 per $100 valuation. That means that if your property is assessed at $300,000, your school tax will be $3,540 next year.
Summary of other action	The board also approved a budget that is $150,000 less than last year's, instructed the superintendent to cut the staff by 25 and approved a set of rules governing student conduct.

Notice that the lead is followed by a paragraph that supports and expands the information in it before the summary paragraph appears. Whether you need a support paragraph before summarizing other action depends on how complete you are able to make the lead.

Checklist for Assembling the Rest of the Inverted Pyramid

- Introduce additional important information you were not able to include in the lead.
- If possible, indicate the significance or "so what" factor.
- Elaborate on the information presented in the lead.
- Continue introducing new information in the order in which you have ranked it by importance.
- Develop the ideas in the same order in which you have introduced them.
- Generally, use only one new idea in each paragraph.

Writing a Story Across Media Platforms

The inverted pyramid can serve you throughout the news reporting and writing process, from tweets to online updates. Most breaking news stories are first tweeted and then developed further online before they are printed in a newspaper or broadcast on television. In fact, the story may never even be printed or broadcast.

One of the most important things to learn as you begin a career in media is how to write the same story across multiple platforms (we'll discuss this more in Chapter 11). The story in the annotated model on the next page "The Classic Inverted Pyramid Story" appeared in print. Let's follow its progress from what the first tweet might possibly look like.

Breaking-News Tweets

If you can write a lead, you can write a tweet, and if you can write a tweet, you can write a lead. The limitation of 280 characters is not much of a problem for journalists. The lead on the accident story is only 95 characters. A journalist at the scene of an accident might send this tweet:

> **EMT crews are working 4-car accident on I-70 near Stadium Blvd. Exit Missouri 41 to avoid traffic backup.**

After the reporter has a chance to talk to an officer at the scene, she could send the next tweet:

> **Police: Four injured in accident on I-70 near Stadium Blvd. No IDs yet. Exit Missouri 41 to avoid traffic backup both directions.**

ANNOTATED MODEL The Classic Inverted Pyramid Story

Note how this story, typical of the inverted pyramid structure, delivers the most important news in the lead and provides fewer essential details toward the end. It also reflects more complete reporting than an earlier web version.

A four-vehicle accident on eastbound Interstate 70 near Stadium Boulevard ended in two deaths on Sunday.

The lead identifies the "what," "where" and "when." The "so what" is that people were killed.

Barbara Jones, 41, of St. Louis died at the scene of the accident, and Juanita Doolan, 73, of St. Joseph died at University Hospital, according to a release from Springfield police. Two other people, William Doolan, 73, of St. Joseph and Theodore Amelung, 43, of Manchester, Missouri, were injured in the accident.

The second paragraph provides details to support the lead and answers "who."

This paragraph shows impact beyond deaths and injuries.

Both lanes of traffic were closed on the eastbound side and limited to one lane on the westbound side as rescue workers cleared the scene.

Authorities said a westbound late-model Ford Taurus driven by Lan Wang of Springfield was traveling in the right lane, developed a tire problem and swerved into the passing lane. A Toyota pickup truck in the passing lane, driven by Jones, was forced over the grassy median along with the Taurus. The two vehicles entered eastbound traffic where the truck struck an Oldsmobile Delta 88, driven by Juanita Doolan, head on.

The "how" is less important than the "what," "where" and "when," so it appears later in the story.

Wang and the one passenger in his car, Kenneth Kuo, 58, of Springfield, were not injured.

An eyewitness account adds sensory details that make the scene more vivid.

John Paul, a tractor trailer driver on his way to Tennessee, said he had to swerve to miss the accident.

"I saw the red truck come across the median and hit the blue car," Paul said. "I just pulled over on the median and called 911."

Jones, who was wearing a seat belt, died at the scene, Officer Stan Williams said. Amelung, a passenger who had been in the truck, was out of the vehicle when authorities arrived, but it was unknown whether he was thrown from the truck or was pulled out by someone else, Williams said.

What's next? This would be higher if the driver, rather than a tire, appeared to be the cause of the accident.

No charges have been filed, but the investigation continues.

Initial Online Story

When the reporter is able to get more information, she might post the first blast for online and mobile devices:

Two people were killed and two others were injured Tuesday in a four-car accident on I-70 near Stadium Boulevard, Springfield police said.

The names of the victims were being withheld pending notification of relatives. All four were state residents.

The two injured were taken to Springfield Hospital.

Authorities said a westbound Toyota pickup truck swerved across the median and collided with an Oldsmobile in the eastbound lane.

Full Story with Ongoing Updates

The next version of this story, shown in the annotated model above, would appear both in print and online. Most publications post the story on the web immediately, even before the newspaper is printed or the news report is aired. The next day, the reporter may be able to update the web version:

> **Two people injured in a four-car accident Sunday were released from Springfield Hospital on Wednesday. The accident claimed the lives of two others.**
>
> **William Doolan, 73, of St. Joseph, and Theodore Amelung, 43, of Manchester, were released. Barbara Jones, 41, of St. Louis, and Juanita Doolan, 73, of St. Joseph, died as a result of the collision.**

This new lead would replace the first three paragraphs of the existing story.

In all versions for all platforms, it is essential to answer and rank the questions that are basic to any inverted pyramid story. If a story is no longer considered breaking news but you have new information, you might decide to write more of a feature story than an inverted pyramid story.

Checking Accuracy

We all can improve our accuracy. Some improvement comes with experience, but most of the errors journalists make involve routine facts. In Chapter 4, you learned the importance of accurately capturing the words that you quote. Here are additional habits you should use to produce more accurate stories. These four habits will help you become more accurate:

1. **Go over your notes at the end of every interview.** Read back the quotes and the facts as you have written them down. Don't assume anything. As you read earlier in the chapter, if someone tells you his name is Smith, ask him how to spell it.
2. **Carefully check your story against your notes and the documents you have collected to be certain you didn't introduce any errors while writing.** We all make typing errors. We make errors because of background noise and commotion. If you recognize that you are not infallible, you will be a more accurate journalist.
3. **When sources give you facts, check them if possible.** During an interview, the mayor may tell you that the city has 50 police officers. Check with the Police Department. The mayor may have the number wrong.
4. **Do a prepublication check.** Some journalists object to prepublication checks because they believe it gives the source too much opportunity to argue over what they will print. Some are afraid sources may approach other media to get their version of the story out even before publication, but those situations are rare.

> **"Selecting the quotes isn't so hard; it's presenting them that causes the trouble. And the worst place to present them is at the beginning. Quote leads deserve their terrible reputation. Yet they still appear regularly in both print and broadcast journalism.**
>
> **"We can make three generalizations about quote leads. They're easy, lazy and lousy. They have no context. The readers don't know who's speaking, why, or why it matters. Without context, even the best quotations are wasted."**
>
> ■ Paula LaRocque, former assistant managing editor, *The Dallas Morning News*

In a study published in the *Newspaper Research Journal*, researcher Duane Stoltzfus found that more newspapers permitted their reporters to check stories or portions of stories with sources before publication than was formerly believed. In all cases, sources are told that they are being asked to check the accuracy of the information.

No journalist should cede authority for decisions about what goes in and what does not. But no journalist should be afraid to take every step possible to ensure accuracy. Some read back quotes; some read back facts gathered from that source. Some even describe information obtained from other sources.

If your publication permits prepublication checks, you will do yourself and your profession a favor by performing them. Verify everything you intend to publish or broadcast. In the online world, where speed is king, verification often is sacrificed in the rush to be first. But being first and wrong is never right, as bloggers will tell you. In an effort to be transparent, some news sites put a note on stories that have been corrected.

CHAPTER RESOURCES

SUGGESTED READINGS

Brooks, Brian S., James L. Pinson and Jean Gaddy Wilson. *Working with Words: A Handbook for Media Writers and Editors.* 8th ed. New York: Bedford/St. Martin's, 2013. This must-have book provides excellent coverage of grammar and word usage and has a strong chapter on "isms."

Gillman, Timothy. "The Problem of Long Leads in News and Sports Stories." *Newspaper Research Journal* (Fall 1994): 29–39. The researcher found that sentences in leads were longer than sentences in the rest of the story.

Kennedy, George. "Newspaper Accuracy: A New Approach." *Newspaper Research Journal* (Winter 1994): 55–61. The author suggests that journalists do prepublication accuracy checks with proper safeguards in place.

Stoltzfus, Duane. "Partial Pre-publication Review Gaining Favor at Newspapers." *Newspaper Research Journal* (Fall 2006): 23–37. The researcher surveyed the 50 largest newspapers to determine their policies toward prepublication review and found that the trend is to permit it.

SUGGESTED WEBSITES

LaunchPad Solo
launchpadworks.com
When you visit LaunchPad Solo for Journalism, you will find research links, exercises and LearningCurve adaptive quizzing to help you improve your grammar and AP style usage. In addition, the site's video collection hosts the videos highlighted in this and other chapters as well as additional clips of leading professionals discussing important media trends.

Axios.com
A news site dedicated to writing news that makes readers smarter faster.

www.documentcloud.org/documents/1995453-graves-nyhan-reifler-mpsa15.html
"Why do journalists fact-check?" is a research study that found the practice of fact checking is spreading.

FactCheck.org
A nonpartisan effort at the Annenberg Public Policy Center at the University of Pennsylvania. Focus on stories involving U.S. politics.

www.stateofthemedia.org
The Pew Research Center's Project for Excellence in Journalism produces an annual "State of the News Media" report that examines journalistic trends and economic trends.

EXERCISES

1. Choose a story that is being widely reported, and compare how The Associated Press, CNN.com, Foxnews.com and *The New York Times* cover it. Do they use inverted pyramid leads? Are they straight news, leads with a flair, summary leads or multiple-element leads?

2. Identify the who, what, where, when, why and how, if they are present, in the following lead:

   The United Jewish Appeal is sponsoring its first-ever walk-athon this morning in Springfield to raise money for the Soup Kitchen, a place where the hungry can eat free.

3. Identify the who, what, where, when, why and how, if they are present, in the following story. Would you move any information higher in the story? If so, why?

   COLUMBIA—A Missouri man died Sunday afternoon after his car hit a utility pole in the 300 block of William Street.

   Police believe the driver had a medical condition prior to the crash that caused the accident, according to a news release from the Columbia Police Department.

   The driver, a 72-year-old man, was not identified in the release because police still have to notify his family.

   According to police, the driver veered off the right side of the road around 2 p.m. and then hit the pole. Medical personnel removed the driver from the car and took him to University Hospital, where he was later pronounced dead.

   Speed, drugs and alcohol were not considered a factor in this crash, the release said.

   Source: "Man Dies in Afternoon Car Accident," June 21, 2015, http://www.columbiamissourian.com/news/local/update-man-dies-in-afternoon-car-accident/article_3c7b35d0-1875-11e5-959b-33961a762765.html.

4. Rewrite the lead in exercise 2 as a "you" lead. Which are better, the third-person or second-person leads? Why are they better?

5. From the following facts, write a tweet of 140 characters or fewer that you could send to tell the story and promote it for a website:

   - **Who:** A nuclear weapon with a yield equivalent to 150,000 tons of TNT.
   - **What:** Detonated.
   - **Where:** 40 miles from a meeting of pacifists and 2,000 feet beneath the surface of Pahute Mesa in the Nevada desert.
   - **When:** Tuesday.
   - **Why:** To test the weapon.
   - **How:** Not applicable.
   - **Other information:** Department of Energy officials are the source; 450 physicians and peace activists were gathered to protest continued nuclear testing by the U.S.

6. **Your journalism blog.** Collect three leads from different internet news sites. Write a blog post in which you identify each type of lead used, and determine what questions each lead answers and what questions it does not. Give your opinion of the effectiveness of each lead. Then review the blog post of at least one other classmate, and post a comment in response.

7. From the following facts, write the first two paragraphs of a news article:

   - **Who:** 40 passengers.
   - **What:** Evacuated from a Delta Airlines jet, Flight 428.
   - **Where:** At the LaCrosse, Wis., Regional Airport.
   - **When:** Monday following a flight from Minneapolis to LaCrosse.
   - **Why:** A landing tower employee spotted smoke near the wheels.
   - **How:** Not applicable.
   - **Other information:** There was no fire or injuries; the smoke was caused by hydraulic fluids leaking onto hot landing brakes, according to Bob Gibbons, an American Airline spokesman.

8. Describe picture and information-graphic possibilities for the story in Exercise 5.

CHAPTER 9

WRITING TO BE READ

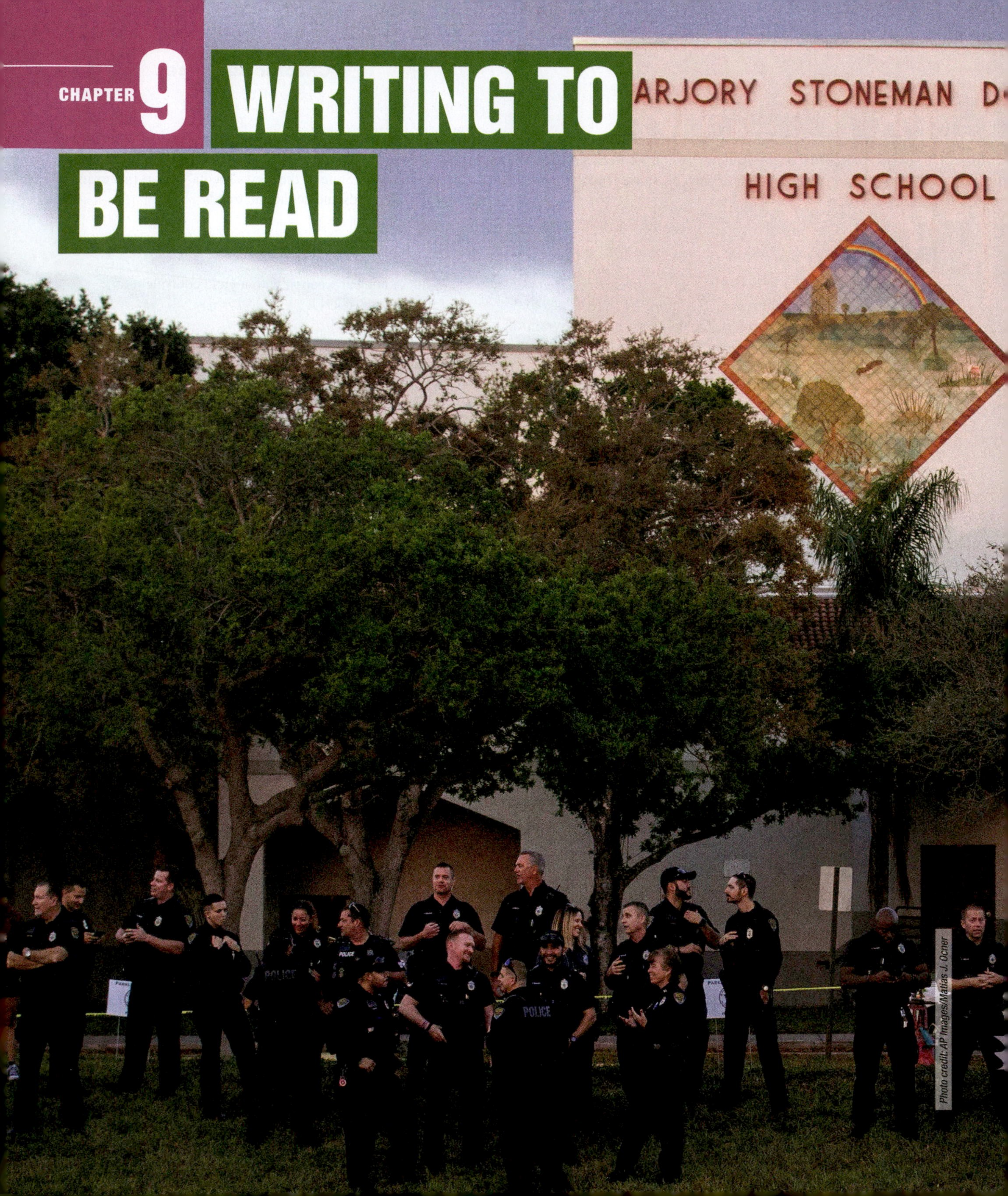

Photo credit: AP Images/Matias J. Ocner

Three months after the shooter at Marjory Stoneman Douglas killed 17 students and staff and injured 17 others in February 2018, Eli Saslow sat down with the only armed officer who had been on the campus. Scot Peterson, the officer, had retired under pressure soon after the massacre. He was treated as a villain because he did not enter the school building when he heard the shots. Members of the community hounded him. A father whose daughter died sued him. He had become a hermit in his own house.

Saslow, who writes in-depth narrative stories for *The Washington Post*, persuaded Peterson to talk to him. Saslow stayed with him for four days. This is how the story opened:

> **Scot Peterson had spent much of the past three months in hiding, but now somebody was walking onto his porch and toward the front door. A motion detector activated an alarm inside his duplex. Peterson, 55, ducked away from the windows and bent out of sight. His girlfriend, Lydia Rodriguez, walked to the entryway and began to pull down a corner of the white sheet that now covered most of their front door. "Oh, please," she said. "What now?"**

Saslow was there to reveal Peterson's life since he had been branded the "Coward of Broward (County)." Saslow's story, built on scenes and dialogue between Peterson and Rodriguez and his interviews, shows Peterson's anguish, confusion and guilt:

> **In his sleep, he was still looking, still scanning the roof, windows and courtyard, only to awaken each morning to the fresh realization of the same result. He had gone to see a psychologist and a psychiatrist after the shooting, and he had come home with a prescription to help him sleep and a sheet describing the symptoms he had begun to experience: "Confusion." "Anxiety." "Guilt." "Grief." "Agitation." "Obsession."**

A good story told well is important to readers. Just because today's newspapers and broadcast reports are gone tomorrow doesn't mean that we should accept a lower level of skill. Comparing the temporal nature of newspapers to a beach, syndicated columnist James Kilpatrick challenged writers: "If we write upon the sand, let us write as well as we can upon the sand before the waves come in."

If Kilpatrick's challenge to your pride is not enough, then the demands of readers and listeners — and of the editors and news directors who are hiring — should be. Editors are looking for those unusual people who can combine reporting and writing talents. The journalist whose prose jerks around the page like a mouse trapped in a room with a cat has no future in the business.

The American Society of News Editors has made the improvement of writing one of its principal long-range goals. Each year, it honors the reporting and writing of journalists in several categories. Some of them go

In this chapter, you will learn:

1. How the skills of reporting make good writing possible.
2. How to add accurate, specific details.
3. How to write a coherent story.
4. How to write with conciseness and simplicity.
5. How to use correct and effective language.
6. How to create scenes, use dialogue and anecdotes and create a sense of person.

launchpadworks.com
WATCH: **"Community Voices: Weekly Newspapers"**

- What are some differences between weekly and daily newspapers, and how might they affect the way weeklies can cover a community?
- In a democratic society, why might having many community voices in the news media be good?

on to win Pulitzer Prizes. Many well-known writers — among them Mark Twain, Stephen Crane, Ernest Hemingway, Alex Haley and Joan Didion — began their careers as journalists. Carl Bernstein and Bob Woodward of *The Washington Post* wrote *All the President's Men*. Rebecca Skloot, a freelance journalist, correspondent and contributing editor, wrote *The Immortal Life of Henrietta Lacks*. Jon Krakauer wrote *Into Thin Air: A Personal Account of the Mt. Everest Disaster*.

At media organizations around the country today, small but growing numbers of journalists are producing literature daily as they deal with everything from traffic accidents to affairs of state. If you have respect for the language, an artist's imagination and the dedication to learn how to combine them, you, too, may produce literature.

We should all attempt to bring quality writing, wit and knowledge to our work. If we succeed, our work will be not only informative but also enjoyable, not only educational but also entertaining, and not only bought but also read.

Good Writing Begins with Good Reporting

Saslow spent four days with Peterson to write the story that opens this chapter. (The link to the story is at the end of this chapter.) He interviewed Peterson in depth, but he also listened and watched. He had Peterson recount moment by moment what he did and what he was thinking. He listened to the sheriff's radio traffic during the shooting. He watched video of Peterson huddled near a wall near the building where the shooting occurred. Without the proper use of participant accounts, personal observation and detail, the best journalist's stories land with a thud. Good writing begins with good reporting. In Chapter 8, we introduced you to this lead:

> **Two people died Thursday when a backhoe fell off a truck's flatbed and sliced off the top of an oncoming vehicle near Fairchild Air Force Base.**

Now let's look at some of the detail found in the story:

> **The top of the Suburban, from about hood height, was shorn off by the backhoe's bucket. The front seats were forced backward, and the dashboard, roof and steering wheel were torn off.**
>
> **Parts of the car lay in a heap of crumpled metal and glass under the overpass. The silver Suburban was identifiable only by a 1983 owner's manual lying in the dirt nearby.**
>
> **Both victims wore seat belts, but in this case, that was irrelevant, (Sgt. Jeff) Sale said. Both suffered severe head injuries.**
>
> **Sleeping bags, a Coleman cooler and fishing equipment scattered on the highway and in the back of the Suburban suggested a camping trip. Unopened cans of Pepsi were jammed behind the front seat of the car.**

Notice that the writer built every sentence on concrete detail. Good reporting makes good writing possible.

ON THE JOB Setting the Hook in the Opening

Courtesy of Amanda Heckert

Justin Heckert, who lives in Charleston, South Carolina, and has written for national publications such as *GQ*, *ESPN The Magazine* and *The New York Times Magazine*, believes one of the most important elements of any story is the first few sentences:

> The experience of reading and being hooked can be because of word play, or rhythm, or a particular style or device. I can recite the first sentences to some of my favorite stories. That's just how they stick with me.
>
> "Those who saw him hushed." That's Colum McCann. "It was a pleasure to burn. It was a special pleasure to see things eaten, to see things blackened and changed." That's Ray Bradbury. "Aye, that face. There's a story about that face, you know. About what he was willing to do with it. With that splatted knob of a nose, that shadowed dent of a mouth. . . ." That's Tom Junod. "It was midsummer, the heat rippling above the macadam roads, cicadas screaming out of the trees, and the sky like pewter, glaring." That's Joyce Carol Oates. These books/stories are nowhere near me as I write this, but I can remember those sentences, and I know I got them right.
>
> This idea has been a huge part of my own writing. I've done it, or tried to, in pretty much every single story I've ever written, be it a success or failure. An example: A few years ago, I reported and wrote a story for *Men's Journal*. I was sitting on top of amazing material. I could've, honestly, probably just written it out like I was talking to a third-grader, and it still would've been an interesting story. But after I talked to my editor and sat down to write it, I sweated forever about how to begin. I sat on the porch and thought about it. I thought about it driving the car. I thought about how to begin while I was watching a football game, before I was going to bed.
>
> The story was about two people who had been pulled out to the sea and had treaded water for hours. The ocean has been written about more than anything since the beginning of time. It was hard to try and think of something new to say about it, to tie it in to the experience of this guy and his son, victims of the ocean, even though they didn't die. How this situation resolved itself is as esoteric as the nature of writing itself: It just came to me.
>
> "The ocean at night is a terrible dream. There is nothing beyond the water except the profound discouragement of the sky, every black wave another singular misfortune." I had stared at the ocean for hours, had thought about how it affected the characters of the story, thought about everything they said about it. I knew it when the words appeared — they came to me the way ideas come to people, inexplicably. I think those are two good sentences. So did my editor. So have a lot of other people who read it. They were that important to me because I wanted them to hook the readers and then keep them with me.

Accurate, Specific Details

Good writing is accurate when it is built on concrete details. When you use language to communicate those details precisely, you inform and entertain your readers. For lawyers, the devil might be in the details, but for writers, clarity is in the details. Echoing your bureaucratic sources, you can write of infrastructures or facilities or learning pods. But try actually touching any of these.

Be specific. You might write that the speaker is big, but compared with what? Abstractions are ambiguous. To someone who is 6 feet tall, someone big might be 6 feet 6 inches tall. To someone who is 5 feet 2 inches tall, 6 feet is huge.

Note the concrete details in the following from Jason Horowitz of *The New York Times*. He was writing about the deadly wildfires in Greece:

> **MATI, Greece—They nearly reached the water.**
>
> **As wind-fueled wildfires that killed at least 80 people in vacation areas outside Athens bore down on their seaside resort, 26 men, women and children gathered in the hope that they could find the narrow path leading to a small staircase down to the water. . . .**
>
> **At sundown, an eyeglass case, a belt buckle, the carcasses of dogs and the shells of cellphones dotted the still-smoldering field where they fell. Amid the burned pine cones and the naked trees, leaning as if slammed by a nuclear wind, lay a large leather sandal and a small blue one with a Velcro strap.**
>
> **All around were the discarded blue rubber gloves of the emergency workers who carried the bodies away.**

The concrete details—eyeglass case, belt buckle, dog carcasses, cellphones and sandals—take you to the scene.

To be concrete, you must have facts. And you must describe those facts in a way that makes readers able to touch, feel or smell them. Lazy reporters create puffballs. Poke their stories, and you'll stick your finger clear through them. Instead of saying "some council members," say "five council members." Instead of writing that a business is "downsizing," report that 150 workers will lose their jobs. Avoid abstractions; covet concrete details.

Show, Don't Just Tell

As you chauffeur the reader through the scenes in your story, you can drive down the road or over the green-laced, rolling hills of Kentucky. You can report that a car hit a skunk, or you can convey the nauseating smell. A word here, a phrase there, and you can hear the plane ripping the tin roof off a house, smell the acrid stench of burning tires, feel the boxing glove's leather rasp against the skin. Good writing appeals to one or more of our five senses: sight, hearing, smell, taste and touch.

Reporting for *The Oregonian*, Steve Duin talked to voters standing in the rain while waiting to vote. He observed: "They arrived in wool hats and sweatpants, in Chuck Taylors and hospital scrubs, with borrowed umbrellas and voter guides and 18-month-olds in their arms."

In addition to the years of anecdotal experience journalists have, there is also statistical support for the common advice to show rather than just tell. For instance, researchers constructed 10 sentences telling information and 10 showing information. College students were divided into two groups and asked to read one of the groups of sentences. Then they were asked to rate the sentences on such qualities as interesting or dull, clear or unclear and engaging or unengaging. The researchers concluded, "The experiment found strong evidence that, as many experts have implied, show sentences are seen as more interesting and engaging than tell sentences."

Saslow is engaging readers as he recreates the scene in Peterson's home when news broke of another school shooting, this time in Texas:

> "I really shouldn't watch this," Peterson said, his voice beginning to crack, but he kept his eyes on the screen. He watched them load the ambulances. He watched a SWAT team enter the school. He watched as the sheriff held his first news conference, promising "accountability and answers." He watched as a somber news anchor came on screen to confirm 10 dead and several more wounded, including a school resource officer in critical condition.
>
> "Unlike in Parkland, this time the deputy went in," the anchor said, and Peterson braced to hear his name.
>
> "A case study in the difference between heroism and cowardice," the anchor said, and now Peterson was shrinking deeper into the couch and into his head.

Saslow doesn't tell you; he shows you by re-creating the scene.

A student writer used her sense of touch to gather information: "After 40 years of working outside, his skin is as leathery as an alligator's." Did she actually touch the tree farmer? "Yes," she says. "I kept looking at his skin. Finally, even though I was embarrassed, I asked him if I could touch his face. He laughed. 'You can tell I don't use no fancy lotions, can't you?'"

The writing is better because the reporters didn't just ask questions and record answers. They looked; they listened; they touched. Readers can see and feel along with the reporters.

Use Words Precisely

Words should mean exactly what you intend them to mean. You should never use *uninterested* when you mean *disinterested*. Nor should you use *allude* for *refer*, *presume* for *assume*, *endeavor* for *try*, *fewer* for *less*, *farther* for *further*. If you report that a fire destroyed a house, you mean the home needs rebuilding, not repair. If you say firefighters donned oxygen masks to enter a burning building, you are either impugning their intelligence or revealing your ignorance. (Oxygen is dangerous around fire; firefighters use air tanks.) You can make the mayor *say*, *declare*, *claim* or *growl*—but only one is accurate.

Coherence

When you write coherently, your writing is understandable. Coherence is built by following a logical order, by matching the content to the appropriate sentence structure, by using the correct coordinating conjunctions and by guiding readers with transitions.

Decide on the Order of Elements

Chronology is the most easily understood of story structures. You start at the beginning and go to the end. A story in the aftermath of Hurricane Sandy began 48 hours

TIPS

Writing a Coherent Story

- Create logical story structures.
- Express the relationship between ideas properly.
- Use language precisely.
- Use transitions.

before the storm hit and continued until the storm passed and the "sun makes a welcome appearance." It was told chronologically. (For more on story structure, see Chapter 10.) Journalists, however, often don't have the luxury of readers' time or publication space to use chronology. That's why it is important to outline a story, even if your outline merely lists the three or four points you expect to make. Your outline is your map. If you know where you are going, your readers will be able to follow.

Here's a list you might make about what happened at a city council meeting:

- Approved one-way streets.
- Raised parking fines.
- Bought snowplows.
- Agreed to study downtown parking facilities.
- Hired audit firm.

To outline the story, first you rank the actions in order of importance. Then you decide whether to focus on one element or to write a summary lead or a multiple-element lead. (See Chapter 8 for more on leads.) After you have done that, you add details to your outline:

1. Single-element lead: one-way streets
2. Summary of other actions
   a. Parking fines
   b. Snowplows
   c. Parking study
   d. City audit
3. Support for lead
   a. The vote
   b. Jones quote
   c. Opposition
4. Support for other actions (in order introduced in second paragraph)
   a. Parking fines
      (i) Amount (ii) Reason (iii) No opposition
   b. Snowplows
      (i) Cost (ii) When delivered
   c. Parking study
      (i) Define problem (ii) When study is due (iii) Who will do it (iv) Dehaven quote (v) Chamber of Commerce request
   d. City audit
      (i) Who will do it (ii) Cost (iii) When due

Outlining might take only five minutes, and it will save you much more time. The outline also creates a structure that flows logically from one idea to the next. Here's how you could start the story outlined above:

The Springfield City Council voted Tuesday to make four streets in the downtown area one-way.

The council also raised parking fines to $5, voted to buy two snowplows, ordered a study of downtown parking facilities and hired a firm to audit the city.

Effective March 1, the four streets that will be one-way are. . . .

Select the Proper Sentence Structure

Within each sentence, you must express the proper relationships between ideas. One way to do this is to think about your sentence structure. Simple sentences express one idea. Compound sentences express two or more ideas of equal importance. Complex sentences subordinate one idea to another. Here are some examples.

Simple The mayor scolded the council.

Compound The mayor scolded the council, and she insisted on a vote.

Compound sentences equate two or more ideas without commenting on them. Complex sentences allow you to show sequence and cause and effect, among other things:

Complex After the mayor scolded the council, she insisted on a vote. (Shows sequence.)

Complex Because the mayor was angry, she insisted on a vote. (Shows cause and effect.)

Both sentences are correct, but the meaning of each is slightly different.

Use the Precise Conjunction

Subordinating conjunctions (such as *if*, *since*, *while*, *after* and *until*) carry different and precise meanings. Choose the subordinating conjunction that expresses the idea you want.

Coordinating conjunctions (*and*, *or*, *but*, *for*, *nor*, *so*, *yet*) also require careful selection. Observe how the meaning changes with the conjunction in these examples:

The mayor insisted that the council vote, and the members ignored her.

The mayor insisted that the council vote, but the members ignored her.

The second example is more coherent because it expresses the council members' reaction more logically.

Six Kinds of Transitions

1. Time
2. Direction and/or place
3. Repetition of words or phrases
4. Numbers
5. Demonstrative adjectives: *this, that, these, those*
6. Relationship connectors: coordinating conjunctions, subordinating conjunctions, and conjunctive adverbs

Use Transitions

Transitions are words, phrases, sentences or paragraphs that show the logical progression of the story structure and the ideas within the structure. Transitions are road signs directing readers through a story. The annotated model "Using Transitions" shows how transitions can be used in a story.

The reference to memory in the next example directs us from the first to the second paragraph:

> **Mr. and Mrs. Lester Einbender are using their memory to project life as it might have been.**
>
> **That memory centers around a son named Michael, a rheumatic disease called lupus and a desire to honor one while conquering the other.**

The use of the word "That" at the beginning of the second paragraph is subtle, but its impact is dramatic. Using "A memory" instead of "That" would not link the reader to the memory already mentioned. Using "The memory" would be more specific, but "That memory" points readers directly to the memory mentioned in the preceding paragraph.

Because the word *a* is good only for general references, it is called an *indefinite modifier*. Because the word *the* is more specific, it is called a *definite modifier*. Because the word *that* is most specific, it is called a *demonstrative adjective*: It demonstrates precisely the word or phrase to which you are referring when you couple it with the noun ("memory"). Other demonstrative adjectives include *this*, *these* and *those*. When you move from indefinite to definite modifier and then to demonstrative adjective, you climb the ladder of coherence.

Another way to write clearly is to use relationship connectors. There are three types:

- Coordinating conjunctions are *and*, *but*, *for*, *nor*, *or*, *so* and *yet*. Choose them carefully to express the relationship.
- Subordinating conjunctions include *although*, *because*, *since* and *while*. Each means something different.
- Conjunctive adverbs include *however*, *therefore*, *accordingly* and *consequently*.

Transitions help you achieve coherence, the logical connection of ideas. They guide you from one sentence to the next, from one paragraph to the next. Writers who are unfamiliar with transitions merely stack paragraphs, like pieces of wood, atop one another. Transitions keep the story, if not the woodpile, from falling apart.

Repeating a word or phrase also helps to keep the story from falling apart. In the preceding example, the writer used a demonstrative adjective and repeated a word.

Parallelism, repetition of a word or grammatical form, is another way to guide readers through a story. Writers frequently use parallelism to achieve coherence.

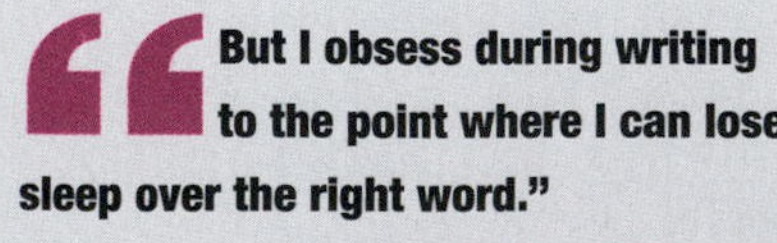

But I obsess during writing to the point where I can lose sleep over the right word."

■ Madeleine Blais, writer

ANNOTATED MODEL Using Transitions

Transitions, like road signs, help readers understand where they have been and where they are going.

On a Monday afternoon, Dr. Glenn Billman pulled back from the autopsy he was performing on a dead girl and stared at the sight before him.

The first four paragraphs focus on Billman, which makes the story easy to follow. Billman's name or a pronoun links the paragraphs.

In his seven years at Children's Hospital, he had never seen anything like it. The girl's colon was severely hemorrhaged, ravaged by bacteria that normally lived in a cow's intestine.

Puzzled and quietly alarmed, Billman notified local health officials. It was the first indication that the lethal strain of bacteria *E. coli* 0157:H7 was on the loose.

The word "But" is a transition that shows the writer is introducing another angle.

But Billman didn't make his discovery at Children's Hospital in Seattle. He made it at Children's Hospital in San Diego, and he made it three weeks before the *E. coli* epidemic struck the Northwest, killing three children and sickening about 500 people.

In December, San Diego was hit by a small *E. coli* outbreak that killed the 6-year-old girl and made at least seven other people sick.

A time reference is used as a transition: "It is now . . ." links the Northwest outbreak to the earlier San Diego outbreak ("In December . . ." in the previous paragraph).

It is now being linked to the Seattle outbreak, but in its early stages, San Diego health officials were slow to recognize the crisis, and they have been sharply criticized for failing to notify the public about the *E. coli* death and illnesses.

"I really believe we need to be safe and not sorry, and the fact is, a girl died in San Diego," said San Diego County Supervisor Dianne Jacob. "I was outraged. The only way I found out was by reading it in the newspaper" after the Northwest outbreak.

Time references ("after the Northwest outbreak" here and "When the first . . ." in the next paragraph) link the two paragraphs.

When the first Washington cases were reported in mid-January, authorities there immediately queried neighboring states, including California, but were not told about the *E. coli* death of the San Diego girl. That information would have alerted them about the bacteria's severity and might have pointed them sooner to the source of the contamination.

Like the patients here, the San Diego girl had eaten a hamburger at a Jack in the Box restaurant days before she got sick and died. The seven other *E. coli* patients had all eaten hamburgers at fast-food restaurants, among them Jack in the Box.

The phrase "Like the patients here" links this paragraph to the preceding one.

The word "That" is a demonstrative adjective that points to the preceding paragraph.

That information was available in early January, according to Dr. Michele Ginsberg, San Diego County epidemiologist. She would not say how many of the seven patients had eaten at Jack in the Box.

"A variety of restaurants were mentioned," she said. "Naming any one of them would create public reaction and perhaps avoidance of those restaurants."

The word "That" again creates a transition from the preceding paragraph.

That reticence angers Jacob, the San Diego County supervisor. "I had a follow-up meeting with county health officials, and I have to tell you, very honestly, I was not pleased with their attitude," she said. . . .

Writing about the complicated subject of nuclear-waste disposal in America, Donald Barlett and James Steele, then of *The Philadelphia Inquirer*, relied on parallelism for coherence and emphasis. Notice the parallel use of "They said . . ." to start sentences and the repeated variations of "It cannot":

> **This assessment may prove overly optimistic. For perhaps in no other area of modern technology have so many experts in the government, industry and science been so wrong so many times over so many years as have those involved in radioactive waste.**
>
> **They said, repeatedly, that radioactive waste could be handled like any other industrial refuse. It cannot.**
>
> **They said that science had most of the answers, and was on the verge of getting the few it did not have, for dealing with radioactive waste permanently. It did not, and it does not.**
>
> **They said that some of it could be buried in the ground, like garbage in a landfill, and that it would pose no health hazard because it would never move. It moved.**
>
> **They said that liquid radioactive waste could be put in storage tanks, and that rigorous safety systems would immediately detect any leaks. The tanks leaked for weeks and no one noticed.**

Barlett and Steele's use of parallelism sets up the story. In the following excerpt from her story about Hurricane Sandy, a storm that devastated parts of the East Coast, Amy Ellis Nutt repeated the word "waiting" for emphasis:

> **Realized or not, we live in constant anticipation. We're always waiting. Waiting to drive. Waiting to turn 21. Waiting for winter break. Waiting to graduate. Waiting for a significant other to come along.**

Chronology and references to time provide other ways to tie a story together. Words and phrases such as "now," "since then" and "two days later" are invaluable in helping readers understand where they have been and where they are going. Chronology is important in everything from reports of automobile accidents (which car entered the intersection first?) to recaps of events that occurred over months or even hours.

Conciseness and Simplicity

Conciseness is a virtue, not only in newspapers and broadcasting where space and time constraints are severe but also online and on social media feeds where you're competing for your readers' attention. Even when you write longer stories, you have to respect readers' time. No one has unlimited time or attention to give you.

Be Concise

Being concise means saying what you need to say in as few words as possible. Some subjects require more details than others. Here are four ways to shorten your stories. (See also the annotated model "Editing for Conciseness" later in this chapter.)

- **Eliminate some subject areas.** Always ask yourself whether all of the subjects need to be included. No doubt, your editor will have a more dispassionate view of what's needed than you will.

- **Eliminate redundancies.** One way to achieve conciseness is to rid your sentences of cabooses — unneeded words or phrases that hitch themselves, like barnacles, onto other words. Delete the barnacles in italics: "remand *back*"; "gather *together*"; "consensus of *opinion*"; "*totally* destroyed"; "*excess* verbiage"; "open *up*"; "fall *down*"; "my own *personal* favorite"; "strangled to *death*."

- **Challenge intensive and qualifying adverbs.** Your job is to select the right word so you don't need two or more. Instead of "really unhappy," perhaps you mean "sad." Instead of "very cold," perhaps you mean "frigid." "Really" and "very" are examples of intensive adverbs. When you say "almost there," you are using a qualifying adverb. You might be near, or you might be a mile away. Be specific.

- **Train yourself to value brevity.** Some of the most notable writing in history is brief: Lincoln's Gettysburg Address contains 272 words; the Ten Commandments, 297; and the American Declaration of Independence, 300.

Writing Clearly

- Keep sentences short.
- Limit each sentence to one idea.
- Favor subject-verb-object sentences.
- Avoid using more than three prepositional phrases in one sentence.
- Avoid using more than three numbers in one sentence.
- Use plain and simple words instead of jargon, journalese or clichés.

■ Paula LaRocque, writing consultant

You will use fewer words when you figure out what you want to say and then express it positively. Enter the following negatively phrased thicket of verbiage at your own risk:

> **The Missouri Gaming Commission has 30 days to appeal a judge's temporary order reversing the commission's decision not to grant a gaming license to a firm that wanted to dock a riverboat casino in Jefferson City.**

The writer is lost in a maze of reversals of negative findings. The lead tries to cover too much territory. Express it in the positive and strip it to its essential information:

> **The state has 30 days to persuade a judge it should not have to license a firm that wants to open a riverboat casino in Jefferson City.**

The writer of this sentence also failed to think clearly:

> **Amtrak, formally the National Passenger Railroad Corp., was created in 1970 to preserve declining passenger train service.**

The writer did not mean that Amtrak was created to preserve *declining* passenger train service. It was created to increase passenger train service.

Keep It Simple

The readers of one newspaper confronted the following one-sentence paragraph:

> **"Paradoxically, cancer-causing mutations often result from the repair of a cell by error-prone enzymes and not the 'carcinogenic' substance's damage to the cell," Abe Eisenstark, director of biological sciences at the university, said at a meeting of the Ad Hoc Council of Environmental Carcinogenesis Wednesday night at the Cancer Research Center.**

> **"Short is beautiful. Short and simple is more beautiful. Short, simple and interesting is most beautiful."**
>
> ■ Don Gibb, educator

ANNOTATED MODEL Editing for Conciseness

To be concise, challenge every word or phrase you write. These examples show how to eliminate 36 of the 127 words. (The replacement words are in italics.)

Bartholow is ~~currently~~ working on other projects, but he ~~has~~ plans to continue ~~with~~ his video game research. ~~In the future~~, he hopes to recruit female subjects—a difficult task because far fewer women than men play violent video games. He's also interested in examining how ~~a person's prior~~ *people's* gaming history affects ~~his or her~~ *their* response to a single exposure to a violent video game.

"Currently" is usually redundant because the verb tense implies it.

"With" is unnecessary.

The plural form gets around the wordy "his or her."

Change "has plans" to "plans" to strengthen the verb.

"In the future" is already implied in the verb.

Pumpkins are everywhere ~~during the fall season~~ *in fall*. They ~~serve as a way to~~ help families and friends ~~to get closer~~ *bond* during the ~~holiday season~~ *holidays*. Whether you're ~~taking a trip~~ *traveling* to the local pumpkin patch ~~to search for the perfect pumpkin~~, or baking ~~up some delicious~~ treats ~~for people to enjoy~~, pumpkins are a ~~strong~~ reminder that comfort isn't ~~too~~ far away.

"Season" isn't required in either sentence in this paragraph.

"Strong" and "too" are unnecessary intensifiers.

No information is lost by eliminating "serve as a way to."

"Traveling" says "taking a trip" in one word.

"Up" is an unnecessary caboose on "baking." Treats are delicious. Whom else do you bake treats for?

If there is a message in those 52 words, it would take a copy editor, a lexicologist and a Nobel Prize–winning scientist to decipher it. The message simply is not clear. Although the sentence is not typical of newspaper writing, it is not unusual either.

The scientist is using the vocabulary of science, which is inappropriate for a general audience. The reporter should say, "I don't understand that exactly. Can you translate it for my readers?" The response may produce an understandable quote, but if it doesn't, paraphrase the statement, and check back with your source to be sure you have paraphrased it accurately.

Too much of what is written is mumbo jumbo. For instance:

> **Approximately 2 billion tons of sediment from land erosion enters our nation's waters every year. While industrial waste and sewage treatment plants receive a great deal of attention, according to the Department of Agriculture the No. 1 polluter of our waterways is "non-point" pollution.**

The writer of this lead contributed some linguistic pollution of his own. The message may have been clear in his mind, but it is not clear in print.

Here's another way to approach this story:

> **Soil carried into the water by erosion, not industrial waste or sewage from treatment plants, is the No. 1 polluter of U.S. waterways, according to the Department of Agriculture.**

Correct and Effective Language

Writing to be read is not easy. Reporters become writers by the sweat of their brows. John Kenneth Galbraith, a best-selling author who was able to make economics understandable to the lay reader, commented on the difficulty of writing well. "There are days when the result is so bad that no fewer than five revisions are required," he wrote. "In contrast, when I'm inspired, only four revisions are needed."

Trying the techniques discussed in this chapter is the first step. Mastering them will be the result of repeated practice.

What's the grammar error in this sentence?

Formerly flying outside the State House in Charleston, South Carolina, state troopers took down the Confederate flag after a vote in the state assembly.

See Appendix 1, Rule 10.

Figures of Speech

Good writers understand how to use literary devices known as figures of speech. Similes and metaphors, two common figures of speech, permit writers to show similarities and contrasts. *Similes* show similarities by comparing one thing to another, often using the word *like* or *as*. Describing her roommate's reaction to the news that she was moving, one writer said, "She stared into space for a few moments, scowling, *as if she were squaring large numbers in her head*." And from a profile of a CEO: "There's barely a picture on the wall or a paper on the desk. It's as clutter-free as a monk's quarters."

Metaphor is the first cousin of simile. A simile says one thing is *like* another, but a metaphor says one thing *is* another: "Michael is a lion with gazelle legs." A metaphor is a stronger analogy than a simile. Describing the radio personality and writer Garrison Keillor, a reporter once wrote, "And there he is. A sequoia in a room full of saplings." The metaphor works on two levels. Keillor is tall enough to tower over most others in the room. Because he is known internationally, his work towers over that of others, too.

With similes and metaphors, writers draw word pictures. These techniques turn the pages of a scrapbook of images in each reader's mind.

> **"The real problem is that misplaced modifiers and similar glitches tend to distract readers. Introduce blunders to an otherwise smoothly flowing story and it's as though a drunk stumbled through a religious procession.**
>
> **What's more, while those errors due to carelessness may not permanently damage the language, they can damage a paper's credibility. Botching a small job sows mistrust about the larger enterprise."**
>
> **■ Jack Cappon, Associated Press senior writer and writing coach**

Careful Word Choice

Freedom in word choice is exhilarating when the result is a well-turned phrase. Here's how one student described the weather in fresh terms: "I rushed off the bus into a downpour of beaming sunlight." Here's Julie Sullivan of *The Spokesman-Review*: "Hand him a soapbox, he'll hand you a homily."

Freedom in word choice is dangerous when it results in nouns masquerading as verbs (*prioritize*, *impact*, *maximize*) or jargon masquerading as respectable English (*input*, *output*, *throughput*).

Precision, however, means more than knowing the etymology of a word; it means knowing exactly what you want to say. Instead of saying, "The City Council wants to locate the landfill three blocks from downtown," to be precise, you say, "Five members of the City Council want to locate the landfill three blocks east of downtown."

Precision also means using the conditional (*could*, *might*, *should*, *would*) when discussing proposals:

Incorrect The bill will make it illegal . . .

Correct The bill would make it illegal . . .

The use of *will* here is imprecise because the legislation has not been passed. By using *would*, you are saying, "If the legislature passes the bill, it would. . . ."

Bias-Free Language

Even when used innocently, sexist and racist language, besides being offensive and discriminatory, is imprecise. Doctors aren't always *he*, nor are nurses always *she*. Much of our language assumes people are male unless they are identified as female. Precise writers avoid *policeman* (*police officer*), *ad man* (*advertising representative*), *assemblyman* (*assembly member*) and *postman* (*postal worker*). In some situations, you can use the plural to eliminate the need for a gender-specific word: "Doctors treat their patients."

Check *The Associated Press Stylebook* to see whether to identify a person's race or ethnicity. Then try to follow the person's own preference and be as specific as possible: *Asian-American* is acceptable but *Chinese-American* may be preferable. *Black* is acceptable for any nationality, but use *African-American* only for an American black person of African descent.

Some words are perfectly precise when used correctly but are imprecise when used in the wrong context. *Boy* is not interchangeable with *young man*, and *girl* is not interchangeable with *young woman*. Not all active retired people are *spry*, which implies that the writer is surprised to find that the person is active. *Grandmotherly* fails when you describe people in their 40s who are grandmothers. It also fails when you use it indiscriminately. When Nancy Pelosi became the first female speaker of the U.S. House of Representatives, many accounts identified her as a grandmother. Although it is true that she's a grandmother, accounts of new male leaders seldom mention that they are grandfathers.

The word *dumb*, as in *deaf and dumb*, is imprecise and derogatory. Instead, use *speech-impaired*. When the terms are used in tandem, use *hearing-impaired and speech-impaired* for parallelism. Because alcoholism is a disease, use *recovering alcoholic* instead of *reformed alcoholic*. *Handicapped* is imprecise; *disabled* is preferred.

The Associated Press recommends *gay* and *lesbian* and sometimes allows *homosexual* but does not permit *queer* and other derogatory terms. AP suggests consulting the National Lesbian and Gay Journalists Association "Stylebook" and "Journalists Toolbox" (www.nlgja.org) for background on this and other similar issues.

Avoiding Carelessness in Word Choice

- Know precisely what you want to say.
- Use the conditional (*could*, *might*, *should*, *would*) when discussing proposals.
- Choose the correct sentence structure to communicate explicitly what you mean.

"I like to say to writers: Write to save your life. Revise to give a gift to the reader. That gift may be insight, entertainment, illumination—better still, let it be all three. The pact between writer and reader is one of trust and generosity."

■ Carol Edgarian, co-founder and publisher of *Narrative* magazine

For example, according to the NLGJA, the preferred term for a person who was identified as female at birth but subsequently came to express a male gender identity is *transgender man*.

The battle over abortion extends to the terms used in news. One side wants to be described as *pro-life*; the other wants to be described as *pro-choice*. The Associated Press prescribes the terms *anti-abortion* and *pro–abortion rights* in an attempt to be neutral.

Some dismiss this concern for language as overly zealous political correctness. That attitude implies that we are afraid to tell the truth. What is the truth about ethnic slang?

The truth is that many words historically applied to groups of people were created in ignorance or hate or fear. During the world wars, American citizens of German descent were called *krauts* to depersonalize them. Over the years, pejorative terms have been applied to immigrants from Ireland, Poland, China and Africa.

We see the same thing happening to more recent immigrants from Latin America, the Caribbean and the Middle East. The adjective Islamic is seldom seen or heard in news reports except to modify *terrorists* or *fundamentalists*. The noun *Muslim* refers simply to an adherent of Islam. As writers concerned with precision of the language, we should deal with people, not stereotypes.

Words are powerful. When used negatively, they define cultures, create second-class citizens and reveal stereotypical thinking. They also change the way people think about and treat others. Writers have the freedom to choose precisely the right word. That freedom can be both exhilarating and dangerous.

Avoiding Sexism in Language

- Use a generic term (*flight attendant*, *firefighter*).
- Participate in the movement to drop feminine endings. (Use *comedian*, *hero*, *actor* and *poet* for both genders.)
- Make the subject plural. ("Reporters must not reveal their opinions.")
- Drop the gender-specific pronoun, and replace it with an article. ("A reporter must not form *a* judgment.")
- Rewrite to eliminate the gender-specific pronoun. ("A reporter must not judge.")
- Write the sentence in the second person. ("You should not form your judgment.")

Correct Grammar and Punctuation

Far too often, grammar and punctuation errors obscure meaning. Consider this example:

> **Watching his parents struggle in low-paying jobs, a college education looked desirable to him.**

Because the participial phrase ("Watching . . .") is followed by the noun "college education," the sentence seems to mean that the college education did the watching. Write the sentence this way:

> **Watching his parents struggle in low-paying jobs, he realized he wanted a college education.**

No one who aspires to be a writer will succeed without knowing the rules of grammar. Dangling participles, subject-verb disagreement, pronoun-antecedent disagreement and misplaced modifiers are like enemy troops: They attack sentences and destroy their meaning, as the authors of a survey discovered.

The personnel director of an Inglewood, California, aerospace company had to fill out a government survey form that asked, among other things, "How many employees do you have, broken down by sex?" After considering the sentence for a few moments, she wrote, "Liquor is more of a problem with us."

Here are some typical errors and ways to correct them:

Pronoun-antecedent disagreement	*Each* of the boys brought *their* sleeping bags.
Correct	*Each* of the boys brought *his* sleeping bag.
Subject-verb disagreement	The *mayor* together with the City Council *oppose* collective bargaining by the firefighters.
Correct	The *mayor* together with the city council *opposes* . . . The *mayor and the city council oppose* . . .
Misplaced modifier	Despite *his* size, *the coach* said Jones would play forward.
Correct	The coach said that *Jones*, despite *his* size, would play forward.

Improper punctuation creates ambiguities at best and inaccuracies at worst. For instance:

> **Giving birth to Cynthia five years earlier had been difficult for Mrs. Davenport and the two parents decided they were content with the family they had.**

Without the required comma before "and," the sentence can easily be misunderstood. A person reading quickly misses the pause and sees this: "Giving birth to Cynthia had been difficult for Mrs. Davenport and the two parents." That's a lot of people in the delivery room. (For more examples of common grammar and punctuation errors, see Appendix 1.)

Most newsrooms used to have two or three people read each story to catch these and other errors. Now, almost all media have reduced the number of copy editors. It is even more important these days for the writer to get it right in the first place.

The Tools of Narration

The tools of narration allow you to build interest in stories. When we use scenes, dialogue and anecdotes, or create a sense of person and place, we are using narrative tools that help make our stories as informative as they are interesting. In exposition, the writer clearly stands between the reader and the information: Journalists have sources who tell them things. Journalists then tell the reader what they heard and saw. Scenes, dialogue and anecdotes allow the reader to see the action.

Scenes

Gene Roberts, former managing editor of *The New York Times*, tells about his first job at a daily newspaper. His publisher, who was blind, had someone read the newspaper to him each morning. One day, the publisher called Roberts into his office and complained, "Roberts, I can't see your stories. Make me see."

> **"The most important thing to any writing, and especially profile writing, is the telling detail."**
>
> ■ **Jacqui Banaszynski, Pulitzer Prize winner**

We should all try to make readers see, smell, feel, taste and hear. One way to do that is to write using scenes as much as possible. To write a scene, you have to be there. You need to capture the pertinent details. Think of yourself as a playwright, not as a narrator standing on a stage. Leave the stage, and let your readers see the action and hear the dialogue. You can see and hear what is happening in the following excerpt. Put yourself in a theater watching the actors on stage:

> **She was in her office getting ready to attend a doctoral candidate's prospectus defense when the call came that would turn her life upside down. The surgeon told her she was very sorry, but it was invasive breast cancer.**
>
> **"Am I going to die?" Carver asked her.**
>
> **"Well, I certainly hope not," the surgeon said.**
>
> **She hung up the phone in a daze but refused to go home. Somehow, she managed to get through the defense. Then she went to see her husband, Bill Horner, a MU political science professor. She walked into his office and shut the door. Horner knew before she had uttered a word.**

A student reporter at South Dakota State University was on a farm to capture this opening scene:

> **Don Sheber's leathery, cracked hands have been sculpted by decades of wresting a living from the earth.**
>
> **But this year, despite work that often stretches late into the evening, the moisture-starved soil has yielded little for Sheber and his family.**
>
> **Sheber's hands tugged at the control levers on his John Deere combine last week as rotating blades harvested the thin stands of wheat that have grown to less than a foot high.**

The writer allows the reader to visit Sheber on the farm. We can see and feel the farmer's hands. We can touch the John Deere combine and the stunted wheat.

To create such scenes, you must use all your senses to gather information, and your notebook should reflect that reporting. Along with the results of interviews, your notebook should bulge with details of sights and smells, sounds and textures. David Finkel, winner of the American Society of News Editors Distinguished Writing Award in 1986 and a Pulitzer Prize in 2006, says, "Anything that pertains to any sense I feel at any moment, I write down." Gather details indiscriminately. Later, you can discard those that are not germane.

David Bacon/The Image Works

"Don Sheber's leathery, cracked hands have been sculpted by decades of wresting a living from the earth." Use descriptive language to paint a vivid picture for readers and to bring a story to life.

Because Bartholomew Sullivan of *The (Memphis) Commercial Appeal* was observing and listening closely at a trial, his readers were able to sit in the courtroom with him:

> **Helfrich banged an index finger on the rail of the jury box as he recalled Thursday's testimony in which a string of Bowers's Jones County friends testified that he was a solid businessman, a Christian—"a gentleman." One of the witnesses was Nix, who called Bowers a "real, real nice man."**
>
> **"They talk of gentlemen," Helfrich whispered. Then, shouting, he said: "These people don't have a gentle bone in their bodies. They were nightriders and henchmen. They attacked a sleeping family and destroyed all they owned."**

Analyze the details: the banging of an index finger, the whisper, the shout. We can see, and we can hear. By creating a scene, the writer transported us to the courtroom rather than just telling us what he saw.

To write a scene, you must be able to capture a sense of place. Show us where the action is taking place. Take us to the courtroom, the basketball court or the city.

Dialogue

The use of *dialogue*—conversation between two or more people, not including the reporter—allows the reporter to recede and the characters to take center stage. When you use quotations, you—the writer—are repeating for the reader what the source said, and the reader listens to you relating what was said. But when you use dialogue, you disappear, and the reader listens directly to the characters. Dialogue is a key element in creating scenes. Compare these examples:

> **During the public hearing, Henry Lathrop accused the council of wasting taxpayers' money. "If you don't stop voting for all this spending, I am going to circulate a recall petition and get you all kicked off the council," he said.**
>
> **Mayor Margorie Gold told Lathrop he was free to do as he wished. "As for us," she said, "we will vote in the best interests of the city."**

That is the traditional way of presenting quotations. The reporter uses quotes but also paraphrases some of what was said. That's telling readers instead of taking them to the council chambers and letting them listen.

Here is that account handled as dialogue:

> **When Henry Lathrop spoke to the City Council during the public hearing, he pounded on the podium. "You folks are wasting taxpayers' money. If you don't stop voting for all this spending, I am going to circulate a recall petition and get you all kicked off the council."**
>
> **Mayor Margorie Gold slammed her gavel on her desk.**
>
> **"Mr. Lathrop," she said as she tried to control the anger in her voice. She looked at him directly. "You are free to do as you wish. As for us, we will vote in the best interests of the city."**

At the hearing, Lathrop and Gold were speaking to each other. The second version captures the exchange without the intercession of the writer.

Anecdotes

The ultimate treats, **anecdotes**, are stories embedded in stories. They can be happy or sad, funny or serious. Whatever their tone, they should illustrate a point. Readers are likely to remember the anecdotes more readily than anything else in a story. You probably remember the stories that your professors tell regardless of whether you remember the rest of the lecture. Long after you've forgotten this chapter, you will probably remember some of the examples from it. Facts inform. Anecdotes inform and entertain.

> **"If history were taught in the form of stories, it would never be forgotten."**
>
> ■ Rudyard Kipling, English writer

As befits something so valuable, anecdotes are hard to obtain. You can't get them by asking your source, "Got any good anecdotes?" But you can get them by asking for examples so you can re-create the scene. To do this, be alert to the possibilities that an anecdote might be lurking in the details. One reporter gathered this quote:

> **"We had one of those coaching nights where we sat up until I don't know when trying to figure it out," Richardson says. "We refer to that as the red-letter day in Spartan football, and since that day, we are 33-15, with three district titles and a conference championship."**

The editor pointed out to the reporter that if it was a red-letter day, the reporter should have asked more questions about that coaching meeting. He did, and he ended up with an anecdote about how the coaches figured out a new strategy that turned out to be successful.

Here's another example. Your source says: "Darren is like a one-man entertainment committee. He's always got something going on. And if nothing is going on, he'll hike up his pants really high and dance to Fetty Wap."

To turn this dry quote into an anecdote, you need to ask, "Can you give me an example of when he acted like an entertainment committee?" or "Tell me about the time he danced to Fetty Wap."

Student reporter Sara Trimble followed up a general comment by asking for specifics. She was doing a profile on a funeral home owner when she was told he was compassionate. Sara asked for an example. She turned the answer into this anecdote:

> **Opportunity would take Millard away from close friends yet again when he moved to Jefferson City to buy his own funeral home after graduating, but it wouldn't be long before his charm would win over another community.**
>
> **"You're just as cute as can be. What are you doing here on a Friday night?" Peggy Talken asked a man sitting across from her. She was attending a fundraiser at her children's school.**
>
> **"Well, you're here too," Millard said.**
>
> **"I've got kids. You don't!" Talken said.**
>
> **That was the first time Talken made Millard blush, and she took great pleasure in doing so. They became great friends after that, but she had no idea just how important his friendship would be until one fateful day in June 2013.**
>
> **"Your daughter's dead. She didn't make it," an ER nurse said.**
>
> **The words a parent never wants to hear, followed by a sight she should never have to see: her daughter, Corrie, in the hospital bed, her hair still matted down with blood and her neck fractured and gashed.**
>
> **Pools of blood stained the floor, and Talken considered taking off her shirt to mop it up herself. She couldn't bear to say her last goodbye to her baby like this.**
>
> **Like an answered prayer, Millard showed up at the hospital.**
>
> **He asked the hospital staff for 15 minutes alone in the room. That's all he needed. In that time, he cleaned the blood off Corrie's face, put a sheet over her neck to cover up the gash and turned the lights down just a little bit.**
>
> **Four days later, over 2,000 people showed up for Corrie's funeral services. How everyone found parking in the small funeral home's lot, Talken still doesn't know. Millard took care of it.**
>
> **He also took care of Corrie's body.**
>
> **"I told him that if even one of her eyelashes looked out of place, I would make them close the casket," Talken says.**

> **The casket remained open.**
>
> **Her neck? Still fractured, but covered with a scarf Millard had found to match the bridesmaid's dress she was buried in. Her fingernails? Cleaned, filed and polished. Her skin? Covered with natural makeup, as if she were attending her cousin's wedding as planned.**
>
> **Doves were released at the gravestone — something else Talken wasn't expecting. But one dove in particular stood out to her. It was dyed pink, Corrie's favorite color.**

Use anecdotes to entertain while you are informing. If the relevance of the anecdote to the larger story isn't obvious, establish the connection in the transition into the anecdote or at the end of it.

Sense of Person

To turn sources into characters, offer your readers a sense of person. Describe the subjects physically and tell us what's in their minds. A student offered this physical description: "Meinke, 48, has the build of Jason Alexander and the voice of Nathan Lane."

Student Megan Farokhmanesh offers a physical sense and helps explain the character's personality:

> **It's Tuesday. The class is discussing Jonathan's Swift's "A Modest Proposal." Some students sit up straight, bright-eyed and attentive, while the eyelids of a few others here and there droop under the weight of their adolescent exhaustion. Overeem, a man of solid build, slowly paces around the room, his steps slow and sure. His Chuck Taylors hit the ground in a smooth, rhythmic pattern. One. Two. One. Two. His glasses zoom repeatedly into his hands and back to his nose as he gestures, continually taking them on and off. Each statement he makes is punctuated with a sharp jump of his eyebrows, as he crumples his forehead in earnest. His voice is level without being monotone, deep without being booming. Even in his excitement he is cool and collected.**
>
> **In a particularly vigorous wave of his hands, his glasses fly off once more as he addresses the class. He opens the discussion to the purpose of existence. The question of whether life is worth living. Some students shift in their seats at the idea. He tells them, "I'd never kill myself. I'm afraid one of the greatest records in the world would be released the next day, and I'd never get to listen to it. And my wife would be left alone." Perhaps his students don't realize it, but Overeem has just bared his soul for them. Just like that, the two loves of his life are out in the open.**

It is clear from this example that the writer was in the room and observed keenly. Good writing always begins with good reporting.

CHAPTER RESOURCES

SUGGESTED READINGS

Hart, Jack. *Storycraft: The Complete Guide to Writing Narrative Nonfiction.* Chicago: Univ. of Chicago Press, 2012. This is as complete a how-to book on writing narrative nonfiction as exists. It practices what it preaches: It is informative and entertaining.

Osborn, Patricia. *How Grammar Works: A Self-Teaching Guide.* New York: John Wiley, 1999. This book will do for you what it promises: It will guide you, step by step, through the basics of English grammar. Its goal is to make you feel comfortable with grammar and the way words work.

Strunk, William, and E. B. White. *The Elements of Style.* 3rd ed. Boston: Allyn & Bacon, 1995. This little book practices what it preaches. For the beginner, it is a good primer; for the pro, it is a good review of writing rules and word meanings.

Tankard, James, and Laura Hendrickson. "Specificity, Imagery in Writing: Testing the Effects of 'Show, Don't Tell.'" *Newspaper Research Journal* (Winter/Spring 1996): 35–48. The authors found that participants in a test said that examples of "show" writing were more interesting and believable.

SUGGESTED WEBSITES

LaunchPad Solo
launchpadworks.com
When you visit LaunchPad Solo for Journalism, you will find research links, exercises and LearningCurve adaptive quizzing to help you improve your grammar and AP style usage. In addition, the site's video collection hosts the videos highlighted in this and other chapters as well as additional clips of leading professionals discussing important media trends.

www.niemanstoryboard.org
This site often interviews the authors of great narrative nonfiction.

www.nytimes.com/2018/07/24/world/europe/greece-wildfire.html?nl=top-stories
Jason Horowitz's story on the wildfires in Greece.

www.washingtonpost.com/national/it-was-my-job-and-i-didnt-find-him-stoneman-douglas-resource-officer-remains-haunted-by-massacre/2018/06/04/796f1c16-679d-11e8-9e38-24e693b38637_story.html?noredirect=on
Eli Saslow's story about the deputy who didn't go into the Marjorie Stoneman Douglas school during the mass shooting.

EXERCISES

1. Underline and count the number of prepositional phrases in the following. Then rewrite to reduce the number of prepositions:

    > I also thought it was interesting that the teacher mentioned that the number of prepositions used in a sentence can also determine the rhythm of your story. We've just gone over the use of prepositions in magazine editing, and they can hurt your work more than they can help it. I've never really paid attention to my use of prepositions before last week's magazine editing lecture, but I will try to limit my use as much as possible.

2. **Your journalism blog.** In the following paragraph, identify the concrete details and the similes. Evaluate what they add to your understanding of the scene. Then list and evaluate the verbs. Write a blog post about your analysis of the paragraph.

    > Boyd is in his truck with Fire Chief James Samarelli, who is at the wheel. They turn right onto Sampson Avenue and are nearly hit by a wooden lifeguard boat slicing through the floodwater. A wall of water is headed directly for them, bringing a second lifeguard boat. Samarelli jerks the truck to the right. A large piece of the boardwalk, ripped away by the waves, slams into the front of the flatbed truck. Boyd looks down at his suddenly cold feet. Seawater is rushing into the cab and a 6-foot-tall swell lifts the truck and begins pushing it sideways, into a telephone pole.

3. Choose the right word:

   a. We need to (ensure, insure) a victory.
   b. Stop (annoying, irritating) your friend.
   c. The attorney won because she (refuted, responded to) the allegations.
   d. The prisoner was able to produce (mitigating, militating) evidence.

4. Write a paragraph in which you give readers a sense of a particular person in your class or a local celebrity. Can your classmates identify him or her?

5. Write a paragraph in which you give readers a sense of a particular place on your campus or in the immediate neighborhood. Can you classmates identify the place?

6. Punctuate the following sentences:

   a. Government officials have come under a newly enacted censorship system and several foreign speakers have been denied permission to enter the country.
   b. It was a Monday night and for the next two days he teetered between life and death.
   c. The council approved the manager's proposals and rejected a tax increase.

7. Use a simile to explain the following numbers:

   The student council's budget is $350,000. The university has 19,000 students. The local city budget is $3 million. The city has 70,000 residents.

8. Calculate the readability levels for a couple of paragraphs you have written and for stories from *The New York Times* and The Associated Press. Compare the readability scores, and account for scoring differences and similarities. You can get the calculation at https://readability-score.com.

CHAPTER 10

ALTERNATIVES TO THE INVERTED PYRAMID

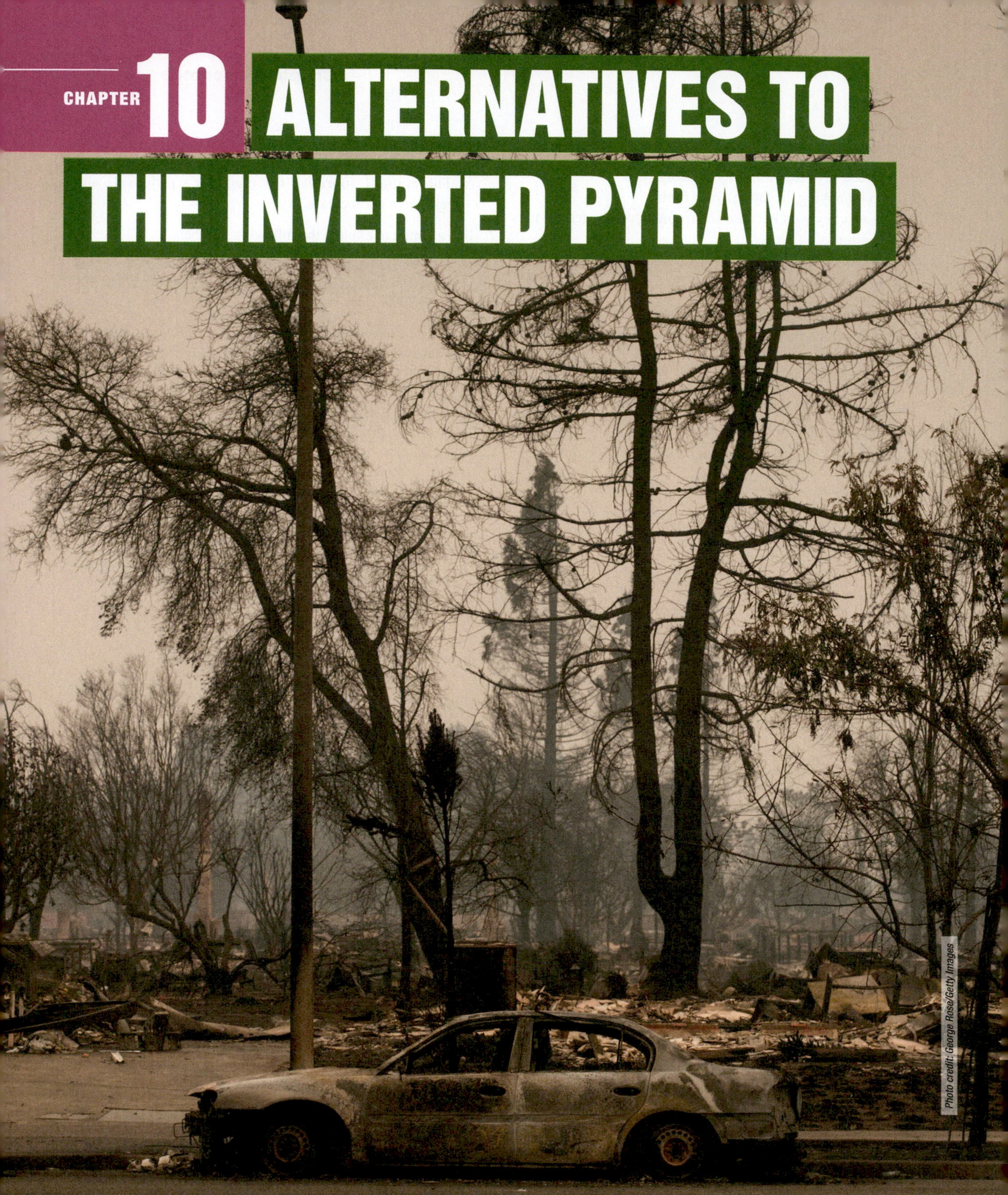

Photo credit: George Rose/Getty Images

God woke you up, you're sure of it.

He kicked you in the head as smoke filled the room. "Look out the back window," came the voice. So you did.

What you saw at 3 a.m. at the Journey's End mobile home park in Santa Rosa was orange light where it shouldn't have been. Row after row of tightly packed units were ablaze along Highway 101.

You didn't want to die, not like this, so you got in your pickup and drove away. Then you turned around.

People were screaming and embers filled the sky. You had firefighting training and knew you could help. Someone handed you a fire hose, and you stayed for hours, until 8:30 in the morning, until the roaring of the flames quieted.

One row of homes survived the night, thanks to you. In the days ahead, you'd be hailed as a savior in the community and in the news, given a spontaneous ovation at the post office.

But if you could relive that night in October, you'd get back in the truck and keep driving.

You'd let it all burn.

There is no who, what, where, when, why and how in this lead by Lizzie Johnson of the *San Francisco Chronicle*. There is a promise that if you keep reading, you will learn why the main character, given a second chance, would have kept on driving. This is narration, the telling of story.

For all its strengths, the inverted pyramid doesn't serve all stories well. That's why journalists use other structures to tell stories in newspapers, magazines, television and websites. Increasingly, journalists are developing new structures to tell stories by taking advantage of the special strengths of the web. Like novelists, they are using characters, not just sources, who encounter complications and eventually reach a resolution.

In Chapter 8, you learned how to rank information from most important to least important. That inverted pyramid structure serves news, particularly breaking news, well. Other structures support other types of stories better. Writers focus on the people involved in issues to tell important stories — health care, cancer research, prayer in schools — in an interesting and informative way.

If time, detail and space are available, consider using the alternative structures we describe in this chapter and summarize in Figure 10.1. Whether you are writing about a car accident, the Boy Scouts' jamboree or wildfires in the western part of the U.S., writing the story will be easier if you know how to use some of the alternative story forms: the chronology, news narrative, focus structure and service journalism formats.

In this chapter, you will learn:

1 How to construct a chronology.

2 How to construct a news narrative story.

3 How to construct a focus structure story.

4 How to deliver information in service journalism formats.

News Story Structures

	Inverted Pyramid	Chronology
What is it?	The lead paragraphs have the most important information, and succeeding paragraphs give details in descending order of importance.	Starting at a particular point of interest, the paragraphs tell a story in chronological order.
When should it be used?	It's best used for hard news, when timeliness is essential and the reader wants to know the important facts right away.	It's good for reporting a detailed sequence of events in a story with controversy or tension and resolution, especially as a follow-up to a news story.
How is it structured?	**Traditional news lead** • Give who, what, when, where, why and how. • Frame the story. **Body: support paragraphs in descending order of importance** • Give additional details about the lead. • Summarize other significant actions or elements relevant to the lead. • Give the impact or effect of the event. • Give the "so what" — the story's importance to the reader. • Give background and history. • Describe relevant physical details. • Narrate relevant sequences of events. • Use quotations from relevant sources. • Give sources of additional information, including links to websites. **Ending** • End with the least significant information, *not* with a conclusion, summary or tie-back to the beginning. The story can be cut from the bottom up without compromising its effectiveness.	**Narrative lead** • Describe a dramatic point in the story. • Create narrative suspense with foreshadowing. **Nut paragraph** • Give the theme of the story. **Body: narrative support paragraphs** • Use foreshadowing. • Pick up the story with a transition back to the beginning of the narrative. • Tell the story in chronological order, highlighting key events found in the timeline. • Describe relevant physical details. • Use narrative techniques like dialogue, flashback and foreshadowing. **Ending** • Give a conclusion to the story. • Resolve the tension or conflict in the story.

FIGURE 10.1

Different structures are useful for different types of news stories.

Chronology

Stories that work best as a chronology are those that have complications or tension and a resolution worth waiting for. In our opening example, the complication is introduced: Why wouldn't the main character go back if he had it to do over? After all, he saved a whole row of houses.

Complications are present even in events like meetings. When a city council faces a contentious issue, such as a proposed smoking ban in public places, you are presented with controversy (supporters and opponents testifying), tension (balancing health and economic interests) and a resolution (the vote). Time

News Narrative	Focus Structure
The story combines elements of inverted pyramid and chronology formats, with an emphasis on either news or narrative.	The story follows one individual as a representative of a larger group.
It's useful for stories when timeliness is somewhat important but the hard news element is not prominent.	It's useful for making complex or abstract stories meaningful to readers.
Narrative lead • Open with an interesting scene or twist that teases the story. ***or*** **Traditional news lead** • Give who, what, when, where, why and how. **Support paragraphs** • Briefly add whatever helps the reader understand the story summarized in the lead. **Body: narrative support paragraphs** • Go back to the beginning, and tell the story in chronological order. **Ending** • Give a conclusion to the story. • Resolve the tension or conflict in the story.	**Narrative lead** • Introduce the subject and describe the person's problem. **Transition** • Create a bridge from the subject to the theme of the story. **Nut paragraph** • Give the theme of the story. **Support paragraphs** • Foreshadow. • Give the "so what" — the story's importance to the reader. • Give the "to be sure" — opposing perspectives. **Body: narrative and expository support paragraphs** • Interweave narrative about the subject with facts about the theme to tell the story. **Ending** • Conclude the story, with a summary or with a tie-back that refers to the beginning of the story.

constraints and tradition often dictate an inverted pyramid structure. But you have other options:

- You could summarize the vote in a sidebar and use chronology to tell the story of the meeting.
- You could write an inverted pyramid version of the story for both the website and the newspaper, and then write a chronological version for the web to replace the earlier version.
- You might use news narrative (see the next section) to report the results and then move to chronology.

What's the grammar error in this sentence?

Rowan County clerk Kim Davis refused to issue marriage licenses to same-sex couples, she spent five days in jail for contempt of court.

See Appendix 1, Rule 2.

Where to Start

Oddly enough, when you use chronology, you don't have to begin at the beginning. Instead, you look for a key moment you can use in the lead to engage readers. To get started, writers often jot down a timeline. In the case of the council meeting, it might look like this:

- **7 p.m.** Opponents and supporters of the smoking ban begin testifying before the council.
  Jones, an opponent, angrily denounces the proposal.
  Smith, a supporter, relates a story about her cancer.
- **8:15 p.m.** Council members begin debate.
  Mayor pounds the gavel to break up an out-of-control argument between two council members.
  Council member Rodriguez is nearly in tears as he urges the council to pass the ordinance.
  Council member Jackson says merchants will face financial ruin.
- **8:47 p.m.** Solinski, a member of the audience, interrupts the debate and is escorted out of the chambers by city police.
  Several in the audience boo, but some cheer.
- **9:10 p.m.** During a recess, no council members mingle with the public, which irritates several of those who are attending.
- **9:30 p.m.** The council votes 5-4 in favor of the smoking ban.
  There are both jeers and cheers.

A Sample Outline

You could begin at the beginning of the timeline given above, with the chamber filling with members of the public, but this lead would not attract much attention. You need a dramatic scene that captures emotion, is short and does not give away the outcome. The removal of a member of the audience has potential; so does the heated argument within the council. Here is a typical outline for a story using chronology:

1. The lead (the scene with Rodriguez).
2. The nut (theme) paragraph.
3. Foreshadowing.
4. A transition back to the beginning of the meeting to pick up the story from that point.
5. The body, highlighting key events found in the timeline. (As with any news story, much of the action is left out; this is a news story, not a secretary's report.)
6. An ending that highlights the vote and the audience reaction.

The Nut Paragraph, Foreshadowing and the "To Be Sure"

Like the lead in an inverted pyramid story, a **nut paragraph** (or *nut graf*) is a paragraph that gives the theme of the story and summarizes the key facts. Unlike the lead in the inverted pyramid format, however, the nut paragraph is not the first paragraph in the story. For the council story, after the first (or lead) paragraph describing the scene with Rodriguez, the nut paragraph might look like this:

> **In a meeting filled with emotional, sometimes angry testimony, citizens and the City Council debated the proposed smoking ban for nearly three hours. Citizens urged — sometimes threatened — council members. The mayor pounded his gavel to bring the council to order several times when some members engaged in heated, personal arguments. In the end, council members voted on the landmark legislation amid jeers and cheers and then left through a back door.**
>
> **From the beginning, it was clear that emotions were running high. . . .**

The nut paragraph both defines the story and foreshadows the heated debate. Even though readers will know the results, many will want to read the blow-by-blow account. It also establishes the "so what": This is a divisive issue, involving landmark legislation, which people care about. Notice that the last line, "From the beginning" creates a transition.

In some stories, you might also need to include a **"to be sure" paragraph**. This paragraph, which gives opposing points of view, is a must when you are focusing on one side of an issue. Before the council vote, you could do a story about a restaurant shift from the perspective of a server. You could follow that with a story from the perspective of a smoker at a bar. In both cases, you would include a paragraph acknowledging that others disagree, especially if that opposing viewpoint is not included elsewhere in the story. For instance:

> **Not everyone agrees with Megan Addison that smoking should be banned. Others, including smokers and business owners, believe that the proposal infringes on their right to smoke or to run their business as they please. But Addison and her fellow servers at the Sports Grill want to work in a smoke-free environment.**

You do not need a "to be sure" paragraph in the council meeting story because all sides are represented in the debate.

The Ending

In the council story, what was the final vote, and how did each council member vote? Readers read a chronology to the end because they want to see how the complications are resolved. For instance, you might be wondering about the outcome of the story introduced at the beginning of this chapter. You will find the rest of the story before you are done here.

News Narrative

In Chapter 8, you saw examples of inverted pyramid stories that didn't have the news in the first paragraph (see "The 'You' Lead" and "Leads with Flair"), but as soon as the writer teased the reader, the news lead appeared. Then the writer arranged the rest of the story in the traditional descending order of importance. Further modification, though, offers writers more choices. The **news narrative** structure combines the inverted pyramid and chronology. Here is an outline of its basic elements:

1. An opening with an interesting scene or twist that teases the story.
2. A traditional news lead.
3. Brief paragraphs that add whatever help readers need to understand the story summarized in the traditional lead.
4. A transition back to the beginning to tell the story in chronological order.

The "news" in "news narrative" implies that the story has a time element and that the story is not a feature. Features, sometimes called "soft stories," can run nearly any time and might be a profile of a stamp collector, a story on a volunteer at the local food bank or an article about riding with a police officer for a shift. A story with a time element usually has to be tweeted, posted on the web and broadcast on the next television news show or published in the next issue of the newspaper.

The "narrative" in "news narrative" means that you can use chronology, one of the most important tools of narrative writing. In the news narrative, you will often find other narrative tools, such as those discussed in Chapter 9: scenes, dialogue, anecdotes and sense of person.

News Narrative with News Emphasis

When the local Sheriff's Department broke an unusual burglary ring, Jane Meinhardt of the *St. Petersburg* (Florida) *Times* elected to use the news narrative structure. In the annotated model "News Narrative with News Emphasis" (Page 211), you can read her story, which follows the outline above. Notice that the story is a news narrative with news emphasis.

This format works well for news that is significant but not earth-shattering. You probably wouldn't use it to report during the first few hours or perhaps even the first couple of days after a major news event like a mass shooting. To relate the chronology, you need to be able to get all the details of how something happened. Immediately following a disaster or other major event, the authorities don't have all the information, and the reporter might not have access to witnesses or documents.

News Narrative with Narrative Emphasis

When the news is less important, the news narrative structure is also useful, but the emphasis is on narrative rather than news. John Tully, a reporter for the *Columbia Missourian*, was asked to look for a story at a horse-riding competition one Sunday

ANNOTATED MODEL News Narrative with News Emphasis

In news narratives with a news emphasis, the writer needs to establish the facts before giving the chronology. This format is associated with breaking news of significance, such as crime.

Source: Jane Meinhardt, "Mother Accused of Being Criminal Ringleader," *St. Petersburg Times*, Oct. 21, 1994.

PALM HARBOR—They carried knapsacks and bags to tote loot. They had a screwdriver to pry open doors and windows.

They used latex gloves.

They acted like professional criminals, but officials say they were teenage burglars coached and directed by a Palm Harbor woman whose son and daughter were part of her gang.

The opening paragraphs set the scene with information that informs and is interesting.

Pinellas County Sheriff's deputies arrested Rovana Sipe, two of her children and two other teens Wednesday after a series of home burglaries.

A traditional news lead gives "who," "what" and "when."

"She was the driver," said Sheriff's Sgt. Greg Tita. "She pointed out the houses. She's the one who said 'Do these.'"

The writer supports the lead with a quote.

Sipe, 38, of 2333 State Road 584, was charged with two counts of being a principal in burglary. She was held Thursday in lieu of $20,000 bail.

The story continues with the breaking news for the next four paragraphs.

Her daughter, Jackie Shifflet, 16, was charged with grand theft. Her son, Ryan Shifflet, 15, was charged with two counts of burglary.

Charles Ruhe, 17, of 1600 Ensley Ave., in Safety Harbor, and Charles Taylor, 16, of 348 Jeru Blvd. in Tarpon Springs, also were held on four counts of burglary each.

"They were very well-prepared to do burglaries, especially with the guidance they were given," Tita said. "We recovered thousands of dollars of stolen items. Anything that could be carried out, was."

The burglary ring unraveled Tuesday, Tita said. A Palm Harbor woman saw a large, yellow car driven by a woman drop off three boys, he said. The three went to the back of her house.

Now that the news has been established, the writer doesn't continue to present the information in order of importance but presents the rest of the story in chronological fashion. Note the important transition from inverted pyramid to chronology: "The burglary ring unraveled Tuesday, Tita said."

They put on gloves and started to pry open a window with a screwdriver, she said. When she tapped on a window, they ran.

She called 911. As she waited for deputies, other neighbors saw the boys walk through a nearby neighborhood carrying bags.

Deputies chased the boys and caught two. The third got into a large yellow car driven by a woman.

The bags contained jewelry, a shotgun and other items deputies say were taken from another house in the neighborhood.

Tita said the boys, later identified as Taylor and Ruhe, told detectives about other burglaries in Dunedin and Clearwater and who else was involved.

At Sipe's house, detectives found stolen VCRs, televisions, camcorders and other valuables. They arrested the other two teens and Sipe.

The story ends with a quote rather than a tie-back or summary.

"We're very familiar with this family and its criminal history," Tita said. "We have found stolen property at the house in the past and made juvenile arrests."

afternoon. Because most of the competitors were not from the newspaper's local area, reporting the results of the competition was not as important as finding a good story.

Tully knew nothing about horse-riding competitions, so he first found people who could explain the judging. He also asked people to suggest interesting competitors. A youth coordinator told him that Cara Walker was competing for the first time since her accident.

After gathering more information from the coordinator, Tully found Walker and her mother — and a story that lent itself to news narrative. Through Tully's story (see the annotated model "News Narrative with Narrative Emphasis" on page 213), readers learned that Walker, who had been seriously injured in a car accident, was able to recover enough to ride again. What they didn't find out until the end was that she won the competition.

Because he had less news to report, Tully was able to go to the chronological format more quickly than Meinhardt, who was reporting the newsier story about the burglary ring. Tully used the outcome of the competition to reward readers who completed the story.

Focus Structure

Applying the Focus Structure

- Focus on the individual.
- Transition to the larger issue.
- Report on the larger issue.
- Return to the opening focus.

For centuries, writers have used the focus structure to tell the story of an individual or a group that represents a bigger population. This approach allows the writer to make large institutions, complex issues and seven-digit numbers meaningful. Not many of us can understand — let alone explain — the marketing system for wheat, but we could more easily do so if we followed a crop of wheat from the time it was planted until a consumer bought a loaf of bread.

The Wall Street Journal knew that not many of us would be attracted to a story about the interaction between pesticides and prescription drugs. That's why a reporter focused on one person to tell a story of pesticide poisoning:

> **Thomas Latimer used to be a vigorous, athletic man, a successful petroleum engineer with a bright future.**
>
> **Then he mowed the lawn.**

Does this opening make you want to read on?

In a quip attributed to him, the Soviet dictator Josef Stalin summed up the impact of focusing on a part of the whole: "The death of one man is a tragedy; the death of millions is a statistic." Think about that the next time you hear that a plane crash killed 300 people. Some events, such as mass shootings or earthquakes, are horrific enough to attract attention in and of themselves. However, when readers have digested the news, you can reach them again by creating a narrative told through the eyes of participants.

ANNOTATED MODEL News Narrative with Narrative Emphasis

In news narratives with a narrative emphasis, less space is devoted to the news, and more narrative techniques are used than in the inverted pyramid format. These types of narratives use fewer quotes and save important information for a strong ending.

Source: John Tully, "Horse Power," *Columbia Missourian*, Nov. 27, 2006.

About five months ago, Cara Walker, 17, was lying in a hospital recovering from the spinal injury she received when she lost control of her car, rolled the vehicle and was thrown halfway through the side window.

Doctors weren't sure she would ever ride again. On Sunday, in a remarkable turnaround, Walker competed in the Midway Fall Classic Quarter Horse Show at the Midway Expo Center. The results were surprising.

The first two paragraphs reveal the news of the injury and the twist that even though doctors were unsure, Cara Walker recovered enough to compete. The horse show is the news event that generated the story. Note that the second paragraph reveals that she competed but only foreshadows how she did.

Last July, Walker, a junior at Rock Bridge High School, was taking a lunch break from riding in preparation for the Fort Worth Invitational, where she qualified in five events. Driving with three passengers on a back road near Moberly, she rolled her car at 50 mph where the paved road turned to gravel without warning. Walker was the only one not wearing a seat belt. Her head and upper body smashed through the side window.

"Last July" is the transition to chronology after the news lead.

Fortunately, she was still in her riding boots. Her spurs got caught on the bar under the seat, which Walker says may have saved her life.

Note that there are no quotes to break the narrative flow. "My spurs got caught on the bar under my seat" and "She first started walking, and going to the mailbox wore her out" (paragraph 8) are paraphrased to stay in storytelling mode.

At the time of the accident, Walker was nationally ranked in the trail-riding event.

Doctors fused her neck in surgery. During the next couple of weeks, she was able to shed her full upper-body cast. Walker returned home to her parents and twin sisters two days after surgery, but her mother, Jane Walker, said doctors told her to stay away from her sport for a few months until she healed.

This background helps establish that she isn't just any rider.

For Walker, the top all-around youth rider in Missouri and the president of the American Quarter Horse Youth Association, the four months following the accident was her first time away from riding.

After returning home she worked to regain strength and mobility from the accident that initially left her right side paralyzed. She walked short distances. Going to the mailbox at the end of the driveway wore her out, her mother recalls.

The story has a surprise ending, which is possible in a chronology. In a straight news story, this would have been the lead.

Walker had to work almost every muscle in her body back into shape. After the accident, the family brought her 10-year-old quarter horse to their barn in Columbia. That motivated Walker to at first walk to the barn and then to start caring for the horse and eventually ride again.

Sunday, the rehabilitation was complete. With ramrod posture and strict horse control, she won first place in the horsemanship class.

Writing the Lead

Issues like health care, budget deficits and taxes don't have much emotional appeal in the abstract. You make them relevant if you discuss the issue by focusing on someone affected by the issue.

For instance, the college student who wrote the following story spoke to Karen Elliott, who willingly told her story to help others with the same disease. The key word is "story." You write articles about diseases; you write stories about people. The lead paragraphs focus on one person in an anecdote that shows her as a character:

> **Karen Elliott, 44, remembers the phone call from Dr. Jonathen Roberts, a general surgeon, as if it had happened yesterday. Dr. Roberts' nurse called one afternoon two years ago and told Karen to hold the line. She froze. She had just had a biopsy on her right breast because of a new lump. It's never good news when the doctor calls at home. Dr. Roberts cut to the chase.**
>
> **"You have atypical hyperplasia," he said.**
>
> **Being a nurse, Karen knew exactly what he meant. No number of breast self-exams could have detected this. Atypical hyperplasia is a life-long condition characterized by abnormal cells. Affecting only 4 percent of the female population, it puts Karen and others at an increased risk for breast cancer. With her family history of the disease, her risk of breast cancer jumps sky-high.**

Reporters working on local stories have just as many opportunities to apply the focus structure as those writing national and international stories. For example, instead of keeping score on the United Way fund drive, focus on the people who will benefit—or will fail to benefit—from the campaign. If the streets in your city jar your teeth when you drive, write about the problem from the point of view of a driver. If a disease is killing the trees in your city, concentrate on a homeowner who has lost several. The focus structure offers the writer a powerful method of reducing institutions, statistics and cosmic issues to a level that readers can relate to and understand.

Advertising agencies use the technique, too. That's why instead of being solicited for money to help the poor and starving, you are asked to support one child for only pennies a day. The technique gives poverty and hunger a face. A starving population is an abstraction; one starving child is a tragedy.

Writing the Setup

After you've completed the opening, you finish the setup to the story. The **setup** consists of the transition to the nut paragraph, foreshadowing the "so what" and the "to be sure." Let's look at each of these elements.

The transition and the nut paragraph

When you open with a scene or an anecdote, you construct a transition that explicitly makes the connection to the nut, or theme, paragraph. "Explicitly" is the key word. If you fail to help readers understand the point of the opening, however interesting it is, you risk losing them. The transition in this example is in italics:

> **Anita Poore hit the rough pavement of the parking lot with a thud. She had never felt such intense, stabbing pain and could barely lift her heavy head. When she reached for the car door, a police officer stared at her and asked her husband, "Is she drunk?" A wave of nausea swept over her, and she vomited.**
>
> **"That's it. Get her out of here!" the officer demanded.**
>
> **Poore was not drunk. She avoided jail, but she faces a life sentence of pain.**
>
> **Now 25, she has suffered migraine headaches since she was in seventh grade.**
>
> ***Not that it is much comfort, but she's not alone.* Health officials estimate that Americans miss 157 million workdays a year because of migraines and spend more than $2 million a year on over-the-counter painkillers for migraine, tension and cluster headaches. Researchers haven't found a cure, but they have found methods to lessen the pain.**

The italicized transition explicitly places Anita Poore among those who miss work, buy painkillers and are waiting for a cure. The material that follows the transition is the theme.

Here's an example of a nut paragraph that follows an opening showing the subject tutoring students. In this one, there is a transition that also works as foreshadowing at the end:

> **She's 73 and has been teaching for 53 years. Lindquist supposedly works part time, but she doesn't plan on slowing down anytime soon. The Lord hasn't told her it's time to quit just yet.**
>
> **So she goes on, taking her therapy dogs to hospitals and rehab centers to see patients, crocheting afghans for those in nursing homes with no families, cooking meals for people she knows are going through a rough time.**
>
> **Lindquist is as reliable as the tides. Her faith gives her endless reserves of empathy. She offers herself as a crutch for those who need it. She cooks meals because it makes life just a smidge easier for others. She knows how gray life can be. *She's been there.***

Those last three words—"She's been there"—are the writer's promise that she will explain Lindquist's experience in a "gray life."

The nut paragraph, says Jacqui Banaszynski, Pulitzer Prize–winning writer, "is like a secret decoder ring—it lets the hapless reader know what your story is about and why they should read it." When you have involved the reader and successfully written the explicit transition to the nut paragraph, you are ready to build the rest of the setup.

Foreshadowing

Foreshadowing can be done in a single line: "The killing started early and ended late." Or you can foreshadow events over several paragraphs. The goal is to assure readers you will reward them if they continue reading.

Moviemakers tease you with the scenes they think will encourage you to buy a ticket. Broadcasters use foreshadowing to keep you from leaving during a

launchpadworks.com
WATCH: **"Narrowcasting in Magazines"**

- Which magazines are good examples of narrowcasting? Why? Do you consider these magazines successful?
- What role might service journalism play in niche publications?

commercial: "Coming up, there's a burglar prowling your neighborhood." Every lead foreshadows the story. The leads that not only tell but promise more good stuff to come are the most successful. Tom Koetting, then of *The Wichita* (Kansas) *Eagle*, spent nine months observing the recovery of a doctor who had nearly lost his life in a farm accident. He produced a story of about 100,000 words. The simple lead promised great things to come: "Daniel Calliendo Jr. had not expected to meet death this calmly."

In the next example, the long opening is packed with promises of great things to come:

> **Deena Borman's relationship with her roommate, Teresa, during her freshman year in college had shattered long before the wine bottle.**
>
> **Weeks had gone by with Teresa drawing further and further away from Deena. Finally, after repeatedly hearing Teresa talk about suicide, Deena says, "I kept telling her how silly she was to want to die."**
>
> **That made Teresa angry, so she threw a full wine bottle at Deena. It shattered against the wall and broke open the simmering conflict between them. That was when Deena tried to find out what had gone wrong with Teresa's life, and that was when Teresa told Deena that she wanted to do something to get rid of her.**
>
> **And that was when Deena began to be scared of her own roommate.**

The writer is promising a great story. What is wrong with Teresa? Does Teresa really try to hurt Deena? Does Deena really have something to be scared about? There is a promise of great things to come. Would you keep reading?

In the opening of the fire story we discussed in the beginning of the chapter, the foreshadowing is in the fact that although the character saved a row of houses, he wouldn't do it again. That foreshadows an as yet unknown complication.

The "so what"

The "so what" tells readers explicitly why they should care. Thomas Latimer was poisoned when he mowed his lawn. Anita Poore almost got arrested for having a migraine headache. Interesting, but so what? Reporters and editors know the "so what," or they wouldn't spend time on the story. Too often, however, they fail to tell it to readers. Latimer's story is interesting, but it's much more important because the writer added the "so what" (in italics):

> **The makers of the pesticide, diazinon, and of Tagamet firmly deny that their products had anything to do with Mr. Latimer's condition. The pesticide maker says he doesn't even believe he was exposed to its product. And in fact, Mr. Latimer lost a lawsuit he filed against the companies. Even so, the case intrigues scientists and regulators because it illustrates the need for better understanding of the complex interactions between such everyday chemicals as pesticides and prescription drugs.**
>
> **Neither the Food and Drug Administration nor the Environmental Protection Agency conducts routine tests for such interactions. Indeed, the EPA doesn't**

even evaluate the synergy of two or more pesticides commonly used together. "We have not developed ways to test any of that," says an EPA spokesman. "We don't know how to do it." And a new congressional report says the FDA lacks both the resources and the enforcement powers to protect Americans from all kinds of poisons.

The "so what" is the impact—the relevance—for people who have no warning that pesticides and prescription drugs may interact to poison them.

In other cases, the "so what" may be included in the theme statement. Let's look at the migraine story again:

Sentence 1: Not that it is much comfort, but she's not alone.

Sentence 2: Health officials estimate that Americans miss 157 million workdays a year because of migraines and spend more than $2 million a year on over-the-counter painkillers for migraine, tension and cluster headaches.

Sentence 3: Researchers haven't found a cure, but they have found methods to lessen the pain.

Sentence 1 is the transition. Sentence 2 is the "so what." The reporter is writing about Anita Poore, but the problem is widespread. Sentence 3 is the theme, which includes foreshadowing. The search for a cure and the intermediate discovery of ways to lessen the pain will be the focus of the story. The "so what" establishes the dimensions of the problem. When you define the "so what," you are establishing the story's impact.

The "to be sure"

To maintain an evenhanded approach, writers must acknowledge that there are two or more sides to a story. We call this the "to be sure," as in "to be sure, there are other opinions." We've seen in the pesticide story that the drug and pesticide makers "firmly deny that their products had anything to do with Mr. Latimer's condition." We see the technique again in an article about the impact of gambling on Tunica, Mississippi.

Writer Jenny Deam opens with a scene in the mayor's store. The mayor says gambling is the best thing that ever happened to the town. At the front counter, a woman is asking for the $85 back she paid on furniture last week because she lost her grocery money gambling. What comes next is a combination theme and "to be sure" statement, highlighted in italics:

And so is the paradox of this tiny Mississippi Delta county, now that the casinos have come to call.

On the one hand, unemployment in a place the Rev. Jesse Jackson once called "America's Ethiopia" has dropped from nearly 24 percent to a low last fall of 5 percent. Anyone who wants a job has one with the casinos. There are more jobs than people to fill them. In a county of about 8,100 people, the number of food stamp recipients fell from 4,218 before the casinos to 2,907 now.

But there is another side. New problems never before seen.

Types of Journalistic Writing

News Writing

- News stories emphasize facts and current events.
- Timeliness is especially important.
- Typical news stories cover government, politics, international events, disasters, crime, important breakthroughs in science and medicine, and sports.

Feature (Soft News) Writing

- Feature stories go into depth about a generally newsworthy situation or person.
- Timeliness is relevant but not critical.
- Typical feature stories are profiles, day-in-the-life stories, how-to stories, and background stories.

Now that you have constructed the setup, you are ready to enter the body of the story.

Writing the Body

Think of readers as people who are antsy to do something else. To maintain their interest, offer them frequent examples to support your main points. Use anecdotes, scenes and dialogue to move the story line. Mix *exposition* (the facts) with *narration* (the story line).

Let's look in on Karen Elliott, who just learned that she has atypical hyperplasia. The writer, Tina Smithers, has been dealing in exposition for a few paragraphs, so she shares an anecdote set in the following scene to keep the readers' interest:

> **Karen was walking downstairs to get the beach ball out of the summer box for Bethany's Hawaiian swim party at Kindercare. Suddenly, Karen fainted and fell down the stairs. She knew she had broken something. Coming to, she blindly made her way upstairs and lay on the bed.**
>
> **"The cat was staring me in the eyes," she mumbled as Bob, fresh from the shower, grabbed ice and a pillow.**
>
> **Karen noticed Bethany crying in the doorway. At this point, Karen realized she had been shouting, "Call 9-1-1! Call 9-1-1!" She didn't want her daughter to see her lose control.**
>
> **She quieted down and told Bethany to come to her bed.**
>
> **"It's okay, honey. Mommy broke her arm, but they'll be over soon to fix it." Later, in the ambulance, one of the paramedics tried to cut off her yellow Tommy Hilfiger sweater.**
>
> **"It's brand new," Karen shouted. "Can't you pull it off?"**
>
> **They gave one small yank, and Karen immediately changed her mind. Every bump along the way was agonizing. Karen pleaded for more morphine. Her wrist, it turned out, was broken in 20 places.**

Writing the Ending

As in the chronology structure, you need a strong ending in the focus structure. The difference is that in chronology, you end with the resolution or outcome. In the focus structure, one device is the **tie-back**, a reference to something that appears at or near the beginning of the story.

TIPS

Ending the Story

- Use anecdotes, dialogue, scenes and good quotes to end the story.
- Be sure the ending wraps up the whole story, not just the last section of the story.

Courtesy of Melissa Rawlins/ESPN Images.

ON THE JOB Know Where You Are Going

Seth Wickersham graduated in 2000 and headed to *ESPN The Magazine*, where he now is a senior writer. He shares a writing tip that works for him:

> I never outline stories. This is no doubt inefficient, but I believe that creative endeavors were never meant to be efficient. You ride the roller coaster of emotions that attend producing a magazine story, but it almost always gets to the right place, and the best version of the story that could be published is published. Tom Junod sums up his writing process this way: "I'm a genius, I'm shit, I'm a genius, I'm shit, I'm a genius, I survived." And that's the thing: You always survive.
>
> My wife, Alison Overholt, who's one of the most decorated editors-in-chief in the industry, always tells me that I have creative amnesia. All of the stress and panic and frustration dissipate forever upon publication. She's right, and while it's not something I've practiced, I'm grateful that it exists.
>
> Look, it's not easy to embrace the creative process and all of its messiness; it takes years of hard work and learning to understand what works for you. One of my sources of inspiration is the box set for Bruce Springsteen's *Darkness on the Edge of Town* album. In it, there's a replica notebook of all of the lyrics that he wrote for the record—and I do mean all. Rough drafts of songs went on for pages—the Boss might experience writer's block, but he refuses to suffer from it—and most of the lyrics were awkward and unusable . . . until he found the few lines that he could stand to sing, and he circled them and moved them over to a new song, and kept at it, and a spare collection of words and ideas that created a song emerged from the rubble. The result was not only one of his best and leanest records.
>
> It was also an endorsement and testament to the creative process. You can't wait for the right words. Sometimes, you've just gotta write and grind through it—to internalize your material, to find the right tone and voice, and yes, to experience the surprising turns the story might take. If I outline, I lose that last, vital part. I like the feeling of an open road—if I know where I'm going.
>
> That's why, while I don't outline, I do have to know exactly how the story ends before I write. The scene, the tone, the lasting lesson. If you've got an ending, you've got a story.

In this profile of a young gay man who performs as a drag queen, writer Kevin Dubouis starts as his subject enters the bar to prepare for his performance. Then he moves back in chronology to retrace his life. Notice that when Paul Reeves arrives at the club, the pronoun is masculine; when Reeves is in costume as a drag queen, the pronoun is feminine.

> **Paul Reeves hadn't been on stage in five months when he arrives at the relocated SoCo Club on a Friday mid-afternoon. He is carrying a large dark handbag and uses his other hand to roll a small wheel suitcase full of his persona's tricks. His gestures convey his excitement. Reeves doesn't know yet what he'll be wearing at night, but he has five hours to figure it out. His eyebrows are already covered with glue stick—just the first step in the long process of disguise.**
>
> **Reeves walks in and greets the staff members he knows.**
>
> **"He is a performer," the hostess says to the man who is standing by the large wooden door. "Let him in."**

The ending ties back to the beginning, where the performer arrived. Now, the performance is over. In between, we have learned about his life.

> **Reeves doesn't think about his future when he is Houston-Boheme. He enjoys the stage and his relationship with the audience. After five months off stage and an eating disorder that still haunts him, the night proved to be a well-deserved break.**
>
> **When the performance is over, Houston-Boheme gets off stage and meets with friends on the rooftop. "It was a good one," she thinks to herself, sipping another cocktail. At the last stroke of midnight, Houston-Boheme knows that she doesn't have to rush home like Cinderella. Now that society is becoming more tolerant and welcoming of her lifestyle, she knows that the magic she has on stage could follow her off-stage. Plus, she gets to keep the shoes.**

The goal in the focus structure is to summarize the theme of the story or tie back to the top of the story. Anecdotes, dialogue, scenes and good quotes can all end the story. Don't just stop writing; construct an ending.

Lizzie Johnson, whose story opens this chapter, went on to describe the quandary of her main character, Robert "Priest" Morgan. He had been a combat medic and a paramedic firefighter, among his many jobs. This day, when he decided that he needed to help rather than flee, he saved a woman in a wheelchair and was credited with saving 40 mobile homes by fighting the fire. So why is this hero struggling? Johnson explains:

> **Ten months later, the residents of those units he saved from the fire are stuck. Those who had insurance can't collect a settlement because the units are standing, and they can't go home because the land is condemned.**

Then Johnson shows Morgan's dilemma:

> **Here is the agony of doing right and then seeing it turned upside down. Morgan is consumed with guilt.**
>
> **"I don't know a single fireman that has ever regretted saving someone's house," he said, crying. "I feel like I should have minded my own business. It's been a thorn for me. The tears, that's not me. I'm a pretty bad-ass dude. But I've seen and suffered and hurt and anguished over this."**
>
> **And so Morgan thinks back to that night, over and over. He is in the truck speeding away, and he doesn't stop. He drives until the glow of Journey's End is a smudge on the dark horizon.**

Then, using a tieback to the opening, Johnson concludes:

> **What did God mean when he kicked Morgan awake? What was the right thing to do? Was there a right thing?**
>
> **"My main worry is one of them is going to die before they get their home back again," Morgan said. "And that's going to hurt. When you get that old, you don't have a whole lot. Your home is your safe place, your castle. And they don't have it."**

And that's the ending you were seeking after you read the opening.

Service Journalism

In Chapter 1, you read that one of the criteria for news is usefulness. Many, if not most, magazines you find on the racks appeal to readers by presenting information they might find useful. More than that, they attempt to present this useful information in the most usable way. This approach to presenting information has been called **service journalism**. You often see it labeled "news you can use." One way to think of this is "refrigerator journalism," information presented in such a way that people can cut it out and put it on their refrigerator or bulletin board. (See Figure 10.2.)

When a man shot and killed 58 people at a music festival in Las Vegas in October 2017, the local and national news media swung into action. Not only did journalists follow the police investigation, but they also told people how and where to donate, where and when vigils were being held, and how to help the victims' families. Readers and listeners could act on that type of information.

A pioneer in service journalism, former Meredith Corp. CEO James Autry liked to call service journalism "action journalism." Its goal is to get readers to use the information. Magazine publishers know that people are more likely to resubscribe to a magazine if they do some of the things the magazine suggests they do.

All media produce service journalism. Providing tips on how to save money on travel is service journalism. A recipe is service journalism. Telling people when and where an upcoming event is and how much tickets are is service journalism. Front-page news stories, too, often contain elements of service journalism, even if it's just a box listing a sequence of events or directing readers to more information. Service journalism is even easier to do on the web. You can provide links to lists, how-to information, time-date-place of events and relevant websites.

In this textbook, you see examples of service journalism in the marginal elements that list the learning objectives for each chapter or that highlight important points. The techniques of service journalism require that you think about content and presentation even as you are reporting.

Ask yourself, "What do readers need so they can act on this information?" The answer might range from a web address to a phone number to instructions on how to fix a lawnmower or make a loaf of bread. As these examples illustrate, you move from simply talking about something to providing the information the reader needs to act on your story.

Much of the basic service journalism information can be presented as sidebars or lists or boxed material. Figure 10.2 uses common service journalism devices to present more information about this topic. Figure 10.3 uses these devices in action.

FIGURE 10.2

Employing the common presentation devices of service journalism, such as boxes and sidebars, this example shows how to highlight information so readers can easily find it and use it.

Service Journalism

In today's digital world, in-a-hurry readers want practical information presented in the most efficient and effective way.

What this means is that you must think not just of a message—the words. You also must think of how those words will appear on the page or screen—the presentation.

Basics

Service journalism is:

- **Useful.** You must inform people, but if you also find ways to demonstrate how your audience can use the information, you will be more successful. Emphasize WIIFM: "What's in it for me?" See how often you can get "you" in the first sentence of your copy.

- **Usable.** Whenever you can, make a list. Lists get more attention and are better understood and more easily retained. You don't have to write sentences. "Tips" is a magical word.

- **Used.** People stop paying attention to information they never use. You should be able to prove that your audience acts on information. To get people to respond, promise them something. Offer a prize; give them something free.

Refrigerator Journalism

10 tips to serve audiences today

1. **Save them time.**
2. **Help them make more money, save money or get something free.**
3. **Address different levels of news interest.**
4. **Address niche audiences more effectively.**
5. **Become more personally useful.**
6. **Make information more immediately usable.**
7. **Become more accessible.** Give people your name, phone number, web address and email address.
8. **Become easier to use.** Learn to layer the news, use cross-references and links, put things in the same place, color-code, tell people where to find things, use page numbers on contents blurbs, use glossaries and show readers where to find more information.
9. **Make effective use of visuals and graphics.** Use photos, videos, slide presentations, interactive graphics, maps, cartoons, comics and other visuals.
10. **Become more engaging and interactive.** Use contests, quizzes, crosswords, games. People remember better if they do something. Give awards to those who send in answers. Give a coffee mug to the person with the best tip or post of the month.

Refrigerator journalism—giving people printouts they can post in a handy place—invites access and participation.

Other Devices of Service Journalism

1. Use blurbs. After a title and before the article begins, write a summary/contents/benefit blurb. David Ogilvy says no one will read the small type without knowing the benefit upfront. Use the same benefit blurb in a table of contents or menu or briefs column. The best word in a benefit blurb is "how." How to, how you, how I do something. Be personal. Use people in your messages. Also, use internal blurbs, little summaries, pull quotes and tips to tease and coax readers into the story.

2. Use subheads. Before you write, outline. Put the main points of the outline into the copy. Perhaps a better word than subhead is "entry point." Let readers enter the copy where they find something interesting.

3. Have a FAQ page or question-and-answer column. A Q&A format allows readers to skip over things they already know or are not interested in.

4. Repeat things in different ways for different people. Don't be afraid to say something in a box or a graphic that you have said elsewhere. Reinforcing a message aids retention.

5. Think more visually. Include pictures and graphics that contain information and are not purely decorative. Remember, being effective and efficient is the only thing that matters. We used to write articles and then look for graphics or photos to enhance the message. Now we put the information in the graphic (where it will get more attention and have more impact) and write a story to enhance the graphic.

"Never be above a gimmick."
—Dave Orman, ARCO

The power of the box

When you can, put some information in a box. Like lists, boxes or sidebars (1) get more attention, (2) increase comprehension, and (3) aid retention. On the web, these kinds of boxes can be linked from the main story:

1. **A reference box.** "For more information, see, read, call, click . . ."
2. **A note box.** Take notes from your articles as if you were studying for an exam. Give them to your readers to complement your message.
3. **A glossary box.** Put unfamiliar or technical terms in a glossary box. Use color or another graphic treatment to indicate which words are defined. Also, teach your audience how to pronounce difficult words.
4. **A bio box.** When you need to say something about where a person lived, went to school and worked, put this information in a box or on a separate linked web page so that your main story is not interrupted.

The 4 goals of the service journalist:

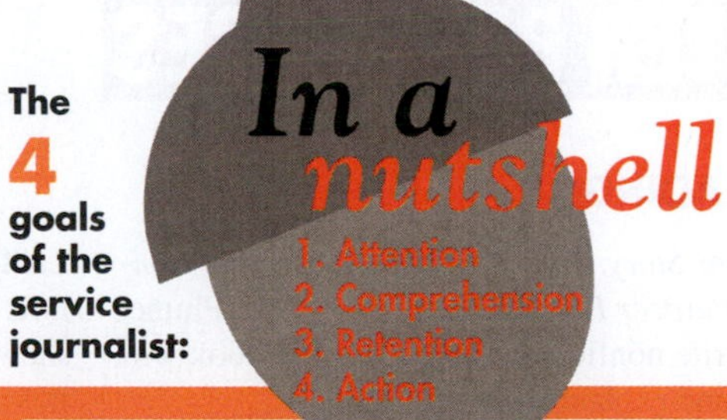

In a nutshell
1. Attention
2. Comprehension
3. Retention
4. Action

PR Tip

Newspapers, magazines, newsletters and websites are doing more and more service journalism. "News You Can Use" and "Tips & Tactics" have become familiar heads. Both newspapers and magazines are becoming more visual. Yet most news releases sent out by PR professionals look the same as they did five and 50 years ago. Why not try refrigerator journalism techniques in your next news release, whether it's sent by mail or digitally?

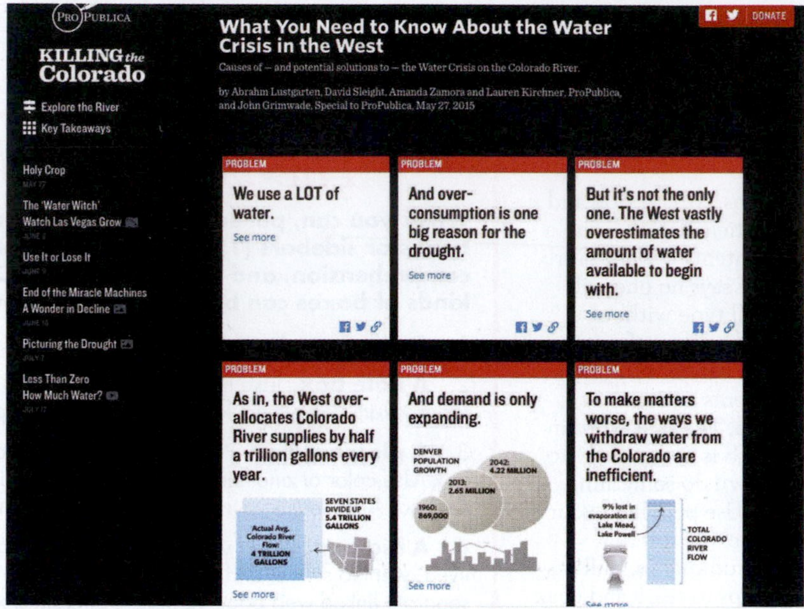

FIGURE 10.3 To break down the complex issue of water usage for readers, ProPublica used boxes to outline problems and solutions.

CHAPTER RESOURCES

SUGGESTED READINGS

Franklin, Jon. *Writing for Story: Craft Secrets of Dramatic Nonfiction by a Two-Time Pulitzer Prize Winner.* New York: Plume, 1994. If you want to write nonfiction narratives, this book will show you the structure and explain all the elements.

Harrington, Walt, and Mike Sager, eds. *Next Wave: America's New Generation of Great Literary Journalists.* The Sager Group at Smashwords, 2012. E-book. This is a collection of literary journalism written by authors under age 40. They are practicing what we describe in Chapters 9 and 10 of this textbook.

LaMott, Anne. *Bird by Bird: Some Instructions on Writing and Life.* New York: Anchor, 1995. LaMott, a best-selling author, shows you how to improve your writing and your life as a writer. It is a classic among writing books.

LaRocque, Paula. *The Book on Writing: The Ultimate Guide to Writing Well.* Oak Park, Ill.: Marion Street Press, 2003. This great book for new writers covers three main topics: mechanical and structural guidelines; creative elements of storytelling; and grammar, usage and punctuation.

SUGGESTED WEBSITES

LaunchPad Solo
launchpadworks.com
When you visit LaunchPad Solo for Journalism, you will find research links, exercises and LearningCurve adaptive quizzing to help you improve your grammar and AP style usage. In addition, the site's video collection hosts the videos highlighted in this and other chapters as well as additional clips of leading professionals discussing important media trends.

www.longreads.com
Longreads offers a selection of stories using the structures described in this chapter.

www.nytimes.com/2018/10/02/us/hurricane-florence-flooding-carolinas.html?action=click

Two weeks after Hurricane Florence, *The New York Times* took readers back to the Carolinas to show the impact of the flooding. The story is full of specific detail, scenes and beautiful phrasing.

www.sfchronicle.com/bayarea/article/Regret-haunts-Wine-Country-fire-hero-I-ve-13071356.php

Lizzi Johnson, whose story is featured in this chapter, is interviewed about the story. The link to the story is in the interview.

EXERCISES

1. From the first few paragraphs of the following story, identify the following:

   a. The nut paragraph.
   b. Foreshadowing.
   c. A sense of person.

   In a story full of sadness, that's another bitter truth. Her name suits her perfectly, summing up her innocence and kind nature. It's a refreshing name, one you don't hear often. But she is a foster child, and the state of Missouri asks us to protect the identities of foster children, so we cannot use her name here.

   So, for this story, she chose a different name: Ariana.

   Her dad lives somewhere in Mexico — not the one in Missouri — and he has never spoken to her. When she was born, he punched a wall in the Boone Hospital Center delivery room. Then, he rushed out. He wanted a boy. Soon afterward, he left the country.

   In the 14 years since, her family has been fractured in other ways. Ariana has five siblings: one older sister, two younger brothers and two younger sisters. Ariana's mom, whom we'll call Jane, lives about five hours away. Her mom's life is improving, but it's still nearly as messy now as it was in the early 2000s, when she was in and out of relationships and battling legal trouble. Her struggles hit their worst in July 2013, when the state took Ariana and one of her sisters, who chose the name Justice, away. Jane has lived without them for the past year and a half. The oldest sister ran away. Her mom still has custody of the other children. They weren't under her care when the state intervened on Ariana and her sister's behalf.

   Ariana and Justice are in limbo, stuck in the foster care system.

   But no matter how bad home was, Ariana still loves her mom and family. Because she loves them, she also suffers.

   Two years ago, when Ariana first came to Coyote Hill, a foster care facility in Harrisburg, she was a hopeless case. She fought every rule and quit in the face of every challenge at school. Then, last summer, she discovered horse riding and, from there, football, cheerleading, quiz bowl and competitive cheer. And she found hope. A girl who never attended school went from failing all her classes to earning A's and B's in her final semester at Harrisburg Middle School.

   She became a new person.

   Ariana has shoulder-length, naturally wavy dark brown hair and rosy cheeks. A seventh-grade boy has a crush on her, and she's not exactly sure what to do about that. She has a few crushes of her own, too, and she got to go to the Harrisburg Middle School dance this spring with one of them. Ariana giggles every time Justice brings that boy up — but, Ariana's quick to point out, Justice has a crush on that boy, too.

2. Christopher Soloman took readers to a sanctuary where bears live in the wild. Only 200 visitors a year, 10 at time, are allowed in and then only under the watchful eyes of a guide. Follow this link — https://www.hcn.org/issues/49.22/alaska-in-the-home-of-the-bear — to read the story. Why did he write it in the first person? What are the strengths and weaknesses of the approach? Which of the writing devices in this chapter are used to keep you reading?

3. **Your journalism blog.** Re-create a scene from one of your classes. For example, you could write about the first day of class or a time when an outside expert visited. Provide the transition into the body of the story, and then stop. Invite your classmates to comment on your story. How closely does it match their recollection of events?

4. Using a chronology, write about eight paragraphs of a story on an aspect of your experience in a journalism class.

5. Write a two- to four-paragraph "sense of person" description of a faculty member who is known to most in your class.

6. Write a two- to four-paragraph "sense of place" description about a location on your campus.

7. Find two examples of service journalism from newspapers, magazines or websites, and analyze them. Find an example of a story that would have benefited from service journalism techniques. Tell what you would have done to make the information more usable for readers.

8. Report on a live event while it is happening. Either tweet or blog short bursts at a time.

CHAPTER 11

WRITING FOR DIGITAL MEDIA

Photo credit: Win McNamee/Getty Images News/Getty Images

In this chapter, you will learn:

1 Why the web is a unique media form.

2 What readers expect from digital media.

3 How to write for the web.

4 How to write with search engines in mind.

5 How to write for blogs.

6 How to use social media.

On the morning of Sept. 27, 2018, when Christine Blasey Ford testified before the Senate Judiciary Committee that Supreme Court nominee Brett Kavanaugh sexually assaulted her when she was a teenager, many news organizations streamed the hearing live from their websites. Television news organizations, such as CNN, provided comprehensive coverage both on television and online. Coverage continued throughout that afternoon when Kavanaugh vehemently defended himself.

The next day, more coverage followed as the committee's Republican leadership forged ahead toward confirmation, ignoring Democrats' request for an FBI investigation of Ford's charges. Sen. Jeff Flake, an Arizona Republican who had been considered undecided about the confirmation, announced he intended to vote for Kavanagh.

Soon after Flake's announcement, CNN captured video footage of a woman confronting Flake in a Senate Office Building elevator as the door was held open. As a sexual assault survivor herself, she gave Flake an impassioned criticism of his decision. Flake, cornered in the elevator, seemed visibly moved. Minutes later, he told the Judiciary Committee of his decision to withhold his support for Kavanaugh on the Senate floor unless the FBI conducted an investigation limited to one week. Faced with insufficient votes to advance Kavanaugh's confirmation, Republicans agreed to a week's delay.

The news of the elevator confrontation and the accompanying video quickly spread online. Some thought the confrontation was the cause of Flake's reversal, and a subsequent *60 Minutes* interview with Flake on CBS confirmed that belief.

These compelling events all unfolded in just over 24 hours. Even though many Americans were at work and were unable to watch the day's events on television, many of them relied on online news media for information about the hearing. They received push alerts on their smartphones with key updates. They watched live streaming of the telecast and video highlights, including CNN's footage of Flake in the elevator. Dozens of stories, photos and links were posted online as soon as possible (see Figure 11.1). All this shows the power of online and mobile media during a breaking news story.

Later in this chapter, we'll focus on CNN to examine in more detail the increasingly sophisticated techniques employed in telling the story of the Kavanaugh hearing. But first, let's take a step back and explore how writing for the web and social media differs from writing for legacy media.

The Web as a Unique Media Form

When it first appeared, web journalism followed a familiar pattern established when radio began to yield to television. As television emerged as a major medium in the post–World War II era, news reports consisted almost entirely of someone sitting at a desk reading written-for-radio news. Many

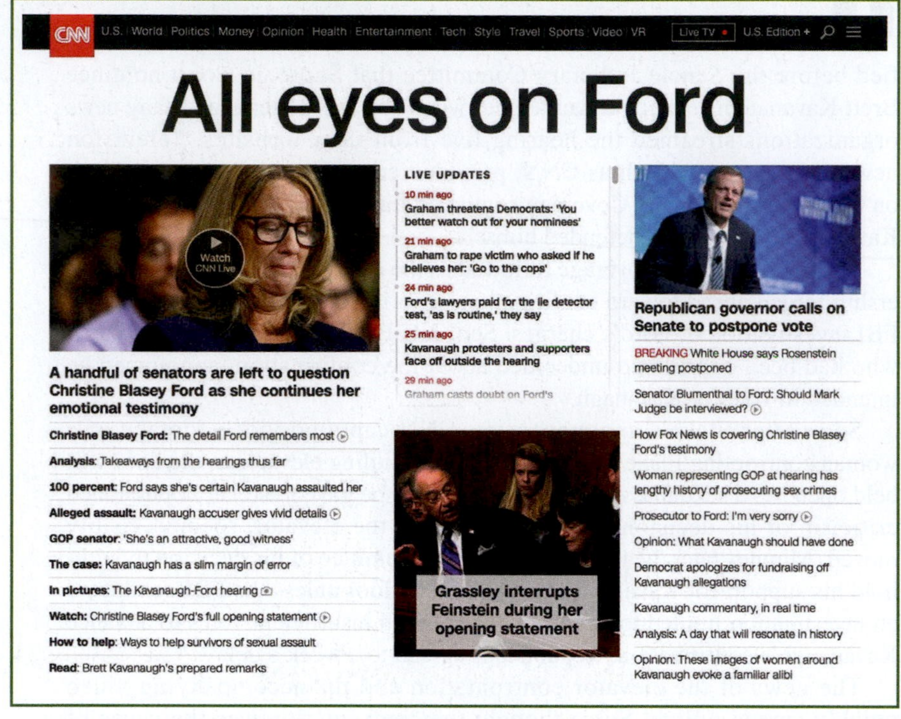

FIGURE 11.1

The CNN home page during Dr. Ford's testimony.

anchors came directly from newspapers, too, and didn't even have expertise in radio news writing. Similarly, when the internet appeared in the mid-1990s, media organizations quickly adopted this same pattern. Regurgitated news, written for traditional media and uploaded to the web, came to be known as **shovelware**. Sites operated by legacy media — newspapers, magazines, radio and television — contained little more than that morning's stories, which had already appeared in print or on the air.

As the internet matured, that began to change. News organizations started to write web-exclusive, or at least web-first, stories. Citizen journalism began to flourish and challenge the dominance of traditional media in disseminating news. Anyone, it seemed, could now become a journalist or even a publisher. Those developments slowly led editors and publishers to conclude that the web was an entirely new medium that demanded a fresh approach.

Most news consumers now receive news on their smartphones or wearables, like the Apple Watch. Others consume news on desktops, laptops or tablets. As we discussed in Chapter 2, these technologies put pressure on news disseminators to deliver breaking news instantly and in bursts, as CNN and other news media did during the Kavanaugh hearing. In addition, by linking to other content and sites within their own articles, reporters now provide users with not only text, photos and graphics but also audio and video that supplements and enhances their original coverage.

When the web first came along, no one knew how to make money with it, an essential ingredient in a country such as the U.S. in which most media are not state-supported. All that has changed. By 2020, online advertising revenue is expected to surpass television in total revenue. It already has become the fastest-growing medium for global advertising. No other medium in recent years has experienced revenue growth even approaching that.

Just as writing for television evolved from its early iterations, so, too, is writing for digital media evolving. The internet is a unique medium that requires a different approach, but that approach is still changing as journalists learn new ways to communicate online. Let's look at the latest techniques on writing for the web as practiced by some of America's top journalists. (See Figure 11.2 for a comparison of print and digital media news stories.)

FIGURE 11.2

Writing for digital media is different in many respects from writing for print newspapers.

Comparison of Print and Digital Media Stories

	Print Stories	Digital Media Stories
Audience	Communication is one-way: from writer to reader. All readers get the same stories.	Communication is two-way: Readers expect to be able to respond online through blogs, forums and so on. Readers customize their reading by specifying preferences and subscribing to newsletters that send coverage of interest straight to their inbox.
Structure	Inverted pyramid predominates, but writers use other structures, too. All of a news event is covered in one major story.	Inverted pyramid, with the key facts up front, is standard; use of suspense is rare. Coverage is layered so that readers can choose how much of a story to read.
Style	Writers sometimes use literary techniques to enhance stories. Stories are mostly written paragraphs with some breakers.	Readers expect stories to be straightforward, crisp and clear, without much use of literary techniques. Writers use a lot of bullets and lists. Editors use a variety of graphic techniques to help readers get the key news points quickly.
Length	Important stories may be lengthy to accommodate in-depth coverage.	Stories are usually short; additional info is "chunked" into linked sidebar stories that readers can click on if they want to know more.
Sidebars	Writers might add short sidebars on one aspect of a story; newspapers may print the text of a speech.	Stories provide links to past stories that are of possible interest and to information on other sites that readers might want.
Visual Appeal	Newspapers use photos, charts, graphs and drawings. Readers expect to see columns of print.	Websites use photos, charts, graphs and drawings, as well as audio, video and animation. Some animations may be interactive. Readers expect sites to be colorful, well-designed, interesting and easy to navigate.
Timeliness	Newspapers are published on a regular schedule, and writers have set deadlines for stories. Readers get news from one medium — the printed newspaper.	Websites are updated throughout the day, and breaking news is posted immediately. Readers get the news at any time on devices such as smartphones.

Readers' Expectations of Digital Media

Before you start to write for digital media, you need to understand readers' expectations of the medium. As a digital media consumer, you are likely already familiar with these expectations, but it is important to acknowledge what they are so you are equipped to begin your first job in writing for this medium.

Every company has a website and a variety of social media accounts. Print-only journalists are a disappearing species; journalists routinely turn in two versions of their stories, one for the newspaper and one for the paper's website. Broadcast journalists produce not only their television stories but also stories for the station website that more closely resemble newspaper stories.

There are still readers who want stories to appear as they are in the newspaper and not be rewritten in some other form. Those readers want to know what readers of the print edition are seeing. Some worldwide readers of *The New York Times*' online edition undoubtedly want to see exactly what the print readers of the New York, national and international editions have read. *The Times* and many other newspapers now produce web-based versions of all or part of their print editions that look exactly like or similar to the print edition. Many such newspapers are available on newspapers.ink. So there's a market for that. But most readers want stories tailored to take advantage of the web's considerable power.

To write effectively for the web, you need to learn a unique way of thinking about writing. Let's begin with these realities about the nature of the web and what readers expect online:

- Readers want the news right away.
- Readers want to have their say.
- Readers want multimedia variety.
- Readers want the news up front.
- Readers want to customize content.
- The audience is international.
- Structure is all-important.

Readers Want the News Right Away

At the *St. Paul Pioneer Press*, all print reporters must file a web story for TwinCities.com (see Figure 11.3) within 30 minutes after witnessing an event or learning about the news. Typically, this story is accompanied by Twitter news bulletins or Facebook posts designed to drive traffic to the story on the newspaper website. Other news sites have similar practices.

One of the first expectations of web-based journalism is immediacy. Years ago, newspapers printed several editions a day and occasionally came out with an

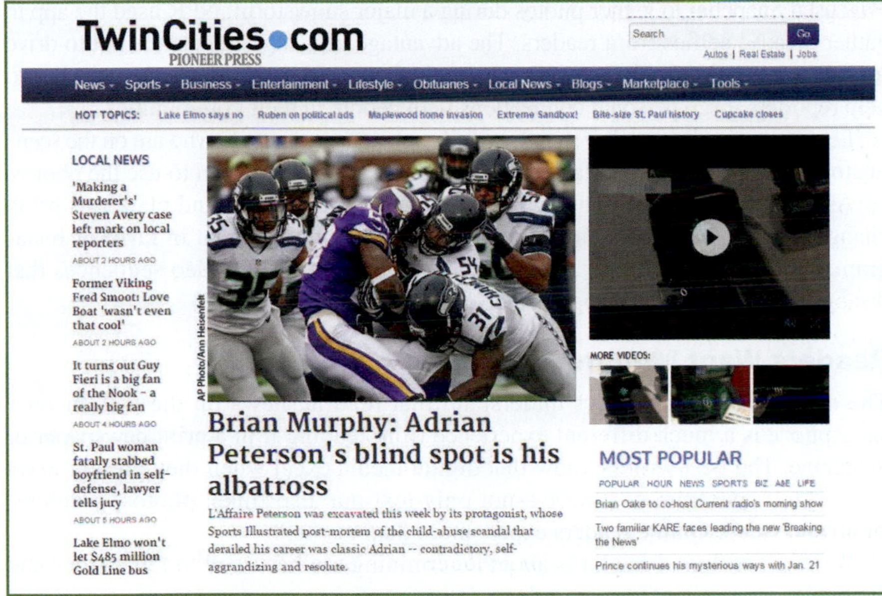

TwinCities.com
PIONEER PRESS

Search Go

Autos | Real Estate | Jobs

News - Sports - Business - Entertainment - Lifestyle - Obituaries - Local News - Blogs - Marketplace - Tools -

HOT TOPICS: Lake Elmo says no | Ruben on political ads | Maplewood home invasion | Extreme Sandbox! | Bite-size St. Paul history | Cupcake closes

LOCAL NEWS

'Making a Murderer's' Steven Avery case left mark on local reporters
ABOUT 2 HOURS AGO

Former Viking Fred Smoot: Love Boat 'wasn't even that cool'
ABOUT 2 HOURS AGO

It turns out Guy Fieri is a big fan of the Nook – a really big fan
ABOUT 4 HOURS AGO

St. Paul woman fatally stabbed boyfriend in self-defense, lawyer tells jury
ABOUT 5 HOURS AGO

Lake Elmo won't let $485 million Gold Line bus

AP Photo/Ann Heisenfelt

Brian Murphy: Adrian Peterson's blind spot is his albatross

L'Affaire Peterson was excavated this week by its protagonist, whose Sports Illustrated post-mortem of the child-abuse scandal that derailed his career was classic Adrian -- contradictory, self-aggrandizing and resolute.

MORE VIDEOS:

MOST POPULAR

POPULAR HOUR NEWS SPORTS BIZ A&E LIFE

Brian Oake to co-host Current radio's morning show

Two familiar KARE faces leading the new 'Breaking the News'

Prince continues his mysterious ways with Jan. 21

FIGURE 11.3

Reporters for the *St. Paul Pioneer Press* file their first stories for TwinCities.com, the newspaper's website and the site's smartphone app.

"extra." Today, newspapers are 24-hour news machines akin to the wire services, which compete with a swarm of emerging, web-only news outlets for the attention of their audience. Web-based journalism is all about getting out the story as quickly—and accurately—as possible. For today's journalist, the message is this: mobile and web first, print and broadcast second. Readers expect to get the news as soon as it breaks. In the view of most editors, however, speed is no excuse to sacrifice accuracy.

launchpadworks.com
WATCH: **"Going Viral: Political Campaigns and Videos"**

- Think of an example of a political video that went viral on the internet. What effect did the video have on events at the time?
- If video images have been important since 1960, is being able to share them on the internet really so significant? Explain.

Readers Want to Have Their Say

A major reason that readers are drawn to digital media is that they want to be active consumers of news, which for the most part is what digital media, as opposed to legacy media, offer. Many web users expect to be active participants in the discussion, proposing their own take on the news, arguing about the impact of the news with their peers and with writers, and perhaps even adding significant information or perspective to the discussion. Indeed, some readers want to provide content by sending in written accounts, photos or videos of things they have witnessed. **Citizen journalism**, also known as **user-generated content**, is alive and well.

The one-way communication paths of the past have given way to the two-way communication paths that the web and social media provide. One social media platform that news organizations use to build community is Snapchat, in which users send photos, videos, text and drawings to friends or acquaintances. *The Washington*

Post used Snapchat to gather photos during a major snowstorm; NPR used the app to gather creative selfies from readers. The advantage of using Snapchat is not to drive traffic to a website (which is the main goal of using Twitter and Facebook) but to help reporters forge personal connections with people in their communities.

Legacy media also monitor social media for photos from people who are on the scene of storms, disasters and similar events. They then seek permission to use the photos.

As with many things in the digital realm, new technologies and platforms bring change. Some users, for example, are now abandoning Snapchat in favor of Instagram Stories, a Snapchat-like feature that creates photo and video sequences that disappear 24 hours after being posted.

Readers Want Multimedia Variety

The most successful writers understand that reading news on the web or on a smartphone is a much different experience from reading it in a print newspaper or magazine. The best writers know that digital media excel when they present news using a full spectrum of assets—not only text but also links, photos, graphics, audio and video. Online readers expect more than just text.

Writing for digital media is about determining the best way to tell a story and then using a variety of media tools to deliver it. This requires an understanding of audio and video production, as well as the use of information graphics. *The New York Times* recognizes this and delivers an enormous amount of multimedia on its website. So, too, do ESPN, CNN and a host of local news sites.

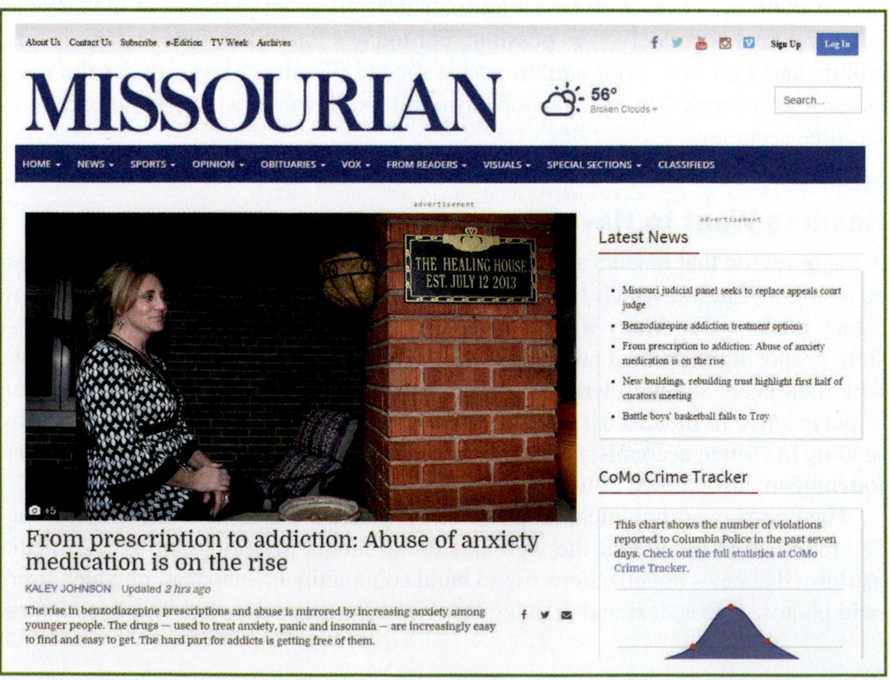

About Us Contact Us Subscribe e-Edition TV Week Archives Sign Up Log In

MISSOURIAN

56° Broken Clouds

Search...

HOME NEWS SPORTS OPINION OBITUARIES VOX FROM READERS VISUALS SPECIAL SECTIONS CLASSIFIEDS

advertisement

From prescription to addiction: Abuse of anxiety medication is on the rise

KALEY JOHNSON Updated *2 hrs ago*

The rise in benzodiazepine prescriptions and abuse is mirrored by increasing anxiety among younger people. The drugs — used to treat anxiety, panic and insomnia — are increasingly easy to find and easy to get. The hard part for addicts is getting free of them.

advertisement

Latest News

- Missouri judicial panel seeks to replace appeals court judge
- Benzodiazepine addiction treatment options
- From prescription to addiction: Abuse of anxiety medication is on the rise
- New buildings, rebuilding trust highlight first half of curators meeting
- Battle boys' basketball falls to Troy

CoMo Crime Tracker

This chart shows the number of violations reported to Columbia Police in the past seven days. Check out the full statistics at CoMo Crime Tracker.

FIGURE 11.4

The *Columbia Missourian* is one of many newspapers that publishes an online edition, updated 24/7.

Writing for the web also requires us to think about changes in the ways media messages are consumed. No longer is the web something you navigate only on a desktop or laptop computer. Today's readers use smartphones and tablets to consume news. Many media organizations have created applications for consuming news on those devices. Other organizations do not have mobile apps but have websites that are "mobile-friendly"—that is, when viewed on a mobile device, the websites display in a different layout that is ideal for small touchscreens.

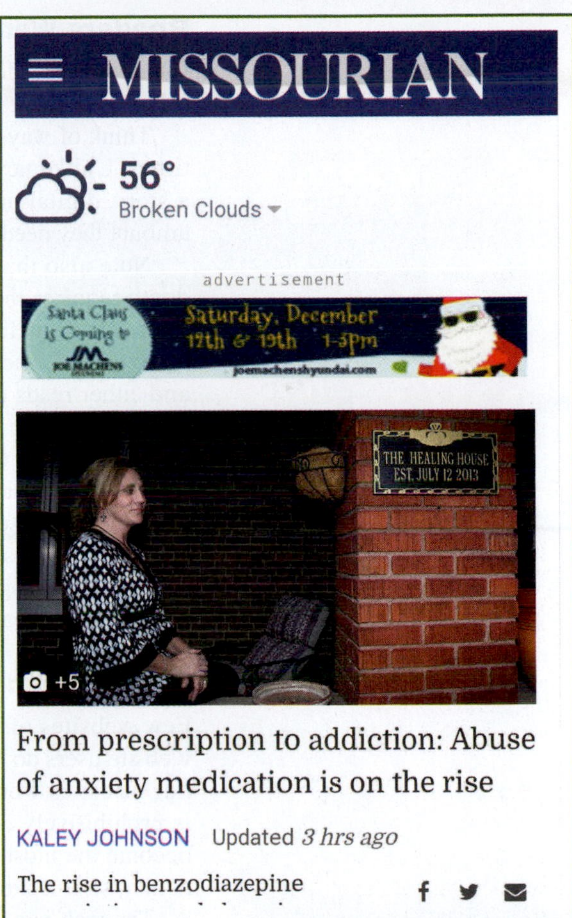

FIGURE 11.5

Viewed on a smartphone, the *Columbia Missourian* uses a layout designed for greater readability on mobile devices. This layout includes a menu button in the top left corner that users can tap to navigate easily to other areas of the site.

Readers Want the News Up Front

On occasion, print journalists writing for newspapers and magazines build a story with a suspenseful ending. Online news writers, however, should not try to withhold information until later in the story. When you're writing online, it's important to surrender control of the story's sequence to the reader. It's also important to remember that web users are surfers and don't remain in one place for long. Write as though you have your audience's attention for 30 seconds or less: If you have only 30 seconds, what you do you need to share with them in that time before they click away?

In Chapter 8, we introduced the most traditional news writing form, the inverted pyramid, which places the most important information in the first paragraph. That technique is exactly what's needed for most brief web stories because the lead is even more important in an online story than it is in print. It literally may be all that appears on the screen, and readers may have to click to get more of the story.

The lead is also important for some search engines, but it's likely that headlines, links within the text and metadata will be even more important for those searching for a story. Sometimes, the lead will be scanned as well, but don't count on it. It's smart to include keywords such as "Maine" and "governor" in the lead or headline of a story concerning the Maine governor to help interested readers find and select your story over others they find among their search results. But your headlines and leads should always be accurate and factual; avoid the temptation to turn them into "clickbait" to draw in your readers.

As we learned in Chapter 10, there is sometimes a place for writing formats other than the inverted pyramid. It would be difficult to argue that a superbly written eight-part series should be condensed for the web, but there are exceptions. Here's what we suggest: For most daily news stories, write briefly in the inverted pyramid format for the digital media. But don't be afraid to give online readers the full measure of your best newspaper or magazine writing—writing that takes advantage of the power of the web by adding multimedia and links, employing ample use of subheads and breaking the story into chunks.

Readers Want to Customize Content

Every reader is different and has different needs. Every reader, therefore, not only will select and choose what to read but also will choose a path that best meets those needs.

Think of ways to present different information for different people at different times. Unlike newspapers and magazines, which must decide how long to make a story, digital media should present information so that readers can choose the amount they need.

Note also that the online reader is active, not passive. Reading stories with depth requires the user to click from place to place, to launch videos, to explore photos and to click on photo galleries. Navigating a website is not linear, as is the reading of newspapers and magazines where a reader begins reading a story and either reads to the end or drops out. In a story with rich media offerings, the reader can jump to related stories, to previous stories on the same subject, to a photo gallery or to a video. The reader becomes much more actively engaged.

Even higher levels of engagement are possible on the web. Allowing users to navigate databases of property values allows them to compare their home values and taxes to those of their neighbors. Interactive maps allow users to see where crime is occurring in their communities. Such engagement makes the media organization more valuable to the reader's life and therefore builds loyalty to the website.

The Audience Is International

Few websites of U.S. media companies are bilingual or multilingual, but many website users do not speak English, Spanish or French as a first language. Ideally, our websites would be multilingual, but hiring a large translation staff usually is prohibitively costly. Fortunately for the English-speaking world, English has become the most commonly used language in international commerce and interaction, so if a site can have only one language, English is usually a safe choice.

The web is a worldwide medium, however, not a local one. Writers can help users around the world understand their content by using plain language and avoiding colloquialisms. Simple writing also allows international users to run a story through online translation programs, such as Google Translate, and make sense of it.

With the growth of Spanish as a second language in the U.S., news outlets need to consider providing content in that language. In the Southwestern states, doing so is already essential.

Structure Is All-Important: Layering and Chunking

Some who write online forget entirely about structure. That's a huge mistake. Even though web stories have a unique structure, they still must be organized in a logical, coherent way. Even though a story may appear on the screen as a mosaic, the way that mosaic is composed will attract readers, keep them and help them follow what for them is the most logical path.

Web writers should consider presenting information in layers (see the annotated model "Layering Content on the Web" later in this chapter). No two readers are alike. You can present the same information with different degrees of detail and support. Writing for the web in layers works like this:

Layer 1. Give readers one or two paragraphs — enough so they can understand the basic story. This first layer is information that is immediately available to readers. Little or no action or effort is demanded of them.

Layer 2. Provide a way for readers to click to continue reading the story. Alternatively, readers should be able to access more information by moving the cursor or by scrolling.

Layer 3. Provide links to earlier stories on the same subject or to related written material.

Layer 4. Use subheads to break up text into chunks, and make ample use of graphic devices such as **pull quotes** — quotations pulled from the text.

Layer 5. Complement the story with video, photos, graphics or audio, or make the video or photo the centerpiece of the story and subordinate the text. This layer may require readers to click on a link that opens up still more information — perhaps audio, video or a source document.

When you write for print, you are concerned with continuity, themes, the inclusion of all aspects of the story into the narrative, and keeping the writing clear and coherent. When you write for the web, you worry less about the structure or flow of the whole piece and more about the relationships of the layers and parts. It's all about understanding what readers want and helping them navigate from place to place to find the information they seek.

Sometimes you may want to take readers down a path that branches into several other paths, a technique called *threading*. The story of a plane crash can lead to various threads: the airline and its safety record, the plane itself and the record of that type of plane, the place of the accident, the people involved, and so forth.

Because most people don't think linearly, writing done for the digital media is more in line with the way people think. It's even more in line with the way today's readers read. For the web, break the story into short, digestible pieces.

The website of the BBC (bbc.com) tackles major international stories in a storytelling form known as **chunking**. Rather than presenting the news in column after column of unrelieved text, the BBC strings together a series of short stories all related to the same subject. The main story is followed by a series of brief related stories, which together give the reader a thorough picture of the event. Each has its own headline, which allows the reader to jump from one item to another in no particular sequence. Chunking gives readers more choices in how they read the story. Readers also can choose to read all the chunks sequentially, an approach that provides all the information a long newspaper-style story would.

A variety of design techniques can be used in creating chunks. In Figure 11.6 on page 236, take a look at some of the techniques CNN used on the web in its coverage of the Brett Kavanaugh hearing mentioned at the start of this chapter.

A Case Study: CNN Covers a Big Story

Over the last 20 years, many reporters and editors have learned that web content — particularly big stories or long stories — must differ from coverage provided in traditional media such as newspapers and television. Readers do not read web content the same way they read newspapers and magazines, and they do not watch the same way they watch television. The web is a distinctly new medium, and it deserves — even demands — a different kind of presentation.

A simple inverted pyramid format is ideal for brief stories that appear on the web. This format gives the readers what they want to know quickly and succinctly. But big stories demand a more complete treatment and some new presentation techniques.

In covering the Senate Judiciary Committee hearing to confirm Brett Kavanaugh to the U.S. Supreme Court in 2018, CNN editors understood how to present news online. In years past, most websites would have offered newspaper-like stories as their primary means of covering such an event. For big stories such as this one, however, CNN now rolls out news in chunks that provide readers with what they want to know about the event. What follows are some of the graphic techniques CNN employed in its website reporting.

The first (see Figure 11.6) is a video link to an important moment in the hearing. It employs a minimum of text and a key pull quote.

25 min ago

Chuck Grassley: The American Bar Association doesn't dictate this committee

Senate Judiciary Committee Chairman Chuck Grassley pushed back against a letter from the American Bar Association urging the Senate to delay a vote on Brett Kavanaugh until the FBI investigates the allegations against him.

Grassley said the ABA will not dictate how the Senate committee operates.

"The ABA is an outside organization, like any other that can send us letters and share their advice — but we're not going to let them dictate our committee's business," Grassley said.

Grassley also noted that the letter was written by the group's president.

"Tis letter is from the president of the ABA, one individual. He doesn't represent the hundreds of thousands of lawyers in the United States," he said.

Watch the moment:

FIGURE 11.6

Video of a key news snippet with minimal text and an attention-getting quote.

There were dozens of chunks like this one tied to video news highlights. Yet another kind of chunk involved was text only, but it summarized an important viewpoint from an anchor of rival Fox News and incorporated a key quotation (see Figure 11.7):

CNN also offered a list of related stories, one with a still photo of President Donald Trump's reaction to the allegations against Judge Kavanaugh.

CNN also compiled a lengthy list of video clips taken from its exhaustive television coverage.

If website users missed the televised hearing, they could click on any of the following video clips to see the highlights.

CNN is first and foremost a cable television news network, but its owners and editors are sophisticated enough to recognize that many Americans now get their news not just from the legacy media (newspapers, radio and television) but also from social media like Facebook and Twitter (see Figure 11.10). They are seeking to satisfy Americans' increasing penchant for receiving the latest news on social media.

With CNN's comprehensive coverage, there was something for everyone on its website.

17 min ago

Fox News host: "This is a disaster for the Republicans"

From CNN's Brian Stelter

The White House says President Donald Trump is watching Christine Blasey Ford's testimony. **If he is watching on his favorite network, Fox News, he may not like what he's hearing.**

Rather than defending Brett Kavanaugh at all costs, like the network's primetime hosts have been doing, Fox's daytime journalists and commentators highlighted Ford's credibility and humanity on display at Thursday's hearing.

"I think Dr. Ford is exceptionally credible," Fox's top legal analyst, Judge Andrew Napolitano, said.

"A lot of folks" are "viewing her as a very credible witness," Supreme Court correspondent and 11 p.m. anchor Shannon Bream said. After the first break at Thursday's hearing, "Fox News Sunday" moderator Chris Wallace said **"this is a disaster for the Republicans."**

Read more about Fox News' coverage here.

FIGURE 11.7

A text-only chunk from CNN's website.

MORE SUPREME COURT NEWS

Matt Damon plays angry Kavanaugh in 'SNL' open

Katie Couric on Kavanaugh-Ford coverage

What will FBI's new Kavanaugh probe include?

Kavanaugh hearing captures the nation's attention

GOP base rallies around Kavanaugh

SE Cupp: Be better than this

Trump mocks Feinstein about Ford's letter

Grassley refers false Kavanaugh allegation to FBI

Actress reacts to Ford, Kavanaugh hearing

Trump: Brett Kavanaugh has suffered

Does the law hear women?

Trump on Kavanaugh: I don't need a backup plan

Jeff Flake's moment: How a reliable conservative cast Kavanaugh's confirmation into doubt

Trump orders FBI probe into Kavanaugh; Senate vote delayed

Lawyer: Kavanaugh accuser cooperating with FBI

Flake: FBI report may change mind on Kavanaugh

FIGURE 11.9

Video highlights from the Kavanaugh confirmation hearing.

Mark Wilson/Getty Images

Trump calls Kavanaugh allegations 'a big, fat con job'

By Kevin Liptak, CNN

- Ginsburg expresses support for #MeToo movement ahead of Kavanaugh hearings
- 21 questions Brett Kavanaugh could face under oath
- Supreme Court is voters' most 'very important' issue
- Republicans and Democrats grapple with Kavanaugh political fallout 7 weeks from midterms
- How Brett Kavanaugh explains his baseball ticket debt
- Clarence Thomas takes jab at Cory Booker over 'Spartacus' comment
- Brett Kavanaugh in his own words: The CNN interviews

FIGURE 11.8

CNN's list of related stories.

CNN Politics @CNNPolitics · 4m

From bars to airplanes, Christine Blasey Ford and Brett Kavanaugh's hearing prompts tears, jeers and personal revelations cnn.it/2OmoRzh

Scott Olson/Getty Images

3 6 8

FIGURE 11.10

People watch Ford's testimony at a bar. This tweet was designed to alert people to the testimony and drive traffic to CNN's telecast or website.

ANNOTATED MODEL Layering Content on the Web

Readers click on a link on the home page or social media feed to get the full story and a photo.

Readers can click on links in the article's sidebar to view videos about other environment-related issues.

More links encourage readers to investigate additional articles on the *Miami Herald*'s website.

The article includes the author's email address so that readers can contact her with questions and comments.

Icons for Facebook, Twitter, email and other social media (including LinkedIn, Google+, Pinterest, and Reddit) allow readers to share and comment on the story.

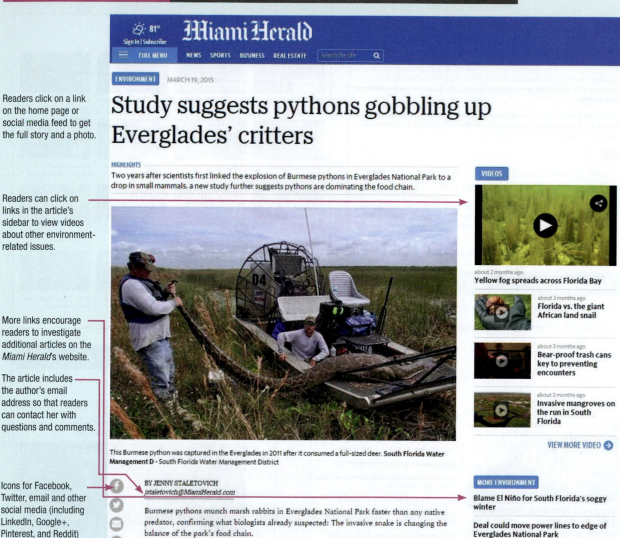

The *Miami Herald* uses layering to draw a reader into a story. Here, the photo and text are complemented by links to additional content.

Stories that require multiple continuous screens of unrelieved text turn off many readers immediately. Many readers hate to scroll on screen. Some exit even before they get to the bottom of the screen. Few will take the time to read a lot of text in one clump. This is not true of highly motivated readers who crave your information or sites like Slate, an online magazine where readers expect long-form stories. You need to know your audience and what your readers expect. In the following section, we'll help to raise your awareness of what readers expect by exploring how to write for the web while employing the best techniques developed by experts, researchers and media practitioners.

Guidelines for Writing and Designing for the Web

Newspaper and magazine editors have long understood that good graphic design helps to attract and hold readers. Readers gravitate to compelling photos and graphics, and well-written headlines give readers the gist of the news and help them decide which stories interest them.

But reading a newspaper or magazine in print is much different from reading it on a computer, tablet or smartphone screen. Researcher Jakob Nielsen found that reading online often does not follow the same left-to-right reading process you learned in school. Instead, readers often scan a web page in an F shape, which indicates online content is not read as thoroughly as print. Users scan across the top of the story, which becomes the F's top bar. Next, users scan down the page and read across in a second horizontal movement that is typically shorter than the first one. Finally, users scan the rest of the page in a vertical movement, completing the F's stem.

Nielsen's conclusion is that the first lines of text receive more gazes than subsequent lines of text on the same page and that the first few words of each line get more attention than subsequent words on the same line. Neilsen notes, however, that there are other scanning patterns:

- A *layer-cake pattern* in which eyes scan heads and subheads without reading the text below.
- A *spotted pattern* in which big chunks of text are skipped as if the reader is looking for something else.
- A *marking pattern* in which the eyes focus on one part of the text as the mouse or finger is used to scroll the text.
- A *bypassing pattern* when people deliberately skip the first words of a line when multiple lines of the text all start with the same words.
- A *commitment pattern* in which people fixate on almost everything on the page. This is rare and is found only when an article is of intense interest to the reader.

Other findings of note regarding how users read on the web include these:

- Nielsen found that readers read only about 20 percent of the text on an average page and spend 69 percent of their time viewing the left half of the page and only 30 percent on the right half.
- Nielsen also found that web users spend 80 percent of their time looking at information above any point where scrolling is required. Thus, brief pages that don't require scrolling are preferred. When longer stories are involved, employing lots of subheads and other graphic devices will help keep readers engaged. In other words, provide the information using layers or chunks.
- According to Chartbeat.com, a web analytics company, 55 percent of page views get only 15 seconds or less of attention.
- About 20 years ago, Nielsen found that it takes 25 percent longer to read online than it does to read on paper. In a recent study, ResearchGate confirmed that result with an estimate of 20 to 30 percent longer.

Some research on web readership consumption is detailed and perhaps not terribly useful to journalists. For example, according to Eyethink.org, which uses eye-tracking technology to observe how readers process writing on the web, the chances that words will be processed by the brain varies greatly depending on whether they are **function words** (like prepositions, articles and conjunctions) or **content words** (including nouns, verbs and adjectives). Content words can normally stand alone; function words cannot. Eighty-five percent of content words and only 35 percent of function words are processed. Because both are useful—even necessary—in journalistic writing, this fact may be interesting but not useful.

What this does show, however, is that news consumers on the web in many cases are scanners, not readers. Although research is not always useful in a production setting, it's important to have as much knowledge as possible about how people are likely to read your website.

With that background in mind, here are some suggestions for writing stories for the web that will compel people to read.

Think Immediacy

As we emphasize throughout this book, speed in handling breaking news is essential. Keeping readers with you means keeping them up-to-the-minute. You must expect to update breaking stories quickly and to add depth whenever it is available. But just because you can easily correct your mistakes does not mean you are allowed to make them. Posting news too quickly could sacrifice quality and damage credibility. Let readers know when you're working to confirm information.

Save Readers Time

Readers' time is finite and, therefore, precious. Whatever you can do to save time for readers is worth *your* time. For many if not most stories, perhaps your chief concern should be this: Have I presented this information in a way that costs readers the least amount of time?

The best way to save readers time is to be clear. Choose the simple word. Vary the length of sentences, but keep them short. Write short paragraphs. Help readers. Perhaps even emphasize key words by highlighting them.

Another reason to use simple words and simple sentences is to enable automated translation programs to translate the text. The simpler the words and sentences, the more likely it is that a foreign-language translation of the story will be accurate and understandable.

Provide Information That's Quick and Easy to Get

The organization of your story must show readers they can get information quickly and easily. Digital media readers have zero tolerance for confusion and no time to be led astray. It's too easy for them to click on something else.

Don't get carried away by your own eloquence. Be guided by what your readers want or need to know. Make it easy for them.

Think Both Verbally and Visually

In the past, writers for print thought little about how their stories were going to appear. Their job was to write the story — period. The designer's job was to make the story fit on the page in a meaningful way. Writers usually did not worry about headlines, subheads, summary quotes, photos, illustrations or anything but the story.

Television news writers know that they must write to the video. Good television has good video, so the visual medium tries to show rather than to tell. Words complement pictures and say what the pictures do not. Sometimes the writer does not make the pictures and is not responsible for getting them, but today's newspaper writers use smartphones and must be prepared to take photos and video or record soundbites if no visual specialist accompanies them. Regardless, the writer still must consider the best way to tell the story, and sometimes visuals convey the story as no amount of text could possibly do.

As a web journalist, you may or may not have to do it all by yourself, but you definitely must *think* both verbally and visually. From the outset, you must be concerned about the most effective and efficient way for the information to appear on the screen. You have to think about how to organize the material, use graphics and audio, be interactive and use online tools.

No one doubts that photos and graphics grab readers' attention. That's why you see icons and information graphics in magazines and newspapers, and that's why you must think, perhaps with the help of graphic designers, of ways to use graphic elements online.

Cut Your Copy

Many digital media consumers simply will not read long stories. In many cases, the best idea for most stories is to get the whole story on one screen. We advise writing no more than 20 lines of text to accommodate small screens. Fortunately, computer

Web Writing Guidelines in a Nutshell

- Get the news online fast.
- Write shorter stories, with subheads if necessary.
- Use sidebars to keep the main story short.
- Include keywords in your lead or introductory blurb.
- Add links, still photographs and video.
- Design a visually appealing and well-organized package.
- Use social media to drive traffic to the website.

programmers are increasingly adept at optimizing web content for screens of varied sizes, from desktop monitors to smartphones, so readers are finding it easier and less frustrating to scroll for more information.

Still, as in broadcast news writing, there's little room online to be cute or even literary. When writing for the web, your goal should always be to create something that is crisp and clear.

Use Lots of Lists and Bullets

In a now-classic study, researcher Jakob Nielsen tested five versions of the same information for usability. He concluded that web pages are most readable when they contain, among other features, bulleted lists. Often you can cut copy by putting information into lists. Whenever possible, make a list. Lists get more attention and allow for better comprehension and more retention than ordinary sentences and paragraphs. (The web-friendly memo-structure story format, illustrated in Chapter 8, has listlike features.)

An entire article structured like a list is sometimes called a **listicle**. When BuzzFeed emerged, most of its content followed a listicle structure because bulleted or numbered lists are scannable and readers can grasp them immediately. Think of information on the web as a database. That's how people use their digital media.

Mark Deuze and Christina Dimoudi of the Amsterdam School of Communications Research conclude in a study that web-based journalism is really a fourth kind of journalism after print, radio and television. They say its main characteristic is "empowering audiences as active participants in the daily news." Web journalists have "an interactive relationship with their audience" and a "strong element of audience orientation" and are "more aware of their publics and service function in society than their colleagues elsewhere."

Write in Chunks

When you can't put material into lists, you can still organize it into chunks of information, as CNN and the BBC do so well. At least put information into sidebars or boxes. Readers will read more, not less, if you break up the information into small bites. Research has also shown that putting some information in a sidebar can give readers better comprehension of the subject. But the main objective here is to write for diverse readers. You don't necessarily know what they want or in what order. Let them decide; they will anyway.

Think of your story as having parts. When writing a story for a newspaper, you need to think of ways to join the various parts of the story. You craft transitions carefully, and you may even add subheads. When writing a story for the digital media, use subheads if necessary. Again, remember the importance of a strong lead in the inverted pyramid form.

Producing Video for the Web

Website users expect multimedia presentation of news, particularly in the case of important news stories. Many web producers are relatively new to video production and editing, so here are some tips for beginners:

- Get instruction from someone who has professional video production skills. You can learn a lot in a day or two.
- Be prepared to go live on television or on streaming video. Today, anchors often cut directly to reporters — even print reporters — to discuss a story. Live video from breaking news events is now an integral part of a publication's video strategy.
- Use good equipment. You won't need cameras and microphones that are capable of producing a Hollywood movie or a CNN broadcast, but the quality of the equipment is still important. Most of today's smartphones shoot video of publishable quality, so quality is easily accessible and most likely already in your hands.
- Eliminate background noise as much as possible. Some naturally occurring background sound is good for an on-site video, but don't record in an atmosphere where the background noise will drown out your message.
- Use digital compression rates that are optimized for the web. Your supervisor or technical support personnel can provide guidelines for specifications expected at your website.
- Employ search-engine optimization techniques so that your video can be found on the web. Use important keywords in headlines, in metadata and even in the name of the file itself.
- Use video to complement other material on your site. Video is best used in conjunction with text, photos, information graphics, links and other material.
- Keep on-demand videos short, no more than two to three minutes. Remember, your audience's time is finite.
- Engage audiences through the use of live video on your website and on social-media platforms. Audiences are eager for live updates during breaking news and will usually participate in talkback interviews with your reporters and editors.
- Brand your videos with your logo, and make it easy for social media users to link to them. Facebook, Twitter, Instagram and other social media networks can drive plenty of traffic to your video and consequently to your website.
- Consider allowing users to rate your video. This, too, can drive more users to the video and to your site.

Use Links

Users of the internet like to feel connected. If you want them to read your copy and come back for more, you must satisfy and enhance that sense of connection. Researcher Jakob Nielsen says that websites must employ scannable text using these elements:

- Highlighted key words, including links.
- Meaningful subheads.
- Bulleted lists.
- One idea per paragraph.
- Half the word count of writing for print.

Being connected means being interactive. Web users want to be actively involved in what they are reading. They are not passive observers. Like video game players, they want to be in control of where they are going and how they get there. Both individual stories and whole pages must be internally and externally interactive.

Internal connections

The most challenging and necessary aspect of writing for the web is making the copy interactive. You begin that process by streamlining your copy and not including everything. Create links that allow readers to access other information on your site, earlier stories on the same subject or even information on another site.

One of the most perplexing problems writers face is deciding when to include the definition of a word. Will you insult some readers by defining a term they know? Will you leave others behind if you do not define the term? A similar problem is whether to tell who a person is. Many readers may wonder how stupid you think they are for telling them that actor Arnold Schwarzenegger once was the Republican governor of California. Other readers may need or want that information.

The web writer can make the word or name a link to a different page so that readers can click on a linked word to find its meaning or read more about it. No longer do writers have to write, "For more information, see. . . ." Academic writers use footnotes. Using **hyperlinks** in the form of **hypertext** linking (which connects readers directly to text) and **hypermedia** linking (which connects them to audio, video and pictures) is much more convenient.

Other techniques can also save space while reducing visual clutter on the screen. Some sites display information only when an interested reader rolls the cursor over an item on the page.

Writing concisely has never been easier. You can stick to the essentials and link to the rest. A story about a homicide can link to a map of where the crime took place, to a chart showing the number of homicides this year compared with last year, to a piece about friends of the victim, to information about violent crimes nationally, and so forth.

Remember, too, that unlike the newspaper, where you may be short of space, and unlike radio and television, where you may be short of time, online you have unlimited space and time to run photos and aspects of stories that could be of real interest to some readers. Sports fans, for example, would probably enjoy seeing a gallery of photos from Saturday's championship game and reading or watching interviews with the stars of the game.

External connections

Don't forget the power of links to different websites. Academic writers include bibliographies. Print journalists often identify sources in their stories. Lazy writers seem to say to readers: "That's all I know about the subject, and I'm not going to tell you where I obtained my information or where you can find more information." Readers now expect links to source material, and you should provide them when writing for the digital media.

You are not expected to lead readers away from your site to a competitor's, especially on a breaking story. Nevertheless, readers will come to rely on your site to help them find more information about subjects that interest them greatly.

The New York Times website made effective use of an external link when it reported on the death of singer Scott Weiland of the band Stone Temple Pilots. It provided a link to YouTube videos of several of Weiland's hit songs, including "Plush" and "Creep." Even those not familiar with his music were able to hear a sample of his talent.

To find appropriate external links, use search engines like Google, Bing and Yahoo Search. Google News is a master of providing links for readers to explore. In addition, consider embedding video links into your story.

Give Readers a Chance to Talk Back

A big part of providing interactive content is allowing readers to comment. The web has leveled the playing field. Everyone can be an owner or a publisher. Some members of the audience feel the right, and often the need, to talk back—if not to the writer of the piece, then to other readers in blogs or simply in the comments section at the end of a story.

The wonderful thing about allowing readers to talk back is that they do. When they do, they will revisit the site again and again. Web readers want to be part of the process. Readers love it when newspapers like the *Miami Herald* include the reporter's email address or Twitter handle in the byline, and many of them respond.

Never has it been easier to find out what is on the minds of your readers. Print and broadcast have mainly been forms of one-way communication. Now, you can get opinions easily and quickly and incorporate them into your story or include links to them. Letters to the editor have always been among the best-read sections in newspapers and magazines. Many readers, especially those reading on the web, want to express their own opinions and love to read the opinions of others. When you publish others' remarks on your website, you should use the same strict standards that you use for publishing in your newspaper or magazine. Even online polls can and have been flooded by advocacy groups. Reporting their results can be meaningless, misleading and certainly unprofessional unless the polls are monitored carefully.

Writing with Search Engines in Mind

It's almost impossible to overemphasize one major consideration in writing for the digital media: If your online story cannot be found, it won't be read. That's why editors of websites emphasize **search-engine optimization (SEO)**—the process of making sure your story will be found when someone searches for its topic on sites such as Google, Bing or Yahoo Search. Generally, putting keywords into the headline increases the likelihood that your story will appear near the top of the search results for that topic.

In fact, search engines tend to rank a story higher if the keywords are repeated in both the headline and the first couple of paragraphs—something newspaper and magazine editors often try to avoid. How does this work with a story in which the lead was not written with SEO in mind? A good solution is to place a summary blurb at the top of the web story for indexing purposes.

Another way to accomplish the same thing is to craft a lead in the form of an extended headline, followed by two or three statements that also read as headlines. If you link the headlines, readers can click on them to read the full version of the story on another page within the website.

Newspapers and magazines are notorious for writing baseball stories that never mention the word "baseball" and hockey stories that never use the word "hockey." That's not a problem if users search for the team name, such as "Atlanta Braves." They'll find your story even if it doesn't include the word "baseball." But what if users search for "baseball"? Your story will not be found unless it contains metadata—that is, tagging information—that includes that search term. Understanding how search engines work is the key to making sure that all possible search terms appear either in the metadata accompanying the story or in the story itself.

Making these search-engine changes may require some extra attention at outlets that try not to repeat words in the headline and lead. But many websites have protocols for ensuring that the proper keywords are used, and several companies now offer services that ensure content is optimized for search engines. These services can be a wise investment for any site looking to increase its readership.

Writing for Blogs

Media organizations use blogs as a great way to allow users to interact with reporters, columnists and even guest writers who don't work for the company. Blogs are analogous to newspaper editorials and columns in many ways because they sometimes allow the writer to express opinions. But unlike those traditional forms of persuasive writing, blogs give readers the chance to answer back and even engage in online discussions with the writer.

Blog entries range from short, inverted pyramid stories that are written quickly by beat reporters to longer essays. Whereas traditional journalism is formal, blogging can be informal. Whereas traditional journalism is dispassionate, much of blogging might be passionate. Whereas traditional journalism is third person (*he*, *she*, *they*), much of blogging might be first person (*I*, *we*). Whereas much of traditional writing is edited by editors, much of blogging is posted without second-party editing.

Wide-Ranging Subject Matter

Political and sports bloggers capture a disproportionate amount of attention, but respected bloggers—some of them independent, many of them working for startups or the traditional media—blog on everything from travel to technology. Even some heads of companies are blogging, and public relations professionals are doing it on behalf of their companies or organizations.

The best blogs are conversational, based in specifics, and full of comparisons, explanations, turns of phrase and links. Although some web writers do not distinguish between fact and fiction, professional journalists must be meticulous about the facts in their blogs. Here are two examples of good blogging.

This excerpt from a blog about women's networking is from the excellent HuffPost blog section. Eleanor Beaton presents facts to back up her opinion that a sports background is beneficial to a woman's career. Notice the reference to Beaton's source material:

> **Research conducted by Ernst & Young and the sports network ESPNW showed a clear correlation between a woman's background in sport and her career potential. Just three percent of the global senior women executives surveyed who occupied c-suite jobs had not played competitive sports.**

The citation of a study conducted by the accounting firm Ernst & Young, which links to the actual report, adds credibility to the blog. Good bloggers in the journalism arena back up their opinions with facts.

Many blogs help readers with popular subjects such as parenting or personal development. Here's an excerpt from "The Art of Manliness," an award-winning blog that in some ways is written like a newspaper column but is based on plenty of research. Here's how one entry begins:

> **Do you sometimes feel like you spend all your time managing crises? That your life is basically spent putting out one proverbial fire after another?**
>
> **At the end of the day do you feel completely sapped and drained of energy, and yet can't point to anything you accomplished of real significance?**
>
> **Yes?**
>
> **Then you, my friend, are probably confusing the urgent with the important.**
>
> **We've talked before about the many leadership lessons that can be gleaned from the life of Dwight D. Eisenhower. Today we're going to talk about another—a principle that guided him through his entire, hugely successful career as general and president:**
>
> **"What is important is seldom urgent and what is urgent is seldom important."**

In this case, the blog gives a link to an earlier blog post mentioned in the current post.

Great blog examples can be found in many places, not just on the sites of newspapers and other traditional media organizations. But wherever they are found, if blogs are to have credibility, they must be fact-based.

Professional Standards in Blogs

Dan Steinberg, who is a full-time sports blogger for *The Washington Post*, has two gripes about blogs. In an interview with Gelf magazine (gelfmagazine.com), he says bloggers shouldn't steal good stuff from journalists who are doing the reporting. He also chafes at the traditional restrictions of taste imposed on him by his newspaper. Steinberg, a former beat reporter, spends a lot of time in locker rooms. He would like to reflect some of the off-color talk he hears there, but his editors impose the same standards on his blog as they do on the rest of the paper.

launchpadworks.com
WATCH: **"Net Neutrality"**

- Why do some people believe net neutrality is important? What are the arguments against net neutrality?
- Do you support net neutrality? Explain.

What's the grammar error in this sentence?

In September 2015, Russia deployed half a dozen tanks and 35 armored carriers to Syria in a move to build up their military presence in the region.

See Appendix 1, Rule 14.

Other bloggers have more freedom. Most are beat reporters who drop news tidbits or humorous observations into a blog about their beats. *The New York Times*, for instance, offers more than 60 blogs, all written by staff writers or columnists. Some bloggers are primarily mini-aggregators. They monitor the web for news of whatever specialty they cover and provide the links for readers. From bursts to full-blown essays, bloggers use a variety of writing styles. There may not be rules or even best practices for bloggers, but there are two worthwhile guidelines: Be interesting, and be accurate.

There are far more bloggers who don't write for media outlets than do write for them. But when bloggers work for media companies, they can expect at least some limitations to be placed on them. When media branding is involved, it's important to retain some semblance of journalistic ethics and responsibility.

The Role of Social Media

Earlier in this chapter, we learned of the tremendous power of the web and social media to assist professional journalists in reporting the news. (Figure 11.11 shows a tweet that alerts a newspaper's readers to an important story.) Citizen journalists armed with mobile phones have become significant contributors to our understanding of the news. But in the hands of biased or unscrupulous people, those tools can be a vehicle for disinformation as well as information.

Verifying Information

As a journalist, your challenge is to embrace audience participation in the news-gathering process while remaining ever skeptical of information provided by others. Our advice is to treat Facebook, Instagram, Twitter and other social media posts as tips, not facts. Find ways to verify the information independently (https://www.poynter.org/news/10-tips-verifying-viral-social-media-videos).

FIGURE 11.11

Tweets can alert readers to important stories as they evolve. A tweet can include photos, links to videos and valuable links to the reporter's story on the web, as this *Roanoke Times* tweet does.

Similarly, view the photos and videos offered to you with a healthy dose of skepticism. Did this really occur when or where the people submitting it suggested? Did they create it or simply share something they found online? Is it real or staged? Does it accurately reflect what occurred at the scene?

Asking such questions is essential to ensuring that your reputation and that of your company are protected. Reporting based on an unsubstantiated social media post or posting a staged video on your site or on the air can be harmful to your company and can endanger your future in the business. Embrace user-generated content, but be suspicious of its accuracy.

> **"In retrospect, the 'Big Bang' inflation of the World Wide Web already looks like a less complicated time, given the meteoric expansion of social media sites like Facebook, Twitter and Instagram and second-generation crowd sourcing sites like Reddit, Newsvine or Wikinews (with Wikipedia being everyone's granddaddy)."**
>
> ■ **James Klurfeld and Howard Schneider**

Reaching Readers

Although social media can be useful as a source of news or tips, they also drive traffic to your company's website. Most journalists today are asked to promote their stories on Facebook, Instagram, LinkedIn or Twitter — or maybe all these. Before or after a writer's story goes live on the website, he or she posts with a tease or link to the piece on various social platforms. This helps drive traffic to the news organization's website. Building the size of the audience enables the organization to charge more for advertising on the site.

Facebook is used in a similar way. Many newspapers, magazines, and radio and television stations have Facebook sites on which reporters post links to their stories and readers comment on them. Some news organizations also are designing stories especially for Facebook that incorporate video, music and clever captions.

Journalists use Twitter primarily for breaking news and promoting their stories, according to a Pew Research Center study, much as television anchors use teases before they break for commercials: "After the break, we'll find out when the snowstorm will arrive." An effective tease gives enough information to pique the reader's interest but does not give away the key elements of the story (see Figure 11.12).

Christine Byers @ChristineDByers

Woman with box cutter boards school bus in St. Louis, attacks teens with box cutter: bit.ly/1kSyDqh

robert paul van beets/Shutterstock

FIGURE 11.12

A tweet from a *St. Louis Post-Dispatch* reporter leads readers to a breaking news story posted on the newspaper's website. Today's reporters are expected to tease their stories on Twitter and other social media sites such as Facebook. A more complete version of the story followed on the website and in the next day's newspaper.

Journalists also use social media to solicit reader suggestions, to talk about the process of news gathering, and to break news before they are able to write even a short story for the web. Journalists covering a developing story may post updates to these platforms throughout to keep their audiences informed—and let audiences know how they can depend on the news organization to stay on top of a story.

In 2015, *The New York Times* launched an account on Instagram, a photo- and video-sharing social network. According to Katie Hawkins-Gaar, a former faculty writer at the Poynter Institute, news organizations use Instagram to showcase exceptional photography, alert readers to upcoming stories and invite viewers to participate in projects. Instagram almost seems tailor-made for delivering news in a new format. NowThisNews.com, for instance, is "the first and only video news network built for people who love their phones and love social media," according to the site's YouTube channel. NowThisNews also integrates its news coverage with Facebook, Snapchat, Tumblr and Twitter.

Writing Effectively and Correctly

Because Facebook, Instagram and Twitter posts don't go through the same editing process as material posted to an outlet's website, you need to reread and edit your own content before sending it. Journalists who send tweets with spelling, grammar and factual errors damage their reputations and those of their employers.

Writing at Poynter.org, Jeff Sonderman reported on research by Dan Zarrella, who studied thousands of tweets to determine what led to the highest click-through rates. Zarrella's advice:

- Write between 120 and 130 characters. Despite Twitter's increase in the size of allowable tweets, longer items will not be read.
- Place links about a quarter of the way through the tweet (not always at the end).
- Tweet only once or twice an hour.

Zarrella also confirmed earlier research that advised writers to use more verbs and determined that tweets are most effective at night or on weekends.

Benefiting as a Journalist

Today's journalists spend a lot of time on social media sites. They do so in part to tease stories they write for websites, newspapers and magazines. But no longer are deadlines daily, weekly or monthly. Social media and websites have made the delivery of news instantaneous, and every minute of the day may provide an occasion to tweet about a breaking news event.

A reporter covering a sporting event might issue as many as 40 tweets during the course of a game, which allows followers who are away from a television to learn what's happening in real time. All the while, that reporter might be crafting a story for the web and perhaps yet another for the next day's newspaper.

Social media also allow that reporter to keep in touch with an editor or colleagues covering the same story or even different ones. And because anyone can follow tweets, there's also an opportunity to see what competitors are reporting. Social media have become essential to today's journalists.

CHAPTER RESOURCES

SUGGESTED READINGS

Bradshaw, Paul. *The Online Journalism Handbook: Skills to Survive and Thrive in the Digital Age.* New York: Routledge, 2018. This excellent book has valuable material on writing for the web.

Filak, Vincent F. *Convergent Journalism: An Introduction.* Burlington, Mass: Taylor & Francis, 2015. A good introduction to online writing.

Friend, Cecilia, and Jane Singer. *Online Journalism Ethics: Traditions and Transitions.* Armonk, N.Y.: M.E. Sharpe, 2015. Friend and Singer have written an excellent treatise on the ethics of online sites.

SUGGESTED WEBSITES

LaunchPad Solo
launchpadworks.com
When you visit LaunchPad Solo for Journalism, you will find research links, exercises and LearningCurve adaptive quizzing to help you improve your grammar and AP style usage. In addition, the site's video collection hosts the videos highlighted in this and other chapters as well as additional clips of leading professionals discussing important media trends.

www.bbc.com/news
Arguably, no news site on the web does a better job than the BBC of presenting news in ideal ways for the medium.

blogs.spjnetwork.org/freelance
The Independent Journalist is a blog for freelancers that was started by the Society of Professional Journalists.

www.espn.com
ESPN.com, one of the best sites on the web, is probably the most extensive internet site for sports fans. It was an early leader in the use of audio and video.

www.mercurynews.com
MercuryNews.com, one of the first comprehensive local news websites, includes area news courtesy of the *San Jose Mercury News.*

www.miamiherald.com
Like many daily newspapers, *The Miami Herald*'s online edition includes most of the stories from its print edition, along with additional online-only posts.

www.newsy.com
This innovative, source of concise, unbiased video news and analysis covers the top stories from around the world.

www.nngroup.com
The Nielsen Norman Group manages this site, which includes the latest research on writing for the web and how users interact with web stories.

PRESSthink.org
Journalist Jay Rosen writes this blog, which covers all facets of journalistic practice. It's entertaining and thorough.

EXERCISES

1. Visit your local newspaper or television station and interview journalists who do the news online. Find out how they were trained and what major challenges they face.
2. Your instructor will assign you a newspaper story. Rewrite it for online use, and indicate any links that you might include.
3. **Your journalism blog.** Compare the websites of three similar news companies. For example, compare three newspaper sites or three broadcast sites. In your blog, describe the differences you see in how well news is presented on the web. Invite comments from your classmates.
4. Find a website that does a good job of linking readers to original source material. In an email memo to your "managing editor," evaluate the use of that technique, and explain why it works for the website.
5. From the BBC website (www.bbc.co.uk), choose one of the major stories of the day. In a one-page memo, outline how the BBC took advantage of different types of media to tell the story.
6. List five differences in how information is conveyed in a newspaper versus how it is conveyed on a website.
7. For each of the following web stories, list multimedia elements, links and sidebars you would use.
   a. A local merchant's group invites kids from a homeless shelter to paint store windows for the holidays.
   b. A star athlete returns to give your college team a pep talk at the beginning of the season.
   c. An explosion of unknown origin destroys a bookstore and café not far from campus.

CHAPTER 12

WRITING NEWS FOR RADIO AND TELEVISION

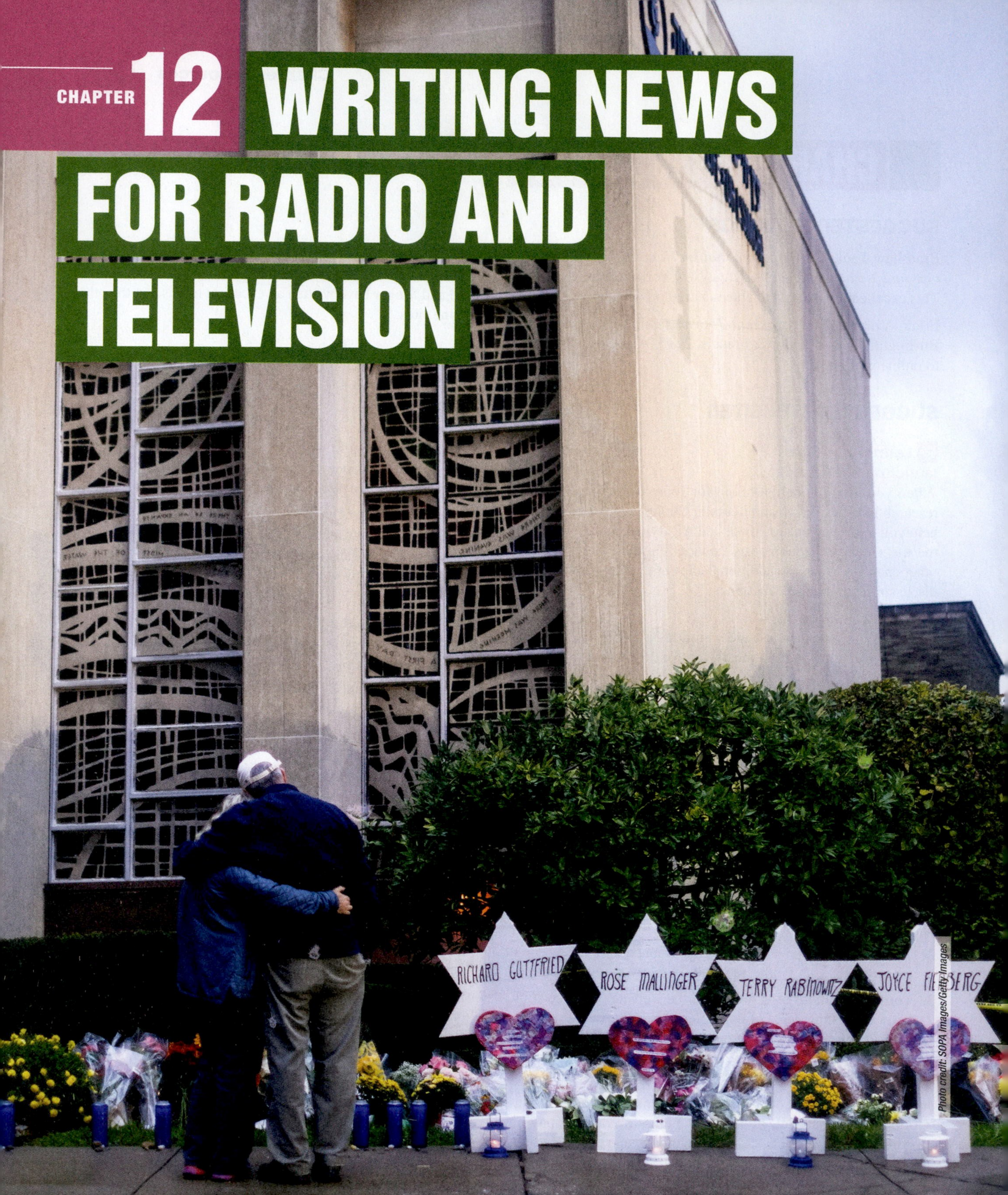

Photo credit: SOPA Images/Getty Images

When the author of frequent anti-Semitic threats opened fire on a Pittsburgh-area synagogue in October 2018, many Americans first heard about the news on social media. The attacks occurred on a Saturday morning, so some of those running errands or enjoying their weekends first learned what was happening through Twitter posts and Facebook links. But the power of live broadcasting and streaming video led Americans to turn to television news channels to see for themselves what was happening. Anchors based their coverage at the scene, and the cable networks devoted all their weekend airtime to the tragic events in Pennsylvania.

Radio and television play a critical role in getting accurate information to the public when time is of the essence — warning the audience of coming dangers, helping them prepare and get to safety, and connecting them with aid after the immediate crisis is past. But perhaps just as crucial is their role in helping the nation take a breath and feel good about itself. It was President George H. W. Bush who said at his inauguration, "We meet on democracy's front porch." This is one reason we go through the time and expense of a second inauguration for two-term presidents. Author Sally Quinn explains, "We want to see the flags wave and the bands play, the parades march along and the leader of the free world standing before our Capitol dome."

Television and online media help us do that.

In this chapter, you will learn:

1. What radio and television do best.
2. How the story selection criteria for radio and television news differ from those for print news.
3. How to write radio and television news.
4. How social media can supplement radio and television content.
5. How to prepare radio and television news copy.

What Radio and Television Do Best

During major news events, radio and television journalists deliver breaking news and then update their audiences as the news develops. If you tune in to CNN or other news channels, you see what's happening and listen to details from journalists, and you see additional headlines streaming below the picture on a ticker. The ticker gives the viewer the chance to find other news and seek it out by continuing to watch CNN or by going online to find more.

Much of the time, journalists must write and report news after it has occurred. Most radio and television stations provide at least some news that is written by journalists working for the wire services, such as The Associated Press or Reuters.

In addition, radio and television journalists are expected to publish updates all day on social media as information is verified. Facebook, Instagram, Snapchat, Twitter and other platforms provide around-the-clock details and updates. Conversely, most broadcast newsrooms routinely take verified content found online or shared by audience members on social media and incorporate it into traditional newscasts.

Even if your primary emphasis is not radio or television news, you will probably find yourself producing content that involves the use of audio and video. And if you are writing for radio or television news, almost certainly you will be required to contribute to the station's website, writing in a style more associated with print journalism.

launchpadworks.com
WATCH: **"Going Visual: Video, Radio and the Web"**

- Why are some radio stations shooting and sharing videos online? What do they hope to accomplish with this?
- Do you visit radio station websites and watch videos? If not, will you do so in the future? Explain.

Radio and television stations also use the web and social media to deliver the news and information they are gathering that cannot find a place on air in the regular newscasts. Rather than interrupt programming with new facts about a developing story, stations publish first on their websites and social media platforms. Almost all local stations, network and cable news operations use this "push" method to deliver news around the clock, 24 hours a day. Audiences do not have to wait for a scheduled news broadcast or hope a broadcaster interrupts regular programming. Instead, information finds them wherever they are, whether on the web, on social media or on mobile devices.

Criteria for Selecting Radio and Television News

Four criteria distinguish the selection of radio and television news from that of print news: timeliness, emphasis on information rather than explanation, audio or visual impact, and emphasis on people rather than concepts.

Timeliness

The radio and television news writer emphasizes one criterion of news value more than any other: timeliness. *When* something happened often determines whether a news item will be used in a newscast and where it will be placed in the news lineup of stories in the newscast, known as a **rundown**. The breaking story receives top priority and often leads the newscast.

Because timeliness is important, a sense of immediacy influences everything in radio news, from what is reported to how it is reported. This often is true of television news, as well. Even when radio and television air documentaries or in-depth segments, the producers typically try to infuse the program with a sense of urgency, a strong feeling of the present, an emphasis on what's happening now.

Information Rather Than Explanation

Airtime is precious, so radio and television reporters are generally more concerned with delivering facts and information rather than spending a great deal of time on explanations of why things are happening. Broadcast stories tend to average only 60 seconds or so and seldom run longer than two minutes; they can be as short as 10 or 12 seconds. A minute of news read aloud is only 15 lines of copy, or about 170 to 180 words. After you subtract time for commercials, a half-hour newscast has only 20 to 22 minutes of **news hole**, which also includes time for weather and sports. So the typical newscast's written content equates to about half of the front page of a newspaper.

That lack of depth on the air used to be a broadcast news weakness that led audience members to turn to newspapers or newsmagazines for background and details. But the internet now allows newscasters to send viewers and listeners to the station's website to find expanded information on the story and an extra perspective. Viewers no longer have to turn to a different news outlet.

Because of their relatively low production costs compared with the costs of producing prime-time scripted dramas and comedies, television newsmagazine formats such as *60 Minutes*, *20/20* and *Dateline NBC* continue to be successful decades after their inceptions. These programs represent a somewhat different challenge to television news writers, but even so, writing for a newsmagazine format resembles writing for television news.

Audio or Visual Impact

Some news is selected for radio because a reporter has recorded an on-the-scene audio report. Some news is selected for television because it is visually appealing or exciting. For this reason, news of an accident or a fire that might appear only in the records column of a newspaper might receive important play on a television newscast. If a television crew returns with good video of an event, that event often receives prominent placement in the next newscast.

One example occurs each year in the American West. Wildfires blanket California, Arizona and other states almost every summer. The story has little news value in print publications, except when large groups of homes are destroyed or people are killed by the fires, as was the case of the 2018 California wildfires—known as the most destructive season in California's history. But television news routinely sends teams of journalists to follow the fires as they crisscross the states. This provides dramatic fire and firefighting video for newscasts each night at a time when the news cycle typically slows down.

Emphasis on People

Radio and television tell the news using people who are affected by the news as central characters more often than print does. Radio and television writers follow the classic focus structure formula of making a problem come alive by finding someone who is dealing with the problem and showing the audience how he or she is doing. (See Chapter 10 for more on the focus structure.) That "someone" can be a representative person or family, a person affected by the story or a chief player. Thus, rather than using abstract concepts, television, in particular, humanizes the story. You can't shoot video of an issue, but you can show the impact the issue has on people. When Don Hewitt, legendary creator of *60 Minutes*, was asked why he didn't do a segment on AIDS, his response was quick and simple: "AIDS is not a story; it's an issue."

Radio and television news writing emphasizes certain characteristics that newspaper and online news writing do not, and because of that, story structure may vary.

Writing Radio and Television News

Although visuals are tops for television and audio rules on radio, writing is the foundation of both media. Broadcast writing varies greatly from other forms of journalism, both in length and in style. Successful broadcast journalists know and follow the rules to make their writing a key part of their stories.

Characteristics of Radio and Television News Writing

Because of the focus on timeliness, radio and television news writers, like journalists writing for digital media, must emphasize immediacy and write conversationally, tightly and clearly.

Immediacy

Radio and television news writers achieve a sense of immediacy in part by using the present tense as much as possible. Note the use of the present, present progressive and present perfect tenses (italicized) in this Associated Press story.

> **GREENVILLE, S.C. (AP)—Sheriffs in five South Carolina counties *are offering* people a chance to turn in explosives, no questions asked.**
>
> **Officials in Abbeville, Anderson, Greenville, Oconee and Pickens counties *have set* aside this week as Explosives Amnesty Week.**
>
> **People in those areas *can call* their sheriff's office to have any explosives, ammunition, weapons, bomb materials or military ordnance removed from their property. Certified bomb technicians will respond to remove and destroy the hazardous materials.**
>
> **Dispatchers will request information about the materials to be collected, including the address where the materials *are stored*.**
>
> **Callers *aren't* required to give their names, and no criminal charges related to hazardous materials reported or collected will be filed against people who *participate*.**

For accuracy, the past tense is sometimes necessary. But radio and television writers like to use the progressive form of the verb ("are offering") to show continuing action and the present perfect tense ("have set") more than the past tense (because the present perfect indicates past action that is continuing). (See the annotated model "Use of Verb Tenses in a TV Story" later in the chapter.)

Radio and Television News Writing

- Emphasizes immediacy.
- Has a conversational style.
- Is tightly phrased.
- Is clear.

Checklist for Writing Radio and Television News

Does My Writing Have Immediacy?

- Uses the present, present perfect and present progressive tenses.
- Uses the word *today* as high in the lead sentences as possible.
- Avoids the past tense, but includes the time element if it must be used.
- In a follow-up story, leads with a new development or a new fact.
- Pushes a "today" angle in the lead of next-day stories.

Does My Writing Feature a Conversational Style?

- Uses simple, short sentences instead of complex sentences.
- Uses active, rather than passive, verbs.
- Uses contractions to add a conversational tone, but avoids any that could be misunderstood.
- Uses sentence fragments sparingly and with effect.
- Uses slang sparingly and only in contexts in which it is widely accepted.
- Doesn't use colloquialisms or vulgar or off-color expressions.
- Uses correct grammar.

Does My Writing Employ Tight Phrasing?

- Uses as few words as possible.
- Uses few adjectives and adverbs.
- Includes carefully selected facts.

Does My Writing Have Clarity?

- Uses familiar words — not jargon or technical terms.
- Avoids unnecessary or confusing synonyms.
- Repeats words or phrases for greater comprehension.
- Avoids foreign words and phrases.
- Avoids phrases like "the former" and "the latter."
- Repeats proper names rather than using pronouns.
- Keeps the subject close to the verb, without many intervening words.
- Avoids clever figures of speech.
- Avoids lists of numbers.
- Breaks down statistics so they are understandable.

Writers want to emphasize the immediacy of stories by indicating that the event covered happened today by including the word *today* as high in the lead sentence as possible. This will sometimes yield copy that loses some conversational tone in order to gain immediacy. For example, this lead seems perfectly fine to indicate a today event:

Seattle police caught the man they say is the so-called "Handsome Robber" today.

But you can move "today" much higher in that sentence to increase immediacy:

Seattle police today caught the man they say is the so-called "Handsome Robber."

Sometimes reporters stress immediacy by saying "just minutes ago" or "this morning." If there is no danger of inaccuracy or deceit, you can omit references to time. For example, if something happened yesterday, you might report it like this:

The latest rash of fires in Southern California is under control.

But if you use the past tense in a lead, you should include the time element:

The legislature sent a welfare reform bill to the governor late last night. It finished just in time before the spring recess.

The best way to avoid the past tense is to avoid yesterday's story. You can do that by updating yesterday's story. By leading with a new development or a new fact, you might be able to use the present tense. So the fire example from above becomes this:

Firefighters are mopping up this morning after bringing the latest rash of fires in Southern California under control.

Remember, radio and television newscasts are almost always delivered live. Your copy must convey that important characteristic.

Conversational style

Although "Write the way you talk" is questionable advice for most kinds of writing, it is imperative for radio and television news writing. "Read your copy aloud" is good advice for most kinds of writing; for radio and television news writing, it is essential. You should read and reread your copy aloud as you write to be sure it's as conversational as possible.

Write so that your copy *sounds* good. Use simple, short sentences, written with transitive verbs in the active voice. Transitive verbs do things to things; they demand an object. People rarely use verbs in the passive voice when they talk; it usually sounds cumbersome and awkward. You don't say, "Guess what I was just told by somebody." "Was told" here is in the passive voice; the subject is being acted on. The preposition "by" also tells you the verb is in the passive voice. "Guess what somebody just told me" is active and more natural, less wordy and stronger. "Told" is in the active voice; the subject is doing the acting.

Because casual speech contains contractions, you should use contractions to give your story a more natural, conversational feel — so long as the person who voices the copy pronounces each contraction clearly. One exception is the negative

> **"Good television journalism presents news in the most attractive and lucid form yet devised by man."**
>
> ■ **Bill Small, author, veteran broadcaster, former president of CBS News**

not, which is more clearly understood when you use the whole word rather than a contraction. For instance, saying that investigators "did not" question the suspect will be much clearer to the listener than saying they "didn't" question the subject. Avoiding the contraction also avoids the risk the listener will mistake "didn't" for "did."

Conversational style also permits the use of occasional fragments. Sentences are sometimes strung together loosely with dashes. They sometimes begin with the conjunction *and* or *but*, as in the following example:

BEAVER FALLS, Pa. (AP) — Police don't plan to cite the drivers of a truck and school bus that crashed in western Pennsylvania.

But only because neither vehicle had a driver when they wrecked.

Conversations often include slang, and conversational writing for radio or television can use slang sparingly. For instance, some broadcasters substitute the word *cops* instead of *police* in their writing. Although some newsrooms would find this use of slang too informal, others embrace its tone as sounding authentic to listeners and viewers. But writing in conversational style does not mean that you may use colloquialisms or incorrect grammar. Nor does it mean that you may use vulgar or off-color expressions. Remember that your audience includes people of all ages, backgrounds and sensitivities.

Tight phrasing

You must learn to write in a conversational style without being wordy. This means you must condense. Use few adjectives and adverbs. Reduce the use of the passive voice to save a couple of words. Make each word count.

Keeping it short means selecting facts carefully because often you don't have time for the whole story. Radio and television newscasters want good, tight writing that is easy to follow. Let's examine how a wire story written for newspapers can be condensed for radio and television. In an Associated Press wire story about the creation of a Space Force by Donald Trump, the print story contained 377 words. However, the broadcast wire contained just 117 words — nearly half the length.

In the broadcast version, listeners are given just the bare facts. They must turn to print or online news sources for the details, and more and more newscasts send their audiences to the station's website for additional content. An online story can be and often is much longer than a broadcast story or a newspaper story.

In radio and television news, tight writing is important even when time is available. Broadcast writers usually strive to waste no words, even in documentaries, which provide in-depth coverage of events.

Clarity

Unlike readers, radio and television news audiences can't go back to reread a passage they didn't quite grasp. Viewers of television newscasts typically see them only once, and they are unlikely to rewatch them. The attention of a broadcast audience waxes and wanes. So you must be clear and precise.

Write simply, in short sentences filled with nickel-and-dime words. Don't look for synonyms. Don't be afraid to repeat words or phrases. Oral communication needs reinforcement. Avoid foreign words and phrases. Avoid phrases like "the former" and "the latter," which are hard for listeners to follow. Repeat proper names in the story rather than use pronouns. The listener can easily forget the person that the pronoun refers to, especially if the story has several subjects.

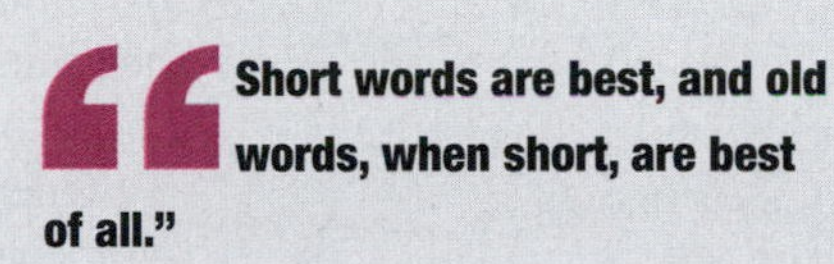

"Short words are best, and old words, when short, are best of all."

■ ***Winston Churchill, British politician***

When you are tempted to write a dependent clause in a sentence, make it an independent clause instead. Keep the subject close to the verb. Close the gap between the doer and the activity. This version doesn't do that:

> **A man flagged down a Highway Patrol officer near Braden, Tennessee, today and told him a convict was hiding in his house. The prisoner, one of five who escaped from the Fort Pillow Prison on Saturday, surrendered peacefully.**

The second sentence contains 12 words between the subject, "prisoner," and the main verb, "surrendered." By the time the broadcaster reaches the verb, many listeners will have forgotten what the subject was.

The story is easier to understand when written this way:

> **A man flagged down a Highway Patrol officer near Braden, Tennessee, today and told him a convict was hiding in his house. The prisoner surrendered peacefully. He's one of five who escaped from the Fort Pillow Prison on Saturday.**

The third sentence is still a complex sentence ("who escaped . . ." is the dependent clause), but it is more easily understood than the original version.

Clarity also requires that you resist a clever turn of phrase. Most viewers and listeners probably will understand it, but a good figure of speech takes time to savor. If listeners pause to savor it, they will not hear what follows. For that reason, clever columnists often fail as radio commentators.

Even more dangerous than figures of speech are numbers. Don't barrage the listener or viewer with a series of numbers. If you must use illustrative numbers or comparative statistics, round them off so they are easier to comprehend. If a school budget is approved at $47,925,345, call it a "48 million dollar budget."

Look for ways to break down numbers so that they are understandable. For example, you should say that one of every seven American adults smokes rather than there are 38 million smokers in the United States. You might be tempted to say how many billions of dollars a federal program will cost, but you will help listeners understand if you say that the program will cost the average wage earner $73 for each of the next five years. Television reporters often supply an on-air graphic illustrating the data given orally to help the audience visually understand the information they are hearing.

Story Structure

Writers must craft radio and television leads somewhat differently from the way they cast print and online leads. They also must construct special introductions and conclusions to video or audio segments and synchronize their words with recorded segments.

Writing the Radio and Television Lead

Like newspaper reporters, radio and television reporters must grab the attention of their audience. Much of what you learned in Chapter 8 on writing the inverted pyramid lead applies to radio and television leads. But be aware that people tend to be doing other things when listening to radio or watching television, so you must strive to attract their attention in different ways.

One way is by preparing your audience for what is to come through *cuing in*. You cue listeners to make sure they are tuned in. You introduce the story with a general statement, something that will pique the interest of the audience; then you go to the specifics. For example:

General statement	Things are far from settled for Springfield's teacher strike.
Specific	School officials and union representatives did not agree on a contract yesterday. They will not meet again for at least a week.

Sometimes the opening sentence will cover a number of news items:

First responders were busy today working several accidents across the Springfield region.

Cuing in is only one method of opening a radio or television story. Other leads go immediately into the what and the who, the where and the when. In radio or television news, the what is most important, followed by who did the what. The time and place may be included in the lead, but seldom is the why or the how. If time permits, the why and the how may come later in the story, but often they are omitted.

The first words of the lead are the most important. Don't keep the listener guessing as to what the story is about. Don't begin with a dependent clause or with a prepositional phrase, as in this example:

In a break from tradition, the U.S. Air Force is asking Congress to increase its size rather than focus on modernizing existing technology.

The opening words are meaningless without what comes later. The listener may not know what you are talking about. Here is a better way to introduce this story:

The U.S. Air Force is breaking with tradition by asking Congress to increase its size rather than modernize existing technology.

Be sure to "tee up," or identify, an unfamiliar name to prepare listeners for a name they otherwise may miss. Do it this way:

Veteran Kansas City, Kansas, businessman and civic leader Kenneth Durban died yesterday in a nursing home at age 83.

Don't mislead. The opening words must set the proper tone and mood for the story. Attract attention; tease a little. Answer questions, but don't ask them. Lead the listener into your story.

Writing Lead-Ins and Wrap-Ups

Radio and television journalists must learn how to write a **lead-in** that introduces a recorded segment from a news source or another reporter or a live report from a journalist in the field. The functions of a lead-in are twofold: to set the scene (by briefly telling the where, the when and sometimes the what) and to identify the source or reporter. The lead-in should contain something substantive. Here's an example:

> **A grand jury decided today not to charge a Cleveland teenager in the killing of his father. Susan Takahashi reports the panel believes the case is one of self-defense.**

Lead-ins should generate interest. Sometimes several sentences are used to provide background, as in the following:

> **It's a long comeback, indeed, and a slow one at that. But as Roberto Martinez reports, some economists continue to be optimistic about the future.**

Be careful not to include in the lead-in what is in the story. Just as a headline should not steal word-for-word the lead of a newspaper story, the lead-in should not parrot the opening words of the correspondent. The writer must know the contents of the segment in order to write a proper lead-in.

After the segment is over, you may want to wrap up the story before going on to the next item. The wrap-up or tag is especially important in radio copy because there are no visuals to identify the person that listeners just heard. If the story reported by Evelyn Turner was about a meeting to settle a strike, you might tag Turner's report by adding this information:

> **Turner reports negotiations will resume tomorrow.**

A tag like this gives the story an ending and clearly separates it from the next story.

Christiane Amanpour is CNN's chief international anchor and the host of Amanpour & Co., *a nightly foreign affairs TV program on PBS. She also works for CNN International. Her authoritative reports from around the world have informed millions.*

Ziv Koren/Polaris

Writing to the Video

Writing for a video report begins with selecting the subject and deciding how it is to be shot. The writing continues through the editing process and is done with the video clearly in mind.

Words and video must be complementary, never interfering with each other and never ignoring each other. Your first responsibility is to relate the words to the video. If you do not, viewers will not get the message because they will be wondering what the video is about.

There is a danger, however, in sticking too closely to the video by pointing out the obvious, giving your report a play-by-play feel. You need to avoid both extremes and use what is commonly called the "touch-and-go" method. This means that at the beginning of a scene or when a scene changes, you must tell the viewer where you are or what is happening by making the words and video "touch."

Suppose the report concerns the continuation of a hospital workers' strike and the opening scene shows pickets outside the hospital. You can explain the video by saying this:

> **Union members are still picketing Mercy Hospital today as the hospital workers' strike enters its third week.**

Viewers now know three things that are not obvious on the video: who is picketing, where and how long they've been picketing. If the video switches to people sitting around a table negotiating, you must again set the scene for viewers:

> **Meanwhile, hospital administrators and union leaders are continuing their meetings—apparently without success.**

After you have related the words to the video, you may add other details of the strike, commenting on the video and providing a clear completion of the story.

Finding the Visuals for TV News

Visuals are the most important element of television news. The medium is strongest when it attracts viewers to watch moving images and listen to accompanying audio. These elements do the following:

- Deliver a sense of presence to the story, putting the viewers on the scene of the news.
- Allow viewers to better understand what happened – or is happening now.
- Allow sources to appear in front of viewers and speak in their own words and voice.
- Provide visual context for what has transpired.
- Make long-lasting memories for viewers.
- When live, give viewers the ability to view big stories remotely as they happen.

Television journalists use a variety of visuals, not all of which are limited to video:

- **Recorded video** of news from the place where the event happened is the most common visual on TV news. TV journalists themselves capture most video shown on newscasts, but video can also come from witnesses who saw and recorded the event or come from social media.
- **Live video** of news as it is happening provides an even more immediate news experience for viewers. Live video is almost exclusively captured by television stations with their live equipment.
- A **photo** can put a face to a name in a story or show news that video cameras were not yet there to capture. Photos can come from official sources like police, from eyewitnesses to news events or even from social media.
- A **graphic illustration** can take many forms on air, such as documents, quotes from someone who does not appear on camera, and data in a table. TV stations have their own tools to create these graphics. Some have a graphics department with artists to build the graphics for use in the daily newscasts, while others expect producers or other journalists to create their own.
- A **map** is often used to show the scene of a news event and typically appears before the station cuts to a reporter on site or a video of the scene of the story. Many stations have mapping software to allow producers to build these maps on their own.
- An **animation** can be used to explain the news through motion, showing more than what a single graphic image can show. For instance, a newsroom might use an animated graphic to show the course of a tornado through a city.

Each type of visual comes with special needs for journalists to verify accuracy and authenticity:

- **Source.** It pays to be skeptical about any video not shot by the news organization itself. You should ask questions about who shot the video and under what circumstances.
- **Authenticity.** Video from social media or other online sources can often be faked. If you're unable to verify a video's authenticity, you should refrain from using it on the air. At the very least, if the decision is made to air unverified video, it is essential to inform the viewers of the lack of verification.

- **No enhancements.** Although enhancing an image to make it easier to see is certainly allowable, you should never alter an image in a way that changes its meaning or what it depicts.
- **No text errors.** Typos and other text errors are far too common in on-air graphics. Be sure to check and double-check all text before airing. Do *not* rely on spell checkers to do that work.
- **No math errors.** In the same way, journalists often make errors in arithmetic, mathematics and statistics. Any graphics with numbers should be checked for accuracy twice before being aired.
- **Permissions.** Video and images that belong to someone else are not always available for newscasts to use without permission of the rights holder. Learn the elements of fair use, and discuss the situation with an editor if you're unsure of your legal right to use a visual in your story.

Visuals properly crafted or chosen can greatly enhance the impact of a news story, so being able to think creatively about the best use of visuals can be a valuable skill to cultivate.

ON THE JOB Successful Reporting Means Watching the Clock

Courtesy of Brian Emfinger

Charged with a coverage area that blankets an entire state, **Alexis Rogers** is a general assignment reporter for WLWT, the NBC affiliate in Cincinnati, Ohio. The job is Rogers' second since graduating from college, where she studied radio and TV journalism.

Rogers says a reporter's days are long.

Before the station's formal assignment meeting, Rogers has already been making calls to find a story. After her assignment is confirmed, she's on her way to a story that could be many miles away. At the same time, she launches into what will be a daylong barrage on social media.

After the story is shot and she's returning to the station or to her live-shot location, Rogers is writing and working with a photographer or editor on her story. Even after she's finished delivering her story, she's back on the web posting her story video and making more calls to set up stories for the next day.

Rogers says she is always watching the clock and timing her day: "You might think it's all going to go right, but there are so many things that go wrong."

Successful reporters leave enough time and have workable back-up plans so they can be sure to make deadline even when problems crop up, she says.

The most important trait she wants the audience to recognize in her is that she is committed to being an expert on the region, Rogers says: "Our viewers are constantly questioning. They don't hesitate to ask you a question to see if you know the area and know what you are talking about."

Rogers' advice to young journalists entering their first jobs is to be the person the newsroom sees as the most dependable employee there.

"In college, you're used to working with a lot of people your own age who work hard. But when I got here, I was the youngest person on air in the market. So the people I worked with questioned whether I could do it," she says.

Her final tip is "Grow your skills." She urges young journalists to learn the skills of the investigative reporter, including computer-assisted and data reporting and visualization, and to learn their local court and government structure so they can go directly to the best sources to find and cover stories.

launchpadworks.com
WATCH: **"Television Networks Evolve: Cable, Satellite, Broadband"**

- What technological changes have challenged the dominance of the terrestrial broadcast networks and cable news for the past several years? How are the latest cellphone technologies again changing the game?
- What is a "broadcaster," and how might different definitions fit in the realm of new digital media?

Using Social Media in Radio and Television

Most newsrooms have merged the traditional "small-screen" delivery of news via television with the even smaller screens of computers and smartphones. This technique, called "second-screen viewing," presents an opportunity for broadcast outlets to deliver additional news content.

Blending Online with On-Air

The dramatic rescue attempts in the summer of 2018 to save 12 boys and their soccer coach from a flooded cave in Thailand captured the attention of people around the world. News organizations quickly began using the Twitter hashtag #ThaiCaveRescue on their own coverage to feature in the stream of social media posts about the attempts to save the boys. The use of a **hashtag** puts broadcast stories into the news stream of social media users. It's a crucial strategy for legacy media to reach an audience that might not consume something as traditional as a television newscast.

Along with real-time interactivity during a live broadcast, radio and television newsrooms use social media to do crowdsourcing (collaborate with the audience to gather information) and collect additional perspectives on daily and long-term projects. The second screen is growing as a way to maintain and increase audience involvement. Most television stations have their own mobile apps that allow users to watch video, interact on social media, interact with weather radar and more. Local stations continue to build the second-screen experience for their audiences. Efforts now focus on giving viewers the chance to use their tablets and laptops to consume value-added content while watching the traditional broadcast on their televisions.

As news consumers continue to explore new places to learn about the news, it is increasingly important for all journalists, in whatever type of newsroom they work, to think about sharing news across many different platforms.

Guidelines for Using Social Media

When a newsroom gathers content from viewers and social media, it must follow these strict guidelines:

- **Verified information.** All information gathered from social media must be verified before being published.
- **Digital first.** Newsrooms should be digital first, meaning that stories and information should be published online and on social media and not held for broadcast newscasts. However, stations may make exceptions for certain promoted or investigative reports designed to deliver audiences to newscasts first.
- **Teaser posts.** Reporters should not use social media posts just to entice audience members to tune in later. Instead, "teaser" posts should contain vital bits of the story being reported and give audience members a reason to watch the later broadcast.

ON THE JOB Be Ready to Meet the Challenge

Courtesy of Lorenzo Hall

Lorenzo Hall is a reporter and anchor at WUSA-TV, the CBS affiliate in Washington, D.C. This follows his assignments as a main anchor at WTIC-TV in Hartford, Connecticut, as well as evening anchor and investigative reporter at WTVR-TV in Richmond, Virginia. Here's his description of today's newsroom:

> We are "on" 24 hours a day, seven days a week. My first job required stories just for television, with the web playing a small role. Now, the web is vital and social media is an equally relevant element. These platforms have created a seemingly incessant connection to our audiences.
>
> I've had to rush and cover breaking news on multiple occasions through our app and Facebook Live. With this standard, having a Rolodex of sources is a must. I also have to be knowledgeable of everything happening locally, nationally and internationally. There's little time to do extended research prior to reporting an event.
>
> With this connection, there's also branding at play. The audience isn't just looking for news content, but also a glimpse into your private life. I have to set boundaries and standards because it's easy to post too much. I've been told by our web manager that a little mystique is still valuable.
>
> Now is an exciting time to be a young journalist. We have so many tools to produce compelling and creative stories outside the traditional television model.
>
> However, I've also learned that the relationship with the audience has to be cultivated. We can't throw information at them because it's reciprocal. Engaging with viewers is key. In fact, like television ratings, a daily log is published internally showing our level of engagement.
>
> This give-and-take relationship is a good way to get an understanding of what's happening in various communities and gauge what people find important. Some of my recent stories have come from viewers sending messages and tips through social media.
>
> There are very few limitations.

- **Audience contributions.** Stations should seek user-generated content from audience members and give viewers a way to supply their own video, stills and audio via the station's website and social media. Any sharing should include terms of service that give the station the right to use the supplied content. Submissions must require contact information in case the newsroom needs additional information about the content.

Preparing Radio and Television News Copy

When you prepare copy to be read by a newscaster, your goals are to make the copy easy for the newscaster to read and easy for the audience to understand.

Format

Almost every station uses newsroom computer system software to prepare rundowns, write copy and produce its newscasts. Details such as line spacing are built into the templates of the NRCS software. But some details are still in the hands of the writers.

> "Writing a silence is as important as writing words. We don't rely on video enough."
>
> ■ John Hart, prize-winning TV news anchor

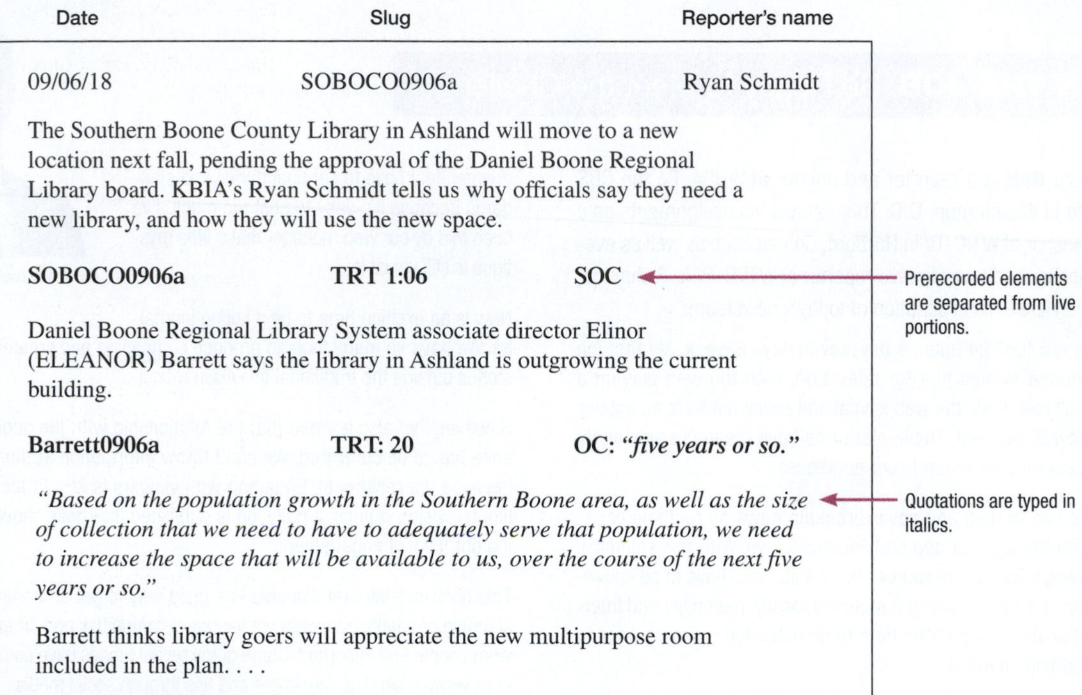

Date
Slug
Reporter's name
09/06/18
SOBOCO0906a
Ryan Schmidt
The Southern Boone County Library in Ashland will move to a new location next fall, pending the approval of the Daniel Boone Regional Library board. KBIA's Ryan Schmidt tells us why officials say they need a new library, and how they will use the new space.
SOBOCO0906a
TRT 1:06
SOC
Prerecorded elements are separated from live portions.
Daniel Boone Regional Library System associate director Elinor (ELEANOR) Barrett says the library in Ashland is outgrowing the current building.
Barrett0906a
TRT: 20
OC: "five years or so."
"Based on the population growth in the Southern Boone area, as well as the size of collection that we need to have to adequately serve that population, we need to increase the space that will be available to us, over the course of the next five years or so."
Quotations are typed in italics.
Barrett thinks library goers will appreciate the new multipurpose room included in the plan. . . .

FIGURE 12.1

In this radio copy, the name Elinor is also spelled ELEANOR, in case the announcer is unfamiliar with the first, less common spelling.

In radio copy, the portion read live is separated from any prerecorded elements (see Figure 12.1). Quotes are italicized. When printing, the system puts each story on a separate piece of paper. That way, the order of the stories can be rearranged, and stories can be added or dropped easily.

In television copy, the stories and pages are numbered, and each story starts on a separate page. Television copy is formatted to put anchor and reporter copy on the right half of the page (see Figure 12.2), while director instructions appear on the left of the page. Each line averages four words, and newscasters average 40 lines per minute. The copy that is read live generally appears in all caps, while recorded audio is in normal upper and lower case. Stations vary with scripting basics.

At most stations, copy is prepared for a **teleprompter**, an electronic device that projects the copy over the camera lens in the studio so the newscaster can read it while appearing to look straight into the camera.

The newscast producer determines the **slug**, or identifying name, for a story and its placement. Some newsrooms have a policy that the slug needs to contain the time of the broadcast to keep track of content when multiple newscasts are in production at the same time. Newsroom computer systems help number the pages and can estimate how long a script might run on the air on the basis of an anchor's read rate.

Names and Titles

In radio and television style, full names are typically used on first reference, with just the surname used in subsequent references. Don't use middle initials unless they are a widely recognized part of someone's name (Samuel L. Jackson) or unless

Story Slug	Time of Broadcast, Reporter
A15.5 - 1 V-5 ENERGY . . .	**15:44:31, Reporter Name**
CAM: 4	((JIM ON CAM)) FOR LOCAL BUSINESSES, SAVING ENERGY ACTUALLY MEANS MAKING MORE MONEY.
TAKE VO *CG [1] 2 LINE: PROVIDENCE ROAD|COLUMBIA	((TAKE VO)) A FORUM IN COLUMBIA TODAY SOLD THIS MESSAGE TO BUSINESS OWNERS. THE ENERGIZE MISSOURI INDUSTRIES FORUM ATTRACTED NINETY PEOPLE FROM BOTH IN-STATE AND OUT-OF-STATE. THE BIGGEST QUESTIONS WERE ABOUT NEW TECHNOLOGY, FUNDING OPPORTUNITIES AND AVAILABLE **RESOURCES.**
A16.5 - 1 S/V-5 ENERGY . . .	**15:45:18, Reporter Name**
TAKE SOT RUNS=7 *CG [1] 2 LINE: GERALD WELK|BUSINESS MANAGER 1-7	((TAKE SOT)) "HAVING AN ACCESS TO THE INFORMATION AND WHERE TO FIND THINGS, I THINK THAT'S THE BIGGEST THING."
VO RESUMES	((JIM/VO)) THE MISSOURI DEPARTMENT OF NATURAL RESOURCES **AND THE U.S. DEPARTMENT OF ENERGY CO-HOSTED THE FORUM.**

"ON CAM" means live on camera with a microphone.

"TAKE VO" means take the video while the anchor reads. ("VO" stands for "voice over.")

"CG" indicates the title is to be shown over video.

"TAKE SOT" means sound should be taken in full. ("SOT" is short for "sound on tape," though now most TV stations use digital rather than rolling videotape.)

"RUNS=7" means sound runs seven seconds.

"1-7" means the title is to be shown for seven seconds after story begins.

FIGURE 12.2

Television copy is typed in two columns — one for text to be read and the other for audio and video directions.

they are necessary to distinguish two people with the same first and last names, as with former presidents George W. Bush and George H. W. Bush.

A title that explains a person's connection to a story should be used during the first reference to that person, and it should precede the name so that listeners are better prepared to hear the name. For example, former Secretary of Defense Jim Mattis at first occurrence and then just Mattis. Broadcast copy typically avoids courtesy titles, such as "Mr." or "Ms." One exception: Most stations prefer to use "President" or "Mr." before all mentions of the current U.S. president's surname.

Pronunciation

You must help the newscaster pronounce the names of people and places correctly. To do this, write out difficult names phonetically in parentheses, putting the syllable with the most emphasis in all capital letters. If you can't find a person's name in an online pronunciation guide, call the person's office to get the proper pronunciation. If the name is of a U.S. town, try calling someone in that town. There is no rhyme or reason to the way some people pronounce their names or to the way some place names are pronounced. Never assume. Never guess. Find out. Here's an example of how to write out difficult names:

> **BAKU, Azerbaijan—The chairman of the Kuwaiti (kuh-WAIT'-ee) National Assembly told parliament members in Azerbaijan (ah-zur-by-JAHN') his country is interested in stronger relations with the former Soviet (SO'-vee-et) republic.**

Perhaps most people know how to pronounce Lima (LEE-mah), Peru, but not everyone can correctly pronounce Lima (LIE-mah), Ohio. You must note the difference between NEW-erk, New Jersey, and new-ARK, Delaware, both spelled "Newark." And who would guess that Pago Pago is pronounced PAHNG-oh PAHNG-oh?

Abbreviations

Generally, do not use abbreviations in your copy. It is easier to read a written-out word than an abbreviation. Do not abbreviate the names of states, countries, months, days of the week or military titles. You may, however, use the abbreviations "Dr.," "Mr.," "Mrs.," "Ms.," "a.m." and "p.m."

When you use abbreviations that contain singly pronounced letters, use hyphens instead of periods to prevent the newscaster from mistaking the final period in the abbreviation for the period at the end of the sentence. You may abbreviate "United States" when you use it as a noun or adjective; "U-S" would be the correct form. If an abbreviation is well-known—"U-N," "G-O-P," "F-B-I"—you may use it. Hyphens are not used in acronyms like "NATO" and "HUD," which are pronounced as one word.

Symbols and Numbers

Do not use symbols—not even $, % and # (for number)—in your copy because newscasters can read a word more easily than a symbol. So "$4,000,000" becomes "four million dollars" in broadcast copy. Use the word "hashtag" for the # symbol in references to Twitter.

Numbers can also be a problem. As in newspaper style, write out numbers one through nine. Also write out eleven, because 11 might not be easily recognized as a number. Use figures for 10 and from 12 to 999, but write out the words "thousand," "million" and "billion." Write out fractions ("two-and-a-half million dollars") and decimals ("three-point-two percent").

Some stations have exceptions. Figures often are used to give the time ("3:20 a.m."), sports scores ("ahead 5 to 2") and statistics, market reports ("an increase in the Dow Jones Industrial Average of 2-point-8 points") and addresses ("3-0-0-2 Grand Street").

As stated earlier in this chapter, you may round off big numbers. Thus, for 48.3 percent, write "nearly half." But when talking about human beings, don't say "more than one hundred" if you know that 104 people died in an earthquake; be precise.

Use "st," "nd," "rd" and "th" after dates: August 1st, September 2nd, October 3rd, November 4th. Make the year easy to pronounce by using numerals: June 9th, 1973.

Quotations and Attributions

Because it is difficult and awkward to indicate to listeners which words are being quoted, use indirect quotes or a paraphrase instead of direct quotations.

If it is important for listeners to know the exact words of a quotation (as when the quoted words are startling, uncomplimentary or possibly libelous), introduce the quote by saying "in his words," "with these words," "what she called" or "he put it this way." Most writers prefer to avoid the formal "quote" and "unquote," though "quote" is used more often than "unquote." Here's an example:

In Smith's words, quote, "There is no way to undo the harm done."

When you must use a direct quotation, the attribution should always precede the quotation. Because listeners cannot see the quotation marks, they will have no way of knowing the words are a direct quote. If by chance they do recognize the words as a quote, they will have no idea who is being quoted. For the same reason, the attribution should precede an indirect quote as well.

If you must use a direct quotation, keep it short. If it is important to use all of a long quote, use a video of the person saying it. If you wish to use a quote of more than one sentence, break it up with phrases such as "Smith went on to say" or "and still quoting the senator." For television, put a longer or more complicated quote on a full-screen graphic display as it is read.

What's the grammar error in this sentence?

China's stock market crisis in August 2015 had a substantial affect on international markets.

See Appendix 1, Rule 19.

Punctuation

In radio and television copy, less punctuation is best. The one exception is the comma. Commas help the newscaster pause at appropriate places. Use commas, for example, after introductory phrases referring to time and place, as in these examples:

In London, three Americans on vacation died today when their car overturned and caught fire.

Last August, beef prices reached an all-time low.

Some newsrooms prefer using three periods in place of a comma. An anchor is less likely to overlook ellipses than commas or confuse a comma for a period. Three periods can also take the place of parentheses and the semicolon. They signal a pause and are easily visible. The same is true of the dash—typed as two hyphens in most word-processing programs. Note the dash in the following example:

> **But the judge grumbled about the news coverage, and most prospective jurors agreed—saying the news coverage has been prone to overstatement, sensationalism and errors.**

To make the copy easier to read, add hyphens to some words even when the dictionary and Associated Press do not use them: "anti-discrimination," "co-equal," "non-aggression."

Stations vary in writing style and in the preparation of copy. But if you learn the guidelines presented here, you will be prepared to work in radio or television. Differences will be small, and you will adapt to them easily.

CHAPTER RESOURCES

SUGGESTED READINGS

Adornato, Anthony. *Mobile and Social Media Journalism: A Practical Guide.* Thousand Oaks, Calif.: CQ Press, 2018. Journalists can use this handbook to navigate using mobile tools to tell stories and reach audiences.

Bliss, Edward Jr., and James L. Hoyt. *Writing News for Broadcast.* 3rd ed. New York: Columbia Univ. Press, 1994. A classic text, often called the Strunk and White of broadcast news writing, this book excels in good writing and sets a superb example for students to do the same.

Block, Mervin. *Writing Broadcast News: Shorter, Sharper, Stronger.* 3rd ed. Washington, D.C.: CQ Press, 2010. This excellent book, written by a former network news writer, is considered the last word in broadcast copy writing.

Freedman, Wayne. *It Takes More Than Good Looks to Succeed at Television News Reporting.* 2nd ed. San Francisco: Wayne Freedman, 2011. Freedman has been called "the best local TV news feature reporter in the country." His book is packed with practical, down-to-earth advice.

Wenger, Deborah Halpert, and Deborah Potter. *Advancing the Story: Broadcast Journalism in a Multimedia World.* 4th ed. Washington, D.C.: CQ Press, 2018. This text continues to be updated online.

White, Ted, and Frank Barnas. *Broadcast News Writing, Reporting, and Producing.* 6th ed. Boston: Focal Press, 2013. This book has excellent coverage on all aspects of broadcast news writing.

SUGGESTED WEBSITES

LaunchPad Solo
launchpadworks.com
When you visit LaunchPad Solo for Journalism, you will find research links, exercises, and LearningCurve adaptive quizzing to help you improve your grammar and AP style usage. In addition, the site's video collection hosts the videos highlighted in this and other chapters as well as additional clips of leading professionals discussing important media trends.

www.advancingthestory.com
Be sure to check out this excellent website companion to Wenger and Potter's textbook.

www.nab.org
The website of the National Association of Broadcasters is a wonderful resource for all kinds of radio- and TV-related information. It includes a career center.

www.newscript.com
This site's purpose is to help radio journalists improve their skills as writers and anchors.

www.rtdna.org
The Radio Television Digital News Association promotes excellence in electronic journalism through research, education and professional training. The site features excellent reports and useful links.

www.rtdna.org/article/social_media_blogging_guidelines
This RTDNA site will help you answer questions about sharing user-generated content. It offers detailed guidelines for newsrooms and journalists to follow when considering the use of social media.

EXERCISES

1. Your instructor will divide your class into five groups. Each group will watch an evening television newscast on the air from one of your local television stations. With the members of your group, make a simple list of the news stories. Then find those stories in the next day's print edition of the local newspaper, and compare the coverage. Be prepared for a good class discussion.

2. **Your journalism blog.** Write a blog post about a complicated local news event. Then boil down the issue, and write a 45-second television piece to present in front of your class. Finally, write a tweet that tells part of your story in 140 characters or less.

3. Check to see if the following story, written for broadcast, follows acceptable broadcast style. Is it technically correct? Does it emphasize immediacy? Change the copy where you think it's necessary.

   Catholic Priest Goes Online to Vow Innocence in Sex Abuse Case
   WORCESTER, Mass.—A Massachusetts priest has gone on the record to say he is innocent of the allegations against him and will fight to clear his name.

   Sixty-four-year-old Father John L. Runnickem was accused by three former altar boys of sexual touching and taking naked pictures.

   Runnickem spoke out in a short, recorded video posted online Wednesday, saying he had done nothing wrong and that God was "on his side."

   Boston archdiocese officials have removed Runnickem from his pastor duties at Our Lady of Snows parish church in Worcester, Massachusetts, and have pledged to cooperate as law enforcement investigates the allegations.

   The three alleged victims are now adults, but ranged in age from nine to 13 years old at the time they say the assaults took place.

   They came forward in October, speaking to media about Runnickem.

   The men said the group Survivors Plus One has helped guide their cases.

4. Rewrite the following newspaper story in broadcast writing style. Assume that the news is current.

   Airplane Makes Emergency Landing, Clogs Interstate
   ORLANDO, Fla.—The pilot of a single-engine Cessna airplane made an emergency landing on busy Interstate 4 Friday, saving those on board the aircraft but stalling busy Walt Disney World traffic for hours.

   Rodney Berwalden, an amateur pilot and owner of a small electronics company in Savannah, Georgia, was flying with his girlfriend Joan Eldishay and her two children en route to Lakeland, Florida, to visit family. The plane was on the last leg of its trip when, Berwalden says, the engine on the 2011 model Cessna Skylane began to fail. Berwalden was following Interstate 4 from Daytona Beach to Lakeland at the time and decided to use the wide swath of concrete as his landing strip.

   "I knew we didn't have much time left in the air, so the interstate seemed like the best option," Berwalden said Saturday. "I saw some open lanes, so I went for it."

   Berwalden put the plane down in the rightmost two lanes of westbound I-4, just east of the Apopka-Vineland Road exit, near the Walt Disney World resort. The highway was clogged with weekend travelers headed for the theme park. Westbound traffic backed up for approximately four miles toward downtown Orlando.

   Orange County Sheriff's deputies and Florida State Highway Patrol troopers responded to check on the well-being of the aircraft's occupants and to try to restore traffic flow.

   "This was a first for all of us," said Cpl. Alice Lowellian of the Florida State Highway Patrol. "Seeing an airplane right in the middle of the road takes some getting used to."

   Officers were able to keep the two leftmost lanes of the interstate open while crews came to load the airplane on a flatbed, but gawkers slowed traffic to a walk. It took crews about two hours to clear the plane from the scene and get traffic back to normal.

   "I'm sorry to cause so many people to be late for their Disney World plans, but I had three people on this plane I had to protect," Berwalden said.

   The National Transportation Safety Board and Federal Aviation Administration have been called in to investigate the cause of the emergency landing. Early reports point to a fuel system problem on the plane, but the agencies said they would not have an official cause for some time.

   "We've just begun the process," said Varda Geister, a spokesperson for the NTSB. "These investigations typically take 90 to 120 days."

   As for Berwalden, he said he and his fellow travelers rented a car at Walt Disney World to finish their trip.

5. Write three paragraphs explaining how learning to write for radio and television makes you a better writer for print.

CHAPTER 13 COVERING A BEAT

Photo credit: Kevork Djansezian/Getty Images

A **beat** is a reporter's assigned area of responsibility. This might be an institution, such as city hall. It might be a geographic area, such as a school district or a county. It might be a topic, such as politics or sports. In any news organization, there are few assignments more important, both to the newsroom and to the public.

Nearly every reporter in a newsroom is assigned to a specific beat. Ashley Zavala is the state government and politics reporter for San Francisco's KRON-TV. Will Schmitt covered the Missouri statehouse for the *Springfield News-Leader* before taking a job reporting on city government at the *The Press Democrat* in Santa Rosa, California.

Chad Day keeps an eye on Capitol Hill as an investigative reporter for The Associated Press, after several years covering crime and juvenile justice for the *Arkansas Democrat-Gazette*. Day's work for the AP covered the Republican presidential campaign of Florida Sen. Marco Rubio, and after the 2016 Republican primaries, he moved to cover Donald Trump's bid for the presidency. He became one of the lead reporters on happenings in and around the Trump administration.

Making the transition from the Little Rock paper to an investigative beat in Washington, D.C., was a bit intimidating and time-consuming for Day. "I didn't have a byline for a month, and they were OK with that," he said. Day explained that the journalistic techniques he used to get acclimated to Capitol Hill were similar to those he employed while preparing to report on crime in Arkansas. "There's a dedicated FOIA (Freedom of Information Act) strategy, trying to read as much as you can about the beat as possible and taking down every single name that you see in a study, a report, a footnote of a court document, whatever, then trying to reach out and call those people," he says.

His advance work has paid off in Washington. Day publishes upwards of 200 stories a year in newspapers across the country and around the world, including *The Washington Post* and *The New York Times*. Although the beat requires him to cover the events of the day — a congressional hearing or a high-profile trial — he prefers talking to sources to dig up stories on his own. That's called working the beat.

In Washington, he said, there are some unique challenges, but it's not as difficult as it might seem. He likes the access. "And one of the best things about covering the Hill is that, at times, if you get in the hallway and you stand outside a room, you're gonna run into five or 10 lawmakers, and you're going to have the opportunity to talk to them. There's a lot of access, a lot of face time with the principal movers and shakers and their staff, and the people they rely on to have the information."

At any level of reporting, whether it's city hall, the crime beat or Capitol Hill, it's important that sources become comfortable with you. They should

In this chapter, you will learn:

1 Why beats are important.

2 Basic principles for covering any beat.

3 How to use social media in covering beat stories.

4 How to apply the basic principles to some of the most common beats.

know and trust that, as a journalist, you want to get the story right. Day cautions, however, that it's a two-way street: "A lot of times it's about me determining whether I can trust them."

The Importance of Beat Reporting

launchpadworks.com
WATCH: **"Agenda Setting and Gatekeeping"**

- What does it mean to say that major television networks and national newspapers are responsible for agenda setting?
- Some feel the rise of the internet cancels out the agenda-setting effect. Do you agree?

The goal of any beat reporter, as Day learned in Little Rock and Washington, is to hold accountable those who occupy positions of power and privilege. That accountability in journalism is vital to the health of the democracy.

Few beat reporters become media stars, as many White House reporters do, but all have been affected by technological and economic changes. Additionally, as you saw in Chapter 1, the definition of news itself is getting broader, which influences the range of beats. Along with standard beats (such as local government, police, business and sports), cultural beats reflect the interests and activities of a changing America — shopping malls, commuting, health, spiritual life and technology.

Covering beats is among the most important work in journalism. Economic pressures have cut the staffs in most newsrooms, print and broadcast, leaving fewer reporters and stretching their assignments over multiple beats. Often, today's reporters are trying to do more, on several platforms, in less time.

Whatever their locale or the size of their newsroom, beat reporters today are expected to tell their audiences what is happening and how to get involved. Stories include telephone numbers, email addresses and often Twitter handles along with the names of decision makers. Much of the most useful reporting is done in advance of public meetings, with the goal of empowering residents to become participants who make their voices heard rather than remain on the sidelines as passive onlookers. Readers are regularly invited to use email or online forums to speak up on public issues. Journalists and officials alike encourage Twitter followers and Facebook friends.

Despite all these changes, beat reporters remain the eyes and ears of their communities. As surrogates for their readers, they keep track of government, education, police, business and other powerful institutions that shape readers' lives.

The principles of good reporting apply to the coverage of any beat. The same principles also apply to specialized publications, including those aimed at particular industries, professions or ethnic groups. A reporter for *Women's Wear Daily* may cover fashion designers. A reporter for *Diario Las Américas* in Miami may cover Cuban exile politics. But each is doing the same job: discovering and writing news that's relevant, useful and interesting to the publication's readers.

Editors and audiences expect reporters on these specialized beats, like those in more traditional assignments, to provide information and understanding that will help readers improve the quality of their lives. That's important and rewarding work. But it's not easy.

Principles for Reporters on a Beat

Whether you cover the public library or the Pentagon, the county courthouse or the White House, the principles of covering a beat are the same. As David Nakamura, who covers the White House for *The Washington Post*, points out: "Ultimately, that's where the White House beat is similar to any other—reporters must be doggedly asking the right questions and relentless in demanding answers. They must be observant and able to identify important shifts in message and tactics, and they must be willing to challenge authority, even at the highest levels."

If you want to succeed as a reporter, you must be prepared, alert, persistent and wary. And on any beat, you must be there. These qualities will help you win the trust of your sources, keep up with important developments on your beat and avoid the trap of writing for your sources instead of your readers. Let's take a closer look at what each of those rules means in practice.

The Successful Beat Reporter Is . . .

- Prepared.
- Alert.
- Persistent.
- Present.
- Wary.

Be Prepared

Where should preparation begin? For you, it has already begun. To work effectively, a journalist needs a basic understanding of the workings of society and its various governments and institutions. You need to know at least the rudiments of psychology, economics and history. That is why the best education for a journalist is broad-based, providing exposure to the widest possible sampling of human knowledge.

But that exposure will not be enough when you face an important source on your first beat. You will need specific information you can acquire by familiarizing yourself with written accounts or records, combing news archives and institutional websites or talking to editors and previous reporters on your beat. Create as comprehensive a database as possible of important contacts. At the *Arkansas Democrat-Gazette*, Day said crime reporters over the years have created a list of phone numbers for every police department, sheriff's department and constable in the state that they hand off to their successors.

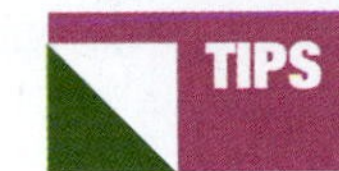

Preparing to Cover a Beat

- Use the internet, especially news archives, to acquire background information and understand context.
- Make note of continuing issues or ideas for stories to come.
- Become familiar with the laws governing the institution you cover.
- Pore over any budgets that are relevant to your beat.
- Look at your state's open-meeting and open-records laws.

Reading for background

In preparing to cover any beat, your first step is to learn as much as possible about the issues and personalities you'll be covering. Google is your friend. General and specialized search engines allow you to read the material that has been produced by your own organization and the relevant stories from other outlets worldwide. Create Google alerts that will automatically update your email about news coming out of your beat. You can often access the contents of major newspapers, magazines, research publications and other reference libraries without regard to physical distance. Use the internet to acquire background and to understand the context of local events and issues.

You'll want to double-check anything you learn from unfamiliar online sources. For example, if your new beat is medicine, you might begin with the website of the Association of Health Care Journalists (healthjournalism.org). If you're covering a local college or university, pay attention to *The Chronicle of Higher Education*. Television and web-only newsrooms are less likely to have their own libraries. Online sources make that less of a handicap. Your local public and university libraries are also valuable resources, with their online catalogs and collections of recent local periodicals.

In your local research, make notes of continuing issues, questions left dangling in previous stories or ideas for stories to come. Go back several years in your preparation. History might not repeat itself, but knowledge of it helps you assess the significance of current events and provides clues to what you can expect.

Library and internet research is only the start of your preparation. You must become familiar with the laws governing the institution you cover. If a governmental organization is your beat, find the state statutes or the city charter that created the agencies you will be covering. Learn the powers, duties and limitations of each official. You might be surprised to discover that someone is failing to do all that the law requires. Someone else might be doing more than the law allows.

Look at your state's open-meetings and open-records laws, too. Every state has such laws, although they vary widely in scope and effectiveness. Knowing what information is open to the public by law — and how to get it — can be a valuable tool for a reporter dealing with officials who may prefer to govern privately. (White House internal documents, as David Nakamura has learned, are exempt from the federal Freedom of Information Act.)

TIPS

Mining Social Media

- Follow the newsmakers on your beat on Facebook, Twitter and other platforms.
- Know the difference between following or "friending" someone on social media and "liking" or "favoriting" their posts.
- Be sure you're projecting a professional image on your own social media accounts.
- Monitor other news media outlets to see what they're reporting.

Mining social media

Today's beat reporters must recognize the value of social media as a tool for reporting the news and a way of monitoring and communicating with their sources. After you've been assigned a beat, it's important that you follow the newsmakers on that beat on Facebook, Instagram, LinkedIn, Pinterest, Snapchat, Twitter and Youtube.

Reporters on the city government beat, for example, should follow the mayor, city council members, the city manager and other department heads on Twitter and add them on Facebook. Many government entities (police and public works departments or school districts, for example) have Facebook pages and Twitter accounts that they use to convey information important to the publics they serve. If you're covering state government, be sure to watch legislators, the governor and other officeholders on social media. If you're a sports reporter, you'll quickly learn that athletes frequently break news through Twitter feeds or Facebook posts. Whatever beat you're working, it's a good idea to follow competing news outlets and journalists so you can keep pace with their reporting.

Journalists should be cautious about how they interact with their sources on social media. Adding people as "friends" on Facebook isn't an act of bias that suggests you agree with their positions or ideologies, but "liking" their posts or "favoriting" their tweets is different. Journalists must be careful not to cross those lines.

Journalists who are newly assigned to a beat need to clean up their social media presence to eliminate any indication of bias or opinion that might undermine their credibility and to ensure that they project a professional image online. That photo of you campaigning for a Republican Senate candidate or attending a rally of abortion rights supporters becomes inappropriate when you begin a career as a journalist. Photos that depict you drinking at a party should be removed. (Be aware that deleting photos from any site does not permanently eradicate the photos; it removes them from the site for the cursory viewer.)

Some journalists choose to have a dual presence on social media, creating two Twitter accounts (one personal and one professional) or separate Facebook pages, for instance. That's an individual decision. Either way, be aware of the public nature of your social media activity, and act accordingly. Consider also how privacy settings on your social media platforms can work for or against you.

Talking to sources

Now you're ready to start talking to people. You should conduct your first interviews in the newsroom with your predecessor on the beat, your assignment editor and any veterans who can shed light on the kinds of things that rarely appear in statute books or newspaper stories. Who has been a good source in the past? Who will lie to you? Who drinks to excess? Who seems to be living extravagantly? Whose friends are big land developers? Who wants to run for national office? Who has been hired, fired or promoted? Who has recently retired or moved to a competing company?

Some understanding of the workings of your own newsroom won't hurt, either. Has your predecessor on the beat been promoted? Has he or she been transferred because of unsatisfactory performance? Will an introduction from your predecessor help you or hurt you with your sources? And what are your boss's expectations? Is your assignment to report almost every activity of government, or will you have time to do some investigative work and analysis?

Only after gaining as much background as possible are you ready to face the people you will be covering. A quick handshake and a superficial question or two might be all you have time for in the first encounter, but within a week you should arrange for sit-down conversations with your most important sources to get acquainted with one another.

You might have noticed that the preparation for covering a beat is similar to the preparation for doing an interview or a single-story assignment. The important difference is that preparing for a beat is more detailed and requires more time and work. Instead of just preparing for a short-term task, you are laying the foundation for an important part of your career. A beat assignment usually lasts at least six months and often two years or more. Understanding that will help shape your first round of meetings with sources.

A story might emerge from those first interviews, but their purpose is much broader. You are trying to establish a relationship, trying to convert strangers into helpful partners in news gathering. To do that, you should demonstrate an interest in the sources as people as well as officials. Ask about their families, their interests, their philosophy, their goals. Make it clear with your questions that you are interested rather than ignorant.

Talking to Sources

- Talk to your predecessor on the beat, your assignment editor and veterans in the newsroom for background.
- Understand your boss's expectations.
- Establish a relationship with sources; demonstrate interest in them.

And be prepared to give something of yourself. If you both like to fish or went to Vassar or have children about the same age, seize on those ties. All of us feel comfortable with people who have something in common with us. This is the time, too, to let your sources know that you know something about their work and that you're interested in it.

Be Alert

Sometimes, being alert means thinking fast and seizing an opportunity. Sometimes, it means recognizing an important story when others don't. Important stories are seldom labeled as such. In many cases, the people involved might not realize the significance of what they are doing. Probably more often they realize it but hope nobody else will. The motivation for secrecy might be dishonesty, the desire to protect an image or a conviction that the public will misunderstand.

ON THE JOB Forming an Understanding of Your Beat

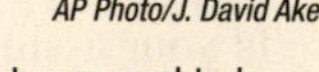

AP Photo/J. David Ake

You've already met **Chad Day**, who covers Capitol Hill as part of The Associated Press' investigative reporting team in Washington, D.C. Day had to climb the ladder to win the prestigious assignment. After earning his degree, Day completed an internship with *The Kansas City Star* in 2009. Then he spent six years at the *Arkansas Democrat-Gazette* in Little Rock, honing his data journalism skills while covering crime, juvenile justice and child mistreatment. He was named Arkansas Young Journalist of the Year in 2010 and has been honored with the state's I.F. Stone Award for investigative reporting.

One of Day's key pieces of advice for any beat reporter is to make open-records requests—whether through the federal Freedom of Information Act or state sunshine laws—for all the blank forms a government agency on the beat uses to collect information. Listen to him describe why and how he does it:

> It allows you to be able to see the data they collect. Not only data but just information about how they think. I did it with the police department in Little Rock. I did it with the juvenile justice system.
>
> You get a lot of pushback at first because people will say, "No, I can't give you those forms." And I say "No, no, no. I don't want the forms that are filled out. I just want the blank forms, and the blanks ones you have to give me because there's nothing on them."
>
> That allowed me to be able to understand a lot—particularly with juvenile justice—about what the data sets are, how they keep that information, the names of the systems they keep it in. You automatically have an internal window into all the jargon that they use, jargon that you're never going to put in a story but that you need to be able to talk to the sources.
>
> When I was covering the juvenile justice system in Arkansas, I knew they weren't going to give me the kids' names, but I also knew that they had all this other information that's recorded on the forms: their race and age range and the gender of the child.
>
> The forms are just a gold mine.
>
> I usually make the requests pretty narrow at first, like asking for all the forms the juvenile justice agency uses to book a child in, the booking packet. I'll go in and talk to them ahead of time and walk them through what I'm asking for. So they would give me that packet and then I would see that it lists some other forms. And then I'd do a follow-up request for those. You start building up a folder of all of these blank forms.
>
> You don't do it all at once. Otherwise you're really going to scare them. You do it little by little over time. I've found that, most of the time, once they understand what you're doing, they'll know: "We can't refuse you."

If your beat is a government agency, you will find that many public officials and public employees think they know more about what is good for the public than the public does. The theory of democratic government is that an informed citizenry can make decisions or elect representatives to make those decisions in its own best interests. If you are the reporter assigned to city hall, the school board or the courthouse, you carry a heavy responsibility for helping your audience put that theory into practice. To discharge that responsibility, you must probe beneath the surface of events in search of the whys and hows that lead to understanding.

When you are presented with a news release or hear an announcement or cover a vote, ask yourself these questions before passing the event off in a few paragraphs:

- **Who will benefit from this, and who will be hurt?** If the tentative answer to the first part suggests private interests or the answer to the second part is the public, some digging is in order.
- **How important is this?** An event that is likely to affect many people for good or ill usually deserves more explanation than one affecting only a handful.
- **Who is for this, and who is against it?** Answers to these questions are often obvious or at least easy to figure out. When you know them, the answers to the first two questions usually become clearer.
- **How much will this cost, and who will pay?** An architect's design for renovating public buildings may look less attractive when the price tag is attached. A campaign by the Chamber of Commerce to lure new industry may require taxpayers to pay for new roads, sewers, fire protection, and even schools and other services for an increased population.

The answers to these questions allow you to judge that most important element of news value—impact.

Be Persistent

Persistence means two things to a reporter on a beat. First, it means that when you ask a question, you do not give up until you get an answer. Second, it means that you must keep track of slow-developing projects or problems.

Insisting on a responsive answer

One of the most common faults of beginning reporters is that they give up too easily. They settle for answers that are unresponsive to their questions, or they return to the newsroom not sure they understand what they were told. In either case, the result is an incomplete, confusing story.

"Why do our fourth-graders score below average on these reading tests?" you ask the school superintendent.

He might reply: "Let me first conceptualize the parameters of the socioeconomic context for you."

The real answer probably is "I only wish I knew."

Insisting on a Responsive Answer

- Cut through the jargon and evasions in search of substance.
- Rephrase technical language in plain English.
- Make sure you understand the answers you're getting before you try conveying them to your audience.

Your job is to cut through the jargon and the evasions in search of substance. Often that is not an easy task. Many experts, or people who want to be regarded as experts, are so caught up in the technical language of their special field that they find it almost impossible to communicate clearly. Many others seek refuge in gobbledygook or resort to evasion when they don't know an answer or find the answer embarrassing. Educators and lawyers are particularly adept at such tactics.

Listen politely for a few minutes while the school superintendent conceptualizes his parameters. When he finishes or pauses for breath, lead him back toward where you want to go. One way is to say, "It sounds to me as if you're saying . . ." and rephrase what he has told you in plain English. At those times when you simply are in the dark — and that may be often — just confess your puzzlement and ask for a translation. And keep coming back to the point: "But how does all that affect reading scores?" "How can the problem be solved?" "What are you doing about it?"

All the while, you must ask yourself, "Does that make sense to me?" "Can I make it make sense to my readers?" Don't quit until the answer is yes. You should not be obnoxious, but you do have to be persistent.

Following up on slow developments

Persistence is also required when you are following slow-developing events. Gardeners do not sit and watch a seed germinate. They do, however, check every few days, looking for the green shoots that indicate growth is taking place. If the shoots are late, they dig in to investigate.

Beat reporting works much the same way. Officials announce a downtown redevelopment plan, say, or a revision in a school's curriculum. The story covers the plans and the hoped-for benefits. The seed is planted. If it is planted on your beat, make a note to yourself to check it in a week or two. And a week or two after that. And a month after that. Start a file of reminders so you won't forget. Such a file often is called a **tickler** because it serves to tickle your memory. Your phone and your laptop will have apps for that.

Like seeds, important projects of government or business take time to develop. Often what happens during the long, out-of-public-view development is more important than the announcements at the occasional news conferences or the promises of the promotional brochures. Compromises are made. Original plans turn out to be impractical or politically unpalatable. Consultants are hired. Contracts are signed. Public money is spent. The public interest may be served, or it may not.

Sometimes the story is that nothing is happening. At other times, the story might be that the wrong things are happening. Consulting contracts might go to cronies of the mayor. Redevelopment might enhance the property values of big downtown landowners. Curriculum revisions might be shaped by influential pressure groups.

Even if nothing improper is taking place, the persistent reporter will give readers an occasional update. At stake, after all, are the public's money and welfare.

Be Present

In beat reporting, there is no substitute for personal contact. Trying to do it all by telephone or email won't work. The only way to cover a beat is to be there as often as possible. Joking with secretaries, talking politics with council members and lawyers, worrying over the budget or trading gossip with the professional staff: You must make yourself a part of the community you are covering. Being present is more than making connections. It's about actively following through while you're with those people — being an active participant in the conversation.

Sometimes, being present provides opportunities beyond the obvious story. Jim Yardley, who reports on the Vatican for *The New York Times*, decided to use Twitter and Instagram to take his readers along when Pope Francis traveled to his native South America.

By using social media, Yardley was able to give his readers a sense of immediacy and involvement — a feeling of being with him at the pope's side — in real time. This is an increasingly common approach, at the *Times* and elsewhere, as reporters try to share with readers not only what the story is but how it was obtained.

Remember that the sources who are most important to you probably are in great demand by others, too. They have jobs to do. Maneuver to get as much of their time as you need, but don't demand too much. Do your homework first. Don't expect a school superintendent to explain basic concepts of education or a city manager to explain how an annual budget is assembled. You can learn that information by talking with an aide or by reading. What you need to learn from the superintendent is how he or she intends to apply those concepts, or why they seem to be inapplicable here.

There are other simple techniques you can use to build and maintain good relationships with the people on your beat. Here are some of them:

- **Do a favor when you can.** As a reporter, you spend much of your time asking other people to do favors for you — giving you their time, sharing information they need not share, looking up records and figures. If a source needs a favor in return, don't refuse unless it would be unethical. The favors asked are usually small things, like getting a daughter's engagement picture or a club announcement in the paper, procuring a print of a picture taken with the governor to decorate the official's wall, bringing in a few copies of a favorable feature you wrote. Day has occasionally relayed contact information for one source to another or helped an attorney get a copy of a courtroom sketch artist's work.
- **Don't shun good news.** One ill-founded but common complaint is that news media report only bad news. Admittedly, there is usually no story when people are doing what they are supposed to do. Sometimes there should be a

story if they do their duty uncommonly well, have done it for a very long time or do it under the burden of some handicap. Sources like these "good news" stories, and so do readers. Watch for opportunities to do profiles or feature stories that emphasize what official actors are doing to benefit their communities.

- **Protect your sources.** Many people in government—politicians and bureaucrats alike—are willing to tell a reporter things they are not willing to have their names attached to in print or otherwise. The same is true of people in private business, who might fear reprisals from their employers, coworkers or competitors. Sometimes such would-be anonymous sources are trying to use you to enhance their own positions. You have to protect yourself and your audience against that possibility. Confer with an editor if you have doubts.

  Most news organizations are properly wary of relying on unnamed sources. Sometimes, though, the requests for anonymity are valid and necessary to protect the source's career. When you have agreed to protect a source, you must do it. Don't tell anyone but your editor.

  An inability to keep your mouth shut can cost you more than a source; it can cost you your reputation. (The protection of sources has legal as well as ethical implications. So-called shield laws in some states offer limited exemptions for journalists from legal requirements to disclose sources; see Chapter 19. But there are no blanket exemptions.)

- **Above all, be accurate.** Inaccurate reporting leads first to loss of respect from sources, then to loss of the sources themselves and finally to loss of the job. If you are a good, tough reporter, not all of the contacts on your beat will love you. But if you are an accurate reporter, they will respect you. Some news providers conduct accuracy checks, reading back to their sources any facts or quotes attributed to them—along with relevant context—to be sure they have things right. They double-check every fact gleaned from documents before they publish. Taking these steps can help both reporters and sources sleep better at night.

Beat reporting is a lot like gardening. Both require you to be in the field every day, cultivating. And in both, the amount of the harvest is directly proportional to the amount of labor invested.

Be Wary

The point of all this effort—the preparation, alertness, persistence and personal contact—is to keep your audience informed. That is an obvious statement, but it needs to be made because every beat reporter is under pressure that can obscure the readers' importance. You must be wary of this problem.

Even with the interactivity offered by online, mobile and social media services, you will have little to do with most of your audience. They will not write you notes when you have done a story they like or call you when they dislike what you have said or written. They will not offer to buy you a cup of coffee or lunch or stop you in the hall to urge you to see things their way. But your sources will.

If you report that city council members are thinking about raising the property-tax levy, you will probably hear complaints from council members about premature disclosure. If you report that the police department is racked by dissension, expect a less-than-friendly reaction from the chief. If you report that the CEO of a major business is looking for a new job, the chances are that he or she will deny it even though the story is true.

All sources have points of view, programs to sell, careers to advance, opponents to undercut. It is likely that they will try to persuade you of the merit of their viewpoint, try to sell their programs through your reporting, try to shape the news to help their careers.

Be wary of sources' efforts to use you. You can lose the critical distance a reporter must maintain from those being covered. When that happens, you start thinking like a participant rather than an observer. You begin reporting for your sources rather than your audience. This is a real danger. No one can spend as much time with sources as a beat reporter does or devote as much effort to understanding them without becoming sympathetic. You may forget that you are a surrogate for the outsiders when you associate so closely with the insiders.

Beat Reporting Across Media Platforms

Online media offer the opportunity for instant reporting. With smartphones, digital cameras and laptop computers, reporters can and do file short reports and even photographs and video for posting on the web as the story unfolds. For newspaper reporters, this is a high-tech return to the distant days of multiple editions, when instead of one deadline a day journalists had many. For radio and television reporters, the online opportunities match those of live reporting over the air.

The Benefits and Challenges of Reporting Across Platforms

The internet and social media, in particular, give journalists the ability to be immediate in their coverage. That ability, however, creates an expectation among audiences that their news sources will provide this immediacy. Rather than wait until an entire city council meeting unfolds to begin writing a report, journalists today can send tweets from the council chamber as the news unfolds. When big news breaks, it can be reported immediately as a news burst or bulletin on your news outlet's website and also on its Twitter account and Facebook page.

Increasingly, newspapers and broadcast outlets have turned to rolling reports in which they continuously update the news online as it's happening and as they learn about it. This in many ways mirrors the longstanding "write-through" practices of wire services—rewriting an original story again and again as information becomes available. The primary difference is that updates today are immediately shared with readers and viewers.

Soon after Will Schmitt completed his master's degree in 2016, he went to work covering Missouri state government for the *Springfield-News Leader* and became the paper's lead reporter on scandals surrounding then-Gov. Eric Greitens, including allegations that he assaulted a woman with whom he had an extramarital affair, blackmailed the woman with a photo of her partially nude, illegally used dark money and a donor list from a nonprofit he created, and improperly used the app Confide, which deletes text messages as soon as they've been read.

Defiant for months, Greitens in May 2018 decided to resign. Schmitt was on vacation and found himself commiting journalism remotely. Using his cell phone and wifi at Kansas City International Airport and on the plane, he was able to report the story immediately on Twitter and for the newspaper's website and print editions.

This experience drives home both the power journalists have to report news from anywhere and also the commitment they must make to their beats. The news never ends, and neither does the job. You have to be ready to report breaking news, no matter the circumstance.

ANNOTATED MODEL A Crime Story Across Media Platforms

A reporter on the crime beat starts reporting instantly via Twitter, follows up with Facebook posts and then revises the story online and in print. Then she writes a blog post highlighting issues raised by the story.

Twitter feed (2 p.m.)
@COPSBEAT Another "bear hug" just reported; this @ Springfield College campus. More soon.

A tweeted news flash contains only bare-bones facts, with the promise of follow-up.

Twitter feed (2:30 p.m.)
@COPSBEAT Suspect described as white man in 20s, reddish beard, bad breath. Composite being circulated @Springfield College and university campuses.

Developing facts are added to the Twitter feed.

Facebook post, shared on relevant campus Facebook pages (2:40 p.m.)
Springfield police are searching for a white man in his early 20s with a reddish beard and bad breath. He is a suspect in three "bear hug" assaults that have occurred in the past two days on the Springfield College and university campuses. Composite sketches of the suspect are being circulated at both schools. Police are asking that anyone with information contact them immediately.

A Facebook post gives additional background to the breaking news and reports a police request.

Web report (3 p.m.)
Springfield College campus police report that an unknown assailant grabbed a female student from behind at 1:25 p.m. on the college campus.

This is the third such assault to be reported in the past two days. The first two both occurred on the university campus. Police suspect the same man is involved.

The suspect is described as a strongly built white male, in his 20s, with a reddish beard and bad breath. Police have produced a composite sketch and are circulating it on both campuses.

In all three instances, the victim was walking alone in a relatively secluded area of the campus during daylight hours. None of the victims was seriously injured. None knew the assailant.

The reporter follows her social media accounts with an online report that includes as many details as are immediately available.

Twitter feed (7:30 p.m.)
@COPSBEAT Police arrest Thomas Albright as suspect in "bear hug" assaults @Springfield College and university campuses.

Tweets continue the updates even after the first web report.

Facebook post, shared on relevant campus Facebook pages (7:45 p.m.)
Thomas Albright has been arrested as the suspect in the Springfield College and university campus "bear hug" assaults.

Important updates can be repeated on several social media platforms.

(continued)

ANNOTATED MODEL A Crime Story Across Media Platforms *(continued)*

Web update (8 p.m.)

The web report is updated with important information.

A university student has been arrested and charged with being the "bear hug" assailant who assaulted women on both the university and Springfield College campuses.

University police gave the suspect's name as Thomas Albright. He is identified as a 20-year-old sophomore from Chicago.

Springfield College campus police reported earlier that an unknown assailant grabbed a female student from behind at 1:25 p.m. on the college campus.

It was the third such assault to be reported in the past two days. The first two both occurred on the university campus.

Police suspect Albright was the culprit in all three assaults. He was arrested after police circulated a composite sketch of the suspect on both campuses and then received an anonymous tip identifying Albright as the assailant.

In all three instances, the victim was walking alone in a relatively secluded area of the campus during daylight hours. None of the victims was seriously injured. None knew the assailant.

Newspaper story (following morning)

A university student has been arrested and charged with being the "bear hug" assailant who assaulted women on both the university and Springfield College campuses.

With the benefit of extra time, the reporter is able to wrap up the story, with additional background and detail. This more complete account will also be posted on the newspaper's website.

University police gave the suspect's name as Thomas Albright. He is identified as a 20-year-old sophomore from Chicago.

A police spokesman said that, after sketches of an unknown suspect were circulated on both campuses, police received an anonymous call naming Albright as the perpetrator. He was taken into custody about 8 p.m. and was identified by at least one of the victims.

The spokesman said Albright denied the accusations but admitted to having tried to find a former girlfriend he believes to be a Springfield College student.

The first incident took place Monday afternoon near the university's recreation center. The victim, a university senior, told police that she screamed and that the man who had grabbed her around the waist from behind turned and fled.

The second assault was later that day, in the Hitt Street parking garage. In that incident, the victim told police the assailant asked her if she was someone whose name she didn't recognize. When she said she wasn't, he mumbled something and released her, she said.

(continued)

ANNOTATED MODEL A Crime Story Across Media Platforms *(continued)*

The third assault was Tuesday afternoon on the Springfield College campus. That victim had much the same experience as in the second incident.

None of the victims was seriously injured.

Albright is in the city jail awaiting a preliminary hearing.

"Cops Beat" blog (later that day)

The blog is where a conversation between reporter and readers can begin. So blog posts can and should be more conversational, more informal than news stories. Notice that a bit of opinion sneaks in, which also would be out of place in a news story. And notice that the reporter, after checking with her editor, is soliciting reader reaction.

The cops are trying to downplay this case of the Bear-Hug Bandit so as to avoid frightening any more women. At least one officer told me as much, but since the comment was anonymous, we didn't use it in the news story. It seems to me and my editor, though, that students and administrators on both campuses should use this as a take-off point for an examination of security, especially in more secluded areas, such as parking garages. Could have been much worse. What do you think?

The need and desire for speed cannot trump the imperative of accuracy. Before you post breaking news on Twitter or Facebook, you have to take the time to verify it. Refrain from retweeting information from social media sources without first making sure it's true. There's no place in journalism for rumor or speculation.

With that opportunity comes obligation. Beat reporters at all levels are expected to blog, send Twitter messages and post updates to social networking sites throughout the day. This takes time and energy and often cuts into the reporter's opportunity for in-depth research or even the conversations that are important in developing sources.

Also, reporters are expected to gather and present to audiences more information, more detail and more points of view online than print, television or radio permit. Citizens who care enough to follow an issue online want and expect to see the source documents reporters use — and that policymakers use. Document Cloud is a free online tool that makes it easy for journalists to share those documents with their readers. Audiences also want and expect links to other websites that offer related information or further background.

But what really sets online and social media apart is interactivity. Social media such as Twitter and Facebook both facilitate interactivity — with sources as well as readers. It's common for a reporter to start covering a beat story with on-the-scene tweets that give the basic facts. Facebook posts offer a little more space and another platform for quickly reporting the news. It's also important that the journalist monitor — and, when appropriate, respond to — any social media conversations that ensue from his or her work.

After taking some time for research, the reporter might follow up with a web story that gives more detail and then update that story as more information becomes available. By the next morning, she or he will have written a print story for the newspaper that contains even more detail and background. Finally, later that day, the reporter might return to the story, this time to write a post for the beat blog that readers respond to. See the annotated model "A Crime Story Across Media Platforms" for an example of how a beat story can progress across media platforms.

This fast-paced use of new media brings its own hazards. It's impossible to be nuanced with a small number of characters, so a reporter in a hurry can easily overstate or misstate something that comes back to bite painfully. In a breaking-news story, authorities don't always have the facts straight, yet the reporter often can't wait for information to be confirmed before getting it out. Finally, tweets are unedited, so the reporter has no editorial "safety net" to catch errors and questionable information. Rereading your tweets at least twice before

Writing Professional Tweets

Because Twitter is such an immediate and informal-feeling medium, it's easy to allow professional standards to slip. Make it a habit to treat your tweets with as much care you do your lengthier texts. Before sending a tweet, check for the following:

- **The information is important, accurate and timely.** Journalists should refrain from flooding readers with unnecessary or repetitive tweets. And although Twitter is an indispensable tool for instant reporting, reporters need to verify information before sharing it with followers. Don't let the desire for immediacy cause you to send out reports that you later will have to correct.
- **Links in the tweet work.** Use a URL shortener such as Goo.gl (https://goo.gl) or Bitly (https://bitly.com) to avoid using too many of your limited characters.
- **Any photos or videos you include have meaning.** Photographs and short videos, even if they're not of the highest professional quality, can convey lots of information without eating up characters. Don't include them unless you are certain they are of value to your audience.
- **Your writing is clear, unambiguous and free of bias and innuendo.** The language of Twitter is casual, but journalists should maintain a professional tone and avoid snarky messages. Occasional humor is acceptable if it doesn't undermine the news you're attempting to convey or stray into the realm of opinion.
- **Your spelling and grammar are correct. Proofread tweets at least twice.** With a 280-character limit, it's common for journalists to use abbreviations or shortcuts in their tweets that they wouldn't use in news reports. Do so sparingly, however.
- **You have used logical hashtags to help audiences follow the subject at hand.** If you're tweeting about the tornado that just swept through town, for example, use #springfieldtwister to convey the news so that others can find it quickly. Refer your website and Facebook audiences to the Twitter hashtag so they can follow along.

hitting Send is critical. All these hazards make it critical for reporters to be as thorough as possible at every stage of a story.

Using Social Media to Find Sources and Audiences

Social media is useful for conveying information and also for going beyond the usual suspects to find additional and interesting sources or to gather information. Search hashtags to see who's posting on Twitter about the news that's occurring, and follow up with those who appear to know what they're talking about or who have been directly affected by the events of the day. Visit the Facebook pages of people in the news to see what sorts of conversations they're having with others. Many newspapers use their content management systems or online services such as RebelMouse to aggregate social media posts and share them with their audiences as a complement to traditional reporting.

Social media also can be a powerful tool for promoting a journalist's work and ensuring the right audiences find it. If you've written a story about a rare sighting of the golden-cheeked warbler in your area, it makes sense to share a link to your story on the Facebook pages of the local chapter of the Audubon Society and the state conservation department. You can also mention the story on your Twitter account, tweet it directly at interested groups and use a hashtag that bird-watchers will quickly discover. If the school board voted to change the attendance zones for your district's elementary schools, posting that story on school and PTA Facebook pages makes a lot of sense. As soon as the story is in front of the most relevant audiences, it's likely to be shared and read by scores of readers who otherwise would not have found it on your web page or in your newspaper or broadcast.

It pays for journalists in the digital age to be nimble in the myriad uses of social media. Those who ignore its potential do so at their own peril.

What's the grammar error in this sentence?

Since the U.S. Supreme Court's decision in Obergefell v. Hodges, *federal law requires that every state issues marriage licenses to same-sex couples.*

See Appendix 1, Rule 18.

Covering the Most Important Local Beats

Your political science courses will introduce you to the structure of government, but from a reporter's viewpoint, function is usually even more important than structure. You must learn who holds the real power, who has the most influence on the power-holders and who are the most likely sources of accurate information. The specifics vary from city to city, but some general principles will help you when covering any type of state or local institution:

- **Information is power.** The holder of information may be a professional administrator (the city manager, school superintendent, police chief or court clerk) or an elected official (the mayor, chair of the county commission or chair of the school board). It might be someone further down the ladder: a city planner, a county road worker, or a school secretary. The job title is unimportant. Find the person who knows in detail how an organization really works, where the money goes and how decisions are made. Get to know that person because he or she will be the most important person on your beat.

launchpadworks.com
WATCH: **"Newspapers and the Internet: Convergence"**

- Careers in journalism have changed with the rise of the internet. How might these changes affect recent journalism graduates?
- How do online news stories and traditional print news stories differ? What new skills does the online world require? What skills are the same?

- **The budget is the blueprint.** This principle is a corollary of the first. Just as detailed knowledge of how an organization works is the key to controlling that organization, a budget is the blueprint for the organization's activities. The budget tells where the money comes from and where it goes. It tells how many people are on the payroll and how much they are paid. It tells what programs are planned for the year and how much they will cost. Over several years' time, the budget tells where the budget-makers' priorities are and what they see as their organization's role in the community.

  Find copies of the last two or three years' budgets for your beat. Learn all you can from your predecessor and from newspaper clips. Then find the architect who drew up this blueprint — the budget director or the clerk or the assistant superintendent — and get a translation. Ask all the questions you can think of. Write down the answers.

  When budget-making time arrives, follow every step. Attend every public hearing and every private discussion session you can. In those dollar figures are some of the most important stories you will write — stories of how much your readers will be paying for schools and roads and garbage pickup, stories of what they will get for their money and stories about public services that might be cut.

- **Distributing power and money is politics.** While looking for your beat's power centers and unraveling its budget mysteries, you also will be absorbing the most interesting part of beat reporting: politics. At any level in any type of organization, power and money go hand in hand with politics. Politics provides the mechanisms through which limited resources are allocated among many competing groups. You will have to learn to spot subtle forms of political maneuvering because neither elections nor political parties are necessary for politics.

  If you are covering city hall, for example, pay close attention as the city budget is being drafted. You may find the mayor's pet project being written in by the city manager. Are the builders influential in town? If so, you will probably find plenty of road and sewer projects in the budget. If the city employees are unionized, look for generous wage and benefit increases. A vocal retirees' organization may account for the proposed senior citizens' center. None of these projects is necessarily bad just because it is political. But you and your readers ought to know who is getting what and why.

  Now suppose an election is coming up, and the builders' campaign contributions will be heavy. A councilman who is running for mayor switches his vote from money for parks to money for new roads. Has a deal been made? Has a vote been sold? That's politics, too. Some digging is in order.

Crucial Factors and Practical Principles for Beat Reporters

- Power: Information is power.
- Money: The budget is the blueprint.
- Politics: Distributing power and money is politics.

Power, money and politics are the crucial factors to watch in any beat reporting. With this in mind, let's take a closer look at the most important local beats.

City and County Government

Most medium-size cities have council-manager governments. The mayor and council members hire a professional administrator to manage the day-to-day affairs of the city. The manager, in turn, hires the police and fire chiefs, the public works director and other department heads. Under the city charter, the council is supposed to make policy and leave its implementation to the manager. Council members are usually forbidden to meddle in the affairs of any department.

Some cities, such as New York and Chicago, have governments in which the mayor serves as chief administrator.

Whatever the structure of your city, you will have a range of good sources to draw on:

- **Subordinate administrators.** They know details of budgets, planning and zoning, and personnel matters. They are seldom in the spotlight, so many welcome a reporter's attention as long as the reporter does not get them into trouble. Many are bright and ambitious and are willing to second-guess their superiors and gossip about politics, again providing you can assure them that the risk of getting into trouble is low. In smaller communities, you might find better access to officials such as police and fire chiefs or planning directors. In larger ones, you'll often be directed toward spokespeople or community relations specialists. Although they can be helpful, you should always strive to get beyond the filtered information they provide and talk directly with the people who have firsthand knowledge of the issues you're exploring.
- **Council members.** Politicians, as a rule, love to talk. What they say is not always believable, and you have to be wary of their attempts to use you, but they will talk. So ask one council member about the political forces behind another member's pet project, and ask the other about the first's mayoral ambitions. This improves the odds that you will learn all there is to know.
- **Pressure groups.** You can obtain an expert view of the city's land-use policies from land developers and a different view from conservationists. The manager or the personnel director will tell one side of the labor-management story. The head of the employees' union will tell the other. How about the city's record in hiring minorities? Get to know the head of the NAACP or of the local Urban League chapter. Public officials respond to pressure. As a reporter, you need to understand what the pressures are and who applies them.
- **Public citizens.** Consumer advocate Ralph Nader made the term "public citizens" popular, but every town has people — lawyers, homemakers, business executives, retirees — who serve on charter commissions, head bond campaigns, work in elections and advise behind the scenes. Such people can be sources of sound background information and useful assessments of officeholders.
- **Opponents.** The best way to find out the weaknesses of any person or program is to talk with an opponent. Seek out the board member who wants to fire the school superintendent. Look up the police captain demoted by the new chief. Chat with the leader of the opposition to the new hospital. There are at least two sides to every public question and every public figure. Your job is to explore them all.

After you have found the sources, keep looking, listening and asking for tips, for explanations, for reactions, for stories. The fun is just starting.

Covering a county government is very much like covering a city government. In both cases you deal with politicians, with administrators, with budgets, with problems. The similarities may be obscured by differences in structure and style, however.

Cities are more likely to have professional administrators, for example. The administration of county governments is more likely to be in the hands of elected commissioners, supervisors or judges. Counties, too, are more likely to have a multitude of elected officials, from the sheriff to the recorder of deeds. City governments are more likely to be bureaucracies. One way to generalize about the differences is to say that city governments are often more efficient and county governments are more responsive.

These differences frequently mean, for a reporter, that county government is easier to cover. More elected officials means more politicians. That, in turn, can mean more talkative sources, more open conflict, more points at which constituents and reporters alike can gain access to the governmental structure.

The principles and the problems of reporting are the same. The budget remains the blueprint whether it is drafted by a professional administrator or an elected officeholder. Knowledge is power, whether it is the city manager or the elected county auditor who knows where the money goes. Politics is politics.

The Schools

No institution is more important to any community than its schools. None is worse covered. And none is more demanding of or rewarding to a reporter. The issues that arise on the school beat are among the most important in our society. If the schools are your beat, be prepared to write about racial tensions, drug abuse, obscenity versus free speech, religious conflict, crime, labor-management disputes, politics, sex—and yes, education.

The process of learning and teaching can be obscured by the furor arising from the more dramatic issues. Even when everyone else seems to have forgotten,

Writing for Readers

What does it mean to write for your audience instead of your sources? It means that you must follow several important guidelines:

- **Translate.** The language of bureaucrats, educators, scientists and lawyers is not the same language most people speak. You need to learn the jargon of your sources, but you also need to learn how to translate it into standard English for your audience.
- **Think of the public pocketbook.** If the tax rate is going up 14 percent, how much will that cost the average homeowner? If teachers are seeking a 10 percent raise, how much will that cost the school district?
- **Get out of the office.** City council or school board votes are important, but many more people will have personal contact with government in the form of a police officer, a clerk or a bus driver than with a council member. Go to where government meets its constituents. You will get a reader's-eye view of your beat, and you may find some unexpected stories.
- **Ask the audience members' questions.** Ask "Why?" "How much will it cost me?" "What will I get out of it?" You are the public's ombudsman.
- **Be prepared, alert, persistent and wary.** If you, as a good beat reporter, always keep in mind the people you are writing for, you'll keep the customers — and the editors — satisfied.

though, you must remember that those are only side issues. The most important part of the school beat is what goes on in the classroom.

Whether those classrooms hold kindergartners or high school students, the principles for covering education remain the same. For the most part, the issues are the same, too. When the schools are private rather than public, you have fewer rights of access.

The classroom is not an easy place to cover. You may have trouble getting into one. Administrators frequently turn down such requests on the grounds that a reporter's presence in a classroom would be disruptive. But a good teacher and an unobtrusive reporter can overcome that drawback easily. Many newspapers, at the start of the school year, assign a reporter to an elementary school classroom. In visiting frequently, they become a part of the classroom community. And that reporter captures for readers much of the sight and sound and feeling of education.

There are other ways, too, of letting readers in on how well — or how badly — the schools are doing their job. Here are some of them:

- **Examine standardized test scores.** The federal No Child Left Behind law, passed under the George W. Bush administration, has forced testing to the core of every conversation about school quality. The Obama administration's Race to the Top program in education has added complications. Every school system administers standardized tests designed to measure how well its students compare either with a set standard or with other students. Insist on learning about the results of such tests. Try to present these scores to your audience in as friendly a graphic format as possible.

  The frequency and importance of standardized testing has become big news. Make sure you know what the context of the controversy is and what the experts say. Find out what decisions are made on the basis of standardized test scores: Do schools with lower scores get additional faculty? Do they get special-education teachers? Are they budgeted to receive more or less money?

- **Be alert to other indicators of school quality.** You can find out how many graduates of your school system go to college, how many win scholarships and what colleges they attend. You can find out how your school system measures up to the standards of the state department of education. National organizations of teachers, librarians and administrators also publish standards they think schools should meet. How close do your schools come?
- **Understand that in education, as in anything else, you get what you pay for.** How does the pay of teachers in your district compare with pay in similar-size districts? How does the tax rate compare? What is the turnover rate among teachers?
- **Get to know as many teachers, administrators, parents and students as possible.** You can learn to pick out the teachers who care about children and learning. One way to do this is to encourage them to talk about their jobs. A good teacher's warmth will come through. Parents often are tapped into emerging issues or activities at the schools and can be invaluable sources of information.

Keeping Up with Issues on the Education Beat

- Subscribe to trade newsletters and magazines.
- Remember the most important part of the beat: what goes on in the classroom.
- Understand what standardized test scores mean.
- Get to know teachers, administrators and students.
- Get acquainted with the parent associations at the schools on your beat.
- Follow relevant organizations and government agencies on social media.

One reason schools are covered poorly is that the school beat often does not produce the obvious, easy stories of politics, personalities and conflict that the city hall and police beats yield. School board meetings usually produce a spark only when a side issue intrudes. Most school board members are more comfortable talking about issues other than education itself, which is often left to the professionals.

The school stories that matter most are those that touch on the most sensitive issues. The ongoing controversy over safety is one. Such stories may help districts prevent a tragedy. Another is the politically charged question of charter schools versus traditional open-enrollment schools. And you can't ignore the classroom complications of race and poverty.

The politics and the budgets of schools are very much like those of other institutions. The uniquely important things about schools are the classrooms and the things that happen inside them. Your reporting will suffer if you forget that fact. So will your audience.

Higher Education

Look around you. Relevant and useful stories are everywhere. From the next meeting of the governing board to the classroom of a popular teacher, the same principles that apply to coverage of primary and secondary schools can be applied on the college campus.

Politics, economics and pedagogy are also prime prospects for examination. Politics may be partisan, especially in public universities with elected or appointed governing boards, or it may be bureaucratic, as individuals or departments compete for power and prestige. The economics of higher education translates to budgets, salaries and tuition costs. Pedagogy, the art and science of teaching, is often overlooked by reporters, but it is really the point of the enterprise.

The Chronicle of Higher Education and campus newsletters are required background reading. *The Chronicle* offers insights into national issues and trends, and newsletters give you insights into the nitty-gritty of local developments.

Suppose, for example, that *The Chronicle* reports a nationwide increase in the average cost of tuition. The obvious local story is what's happening on your campus and how that compares with the situation at peer institutions. A less obvious story may be how students are scraping together tuition money. And an even better, though more difficult, story would be how rising costs affect who can afford to attend and therefore the composition—by race, ethnicity, social class, even geography—of the student body.

To cover your campus, you'll have to overcome the natural hesitancy of many students to challenge professors, administrators and other authority figures. Try to think of them as sources and possible subjects of stories, and treat them respectfully. If your campus is state-supported, they are public officials, after all. That means, among other things, that state laws governing open meetings and records apply.

Here are a few of the topics that should yield good stories on most campuses:

- **Politics.** Who are members of the governing board, and how are they chosen? What's their agenda? Within the campus, which are the favored departments? How much clout do different student organizations wield with the campus administration or alumni? In an institution founded on free inquiry, just how free is speech for students, faculty and staff?

- **Finances.** How much is the president paid? The faculty? The janitors? Where does the money to support the institution really come from? The state? Tuition? Alumni giving? Research grants and contracts? Where does that money go? How much is spent on intercollegiate athletics? How much on the English and history departments?
- **Pedagogy.** Who are the best (and worst) teachers on campus? Is good teaching rewarded as much as research is? Among the faculty, who receives tenure, and who doesn't? Who does the teaching, anyway? Senior faculty? Graduate students? Part-timers?
- **Research.** What sorts of cutting-edge studies are the faculty engaged in? Who are the experts on emerging issues involving the environment, medicine, the economy, or agriculture? Who is funding their research and why?

You can practice good reporting without leaving your campus.

Police

The police beat probably produces more good, readable stories per hour of reporter time than any other beat. It also produces some of the worst, laziest reporting and generates many of our most serious legal and ethical problems. It is the beat many cub reporters start on and the beat many veterans stay on until they have become almost part of the police force. It offers great frustrations and great opportunities. All these contradictions arise from the nature of police work and of reporting.

If you are going to be a police reporter — and nearly every reporter is, at least briefly — the first thing you have to understand is what police officers are and what they do. We hire police officers to protect us from one another. We require them to deal every day with the dregs of society. Abuse and danger are parts of the job, as is boredom. For the most part, we pay police officers mediocre wages and accord them little status. We ask them to be brave but compassionate, stern but tolerant.

When you walk into a police station as a reporter for the first time, expect to be met with some suspicion, even hostility. Police officers often perceive young reporters as being radical, unkempt, anti-authority. How closely does that description fit you and your classmates?

Police departments are quasi-military organizations, with strict chains of command and strong discipline. Their members are sworn to uphold the status quo. The reasons that police and young reporters are mutually suspicious should be clear by now.

Then how do you cover the police?

- **Educate yourself in police lore.** Take a course in law enforcement, if you can, or take a course in constitutional law. You also might read Joseph Wambaugh's books for a realistic portrait of the police.
- **Try to fit in.** Keep your hair neat, dress conservatively and learn the language. Remember that police officers, like the rest of us, are usually quicker to trust people who look and act the way they do.

Covering the Police Beat

- Educate yourself in police lore.
- Try to fit in.
- Lend a sympathetic ear.
- Encourage gossip.
- Talk with other police watchers.

- **Lend a sympathetic ear.** You enjoy talking about yourself to somebody who seems to be interested; so do most police officers. They know they have a tough job, and they like to be appreciated. Open your mind, and try to understand even the points of view with which you may disagree strongly.
- **Encourage gossip.** Police officers may gossip even more than reporters do. Encourage such talk over a cup of coffee at the station, while tagging along in a patrol car or over a beer after the shift. The stories will be one-sided and exaggerated, but you may learn a lot. Just don't print anything you haven't verified.
- **Talk with other police watchers.** Lawyers can be good sources, especially the prosecutors and public defenders who associate every day with the police. Other law enforcement sources are good, too. Sheriff's deputies, for example, may be eager to talk about dishonesty or inefficiency in the city police department, and city police may be eager to reciprocate.

One important reason for all this work is that little of the information you need and want as a police reporter is material you are entitled to see under public-records laws. By law, you are entitled to see only the *arrest sheet* (also called the *arrest log* or **blotter**). This record tells you only the identity of the person arrested, the charge and the time the arrest took place. You are not entitled by law to see the arrest report or to interview the officers involved.

Writing a story depends on securing more than the bare-bones information. Finding out details depends on the goodwill you have generated with the desk sergeant, the shift commander and the officers on the case.

Chad Day, the Associated Press reporter in Washington, D.C., was assigned to the night police beat when he first went to work for the *Arkansas Democrat-Gazette*. Working from late in the afternoon up until midnight, he often found himself at crime scenes where he talked directly with detectives. Public information officers, known as PIOs, often don't want to deal with news that breaks late at night. That kind of access can lead to inside details about the crime news of the day and conversations about the police union or the political climate of the department.

Sometimes the police themselves are the story. More frequent use of cellphone videos by bystanders and body cams by police has led to more questions than answers. For example, after the director of the FBI suggested that sensitivity to the presence of video might inhibit police from cracking down on violent crime, he admitted that there was no evidence to support that hypothesis. In another case, a black educator wrote an opinion piece complaining that local police had accused her of "walking while black." In response, the police released a video of the encounter that seemed to show a calm and respectful encounter.

Seeing isn't always believing. On the other hand, police body cams and dashboard cams have played a central role in stories about police shootings of young African-American men and the Black Lives Matter movement. Like all other information, videos need to be vetted for accuracy by journalists before they are used in a story.

The dangers — of being unfair, of damaging your reputation and that of your organization — are ever-present. Good reporting requires that you know what the dangers are and how to avoid them.

Sports

A good sports reporter is a good reporter. That's not always obvious, especially to beginners, because the love of sports lures them to the field in the first place. Most sports reporters were sports fans before they were journalists. That's not typical of other specialties. Reporters who cover government seldom attend city council meetings for fun. Medical reporters don't usually spend their days off observing operations. (Instead, they may watch a sports event.)

As a sports reporter and writer, you are likely to find your workplace organized in much the same way as the news department. Typically, in the sports department of a newspaper, there will be reporters, copy editors and an editor. The difference is likely to be the scale. On small papers, the sports editor may double as a writer and may even take the photographs. He or she might be responsible for designing the print edition. On medium-sized papers, the sports reporters usually don't specialize as the news reporters may. One day you may be covering high school swimming; the next, football or a visiting rodeo.

At small and medium-size broadcasting stations, a "sports department" is likely to consist of one person who serves as writer, photographer and sports anchor at various times of the day or night. The big crews (the "guys in the truck" you hear mentioned on ESPN) are at the network level. At most local stations, you'll be expected to report, write, shoot video and deliver your work on camera. When time pressure is great or the game is big, you'll go on the air live, summarizing a game that has just ended or that may even be in progress. Then your skills at ad-libbing will be tested, a challenge that print reporters don't face.

In the multiplatform world, you should be prepared to do it all, including tweeting during the event and engaging with your audience during and after.

One more thing: Don't confuse sports reporters with play-by-play announcers. The latter may be reporters in a literal sense, but they usually aren't journalists. Their skill is in instant description, not the behind-the-scenes digging or the after-the-fact analysis expected of print and broadcast reporters.

To get to the why and how of a game's outcome, reporters need to dig beneath the mere results. They can bring a story to life by getting out of the press box to find an interesting story angle or to secure compelling quotes from players and coaches.

Sports reporting is beat reporting

Before you even thought about sports reporting, chances are good that you were reading about, watching and playing sports. In that sense, at least, preparing to be a sports reporter is easier than preparing to cover city hall. But there is more to preparation than immersing yourself in sports.

Competition pushes people to their limits, bringing out the best and worst in them. So you need to know some psychology. Sports has played a major role in the struggles of black communities and women for equality. So you need to know some sociology and history. Sports, professional and amateur, is big business. So you need a background in economics and, if you're covering high school or collegiate sports, a working knowledge of the athletics budget. Some of our greatest writers have portrayed life through sports. So you need to explore literature.

And you need to know the law, especially Title IX of the federal code. This law forbids discrimination and abuse based on gender. Too often, the headlines today show prominent athletes, especially at the college and professional levels, being accused of or punished for violations. Life in sports is real life.

ON THE JOB Transferring Skills Across Beats

Courtesy of Ashley Zavala

Ashley Zavala is the state government and politics reporter for San Francisco's KRON-TV. Before moving to California, Zavala worked at central Missouri's CBS affiliate, KRCG, as a general assignment reporter, and she helped launch the station's investigative unit as its lead reporter. While there, she won two Edward R. Murrow awards and was one of the few bilingual broadcast journalists in Missouri. Zavala began her career in college at the University of Missouri shooting high school football highlights for the local NBC affiliate, KOMU. There, she filled in as a sports anchor and reporter before joining Comcast Sports Southeast in Atlanta as a Mizzou athletics correspondent. The skills she learned covering sports translate to what she's doing now. Zavala explains:

Covering a sports team was one of the most valuable experiences I've ever had as a reporter. It provided me with fundamental journalism tools. Sports beat reporting required me to memorize and perfect the names and roles of players and coaches, and encouraged me to get to know them as human beings. I spent three full years covering the Mizzou football team. Covering the same team and sport every day forced me to get creative with story ideas and pushed me to come up with content that the competition wouldn't have. As a football beat reporter, I was expected to turn at least one story a day, and that can get difficult when the team plays one game a week.

Engaging with the team, understanding personalities, remembering a birthday or accomplishment, and simply just showing up helped me develop sources. Those sources translated into my breaking some of the bigger stories, including the star quarterback's secret injury that would end up keeping him sidelined most of the season. Those sources also felt comfortable enough opening up to me about topics they might not share with other reporters: the player who was determined to set an example for his young nephew born into a complicated situation, or the player who felt different from his teammates because of his devotion to his religion. In my role as a beat reporter, I also felt responsible for holding team leaders accountable for concerning behavior or questionable decision making.

These skills are important when reporting anything in news. As a reporter, I've applied what I learned from sports reporting to every story I'm assigned, including city and state government, law enforcement, courts and crime. The city council or state legislature is the team, the mayor or governor is the coach, and breaking big stories or finding that great human-interest story relies on how engaged you are in your beat and the sources developed. Leaders of governmental bodies, departments and other organizations all need to be held accountable for concerning behavior or questionable decision-making.

Here are a few tips to help you be alert to stories that go beyond the cliché:

- **Look for the losers.** Losing may not — as football coaches and other philosophers like to assert — build character, but it certainly bares character. Winners are likely to be full of confidence, champagne and clichés. Losers are likely to be full of self-doubt, second-guessing and surliness. Winners' dressing rooms are magnets for sports writers, but by seeking out the losers, you usually can tell your readers more about the game and those who play it.
- **Look for the benchwarmers.** If you follow the reporting crowd, you'll end up in front of your local version of Aaron Rogers, Lebron James or Serena Williams every time. Head in the other direction. Talk to the would-be football player who has spent four years practicing but never gets into a game. Talk to the woman who dreams of being a professional golfer but is not yet good enough. If you do, you may find people who both love their sport more and understand it better than the stars do. You may find less press agentry and more humanity.

- **Look beyond the crowds.** Some of the best and most important sports stories draw neither crowds of reporters nor crowds of fans. The so-called minor sports and participant sports are largely untapped sources of good stories. More Americans watch birds than play football. More hunt or fish than play basketball. More watch stock-car races than watch track meets. But those and similar sports are usually covered—if at all—by the newest or least talented reporter on the staff. Get out of the press box. Drop by a bowling alley, a skeet-shooting range, the local college's Ultimate Frisbee tournament. Anywhere you find people competing—against each other, against nature, against their own limits—you can find good stories.

Developing contacts

Being there is half the fun of sports reporting. You're there at the big games, matches and meets. You're there in the locker rooms and on team buses and planes, with an inside view of athletics and athletes that few fans ever get. If you are to answer your readers' questions and provide insights and anecdotes, you must be there and be present.

Sometimes you should be where the fans are. Plunk down $20 (of your boss's money) for an end-zone seat, and write about a football game from the average fan's point of view. Cover a baseball game from the bleachers. Cold hot dogs and warm beer are as much a part of the event as is a double play. Watch a weekend sports show on television, and compare the way it presents a track meet or a fishing trip to the way it is experienced in person.

Be sure to follow the social media activities of athletes and coaches on your beat. College and professional athletes, in particular, are among the most prolific users of Twitter as they seek to connect with their fans. They can tip you off to stories you might not find anywhere else.

Go also beyond the players, coaches and administrators. Trainers and equipment managers have insiders' views and sometimes lack the fierce protectiveness that often keeps players from talking candidly.

Alumni can be excellent sources for high school and college sports stories. If a coach is about to be fired or a new fund drive is being planned, important alumni are sure to be involved. You can find out who they are by checking with the alumni association or by examining the list of major contributors that every college proudly compiles.

The business managers and secretaries who handle the money can be invaluable for much-needed but seldom-done stories about the finances of sports at all levels. Former players sometimes will talk more candidly than those who are still involved in a program. As on any beat, look for people who may be disgruntled—a fired assistant coach, a benched star, a big contributor to a losing team. And when you find good sources, cherish them. They are your lifeline.

Digging for the real story

It is even harder for a sports reporter than it is for a political or police reporter to maintain a critical distance from the beat. The most obvious reason is that most of the people who become sports reporters do so because they are sports fans. To be a fan is precisely the opposite of being a dispassionate, critical observer. It's probably not appropriate to wear the ball cap or jersey of the team you're paid to cover.

Contacts for the Sports Beat

- Players, coaches, administrators.
- Trainers.
- Equipment managers.
- Alumni (for high school and college sports).
- Business managers and secretaries who handle money.
- Former players.
- People who are disgruntled.

Digging for the Real Story

- Maintain your distance from the people you cover.
- Keep readers in mind.
- Answer readers' questions about the story behind the story.
- Follow the money.
- Find the real "why."
- Find the real "who."
- Pay attention to athletes' tweets.

In addition, athletics—especially big-time athletics—is glamorous and exciting. The sports reporter associates daily with the stars and the coaches whom others, including cynical city hall reporters and hard-bitten managing editors, pay to admire at a distance.

Finally, sports figures ranging from high school coaches to owners of professional baseball teams deliberately and persistently seek to buy the favor of the reporters who cover their sports.

We are taught from childhood not to bite the hand that feeds you. Professional teams and many college teams routinely feed reporters. Major League Baseball teams even pay reporters to serve as official scorers for the game. In one embarrassing incident, the reporter-scorer made a controversial decision that preserved a no-hit game for a hometown pitcher. His story of the game made little mention of his official role. The reporter for a competing paper wrote that if it had been his turn to be scorer, he would have ruled the other way.

Sports journalism used to be even more parasitic toward the teams it covered than it is now. At one time, reporters routinely traveled with a team at the team's expense. The good news organizations pay their own way today.

Even today, however, many reporters find it rewarding monetarily as well as psychologically to stay in the favor of the teams and athletes they cover. Many teams pay reporters to write promotional pieces for game programs. And writing personality profiles or "inside" accounts for the dozens of sports magazines can be a profitable sideline.

Anywhere athletics is taken seriously, from the high schools of Texas to the stadiums of the National Football League, athletes and coaches are used to receiving special treatment. Many think of themselves as being different from and even better than ordinary people. Many fans agree. Good reporters, though, regard sports as a beat, not a love affair.

Those sports reporters maintain their distance from the people they cover, just as reporters on other beats do, by keeping their readers in mind. Readers want to know who won and how. But they also want to know about other sides of sports that may require some digging to expose. Readers' questions about sports financing and the story behind the story too often go unanswered.

When a key player is traded or when a city manager is fired, readers have a legitimate interest in the real why. When athletes leave school without graduating, find out why. When the public is asked to pay for the expansion of a stadium, find out why. The whys of sports are frequently as hard to discover as they are in any other area, so it becomes the responsibility of the reporter to fill in the gaps in the public's mind that scores cannot.

CHAPTER RESOURCES

SUGGESTED READINGS

Crouse, Timothy. *The Boys on the Bus.* New York: Random House, 1973. A hard-hitting, insightful and humorous look at journalistic coverage of the 1972 presidential campaigns of Richard Nixon and George McGovern.

Houston, Brant, and Investigative Reporters and Editors, Inc. *The Investigative Reporter's Handbook.* 5th ed. New York: Bedford/St. Martin's, 2009. This comprehensive guide to using public records and documents, written by members of Investigative Reporters and Editors, is a must for serious reporters. See also the suggested readings at the end of Chapter 17. They'll be useful in beat reporting, too.

Royko, Mike. *Boss: Richard J. Daley of Chicago.* New York: New American Library, 1971. This is a classic, brilliantly written study of urban machine politics.

Schulte, Henry H., and Dufresne, Marcel. *Getting the Story: An Advanced Reporting Guide to Beats, Records, and Sources.* New York: Macmillan, 1994. This is an excellent exploration of practical strategies for effective public affairs reporting as well as the evolution of the field.

Silverman, Craig, ed. *Verification Handbook: An Ultimate Guide on Digital Sourcing for Emergency Coverage.* European Journalism Center. This work is licensed under a Creative Commons Attribution-NonCommercial-NoDerivatives 4.0 International License. You can download this manual free of charge at http://verificationhandbook.com/downloads/verification.handbook.pdf. It is edited by the founder and editor of "Regret the Error," a Poynter Institute blog about media errors, accuracy and verification.

SUGGESTED WEBSITES

LaunchPad Solo
launchpadworks.com
When you visit LaunchPad Solo for Journalism, you will find research links, exercises and LearningCurve adaptive quizzing to help you improve your grammar and AP style usage. In addition, the site's video collection hosts the videos highlighted in this and other chapters as well as additional clips of leading professionals discussing important media trends.

www.espn.go.com
As every sports fan knows, here you'll find multimedia reporting, commentary, statistics and lots of good story ideas.

joymayer.com
Joy Mayer's Journalism+Community blog offers strategies for how beat reporters and news organizations can mine social media, engage audiences and build trust in their reporting.

media.twitter.com/news
Twitter provides useful guidelines for how journalists and newsrooms can best use the popular social media platform to cover their beats and inform their audiences.

www.pewstates.org/projects/stateline
This site, a service of the Pew Charitable Trusts, provides story tips and background information on state government and state-level issues.

www.poynter.org
We recommend this site repeatedly because it is useful in many ways. One feature is its links to nearly every professional journalism organization.

www.rjionline.org
The Donald W. Reynolds Journalism Institute's website offers an array of resources and tips for journalists covering any beat for any platform.

EXERCISES

1. In most communities, the local newspaper is likely to have reporters assigned to specific beats. By following the news, identify one of those beat reporters. Interview her or him. How do the principles outlined in this chapter seem to apply in the reporter's real life?

2. After you have met a beat reporter, stay in touch. Get yourself invited to accompany your new friend on part of her or his daily rounds. What do you learn?

3. With your classmates, form the class into a newsroom. Decide on the essential beats to cover. Assign a pool of reporters to each beat. Working with the other members of your group, take the necessary first step toward successful coverage by producing a background memo that identifies key issues and sources for your beat. Be sure to include relevant sources' Twitter handles and Facebook pages. Present your memo for class discussion. Listen to and comment on other groups' work.

4. Now get out of the classroom, and spend some time actually covering one of these beats. Get acquainted with some of the sources your group has identified. Write a beat memo that describes several story ideas, with likely sources.

5. Complete the job by reporting and writing one of the stories you've identified. This would be a good opportunity for peer critiquing of one another's work.

6. **Your journalism blog.** Spend some time exploring the coverage of one specific beat on a news website. In a blog post, compare the news coverage and the features of the website with the content of the newspaper and the television outlet that cover the same beat. Which of the three is more useful, more satisfying, more fun?

CHAPTER 14 SPEECHES, NEWS CONFERENCES AND MEETINGS

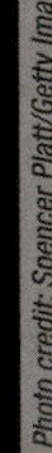

At his 2017 debut before the United Nations General Assembly, U.S. President Donald Trump declared, "Rocket Man is on a suicide mission for himself and for his regime." The reference to North Korean leader Kim Jong Un and his country's pursuit of nuclear weapons created a Twitter frenzy and drew headlines across the globe. Months later, the two leaders met in Singapore for an unprecedented summit. Trump and his supporters argued that Trump's tough rhetoric helped make the meeting possible.

On Sept. 25, 2018, Trump addressed the General Assembly again. As was the case in 2017, the president covered numerous topics: Iran, North Korea, trade and more. What did journalists rate as most newsworthy?

For the United States' premier business publication, *The Wall Street Journal*, the top news was Trump's defense of his "hard-line trade policies."

The global news agency Reuters transmitted multiple stories, one on Trump's promise to impose more sanctions against Iran and another on his comments on North Korea: "U.S. President Donald Trump praised North Korea's leader Kim Jong Un on Tuesday for his courage in taking steps to disarm, but said much work still had to be done and sanctions must remain in place on North Korea until it denuclearizes."

USA Today journalists John Fritze and Deirdre Shesgreen crafted a double-pronged lead, focusing on both Iran and Trump's world view: "President Donald Trump blamed Iranian leaders for sowing 'chaos, death and destruction' in a steely speech to the United Nations General Assembly on Tuesday that heavily emphasized the president's support of national sovereignty over globalism."

Both *The Washington Post* and *The New York Times* also highlighted Trump's world view in their leads. Although *The Times*' front-page headline noted Trump's "scorn for Iran, praise for Kim," writer Mark Landler verged into analysis in his second sentence, saying Trump "sounded as eager to claim credit for his achievements after 20 months in office, as he was to disrupt the world order." Three paragraphs later, Landler noted that many world leaders laughed when Trump said, "In less than two years, my administration has accomplished more than almost any administration in the history of our country."

This appeared in *The Times*' main print and online story about the speech. *The Times* and *The Washington Post* also posted separate stories featuring an Associated Press video clip from the speech on their websites. *USA Today* posted the same clip on its site.

Did the General Assembly's reaction to one line in Trump's speech merit much attention? Fritze and Shesgreen waited until the ninth paragraph of *USA Today*'s main story to mention what they deemed "an awkward moment." Vivian Salama of *The Wall Street Journal* noted the laughter in her 21st paragraph — after she included the Iranian, French, Turkish and Mexican presidents' responses to the substance of Trump's speech.

In this chapter, you will learn:

1. How to distinguish among speeches, news conferences and meetings.
2. How to prepare to cover speeches, news conferences and meetings.
3. What's involved in covering these events.
4. How to structure and write stories about them.

Odds are that history will show the United States' evolving policies toward Iran and North Korea were more important than a few moments of laughter, no matter how amusing to Trump's critics. The best reporters identify the most important news and build their speech stories around that content.

To produce complex and important stories, reporters have to be knowledgeable about the topics and to be there.

You might not be covering the White House or United Nations, but whatever your beat, you must be prepared to cover three basic assignments: speeches, news conferences and meetings.

LaunchPad Solo
macmillan learning

launchpadworks.com
WATCH: **"What Makes Public Television 'Public'?"**

- Are public television and radio at an advantage or a disadvantage in covering speeches, news conferences and meetings? Why?
- Now that people can tune in to hundreds of commercial channels, is there still a role for public systems like PBS? Explain.

Distinguishing among Speeches, News Conferences and Meetings

A *speech* is a public talk. Someone speaks to an audience in person or through the media, often reading from a prepared text. Regardless of the medium, a speech can generally be regarded as a one-way communication in which the speaker talks to a listening audience.

Speakers are usually invited and sometimes paid to address an audience. That is not the case with those who hold a *news conference*. People "call" or "hold" news conferences. They do not send invitations to the general public, but they do alert members of the news media. Journalists respond because of the importance of the person calling the news conference and because the person might have something newsworthy to say. The person holding the news conference often begins with an opening statement or announcement and usually accepts questions from reporters. A news conference is meant to be two-way communication. Many politicians, who often would rather not take questions, are using social media, particularly their websites, Twitter and Facebook, to make announcements.

Unlike speeches and news conferences, *meetings* are not held with an audience in mind, although an audience might be present and allowed to participate. A meeting is primarily for communication among the members of a group or organization, whether a local parent-teacher association or the U.S. Congress. Reporters who are permitted to witness a meeting tell the public what is of interest and importance.

Getting Ready to Cover the Story

Good reporters know that preparation makes covering a story much easier, and they always do their homework. The preparation for speeches, news conferences and meetings is similar. Because these events are usually announced in advance, you often have time for thorough preparation.

Preparing for the Speech Story

Not every speech demands a great deal of research. Many speakers give dry and routine speeches. Often, the person giving the speech is someone you know or someone you have covered before. If you are working for campus media, the speaker could be a university official. If you are working for the professional press, it could be the mayor or the director of the local United Way. At other times, you might get an assignment on short notice and be forced to find background information after hearing the speech. In either case, never take the speaker or the topic for granted. Failure to get enough background almost guarantees failure at writing a comprehensive speech story.

If you have not covered the speaker before, the first step in your research is to identify the person correctly. Middle initials are important, but sometimes they are not enough. *USA Today* had to print a "clarification" after reporting that Larry King had made a $1,000 donation to a presidential campaign. The donor was Larry L. King, author and playwright, not Larry King, the former CNN TV show host.

Before doing research on the speaker, contact the group sponsoring the speech, and ask for the topic. You might find you need to do some reading to prepare yourself to understand the subject. Ask for an advance copy of the speech, too; you might get lucky. Next, check your organization's own archives and other online sources to see what other reporters have written about the speaker and the topic. You may find useful information.

If the speech is important enough, you might want to contact the speaker ahead of time for a brief interview. If he or she is from out of town, you might plan a meeting at the airport. You might also arrange to interview the speaker after the speech in case you have questions or points to clarify.

Not every speech demands this much effort. But even the most routine speech assignment requires preparation. Sooner or later, you may be called on to cover speeches by major political figures, perhaps even the U.S. president. For this task, too, you will need background—lots of it. You must keep up with current events by regularly reading or listening to the news. Subscribe to news alerts from several major news organizations, such as CNN or *The New York Times*, and follow them on Twitter. On Facebook, follow the pages of big news organizations so you get postings from them. You can also sign up for one of the online aggregators of articles from a variety of sources.

Preparing for the Speech Story

- Be sure you have the right person.
- Contact the group sponsoring the speech, and ask for the topic and a copy of the prepared speech if available.
- Check your news organization's archives and online sources for background on the speaker.
- If the speech is important enough, contact the speaker for a brief interview.

Preparing for the News Conference Story

Preparing for a news conference is similar to preparing for a speech. You need up-to-date background on the person giving the news conference, and you must try to learn why the news conference is being held. Often the person holding the news conference has an announcement or an opening statement. Unless that statement is leaked to the press, you will not know its content ahead of time, but you can make some educated guesses. What's been happening on that beat? Are there any

Preparing for the News Conference Story

- Get up-to-date background on the person holding the news conference.
- Learn why the conference is being held.
- Check out any rumors beforehand.
- Try to arrange an interview before or after the news conference.

unresolved issues? Check out any rumors. Call the person's associates, friends or secretary.

Consult your editor and other staff editors about specific information they want. Then draw up a list of questions to ask at the news conference. When the news conference begins, you will not have time to think of questions; recording responses to other reporters' questions will keep you busy. The better prepared you are, the better chance you will have of coming away with a coherent, readable story.

It may be impossible to arrange an interview before or after the news conference. If the person holding the news conference wanted to do interviews with individual reporters, he or she probably would not have called the news conference. But you can always ask: You might end up with some exclusive information.

Preparing for the Meeting Story

- Contact some of the key figures.
- Try to find out what the meeting is about. Most governmental bodies are required to post agendas.
- Study and investigate issues before arriving.

Preparing for the Meeting Story

Often the meetings of important organizations are preceded by an agenda. Look online: Government officials often post a detailed agenda with links to related reports and other supporting documents. Another reporter also might have written an advance — a report outlining the subjects and issues to be covered during the upcoming meeting.

However, with nongovernmental and even some governmental meetings, you often do not know what to expect, so you must do your best to prepare. Who is holding the meeting? What kind of organization is involved? Who are the key figures? Again, the news archives should be your first stop, and online research will yield more information. Then contact some of the key figures.

If there is no agenda, talk to the organization's leader to find out the purpose of the meeting. If you know the main subject to be discussed, you will be able to study and investigate the issues before arriving. Knowing what to expect and being familiar with the issues will make covering the meeting much easier.

Covering Speeches, News Conferences and Meetings

Preparing to cover an event is only the beginning. Knowing what to do when you get there is equally important. You must cover the entire event — the content of the speech, news conference or meeting; the time, place, circumstances and number of people involved; and the possible consequences.

A news conference is the most challenging of the three events because reporters become participants rather than just observers. You must be prepared to ask questions and capture the answers.

Sometimes the question — or the reporter — becomes the story, which has happened to CNN's Jim Acosta on multiple occasions during Trump's news conferences. During a news conference related to Supreme Court Justice

Brett Kavanaugh's nomination to the court, Acosta made headlines for asking the president to take a question from a female reporter after he answered Acosta's question. Trump ultimately did so — but not before Acosta asked the president why he "always" seems to take the side of men who have been accused of sexual assault, rather than the female accusers. Trump disputed Acosta's assertion.

It was not the first time the two had tangled. In July 2018, a *New York Times* writer referred to Acosta as "a preferred punching bag of Trump supporters" and reported that Trump declined to answer one of Acosta's questions because, Trump said, "CNN is fake news." Later in 2018, Acosta temporarily lost his White House press credentials.

Concerns about attitudes toward the press have sometimes prompted journalists for competing news organizations to work together. *New York Times* reporter Michael M. Grynbaum wrote this about another news conference:

> **Hallie Jackson, a correspondent for *NBC News*, was grilling the press secretary, Sarah Huckabee Sanders, about President Trump's credibility, given his attempts at damage control after a Helsinki summit meeting with President Vladimir V. Putin of Russia.**
>
> **Ms. Sanders, eager to move on, invoked a tried-and-true spin doctor tactic: Next question, please.**
>
> **"I'm going to keep moving," she said, interrupting Ms. Jackson and turning to Jordan Fabian of *The Hill*. "Jordan, go ahead."**
>
> **Undeterred, Ms. Jackson said she had a follow-up question. "Sorry, you've asked two," Ms. Sanders said, speaking over her. "I'm going to move on to Jordan."**
>
> **A brief silence fell over the room, before Mr. Fabian spoke up.**
>
> **"Hallie," he said, "go ahead if you want."**

Jackson showed perseverance and was able to ask her follow-up question — a good reason to make the news.

> **"Just because the White House is uncomfortable with a question regarding the news of the day doesn't mean the question isn't relevant and shouldn't be asked. This decision to bar a member of the press is retaliatory in nature and not indicative of an open and free press. We demand better. As a member of the White House press pool, Fox stands firmly with CNN on this issue of access."**
>
> ■ Bret Baier, Fox News anchor, after CNN White House reporter Kaitlan Collins was banned from a White House event

The Medium Matters Less These Days

Increasingly, what you need to do at a speech, news conference or meeting is the same whether you're working for a newspaper, broadcaster or digital-only news organization.

If it is a high-interest event, you probably will be live tweeting and posting updates. Tweeting gets the public conversation started while the event is under way. Your tweets also provide a good chronology of a major address or council meeting as it unfolds. Just be sure your tweet has enough context so that audience members who haven't been following your tweets can understand it if they jump on Twitter midstream.

In some cases, you'll want to post photos and even videos on your organization's social media platforms. In April 2018, just before Missouri lawmakers released a graphic report related to then-Gov. Eric Greitens' extramarital affair, Greitens scheduled a news conference. The *Columbia Missourian* used Facebook to livestream the conference, earning the small newspaper 3,900 views. When Greitens announced his resignation, KOMU television posted a livestream on its Facebook pages. The video was viewed more than 25,000 times.

Whether you're working in broadcast or for a newspaper, you likely will need to write a web story. The print reporter also will be likely to be expected to supply an audio clip, a video clip or a photograph. And at sophisticated news organizations, the copy you write for the web and social media will differ from what you write for print. The social media headlines will be more conversational, and the summaries for the web will be primed for search-engine optimization. If you are working for a television station, you might be shooting coverage of the event, interviewing people afterward, editing the video and writing a broadcast script. (You'll have already tweeted and written a quick web story.)

More and more news organizations are adding video to their websites, which means you have to learn something about videography. With today's many ways of distributing news, you need to learn to become a multimedia journalist. Doing so will make you more valuable to your employer.

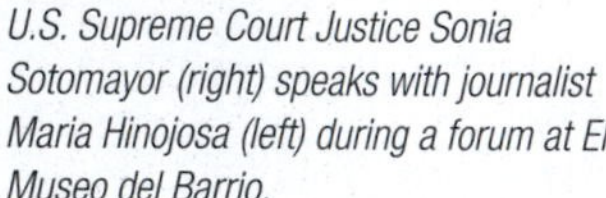

U.S. Supreme Court Justice Sonia Sotomayor (right) speaks with journalist Maria Hinojosa (left) during a forum at El Museo del Barrio.

Reuters/Keith Bedford

Getting the Content Correct

You may find a digital audio recorder and your smartphone useful for covering the content of speeches, news conferences and meetings. Practice using your equipment until you are familiar with its idiosyncrasies. Make sure your phone is fully charged and ready to go.

When someone says something newsworthy, note the counter on the recorder (or the time) so you can find the quote quickly. Even if you record an event, take notes. Malfunctions can occur, even with the best recorders, at the most inopportune times. (See Chapter 4 for more on recording audio and video interviews.)

Develop your own note-taking shortcuts. Learn to abbreviate (for example, *wh* for "which," *th* for "that," *bk* for "book," *st* for "street," *bldg* for "building," etc.) and use signs (*w/* for "with," *w/o* for "without," *acc/* for "according to"). Taking notes is most crucial when you wish to record direct quotes.

As you learned in Chapter 5, putting someone's words in quotation marks means you are quoting the exact words the person spoke. Speeches, news conferences and meetings all demand that you be able to record direct quotes. Your stories will be lifeless and lack credibility without them. A speech story, for example, should contain several direct quotes.

Whether covering a speech, a news conference or a meeting, be careful to quote people in context. For example, if a speaker gives supporting evidence for an argument, you would be unfair not to report it. Quotes can be misleading if you carelessly or deliberately juxtapose them. Combining quotes with no indication that something was said in between them can lead to inaccuracies and to charges of unfairness. Suppose, for example, someone says this:

> **"Cutting down fuel costs can be an easy thing. If you have easy access to wood, you should invest in a good wood-burning stove. With little effort, you can cut your fuel bills in half."**

A reporter who omits the middle sentence of that quote, even inserting an ellipsis, makes the speaker look ridiculous:

> **"Cutting down fuel costs can be an easy thing. . . . With little effort, you can cut your fuel bills in half."**

Describing the Participants

An audio recording does not capture a speaker's facial expressions and gestures. These are sometimes more important than the words themselves.

Simply reporting the words of a speaker does not indicate the volume and tone of voice, inflections, pauses, emphases and reactions to and from those in attendance. You might note that a speaker deliberately winked while reading a sentence. Or you might notice unmistakable sarcasm in the speaker's voice.

Achieving Total Coverage of Content and Event

- Get the content correct. Recorders can be helpful, but always take good notes. Quote people exactly and in context.
- Note the background, personal characteristics and mannerisms of the main participants.
- Cover the event holistically. Look at the audience (size, reactions, composition) and sometimes at what is happening outside the building.
- Get there early, choose a good vantage point and hang around afterward.

What's the grammar error in this sentence?

It was Nikki Haley who became the first female governor of South Carolina in 2011, and it was her who resigned as the U.S. ambassador to the United Nations in 2018.

See Appendix 1, Rule 17.

Using a Digital or Smartphone Recorder

- Be familiar with the device. Practice using it. Make sure you understand its peculiarities. Check its sound capabilities.
- Set it where you can see that it's working. Use the digital counter or time to note newsworthy quotes.
- Take notes. The recorder might not be working, or it might not have captured the voices clearly.

Covering an Event

- Be sure to record what the digital recorder misses — gestures and facial expressions.
- Remember that a person's words often must be measured against his or her background.
- Take note of the tone of questions.
- Note the size of the audience.

Even if you're not taking photos for publication, consider using your phone camera to help you record details you'll want to write about later.

Regardless of who the speaker is, you should always note the speaker's background. For example, if a former Communist is speaking on communism, this fact might have a bearing on what he says. If a former CIA agent is speaking about corruption in the CIA, you cannot adequately report her message if you do not mention her background.

Sometimes, physical facts about the speaker might be relevant to the story — particularly if the speaker indicates this is the case. A blind person pleading for funds to educate the blind might do so, as might a veteran who lost a limb and now speaks out about the hell of war. Beware, however, of including gratuitous descriptions; there's no need, for example, to point out the race of a state senator advocating for gun control.

You also should note what the person who introduces a speaker says. This may help you understand the significance of the speaker and the importance of what he or she has to say. (Better yet, interview the organizer beforehand.)

Being Observant

Keep an eye on the audience and on what's happening around the edges. Measure the mood of the audience by noting the tone of the questions. Are they sharply worded? Is there much laughter or applause? Perhaps members of the audience boo. Does the speaker or the person holding the news conference or the person presiding over the meeting remain calm and in control? Is the audience stacked with supporters or detractors?

Sometimes the real action takes place outside in the form of a picket line or protest. Sometimes police manage to keep protesters away from the site. Sometimes, who is *not* there is news.

Don't overlook the obvious. For example, you should note the size of the audience. Reporting a "full house" means little unless you indicate the house capacity. One way to estimate is to count how many people are sitting in a row or in a typical section. Then you multiply that number by the number of rows or sections in the hall. Use good judgment and common sense to adjust for some sections being more crowded than others. For large venues, you can find out the seating capacity ahead of time. Some local fire departments require all public venues to post the maximum capacity of the space.

Arriving, Positioning Yourself and Staying On

Most reporters arrive early. At some events, special seating is set aside for reporters, but you should probably not count on that unless you know for sure.

At a speech, sitting in the first row is not necessarily best. Instead, choose a location that lets you see the reaction of the audience. If there is a question-and-answer period, you might want to be able to see the questioner. And you certainly want to be in a good position to ask questions yourself.

At a news conference, your location might help you get the attention of the person holding the conference. You should have your questions prepared, but preparing them is not enough. You have seen presidential news conferences on television, and you know how difficult it is to get the president's attention. Sometimes a list shows the order in which reporters will be recognized. All news conferences present the reporter with similar difficulties, though on a smaller scale. You have also seen how difficult it is for reporters to follow up on their own questions. At some news conferences, you will not be called on twice.

But you must do more than try to get your own questions answered. You must listen to others' questions and be able to recognize the making of a good story. Listen for what is newsworthy and pursue it. Sticking with an important subject will make the job of writing the story easier. Remember, when the news conference is finished, you will have a story to write. Piecing together notes on dozens of unrelated topics can be difficult, if not impossible.

At a meeting, you should be able to see and hear the main participants. Before the meeting starts, you should know which members are sitting where. You might want to assign each participant a number so you do not have to write the person's name each time he or she speaks. You also can draw a sketch or take a photo of where members are sitting. This way you will be able to quote someone by number and if necessary find out his or her name later. Know who the officers are. Organizations' websites often will include photos of their top officials you can use to recognize people. After a meeting, the secretary might be able to help you fill in missing words or information.

As a general rule, when the speech, news conference or meeting is over, do not rush off unless you are on deadline. Some of the best stories happen afterward. You might have some questions to ask. You might need clarification or want to arrange an interview with a key spokesperson. Listen for and seek out reactions from those in attendance.

White House press secretary Sarah Huckabee Sanders at a July 2018 briefing. When she tried to stop a follow-up question from Hallie Jackson of NBC News by calling on Jordan Fabian of The Hill, *Fabian offered his time to Jackson.*

Al Drago/The New York Times/Redux

Five Ways to Master the Meeting Story

- Do your homework.
- Arrive early.
- Listen to others' questions.
- Pursue what is newsworthy.
- Don't rush off. Some of the best stories happen afterward.

Structuring and Writing Your Story

Writing the lead for the speech, news conference or meeting story is no different from writing the lead for any other story. All of the qualities of the inverted pyramid news lead discussed in Chapter 8 are important here, as well.

What was the most important thing that happened? What was the main point of the speech? You must be careful not to emphasize an interesting but minor point that does not lead into the rest of your story. It's tempting, for example, to lead with a striking quote. But rarely does a speaker or someone holding a news conference highlight the content or the main point in a single, quotable sentence. Of course, there are exceptions. As a lead for one of Dr. Martin Luther King Jr.'s most famous addresses, a good reporter might have begun with "I have a dream."

Because of the nature of the inverted pyramid news story, rarely should you follow the chronology of the event you are covering. But the flow of your story might demand at least *some* attention to chronology (see Chapter 10). If you pay no attention to chronology, you might distort or cause readers to misinterpret the meaning of the event.

Writing the Speech Story

Although you might not soon be called on to cover the speeches of well-known politicians, you can learn a lot from the way the pros handle important political addresses. The annotated model "Analyzing a Speech Story" shows the first 361 words of *The Wall Street Journal*'s coverage of a speech by Vice President Mike Pence that criticized the Chinese government for censorship and alleged meddling in U.S. elections, as well as Google for working with China. In its web story, *The Journal* provided links to earlier related stories and a video in which Gerald F. Seib, *The Journal*'s Washington bureau chief, explains the rising tensions between the United States and China.

The approach for a video reporter is somewhat different. For television or video on the web, you'll introduce the subject and the speaker and then cut in video snippets of the speech itself. You might end the piece with an interview of someone who attended and thereby get some audience reaction.

Writing the News Conference Story

Writing the news conference story might be a bit more challenging than writing the speech story. Because you might go to the conference with different questions in mind than your peers, you might come away with a different focus than other reporters.

ANNOTATED MODEL Analyzing a Speech Story

Pence Cautions Google on China: Vice President Warns Against Aiding Chinese Censors as Trade Tensions Simmer

By Michael C. Bender and Dustin Volz
The Wall Street Journal

The reporters summarize what they viewed to be the most important message in the speech. →

WASHINGTON—The Trump administration took aim at Google, calling on the tech giant to halt development of a project it said would accelerate censorship efforts in China.

Additional details support the lead and let readers know that the vice president addressed multiple issues. →

In a speech on Thursday that outlined the White House's long list of frustrations and grievances with Beijing, Vice President Mike Pence called on companies to reconsider business practices in the world's second-largest economy that involve turning over intellectual property or "abetting Beijing's oppression."

The quote provides details to support the first two paragraphs. The writers also weave in information about Pence's audience. →

"For example, Google should immediately end development of the Dragonfly app that will strengthen Communist Party censorship and compromise the privacy of Chinese customers," Mr. Pence said in his speech at the Hudson Institute, a conservative think tank focused on security and economic issues.

← Note that *The Wall Street Journal* uses courtesy titles on second reference while The Associated Press does not.

The journalists provide the larger context for the speech. →

Mr. Pence's speech was the latest sign from the White House that the warm relations between President Trump and Chinese President Xi Jinping haven't trickled through the administration ranks. Trade tensions between the two countries have been escalating for months, and disputes continued over military cooperation, espionage and territorial claims in the South China Sea.

The reporters introduce another element of Pence's speech. It supports the assertion from the previous paragraph that tension is rising between the two countries. →

Mr. Pence said Thursday that China is working to remove Mr. Trump from office and described a broad effort to influence political opinion and manipulate academic institutions and U.S. companies.

← The time reference provides a transition, and the paragraph provides more history.

Last week, Mr. Trump accused China of trying to interfere in the U.S. midterm elections in November to hurt him and the Republican Party in retaliation for his stance on trade.

← The online version of the story includes a hyperlink to coverage of Trump's speech.

Although the journalists are covering Pence's speech, they introduce information from sources who did not attend but have a stake in the issues addressed. To keep the story flowing, the writers use delayed identification for the Senate Democrats. →

Senate Democrats asked the Trump administration on Thursday for evidence to support assertions of election meddling. In a letter to Director of National Intelligence Dan Coats, three senators asked whether the accusation from Mr. Trump "aligns with the intelligence community's assessments of Beijing's intentions, plans and activities."

(continued)

ANNOTATED MODEL Analyzing a Speech Story *(continued)*

The senators, as well as their relevant committee memberships, are identified.

Sens. Ron Wyden of Oregon, Martin Heinrich of New Mexico and Kamala Harris of California, who all serve on the Senate Intelligence Committee, asked for a response by Oct. 8 "so that the public and members of Congress have the information in advance of the election."

Other sources are brought into the story for balance.

A spokeswoman for the Office of the Director of National Intelligence said the letter had been received and that Mr. Coats would respond to it. Chinese officials have said they don't interfere internally in other countries.

Source: Michael C. Bender and Dustin Volz, "Pence Cautions Google on China: Vice President Warns Against Aiding Chinese Censors as Trade Tensions Simmer," *The Wall Street Journal*, Oct. 5, 2018, page A18, retrieved via the Factiva Database on Oct. 14, 2018. Only the first nine paragraphs appear here.

A news conference often covers a gamut of topics. Often it begins with a statement from the person who called the conference.

For example, when the mayor of Springfield holds a news conference to announce her candidacy for a second term, you can be sure that she will begin with a statement to that effect. Although her candidacy might be news to some people, you might want to ask her questions about the location of a new landfill that the city is rumored to be planning. Most citizens will admit the need for landfills, but their location is always controversial. And then there's that tip you heard about the city manager possibly resigning to take a job in a larger city.

Other reporters will come with other questions. Will there be further cuts in the city budget? Will the cuts mean that some city employees will lose their jobs? What happened to the plans to expand the city jail?

After you leave a news conference that covered many topics, you have the job of organizing the material in some logical, coherent order. You can choose to write a multiple-element lead (see Chapter 8). But usually you will treat the most newsworthy subject first and deal with the other subjects in the order of their importance. Rarely would you report on them in the chronological order in which they were discussed.

Suppose you decide the location of the landfill is the most important item of the news conference—especially if the mayor revealed the location for the first time. You might begin your story this way:

The city will construct its new landfill near the intersection of State Route 53 and Route E, four miles north of Springfield, Mayor Juanita Williams said Tuesday.

"After nearly a year of discussion and the best advice we could obtain, we are certain the Route E location is best for all concerned," Williams said at a news conference.

The mayor acknowledged there would be continued opposition to the site by citizens living in the general area, especially those in the Valley High Trailer Court. "No location will please everyone," Williams said.

Williams called the news conference to make the expected announcement of her candidacy for a second term.

Now you have to find a way to treat the other topics of the conference. You might want to list them first in a series of bullet points:

In other matters, Williams said:

- **City Manager Diane Lusby will not be resigning to take another post.**
- **Budget constraints will not permit any new construction on the city jail this year.**
- **Budget cuts will not cost any city employees their jobs. However, positions vacated by retiring personnel will not be filled.**

After this list, you will either go back to your lead, giving more background and quoting citizens or other city officials on the subject, or go on to discuss, one at a time, the matters you listed. Pay particular attention to making proper transitions from paragraph to paragraph so your story is coherent: "On other subjects, the mayor said . . ."; "The mayor defended her position on . . ."; "Again she stressed. . . ."

If one of the subjects is of special interest, you may want to write a **sidebar** — a shorter piece to go with your main story. For this story, you could do a sidebar on the mayor's candidacy, her record, her possible opponents and the like.

With a longer or more complicated story, you may want to make a summary list of all the main topics covered and place the list in a box or sidebar. In a digital story, items in the list could be links to other stories or to additional source material.

You probably wrote a story before the news conference to say the mayor was expected to announce her candidacy. You tweet the announcement when she makes it. You probably also tweet the location where the city plans to locate the landfill.

Remember, your job is to give readers the news as simply and clearly as possible. Cover the event itself, as well as the context. Perhaps some picketers protested the mayor's remarks about a local abortion clinic. Sometimes what happens at a news conference is more newsworthy than anything the person holding the conference says.

Writing the Meeting Story

Readers want you to take their place at the meeting you are covering. Let's look at a simple meeting story—in this case, a meeting of a local school board:

> **The decision of three national corporations to protect a formula used to compute their property taxes is causing more than $264,000 to be withheld from the Walnut School District's operating budget for the 2019–20 school year.**
>
> **Superintendent Max Schmidt said at Monday's school board meeting that International Business Machines Corp., ACR Corp. and Xerox are arguing that the method used in computing their property taxes was no longer valid. Nine California counties are involved in similar disputes.**
>
> **The taxes, totaling $264,688, are being held in escrow by the county until the matter is resolved. Some or all of the money eventually may be returned to the district, but the administration cannot determine when or how much.**
>
> **"If we take a quarter million dollars out of our program at this time, it could have a devastating effect," Schmidt said. "Once you've built that money into your budget and you've lost it, you've lost a major source of income."**
>
> **Mike Harper, the county prosecuting attorney, and Larry Woods, the school district attorney, advised board members to take a "wait-and-see attitude," Schmidt said. He said that one alternative would be to challenge the corporations in court. A final decision will be made later.**
>
> **The board also delayed action on repayment of $80,000 to IBM in a separate tax dispute. The corporation claims the district owes it for overpaid 2015 property taxes. The County Commission has ruled the claim is legitimate and must be repaid.**
>
> **A possible source of additional income, however, could be House Bill 1002, Schmidt said. If passed, this appropriations bill would provide an additional $46 million for state education, approximately $250,000 of which could go to the Walnut School District.**
>
> **Charles Campbell, the district architect, said plans for the area's new vocational technical school to be built on the Rock Bridge High School campus will be given to contractors in February. Bids will be presented at the March 15 board meeting.**
>
> **The board voted to have classes on Presidents Day, Feb. 15, to make up for time missed because of the teachers strike.**

The issue of the meeting was money problems—a subject that concerns every taxpayer. The writer jumped right into the subject in the lead, giving the "what" in the first paragraph and then in the second paragraph giving us the "who," "when" and "where." The reporter then dealt with specifics, naming names and citing figures, and quoted the key person at the meeting. In the last two paragraphs, the writer dealt with other matters discussed in the meeting.

The issues discussed at a meeting are not your only considerations in covering a meeting story. Others: Who was there? Who represented the public? How did people react after the meeting was over?

ON THE JOB Reporting in the Era of Social Media

Courtesy of Politico

Darren Samuelsohn, a senior White House reporter at Politico, covers plenty of speeches, news conferences and meetings. He takes his work seriously but himself less so. Here he shares some of what he has learned about Washington reporting in the era of social media:

> Golden Journalism Rule No. 1: Post your stories on Facebook so your mom knows what you're writing about.
>
> Yes, it can be a bit embarrassing when she forwards those posts to her friends with ALL CAPS declarations of how awesome her son or daughter is. But still, she's your mom. And Facebook for me (and I bet most journalists) has become the best way yet to share my work with my No. 1 fan.
>
> Depending on what you're writing about, Facebook can also be a great way to make all your old high school classmates jealous. All joking aside, social media have become a routine part of my daily journalism life.
>
> At various moments over the day, I check the feeds on my phone or with a dashboard like Hootsuite to see what people are talking about. What have I found? A small sample: on-the-record comments, press releases, story ideas, details on where a lawmaker or agency official is speaking at a public event.

Twitter, Facebook and Snapchat are no substitute for phone calls, physically going to the Capitol for a hearing, meeting sources for coffee or lunch, and interviewing lawmakers. But all of these platforms have become another source of information to help with reporting out stories.

I can't stress enough this important reminder: *Any information you find on social media—especially during breaking big big big news moments—must be verified.*

We have some basic rules at Politico on social media that I don't mind sharing. Post away when it comes to links to your own work or of your colleagues. Pull out the best quotes and other nuggets and give them their own separate posts to make sure they get noticed. On Twitter, it never hurts to post the same item a couple of times considering how fast streams move.

Tweeting about a live event in real time is good, too. But there's a hard and fast rule that I live by and think other journalists should, too: Don't scoop yourself. If you have something exclusive, publish it first with your news organization. Get the byline and the link. And then share away on social media and take a brief victory lap for the scoop.

One reporter began her meeting story in this way:

> **Even though they are footing the bill, only one of Boone County's residents cared enough to attend a Tuesday night hearing on the county's budget.**

> **With an audience of one citizen plus two reporters, County Auditor June Pitchford presented her official report on the $21 million budget to the Boone County Commission in a silent chamber.**

Even when covering routine, boring events, you are allowed to use your creativity. In addition to getting all the facts, your job is also to be interesting, to get people to read the story. Remember, two of the criteria for news are that it needs to be relevant and useful. Another criterion is that it needs to be interesting.

If you're a video reporter, your approach to a meeting story will be quite different. There's almost nothing as boring as video of a council meeting, so telling the story creatively is important. If you know the council will be debating increased garbage pickup rates, get some video of garbage trucks to show while you're narrating the gist of the story. You can use interviews with council members or members of the public to complete the story.

Regardless of your media platform, you will be expected to write well—even for a common event like a speech, news conference or meeting. You'll also be expected to produce more than a written story.

CHAPTER RESOURCES

SUGGESTED READINGS

Biography and Genealogy Master Index. Detroit: Gale Research, 1981 to present. This compilation of biographical directories lists people whose biographies have been written and indicates the date and volume of those reference books to consult for the actual biography.

Biography Index Past and Present. New York: H.W. Wilson, 1946 to present. This reference helps you locate biographical articles that have appeared in 2,000 periodicals and journals, as well as in biographical books and chapters from collective biographies.

Current Biography. New York: H.W. Wilson, 1940 to present. This monthly publication about people in the news includes a photo of each subject. It is an excellent source for people not included in more formal biographical sources.

SUGGESTED WEBSITES

LaunchPad Solo
launchpadworks.com
When you visit LaunchPad Solo for Journalism, you will find research links, exercises and LearningCurve adaptive quizzing to help you improve your grammar and AP style usage. In addition, the site's video collection hosts the videos highlighted in this and other chapters, as well as additional clips of leading professionals discussing important media trends.

journalistsresource.org
This website is part of Harvard's Shorenstein Center on Media, Politics and Public Policy. You can search for tip sheets on how to cover government, for example, as well as up-to-date background information on public policy issues. You can also sign up for a weekly compilation of timely resources.

EXERCISES

1. Find out when your university's faculty council or similar faculty representative group is having its next meeting. Plan the steps you will take to prepare for the meeting. Then cover the meeting, taking notes. Write the story. If classmates are covering the same event, compare their work with yours. How similar are the leads and the story structures? How do they differ? Are direct quotations used effectively? How could the stories be improved?
2. An official transcript of President Donald Trump's Jan. 30, 2018, State of the Union address is available on an official White House website (https://www.whitehouse.gov/briefings-statements/president-donald-j-trumps-state-union-address), but an annotated transcript also appears on *The New York Times*' website (https://www.nytimes.com/interactive/2018/01/30/us/politics/state-of-the-union-2018-transcript.html). What, if anything, has

The New York Times done to enhance the value of the transcript? Discuss in class what you would use for your lead and why.

3. The site that contains the text of the State of the Union speech mentioned in exercise 2 also contains the video, which is also available on YouTube. After watching the video, decide what observations about the president's demeanor or delivery, audience reaction, or setting you would add to your story.

4. To practice covering a speech, do a Google search for TED Talks by journalists Sebastian Junger and Megan Kamerick. Listen, record and take notes, and write a 250-word story. Be sure to use at least two direct quotes. Compare your lead to those of your classmates. Did you agree on the main message? Also, check your direct quotes against the transcript. How accurate were you?

5. Find out when a public figure in your area — a government official or a college administrator, for example — plans to give a speech on a specific topic. Prepare for and cover the speech, using a digital recorder. Send at least two tweets from the speech itself. Then write two versions of your news story: one for immediate posting on a website and one for the print edition of a newspaper. For the web version, what specific links would be useful? Suggest at least one possible sidebar.

6. **Your journalism blog.** Attend a speech, news conference or meeting — preferably one occurring at the school you are attending. Then on your blog, post a 300-word item about the event, including its content. Be sure to include links to pertinent social media and other sites. Invite your classmates to comment on your blog.

7. Prepare for and cover a meeting of a local government agency or committee — the school board, the city council or a similar group. Try to interview one of the participants before or after the meeting. Then write your story in two versions — one for a website specializing in local events and one for a local radio news broadcast. How do the two stories differ? How does each story meet the criteria of usefulness, relevance and interest?

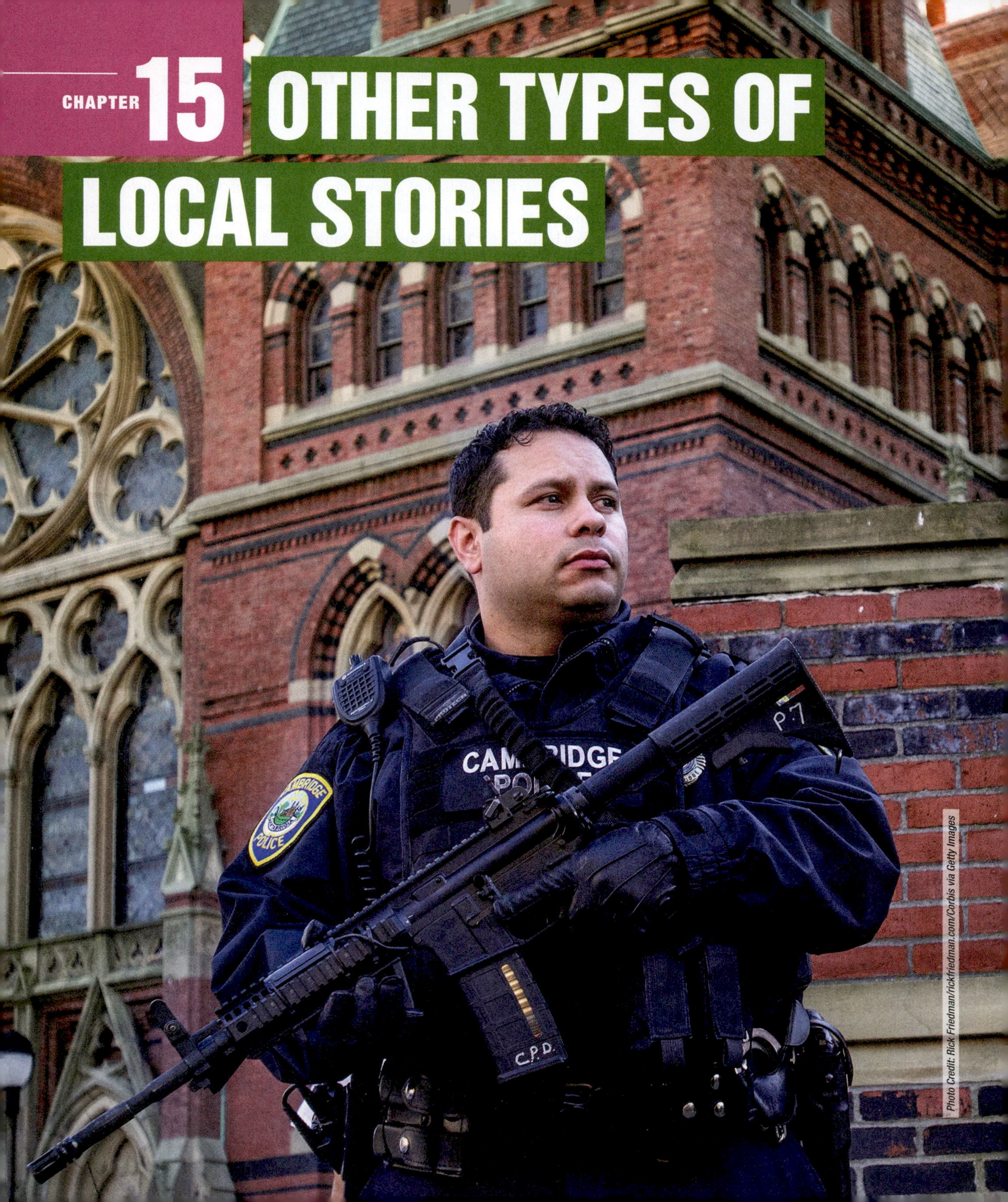

CHAPTER 15 OTHER TYPES OF LOCAL STORIES

Photo Credit: Rick Friedman/rickfriedman.com/Corbis via Getty Images

Much of reporting on local stories can involve speaking with police departments or law enforcement agencies in your area. With the rise in bomb and gun threats on campuses in recent years, police presence in those areas has increased especially. As the number of reported sexual assaults rose in Missouri, student reporter Anna Brett grew curious about why so few cases were prosecuted. She was studying to become an investigative reporter, and she used the skills she learned to produce a story for the *Columbia Missourian* that would have major implications for the state. Here's the top of it:

> No one knows the total number of untested sexual assault evidence "kits" in Missouri. Not the Missouri State Highway Patrol. Not the Missouri Coalition Against Domestic and Sexual Violence. Not the Office of the Attorney General.
>
> Missouri is in the minority of states that has never done a statewide audit; 32 already have.
>
> MU Police, the Boone County Sheriff's Department and the Columbia Police Department have all said their agencies don't send evidence to be tested unless the survivor wants to go forward with possible charges.
>
> But that makes it harder to link repeat offenders to more than one victim. And they can't match unknown perpetrators to DNA profiles that might already be in the system.
>
> During her testimony last summer in a Columbia sexual assault case, a Highway Patrol lab technician said there is a 900-case backlog at the lab, which includes DNA from crimes against property and people. The patrol says this does not include sexual assault evidence because all of those cases are started within 30 days. From start to finish, it takes an average of 35 days to process the evidence, Highway Patrol Captain John Hotz said in an email.
>
> But that's if it even makes it to the lab. There is evidence collected at hospitals that has never been sent to police departments and evidence at police departments that has never been sent to the lab. No law requires that any of these agencies audit the number of unprocessed kits they are storing, so many don't.
>
> The frequency of the practice remains unknown, said Jennifer Carter Dochler, director of public policy at the Missouri Coalition Against Domestic and Sexual Violence.
>
> "You would have to ask every law enforcement agency in the state how many kits they have," she said. "You would have to ask every hospital in the state how many kits they have, and you would have to ask every crime lab in the state how many kits they have."
>
> This is the kit distributed by the Missouri State Highway Patrol Crime Lab. Most hospitals and medical clinics use it, but some are still transitioning after a statewide effort to standardize it.
>
> The attorney general's office doesn't oversee the Crime Lab, nor does it keep statistics "related to the processing of sexual assault kits," according to an email from Loree Ann Paradise, deputy chief of staff for the attorney general. But, she added, the office is willing to assist prosecutors "to ensure kits are processed in a timely manner." . . .

In this chapter, you will learn:

1. How to gather information for stories about crimes, accidents and fires, and court proceedings.
2. How to write such stories.
3. How to report a criminal court case step by step.
4. How to recognize special problems of crime and court reporting.
5. How to report and write obituaries and life stories.

Brett's story caught the attention of state officials, and months later the state's attorney general released an audit that showed the extent of the problem. It showed that law enforcement agencies and health care providers in Missouri never sent 4,889 sexual-assault evidence kits for testing. Later that year, legislators passed a law requiring the state to develop procedures for gathering, transmitting and storing rape kits.

Brett's impactful reporting was launched after a newsroom conversation about why so many cases of rape and other forms of sexual abuse are never reported to authorities, much less prosecuted. Such crimes often are never reported in news columns, either. When they are, brief items such as this often appear:

A 19-year-old university sophomore reported to police early Sunday morning that she had been sexually assaulted at an apartment near the campus on University Avenue. The woman said she was attending a party and was assaulted by another partygoer whose name she did not know. Police are investigating.

Although important stories like Brett's lead to important changes in the way authorities conduct business, they unfortunately are rare. Much more common are bare-bones crime stories like the one above. Often, the reporter is given almost no information that could lead to pursuit of a more complete story.

Early in their careers, most reporters are assigned to cover bread-and-butter stories of this type that represent the worst of the human condition—crimes, accidents, fires and court proceedings. They also are asked to chronicle the lives of a community's citizens, and they sometimes write obituaries that serve as the final chapters in those citizens' lives.

As an aspiring journalist, you are likely at some time to find yourself covering crime, chasing fire trucks, trying to make sense of court proceedings or writing an obituary. This chapter will help.

Your Preparation

When news breaks, you won't have much time to prepare before rushing out the door or picking up the phone. However, there is some instant research you can do, even if it requires using your smartphone on your way to the scene (preferably with someone else driving).

Begin as you would with any other story—by checking your newsroom's archive. There you'll learn whether a similar crime has occurred before, whether accidents are common at the location of the latest one, whether similar suspicious fires have occurred or whether the person charged with the crime has been in trouble before.

Preparing for the Crime Story

Meetings, news conferences, speeches and court proceedings are usually scheduled events, so usually you will have ample time beforehand to do background research on the individual or topic to be covered. Obituaries also call for a check of the television station or newspaper archive.

But crime reporting may be different. If the police radio reports a murder in your area, you may be dispatched to the scene as the story is breaking. At this point, no one will know who is involved or what happened. There will be no time to check the library and probably little useful information there anyway, and you will have to do your initial reporting at the scene.

Most information about crimes comes from three sources:

- Police officials and their reports.
- The victim(s).
- The witness(es).

The circumstances of the crime may determine which of these three is most important, which should be checked first or whether they should be checked at all. If the victim is available, you should make every effort to get an interview. If the victim and witnesses are unavailable, the police and their reports become primary sources.

In the era of convergence, you'll need more than a pencil and notebook to gather information at the scene of a crime. A digital or smartphone recorder will allow you to record your interviews for publication on your news organization's website, and a smartphone camera might help record what happened at the scene. That's particularly true if you are covering the event alone without the help of a photojournalist or videographer. A smartphone also will make it possible for you to tweet instant updates from the scene.

The point at which your editor assigns you to a crime story is important. If you are dispatched to the scene of the crime as it happens or soon afterward, you should attempt to interview the victim and witnesses first. Depending on when the crime occurred, a police report may or may not be available.

The timing also affects what kinds of material you will be able to gather and which medium might be used. A major breaking story might warrant a mobile phone news bulletin or a television report. Something that happened the night before might require more sophisticated work, such as gathering information for a detailed information graphic of a crime scene.

A police officer investigating a crime covers much of the same ground as you. The officer is interested in who was involved, what happened, when, where, why and how. When you write about crime, always check the police report. It is often the source of basic information, such as the following:

- A description of what happened.
- The location of the incident.
- The name, age and address of the victim.
- The name, age and address of the suspect, if any.
- The offense police believe the suspect has committed.
- The extent of injuries, if any.
- The names, ages and addresses of witnesses, if any.

If you arrive at the scene of a crime as it is taking place or immediately afterward, you have the advantage of being able to gather much of the required information firsthand. When timely coverage is impossible, however, the police report allows you to catch up quickly. The names of those with knowledge of the incident usually appear on the report, and the reporter uses that information to learn the story.

Reporters sometimes write crime stories from the police report alone. Good journalists, however, demand more because police reports are frequently inaccurate. Most experienced reporters have read reports in which the names of those involved were misspelled, ages were wrong and other basic information was inaccurate. Sometimes such errors are a result of sloppy reporting by the investigating officer or mistakes in transcribing notes into a formal report. Whatever the reason, you should do your own reporting and not depend solely on a police officer's account. Remember that editors frown on single-source stories of any kind.

Often, you will want to post the police report itself on your organization's website. The public has a right to see primary sources of this type. But be careful to protect the privacy of victims where appropriate. After a newspaper posted the police account of interviews with the victim of a sexual assault, editors were horrified to discover that the police had failed to remove the victim's name in several places. (Most news organizations protect the identities of sex crime victims.) Another thing to remember is that police reports often contain graphic details some civilians find offensive.

For crime stories, you will usually do a background check in the newsroom's archive after you return to the office. Check whether the archive contains relevant information about those involved in the crime, for example. Most states also have online archives of criminal activity you can check. Has the suspect been arrested before? Has the store been robbed before? The archives might help answer those kinds of questions.

TIPS

What to Do at the Scene of an Accident

- Question the person in charge of the investigation.
- Try to find and interview witnesses.
- Try to find friends or relatives of the victims.
- If possible, interview the victims.
- Talk with others at the scene.
- Be sensitive to victims and their families.

Preparing for Accident and Fire Stories

If you are assigned to cover an accident or a fire, you can expect some of the same problems you'd encounter in covering a crime. Much depends on whether the police or fire report is available before you are assigned to the story. It will give you most of the basic information you need and lead you to other sources.

If you are sent to the scene of an accident or a fire, your job is to collect much of the basic information yourself. As for crimes, the basic information you'll need includes the following:

- A description of what happened.
- The location of the incident.
- The name, age and address of the victim or victims.

- The extent of injuries, if any.
- The names, ages and addresses of witnesses, if any.

Preparing for the Court Story

Most court stories you are likely to cover will be follow-ups to earlier stories. If a murder suspect is appearing for a preliminary hearing, details of the crime probably were reported earlier, and a check of the newsroom's archive may give you ample background information as you prepare for your visit to the courtroom. Otherwise, a chat with the district attorney or the police chief or one of their assistants might provide some preliminary background.

Court stories are often difficult for beginners who do not understand the complex process used in criminal prosecutions. In addition, reporters might be asked to cover civil court proceedings, which are lawsuits that charge an individual or company with harming another. Here's our best advice on how to approach court stories: Ask plenty of questions of the judge and attorneys before or after the court proceeding or during recesses. It's much better to admit your lack of knowledge about the court process than to make a serious error in a story because you didn't understand what was happening.

Writing the Story

Rex Huppke, a reporter and columnist for the *Chicago Tribune* (see the "On the Job" box on page 333), offers useful suggestions that apply to reporting crimes, fires or any other breaking news:

> **First make sure you nail down the essential information you'll need: in essence, the classic "who, what, when, where and why." At the very least you need to be able to write a simple story that details whatever has happened. Once you've got the basics covered, assuming you have time, open your eyes and ears and start taking notes. Capture a mental picture of the scene and put it in your notepad.**
>
> **When you sit down to write the story, take a quick moment to consider what you've just witnessed. Is there an anecdote that jumps out? Is there a scene you can re-create that gets at the heart of the story?**
>
> **If nothing comes to you, just start writing the straightforward story — lay out the basics. You have a deadline looming, and you must at least make sure you've got a story in place. Once that's done, if there's still time, take another moment. Look at the simple house you've built. What can you do to jazz it up? Is there a more interesting way to get into the story, one that tells the news more vividly? Are there some details you can sprinkle in among the facts and quotes, tidbits that will boost the reader's mental image of the scene? If so, get them in there.**
>
> **Once you've done this several times, you'll start to relax more. Knowing that you've got the basics that you need for a story provides a calm, and that calm allows you to soak in more of the surroundings. The soaking part usually will yield the best material.**

Notice that Huppke emphasizes the role of revision. Often, under the pressure of a deadline, you won't come up with details, quotes and anecdotes that really engage a reader. Only after you've written a first draft and have the chance to review it will interesting "tidbits" come to mind. If that happens, don't hesitate to revise to make your story more effective.

The Crime Story

Solid reporting techniques pay off for crime stories just as they do in other types of reporting; then it is a matter of writing the story as the facts demand. Sometimes the events are most effectively told in chronological order, particularly when the story is complex (see Chapter 13). More often, a traditional inverted pyramid style works best. The amount of time the reporter has to file the story also influences the approach. Let's take a look at how two accounts of a crime were developed over time and why a different writing style seemed appropriate for each.

Gathering facts from the many sources available and sorting through conflicting information can be time-consuming tasks. Sometimes, especially when you are posting online, you may have to write the story before all the facts are gathered. The result is a bare-bones account. The breaking news story shown at the top of the annotated model "Comparison of a Breaking News Story and a Follow-Up Story" later in this chapter illustrates this kind of treatment.

After meeting the deadline, the reporter had enough time to gather material for the follow-up story, also shown in the annotated model. That second story uses a chronology structure with a narrative emphasis to give a fuller picture of the sequence of events.

If several people witnessed or were affected by a crime, you can supplement the main story with a sidebar that deals with the personal impact of the crime — the "so what." The writer of the follow-up story shown in the annotated model also decided to write a separate story on nearby residents who had little to add to the main story but became a part of the situation nonetheless:

In the grass at the edge of a woods near Pierpont Friday afternoon, the only remaining signs of James Phipps were a six-inch circle of blood, a doctor's syringe, a blood-stained button and the imprints in the mud where Phipps fell after he was shot by a Highway Patrol officer. Elsewhere in the area, it was a quiet, sunny, spring day in a countryside dotted by farms and houses. But inside some of those houses, dwellers still were shaken by the morning's events that had forced a police order for them to evacuate their homes.

Mrs. James G. Thorne lives on Cheavens Road across the clearing from where Phipps was shot. Mrs. Thorne had not heard the evacuation notice, so when she saw area officers crouching with guns at the end of her driveway, she decided to investigate.

"I was the surprise they weren't expecting," she told a Highway Patrol officer Friday afternoon. "I walked out just before the excitement."

When the officers saw Mrs. Thorne, "they were obviously very upset and shouted for me to get out of here," she said. "I was here alone and asked them how I was supposed to leave. All they said was, 'Just get out of here!'"

Down the road, Clarence Stallman had been warned of the situation by officers and noticed the circling airplane and helicopter. "I said, 'Are they headed this way soon?' and they said, 'They're here,'" said Stallman.

After Stallman notified his neighbors, he picked up Mrs. Thorne at her home and left the area just before the shooting.

On the next street over, Ronald Nichols had no intention of running.

"I didn't know what was happening," Nichols said. "The wife was scared to death and didn't know what to do. I grabbed my gun and looked for them."

Another neighbor, Mrs. Charles Emmons, first was alerted by the sound of the surveillance plane. "The plane was flying so low I thought it was going to come into the house," she said. "I was frightened. This is something you think will never happen to you."

Then Mrs. Emmons flashed a relieved smile. "It's been quite a morning," she said.

The techniques of writing in chronological order and separating the accounts of witnesses from the main story worked well in this case. More often, however, crime stories are written in the classic inverted pyramid style because of time and space considerations.

Accident and Fire Stories

When you are assigned to cover an accident or a fire, many of the facts and all of the color are gathered at the scene. You must observe the scene, but you must also actively solicit information from those who are present. Keep a digital recorder or smartphone at hand. You may be asked to prepare stories for multiple media.

When you are dispatched to the scene of an accident, move as quickly as possible to collect this information:

- The names, ages, addresses and conditions of the victims.
- Accounts of witnesses or police reconstructions of what happened.
- When the accident occurred.
- Where it occurred.
- Why or how it happened or who was at fault, as determined by officials in charge of the investigation.

If this list sounds familiar, it should. You could simplify it to read "who, what, when, where and why." As in any news story, that information is essential. You must gather it as quickly as possible after being assigned to the story.

Source Checklist for Accidents, Fires and Disasters

- Civilian witnesses.
- Victims of personal injury, if they can be interviewed.
- People who were involved but escaped injury.
- Victims of property damage, including property owners, tenants and employees.
- Neighbors and passers-by.
- Relatives and neighbors of victims.
- Rescue workers (firefighters, police, EMS workers, hospital personnel, etc.).
- Government regulatory agencies (local, state and federal).

Just as important is knowing what to do when you arrive on the scene of an accident. These suggestions will help:

- **Question the person in charge of the investigation.** This individual will attempt to gather much of the information you want. A police officer, for example, needs to know who was involved, what happened, when it happened and who was at fault. If you are able to establish a good relationship with the investigator, you may be able to secure much of the information you need from this one source, though single-source stories are usually inadequate.

  Remember that the spellings of names, addresses and similar facts must be verified later. Any veteran reporter can tell you that police officers and other public officials often make errors in recording the names of victims. To avoid such errors, call relatives of the victims or consult the city directory, telephone book or other sources to check your information.

- **Try to find and interview witnesses.** Police and other investigators may lead you directly to the best witnesses. The most accurate account of what happened usually comes from witnesses, and the investigators will try to find them. You should, too. Listen in as investigators interview a witness, or approach the witness after they are finished. If there is time, try to find your own witnesses. Social media may reveal the identity and contact information of some witnesses.

- **Try to find friends or relatives of the victims.** These sources are helpful in piecing together information about the victims. Through them you often get tips about even better stories.

- **If possible, interview the victims.** Survivors of an accident may be badly shaken, but if they are able to talk, they can provide firsthand details that you won't find in an official report. Make every attempt to interview those involved.

- **Talk with others at the scene.** If someone died at the scene of the accident, an ambulance paramedic or the medical examiner may be able to give you some indication of what caused the death. At the least you can learn where the bodies or the injured will be taken, and hospital officials may be able to provide further information.

- **Be sensitive to victims and their families.** You have a job to do, and you must do it. That does not mean, however, that you can be insensitive to those involved in an accident or a fire.

- **Sketch elements of the scene on a piece of paper or take photos with your phone.** The sketch or photos may be useful in helping an information graphics artist re-create the scene.

- **Record your interviews.** You might need a recording for your website or to help you make sure the information is correct.

ANNOTATED MODEL Comparison of a Breaking News Story and a Follow-Up Story

With breaking news, a reporter might post the basic facts online immediately in an inverted pyramid story. After the basic news is posted, the reporter has time to gather additional facts and craft a chronological narrative that gives readers the full story.

Breaking News Story

A Highway Patrol marksman shot and killed a Kansas man in a rural area south of Springfield this morning after the victim threatened to blow off the head of his apparent hostage.

A short, inverted pyramid story may be posted online immediately after the news breaks.

The summary lead captures the action and some of the drama.

A hitchhiker reportedly told police earlier this morning that his "ride" had plans to rob a service station on Interstate 70. That tip apparently followed an earlier report of a van leaving a station at the Millersburg exit of I-70 without paying for gasoline.

An ensuing hourlong chase ended at 9:30 a.m. in an isolated meadow in the Pierpont area when Capt. N.E. Tinnin fired a single shot into the stomach of the suspect, identified as Jim Phipps of Kansas City, Kansas.

Phipps, armed with a sawed-off shotgun, and his "hostage," identified as Anthony Curtis Lilly, 17, also of Kansas City, Kansas, eluded police by fleeing into a rugged, wooded area at the end of Bennett Lane, a dead-end gravel road off Route 163.

Then comes a chronological reconstruction but without much detail or background.

Tinnin said he fired the shot with a .253-caliber sniper rifle when it appeared Phipps was going to shoot Lilly. Two troopers' efforts to persuade Phipps to throw down his weapon and surrender were unsuccessful, Tinnin said.

Follow-Up Story

With more time to learn the full story, the reporter can give readers a more complete account, either online or in print.

James Phipps and Anthony Lilly, a pair of 17-year-olds from Kansas City, Kansas, were heading west on Interstate 70 at 7:30 a.m. Friday, returning from a trip to Arkansas.

The reporter can use narrative to bring interest to an ongoing story.

Within the next hour and a half, Phipps had used a sawed-off shotgun stolen in Arkansas to take Lilly hostage, and, after holding that shotgun to Lilly's head, was shot and killed by a Highway Patrol captain on the edge of a rugged wooded area south of Springfield.

As the episode ended, local officials had only begun to piece together a bizarre tragedy that involved a high-speed chase, airplane and helicopter surveillance, a march through a wooded ravine and the evacuation of several frightened citizens from their country homes.

After the lead (the first two paragraphs) comes a paragraph of scene-setting and foreshadowing.

One attribution (underlined) allows the reporter to narrate the story without repeating the source.

As police reconstructed the incident, Phipps and Lilly decided to stop for gas at the Millersburg exit east of Columbia at about 7:30 a.m.

With them in the van was Robert Paul Hudson Jr., a San Francisco–bound hitchhiker.

Hudson was not present at the shooting. He had fled Lilly's van at the Millersburg exit after he suspected trouble.

(continued)

ANNOTATED MODEL Comparison of a Breaking News Story and a Follow-Up Story (*continued*)

The trouble began when Lilly and Phipps openly plotted to steal some gasoline at Millersburg, Hudson told police. He said the pair had agreed to display the shotgun if trouble arose with station attendants.

Here is a necessary bit of explanation.

Hudson said he persuaded Phipps to drop him off before they stopped for gas. He then caught a ride to Springfield and told his driver of the robbery plans he had overheard. After dropping Hudson off near the Providence Road exit, the driver called Springfield police, who picked up Hudson.

Then the narrative begins.

Meanwhile, Phipps and Lilly put $8.90 worth of gas in the van and drove off without paying. The station attendant notified authorities.

As he approached Springfield, Phipps turned onto U.S. 63 South, where he was spotted by Highway Patrol troopers Tom Halford and Greg Overfelt. They began a high-speed chase, which ended on a dead-end gravel road near Pierpont.

Transitions orient the reader and keep the story moving.

During the chase, which included a U-turn near Ashland, Phipps bumped the Highway Patrol car twice, forcing Halford to run into the highway's median.

Upon reaching the dead end, the suspects abandoned the van and ran into a nearby barn. At that point, Phipps, who Highway Patrol officers said was wanted in Kansas for escaping from a detention center, turned the shotgun on Lilly.

When Halford and Overfelt tried to talk with Phipps from outside the barn, they were met with obscenities. Phipps threatened to "blow (Lilly's) head off," and vowed not to be captured alive.

The reporter uses a direct quote to add color to the narrative.

Phipps then left the barn and walked into a wooded area, pressing the gun against Lilly's head. Halford and Overfelt followed at a safe distance but were close enough to speak with Phipps.

While other officers from the Highway Patrol, the Lincoln County Sheriff's Department and Springfield police arrived at the scene, residents in the area were warned to evacuate their homes. A Highway Patrol plane and helicopter flew low over the woods, following the suspects and the troopers through the woods.

The four walked through a deep and densely wooded ravine. Upon seeing a partially constructed house in a nearby clearing, Phipps demanded of officers waiting in the clearing that his van be driven around to the house, at which time he would release his hostage. Halford said, "They disappeared up over the ridge. I heard some shouting (Phipps' demands), and then I heard the shot."

Another direct quote lends authenticity while giving the story a dramatic conclusion.

After entering the clearing from the woods, Phipps apparently had been briefly confused by the officers on either side of him and had lowered his gun for a moment.

That was long enough for Highway Patrol Capt. N.E. Tinnin to shoot Phipps in the abdomen with a high-powered rifle. It was about 8:45 a.m. Phipps was taken to Boone County Hospital, where he soon died.

The story is wrapped up in the final paragraph.

Your deadline will have a major impact on the amount of information you are able to gather. If you must meet a deadline soon after arriving at the scene, you probably will be forced to stick to the basics of who, what, when, where, why and how. Thus, it is important to gather that information first. Then, if you have time, you can concentrate on more detailed and vivid information to make the story highly readable.

Accidents and fires present similar problems for the reporter, but at a fire of any size you can expect more confusion than at the scene of an accident. One major difference is that the officer in charge will be busier. At the scene of an accident, the damage has been done, and the authorities are usually free to concentrate on their investigation. At a fire, the officer in charge is busy directing firefighters and probably will be unable to talk with you. In many cases, the cause of the fire will not be known for hours, days or weeks. In some cases, it may never be known.

Another problem is that you may not have access to the immediate area of the fire. Barriers often are erected to keep the public—and representatives of the news media—from coming too close to a burning structure. You may not be able to get close enough to firefighters to learn about the problems they are having or to obtain the quotes you need to improve your story.

These problems usually make covering a fire more difficult than covering an accident. Despite the difficulties, you cover a fire in much the same way, interviewing officials and witnesses at the scene. When covering a fire, you must learn the following:

- The location of the fire.
- The names, ages and addresses of those killed, injured or missing.
- The name of the building owner or, in the case of a grass fire or forest fire, the landowner.
- The value of the building and its contents or the value of the land.
- Whether the building and contents were insured for fire damage. (Open land seldom is.)
- Who reported the fire, when the fire started, and how many firefighters and pieces of equipment were called to the scene.
- What caused the fire, if known.

As in any story, the basics are who, what, when, where, why and how. But the nature of the fire will raise other questions that must be answered. Of primary importance is whether life is endangered. If it is not, the amount of property damage becomes the major emphasis of the story. Was arson involved? Was the building insured for its full value? Was there an earlier fire at the same location? Did the building comply with fire codes? Were any rare or extremely valuable objects inside?

Your job is to answer these questions for your readers or viewers. You may be able to obtain some of this information later on from official fire reports if they are ready before your deadline. But most information will come from interviews that you conduct at the scene with the best available sources. Finding your sources may not be easy, but you can begin by looking for the highest-ranking fire official. Large departments may have a designated press officer whose job is to deal with you and other reporters.

> **"The news is no longer the news. . . . It's all about luridness. Body bags will be seen at 7, chasing ambulance at 8, victim's family at 9."**
>
> ■ Oliver Stone, film director

Another important source is the fire marshal, whose job is to determine the cause of the fire and, if arson is involved, to bring charges against the arsonist. You should make every effort to talk with the fire marshal at the scene.

It is important to verify information received at the scene to the maximum extent possible. One way to do that is to see if two sources agree on the same version of what happened. Remember, when news is breaking, confusion reigns. Be cautious, especially if you are tweeting immediate events from the scene. Even official sources can be mistaken about what happened. Verify to the extent possible, and attribute all information to the source from whom you received it.

The Court Story

Criminal justice proceedings can be complicated as a case moves through a number of stages—from occurrence of the crime, to police investigation, to actions by prosecutors and defense attorneys, to actual criminal trials, to legal punishments like incarceration and execution.

Throughout this cycle of events, a reporter has numerous opportunities to write stories. The extent to which the reporter does so depends on the importance of the case and the amount of local interest in it. In a major case, the filing of every motion may prompt a story; in other cases, only the verdict may be important. NEWS value is the determining factor.

Avoiding libelous statements

Accuracy is also important, as in any form of reporting. Perhaps no other area of writing requires as much caution as the reporting of crime and court news. The potential for libel is great.

Libel is damage to a person's reputation caused by a written statement that brings the person into hatred, contempt or ridicule or that injures a person's business or occupational pursuits (see Chapter 19). Reporters must be extremely careful about what they write. One of the greatest dangers is the possibility of writing that someone is charged with a crime more serious than is the case. Suppose that after checking clippings in the newsroom library, for example, a reporter writes the following:

> **The rape trial of John L. Duncan, 25, of 3925 Oak St. has been set for Dec. 10 in Jefferson County Circuit Court.**
>
> **Duncan is charged in connection with the June 6 rape of a Melton High School girl near Fletcher Park.**

Duncan originally was charged with rape following his arrest. However, the prosecutor later determined that the evidence was insufficient to win a

ON THE JOB "Every Story Is Important"

Earlier in this chapter, we introduced you to **Rex Huppke**, a reporter and columnist for the *Chicago Tribune* and chicagotribune.com. This isn't the job he landed fresh from school. In fact, he majored in chemical engineering, only to discover six months into his first job that he had made a big mistake. Eventually, he returned to graduate school, this time in journalism. His first reporting job was in Colorado. Then later on in Indiana, he joined The Associated Press while his wife earned her law degree. He has never forgotten a lesson learned on his first assignment in Colorado Springs:

> I was dispatched to a county fair with the mission of finding something "cute" to put in the next day's paper. There was, without question, a part of me that felt I was above such a simple assignment. I was a journalism school graduate, after all.
>
> But I went and found two sisters prepping their goats for a 4-H competition, and wound up spending about an hour with the girls and their mother learning the intricacies of goat upkeep and show prep. The family was so excited to have a reporter in their midst that the mother insisted I pose for a picture with the girls and their goats.
>
> I did, then went back to the newsroom and, charmed by the family, put together a nice feature story that ran inside the next day's feature section. About a week later, I received a letter and opened it to find a copy of the picture the mother took with a note that gushed about how much the article meant to those girls. It was something, the mother wrote, that they would keep forever.
>
> I have kept that photo, and I look at it now and then to remind myself what matters in this business. Every story is important. You are never greater than the people who let you into their lives, whether it's at a time of triumph or tragedy or simple day-to-day existence.
>
> Start each story with that one truth—every story is important—and you will do fine.

rape conviction and reduced the charge to assault. The newspaper had to print a correction that identified the correct charge.

Many courts handle both civil and criminal cases. Media coverage often focuses on criminal cases, although civil actions—lawsuits involving disputes of one type or another—are often excellent sources of stories.

Any story involving arrests should raise caution flags. You must have a working knowledge of libel law and understand what you can and cannot write about an incident. This is covered in more depth in Chapter 19. Any reporter who writes the following, for example, is asking for trouble:

> **John R. Milton, 35, of 206 East St. was arrested Monday on a charge of assaulting a police officer.**

It would be safer, and more accurate, to write that he was arrested "on suspicion of" the assault. Only a prosecutor, not a police officer, may file charges. Many journalists prefer to release the name of an arrested person only after the charge has been filed.

Reporters who cover court news encounter many such dilemmas. They are not trained as attorneys, and it takes time to develop a working knowledge of legal proceedings. The only recourse is to ask as many questions as necessary when a point of law is not clear.

However, anything said in open court is fair game for reporters. If, in an opening statement, a prosecutor says the defendant is "nothing but scum, a smut peddler bent on polluting the mind of every child in the city," then by all means report the comment in context in your story. But if a spectator makes that same statement in the hallway during a recess, you probably would not report it. Courts do not extend the qualified privilege to report court proceedings beyond the context of the official proceeding.

Types of Courts and Cases

The U.S. has two main court systems: federal and state. Federal district courts handle violations of federal crime statutes, interpret the U.S. Constitution, and deal with civil rights, election disputes, commerce and antitrust laws, postal regulations, federal tax laws and similar issues. They also handle actions between citizens of different states when the disputed amount exceeds $50,000.

Each state has its own system, with many similarities from state to state. The average citizen is most likely to encounter city or municipal courts, which have jurisdiction over traffic and other minor violations. News from these courts is handled as a matter of record in some newspapers.

Violations of state statutes usually are handled in the state trial courts. These *courts of general jurisdiction* (often called *circuit* or *superior courts*) handle civil cases, such as contract disputes, as well as criminal cases.

Most state crimes are either misdemeanors or felonies. A *misdemeanor* is usually punishable by a fine, a county jail term not to exceed one year, or both. *Felonies* are punishable by a fine, a state prison sentence of more than one year, or death.

Reporting a Case Step-by-Step: An Example

Let's trace a sample criminal case from the time of arrest through the trial to show how a reporter might cover each step.

A Breaking-News Tweet

When arrested, a suspect is taken to a police station for fingerprinting, photographs and perhaps a sobriety test or a lineup. The police may take statements as evidence only if the person is informed of and waives the Miranda rights, which include the right to have an attorney and the right to remain silent. A charge must be filed, or the person must be released, usually within 24 hours.

The first report of a story could come as a tweet as soon as the arrest is confirmed:

Arrest made in death of Springfield woman. More to come.

A Typical First Story

Next would come a more detailed version of the story for the web. You'll notice that unanswered questions remain. This bare-bones story, however, provides a glimpse of several key points in covering arrest stories:

> **An unemployed carpenter was arrested today and charged with the Aug. 6 murder of Springfield resident Anne Compton.**
>
> **Lester L. Rivers, 32, of 209 E. Dillow Lane was charged with first-degree murder, Prosecuting Attorney Mel Singleton said.**
>
> **Chief of Detectives E.L. Hall said Rivers was arrested on a warrant after a three-month investigation by a team of three detectives. He declined to comment on what led investigators to Rivers.**
>
> **Compton's body was found in the Peabody River by two fishermen on the morning of Aug. 7. She had been beaten to death with a blunt instrument, according to Dr. Ronald R. Miller, the county medical examiner.**

Notice that the reporter carefully chose the words "arrested … and charged with" rather than "arrested for," a phrase that may carry a connotation of guilt.

Another important element of all crime and court coverage is the tie-back sentence. This sentence relates a story to events covered in a previous story — in this case, the report of the crime itself. It is important to state clearly — and near the beginning of the story — which crime is involved. It is also important to provide enough information about it so that the reader recognizes it. In this story, the reporter identifies the crime in the lead and then at the end gives more details to help the reader recall the event. Clarification of the crime is important even in major stories with ready identification in the community. This story does that by recounting when and where Compton's body was found and by whom. It also tells that she died after being hit with a blunt instrument.

Writing the Court Story

- Possess a strong working knowledge of libel law.
- Ask questions when a point of law is unclear.
- Know that anything said in open court is fair game.
- Early in the story, state clearly which crime is involved, and provide enough information so the reader recognizes it.
- Don't overstate facts.
- Take good notes. Trial coverage is greatly enhanced with direct quotations of key exchanges.

Follow-Up Story: First Court Appearance

After the district attorney, who argues for the state, files charges, the defendant is usually brought before a judge, informed of the charges and reminded of the Miranda rights. Bail may be set.

For a *misdemeanor*, if the defendant pleads guilty, the judge usually handles the case immediately with a sentence or fine. If the plea is not guilty, a trial date is set.

For a *felony* — a much more serious offense — the defendant does not enter a plea. The judge sets a date for a preliminary hearing, unless the defendant waives the right to such a hearing. A defendant who waives this hearing is bound over to the general jurisdiction trial court; that is, the records of the case are sent to the trial court.

In the Rivers case, the following morning the suspect was taken to Associate Circuit Court for his initial court appearance. Here is part of the story that resulted:

> **Lester L. Rivers appeared in Associate Circuit Court today charged with first-degree murder in connection with the Aug. 6 beating death of Springfield resident Anne Compton.**
>
> **Judge Howard D. Robbins scheduled a preliminary hearing for Nov. 10 and set bail at $10,000. Robbins assigned Public Defender Ogden Ball to represent Rivers, 32, of 209 E. Dillow Lane.**

Rivers said nothing during the 10-minute session as the judge informed him of his right to remain silent and his right to an attorney. Ball asked Robbins to set the bail at a "reasonable amount for a man who is unemployed." Rivers is a carpenter who was fired from his last job in June. Despite the seriousness of the charge, it is essential that Rivers be free to help prepare his defense, Ball said.

Police have said nothing about a possible connection between Rivers and Compton, whose body was found in the Peabody River by two fishermen on the morning of Aug. 7. She had been beaten to death.

The reporter clearly outlines the exact charge and reported on key points of the brief hearing. Again, the tie-back helps readers recognize and remember details of the crime.

Follow-Up Story: Preliminary Hearing

Next comes the *preliminary hearing*, where the evidence linking the defendant to the crime is first revealed.

The hearing is usually held before a magistrate or a lower-level judge. The prosecutor tries to convince the judge that there is *probable cause* to believe the defendant committed a crime. Because preliminary hearings are often one-sided, reporters must be careful to write a well-balanced story.

If the judge finds probable cause, the prosecuting attorney must file, within a short time period (usually 10 days), what is called an "information" based on the judge's finding.

Here's the story that resulted from Rivers' preliminary hearing:

Lester L. Rivers will be tried in Jefferson County Circuit Court for the Aug. 6 murder of Springfield resident Anne Compton.

Associate Circuit Judge Howard D. Robbins ruled today there is probable cause to believe a crime was committed and probable cause that Rivers did it. Rivers was bound over for trial in Circuit Court.

Rivers, 32, of 209 E. Dillow Lane is being held in Jefferson County Jail. He has been unable to post bail of $10,000.

At today's preliminary hearing, Medical Examiner Ronald R. Miller testified that a tire tool recovered from Rivers' car at the time of his arrest "could have been used in the beating death of Miss Compton." Her body was found floating in the Peabody River Aug. 7.

James L. Mullaney, a lab technician for the FBI crime laboratory in Washington, D.C., testified that "traces of blood on the tire tool matched Miss Compton's blood type."

In reporting the testimony, the reporter is careful to use direct quotes and not to overstate the facts. The medical examiner testified that the tire tool "could have been used" in the murder. If he had said that it "had been used," the reporter would have needed a stronger lead.

Defense attorneys usually use preliminary hearings to learn about the evidence against their clients and do not present any witnesses. This allows them to build a stronger case for their clients during the trial.

In most states, a person can also be brought to trial by a grand jury indictment. In federal courts, the Constitution requires indictment by a grand jury in felony cases.

In some states, grand jury hearings are secret, and potential defendants are not allowed to be present when testimony is given. The district (or prosecuting) attorney presents evidence that determines whether there is probable cause to prosecute.

A grand jury returns a "true bill" if it finds probable cause and "no true bill" if not. The jury foreman or forewoman and the prosecuting attorney must sign the indictment, which then is presented in open court to a trial judge.

If the defendant is not already in custody, the judge orders an arrest warrant. Arraignment in the trial court follows.

Follow-Up Story: Arraignment

Arraignment, conducted in open court, is the first formal presentation of the information or the indictment to the defendant. The defendant enters a plea to the charge: guilty, not guilty, or not guilty by reason of mental disease or defect.

In the Rivers case, the prosecutor filed an information, as state law required. The defendant was arraigned in Circuit Court, and the result was a routine story that begins as follows:

> **Circuit Judge John L. Lee refused today to reduce the bail of Lester L. Rivers, who is charged with first-degree murder in the Aug. 6 death of Springfield resident Anne Compton. Rivers pleaded not guilty. Repeating a request he made earlier in Magistrate Court, Public Defender Ogden Ball urged that Rivers' bail be reduced from $10,000 so he could be free to assist in preparing his defense.**

The not-guilty plea was expected, so the reporter concentrated on a more interesting aspect of the hearing—the renewed request for reduced bail.

At this point in criminal proceedings, *plea bargaining* sometimes occurs. A defendant changes a plea from not guilty to guilty in return for a lighter sentence, typically pleading guilty to a lesser charge. To save the time and expense of a trial, prosecutors often agree to this if they believe justice is served.

If the defendant enters a guilty plea, the judge may impose a sentence immediately, or a *presentencing investigation* of the defendant's background may be ordered to help the judge set punishment. If the defendant enters a plea of not guilty, the judge sets a trial date. Most jurisdictions require speedy trials.

As the prosecutor and defense attorney prepare for trial, they may file motions for disclosure of evidence, suppression of evidence and similar rulings. A defense attorney who feels that pretrial stories in the local media may prejudice potential jurors will often ask for a **change of venue**, which moves the trial to a county other than the one where the crime occurred.

Follow-Up Story: First Day of the Trial

On the first day of a trial, a jury, usually 12 jurors and at least one alternate, is selected during a process called *voir dire* (vwar DEER). The prosecutor and defense attorney, and sometimes the judge in the federal system, question the prospective jurors to identify jurors they hope will be sympathetic to their positions.

Each attorney can eliminate a certain number of people as jurors without having to state a reason and can dismiss an unlimited number *for cause* (if, for example, the prospective juror is related to the accused).

In the Rivers case, after a series of motions was reported routinely, the trial began. Here's the story written on the first day:

> **Jury selection began today in the first-degree murder trial of Lester L. Rivers, who is charged with the Aug. 6 beating death of Springfield resident Anne Compton.**
>
> **Public Defender Ogden Ball, Rivers' attorney, and Prosecuting Attorney Mel Singleton both expect jury selection to be complete by 5 p.m.**
>
> **The selection process started after court convened at 10 a.m. The only incident occurred just before the lunch break as Singleton was questioning prospective juror Jerome B. Tinker, 33, of 408 Woodland Terrace.**
>
> **"I went to school with that guy," said Tinker, pointing to Rivers, who was seated in the courtroom. "He wouldn't hurt nobody."**
>
> **Singleton immediately asked that Tinker be removed from the jury panel, and Circuit Judge John L. Lee agreed.**
>
> **Rivers smiled as Tinker made his statement, but otherwise sat quietly, occasionally conferring with Ball.**

The testimony is about to begin, so the reporter sets the stage here, describing the courtroom scene. Jury selection is often routine and becomes newsworthy only in important or interesting cases.

After the jurors are sworn in, the prosecutor makes an opening statement that outlines how the state expects to prove each element of the crime. The defense attorney may follow with a statement, may wait until after the prosecution has introduced its evidence to make a statement, or may waive an opening statement altogether.

Follow-Up Story: Trial Testimony

A basic tenet of criminal law is that the prosecution must prove the defendant guilty beyond a reasonable doubt. The defendant is not required to prove anything or even to testify.

To establish what happened and to link the defendant to the crime, the state calls witnesses to testify. First, the prosecutor asks questions, and the witness responds. The defense attorney then cross-examines the witness.

When the defense attorney finishes cross-examination, the prosecutor conducts *redirect examination* to clarify certain points or to bolster a witness's credibility. Cross-examination and redirect examination continue until both sides have asked the witness all their questions.

Trial coverage can be tedious, but when the case is interesting, the stories are easy to write. As the Rivers trial progressed, the reporter picked the most interesting testimony to use in leads:

> **A service station owner testified today that Lester L. Rivers offered a ride to Springfield resident Anne Compton less than an hour before she was beaten to death Aug. 6.**
>
> **Ralph R. Eagle, the station owner, was a witness at the first-degree murder trial of Rivers in Jefferson County Circuit Court.**

"I told her I'd call a cab," Eagle testified, "but Rivers offered her a ride to her boyfriend's house." Compton had gone to the service station after her car broke down nearby. Under cross-examination, Public Defender Ogden Ball, Rivers' attorney, questioned whether Rivers was the man who offered the ride.

"If it wasn't him, it was his twin brother," Eagle said.

"Then you're not really sure it was Mr. Rivers, are you?" Ball asked.

"I sure am," Eagle replied.

"You think you're sure, Mr. Eagle, but you really didn't get a good look at him, did you?"

"I sold him some gas and got a good look at him when I took the money."

"But it was night, wasn't it, Mr. Eagle?" Ball asked.

"That place doesn't have the best lighting in the world, but I saw him all right."

The reporter focuses on the key testimony of the trial by capturing it in the words of the participants.

After the prosecution witnesses have testified and the state rests its case, the defense almost always makes a motion for acquittal, arguing that the state has failed to prove its case beyond a reasonable doubt. Almost always, the motion is denied.

The defense then calls witnesses to support its case, and the prosecutor cross-examines them. Finally, when all witnesses have testified, the defense rests. In some cases, rebuttal witnesses may be called in an attempt to discredit defense witness testimony.

Follow-Up Story: Verdict

After these witnesses have testified, the judge instructs the jury about possible verdicts and key points of law. The prosecuting and defense attorneys then present their closing arguments. In the federal system, closing arguments precede the judge's instructions to the jury. The jury then retires to deliberate.

For the journalist covering the trial, there is eventually the verdict story, which is usually one of the easiest to write. Here's the verdict story in the Rivers case:

Lester L. Rivers was found guilty of first-degree murder today in the Aug. 6 beating death of Springfield resident Anne Compton.

Rivers stood motionless in Jefferson County Circuit Court as the jury foreman returned the verdict. Judge John L. Lee set sentencing for Dec. 10.

Rivers, 32, of 209 E. Dillow Lane could be sentenced to death in the electric chair or life imprisonment in the State Penitentiary.

Public Defender Ogden Ball, Rivers' attorney, said he will appeal.

After the verdict was announced, Mr. and Mrs. Lilborn O. Compton, the victim's parents, were escorted from the courtroom by friends. Both refused to talk with reporters.

What's the grammar error in this sentence?

With the melting of glaciers around the world. Some areas are dealing with the threat of decreased water supply.

See Appendix 1, Rule 3.

Because a criminal trial requires a unanimous verdict, deliberations often are protracted. If jurors fail to agree (a *hung jury*), the judge may order a mistrial; then the entire case will be retried with a new jury. If a verdict is reached, the jury returns to the courtroom, where the verdict is read.

Sentencing and Appeals

In some states, juries may recommend sentences in guilty verdicts. But the judge almost always makes the final decision unless a crime carries a mandatory sentence. For a really important criminal trial, reporters might be assigned to cover a sentencing hearing.

The defense often files a motion asking that a guilty verdict be set aside or requesting a new trial. These motions, though usually denied, are often prerequisites to the filing of an appeal. Appeals often follow guilty verdicts. Except in cases involving serious crimes, judges often permit a defendant to be released on bail pending the outcome of appeals.

Many other types of stories can be written about a trial. Lengthy jury deliberations, for example, might prompt stories about the anxiety of the defendant and attorneys and their speculations about the cause of the delay.

Covering court news requires care and good reporting. As in any kind of reporting, you must be well prepared. If you understand the language of the courts and how they are organized, your job is simplified.

Other Issues in Crime and Court Reporting

Covering crime and the courts is not a simple matter. The complexity of court proceedings can be baffling to a beginning reporter, but there are other pitfalls as well.

The Free Press/Fair Trial Controversy

The 1954 murder trial of Dr. Samuel Sheppard in Cleveland was the landmark case involving the perceived conflict between a defendant's right to a fair trial and the public's right to know. Sheppard was accused of murdering his wife. News coverage in the Cleveland newspapers, which included front-page editorials, was intense. In 1966, the U.S. Supreme Court said the trial judge had not fulfilled his duty to protect the jury from the news coverage that saturated the community and to control disruptive influences in the courtroom. The court overturned Sheppard's conviction, and he was acquitted after a second trial.

That case, more than any other, ignited what is known as the **free press/fair trial controversy**. It continues more than 50 years later, and it's most often an issue when famous individuals are charged with crimes. When NFL superstar O.J. Simpson was prosecuted for the June 12, 1994, murder of his wife, Judge Lance Ito often threatened to end television coverage of court proceedings to protect Simpson's rights. Lawyers charged that the media were threatening the Sixth Amendment right of the accused to an impartial jury. The media countered with charges that lawyers were threatening the First Amendment.

More recently, the high-profile prosecution of comedian Bill Cosby on multiple sexual assault charges raised similar questions about whether an impartial jury could be impaneled after nationwide publicity about the case. Cosby was convicted in 2018, but he appealed. One point in the appeal is the defense attorneys' claim that one jury member should have been rejected after he allegedly told a rejected juror, "I just think he's guilty, so we can all be done and get out of here." That shows the difficulty of impaneling an unbiased jury, particularly in high-profile cases.

Editors realize that coverage of a crime can make it difficult to impanel an impartial jury, but they argue that courts have available many remedies other than restricting the flow of information. In the Sheppard case, for example, the Supreme Court justices said a change of venue, which moves the trial to a location where publicity is not as intense, could have been ordered. Other remedies suggested by the court in such cases are to "continue" (delay) the trial, to grant a new trial or to head off possible outside influences during the trial by sequestering the jury. Editors also argue that acquittals have been won in some of the most publicized cases in recent years.

> **"To make inroads into the mind-set that 'if the press reported it, it must be true' is the lawyer's most challenging task."**
>
> ■ **Robert Shapiro, attorney**

Gag Orders and Closed Trials

Despite the remedies the Supreme Court offered in the Sheppard case, trial judges continued to be concerned about impaneling impartial juries. Judges issued hundreds of gag orders in the wake of the Sheppard case.

Finally, in 1976, in the landmark case of *Nebraska Press Association v. Stuart*, the Supreme Court ruled that a gag order was an unconstitutional prior restraint that violated the First Amendment to the Constitution. The justices did not rule that all gag orders are invalid. But in each case, the trial judge has to prove that an order restraining publication would protect the rights of the accused and that no other alternatives would be less damaging to First Amendment rights.

The *Stuart* ruling did not end the concerns of trial judges. Rather than issue gag orders restricting the press from reporting court proceedings, some attempted to close their courtrooms. In the first such case to reach the U.S. Supreme Court, *Gannett v. DePasquale*, the press and public suffered a severe but temporary blow. On July 2, 1979, in a highly controversial decision, the justices said, "We hold that members of the public have no constitutional right under the Sixth and Fourteenth amendments to attend criminal trials." The case itself had involved only a pretrial hearing.

As a result of the decision and the confusion that followed, the Supreme Court of Virginia sanctioned the closing of an entire criminal trial. The accused was acquitted during the second day of the secret trial. The U.S. Supreme Court agreed to hear the appeal of the trial judge's action in a case known as *Richmond Newspapers v. Virginia*. On July 2, 1980, the court said that under the First Amendment "the trial of a criminal case must be open to the public." Only a court finding of an "overriding interest," which was not defined, would be grounds for closing a criminal trial.

Covering Sex Crimes

The reporting of sex crimes often causes controversy. Most news executives think of their products as family newspapers or broadcasts and are properly hesitant about reporting the lurid details of sex crimes.

Sex crime victims

One problem in reporting on sex crimes is the question of how to handle rape victims. Too often, rapes are not reported to police because victims are unwilling to appear in court to testify against the suspects. Defense attorneys sometimes use such occasions to attack the victim's moral character and imply that she or he consented to sexual relations. Many victims decline to press charges because of fear that their names will be made public in the media. There is, after all, still a lingering tendency to attach a social stigma to the rape victim, despite increasing public awareness of the nature of the crime. In some states, "rape shield" statutes prohibit a defendant's attorney from delving into the rape victim's prior sexual activity unless some connection can be shown with the circumstances of the rape charged.

Sex crime offenders

In Massachusetts, a judge excluded the public and press from the entire trial of a man accused of raping three teenagers, enforcing a state law that provided for the mandatory closing of trials involving specific sex offenses against minors. In 1982, the U.S. Supreme Court held in *Globe Newspaper Co. v. Superior Court* that the mandatory closure law violated the First Amendment right of access to criminal trials established in the *Richmond Newspapers v. Virginia* case. The justices ruled that when a state attempts to deny the right of access in an effort to inhibit the disclosure of sensitive information, it must show that the denial "is necessitated by a compelling governmental interest." The court indicated in the opinion that in some cases *in-camera proceedings* (proceedings that take place in a judge's chambers outside the view of the press and public) may be appropriate for youthful witnesses.

In *Press-Enterprise v. Riverside County Superior Court*, the U.S. Supreme Court ruled in 1984 that a court order closing the jury-selection process in a rape-murder case was invalid. The court ruled that jury selection has been a public process with exceptions only for good cause.

In a second *Press-Enterprise v. Riverside County Superior Court* case, the U.S. Supreme Court said in 1986 that preliminary hearings should be open to the public unless there is a "substantial probability" that the resulting publicity would prevent a fair trial and there are no "reasonable alternatives to closure."

In 1993, the Supreme Court continued its emphasis on the importance of open court proceedings. It struck down a Puerto Rican law that said preliminary hearings "shall be held privately" unless the defendant requests a public preliminary hearing.

Press-Bar Guidelines

The previous cases appear to uphold the right of the press and the public to have access to criminal proceedings. Judges, however, also have a duty to protect the rights of the accused.

The Supreme Court of the state of Washington, in *Federated Publications v. Swedberg*, held in 1981 that press access to pretrial hearings may be conditioned on the agreement of reporters to abide by the voluntary guidelines for representatives of the press and the bar that exist in some states. The decision involved a preliminary hearing in a Bellingham, Washington, murder case tied to the "Hillside Strangler" murders in the Los Angeles area. The state Supreme Court ruled that the lower-court order was "a good-faith attempt to accommodate the interests of both defendant and press." The lower court had required reporters covering the hearing to sign a document in which the reporters agreed to abide by press-bar guidelines. The state Supreme Court said the document should be taken as a moral commitment on the part of the reporters, not as a legally enforceable document.

The U.S. Supreme Court in 1982 refused to hear an appeal of that case. Fortunately, many states have statutes to the effect that "the setting of every court shall be public, and every person may freely attend the same." When such statutes are in place, the closed-courtroom controversy appears to be moot. In states that have no such statute, the result seems to be that (1) a criminal trial must be open unless there is an "overriding interest" that requires part of it to be closed and (2) judges must find some overriding interest before closing pretrial hearings.

One effect of the Washington decision is that many media groups are withdrawing from state press-bar agreements in the few states that have such guidelines. Their reasoning is that the voluntary guidelines in effect could become mandatory.

Cameras in the Courtroom

In 1994, the U.S. Judicial Conference ended its three-year experiment with cameras in federal courts by banning them. Two years later, the Judicial Conference agreed to permit cameras in some lower federal courts. And most states do allow cameras in at least some state courtrooms. Only Indiana, Mississippi, South Dakota and the District of Columbia ban courtroom cameras.

Judges have many ways to protect the rights of the accused without trampling on the right of the press and public to attend trials and pretrial hearings. Most editors

launchpadworks.com
WATCH: **"Fake News/ Real News: A Fine Line"**

- *Onion* editor Joe Randazzo suggests that fake news outlets like *The Onion* do better at getting at "the truth" than traditional media companies do. Do you agree? Explain.
- Think about the ways you get your news. How do you decide which sources to consult? How much do you trust what they tell you?

are sensitive to the rights of the accused and exercise self-restraint when publishing or broadcasting information about a crime. And most have attempted to establish written policy on such matters, although others insist that individual cases must be judged on their merits.

Coverage of Minority Groups

Reporters and editors must share with judges the burden of protecting the rights of the accused. They also must ensure that certain groups within our society are not treated unfairly, either by the courts or in the media.

In a study of crime reporting he conducted at the Gannett Center for Media Studies, Robert Snyder discovered that minorities tend to be covered by the media mainly in the context of crime news. Crime reporting is a staple of urban news, and urban areas are where minorities are concentrated. In large cities like New York and Los Angeles, some areas of the city often make news only because of crime.

As it is reported now, Snyder says, crime is almost always a conversation about race. He concludes that if the media are to change that perception, they must cover minorities more broadly and sympathetically. The real story of crime, Snyder says, should be the "breaking down of communities and the real weakening of the social structure."

Many editors are concerned about the ways minorities are portrayed in crime stories. In fact, many newspapers and broadcast stations studiously avoid gratuitous mentions of race. Their reporters are allowed to mention the race of a suspect only as part of the complete identification of a fugitive. For many years, it was common to read or hear references to a "six-foot-tall black man" who was wanted for a crime. Today such a description would be considered unacceptable. Too many men fit that description, and the racial reference merely reinforces stereotypes. However, if a complete description of a fugitive might help lead to an arrest, it is appropriate to mention race as a part of that description. Only when race becomes the central theme of a story should it be emphasized.

Similarly, most editors consider a person's sexual orientation off limits unless the story focuses on heterosexuality or homosexuality. Tastefully handling crime news that involves homosexual crimes often proves to be difficult. This was never more true than in the sensational 1992 murder trial of Milwaukee's Jeffrey Dahmer, convicted of sexually molesting young boys and men, killing them and eating parts of their bodies. In such cases, the press walks a fine line between responsibly informing the public and pandering to its seemingly insatiable appetite for sensational crime news.

Crime and Social Media

Citizens who witness a crime or encounter a crime scene after the fact are prone to post about it on social media. It's important to remember that such reports can be and often are wildly inaccurate. Make sure not to quote information from social media reports without verifying that information with better sources.

Issues of Taste and Ethics

News editors ponder a number of major issues involving taste and ethics in crime and court reporting:

- When should the media reveal details of how a murder or another crime was committed?
- When should the media reveal details about sex crimes or print the names of sex crime victims?
- When should the media reveal a suspect's confession or even the fact that the suspect confessed?
- When should the media reveal a defendant's prior criminal record?
- When should the media reveal the names of juveniles charged with crimes?

None of these questions can be answered to everyone's satisfaction, and it is doubtful whether rules can be established to apply in all such situations.

Reporting details of a crime

Some have charged that when the media reveal details of a murder, some people use the techniques described to commit additional murders. This charge is directed most frequently at television, but newspapers have not been immune, and online media may also face this issue.

Reporting confessions and prior convictions

Many editors will not publish or broadcast details of a suspect's confession in an effort to protect the suspect's rights. Revealing such information blocks the way for a fair trial perhaps more than anything else the media can do. Some newspapers and broadcast stations, however, continue to reveal assertions by police or prosecutors that a confession was signed. Many critics question whether such information isn't just as prejudicial as the confession statement itself.

Occasionally, journalists question whether to suppress an unsolicited confession. After a youth was charged with a series of robberies and was certified to stand trial as an adult, a newspaper reporter phoned the youthful defendant, who was free on bail, for an interview. The defendant admitted to committing two other robberies in what amounted to a confession to the newspaper and its readers. The editor, who would not have printed a statement by police that the defendant had confessed to the crimes, printed this one. Why? The editor reasoned that information about a confession to police amounts to secondhand, hearsay information. The confession to a reporter, however, was firsthand information obtained by the newspaper directly from the accused.

Lawyers also view as prejudicial the publication of a defendant's prior criminal record. Even if authorities refuse to divulge that information, much of it may be in the newspaper's morgue. Should it be reported? Most journalists believe it should be, particularly if a prior conviction was for a similar offense. Most attorneys disagree.

Identifying juveniles

Whether to use the names of juveniles charged with crimes is a troublesome issue as well. Most states prohibit law enforcement officers and court officials from releasing the names of juveniles, which in most states refers to those under the age of 18. The reasoning of those who oppose releasing juveniles' names is that the publicity marks them for life as criminals. Those who hold this view argue that there is ample opportunity for these individuals to change their ways and become good citizens—if the media do not stamp them as criminals. Others argue that juveniles who commit serious offenses, such as rape and armed robbery, should be treated as adults.

Questions such as these elicit divergent views from editors, some of whom regularly seek the advice of their lawyers. Little guidance for the reporter can be offered here. Because the decision to publish or not to publish is the editor's, not the reporter's, consultation is necessary. Each case must be decided on its merits.

Obituaries and Life Stories

In the online world, obituaries are big business. Websites sell advertising to funeral homes and auxiliary services because they have found that readers search for obituaries frequently. Even former residents of a city monitor obituaries. Some websites are devoted to obituaries and provide resources for readers and advertisers. One, legacy.com, which is partially owned by a newspaper, provides links and a searchable database to hundreds of newspapers, sells advertising to the funeral industry, and allows readers to post memorials to friends and family members who have died.

Newspaper editors have known about the drawing power of obituaries for years. Chuck Ward, publisher of the *Olean* (New York) *Times Herald*, once told his readers about the time his editor asked whether they should do a special obituary on the father of one of their employees: "My response was that unless the father (or any relative) of the employee met the criteria for a glorified obituary, the obituary should be treated as 99 percent of our obituaries are."

He then recounted that when he went to the visitation that evening, the line extended 50 yards outside the mortuary. He returned in an hour, and the line was still long. That got Ward thinking about his question earlier in the day: "What did he do?"

"All he did, apparently, was live a wonderful, loving life with a splendid family. During the course of that life, he must have touched the lives of countless people in our community. And they all were there to say goodbye."

Ward learned that people don't have to be public figures to deserve well-reported obituaries. Too many obituaries read as if they were written by a computer program—efficient but lifeless. This tendency persists despite readership surveys that show that about 50 percent of readers look at obituaries, about twice as many as those who look at most other features.

And obituaries are read critically. If the deceased belonged to the Shiloh Baptist Church, count on a phone call if you say she was a member of Bethany Baptist. Writing obituaries is important work, and you must get it right.

Despite this importance, many newspapers and television news stations today do not publish a news obituary unless the person who died was well-known. You're more likely to find staff-written obituaries in local publications, in print and online. Jim Nicholson of the *Philadelphia Daily News*, who wrote obituaries full time and won the American Society of News Editors Distinguished Writing Award, explained that readers want to know, "How did someone live a good life? How did they get through this world?"

Although most obituaries are now paid stories, often written by someone at the mortuary and someone in the family, some newspapers, mostly smaller ones, still write obituaries. An obituary is a news story. You should apply the same standards to crafting a lead and building the body of an obituary as you do to other stories.

Five Safeguards for Obit Writers

- Confirm spellings of names on the mortuary form.
- Check the addresses. If a telephone book or city directory lists a different address, contact the mortuary about the discrepancy.
- Check the birth date against the age, noting whether the person's birthday was before or after the date of death.
- Verify with the mortuary or family any obituary sent to the newspaper.
- Check your newspaper's library for stories about the deceased, but be sure you don't pull stories about someone else with the same name.

Crafting a Lead

You begin by answering the same questions you would answer in any news story: who (Michael Kelly, 60, of 1234 West St.), what (died), where (at Regional Hospital), when (Tuesday night), why (heart attack) and how (while jogging). With this information, you are ready to start the story.

The fact that Kelly died of a heart attack suffered while jogging may well be the lead, but the reporter does not know this until the rest of the information essential to every obituary has been gathered. You also must know the following:

- Time and place of funeral services.
- Time and place of burial.
- Visitation time (if any).
- Survivors.
- Date and place of birth.
- Achievements.
- Occupation.
- Memberships.

Any of these items can yield the nugget that will appear in the lead. However, if none of these categories yields notable information, the obituary will probably start like this:

> **Michael Kelly, 60, of 1234 West St., died Tuesday night at Regional Hospital.**

Another standard approach could be used later in the news cycle:

> **Funeral services for Michael Kelly, 60, of 1234 West St., will be at 2 p.m. Thursday at St. Catherine's Roman Catholic Church.**

However, good reporters often find distinguishing characteristics of a person's life. It may be volunteer service, an unusual or important job, service in public office or even just having a name of historical significance. Whatever distinguishes a person can be the lead of the obituary.

Building the Story

You will find most of the obituary information on a standard form from the mortuary. When the reporter relies only on the form, this is usually what results:

> **Michael Kelly, 60, of 1234 West St. died Tuesday night at Regional Hospital.**
>
> **Kelly collapsed while jogging and died apparently of a heart attack.**
>
> **Services will be at 2 p.m. Thursday at St. Catherine's Roman Catholic Church. The Rev. Sherman Mitchell will officiate. Burial will be at Glendale Memorial Gardens in Springfield.**
>
> **Friends may visit at the Fenton Funeral Chapel from 7 to 9 p.m. Wednesday.**
>
> **Born Dec. 20, 1956, in Boston to Nathan and Sarah Kelly, Kelly was a member of St. Catherine's Roman Catholic Church and a U.S. Navy veteran. He had been an independent insurance agent for the last 25 years.**
>
> **He married Pauline Virginia Hatfield in Boston on May 5, 1974.**
>
> **Survivors include his wife; a son, Kevin, of Charlotte, North Carolina; and a daughter, Mary, who is a student at the University of North Carolina at Chapel Hill.**
>
> **Also surviving are a brother, John, of Milwaukee, Wisconsin, and a sister, Margaret Carter, of Asheville, North Carolina.**

Writing Life Stories

The Kelly obituary is a dry biography, not a story of his life. There is no hint of Kelly's impact on friends, family or community. Good reporting produces stories of life, such as this one:

> **Frank Martin loved to garden and loved to share.**
>
> **"When the ground began to thaw, he'd try to figure out how to grow things," friend and co-worker Walter Begley recalled.**
>
> **Another friend, Caroline Newby, said he would come to her home to help take care of her small vineyard. He made wine from the grapes to share with his family during the holidays. When she had problems with her crop, Mr. Martin would drive over and open the trunk of his old Dodge to reveal a nursery of soil and gardening tools.**
>
> **On the back of that car was a bumper sticker that read "Practice Random Acts of Kindness and Senseless Acts of Beauty." Newby said Mr. Martin lived by that phrase. . .**

The more traditional biographical information, along with information about visitation and funeral services, appears later in the story.

When writing a life story, you ask people what was important to the deceased and what the evidence for that is. If the subject volunteered, find out where and why, and talk to the people served. Your goal is to capture the theme of the person's life.

Sources of Information

Writing an obituary or a life story is like writing a feature story. You seek anecdotes that reveal the person. Your sources include the mortuary form, your publication's own library, and family and friends of the deceased (and possibly their paid funeral notices).

The mortuary form

For many reporters, the standard form from the mortuary is the primary source of information. The mortuary can be of further help if you need more information. It can usually provide anything from a picture of the deceased to clarification on any conflicting information you may have.

Writing obituaries from the mortuary's information alone is a clerk's work. As a reporter, you should go beyond the form. You should also confirm every fact on the sheet. Mortuary forms are often notoriously inaccurate.

The newsroom library

In the newsroom archive, you may find an interview with the deceased, an interesting feature story or clips indicating activities not included on the mortuary form. In an interview or a feature story, the person may have made a statement about a philosophy of life that would be appropriate to include in the obituary. The subject also may have indicated his or her goals in life, against which later accomplishments can be measured. You can find the names of friends and co-workers in the clips as well. These people are often the source of rich anecdotes and comments about the deceased.

Your newsroom files are not the only source for information on people who have state or national reputations. You or your librarian should also search electronic databases for stories that have appeared elsewhere.

Sources for Obits

- Mortuary forms.
- Paid funeral notices.
- The newsroom's library.
- Interviews with family and friends of the deceased.

Interviews with family and friends

Journalists treat public figures in more detail than private citizens not only because they are newsworthy but also because reporters know more about them. Even though private citizens are usually less newsworthy, many good stories about them are never written because the reporter did not—or was afraid to—do the reporting. The fear is usually unfounded.

Choosing Your Words

- Avoid euphemisms; such terms are out of place in a news story. People don't "pass away." They die. If a "lingering illness" was cancer, say so.
- Watch your language as you report the cause and circumstances of the death.
- Be careful with religious terms.

Cause of Death

If the person who died was not a public figure and the family does not wish to divulge the cause of death, some news organizations will comply. That is questionable news judgment. The reader wants to know what caused the death. A reporter should call the mortuary, the family, the attending physician and the appropriate medical officer. Only if none of these sources will talk should you leave out the cause of death.

A death certificate must be filed for each death, but obtaining it often takes days, and some states do not make the cause of death part of the public record. Even if the state lists the cause of death and the reporter has timely access to the death certificate, the information is often vague.

If the deceased was a public figure or a young person, most newspapers insist on the cause of death. If the death is the result of suicide or foul play, reporters can obtain the information from the police or the medical examiner. Some

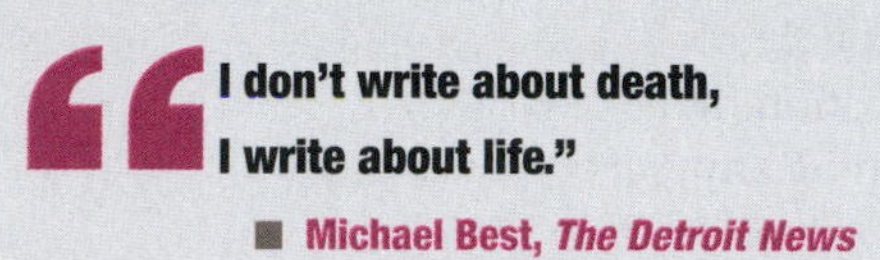
"I don't write about death, I write about life."
Michael Best, The Detroit News

newspapers include suicide as the cause of death in the obituary, others print it in a separate news story, and still others ignore it altogether. This is one way to report a suicide:

> **Services for Gary O'Neal, 34, a local carpenters' union officer, will be at 9 a.m. Thursday in the First Baptist Church. Coroner Mike Pardee ruled that Mr. O'Neal died Tuesday of a self-inflicted gunshot wound.**

CHAPTER RESOURCES

SUGGESTED READINGS

Bayles, Fred. *Field Guide to Covering Local News: How to Report on Cops, Courts, Schools, Emergencies and Government.* Thousand Oaks, Calif.: CQ Press, 2012. A guide to covering the most common types of stories.

Loci, Toni. *Covering America's Courts: A Clash of Rights.* New York: Peter Lang, 2013. Tips on how to cover the courts effectively.

Pulitzer, Lisa Beth. *Crime on Deadline: Police Reporters Tell Their Most Unforgettable Stories.* New York: Boulevard, 1996. Real stories from nine of the nation's top crime reporters are featured in this book.

Siegel, Marvin, ed. *The Last Word:* The New York Times *Book of Obituaries and Farewells: A Celebration of Unusual Lives.* New York: Quill, 1998. Examples abound of well-written and compelling obituaries from *The New York Times*.

Singer, Eleanor, and Phyllis M. Endreny. *Reporting on Risk: How the Mass Media Portray Accidents, Diseases, Disasters and Other Hazards.* New York: Russell Sage Foundation, 1993. The authors take a critical look at media reporting of accidents and disasters.

SUGGESTED WEBSITES

LaunchPad Solo
launchpadworks.com
When you visit LaunchPad Solo for Journalism, you will find research links, exercises and LearningCurve adaptive quizzing to help you improve your grammar and AP style usage. In addition, the site's video collection hosts the videos highlighted in this and other chapters as well as additional clips of leading professionals discussing important media trends.

www.fbi.gov
The FBI website provides useful information about crime.

www.fema.gov
The Federal Emergency Management Agency, part of the U.S. Department of Homeland Security, provides assistance during major emergencies. This site provides useful background information and contacts.

www.ntsb.gov
The National Transportation Safety Board website is an excellent source of accident information.

www.ojr.org
The Online Journalism Review has useful tips, articles and information about tools and techniques for reporting and storytelling online.

www.supremecourtus.gov
The U.S. Supreme Court is the nation's highest court. The Supreme Court's website outlines its operation.

EXERCISES

1. Working in teams, analyze the coverage of a major national crime, accident or fire story. Each team member should scrutinize the coverage of the story by a different news organization—print, online or broadcast. Then meet with the other members of your team to compare notes, and discuss which stories are most satisfactory and why.
2. **Your journalism blog.** Monitor a day of local news. Take note of how many of the stories are the types covered in this chapter. Do they provide an accurate picture of your town? Do these stories meet the standards you've just learned? If not, how could they be improved? Write a blog entry of at least 500 words to report your conclusions.
3. Find an accident story in a local newspaper. List all the sources the reporter used in obtaining information for the story. List additional sources you would have checked.
4. Talk with a firefighter in your local fire department about the department's media policy at fire scenes. Using what you learn, write instructions for your fellow reporters on what to expect at fires in your city or town.
5. Cover a session of your local municipal or circuit court. Write a story based on the most interesting case of the day.
6. Research the coverage of constitutional rights as they pertain to terrorism suspects. Evaluate whether the media have done an adequate job of covering this issue. If you find fault with the coverage, describe what you would do differently.
7. Research and write the life story of a resident of your city.

CHAPTER 16 BUSINESS AND CONSUMER NEWS

Photo credit: Bloomberg/Getty Images

Business news is now big news. Stories about job creation, trade deals or the latest tech innovation lead local and national newscasts. On satellite or cable television in any country around the world, 24-hour channels like CNBC or Bloomberg News follow the world stock markets and broadcast that information in English, Chinese, Arabic, Spanish, Portuguese and German. Apps give business news on your smartphone or tablet. The speed of these tech innovations complicates an already hard-to-understand topic.

The demand for business journalists is so high that many recent grads find themselves at the center of the world's most important stories. Weeks after donning her cap and gown, Jessica Smith landed a job with the Fox Business Network as a production assistant for *Countdown to the Closing Bell*. Her job — lining up interviews with investors, CEOs and billionaires to talk with the on-air anchors about what made the market crash or soar that day — required Smith to use her training and a bit of poise and moxie.

This training was put to good use in 2018 when Smith, now a Washington correspondent for Nexstar Television, asked then-Environmental Protection Agency Secretary Scott Pruitt about using his influence as a Cabinet secretary to win a fast-food franchise for his wife, Marlyn.

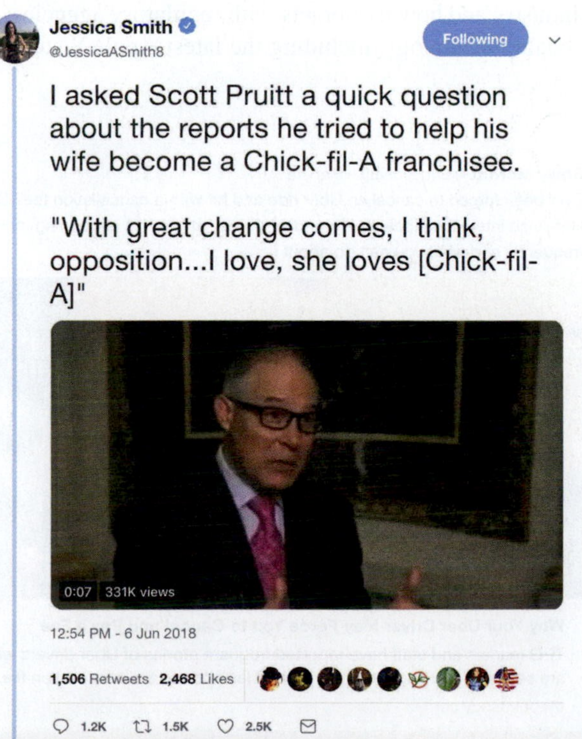

In this chapter, you will learn:

1. Why business journalism is growing in importance.
2. How to report business stories.
3. Where to find business stories.
4. How to understand business numbers.
5. How to find and report consumer news.

Smith tweeted out the interview, prompting other journalists to retweet her and note that Pruitt tried to dodge Smith's question. Under fire for many questionable business dealings and purchases while EPA chief, Pruitt later resigned his Cabinet post.

Despite declines in some sectors of journalism, business news has seen growth, and knowledgeable young journalists have attractive job prospects. It's a natural for journalists who want to live and work in world financial capitals. Shelly Hagan joined Bloomberg News shortly after her 2018 graduation. As part of her first year, Hagan rotated through various beats, from the stock market to consumer news, at the media outlet's world headquarters in New York. Linly Lin works in Bloomberg's London office, monitoring social media written in her native Chinese as well as in English. Her role is to spot trending topics or emerging issues that might result in stories that affect global business or stock markets.

Business job opportunities happen on Main Street as well as Wall Street. When Jacob Steimer graduated in 2016, he walked into a job in his home state of Tennessee covering the music industry for the *Nashville Business Journal* and later transferred closer to home to cover retail at the *Memphis Business Journal*. After college, Austin Alonzo moved back to his hometown of Kansas City and worked there remotely covering the poultry industry for WattAgNet.

Business reporters also cover Washington and its effect on business. Danny al Faruque works for Informa, a subscription web portal that covers the $156 billion medical device industry and how it interacts with regulatory agencies. That industry includes digital health technology, including the latest Apple Watches that monitor hearth rhythms.

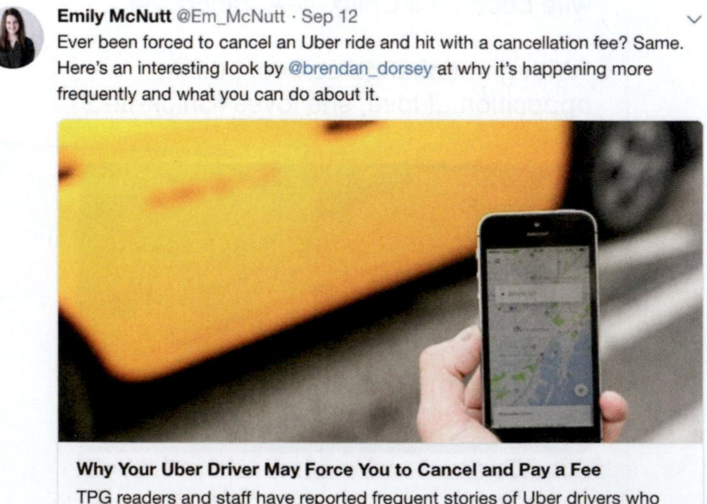

Emily McNutt @Em_McNutt · Sep 12
Ever been forced to cancel an Uber ride and hit with a cancellation fee? Same. Here's an interesting look by @brendan_dorsey at why it's happening more frequently and what you can do about it.
Why Your Uber Driver May Force You to Cancel and Pay a Fee
TPG readers and staff have reported frequent stories of Uber drivers who are seemingly forcing them to cancel rides and eat the cancellation fee.
thepointsguy.com

PAU BARRENA/Getty Images

Business coverage also includes at-work lifestyle. Thepointsguy.com, a digital-only publication, caters to business travelers who want to maximize frequent flyer and credit card miles. Emily McNutt covers the travel industry for the web publication, which has grown since its debut in 2010 to cover the entire travel industry. Using the website as well as Twitter, she offers consumer advice such as how business travelers can avoid cancellation fees from the ride-sharing service Uber. In one week, she'll write, tweet and even shoot video about airline fare sales, hotel perks, an aborted takeoff at JFK airport, and business credit card rates.

How do you get started covering business news? First, you need to understand business terminology and basic math. You also need to learn how to read financial statements, which is surprisingly easy. Beyond that, you need the skills of any journalist: perseverance, curiosity and an ability to ask questions and get answers.

The Importance of Business Journalism

In November 2016, Americans elected Donald Trump, a businessman, as president. That election raised questions about the connections between business and politics as Trump revised old trade deals, changed regulations and convinced Congress to lower tax rates for businesses. The business upturn during 2018 sparked even more business coverage.

Nearly all stories can have a business angle. A glance at an edition of *The Wall Street Journal* shows the breadth of news with economic components—the U.S. brandy industry's attempts at increasing consumption, the retail giant Amazon's search for a location for a second headquarters, the economic damage suffered by businesses when hackers steal and leak customer data.

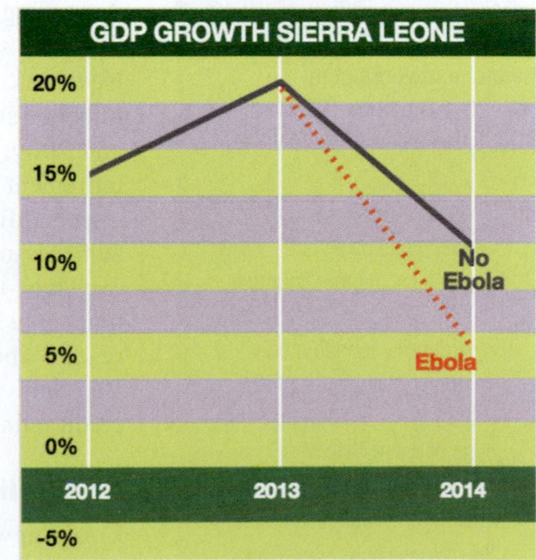

CDC/Centers for Disease Control, https://www.cdc.gov/vhf/ebola/pdf/impact-ebola-economy.pdf

Health care is an important business topic. Americans are concerned about the rising costs of prescription drugs and doctor visits, and reporters covering health reform legislation need to understand the business side of medical care so they can explain these changes to audiences. Health care is an important cost for business. Beyond the cost of medical insurance, the Centers for Disease Control and Prevention estimates that flu outbreaks cost $10.4 billion annually between medical costs and lost work.

Even more financially concerning was the Ebola epidemic of 2014 to 2016. The CDC reported that the West African country of Sierra Leone lost 50 percent of its workforce to the epidemic, which is projected to cripple the country's gross domestic product for years to come.

Yet many news directors and editors still struggle with the focus of business news. Who is the audience? Is it consumers, investors, local business executives or job hunters? When oil prices rise, should reporters in Houston emphasize the higher prices that motorists are paying at the pump? Or should they focus on how those higher prices

translate into jobs or new drilling in the Texas oil industry? Or focus on the politics of changing restrictions to allow the U.S. to export more oil? This array of ways to focus business stories provides an opportunity in the field of business journalism.

Business journalism adapted to the digital world rapidly because the internet delivers news faster, which is important to market traders. Financial news, including up-to-the-second stock prices, is available on mobile devices. The instant nature of social media demands that today's business journalists be skilled in using Facebook, Instagram, LinkedIn, Snapchat and Twitter.

Business executives use Twitter to communicate directly to customers, and the number of business-related Facebook, Instagram and Snapchat sites continues to grow. In 2017, a Nevada teenager tweeted at fast-food giant Wendy's, seeking a free order of chicken nuggets. The restaurant chain responded that Carter Wilkerson needed 18 million retweets to win a year's worth. He asked for help from the Twitter community and set a record for the most retweets, about 3.6 million. Although Wilkerson fell short of the goal, he garnered enough press coverage that Wendy's sent him a year's worth of nuggets. In 2017 and 2018, United Airlines had several customer service mishaps that were either tweeted about or videoed, including disagreements over seating, disputes over the handling of pets and even a passenger being dragged from an oversold flight. Because such videos and tweets become a focus of news coverage and provide a glimpse inside the customer service operations of major companies, business journalists monitor social media to discover important trends and to disseminate news.

The increasing number of business news outlets in print, online and on radio and television is just one reason that business-trained journalists are in high demand. According to the salary website Glassdoor, business reporters are paid a premium for their skills, whether they report from Middle America, Silicon Valley or New York. Business journalism training is also important for those who seek jobs in corporate communications. Despite a decline since the Great Recession of 2008 and 2009, about half of all Americans own stock, mostly through their 401(k) retirement plans.

In addition, companies employ journalists to write about investor and consumer issues. In 2018, Chris Dieterich left *The Wall Street Journal* to blog about exchange-traded funds for New York–based BlackRock Investments. His blogs are much like his news coverage was at *The Journal* and inform BlackRock newsletter readers about this popular investing topic. Longtime freelance consumer reporter Bob Sullivan wrote a story about scams that target senior citizens for the website of credit rating agency Experian as part of its education efforts.

launchpadworks.com
WATCH: **"The Money Behind the Media"**

- The U.S. media industry is dominated by private companies. In other countries, the media system is dominated by a publicly funded media company, such as the BBC in Britain. What are the pros and cons of each system?
- Some people say commercials make them "feel good about the free and open commerce . . . in America." Why?

Specialized Business News

Local newspapers are shedding business staff members as part of a major employment decline, but those reporters are finding job opportunities at the weekly business journals that have grown and expanded in all major U.S. cities—from Fresno, California to Louisville, Kentucky to Hartford, Connecticut. American City Business Journals, based in Charlotte, North Carolina, publishes profitably in some 40 U.S. cities, with a total readership for print and digital of 16 million.

Pick an industry, and it is covered by a magazine, an internet news site, a newsletter or a newspaper that specializes in it. Far from sleepy operations, these publications often are in the midst of breaking news. *CFO* magazine—whose audience of 440,000 subscribers is comprised of financial professionals in a wide range of industries—doesn't shy away from covering the scandals that have rocked the finance industry. Watt Global Media, based in Rockford, Illinois, has covered agribusiness for nearly a century. Its *Poultry USA* publication has covered the bird flu epidemic and the resulting rise in egg prices. Its *Poultry International* publication, also available digitally, is sent to 45,000 professionals in 160 countries and includes a Chinese-language edition.

Global Reach

Business journalism is a growing global industry. Business newspapers are now prevalent in China's major cities. *Shanghai Securities News*, founded in 1991, focuses on covering the Shanghai and Hong Kong stock exchanges as well as Asian economic news. American business media outlets have bureaus in major Asian cities and employ multilingual reporters.

Business journalists who work for mainstream organizations must acknowledge the often-conflicting outcomes of economic events. President Trump started a trade war with China in an effort to boost the U.S. steel industry, but it ended up hurting Midwestern soybean farmers when China slapped them with retaliatory tariffs.

And business journalists must be able to see the big picture. Although many Americans have lost jobs that went to workers in India and Mexico, more Americans now work for global employers. It surprises many that the U.S. has often led the world in foreign direct investment; funds from other countries are building businesses in every state. Workers in South Carolina make small refrigerators for Chinese-owned Haier Group. Autoworkers in southern Indiana learn Japanese manufacturing techniques while manufacturing SUVs and minivans for Toyota. When the United Kingdom voted in 2016 to end its relationship with the European Union, it rocked world markets and sent the pound sterling plummeting. The decision continues to reverberate in global business decisions and has spawned special coverage by British financial media of how Brexit will affect their homeland.

A Wide Range of Topics

The range of possible business stories is as broad as business itself. Some business stories are about a company's promotions and retirements, and some concentrate on company profits, which are of interest to investors and potential investors in that company. Other business stories cover personal finance issues that are of interest to lay readers rather than investment community insiders. Business journalists use stories, lists, photos and graphics to communicate. Larry Buchanan, a graphics editor for *The New York Times*, used his coding skills to create an interactive web feature for readers to determine how their taxes would change under the 2018 tax rules change.

Personal finance news is so popular that there are scores of websites devoted to this topic, such as Cheddar, focused on millennials and money, as well as CNN's MONEY and the venerable Kiplinger, which started as a newsletter and now is a robust website. A business story might also be about new products, like the array of tablets or smartwatches released before every holiday season. These stories interest shareholders of the company as well as potential consumers. How does the latest smartphone stack up against its competitors? What does that mean for investors? Interest in new generations of Apple's iPhone and Apple Watch pushed the company's stock to record highs and made the Cupertino, California–based tech firm one of the world's most valuable companies.

Many stories are both global and local. A story about a decision by the Federal Reserve Board's Open Market Committee to expand or tighten the money supply may seem far removed from your audience. But this decision can affect the interest rate your readers pay for a car or mortgage loan. A sizable trade deficit for the U.S. may weaken the value of the dollar and increase the price of a Korean-made TV, a Volkswagen car or a bottle of Cutty Sark scotch whisky. It takes skill, but a good business journalist can make these seemingly esoteric stories clear and relevant to the audience.

Many important corporate and economic decisions that affect us all are made in Washington, New York, Chicago and a few other major metropolitan centers. But those cities do not have a monopoly on the creation and coverage of business news. Even in towns of a few thousand residents, businesses will open or close, and manufacturing plants will increase or decrease production, hire or fire employees. Local residents will spend money for houses, cars, vacations or tablets or sock it away in local banks or savings and loan associations. There is a business story in every such development.

Increasingly, economics plays a strong role in disaster coverage, second only to coverage of the loss of life. Hurricane Florence, which flooded the Carolinas for a week in September 2018, will cost between $17 billion and $22 billion, according Moody's Analytics Chief Economist Mark Zandi. The wildfires in California in 2018 are etimated to have caused up to $18 billion in damage.

Hurricane Katrina caused at least $125 billion in economic damage when it swamped coastal areas in Alabama, Florida, Louisiana and Mississippi in August 2005. Only half of the damage was covered by insurance. Hurricane Sandy, which devastated coastal areas in New Jersey, New York and Connecticut in October 2012, cost that region more than $50 billion.

The most expensive natural disaster in world history was the March 2011 Tohoku earthquake and tsunami, which resulted in more than $235 billion in losses to the Japanese economy, according to the World Bank. The disaster, including the related meltdown of three nuclear reactors at the Fukushima Daiichi power plant, rocked manufacturing in Japan, caused parts shortages in Toyota plants worldwide and affected investment in the Japanese economy.

The economic risk of natural disaster is of paramount interest to investment professionals, who abide by the investing wisdom "Buy on rumor and sell on news." Two days before Katrina hit, financial news outlets like Bloomberg News and Dow Jones Newswires were already reporting the potential impact on oil drilling and gasoline refineries in the Gulf of Mexico.

Taxes are also a mainstay in business coverage, including stories aimed at consumers as they file taxes each spring. But taxes are a big part of every business. A global team of reporters won the Pulitzer Prize for a data-driven series on the Panama Papers, which were leaked by an anonymous source in 2015. The reporting exposed a global effort by individuals and businesses to avoid taxes and public scrutiny by using anonymous companies and bank accounts in offshore "tax havens" that don't reveal account holder names or amounts.

Reporting Business Stories

- Use language readers will understand, but don't oversimplify.
- Be fair. You will win the trust and confidence of businesspeople — or at least their grudging respect.
- Appearances count. It may help you to dress as businesspeople do.
- The more you can demonstrate that you understand a business, the more likely you are to generate trust and draw out the information you seek.
- There are many sides to business stories — and you need to understand the viewpoints of shareholders, customers, competitors, suppliers and workers.
- Always remember that a company, government agency or pressure group may be using you to plant stories that serve a special interest.

How to Report Business Stories

Business stories use the same structures as other types of stories: inverted pyramid, chronology, news narrative and focus. The preparation is the same as for any other beat, but business writers also have some unique challenges.

Finding the "So What" and Avoiding Jargon

What separates a business story from a soccer story — or a soccer story from a story about atomic particles — is the knowledge and language required to ask the right questions, to recognize the newsworthy answers, and to write the story in a way that readers without specialized knowledge will understand. A reporter who understands the subject can explain what the jargon means.

Business reporters must use understandable language. Bloomberg News reporters use *The Bloomberg Way*, a handbook written by former Editor-in-Chief Matthew Winkler. The handbook offers this example of how to avoid the jargon often used in the business world:

Before: ModusLink has retained Goldman Sachs to review strategic alternatives, including the disposal of certain assets.

After: ModusLink hired Goldman Sachs to review options, including the sale of some assets.

Rather than imposing on busy readers, business reporters should develop the expertise to translate or explain technical terms. You may even have to do some math. For example, if banks change lending rates, the personal finance reporter might be the person to write the story explaining that an increase of 1 percentage point could result in higher interest rates for car or home loans.

If West Coast longshoremen go on strike, a reporter covering local corporations might explore the strike's impact on the delivery of supplies to a local manufacturer, while a retail reporter might talk to store owners about whether they'll have this year's most popular toy on their shelves in time for Christmas.

TIPS

Accuracy Checklist for Business Reporting

- Are titles and names correct, including initials?
- Did you check percent increases and decreases?
- Did you read back quotes to the source?
- Do you have the correct stock ticker and stock price?
- Did you compare all financial facts to the same period last year? For example, sales from the third quarter with the third quarter of last year?
- Did you avoid using lazy adjectives like *cheap* or *big*? Instead, be specific with items like "a $2 cigar" or "a 22-foot video wall."

Putting Sources at Ease

Sourcing presents a challenge for business reporters: How do you get information from someone who does not legally have to tell you anything? It often takes more creative reporting skills to coax a story from a business source than from a government official. Almost all government information is public. Many business records are not.

The mistrust that many businesspeople have of the press can make it difficult to cover stories adequately, even when it would be in the business's interest to have the story told. If executives are willing to talk, they may become angry if the reporter quotes an opposing point of view or points out a flaw in the company's public image. And businesses know they can often sell their "spin" on a story by reaching the public directly through their websites and social media outlets.

The best antidote for an uncooperative attitude is to report fairly and accurately what a business is doing and saying. By always being fair, you can win the trust and confidence of businesspeople — or at least their grudging respect.

Because business executives tend to be cautious when talking with reporters, it may help you to dress more like a business manager than a concert reviewer. Appearances count. Businesspeople, like reporters, feel more comfortable with their own kind. The more you demonstrate that you understand their business, the more likely you are to generate trust.

Public relations people can provide background information and direct you to executives who can offer other comments and information, but you should try to get to know as many company executives as you can. Sometimes you can do this best through a background interview, one not generated by a crisis but intended to provide information about what the company is doing. Perhaps you can arrange to have lunch to see what the managers are thinking about and to give them a chance to see that you are probably not the demon that they may have thought you were.

TIPS

Libel and Legal Considerations in Business Reporting

- Use the precise name of the company because different companies often have similar names. Also include the location.

(continued)

Watching Out for Biases and Conflicts of Interest

Always remember that a company, government agency or pressure group may be trying to use you to plant stories that serve a special interest. Companies want stories that make them look promising to investors, drive up the price of their stock or attract merger partners. If you are suspicious, talk to competitors and analysts, and ask detailed questions. You don't have to write a story just because a company or some other group is pushing it.

Business journalists face conflict-of-interest challenges because they often write stories, some of which are unfavorable, about companies that buy advertising dollars from their media companies. Business editors across the country have become increasingly concerned as advertisers threaten to pull advertising over unfavorable coverage. For instance, a story in the *Orlando Sentinel* on the shoddy practices of homebuilders cost the newspaper $700,000 in canceled advertisements.

Because business news can affect market prices, business journalists must adhere to a strong code of ethics to avoid the appearance that their stories are being influenced. In addition, business journalists can be fined or even jailed if they violate U.S. securities laws and face jail time if they trade stocks based on inside information uncovered during the reporting process. In a famous case, R. Foster Winans, a former reporter for *The Wall Street Journal*, was convicted in 1985 of illegal insider trading and mail fraud for tipping off a stockbroker to information he later published in his "Heard on the Street" columns. He served nine months in federal prison.

- Libel damages are based on economic loss, which is often easy to prove in business.
- Double-check the math: Even the original source can be wrong in math, so do calculations yourself.
- Use the correct names and titles of business executives. Check corporate websites for exact names and titles. Some executives have more than one title.

ON THE JOB Learning to Be Nimble and Be First with a Story

Courtesy of Justin Stark, Nucleus Pictures.com

It was a college internship at *The Kansas City Star* and another at Bloomberg News that convinced **Allison Prang** that she loved the business world. Her first postgraduation job was as a business reporter for the *Charleston* (South Carolina) *Post and Courier*, covering the local tech and tourism industries. Months later, she moved to New York to cover community banks for *American Banker*, the industry publication for financial services. A little more than a year after that, she joined the breaking-news desk of *The Wall Street Journal*.

Says Prang: "Business reporting for a metro paper is different in that you are writing for average citizens and local business leaders. At *American Banker*, you're writing for financial professionals, and you assume your readers know the topics you're covering. *The Journal* is a mix of that. Many *WSJ* readers are business-focused and well educated, so you're obviously writing for that audience. But *The WSJ* is the largest circulation paper in the U.S. and has tremendous reach, so you want to write in a way that the average person can understand. For example, if we mention a company, it's helpful to say what the company does."

The WSJ aggressively uses push notification via RSS and social media to drive readers to breaking news, which has a more general audience than *The WSJ* print publication or subscriber website. Says Prang: "You're just trying to get the news out as fast as possible." On a recent week, she wrote a longer data-driven story about how midterm elections are good for the stock market, regardless of which party is in power. She has also covered employment reports and jumped in to cover breaking news on embattled Tesla founder Elon Musk.

Business journalism's complexity can be intimidating, but Prang says "that's all the more reason we need reporters who want to understand it."

"One of the neatest parts of a journalist's job is how much we get to learn," she says. "I'm always learning in this job."

Where to Find Business Stories

The starting point in writing a business story is similar to the first step in reporting any story: understanding the subject you're writing about. For the business reporter, that almost always means some basic research into the subject. For openers, check your organization's archives to learn what's been written locally about your topic or company.

A broad spectrum of internet-accessible databases provides lists and summaries of stories published on a wide range of subjects. The truly adept can plumb raw data, including stock market transactions, to track the impact of announcements, mergers and personnel changes on stock prices. But everyone can use simple internet searches to access annual reports, stock analyses, press releases and other announcements. And now, many of these resources are available on mobile phone apps. Journalists can use Yahoo Finance's app to find stock quotes and business statistics in the field or grab national or international economic statistics from the upgraded app from the Federal Reserve Economic Data, or FRED—the branch of the U.S. Federal Reserve Bank based in St. Louis.

Any internet search of news sites will help you find stories you need for research. Bloomberg Business News, Dow Jones Factiva and Reuters provide detailed and extensive databases of background information on companies and securities, historical prices and real-time news on business and economic issues. In addition, companies like Business Wire and Cision's PR Newswire handle thousands of news releases daily from companies and nonprofit organizations, pumping out public relations news and videos through the internet and social media. Sometimes that information causes investors to sell or buy stocks or bonds, even before journalists have the time to check it for accuracy or "spin."

Journalists now rely on an array of aggregation websites focused on information for investors. Two examples are MarketWatch and Yahoo Finance, which compile news on companies and provide links to government-required Securities and Exchange Commission filings and charts of historical stock prices.

Where to Find Business Stories

- Conduct some basic research into the subject. Check internet and paper archives to learn what's been written about the topic or company.
- Turn to your computer. From a broad spectrum of databases, you can obtain lists and summaries of stories published on a wide range of subjects. LinkedIn provides autobiographical employee profiles. You can even search Facebook, where users often disclose their workplace.
- Read print sources to find stories about your business or industry. Many trade journals are available online.

Records and Reports

Here are some sources of information that you will find invaluable when writing business stories. Many of these can be accessed through various online databases, so you can log on and find the information you need right away.

Corporate data

Basic information on corporations can be found online, either on the company's own website or through government filings. Independent sources include Dun & Bradstreet Credibility Corp., which provides online information on large and small businesses. D&B also owns Hoovers.com, another business database. S&P Global investigates the creditworthiness of companies and issues analysts' reports. To find suppliers and product news, check out ThomasNet.com's database of American manufacturers.

Investment data

To get specific information about the financial performance of a company or an industry, check reports prepared by S&P Global, as well as ratings competitors Fitch Ratings and Moody's Investors Service. Morningstar, Thomson First Call and Value Line discuss company prospects, forecast earnings and predict major trends. Also helpful are annual corporate scoreboards prepared by Bloomberg, *Forbes* and *Fortune*, such as information on the wealth of individuals (Forbes World Billionaires).

Financial ratios

To assess a company's financial picture and management, compare your subject's financial data with averages for other firms in the same industry. Industry ratios and averages can be found in a number of trade journals, on Yahoo Finance and in reports prepared by Dun & Bradstreet, Moody's and S&P Global.

Company filings

The U.S. Securities and Exchange Commission mandates that companies that sell shares to the public must file detailed financial performance records. You should start with the annual report, which gives an overview of the company's operations and finances. The SEC's 10-K form, a more detailed version of the annual report required by the SEC, will also give you the number of employees, a list of major real estate and equipment holdings, and information on any significant legal proceedings. Many other important documents, such as labor contracts, are listed by reference and can be acquired through the company, a Freedom of Information Act request or a private service such as Disclosure Inc. Annual reports often show up on the nightstands of business reporters.

Most filings are available free of charge through the SEC's online EDGAR system, but journalists often use the pay service DisclosureNet or the newer Intelligize. Other free outlets, such as MarketWatch and Yahoo Finance, will let you set up alerts notifying you of news and filings on companies of interest.

Another SEC filing, the *proxy statement*, which goes to shareholders before the annual meeting or other important meetings, provides executive salaries, an outline of issues to be voted on, and information on the company's board of directors. The proxy also sometimes contains leads about the company's business dealings. Interesting nuggets are found under mundane headings such as "Other Matters" or "Legal Proceedings." For example, now-bankrupt Enron Corp. disclosed some hints about its offshore partnerships in the footnotes of its SEC filings. Those footnotes generated some stories, but company officials did not disclose the true extent of the company's financial problems. In any filing, always read anything pertaining to lawsuits, which can lead you to public documents regarding a particular suit.

All publicly traded companies now release their annual report, 10-K form and proxy statement on their websites, and materials can be downloaded.

Trade press

Beyond the newspapers and magazines you already know and read, there is another segment of journalism known as the *trade press*. In these journals and house organs, you can find grocers talking with grocers, undertakers talking with undertakers and bankers talking with bankers. You will learn what the important issues in a field are, how an industry markets its products and services, and what legislation it fears and favors.

A number of trade publications are independent and objective. Among them are *Advertising Age*, *American Banker*, *Aviation Week*, *Editor & Publisher*, *Institutional Investor*, *Variety* and *The Wrap*. Although many are very pro-industry, they are valuable for learning about current issues, marketing and lobbying strategies. To find trade publications, consult the *Standard Periodical Directory* or *Ulrich's International Periodicals Directory*. Most trade publications offer online versions, like www.ogj.com, the online version of the comprehensive trade publication *Oil & Gas Journal*.

Newsletters

Newsletters, which have morphed into subscription and free topic websites, have become an important source of inside information in recent years. Some are purely ideological, but others can be valuable. Among the best are Education Daily, The Energy Daily and Platts Nucleonics Week. Peter Zollman, a former wire service reporter, runs a subscription-only print and online newsletter, *Classified Intelligence Report*, which covers the $10 billion online classified and recruitment industry, which includes such companies as Craigslist and Indeed.com. Other newsletters can be found by accessing the *Oxbridge Directory of Newsletters*.

Court records

Most companies disclose only information required by the SEC. But when a corporation sues or is sued, an extensive amount of material becomes available. Likewise, a criminal action taken against principals in a firm can lead to a good story. It is important to check court testimony and records at all levels, including those of bankruptcy and divorce courts, all of which can be found on Pacer.gov or USCourts.gov. States also offer court records online through such sites as Iowa's www.iowacourts.state.ia.us. Journalists found information about the pay package and executive perks of former General Electric CEO Jack Welch in his divorce filing.

Local regulators

Frequently, businesses want to enlarge facilities or expand into new markets. To do so, they may seek funds from an industrial bond authority, which helps companies obtain large sums of money at below-market rates. When an institution such as a hospital wants to expand its services, often it must make a case for the expansion before a regional or local agency. In either case, documents filed to support the request may be revealing and may put into the public record information that previously was unobtainable. Local reporters who know how to find business plan filings in the county or city planning commission office gain insights into their area's economic development. These records are public but are often underutilized by reporters.

Other sources

The preceding lists are certainly not exhaustive. Other relevant materials may be found at local tax and record-keeping offices, as well as in filings with the Bureau of Labor Statistics, the Federal Communications Commission, the Federal Trade Commission, the Food and Drug Administration, and the Interstate Commerce Commission. In addition, various state agencies, such as the secretary of state's office, compile information on businesses registered in the state.

Don't overlook the Federal Reserve — the central bank of the U.S. — which employs scores of economic analysts at each of its 12 regional banks. Eight times a year, the Fed publishes a comprehensive book of regional statistics and analysis, nicknamed the "Beige Book," which is available online at www.federalreserve.gov. FRED, based at the St. Louis Federal Reserve Bank, continues to add business indices and economic data to its massive collection. The Consumer Confidence Index, a survey of 5,000 sample households by the Conference Board, gauges consumer sentiment on the U.S. economy. This important monthly index is followed by market watchers as well as the Federal Reserve in setting interest rates.

The Department of Commerce's Bureau of Economic Analysis (www.bea.gov) allows reporters to generate economic data by county, region or state. The BEA uses data from agencies that don't issue public reports, such as the Internal Revenue Service. The Census Bureau (www.census.gov) provides timely data on many

Publicly Held Company SEC Filings: Essential to Business Reporters

The following is a list of places to look for the SEC filings of publicly held companies:

- **Schedule 13D.** A filing that includes a list of the owners of more than 5 percent of the voting stock of a company. It must report increases and decreases of holdings and be filed within 10 business days.
- **Form 13-F.** The quarterly report of ownership by institutional investors. It includes holders of less than 5 percent of the company.
- **Form 8-K.** A report of a significant incident.
- **Form 10-Q.** A quarterly financial statement.
- **Form 10-K.** The annual financial statement. It includes number of employees, major real estate and equipment holdings, and significant legal proceedings. Many other important documents, such as labor contracts, are listed by reference and can be acquired through the company, a Freedom of Information Act request or a private service.
- **Proxy statement.** A statement that contains executive salaries, director information and shareholder voting issues.
- **Annual report to shareholders.** A report that may lack much of the data found in the 10-K form.
- **Securities registration statement/prospectus.** A statement submitted when new stock is to be issued. It usually contains the same information as the 10-K form and proxy statement but is more up to date.

economic functions, including business inventories and monthly retail sales. Check out the bureau's Business and Industry portal. The bureau also has a smartphone app that allows reporters to access this information in the field. Graphic artists can use the Census Bureau's data visualization tools to create information graphics.

Human Sources

Who are the people you should talk to on the business beat? Here are some who are important sources of information.

Company executives

Although many public relations people can be helpful, the most valuable information will probably come from the head of the corporation or corporate division. Chief executive officers are powerful people, either out front or behind the scenes, in your community. They are often interesting and usually well informed. Not all of them will be glad to see you, although many executives value open communication with the press.

For more than a decade, companies have released quarterly financial information via electronic news services like Business Wire and PR Newswire. They also discuss those results with analysts on web-based public conference calls that journalists can listen to but not ask questions on. Transcripts of those calls are usually available from third parties, such as Seeking Alpha, or are on the companies' own websites.

Public relations sources

Many people working in corporate communications and public relations are professionals, and providing information to journalists is part of their job. They are paid to make the company look good, though, so they are likely to give you the company's viewpoint. Public relations professionals aren't objective, but that doesn't mean that the information they provide is untrue. Instead, you should assume that it is being packaged to show the company in its best light. Can't reach a company? Try sending a tweet to the corporate account.

Academic experts

Your college or university has faculty members with training and experience in business and economics. They can be good sources for local reaction to national developments or analysis of economic trends. If you are writing about small business or agriculture, state universities operate extension services that have regional outreach offices that can be sources.

Trade associations

Although trade associations clearly represent the interests of their members, they can provide expert commentary on current issues or give explanations from the perspective of the industry. When *The New York Times* reported on the revival of the moving industry, the Household Goods Carriers' Bureau, a major trade group, proved to be an important source. To find trade associations, check the federal USA .gov site, which maintains an alphabetized list.

Ted Soqui/Getty Images

Union meetings such as this one can be an excellent source of labor stories.

Chamber of commerce officials

Chamber of commerce officials are pro-business. They will seldom make an on-the-record negative comment about business, but they usually know who is who and what is what in the business community. The chamber may be involved in such projects as downtown revitalization and industry recruiting. State and regional areas all have economic development agencies that receive tax funds and are required to file reports of recruitment activities.

Former employees

Many business reporters say former employees can be valuable sources. Business reporter and analyst Chris Welles writes, "Nobody knows more about a corporation than someone who has actually worked there." He warns, "Many, probably most, have axes to grind, especially if they were fired; indeed, the more willing they are to talk, the more biased they are likely to be." The good reporter will exercise care in using information obtained from former employees. A quick way to search is through LinkedIn. The site offers a tutorial for journalists.

Labor leaders

For the other side of many business stories and for pieces on working conditions, contracts and politics, get to know local union officials. The workings, legal and otherwise, of unions make good stories, too.

Other sources

Don't overlook the value of a company's customers, suppliers and competitors. You may also want to consult with local bankers, legislators, legislative staff members, law enforcement agents and regulators, board members, oversight committee members

What's the grammar error in this sentence?

Relations between North and South Korea use to allow for occasional "reunion" meetings for families separated during the 1950–53 Korean War.

See Appendix 1, Rule 20.

and the like. Don't forget those ubiquitous consultants, who are usually well informed and often willing to talk, if only for background. If the company you are covering is publicly traded, investor sites like Yahoo Finance offer a list of peer companies.

Announcements and Meetings

A company announcement can be the source of much business news and the starting point for many good stories. It might introduce a new product or explain the firm's reaction to an action taken by a government agency. News conferences can take many forms—in person or via a webcast. Companies also send out news releases via electronic outlets like Business Wire or Cision's PR Newswire, or a corporate communications office might send news to a reporter directly by email.

If you work in a city where one or more corporations are based, you may have the opportunity to cover an annual meeting, which invariably produces some news. Many companies will restrict those meetings to shareholders, but some—particularly Warren Buffett's company, Berkshire Hathaway, based in Omaha, Nebraska—allow the media to observe.

Reporter Enterprise

As in other areas of journalism, the best business news stories often are generated by a reporter's initiative, sparked by a hunch or a tip passed along by an editor, a shareholder or a disgruntled employee or customer.

In other cases, a news release may raise questions that turn into stories. For example, a routine announcement of an executive appointment may lead a curious reporter to a story about the financial problems that produced the change in leadership. Or a stockholder's question may result in a story about a new trend in corporate financing or a shift in emphasis on operations within the company. Or a former employee's call that a company is quietly laying off workers may produce a story about the firm's declining fortunes.

Looking at the Numbers

An understanding of the numbers that a business generates is essential to any intelligent analysis of a company or an industry.

More than 100 million copies of annual reports are pumped out each year, and almost all annual reports can be downloaded from the internet, as can recent recordings of "conference calls"—or the conversations that company executives have with investment analysts.

Annual reports can be complicated, and new journalists should look first at Microsoft's reports, which feature easy-to-read financial statements. A typical annual report includes the following:

- An opening letter from the CEO.
- Key financial data.
- Results of continuing operations.
- Market segment information.

- New product plans.
- Subsidiary activities.
- Research and development activities on future programs.
- Summarized disclosures from the 10-K report.

Most veteran reporters, such as Diana Henriques, a contributing business writer for *The New York Times*, start with the auditor's statement, which is generally located near the back of the annual report, and also examine basic financial data, footnotes and supplementary financial information. The basic auditor's report, from one to four paragraphs long, states that the material conforms to generally accepted auditing standards and that it fairly presents the financial condition of the company. But read the report closely. Sometimes auditors hint at trouble by deviating from the standard language.

Next, move on to the footnotes, where the seeds of many fascinating stories may be germinating among the innocuous prose and numbers that follow and supplement the company's basic financial data. Then turn to the front of the annual report to find the report from the CEO. It is usually addressed "To our shareholders" and should give an overview of the company's performance.

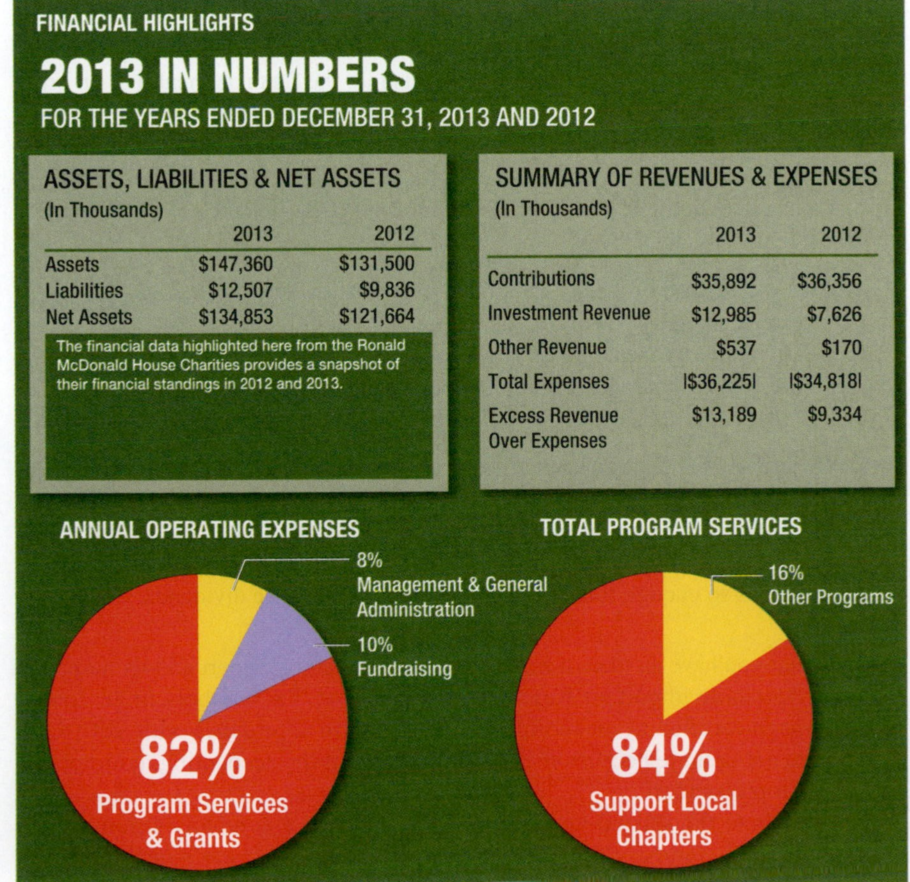

	2013	2012
Assets	$147,360	$131,500
Liabilities	$12,507	$9,836
Net Assets	$134,853	$121,664

	2013	2012
Contributions	$35,892	$36,356
Investment Revenue	$12,985	$7,626
Other Revenue	$537	$170
Total Expenses	($36,225)	($34,818)
Excess Revenue Over Expenses	$13,189	$9,334

A "Financial Highlights" snapshot can provide employees and investors with a quick overview of a company's financial reports.

Cautions When Examining an Annual Report

- Remember that the numbers on an annual report are not definite.
- Look at the company's numbers in the context of its industry, and compare the numbers with several years' performance.
- Remember that cash flow from operations — which are funds that companies earn from products or services they sell and not from the sale of assets — is the true measure of a company's performance. Earnings can also come from the sale of assets or from financing, which can make the balance sheet look good but aren't sustainable.
- Use the knowledge you gain in this chapter to reach preliminary conclusions that you can pursue with experts and company officials.
- The return on sales will tell you how much profit after expenses was produced by each dollar of sales. Reporters should remember that average percentages can vary widely by industry, but generally the higher the percentage, the better.

After that, you're ready to look at the numbers. Here are a few things to watch for:

- **Balance sheet.** This report is a snapshot of the company on one day, generally the last day of the fiscal year. The left side of the balance sheet lists the *assets*, or what the company owns. On the right side are the *liabilities*, or what the company owes, and the *shareholders' equity*, or the dollar value of what stockholders own. The two sides must balance, so the balance sheet can be summarized with the following equation: assets equal liabilities plus shareholders' equity. The balance sheet shows how the year in question compares with the previous year. Reporters should note any significant changes that might be worth exploring for a possible story.
- **Income statement.** This report, also referred to as an *earnings statement* or *statement of profit and loss*, answers this key question: How much money did the company make for the year? Look first at *net sales* or *operating revenues*, and determine if they went up or down. If they increased, did they increase faster than they did last year and faster than the rate of inflation? If sales lagged behind inflation, the company could have serious problems.
- **Return on sales, or ROS.** Company management and financial analysts calculate a number of ratios to gain better insights into the financial health of an organization. One important test of earnings is the relation of net income to sales, which is obtained by dividing net income by sales and multiplying the result by 100. For example, suppose a company has sales of $150,000 and, after expenses, has a net income of $30,000: ROS = ($30,000/$150,000) × 100 = .2 × 100 = 20 percent.
- **Return on equity, or ROE.** This ratio, which shows how effectively a company's invested capital is working, is obtained by dividing net income minus preferred dividends by the common stockholders' equity for the previous year. ROE ratios are best compared within an industry, but generally speaking, between 15 and 20 percent is considered a good ROE.
- **Dividends.** These payments to shareholders are declared quarterly and generally are prominently noted in the annual report. Dividends are an inducement to shareholders to invest in the company. Because companies want to see dividends rise each quarter, they sometimes change their accounting or pension assumptions so enough funds will be available to increase dividends.

Now that you have an idea of how to examine an annual report and its numbers, it is time for some important words of caution. First, the numbers in an annual report, though certified by an auditor and presented in accordance with SEC regulations, are not definite because they are a function of the accounting assumptions used in their preparation.

This leads to the second and third points: Look at a company's numbers in the context of its industry for one year, and compare one year's numbers with several years' performance. To understand how well a firm is performing, examine the numbers along with those of other firms in the same industry. Look at how the company has performed for the last five to 10 years. Then you will discern trends instead of basing your conclusions on one year's performance, which may be atypical.

Covering Consumer News

The phrase "consumer news" might seem arbitrary and redundant. All economic news is, directly or indirectly, about consumers. A story about the stock market may be of interest to "consumers" of stocks and bonds even though those items aren't consumed like cornflakes. Journalists write about crude oil prices because oil is in the things we use every day, like gasoline or plastics. A lack of rain in Kansas could hurt the wheat crop and drive up the price of hotdog buns.

Credit score websites like Credit Karma and Credit Sesame have readers interested in understanding borrowing and credit cards. You can even learn about the average credit score in your state by visiting Experian.com, the credit agency. Figure 16.1 shows how credit scores can be judged.

Many news outlets, especially local and network television, run "consumer target" features that respond to consumer complaints of alleged fraud or unfair treatment by merchants or landlords. For the *Chicago Tribune* investigative series "Dangerous Doses," a team of reporters tested 255 pharmacies to see how often pharmacies dispensed dangerous drug combinations without warning patients. Only a few passed the test, and the series brought legislative change.

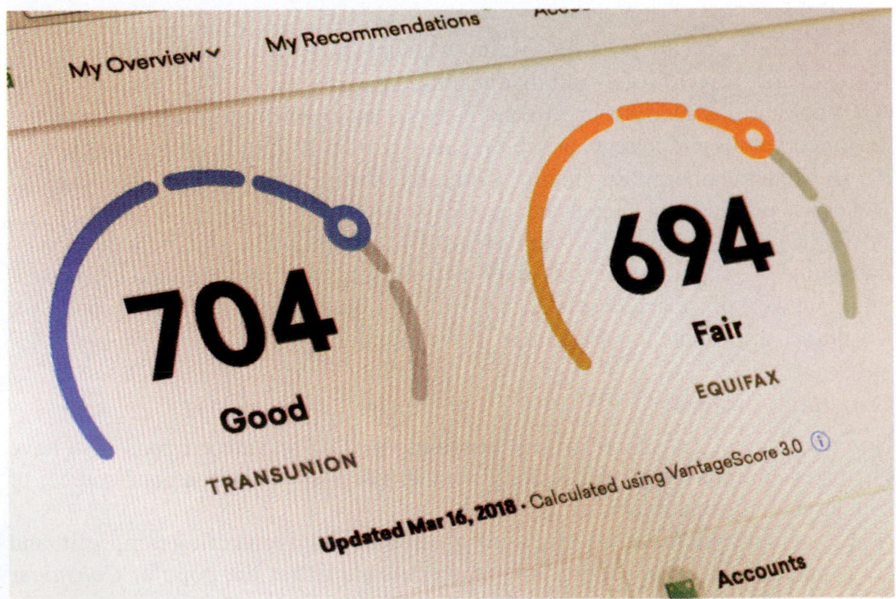

B Christopher/Alamy

FIGURE 16.1

Credit score websites have many tools to help you understand your credit, and what makes a good credit score.

Where to Find Consumer News

Sources of consumer news fall into three general categories: government agencies, consumer groups and private businesses. Let's consider each of these groups.

Government agencies

Many municipalities, especially large cities, have a consumer advocate who calls public attention to problems that affect consumers, including rental apartments. Most county prosecuting attorneys' offices also have a person or even a whole department that challenges business practices of questionable legality. These offices handle cases of consumer fraud in which people pay for something they do not receive or pay for something of a certain quality and receive something less.

Most states have a consumer affairs office that investigates consumer problems and orders or recommends solutions. In addition, state attorneys general investigate and prosecute cases of consumer fraud. Most states also have regulatory commissions that represent the public in a variety of areas. The most common commissions regulate rates and practices of insurance companies, rates and levels of service of utilities and transportation companies, and practices of banks and savings and loan associations. Another source is the state auditor's office, which may also uncover fraud and wrongdoing within government or government contracts.

At the federal level, government regulatory agencies involved in consumer affairs have the power to make rules and to enforce them:

- The Federal Trade Commission oversees matters related to advertising and product safety.
- The Food and Drug Administration watches over prices and safety rules for food, drugs and a variety of other health-related items.
- The Securities and Exchange Commission oversees the registration of securities for corporations and regulates the exchange, or trading, of those securities.
- The Federal Energy Regulatory Commission regulates the rates and levels of service provided by interstate energy companies.
- The Occupational Safety and Health Administration has inspectors who routinely visit and report on safety in workplaces and factories and who investigate workplace accidents. They maintain a database of such information for journalists to mine for stories.

Consumer groups

Nongovernment consumer groups are composed of private citizens who have organized to represent the consumer's interest. They, too, are often good sources of background information or comment.

Consumer Federation of America, an advocacy and education nonprofit, and Consumers Union, an independent group that publishes the popular *Consumer*

Reports, are general in nature. Many states have public-interest research groups. Other organizations, such as the Sierra Club, which concentrates on environmental matters, are such strong advocates that their information might, at times, be anti-business. Other groups may be more local in scope. They may try to enact legislation that promotes recycling, or they may fight what they perceive as discrimination in the way banks and savings and loan associations make housing loans.

Private businesses

Almost all large corporations and many smaller ones have public relations departments that try to present the company in the most favorable light and attempt to mask mistakes as much as possible.

Because of the successes of the consumer movement, a number of companies have taken the offensive and have instituted programs they deem to be in the public interest. Oil companies tell drivers how to economize on gasoline, electric utilities tell homeowners how to keep their electric bills at a minimum and even to use solar and wind power, and credit card companies suggest ways to manage money better.

A new breed of websites, like Bankrate.com, are independent sources of information for consumers on lending rates and credit cards, though their advertising support comes from the credit industry.

How to Report Consumer Stories

Consumer stories may be exposés that bring to light dangerous practices or price increases for a product or service. Research for such stories can be simple and inexpensive to conduct, and the findings may arouse intense reader interest. The project can be something as simple as buying hamburger meat at every supermarket in town to see if all purchases weigh what they are marked.

Theo Keith, while a reporter at WISC-TV in Madison, Wisconsin, found that 50 local gas stations with faulty meters were shorting customers on gasoline purchases. For Crain's New York Business, Jeff Koyen and Jeremy Smerd went to the streets to look into the economics of street hot dog vendors. Despite long hours, the vendors—often immigrants—have to give most of what they receive for a hotdog to a person who controls mobile food permits.

Informative consumer stories are intended to help readers make wiser or less expensive purchases. Cautionary consumer stories warn readers of impending price increases, quality problems with products or questionable practices of business or consumer groups. Such stories can have great impact. TV reports on food safety recalls because of contamination can save lives.

And last, consumer stories can sometimes put news organizations at odds with advertisers. A consumer story led to a lawsuit against *The Denver Post* when it published a story about a dry cleaner that consistently lost customers' clothes.

CHAPTER RESOURCES

SUGGESTED READINGS

Cohen, Sarah. *Numbers in the Newsroom: Using Math and Statistics in the Newsroom.* 2nd ed. Available in an e-edition from Investigative Reporters and Editors. http://store.ire.org/products/numbers-in-the-newsroom-using-math-and-statistics-in-news-second-edition-e-version

Cuillier, David, and Charles N. Davis. *The Art of Access: Strategies for Acquiring Public Records* 2nd ed., Washington, DC: CQ Press, 2011. How to navigate public records, which is especially helpful in getting information on businesses. Includes information on Freedom of Information requests.

Houston, Brant, and Investigative Reporters and Editors. *The Investigative Reporter's Handbook: A Guide to Documents, Databases and Techniques.* 5th ed. New York: Bedford/St. Martin's, 2009. This valuable guide should be on every reporter's shelf. See especially the chapter on business.

Lewis, Michael. *The Big Short: Inside the Doomsday Machine.* New York: Norton, 2010. Lewis provides a gripping explanation of the housing and credit bubbles of the 2000s.

Morgenson, Gretchen. *The Capitalist's Bible: The Essential Guide to Free Markets—and Why They Matter to You.* New York: HarperCollins, 2009. This guide offers a good discussion of business terms and concepts.

Sviokla, John, and Mitch Cohen. *The Self-Made Billionaire Effect: How Extreme Producers Create Massive Value.* New York: Portfolio, 2014. The authors studied 800 self-made billionaires, including Mark Cuban, to determine what makes them successful in adding value to their companies.

Taparia, Jay. *Understanding Financial Statements: A Journalist's Guide.* Chicago: Marion Street Press, 2004. Taparia, a popular trainer in business journalism, walks journalists through complicated financial statements.

Wilkins, Lee, Martha Steffens, Esther Thorson, Greeley Kyle, Kent Collins and Fred Vultee. *Reporting Disaster on Deadline: A Handbook for Students and Professionals.* New York: Routledge, 2012. This handbook describes how to cover disasters in today's internet age. See the chapters on economic damage and consumer fraud.

SUGGESTED WEBSITES

LaunchPad Solo
launchpadworks.com
When you visit LaunchPad Solo for Journalism, you will find research links, exercises and LearningCurve adaptive quizzing to help you improve your grammar and AP style usage. In addition, the site's video collection hosts the videos highlighted in this and other chapters as well as additional clips of leading professionals discussing important media trends.

www.bea.gov, www.bls.gov and www.census.gov
These sites, from the U.S. Department of Commerce and the U.S. Department of Labor, offer overviews of the U.S. economy and exhaustive studies about each segment of the economy.

www.business.com
This directory of business websites offers information about individual companies and industries.

www.businessjournalism.org
This website, funded by the Donald W. Reynolds National Center for Business Journalism, at the Walter Cronkite School of Journalism and Mass Communication at Arizona State University, offers tips and tutorials for business journalism professionals and students.

www.finance.yahoo.com
This portal is an accessible and free index of corporate financial filings, stock prices and corporate news.

www.investorwords.com and investopedia.com
These sites offer reliable definitions of the words and processes used in finance.

www.ire.org/nicar/database-library
The National Institute for Computer-Assisted Reporting provides access to databases and training in how to use them to analyze business, economic and regulatory information.

www.sabew.org
The Society of Advancing Business Editing and Writing can be a good source for contacts, story ideas and student training opportunities. Students can join the organization for a modest fee and win prizes for student publication work in the SABEW annual contest.

EXERCISES

1. Jobs are the lifeblood of an economy because workers as well as businesses pay taxes. Journalists must understand unemployment rates.
   a. Find the BLS press release on the latest monthly job numbers. Find the states with the highest and lowest rates. Now find how those statistics have changed from month to month and year to year.
   b. Thinking critically, what would "seasonal adjustment" mean in employment statistics?
   c. How does employment differ by age, race and gender?
   d. Find your state, and write two paragraphs on your findings. Also think what you would do next to tell the story through people.
2. Many websites use "price discrimination," an economic term that means that different consumers are given different prices. With your laptop, visit a travel booking website, and find the prices for a hotel room in Paris three months from today. Now have a friend use his or her phone to do the same thing. Is the price the same for mobile users and for laptop users? (You won't be able to do this by yourself because your phone and your computer may have similar browsing histories.) Write about what you find.
3. Identify a local business reporter. Study her or his work, and then interview the reporter. Ask about sources, story ideas and career opportunities. Follow the reporter's Twitter account.
4. Download a prospectus on a mutual fund, and study its investment rationale. Or read a prospectus on a stock offering, and study its price-earnings ratio, yield on dividends and other value indicators. Find commentary on the fund or stock on the web, and explain its performance.
5. Go to Yahoo Finance, and type in the name of a local company that is traded on a stock exchange. What is that company's market capitalization? What price is its stock trading for? Find all that you can about that company through this web outlet.

CHAPTER 17

INVESTIGATIVE AND DATA-DRIVEN REPORTING

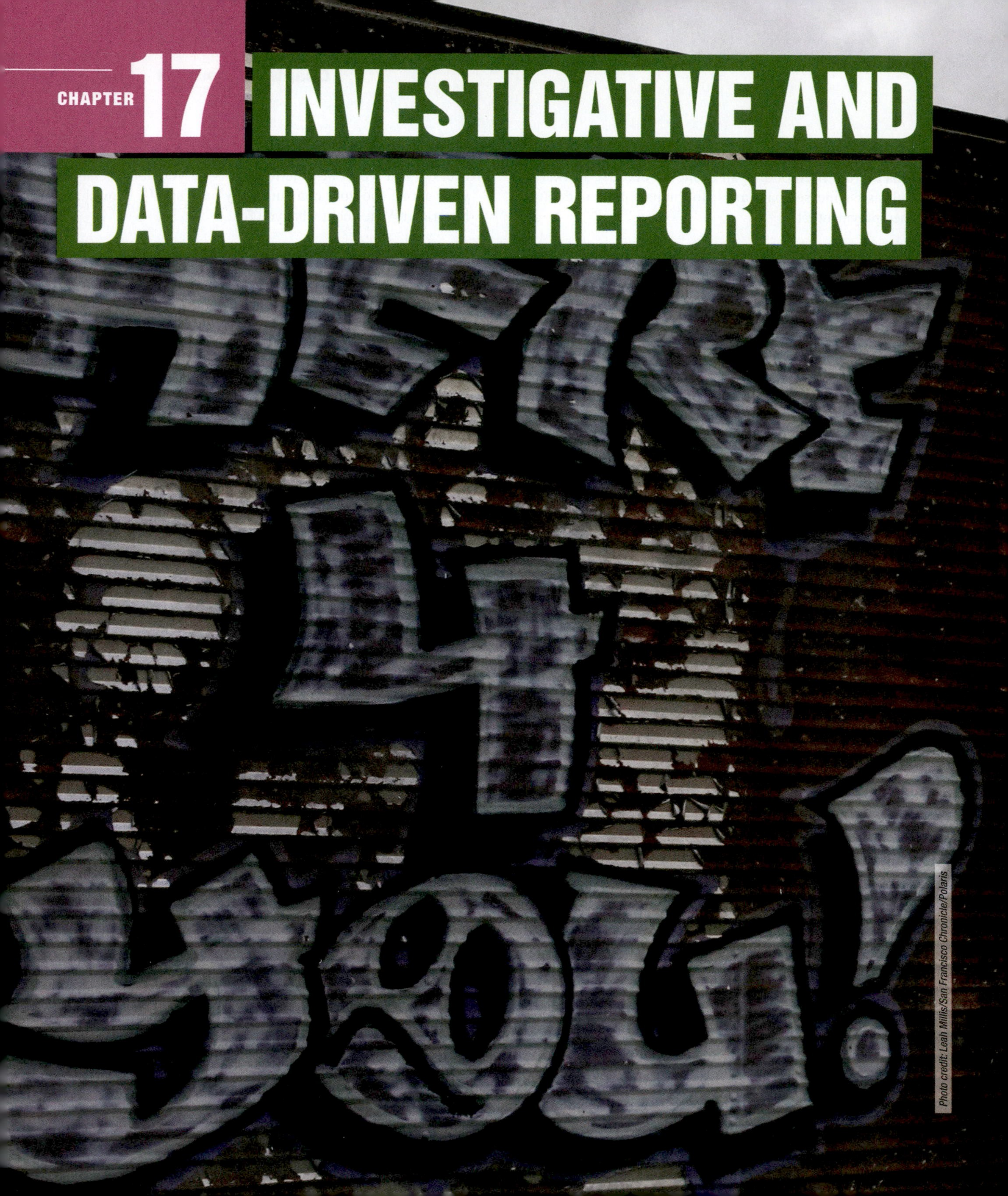

Photo credit: Leah Millis/San Francisco Chronicle/Polaris

In-depth reporting that uses documents and data to supplement human sources is in demand. As Doug Haddix, executive director of Investigative Reporters and Editors, a global membership organization, reports:

> **Even with budget cuts, more and more newsrooms are seeking journalists with skills in using public records and data to get closer to the truth.**
>
> **Public trust in the news media has eroded in recent years but can be restored through the tenets of strong accountability reporting: facts, data, documents and other verifiable information. Journalists with skills in investigative reporting continue to produce stories with high impact in communities large and small across the United States and beyond. In response to business pressures, more and more newsrooms are collaborating to harness more firepower for investigative stories.**
>
> **New models—including legacy media, broadcast, universities and nonprofits—offer hope for continued robust investigative reporting.**

A few examples, taken from the IRE Awards presented for 2017, show how journalists are producing exemplary, in-depth multimedia projects with human sources, documents and data:

- The *San Francisco Chronicle* won for uncovering questionable arrests of children at California's foster care shelters. The reporting team found children as young as 8 years old arrested after emotional and other minor outbursts. The team built a database of 14,000 police calls to the foster shelters over two years so it could document the extent of the problem. The *Chronicle*'s web report included a text story, video, information graphic and map showing the number of calls for service by shelter location. The *Chronicle*'s reporting had an immediate impact: A week after the stories ran, the state attorney general's office started an examination of shelter arrests. Also, the state closed an intake center where children were victimized by human traffickers and had to sleep on the floor.
- NPR and ProPublica, a nonprofit investigative news organization, won for reporting how workers' compensation insurers in Florida had taken advantage of state law to deport immigrants who had filed workplace injury claims. ProPublica and NPR analyzed 14 years of state insurance fraud data and thousands of pages of court records for their story. NPR reported the story on its *All Things Considered* radio program. Both news organizations published text stories, along with photos of workers who had been targeted by their former employers.
- BuzzFeed News won the Tom Renner Award for crime reporting for its series that linked Russian assassins to murders in the United Kingdom and United States. BuzzFeed relied on human sources, documents and secret recordings to stitch together details about how Russian intelligence operatives killed enemies of the Kremlin. BuzzFeed published long-form text stories supported with rich multimedia elements, such as evidence photos and interactive graphics that gave readers more details about each victim. After the stories ran, a U.S. Senate Foreign Relations Committee staff report cited the revelations in a warning sent to other Western governments.

In this chapter, you will learn:

1. How the tradition of investigative reporting grew.
2. What the process of investigative reporting is.
3. How to find and use human and written sources.
4. What the importance of data analysis in investigative reporting is.
5. How investigative stories are being presented on multiple platforms and produced by teams.

launchpadworks.com
WATCH: **"Investigative Reporting Resources"**

- How does investigative reporting differ from the usual reporting journalists do?
- What different challenges do government, nonprofit and commercial sources pose for investigative reporting?

Investigative Reporting: An American Tradition

Investigative reporting has a rich history in American journalism. The fiercely partisan editors of the Revolutionary War era dug for facts, as well as the mud they hurled at their opponents. In the early 20th century, investigative reporting flowered with the "muckrakers," a title bestowed angrily by President Theodore Roosevelt and worn proudly by journalists. Lincoln Steffens explored the undersides of American cities, laying bare the corrupt combinations of businessmen and politicians that ran them. Ida Tarbell exposed the economic stranglehold of the oil monopoly. And Theodore Dreiser, Upton Sinclair and Frank Norris revealed the horrors of working life in factories and meatpacking plants.

Just as the work of the muckrakers appeared in magazines, nonfiction books and even novels, the work of today's investigative reporters is produced beyond traditional newsrooms. One prominent example of 21st-century muckraking is ProPublica, which was established in 2007. Funded initially by foundation grants and led by a former editor of *The Wall Street Journal*, ProPublica tackles major investigations of national significance, often in partnership with traditional news organizations.

As economic pressures force staff cuts in traditional newsrooms, other investigative innovations are emerging at local and regional levels. For example, reporter Andy Hall, who left his newspaper when the staff was reduced, launched the

Courtesy of the Ida M. Tarbell Collection, Special Collections, Pelletier Library, Allegheny College

Ida Tarbell, one of the original muckrakers, helped set the pattern for investigative reporting with her exposé of Standard Oil.

Wisconsin Center for Investigative Journalism (WisconsinWatch.org), a nonprofit cooperative that seeks to pick up where diminished newsrooms are leaving off. Similar efforts are underway across the country. Many startup news organizations rely on multimedia and interactive storytelling to connect with their primarily online audiences.

Today's investigators, like the original muckrakers, are not satisfied with uncovering individual instances of wrongdoing. They look at organizations as a whole, as entire systems, often analyzing computer databases to gain a better understanding of their workings. They seek to both expose and explain, and in many cases, they seek solutions for the problems and abuses they reveal. Most investigative reporters think of themselves as more than chroniclers of fact or analysts. They also see themselves as catalysts for reform. This, too, was true of the muckrakers.

The drive to expose abuses is something the public welcomes and expects from journalists. Studies have shown that the consumers of journalism support investigative reporting when it leads to reforms. There's no conflict between investigative reporting and the journalistic standard of objectivity, either. You'll remember from Chapter 1 that objectivity doesn't have to mean neutrality. In journalism, as in science, objectivity is the method of searching for the truth. Just as scientists are not expected to be neutral about the desirability of curing disease, journalists don't have to be neutral about exposing wrongdoing. What objectivity does require is honest, open-minded investigation and truthful reporting of the results of that investigation.

The Process

Most investigations start with a hunch or a tip that something or someone deserves a close look. If a preliminary search supports that expectation, a serious investigation begins. When enough information has been uncovered to prove or modify the reporter's initial hunch, it's time to analyze, organize and produce the story.

Beginning the Investigation

No good reporter begins an investigation unless there is some basis for suspicion. That basis may be a grand jury report that leaves something untold or a tip that a public official is on the take. It may be a sudden upsurge in drug overdoses, or it may be long-festering problems in the schools. If you don't have some idea of what to look for, an investigation is likely to turn into a wild-goose chase.

Acting on a tip or suspicion, together with whatever background material you have, you form a hypothesis. Reporters hardly ever use that term, but it shows the similarity between the processes of investigative reporting and scientific investigation. In both, the hypothesis is the statement of what you think is true. Your

TIPS

Carrying Out the Investigation

- **Be organized.** Careful organization keeps you on the right track and prevents you from overlooking anything important.
- **Draw up a plan of action.** Write out a plan. Then go over it with your editor, news director or producer.
- **Carry out your plan.** Keep your hypothesis in mind as a guidepost, but allow flexibility for the unexpected twists that most investigations take.
- **Be methodical.** The method you use isn't important as long as you understand it and are consistent.

informal hypothesis might be "The mayor is a crook" or "The school system is being run incompetently." It is a good idea to state your hypothesis clearly when you begin your investigation. By doing so, you focus on the heart of the problem and lessen the possibility of any misunderstanding with your editor or co-workers.

As soon as the hypothesis is stated, the reporter — like the scientist — sets out to support it or show that it is not supportable. You should be open to the possibility that your first assumption was wrong. Reporters — like scientists — are not advocates. They are seekers of truth. No good reporter ignores or downplays evidence because it contradicts his or her assumptions. In journalism, as in science, the truth about a situation is often sharply different from what is expected. Open-mindedness is an essential quality of a good investigative reporter. And even if your hypothesis is not supported, you may still have a good story.

Carrying Out the Investigation

The actual investigative work usually proceeds in two stages. The first is what Robert W. Greene, a legendary reporter and Pulitzer Prize–winning editor for *Newsday*, named the **sniff**. After you form a hypothesis, you nose around in search of a trail worth following. If you find one, the second stage, serious investigation, begins.

Preliminary checking should take no more than a day or two. Its purpose is not to prove the hypothesis but to determine the chances of proving it. You make that effort by talking with the most promising source or sources, skimming available records and data, and consulting knowledgeable people in your newsroom. The two questions you are trying to answer are (1) "Is there a story here?" and (2) "Am I going to be able to get it?" If the answer to either question is no, then there is little point in pursuing the investigation.

When the answer to both questions is yes, the real work begins. It begins with organization. Careful organization keeps you on the right track and prevents you from overlooking anything important as you go. Many reporters take a kind of perverse pride in their illegible notebooks and cluttered desks. As an investigative reporter, you may have a messy desk, but you should arrange your files — paper and electronic — clearly and coherently. Begin organizing by asking yourself these questions:

- Who are my most promising sources? Who is likely to give me trouble? Whom should I go to first? Second? Last?
- What records and data do I need? Where are they? Which are public? How can I get to the ones that are not readily accessible?
- What is the most I can hope to prove? What is the least that will still yield a story?
- How long should the investigation take?

Then draw up a plan of action, such as the one shown in Figure 17.1. Experienced reporters might do this mentally. But when you are a beginner, it's a good

2/26/19 Plan for Mayor Jane Jones story

Hypothesis: Mayor Jones accepted improper campaign contributions from Top Construction as a council member, and as mayor, she later awarded the company a contract to build a new community center.

Initial source: In a conversation, XX casually suggested info about the campaign contribution.

Draft: Due 3/7/19.

Questions:
- How much of this hypothesis can I prove?
- Is XX trustworthy? What does XX have to gain? Will XX go on the record?
- Will documents or data support the hypothesis? What records are important?
- What other people should I interview—on both sides?
- Will I have at least two credible sources for each fact?
- How can I make sure the story is relevant, useful and interesting?
- Is this one story or a series?

Plan:

1. Request and review relevant documents and data:
   - Any docs from XX.
   - Campaign contribution records; get Stacy to help w/ this.
   - Contract bids for community center; ask Manuel how to compare.
2. Interview major people:
   - XX, to follow up on initial info.
   - City auditor about bids.
   - Mayor's campaign manager (Roberts?) about contributions.
   - Pres. of Top Construction (Smythe?) about contributions.
   - Mayor.
3. Write outline:
   - What's the lead?
   - Story structure: inverted pyramid?
   - Enough facts? details? anecdotes? quotes?
4. Build multimedia team for presentation:
   - How do we want to present the story?
   - What video, audio, print and interactive elements do we need to create or gather?
   - Involve other journalists, as needed, to help with digital storytelling.
5. Write draft:
   - Is the story complete?
   - Easy to follow?
   - Convincing?
   - Compelling?
6. Next steps:
   - Editor? legal department?
   - Need more facts? Details?
   - Revise and finalize draft?
   - With editors, schedule print, broadcast and digital publication and social media use.

FIGURE 17.1

A plan of action lists the hypothesis and the steps the journalist will take to gather information and draft a story.

idea to write out a plan and go over it with your editor, news director or producer. Your supervisor may spot some holes in your planning or have something to add. And an editor, a news director or a producer is more likely to give you enough time if he or she has a clear idea of what has to be done.

Allowing flexibility for the unexpected twists that most investigations take, carry out your plan. During your first round of interviews, keep asking whom else you should interview. While you are checking records, look for references to other files or other people.

Be methodical. Many investigative reporters spend an hour or so at the end of every day adding up the score — going through their notes and searching their memories to analyze what they have learned and what they need next. Some develop elaborate, cross-indexed files of names, organizations and incidents. Others are less formal. Nearly all, however, use a code to disguise the names of confidential sources so that those sources will remain secret even if the files are subpoenaed.

The method you use isn't important as long as you understand it. What is vitally important is that you have a method and use it consistently. If you fail to keep careful track of where you're going, you may go in the wrong direction, or in circles. Many investigative journalists will keep notes in a file format, such as Word, that can be easily searched.

Getting It Right

The importance of accuracy in investigative reporting cannot be overstated. It is the essential element in good journalism of any kind. But in investigative reporting especially, inaccuracy leads to embarrassment, to ruined reputations and sometimes to lawsuits. The reputations ruined are often those of the careless reporter and the news organization. Most investigative stories have the effect of accusing somebody of wrongdoing or incompetence. Even if the subject is a public official whose chances of suing successfully for libel are slim (see Chapter 19), fairness and decency require that you be sure of your facts before you report them.

Many experienced investigators require verification from two independent sources before they include an allegation in a story. That is a good rule to follow. People make mistakes. They lie. Their memories fail. Documents can be misleading or confusing. Check and double-check. There is no good excuse for an error.

Writing the Story

Most investigative stories require review by the media company's lawyer before they are published, posted online or broadcast. The lawyer will advise on what you can publish safely and what you cannot.

Most editors, producers and news directors heed their lawyers' advice. If you are lucky, the lawyer will understand and sympathize with good, aggressive journalism. If he or she does not, you may find yourself forced to argue for your story. You will be better equipped for such an argument (few reporters go through a career without several) if you understand at least the basics of libel and privacy law. Chapter 19 outlines those fundamentals, and several good books on law for journalists are listed in the Suggested Readings at the end of that chapter.

The last step before your investigation goes public is the writing and rewriting of the story. After days or weeks of intense reporting, the actual writing strikes some investigative reporters as a chore — necessary but unimportant. That attitude is disastrous. The best reporting in the world is wasted unless it reaches an audience. Your hard-won exposé or painstaking analysis will disappear without a trace unless your storytelling attracts the audience and maintains its interest. Good investigative reporters recognize this. They stress engaging storytelling almost as much as solid reporting.

> **"Our collaborative model is based on the idea that many journalists working together can reveal a global truth, a truth that is discovered, questioned, checked and checked again — not by a single reporter but by teams of talented journalists and news organizations working toward a common goal. By putting aside rivalries and blocking out commercial pressures, we can devote ourselves to finding and sharing true stories of genuine significance to the world."**
>
> ■ **from International Consortium of International Journalists, Manifesto**

Selecting an effective story structure and lead

How do you tell the results of a complicated investigation? The general rule is, as simply as you can. One approach is to use a **hard lead** (an inverted pyramid lead that reports newly discovered facts), displaying your key findings in the first few paragraphs. Another option is to adopt one of the alternative approaches to storytelling explained in Chapter 10.

Amy Julia Harris and Shoshana Walter, reporters for Reveal, the nonprofit Center for Investigative Reporting's website, public radio program, podcast and social media platform, reported in 2017 that judges had sentenced petty thieves with no drug and alcohol problems to rehabilitation centers that are really work farms. Here's how they started their story:

> The worst day of Brad McGahey's life was the day a judge decided to spare him from prison.
>
> McGahey was 23 with dreams of making it big in rodeo, maybe starring in his own reality TV show. With a 1.5 GPA, he'd barely graduated from high school. He had two kids and mounting child support debt. Then he got busted for buying a stolen horse trailer, fell behind on court fines and blew off his probation officer.
>
> Standing in a tiny wood-paneled courtroom in rural Oklahoma in 2010, he faced one year in state prison. The judge had another plan.
>
> "You need to learn a work ethic," the judge told him. "I'm sending you to CAAIR."
>
> McGahey had heard of Christian Alcoholics & Addicts in Recovery. People called it "the Chicken Farm," a rural retreat where defendants stayed for a year, got addiction treatment and learned to live more productive lives. Most were sent there by courts from across Oklahoma and neighboring states, part of the nationwide push to keep nonviolent offenders out of prison.
>
> Aside from daily cans of Dr Pepper, McGahey wasn't addicted to anything. The judge knew that. But the Chicken Farm sounded better than prison.

What's the grammar error in this sentence?

Critics in Congress slammed the White House for what they say is its ineffective disorganized campaign to train a Syrian rebel army against ISIS.

See Appendix 1, Rule 7.

A few weeks later, McGahey stood in front of a speeding conveyor belt inside a frigid poultry plant, pulling guts and stray feathers from slaughtered chickens destined for major fast food restaurants and grocery stores.

There wasn't much substance abuse treatment at CAAIR. It was mostly factory work for one of America's top poultry companies. If McGahey got hurt or worked too slowly, his bosses threatened him with prison.

And he worked for free. CAAIR pocketed the pay.

"It was a slave camp," McGahey said. "I can't believe the court sent me there."

The best stories are usually about people, and Walter and Harris used one person's troubles to introduce readers to the bigger story. A few paragraphs later, they reveal that big picture:

Soon, it would get worse.

Across the country, judges increasingly are sending defendants to rehab instead of prison or jail. These diversion courts have become the bedrock of criminal justice reform, aiming to transform lives and ease overcrowded prisons.

But in the rush to spare people from prison, some judges are steering defendants into rehabs that are little more than lucrative work camps for private industry, an investigation by Reveal from The Center for Investigative Reporting has found.

Moving from the particular to the general is a logical progression and an effective way to show readers the humanity and the full scope of the investigation.

Including proof of the story's credibility

Throughout their story "All Work. No Pay," Harris and Walter showed readers how they verified the story. When they wrote, "The judge had another plan," that sentence included a hyperlink to the court document signed by the judge. Similarly, when they reported that the judge knew McGahey did not have an addiction problem, that sentence included a hyperlink to another court document that included that assessment provided to the judge. And when Harris and Walter told readers, "Chicken processing plants are notoriously dangerous and understaffed," they gave readers a hyperlink to a report from the federal Occupational Safety and Health Administration with the headline "Poultry Processing Among Most Dangerous Industries."

Later in the story — after readers have been hooked by the narrative — the reporters describe their methods: "To unearth this story, Reveal interviewed scores of former participants and employees, court officials and judges and reviewed hundreds of pages of court documents, tax filings and workers' compensation records."

That's important, too, if you want to be believed. You owe it to your audience to be as open as possible about not only what you know but how you know it. By the way, in response to Reveal's reporting, at least three class-action lawsuits have been filed, and the program is being investigated by the American Civil Liberties Union.

Striving for clear, simple explanations

Writing an investigative story that will have an impact on its audience takes the same attention to organization and detail as does any good writing. Here are a few tips that apply to all types of storytelling but especially to investigative stories:

- **Get people into the story.** Any investigation worth doing involves people in some way. Make them come alive with descriptive details, like the kind we were given in the story about the chicken processing plant. Not only was McGahey featured in the top of the Reveal story, but the team also produced a compelling video about his recovery from a terrible accident at the plant.
- **Keep it simple.** Look for ways to clarify and explain complicated situations. When you have a mass of information, consider spreading it over more than one story — in a series or in a main story with a sidebar. Think about how videos, photos, charts, graphs, interactives or lists can be used to present key facts clearly. Don't try to include everything you know; include just enough to support your conclusions. More than that is too much. Link to documents and other source materials referenced in your reporting.
- **Tell the audience what your research means.** Sometimes journalists are tempted to just lay out the facts and let people draw their own conclusions. That is unfair to both you and your audience. Lay out the facts, but explain their impact. A team of Chicago Tribune reporters who investigated the deplorable conditions in juvenile treatment centers wrote this lead: "In residential treatment centers across Illinois, children are assaulted, sexually abused and running away by the thousands — yet state officials fail to act on reports of harm and continue sending waves of youths to the most troubled and violent facilities, a *Tribune* investigation found." If the facts are there, drawing the obvious conclusions is not editorializing. It is good and helpful writing.
- **Organize before you write.** Careful organization is as important in writing the investigative story as it is in reporting it. The job will be easier if you have been organized all along. When you are ready to write, review your notes. Make an outline. Pick out your best quotes and anecdotes. Some reporters, if they are writing more than one story, separate their material into individual folders, one for each story. However you do it, know what you are going to say before you start to write.
- **Suggest solutions.** Polls have shown that readers prefer investigative stories that show how to correct the problems identified. Are new laws needed? Better enforcement of present laws? More resources? Better training? Remember that the progressive movement of the early 20th century with the original muckrakers produced reforms, not just good stories.

ON THE JOB Getting Visual for Investigations

Judd Slivka, courtesy of Jamie Grey

Jamie Grey is an investigative journalist who has worked as a multimedia journalist, reporter and producer for television stations from New Orleans to Boise, Idaho. She is a Missouri-based national investigative producer for Raycom Media's Investigate TV, which generates stories for dozens of local television stations and streaming devices. Before that, she taught advanced broadcast reporting at the Missouri School of Journalism.

For Grey, working with video is powerful. It allows viewers to see and hear how the subjects of investigations are saying things and brings the audience right into the story. Often, Grey says, the tricky part of investigative reporting is working with "nonvisual" stories that include lots of documents, data or flat photos.

To showcase those more boring visual elements, Grey suggests thinking creatively. For instance, find ways to use unusual lighting on documents (even a smartphone light can make an interesting targeted beam to showcase a word on a page). Shoot things from different angles or in related environments (borrow a courtroom for a few minutes to lay out legal documents near a gavel).

Journalists have had to change their visual styles to account for online audiences, Grey says. For example, she makes shorter versions of stories and layers in text so the pieces work well on social media, where many people watch videos on mute. For streaming audiences, Grey and her co-workers streamline video packages with sleek, documentary-style graphics and often break up stories differently to account for ad spaces or viewers who use autoplay functions.

When it comes to using numbers, Grey offers these tips. Make sure visual elements with text or numbers match what the reporter is saying. Viewers will favor their eyes, so if the sound and visuals are different, they're likely to forget what was said. For numbers, avoid talking about more than three at a time. That's about the limit for viewers. Also, keep measurements in the same formats: If you've been using percentages, don't switch to fractions.

Grey says the most important thing she's learned is harnessing the power of pacing. When stories are tough visually but have dramatic findings (often the case in investigative work), pick up the pace of writing and editing. Think short tracks, short bites, short shots. That technique can help hold viewers' attention on an important story.

- **Use the web to support your story.** Your audience is skeptical. People want to be shown, not just told. So even if your story is aired first on television or radio, use your organization's website to post supporting documents, photographs, audio or transcripts of key interviews. In addition, use the web to visualize your data. Create news applications that allow your audience to interact with and find information that's meaningful to them.
- **Be fair.** Your reporting should include any responses or defenses offered by the people or institution you're examining. Fairness is essential.

Think of writing as the climax of a process that begins with a hypothesis, carefully tests that hypothesis, checks and double-checks every fact, and satisfies the concerns of your supervisors and lawyers. Every step in that process is vital to the success of any investigative story.

Planning the Multimedia Aspects of the Story or Series

As seen in the examples throughout this chapter, news organizations have been presenting more of their stories digitally. Traditional news organizations, such as newspapers and television, are using online platforms to build on the print or broadcast reporting that they've always done. Nontraditional news organizations — such as ProPublica, The Center for Investigative Reporting (based in California), and the International Consortium of Investigative Journalists (based in Washington, D.C.) — exist primarily on the web and use digital tools extensively in their storytelling.

ICIJ, for example, uses visualizations and news applications to allow its audience to interact and engage with its databases. In 2017, ICIJ created a tool as part of "The Paradise Papers: Exposing the Rogue Offshore Finance Industry," its project on offshore banking accounts, to allow visitors to explore the offshore connections of Queen Elizabeth II, Donald Trump and other global leaders.

News organizations that produce digital investigative journalism are relying on teams to get the job done. No one journalist — let alone an investigative reporter — has all the skills needed to create a rich interactive experience for the audience. Multimedia investigative packages often require help from videographers, digital photographers, web producers, news application developers, interactive designers, graphic artists, reporters, editors and more.

More than 20 journalists at *The Miami Herald* worked on its "Fight Club" series — an exposé of abuse inside Florida's juvenile justice system that ran in 2017. The team included reporters, data analysts, and story, video and visual editors. The multimedia team created a scrolling story on the landing page that featured video of juveniles forced by guards to fight each other.

The Arizona Republic and USAToday Network employed multimedia storytelling for their 2017 project "The Wall: Unknown Stories, Unintended Consequences." The package includes traditional text stories, podcasts and an interactive map. Plus, the team created traditional and virtual reality videos to help show the story about Trump's proposed border wall. The newspaper says "scores" of its journalists spent nine months creating the multimedia package. Their work won the 2018 Pulitzer Prize for explanatory reporting, the same category ICIJ won in 2017 for the Panama Papers project.

Successfully executing a digital investigative project takes time, planning and teamwork. Early in the process, reporters should talk to their editors or producers to determine the best way to present the story and work to put a team together. Good editors will ensure that all the key players are able to contribute their thoughts early.

Investigative storytelling is a process that takes collaboration. Because the story can change as the reporters develop more information, it's important for the team to meet regularly about any progress or obstacles.

EXPLORE OFFSHORE CONNECTIONS OF POLITICAL POWER PLAYERS

Explore the offshore connections of world leaders, politicians and their relatives and associates.

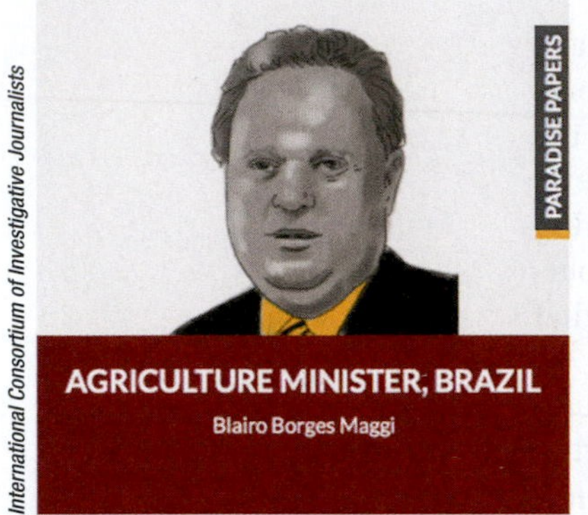

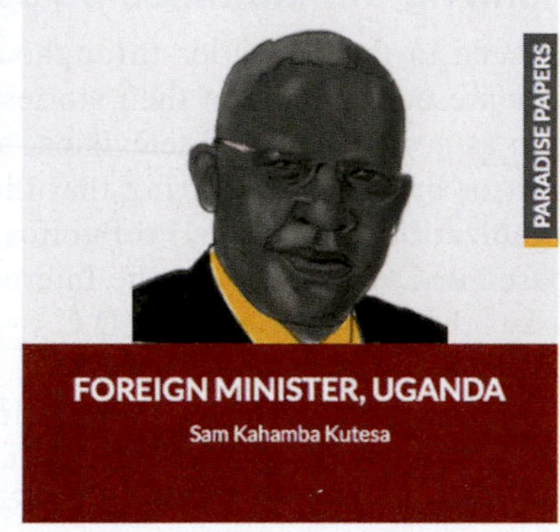

International Consortium of Investigative Journalists

FIGURE 17.2

Journalists at the International Consortium of Investigative Journalists created this interactive graphic to allow the audience to explore the offshore connections of political power players around the globe. To see the graphic, go to https://www.icij.org/investigations/paradise-papers/explore-politicians-paradise-papers/.

The Sources

Investigative reporters get their information from people, documents or data. The perfect source is a person who has the pertinent documents and is eager to tell you what those documents mean. Don't count on finding the perfect source. Instead, expect to piece together the information you need from a variety of people and records. Some people will not be eager to talk to you, and some records will be difficult to obtain—and, if you do gain access to them, difficult to understand. Let's consider human sources first.

Human Sources

Suppose you get a tip that the mayor received campaign contributions under the table from the engineering firm that just won a big city contract. Who could be a good source?

- **Enemies.** When you are trying to find out anything bad about a person, his or her enemies are usually the best sources. More often than not, the enemies of a prominent person will have made it their business to find out as much as possible about that person's misdeeds and shortcomings. Frequently, they are happy to share what they know with a friendly reporter. However, because of the stake they hold in wanting to "out" your subject, it's vital to weigh their reliability and confirm any information they provide.
- **Friends.** Friends are sometimes nearly as revealing as enemies. In trying to explain and defend their friend's actions, they may tell you more than you knew before. Occasionally, you may find that someone your subject regards as a friend is not much of a friend after all.

- **Losers.** Like enemies, losers often carry a grudge. Seek out the loser in the last election, the losing contender for the contract, the loser in a power struggle. Bad losers make good sources. However, as with enemies, check their reliability.
- **Victims.** If you are investigating a failing school system, talk with students and their parents. If your story is about nursing home abuses, talk with patients and their relatives. The honest and hardworking employees caught in a corrupt or incompetent system are victims, too. They can give you specific examples and anecdotes. Their case histories can help you write the story. Be wary, though. One thing enemies, losers and victims have in common is that they have an ax to grind about your subject. Confirm every allegation they make.
- **Experts.** Early in many investigations, there may be a great deal that you don't understand. You may need someone to explain how the campaign finance laws could be circumvented, someone to interpret a contract, someone to decipher a set of bid specifications. Lawyers, accountants, engineers or professors can help you understand technical jargon or complicated transactions. If they refuse to comment on your specific case, fit the facts you have into a hypothetical situation.
- **Police.** Investigative reporters and law enforcement agents often work the same territory. If you are wise, you will make friends with carefully selected agents. They can — and frequently will — be of great help. Their files may not be gold mines, but they have investigative tools and contacts you lack. When they get to know and trust you, they will share. They know, too, that you can do some things they cannot. You need less proof to print that the mayor is a crook than it may take to convince a jury. Most police investigators want to corner wrongdoers any way they can. You can use that attitude to your advantage.
- **People in trouble.** Police use this source, and so can you. However, unlike prosecutors, you cannot promise immunity or a lesser charge. A classic case is the Watergate affair, in which members of President Richard Nixon's administration recruited five men to break into the headquarters of the Democratic National Committee to wiretap phones illegally. When the Nixon administration started to unravel, officials trying to save their careers and images began falling all over one another to give their self-serving versions of events. People will react similarly in lesser cases.

As an investigative reporter, you cultivate sources in the same ways a reporter on a beat does. You just do it more quickly. One excellent tactic is to play on their self-interest. Losers and enemies want to reveal hidden truths about your subject, and thus you have a common aim. Friends want their buddy's side of the story to be explained. So do you. Keep in mind that no matter how corrupt your subject may be, he or she is still a human being. That attitude may also help ensure that you treat the subject fairly.

Experts want to explain the problem as you present it. And you want to understand. People in trouble want sympathy and some assurance that they still merit respect. No reporter should have trouble conveying either attitude.

Another way to win and keep sources is to protect them. Occasionally a reporter faces jail unless he or she reveals a confidential source. Even jail is not too great a price to pay to keep a promise. More often, the threats to confidentiality are less dramatic. Other sources, or the subject of the investigation, may casually ask, "Where'd you hear that?" Other reporters, over coffee or a beer, may ask the same question. Hold your tongue. The only person to whom a confidential source should ever be revealed is your editor.

Human sources both pose problems and help solve them. To hurt an enemy or protect a friend, to make themselves look better or someone else look worse—and sometimes simply for fun—people lie to reporters. No reporter is safe, and no source is above suspicion. They may use you, too, just as you are using them. The only reason most people involved on any side of a suspicious situation will talk about it is to enhance their own position. That is neither illegal nor immoral, but it can trip up a reporter who fails to take every self-serving statement with the appropriate grain of salt.

And sometimes sources change their stories. People forget. Recollections and situations change. Pressure is applied. A source may deny tomorrow—or in court—what he or she told you today.

Finally, sources seldom want to be identified. Enemies of a powerful person are often reluctant to see their names attached to their criticisms in print. Even friends may be reluctant to be identified. Experts might be willing to provide background information but often cite their codes of ethics when you ask them to go on the record. Stories without identifiable sources have less credibility with readers, with editors and even with colleagues.

Written Sources

Fortunately, not all sources are human. Records and documents neither lie nor change their stories, they have no axes to grind at your expense, and they can be identified in print. Many useful documents are public records, available to any citizen on request. Others are nonpublic but still may be available through your human sources.

Remember that most, if not all, of the relevant documents—especially the public records kept by government agencies—are likely to be accessible online. Google and other search engines shouldn't be your only tools, but they are powerful ones. Use them early and often. And don't overlook the revelations, some of them unintentional, that turn up on social networking services like Facebook, LinkedIn and Twitter.

Public records

You can learn a great deal about individuals and organizations through paper and electronic records. Most can be found online in nearly every jurisdiction. Some are even available for download in a file that you can import into a spreadsheet or database manager for analysis.

- **Property records.** Many investigations center on land — who owns it, who buys it, how it is zoned, how it is taxed. Your county recorder's office (or its equivalent) has on file the ownership of every piece of land in the county, as well as the history of past owners.
- **Corporation records.** Every corporation must file a document showing the officers and principal agent of the company. This document must be filed with the state in which the corporation is formed. The officers listed may be only "dummies" — stand-ins for the real owners — but this record is a start.

  Publicly held corporations must file annual reports with the Securities and Exchange Commission. The reports list officers, major stockholders, financial statements and business dealings with other companies owned by the corporation. Nonprofit corporations — such as foundations and charities — must file a Form 990 with the Internal Revenue Service. Those with annual revenues of more than $50,000 a year must show how much money came in and where it went. In many states, similar statements must be filed with the state attorneys general.

  Corporations often are regulated by state or federal agencies and file regular reports with the regulating agency. Find out which ones.

  After you have obtained corporation records, you must interpret them. Your public library has books that tell you how. Your news organization's own business experts also may be willing to help.
- **Court records.** Few people active in politics or business go through life without becoming involved in court actions of some sort. Check the offices of the state and federal court clerks for records of lawsuits. The written arguments, sworn statements and answers to questions (*interrogatories*) may contain valuable details or provide leads to follow. Has your target been divorced? Legal struggles over assets can be revealing. Probate court files of your subject's deceased associates may tell you something you need to know.
- **Campaign and conflict-of-interest reports.** Federal — and most state — campaign laws require political candidates to disclose, during and after each campaign, lists of who gave what to whom. Those filings can yield stories on who is supporting the candidates. They also can be used later for comparing who gets what from which officeholder.

  Note, however, that although individuals face limits on how much they can give directly to a political candidate, nonprofits that wish to influence politics may receive unlimited donations from individuals, corporations or other groups. The money those nonprofits spend is often called "dark money" because the nonprofits are not required to identify the donors. As of November 2018, critics and proponents of undisclosed donations were fighting over the issue in the nation's courts.

  In addition to campaign reports, many states also require officeholders to file statements of their business and stock holdings. You can check these for possible conflicts of interest or use them as background for profile stories.

- **Loan records.** Commercial lenders usually file statements showing property that has been used as security for loans. Known as *Uniform Commercial Code filings*, these can be found in the offices of state secretaries of state and sometimes in local recorders' offices.
- **Minutes and transcripts.** Most elected and appointed governing bodies, ranging from local planning and zoning commissions to the U.S. Congress, are required by law to keep minutes or transcripts of their meetings.

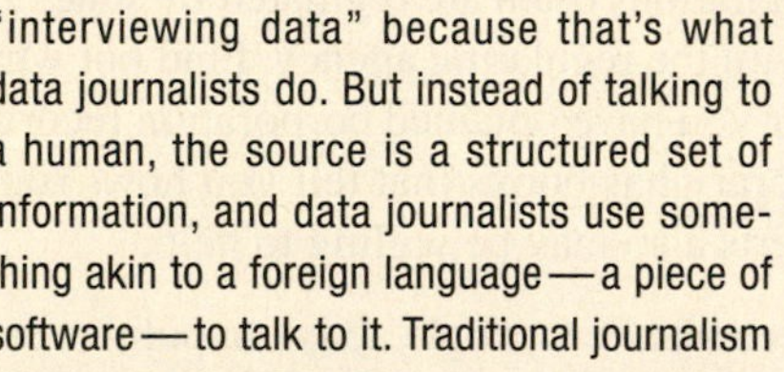

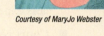

Courtesy of MaryJo Webster

As a data journalist for more than two decades, **MaryJo Webster** has seen computers become more powerful, software improve and government data become more accessible. But one thing hasn't changed: the amazing, powerful stories that are often possible only as a result of journalists doing their own data analysis.

Webster, data editor for the *Star Tribune* in Minneapolis, has used data to show that police failed to fully investigate reports of sexual assault and that laws aiming to reduce pollution from underground gasoline storage tanks were flawed. Using decades of demographic data, she also showed that Minneapolis and St. Paul schools had returned to being segregated despite integration 20 years earlier.

Webster loves that she gets to work on a wide range of stories. She covered politics while at the Center for Public Integrity, a nonprofit newsroom in Washington, D.C., then switched to sports at *USA Today*. And as the data editor for nine years at the St. Paul *Pioneer Press* and now in Minneapolis, she's worked on stories on almost every beat.

Sometimes it's serious, important stories that help change laws. Other times it's run-of-the-mill explanatory journalism. And occasionally it's something fun. One year she used demographic data for a lighthearted piece about where the best Halloween trick-or-treating might be. Another year she used historical football game prediction data to show that the Minnesota Vikings were one of the teams with a long track record of disappointing fans by losing games they were favored to win.

Analyzing data should really be called "interviewing data" because that's what data journalists do. But instead of talking to a human, the source is a structured set of information, and data journalists use something akin to a foreign language — a piece of software — to talk to it. Traditional journalism skills, including a healthy dose of skepticism, play a big role in asking good questions, interpreting the answers, and then consulting other sources to double-check the results.

Webster has also learned that analyzing data yourself, instead of relying on summarized data from a government agency, gives you more insights. It allows you to ask questions you hadn't initially thought about and can even lead you to a different story. The best part, though, is that the source you're interviewing won't kick you out of his or her office or hang up on you.

The data analysis gives the story a strong backbone to support the other reporting. For the *Star Tribune* story about police failing to investigate sexual assault cases, Webster and a team of reporters read thousands of police case files. They also built a database to document whether police had taken basic investigative steps and if the case ended in a conviction. The data showing systemic failures across police agencies, paired with powerful, heartbreaking stories from victim/survivors, resounded with readers and policymakers, who launched corrective actions within days of the first story. The victims' stories alone, without the data backbone, wouldn't have been enough.

The states and the federal government have laws designed to ensure access to public records. Many of these laws — including the federal **Freedom of Information Act**, which was passed to improve access to government records, and similar state **open-records laws** — have gaping loopholes and time-consuming review procedures. (Read more about them in Chapter 19.) Still, they have been and can be useful tools when all else fails. You can obtain information on access laws and their interpretations by contacting your state's open government group.

launchpadworks.com
WATCH: **"Shield Laws and Nontraditional Journalists"**

- Why are shield laws important to journalists and the practice of journalism? How would journalism be different without them?
- Should citizen journalists have the same shield law protections as professional journalists working for a traditional news entity? Explain.

Nonpublic records

Nonpublic records are more difficult, but often not impossible, to obtain. To get them, you must know that they exist, where they are and how to gain access. Learning those things requires good human sources. That said, here are some of the most valuable nonpublic records:

- **Investigative files.** The investigative files of law enforcement agencies can be rich in information. You are likely to see them only if you have a good source in a particular agency or one affiliated with it. If you do obtain such files, treat them cautiously. They will be full of unsubstantiated allegations, rumor and misinformation. Be wary of accepting as fact anything you have not confirmed yourself.
- **Past arrests and convictions.** Records of past arrests and convictions increasingly are being removed from public scrutiny. Usually these are easier than investigative files to obtain from friendly police or a prosecuting official. And usually these records are more trustworthy than raw investigative files.

"Spotlight" on Investigative Reporting Methods

For a realistic depiction of investigative reporting, check out the 2015 film *Spotlight*, about *The Boston Globe*'s exposé of sexual abuse by Roman Catholic priests. The movie follows members of the *Globe*'s Spotlight investigative team as the journalists document crimes against hundreds of children, crimes that were later covered up by Cardinal Bernard Law and others in the church leadership.

The movie shows how the four members of the Spotlight team methodically developed the story, initially by meeting with the leader of a group for survivors of sexual abuse by priests. Getting leads from the head of the group, a survivor himself, they slowly gather information that begins to snowball.

Reporter Matt Carroll, played by Brian d'Arcy James, has a breakthrough while looking at directories of the archdiocese of Boston to research church assignments of priests. He discovers that priests who've been removed because of sexual abuse complaints no longer have church assignments in the following year. Instead, he finds their assignments are listed cryptically, such as with the words "on leave."

Carroll, a computer-assisted reporting specialist, entered the names of the priests who had been placed on leave from 1983 to 2001 into a database, which became a key reporting tool for the team. The *Globe*'s 2002 stories won the Pulitzer Prize for public service the following year.

launchpadworks.com
WATCH: **"The Power of Images: Amy Goodman on Emmett Till"**

- It's easy to form a mental image of Emmett Till based on Goodman's description. Can you think of another historical image that is similarly powerful?
- Because they can evoke strong feelings, images can be used to persuade people. Think of a media image that changed your mind about something. Why was it effective?

- **Bank records.** Bank records would be helpful in many investigations, but they are among the most difficult types of records to get. Bankers and the government agencies that regulate banks are trained to keep secrets. A friend in a bank is an investigative reporter's friend indeed.
- **Income tax records.** Except for those made public by officeholders, income tax records are guarded carefully by their custodians. Leaks are rare.
- **Credit checks.** Sometimes you can get otherwise unavailable information on a target's financial situation if someone leaks information from a credit check. Credit reports may reveal outstanding debts, a big bank account, major assets and business affiliations. Use that information with care. It is unofficial, and companies that provide it intend it to be confidential.

Problems with written sources

Even when you can obtain them, records and other written sources can present problems. They are usually dull and unable to fill in between the lines of a given situation. Records give you names and numbers, not anecdotes or sparkling quotes. They are bare bones, not flesh and blood.

Documents and data also can be misleading and confusing. Many highly skilled lawyers and accountants spend careers interpreting the kinds of records you may find yourself pondering. Misinterpreting a document is no less serious an error than misquoting a person. And it's easier to do.

Documents usually describe without explaining. You need to know the "why" of a land transaction or a loan. Records tell you only the "what." It's important to go into these documents having done as much homework as possible beforehand. Understand what you're looking at before reporting on it.

Most investigative reporters use both human and documentary sources. People can explain what documents cannot. Documents and data can help prove what good quotes cannot. You need people to lead you to documents and data, and you need people to interpret what those mean. And you need documents and data to substantiate what people tell you. The best investigative stories combine all types of sources.

Computer-Assisted Reporting

For decades, journalists have used computers to analyze data and to create knowledge that nobody had before. Computers assist reporting in two main ways:

- Journalists can access digital information from databases on the internet. (See Chapter 3 for more about these resources and ways you can tap them.)
- Journalists can become knowledge creators by compiling and analyzing information that was previously not collected or not examined. (See Chapter 7 for more about using numbers.)

David Herzog, academic adviser to the National Institute for Computer-Assisted Reporting, teaches University of Missouri students and hundreds of practicing journalists from all over the world how to use their computers as more than word processors. His students learn how to acquire data from government agencies, nonprofit organizations and other researchers. Then they place the information into a searchable database, such as an Excel spreadsheet, so they can analyze the data. Often they match information from two or more databases to find something even policymakers didn't know. To learn more or to get help with your own reporting, go to www.ire.org/nicar. There you can benefit from computer-assisted learning.

Take, for instance, the topic of police shootings. Jo Craven McGinty was a graduate student at the University of Missouri who mastered analytic techniques and worked part time for NICAR, helping professional journalists tell statistics-based stories. She came across an FBI database on the use of weapons by police officers. When she accepted an internship at *The Washington Post*, she already had a great story idea. Months later, as part of *The Post*'s investigative team, she helped tell the story that Washington police used their guns to shoot civilians more often than police in any other city. The story won a Pulitzer Prize for *The Post*. She later joined *The Wall Street Journal*, where she writes a column, "The Numbers."

Not all computer-assisted reporting leads to Pulitzers, but much of it reveals important information that otherwise would remain hidden in bureaucratic files. Sometimes those stories are hidden in plain sight, and the data must just be appropriately configured to be understood.

Herzog also teaches computer mapping, which is the use of special software programs to display information in maps to reveal significant patterns. Crimes, for example, can be mapped to show the truly dangerous areas of a city. Outbreaks of disease can be mapped to help identify sources of infection. Patterns of immigration or unemployment or voting can be demonstrated more clearly with interactive maps than words alone could describe.

By harnessing increasingly sophisticated computers and software, traditional reporting skills and the multimedia power of the web, investigative journalists can reveal problems and spark reforms.

CHAPTER RESOURCES

SUGGESTED READINGS

Hamilton, James T. *Democracy's Detectives: The Economics of Investigative Journalism*. Cambridge: Harvard University Press, 2016. This award-winning, brilliantly researched book shows the huge economic impact investigative journalism has on society. Hamilton also includes an in-depth case study on Pat Stith, a Pulitzer Prize–winning journalist whose investigations have led to changes in North Carolina state laws.

Hersh, Seymour M. *Reporter: A Memoir*. New York: Knopf, 2018. Veteran investigative reporter Hersh reflects on his career in newspapers, magazines and books. He takes readers behind the scenes and shows how he reported some of his biggest stories.

Herzog, David. *Data Literacy: A User's Guide*. Los Angeles: Sage, 2016. This hands-on book introduces journalism students to fundamental data skills. Herzog, a professor at the Missouri School of Journalism, based the book on his experience teaching student and professional journalists.

Houston, Brant. *Computer-Assisted Reporting: A Practical Guide*. 4th ed. New York: Routledge, 2015. Houston, holder of the Knight Chair in Investigative and Enterprise Reporting at the University of Illinois, has written an invaluable how-to guide for using the newest and most powerful reporting tools.

Houston, Brant, and Investigative Reporters and Editors. *The Investigative Reporters' Handbook: A Guide to Documents, Databases and Techniques*. 5th ed. New York: Bedford/St. Martin's, 2009. This handbook tells you how to get and how to use the most important records and documents.

The IRE Journal. A publication of Investigative Reporters and Editors Inc., 141 Neff Annex, Missouri School of Journalism, University of Missouri, Columbia, MO 65211. Every issue has articles on investigations, guides to sources and documents, and a roundup of legal developments.

SUGGESTED WEBSITES

LaunchPad Solo
launchpadworks.com
When you visit LaunchPad Solo for Journalism, you will find research links, exercises and LearningCurve adaptive quizzing to help you improve your grammar and AP style usage. In addition, the site's video collection hosts the videos highlighted in this and other chapters as well as additional clips of leading professionals discussing important media trends.

www.icij.org
This site takes you to the work of the International Consortium of Investigative Journalists. The site is a great resource for examples of groundbreaking cross-border investigative projects.

www.ire.org
Begin here. Investigative Reporters and Editors, based at the University of Missouri, is the world's leading source of expertise, story ideas and professional and personal support for investigative reporters.

www.ire.org/nicar
The National Institute for Computer-Assisted Reporting, a partnership of IRE and the Missouri School of Journalism, teaches the skills and provides the consulting you'll need to get and analyze the data for richer, more revealing stories.

www.opensecrets.org
The Center for Responsive Politics specializes in collecting, analyzing and making available information on money and politics in elections for federal offices. The center's handbook, *Follow the Money*, is an invaluable resource for any reporter interested in the impact of money on self-government.

EXERCISES

1. School board member Doris Hart reported at last week's meeting of the board that major flaws, including basement flooding and electrical short circuits, have plagued the new elementary school. She noted that this is the third straight project designed by consulting architect Louis Doolittle in which serious problems have occurred. School Superintendent Margaret Smith defended Doolittle vigorously. Later, Hart told you privately that she suspects Doolittle may be paying off Smith to keep the consulting contract, which has earned the architect more than $100,000 per year for the past five years. Describe how you will investigate the following:
   a. The sniff.
   b. Human sources. Who might talk? Where should you start? Whom will you save for last?
   c. What records might help? Where are they? What will you be looking for?
   d. What is the most you can hope to prove? What is the least that will yield a story?
2. **Your journalism blog.** Use your blog to share discoveries, frustrations and lessons learned while designing your project. Invite other classmates to compare their experiences.

3. Examine three stories from MaryJo Webster's archives at the *Star Tribune* (http://m.startribune.com/index.php/maryjo-webster/303594441/). What can you learn about the stories that she's involved with, her methods and her challenges? Would you like to have a job like hers? Why or why not?

4. Go to www.ire.org, and find the stories that have won recent IRE awards. Choose one story from each of at least three categories. Compare the sources and techniques used. What similarities and differences do you find in different media? Which stories seem to you most complete and most satisfying? Why?

5. Choose a public official in your city or town, and compile the most complete profile you can, using only public records.

6. Use opensecrets.org and the computer databases described in Chapter 3 to learn as much as you can about your representative in Congress. Write the most complete investigative profile you can from the databases. In a memo, explain what additional information you'd need to complete your story and where it might be found.

7. Visit the open-data portal for the federal government (www.data.gov) and the one for your state. Identify one database on each site, and write a few paragraphs about how you could use each for further reporting.

CHAPTER 18 PUBLIC RELATIONS

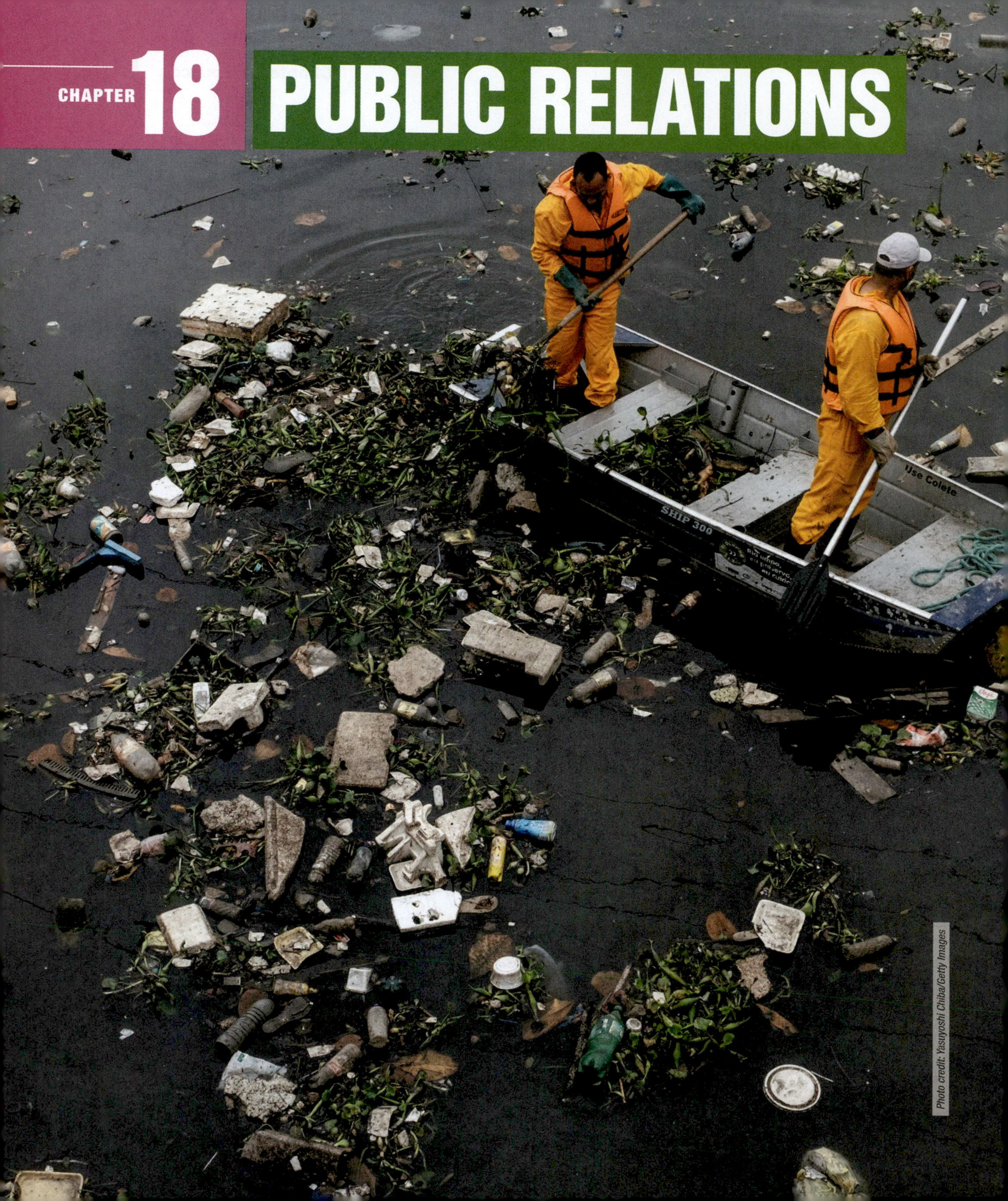

Photo credit: Yasuyoshi Chiba/Getty Images

A mountain of plastic trash the size of France is floating in the Pacific Ocean endangering and killing hundreds of species. LadBible, a social media platform aimed at young people, engaged creative agency AMV BBDO in London to take on the challenge of raising awareness of this pollution and to encourage young people to make their voices heard to the United Nations.

To highlight the problem, the agency created the the imaginary nation of Trash Isles and many of the items that a country should have: passports made of recycled materials, a flag and even an official money called "Debris." It recruited citizens and signed up celebrities: Former U.S. Vice President Al Gore became the first honorary citizen, British actor Dame Judi Dench offered to be queen, and actor and former pro wrestler Dwayne "The Rock" Johnson volunteered to be Secretary of Defense. More than 100,000 people became "citizens" in the first week of the campaign alone. It ultimately reached half a billion people and spurred a big increase in Google searches for "plastic pollution."

How did the campaign's creators do it, and why is this considered public relations? Their strategy included an impressive range of tactics using LadBible's websites, videos, social media platforms and events. They also used more traditional publicity tools to gain coverage in broadcast, digital, and print media and even sent out old-school postcards. Rather than using advertising, generally defined as paid space and time, they used public relations approaches to get the word out in an intriguing and surprising way.

The campaign won the top PR award at the Cannes Lions International Festival of Creativity. The festival is the gold standard for creative competition in the advertising world. With over 30,000 members, the Public Relations Society of America is the largest organization in the U.S. serving communication professionals and has its own awards program, the Silver Anvils. But PR was not included as a category at Cannes until 2009. For many, this new category was a proper acknowledgment of the scope and influence of PR in the 21st century. Stuart Smith, Ogilvy global PR CEO, served as the Lions jury chair in 2018 and commented in a *PRWeek* article that in the 10 years since the establishment of the Lions, the immense changes in media have made PR more relevant than ever: "We have moved from a defensive position on paid [advertising] to a more proactive stance on the central role of earned influence in building brands, enhancing reputations, and driving demand. Some would say 'everything is PR.'"

The strategies and tactics included in the Trash Isles initiative reveal that if you intend to work in any area of public relations, you need to have expertise in the ever-expanding landscape of media. This includes communicating with news, general interest and entertainment publications. Increasingly, PR also involves a broad array of direct-to-consumer approaches through social media, email marketing, content marketing, promotional events and experiences. The Trash Isles example shows how PR professionals developed a holistic approach to communicating about an environmental issue. Further, it shows how they developed specific metrics or measurements to evaluating their success.

In this chapter, you will learn:

1. How public relations differs from journalism and advertising.
2. Why message, audience and media, including social media, are important in public relations writing.
3. Why research-based public relations plans are necessary for effective messaging.
4. How to write persuasively.
5. How to write a news release that gets attention.
6. How to put together a digital news release.

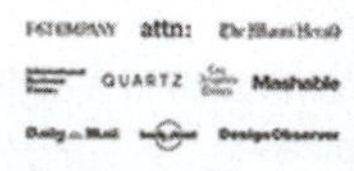

FIGURE 18.1

The "Trash Isles" campaign drew attention to a growing environmental issue in a creative way, earning a PR award.

Public Relations Skills

The "Global Communications Report 2017" put out by the University of Southern California Center for Public Relations provides the results from three surveys—one for students, one for in-house corporate executives and one for marketing professionals. The studies reveal that among PR professionals, the top required skills are strategic planning, written communication, social media, multimedia content development, verbal communications, analytics, media relations, business literacy and search engine optimization.

Many of these skills are linked. In order to write effectively and develop content, the writer needs to have insights based on research and a well-crafted plan. Today's PR pros need writing and planning skills for different media platforms tailored for different audiences.

Journalism schools traditionally require a course in news writing for students interested in public relations, and many public relations professionals like to hire people with some news writing experience. Studying news and the ways news and media organizations operate will help you be successful in public relations or in offices of public information. For example, knowing how reporters deal with news releases will help you write better releases. Studying the news and media also helps you enormously in the advertising world and in what is now frequently called *strategic marketing* or *strategic communication*.

The News Release

Not only do skilled public relations or public information practitioners know how to write news, but they also apply all the principles of good news writing in their news releases. Thus, a good news release meets the criteria of a good news story. Like a good story, it should have some staying power because organizations often keep recent news releases available on their websites.

You can see a typical news release in Figure 18.2. Notice that the release begins with the name of the organization that put out the release and includes the contact person's name, title, phone number and email address. In the past, if the news was for immediate release, the writer would say so or provide a release date. Today, however, most news releases live on organizational websites

FIGURE 18.2

A traditional news release follows AP style. Note that this release includes the line "For immediate release" at the top. The release also indicates whom to contact, and how, for more information. It also includes social media links. This release is distributed both as a PDF (shown) and in a text (HTML) version on the organization's website.

NEWS RELEASE

FOR IMMEDIATE RELEASE: December 7, 2015 No. 15-26

MEDIA CONTACT: GARY SOMERSET 202.512.1957 | **mb** 202.355.3997 | gsomerset@gpo.gov

NEW MEXICO LIBRARY JOINS GPO PROGRAM AS ALL-DIGITAL MEMBER

WASHINGTON—The U.S. Government Publishing Office (GPO) designates The Institute of American Indian Arts (IAIA), a land-grant institution of higher learning in Santa Fe, NM, as the newest all-digital member of GPO's Federal Depository Library Program (FDLP). The Institute will provide patrons with digital-only access to Federal Government publications at no cost.

###

U.S. GOVERNMENT PUBLISHING OFFICE | KEEPING AMERICA INFORMED | **OFFICIAL | DIGITAL | SECURE**

732 North Capitol Street, NW, Washington, DC 20401-0001 | **www.gpo.gov** | **www.fdsys.gov**

Follow GPO on **Facebook** http://www.facebook.com/USGPO, **Twitter** http://twitter.com/USGPO, **Pinterest** http://pinterest.com/usgpo/, and on **YouTube** http://www.youtube.com/user/gpoprinter.

and such distribution hubs as BusinessWire, IReach and PRNewswire, and tend not to have delayed release dates.

Public relations professionals also know that doing internal and external communications for an organization demands strategic planning, a specific perspective and, in many cases, a specific kind of writing. But good writing is good writing, and what you have learned so far applies to public relations writing. You also will be called on to do writing that is different from the kinds of writing journalists do.

Defining Public Relations

Rex Harlow, called by some the "father of public relations research" and perhaps the first full-time public relations educator, found 472 definitions of public relations. One definition, in use from 1982 to 2012 according to the Public Relations Society of America, was simple: "Public relations helps an organization and its publics adapt mutually to each other."

In 2012, PRSA selected this definition by a public vote: "Public relations is a strategic communication process that builds mutually beneficial relationships between organizations and their publics." Possibly the definition that best reflects today's practice is that offered by Paul Holmes, founder and chair of the Holmes group: "Public relations is the discipline of managing the relationship between an organization and the people upon whom it depends for success and with whom it interacts, and ensuring that those relationships facilitate the organization's strategic objectives."

In *Public Relations: Strategies and Tactics*, Dennis Wilcox, Glen Cameron and Bryan Reber write that these key terms are essential to understand:

- **Deliberate.** The "activity is intentional . . . designed to influence, gain understanding, provide feedback, and obtain feedback."
- **Planned.** "organized . . . systematic, requiring research and analysis."
- **Performance.** "based on actual policies."
- **Public interest.** "mutually beneficial to the organization and to the public."
- **Two-way communication.** "equally important to solicit feedback."
- **Management function.** "an integral part of decision-making by top management."

As defined by the American Marketing Association, "marketing is the activity, set of institutions, and processes for creating, communicating, delivering, and exchanging offerings that have value for customers, clients, partners, and society at large." Advertising uses paid space and time to persuade and promote a product, service or idea. Specialists in integrated marketing communication and in strategic communication develop strategies to link all of these approaches together.

Margaret Duffy, former marketing executive and executive director of the Novak Leadership Institute, says strategic communication "uses research-based evidence to create strategies and tactics aimed at achieving a desired response from a given audience. Communicators seek to maximize effects by coordinating the optimal combinations of media social digital or interpersonal tactics to accomplish organizational goals."

The "Global Communications Report 2017" found that "almost half of PR professionals and more than 60 percent of marketing executive believe that their two disciplines will become more closely aligned in the next five years." In addition, nearly nine out of 10 PR executives said that the definition of public relations would change in the next five years. It's clear that those seeking careers in PR and related fields must be avid learners who are always adapting to an ever-changing work environment.

Now that you have a broad understanding of how media professionals work, you can begin to appreciate and learn the skills and background you'll need to be successful.

A Range of Interests

If you want to write in the field of public relations, you have many choices:

- **Media relations.** Seeking publicity and answering questions posed by the media.
- **Publicity.** Working to help individuals provide opportunities through media, personal appearances and events to build their reputations and visibility.
- **Government affairs.** Spending time with legislatures and regulatory agencies, sometimes including lobbying.
- **Industry relations and trade publications.** Relating to other firms within the industry and to trade associations.
- **Investor, financial or shareholder relations.** Working to maintain investor confidence and good relationships with the financial world.
- **Research.** Conducting investigations into target audiences to discover their habits, preferences, media choices, developing insights into optimal strategies, and reporting findings.
- **Internal communication.** Creating and disseminating messages to organizational employees or members in order to inform, attract and retain staff members.
- **Philanthropy.** Writing, managing and publicizing an organization's charitable programs.
- **Social media.** Planning and executing strategies for various social media platforms.
- **Content marketing.** Creating blogs, white papers, case studies and e-books to promote an organization or cause by providing useful information to clients and potential clients.
- **Business-to-business communication.** Developing messaging and selling products and services from one business to another.
- **Owned media.** Developing strategies and messaging for organizational websites, Facebook or Instagram, Twitter, blogs and mobile sites.

- **Event planning.** Planning, proposing and executing promotional events using a variety of media and tactics.
- **Speech writing.** Researching and writing materials for delivery by key organizational members, policymakers and political candidates.
- **Account planning.** Researching and developing consumer insights, preparing creative briefs and campaign reports.
- **Crisis communication.** Preparing readiness plans and communicating swiftly and accurately to stakeholders in the event of a personnel problem, production failure, environmental issue or similar problematic situation.

As Ronald Smith explains in *Strategic Planning for Public Relations*:

> **It's no longer enough to know *how* to do things. Today, the effective communicator needs to know *what* to do, *why* and how to *evaluate* its effectiveness. Public relations professionals used to be called upon mainly for tasks such as writing news releases, making speeches, producing videos, publishing newsletters, organizing displays and so on. Now the profession demands competency in conducting research, making decisions and solving problems. The call now is for strategic communicators.**

In short, the strategic communicator must take a more scientific approach, do solid research, make careful choices and, when finished, evaluate the effectiveness of the completed program. Such a communicator would certainly be expected to write clearly and precisely, but differently from reporters.

Objectivity and Public Relations Writing

In traditional reporting, journalists strive to remain unbiased. They should not set out to prove something or to be advocates for a point of view. They should get the facts and let the facts speak for themselves.

By contrast, columnists and editorial writers do have a point of view, and good ones find ways to support it convincingly. Editorial writers use facts to persuade people to change their minds, to confirm their opinions, or to get people to do something or to stop doing something. (See Figure 1.1 in Chapter 1 for a comparison of how reporters and commentators approach accuracy, fairness and bias in writing.)

That's also what public relations writers do. Although sometimes they wish only to inform their audiences, they most often want to do what editorial writers do: persuade the audience to accept a particular position.

However, there's one major difference. News commentators serve the public. Public relations writers work for an organization or for a client other than a news operation. Their job is to serve as advocates.

But this doesn't mean that effective public relations writers should ignore facts, even when the facts are harmful or detrimental to the cause they are promoting. Because they are promoting a cause or looking out for the best interests of the people for whom they are working, however, they will generally interpret news and events through the lens of an advocate. Public relations writers work much the way attorneys work for clients. They should not lie or distort, but they might play down certain facts and emphasize others.

In its "Official Statement on Public Relations," the Public Relations Society of America says this:

> **Public relations helps our complex, pluralistic society to reach decisions and function more effectively by contributing to mutual understanding among groups and institutions. It serves to bring private and public policies into harmony. . . . The public relations practitioner acts as a counselor to management and as a mediator, helping to translate private aims into reasonable, publicly acceptable policy and action.**

The PRSA has a code of ethics for the practice of public relations. The code, given in full on its website (www.prsa.org), requires members to "adhere to the highest standard of accuracy and truth," avoiding extravagant claims or unfair comparisons and giving credit for ideas and words borrowed from others. It also requires members not to "knowingly disseminate false or misleading information." However, in today's media landscape, it is a greater challenge to win media audience's trust.

Fake News?

The use of the term *fake news* became widespread following the 2016 presidential election. Fake news is disinformation that may be partially or entirely false. It may be created to enhance or discredit individuals, political parties and organizations. It's generally presented in social media as reporting, although many fake news sites use names (like NBCNews.co) that mimic actual news sites and use URLs and graphics that copy those of the genuine site.

The phenomenon has created serious problems for news organizations because it has eroded trust in traditional media. Because today it's easy and cheap for relatively unskilled people to fabricate photos, videos and textual material, fake news can spread easily through social media: In 2018, Pew reported almost 70 percent of people in the U.S. get at least some of their news on social media.

PR professionals today must, along with their journalistic colleagues, be meticulous about their sources and confirm the accuracy of the information they provide. They must know the difference between advocacy and misinformation. This is important because it's the right thing to do, but it's also practical to keep trust in media. Distrust of media hurts PR efforts just as it hurts legitimate news.

The Main Focus of Public Relations Writing

Public relations personnel are concerned with three things: the message, the audience and the media used to deliver the message.

The Message

To be an effective public relations professional, you must know the message your organization wants to send. That message might focus on a product, a program or the organization itself. For every message you work on, you must first know what you hope to accomplish, even if your purpose is just to inform.

The Audience

As important as knowing all you can about the message is knowing the audience you're trying to reach. This research will also inform your messaging. The better you target your audience, the more effective you will be. As in advertising, the demographics and psychographics (the interests, attitudes and opinions) of your target audience determine the way you write your message, the language you choose and the simplicity or complexity of the piece you create.

Who are these people, what are their attitudes, and what do they do for work and recreation? You will answer these questions somewhat differently if you write for internal audiences (employees or managers) or external audiences (the media, shareholders, constituents, volunteers, consumers or donors).

The Media

After you have used research and insights to shape the message or campaign and targeted the audience, you have to choose the media through which to deliver that message. Research is also important in media planning because you want to use media that your target audience prefers and that can be deployed within budgets. PR isn't free. It requires investment in fact finding, audience analysis, content creation, development of metrics and coordination with other campaign elements.

Effective public relations people, like those in advertising, think in terms of campaigns and strategies. A campaign assumes that you can't tell an audience only once what you want them to learn, retain and act on. It's usually more effective to send the message in a mix of media in a carefully timed or orchestrated way. To do this, you must learn what each medium does best.

Television, radio and newsstand publications

For a message that nearly everyone wants or needs to know, television and other traditional media still might be your best medium. Although audiences' use of digital media continues to grow, even younger people spend considerably more time with ad-supported TV content on sites like Hulu and YouTube. According to the media measurement company Nielsen, the 18- to 34-year-old segment spends significantly more time with TV content, though this can often be on multiple screens (tablets and mobile phones) and may involve time shifting. This underscores the importance of learning about your targets' media choices and habits.

Radio listeners usually are loyal to one radio station. They will listen to your message over and over. The more often they hear it, the more likely they are to retain it.

Print media such as newspapers and magazines are better for complicated messages and sometimes for delicate messages. People can come back again and again to a print message. Some argue that print still has more credibility than other media despite the trend toward digital. Even though some PR professionals may not use much traditional media, it's dangerous to assume that one's own preferences apply to other audiences.

ON THE JOB A PR Storyteller and Story Miner

Courtesy of Dan Pierce

Dan Pierce's first job out of college was as a communications intern for the Cleveland Indians baseball team. Twenty years and several jobs later, he's a senior manager with General Motors' Global Connected Experience team, which tells the world about GM's Onstar safety and security system. He also is responsible for creating awareness for the technology in the company's vehicles, including "infotainment" systems and Wi-Fi.

His career path led him from sports to the global PR agency FleishmanHillard in Kansas City, where he recalls that "working in an agency opened my eyes to what PR could be. It gave me the chance to see a variety of different clients' business perspectives, including learning how important employee communication was to a firm's success."

Pierce's networks and relationships brought him to the position of director of international communications for Budweiser: "My experience with AB InBev strengthened my belief that strategies based on customer insights are at the heart of effective communication, especially when my team and I were developing campaigns for Budweiser's FIFA World Cup and the Olympics sponsorships. We really had to understand the market and consumer. This was also important when we had the challenge to launch Budweiser, a classic American brand, in places like Russia and India. We had to figure out PR ideas that could be executed globally."

When Budweiser launched in Russia, Pierce's team developed a range of approaches to tell the story, thus again highlighting the importance of shaping messages for the audience: "For this launch, we wanted to tell two different stories. The first story was business focused, with our senior executives explaining why brewing and selling Budweiser in Russia made sense to shareholders, business publications and financial analysts. The second story was consumer focused."

Because Budweiser is perceived as a premium beer outside the U.S., Pierce's team had a brewmaker work with top chefs in Russia to put on dinners for the media. The chefs included Budweiser as ingredients in each course. They also paired food with the beer to appeal to those who like fine dining and premium beers.

Pierce emphasizes how much the changing media landscape has allowed for quicker and more targeted storytelling: "We need to make sure we're finding and disseminating compelling stories, which is why the best PR people are both storytellers and story miners. For instance, we talked with a physician who trains our OnStar emergency services adviser — the employees who speak with customers involved in a crash who are waiting for first responders. We discovered that these well-trained people are being educated about how to help deliver babies, talk people through how to save someone undergoing cardiac arrest, and giving instructions on saving someone from choking. The story was front page news in the *Detroit Free Press* and widely shared on social media." (See the URL in the website listings at the end of this chapter.)

The internet: An all-in-one medium

Perhaps the best way to do public relations today is through digital media. More and more people are getting the information and products they need online — from laptops, desktop computers, smart speakers (Amazon Echo, Google Home, Sonos One), smartphones or tablets. With computers and smart devices, you gain advantages of every medium — print, video and audio — all in one.

People who spend a lot of time online generally are better educated and more affluent than those who do not. They love the control they have over the messages they find online. They can click on only the information they want, and they can do so in any order they choose. They can be involved and engaged and can respond to one another.

One challenge of digital media is the high degree of individualization. The online world is one of "mass customization." You must present the message at different levels to different people so that every person feels as if you are writing only to him or her. It's all about providing individual choices and involving your readers so they will interact with you. As opposed to "interruption marketing" (such as when an ad cuts into your game or program), good messaging provides customers with information and entertainment they will appreciate. As web usability expert Jakob Nielsen puts it, online readers are "selfish, lazy and ruthless," meaning digital consumers are able to be picky about their interactions. Successful communication online means making use of print, audio and video to get your story across. (For more about writing for the digital media, review Chapter 11.)

Social media

It's no exaggeration to say that social media have radically changed the way professionals do public relations. David Avitabile, president of JFK Communications, says, "In many ways, social media was made for public relations and vice versa." The advantages are enormous. "The ability to develop a story over time, to weave in new messages, to engage with customers in meaningful ways and respond to their feedback are all features of social media," says Avitabile.

According to recent studies, 88 percent of companies surveyed use social media outlets for PR purposes. Social media coach Sally Falkow says, "If you are looking for a job in PR or marketing, social media training and experience would be your best bet."

Tumblr, Twitter and other microblogging sites make it possible to send short text messages and internet links to large groups of subscribers instantaneously. In addition, social media giants like Facebook have the capacity to reach large groups with targeted messages.

YouTube can also be a source of attention, especially if your advertisement goes viral. In 2014, a clothing company called Wren posted a video titled "First Kiss" to YouTube. The premise of the short film was fairly simple: Twenty strangers were asked to kiss for the first time. The video quickly amassed hundreds of millions of views on the original video alone. But soon after, people learned it was actually an advertisement for a clothing company and felt deceived. However, it also boosted Wren's clothing sales shortly after and sales of the song played in the video.

All of this developed rapidly, and most experts believe that we've seen only the beginning. Print will not disappear, but the arrival of the microblog is already changing way we write nearly everything.

The Super Bowl is the largest mass audience event in the U.S. and drew more than 103 million viewers in 2018. Tide detergent's paid advertising used humor with ads that looked like traditional ads for cars, beer and deodorant but, in a twist, turned all those ads into Tide ads. For many viewers, it felt as if Tide had taken over the Super Bowl. Social media was a major component of Tide's overall campaign in extending its reach beyond traditional TV.

TIPS

Avoid Overused Words

Some PR workers consider certain words and phrases overused in news releases. Here are some examples you might want to avoid:

- Announcement
- Award-winning
- Cutting-edge
- Exciting
- Exclusive
- Groundbreaking
- Innovative
- Proactive
- Revolutionary
- Unprecedented

Alan Lin, Saatchi & Saatchi digital social director, told *AdWeek*: "Our #TideAd work on social media was not just a lift from our in-game broadcast. . . . Rather, we used the medium to comment on advertising conventions and other ads to both plant the seed that if the next ad they see has clean clothes it could be a #Tide Ad." Tide used actor David Harbour of the hit web television series *Stranger Things* as the commentator who drew all of the ads together. Social media can encourage stronger connections with audiences because the messages feel more personal, and people can participate by commenting, retweeting and even creating funny memes.

The streaming music service Spotify devised an imaginative paid+social strategy with its 2018 New Year's Resolution campaign. Using data gathered from Spotify listener habits, the promotional team took insights and turned them into clever and sometimes provocative headlines for billboard ads: "Be as humble as the person who got an entire billboard for listening to HUMBLE. 1251 times. *Spotify*." And "Exercise more conventionally than the 46 people who put 'slow hands' on their running playlists. *Spotify*."

Spotify CMO then Seth Farbman said, "Out-of-home gives that hyperlocality that gives those 'aha' moments to people. And it allows the digital community to feel connected in a physical way This is happening here, we're all seeing this and remembering this moment together." Another aspect offered cutouts, shapes, images and letters that extend beyond the traditional shape of a billboard. This campaign featured musicians like Bruno Mars pictured with a vintage car, champagne and lobster, and read, "Be something that Bruno Mars likes." The campaign went full circle from online data to outdoor media to social media. Musicians and listeners took selfies of billboards and shared them on social media. The integration of all of these elements illustrates how carefully using multiple touchpoints can amplify the effect of a promotion.

Internal publications, brochures and signage

As with any effective PR effort, internal communication requires research and thoughtful strategies to be effective. In addition, studies show that fostering a positive culture is crucial to the long-term success of an organization. David Novak is co-founder and retired CEO of YUM! Brands (KFC, Pizza Hut and Taco Bell), one of the world's largest restaurant chains. Novak, credited with creating record profits through a culture of positive energy and recognition at YUM!, believes that effective communication is at the heart of any organization's success. In particular, he says that a people-first culture that celebrates employee accomplishments and offers recognition is crucial. Internal communication plays a central role in this.

It's also important to use the right tools and methods: You can't communicate everything, and different employee audiences often require different approaches. U.S. Army leadership at Fort Leonard Wood in Missouri recognized that traditional communication channels were not as effective as they should be and asked strategic communication researchers at the Missouri School of Journalism to conduct a communication audit and recommend best practices for enlisted soldiers and officers, staff and family members. With that information, the commanding general and staff were able to reallocate their resources, improve information dissemination and increase esprit de corps.

Insurance giant USAA learned through research that its 30,000 employees had only eight minutes each day to devote to news and information about the firm.

As reported by *PRWeek*, communicators developed five strategy guidelines—listen, collaborate, simplify, target and engage. Important tactics included reimagining its social engagement program and refocusing its communication team. The company saw an increase of almost 9 percent in employees' consumption and understanding of essential company information.

Many corporations are now communicating with employees throughout the day using various online services and apps accessible only to employees. For messages that need more explanation or study, such as health care matters, sometimes a printed brochure or printable PDF will do the job best. Company chat software (such as Slack and Yammer) or proprietary platforms are also possibilities.

Internal communicators will also want to strike the right tone for messaging. Avoid dull and preachy. Use conversational language, and build in fun where it's appropriate. Today's audiences are also conditioned to expect channels for

ON THE JOB Building Authentic Relationships

Courtesy of Alexis Johnson

Ten days after she graduated from college in 2015, **Alexis Johnson** flew to Los Angeles to become an intern at Ketchum, a global public relations agency and communication consultancy. This began her path in the PR world and was followed by a stint at the NFL's digital properties promoting a range of media programs and events. She then moved to Complex Media, which was founded as a magazine and has evolved into a broad portfolio of digital brands, videos, hosted shows, viral web series and other pop culture–oriented content.

Johnson explains: "We're the leading youth culture brand that embraces music, fashion, food, cultural trends and celebrity news. I promote all the original content that comes out of Complex Networks. For example, 'Sneaker Shopping' is a web series featuring celebrities like Kevin Hart, Lakeith Stanfield and Charlize Theron shopping for shoes." Complex.com's programming attracts more than 50 million unique visitors a month.

Her responsibilities involve obtaining publicity through press tours, television interviews, and placements on late night and daytime television programs and elevating the profiles of internal talent. Social media are major tools for influencing and offering information. "Performing on social media is crucial," Johnson says, "and we closely monitor the metrics on what's effective and how we can develop our strategies for future efforts. This means we need to set clear goals for what we want to accomplish."

Complex.com's offerings are youthful, brash and trendy, but many of Johnson's responsibilities will sound familiar to other public relations professionals publicizing more traditional offerings: "Mostly my work involves media relations and communicating with carefully targeted lists of outlets and reporters. Even in this digital world, much of my work is developing relationships and often meeting with reporters in person to better understand their interests and needs."

Johnson's job begins with conducting research on publications, publishers and reporters. She pores over archives to discover writers' preferred subjects, tones and styles. She also searches Twitter and other media to learn reporters' beliefs and attitudes about PR, their preferred means of communication and even their pet peeves.

Her advice to aspiring PR people? "The No. 1 skill? Write well! Write as if you're the reporter. Those writing skills, spelling, grammar and accuracy, are crucial. Make sure it's right: It's better to be right than first."

Johnson says it's not all glamorous: "While events and celebrities may be exciting, it's important to be patient and present in the work you're doing—actually doing the work, not just talking about it."

feedback. That feedback can give communicators vital information on what's resonating and what isn't. Lastly, emphasize recognition for jobs well done. Research commissioned by Novak's new venture, oGolead, found that more than 80 percent of people don't feel recognized by their supervisors for their work, 60 percent reported they value recognition as much as compensation, and 40 percent say they would put more effort into their work if they received more recognition.

Persuasive Writing

Most of the time in PR writing, you will write to try to persuade people. To succeed, you must study the techniques of persuasion and use them carefully. Before going further, it's important to explore persuasion itself and situate it as a communication element.

Your Attitude

To persuade people ethically, you need to believe three things:

- **People are essentially good.** If you are convinced of this, you will appeal to people's basic goodness and fairness.
- **People are intelligent and can learn.** Don't talk down to people. Don't assume that you can trick or fool them. But also don't assume that because they are intelligent and educated, they know the subject matter as well as you do. Never underestimate the intelligence of your audience, and never overestimate what they know. A college professor with a Ph.D. in philosophy might be brilliant in that field but know nothing about the financial markets.
- **People are changeable, and you can gain their attention and acceptance.** You can use effective and ethical strategies to increase awareness of your product, service, or idea; to shape attitudes; and even to encourage certain types of actions. Henneke Duistermaat, writing expert, shared her best tips in *Inc.* magazine. She says writing persuasively begins with developing a clear objective regarding what you hope to accomplish: "From there, work backwards. Think about what objections you need to overcome, what questions you need answered, and what you need to do to make the reader [or viewer] believe you."
- The best persuasive writers, like the best salespeople, are good listeners. They listen to how their audiences describe their challenges, wants and worries. They use words and phrases that are familiar to audiences and address their concerns. A good writer is empathetic and authentically seeks to understand other's points of view and see things from their perspective.

Duistermaat also highlights the importance of communicating the benefits of what you're trying to communicate rather than the features of a product, service or idea. For example, a pair of red rubber boots has features of having a certain color, being made of a particular material and being footwear. The benefits of red rubber boots might be dry feet and a perhaps a fashion statement.

How does this translate to PR writing? Let's assume you've been tasked with helping raise awareness of a new incentive-based wellness program at your company with the goal of increasing participation, improving health, and reducing sick days and employee illness.

You'd want to start with data about your employees and conduct qualitative and quantitative research to learn their perceptions and behaviors: How do they perceive their current health? What diet and exercise activities do they engage in? What barriers do they face in adopting more healthful behaviors? What incentives or rewards are the most appealing?

From there, you'd think about the features of the new plan — a $450 annual reward for completing certain activities, group wellness programs, cooking classes, a varied menu of ways to gain rewards.

The next step is dramatizing the benefits, which could include an employee's ideas about how she might spend her rewards, the fun in meeting new people and socializing, or the enjoyment of learning new recipes and sharing with friends. The persuasive writer would prioritize those benefits and possibly segment them for different employee audiences.

Credibility and Trust

More than anything else, you need to establish and maintain your credibility and the credibility of the organization you represent. Aristotle wrote that the character of the speaker is the most essential and powerful component of persuasion. Without a doubt, character is the most important attribute public relations people need to have and to develop. A sterling reputation takes a long time to build, and it can be lost in an instant. Journalists and audiences will trust you if you tell the truth even when there is difficult news about your organization.

It's easy to become frustrated when audiences don't respond positively to your messages, and it's tempting to lash out. But you can't persuade people by insulting them or by calling them names. It isn't useful to view a client or the public as your enemy. This is particularly true regarding your attitude toward journalists. For some public relations professionals, members of the press are the enemy, are not to be trusted with the truth and need to be stonewalled at every opportunity. This can

Six Alternatives to Sending a News Release

PR professional Claire Celsi, the Public Relations Princess, suggests you write a news release to gather your thoughts but then not send it. Instead, do one of the following:

- Send an email pitch. More than 90 percent of reporters say they want email pitches.
- Post on a website.
- Send a tweet.
- Send a Facebook message.
- Call.
- Offer to meet the reporter for coffee if you're in the same city.

work in the short term, but it rarely is a good long-term strategy. Journalists and PR professionals are members of the same team when it comes to getting information out to an audience; a little mutual respect can take you a long way.

News Releases That Get Attention

News releases, whether in traditional, social or digital forms, are still the staple for most PR campaigns. In an article titled "Not So Fast" on WiredPen.com, Kathy Gill wrote, "What press releases — or blog posts — can do is provide an accessible back story that cannot or will not be included in a 30-second TV news story or a six-column-inch news story. One thing tweets do well is provide a link to more detailed information: the press release, whether its form is a classic release or the modern blog post."

A 2014 "Disrupting the Press Release" study by Green Target surveyed 100 journalists and conducted a series of focus groups with reporters and editors in Chicago and New York. It found that 41 percent of journalists considered news releases "sometimes valuable," 25 percent "valuable," and 22 percent "very valuable." That means 88 percent of journalists find value in news releases.

Journalists indicated that the news releases had three seconds to get their attention, and nearly 70 percent said they spent less than one minute reading them. Not surprisingly — but seldom seen in news releases — 53 percent of the journalists said they would find it helpful if the key information would be presented in the form of bullet points. Another 36 percent were open to the idea, 68 percent want only the facts, and 79 percent say a good subject line gets them to open your news release.

Even the smallest newspaper or radio or television station gets dozens of news releases weekly. Myriads of print and electronic publications such as those in the American Business Media and the Specialized Information Publishers Association also receive dozens of public relations releases weekly. Most releases are now sent electronically or through public relations wire services.

Regardless of how you send your news, your problem is still the same: How do you break through the clutter and attract the attention of the gatekeepers at these publications? Here are some guidelines to help you get your message to your intended audience.

Know What News Is and How to Write It

The news media will not pay attention to puffery — copy that's full of exaggerations or self-serving quotations. They might make fun of your work and discard it immediately. Even worse, they may save it, as several journalists have, on a "wall of shame." Avoid statements such as, "Moonfield College is recognized as the foremost and most prestigious college of liberal arts in the entire Midwest." Who says?

To write for most publications, certainly for news media and the majority of print and electronic publications, you need to know Associated Press style. (See Appendix 2 for a summary of the style that is followed by most news publications.) Correct spelling, usage and grammar are essential, but adhering to AP style is just

What's the grammar error in this sentence?

New York hedge fund manager Martin Shkreli increased the price of his newly-acquired drug, Daraprim, by 5,455 percent.

See Appendix 1, Rule 11.

as important. Why should news editors take you seriously if you don't bother to write in the style of their publications? That includes knowing how to write in the inverted pyramid format (see Chapter 8). Later in this chapter you will learn different approaches to writing news releases.

Some newspapers and magazines have their own stylebooks. Quite a few magazines follow *The Chicago Manual of Style*. Be sure you know which rules to follow.

Know the Structure and Operations of Newsrooms

If you don't get experience in a television, radio, newspaper or convergence newsroom in college, find other ways to spend some time in at least one of these. Use your public relations skills to get inside and experience what goes on there.

The simplest and most important thing you can learn about newsrooms is that they have deadlines. Learn the deadlines of the media in your area, and respect them. This means that you should not call in a story to a television news station a half-hour before airtime. Not only will the station not use your story, but frustrated station employees won't forget the interruption at a critical time. News organizations will tell you the time for submitting a story to make the news that day.

Be sure that you make yourself available — in person, online, or by phone, email or text — 24 hours a day. Nothing is more important for a public relations practitioner. A reporter on deadline will write the story with or without you. It's *always* best that you talk to the reporter.

> **"Employers want people who can write and communicate ideas — who can pull complex or fragmented ideas together into coherent messages. This requires not only technical skill but also intelligence. It also requires a love of writing."**
>
> ■ Thomas H. Bivins, *Public Relations Writing: The Essentials of Style and Format*

Know the People in the News Media and the Jobs They Hold

It's especially important to know who does what at the newspapers you contact. Sending a release addressed simply to a newspaper can be a waste of time and make you look as if you do not know what you are doing. Sending a release to the business editor or to the features editor makes more sense. Addressing the editor of the section in which you wish the story to appear works best.

Read what Chris Anderson, former editor-in-chief of *Wired* magazine, had to say on this subject in his blog:

> **Sorry, PR people: you're blocked.**
>
> **I've had it. I get more than 300 e-mails a day and my problem isn't spam . . . it's PR people. Lazy flacks send press releases to the Editor in Chief of *Wired* because they can't be bothered to find out who on my staff, if anyone, might actually be interested in what they're pitching. . . . So fair warning: I only want two kinds of e-mail: those from people I know, and those from people who have taken the time to find out what I'm interested in and composed a note meant to appeal to that (I love those e-mails; indeed, that's why my e-mail address is public).**

If the people to whom you send news releases know and trust you, they are more likely to pay attention to your releases. Sometimes you can call them with a story idea and let them write their own stories. There's nothing writers like more than to get wind of good stories. Remember, your job is to help reporters write good stories. If you can help them do that and at the same time serve your client's interests, you will be a successful public relations practitioner.

Know the Style of Writing That Fits the Medium

Do not make the mistake of sending to a radio or television station the same news release that you send to a newspaper. Do not expect busy journalists to translate your newspaper release into broadcast copy. If you can write radio or television copy (see Chapter 12), you have a much better chance of getting the copy read over the air. Remember, too, that writing for digital media (see Chapter 11) differs from writing for print.

In our social media world, sometimes you can tweet a news release. Your headline must inform and grab, but keep it well below 280 characters so that people can retweet it with a brief comment.

Become acquainted with Google AdWords, Google Insights, Keyword Discovery and Wordtracker for help with choosing the right words. Vanessa Bugasch, of the PR software and services company Cision, warns against overlinking, which might cause confusion. But she does advise writers to use one or two keywords in the headline or subhead. She tells us that using them in the first two paragraphs has more impact than placing them lower in the release and cites research that shows that news releases "with pictures, video and other multimedia get at least 80 percent more search traffic than text-only releases."

According to MediaPost, firms often use influencer media packages in order to gain airtime on broadcast news programming. These are similar to video news releases, which were both popular and controversial. Just as some newspapers will use your news releases almost verbatim — some have sections of verbatim releases about events, promotions and so on — some radio and television stations will use your audio and video releases without editing them.

Doug Simmons, president of a video communications firm, told Media Post that his company provides free video to television stations and provides the example of a client presenting new guidelines for treating low back pain. The package included B-roll footage (supplementary video that news organizations can edit for their needs), sound bites, and a more highly produced video story. Simon reported that the package resulted in 638 broadcasts in local and major network shows.

Influencer packages tend not to have publicists posing as reporters, but the practice remains controversial in that it appears to most viewers as if the on-air piece were the result of independent reporting, not a PR effort.

Know How to Distribute Information Online

Not even the largest newspapers or radio or television networks can reach as many people as digital media can. With millions of websites, there are practically no limits to the audiences that can be reached on the internet. First, you must establish your own credible, up-to-date, interactive website. Second, you must be thoroughly familiar with websites such as Definition6 and PR Newswire so that you can distribute your releases online and keep up with what's happening in public relations. Third, you must become expert at using digital media to get across your organization's messages (see Chapter 11).

Digital News Releases

To be effective in their jobs, writers of news releases need to learn all the techniques that journalists use in writing news stories. The straight, no-nonsense inverted pyramid news release remains the staple of the public relations professional. Some believe that news professionals will not take any other approach seriously. (See Chapter 8 for more on the inverted pyramid.)

Despite the continued use of traditional news releases, today's savvy public relations professionals are sending social media news releases. Here are some of the steps, summarized and condensed, that digital PR expert Sally Falkow recommends for successful social media news releases:

- Write a short, concise headline.
- Answer the five W's in the first paragraph.
- List the core news facts in bullet points.
- Add approved quotes.
- Write the rest in narrative form; use relevant keywords so that journalists and others can find the release through search engines or social sites.
- Add links to research, facts, statistics or trends.
- Include an original, high-quality image that tells the story.
- Provide the source URL for the image so that bloggers and journalists can use it easily and quickly.
- Add more images, icons and, if possible, a short video, plus more supporting materials, such as charts and infographics.
- Provide an embed code with these items so that they can be easily republished. (An embed code acts like a link to video content.)
- Add the "About Us" boilerplate and contact person.
- Make the release available in an RSS news feed.
- Add sharing buttons so that the release can be shared through social networking sites.

Study the annotated model "Social Media News Release" for an example. Notice how the information leaps out at you, and note how many choices the release gives the readers and how many connections it provides.

The social media news release has changed the way public relations professionals think about doing news releases. And social media have changed the way they think about doing public relations.

What Professionals Look for When Hiring a PR Person

- Kindness
- Creativity
- Passion
- Hustle
- Smarts

■ Kathleen Henson, PR News

Some Final Advice

In addition to writing news releases, public relations professionals are involved with many other important functions that increase the value of public relations, including planning and carrying out successful news conferences and dealing with the foreign press.

You might be hired to be a speechwriter or to do something as specialized as write an organization's annual report. Corporations and institutions such as hospitals and universities hire thousands of communicators to get their messages out to the public. Or you might work for an agency hired to do this work for organizations. Many people make a good living working out of their homes for just a half dozen or fewer clients. No matter where you work, public relations demands that you never stop developing your skills and continuing your education.

Jon Cook is global chief executive of VMLY&R, one of the top full-service marketing communication agencies in the world with more than 7,000 employees. He notes that the traditional labels of PR and advertising are becoming less relevant: "At VMLY&R, we're working with some of the most iconic and vibrant brands. But we're not just doing 'advertising' or 'PR.' We're working in virtual reality, engaging with internet influencers, using smart speaker technology, and even producing original music. For Wendy's we created a hip-hop mix tape that made Spotify's global viral 50 rating and reached No. 3 on Apple Music hip-hop charts. We got great social traction and word-of-mouth."

Cook points out that while a hip-hop tape isn't traditional PR writing, the project is relevant because it emphasizes the importance of research, clear messaging, creativity and effective methods of reaching a target audience: "With every project, we're creating a connected brand and memorable consumer experiences. We plan, write and create with three major goals in mind: first, to inspire prospective customers and raise awareness for the brand. Second, we discover ways to engage customers and lead them to a purchase. Third, once they've enjoyed our product, we find ways to keep them involved through messaging, loyalty programs and subscriptions."

Cook advises that an aspiring PR professional should "show up and follow up." He explains that this goes beyond working on an assignment: "Make your mark. Be as prepared as possible and develop a reputation for being the one who shows up. People will know that as the result of your contributions, better things happen and you bring out the best in others. 'Following up' means that you see things through and continue to take action. Whether you're an intern or a CEO, the advice is the same: no matter your profession or your job, there's always an opportunity to go one step further."

CHAPTER RESOURCES

SUGGESTED READINGS

Bivins, Thomas H. *Public Relations Writing: The Essentials of Style and Format*. 8th ed. New York: McGraw-Hill, 2013. Bivins covers the wide variety of writing expected of public relations professionals.

Brown, Rob. *Public Relations and the Social Web: How to Use Social Media and Web 2.0 in Communications*. Philadelphia: Kogan Page, 2009. This book discusses the whole range of social media, including social media releases, Twitter and wikis.

Carnegie, Dale. *How to Win Friends and Influence People*. Rev. ed. New York: Pocket Books, 1982. The classic: absolutely guaranteed worthwhile reading for anyone in public relations.

Howard, Carole, and Wilma Mathews. *On Deadline: Managing Media Relations*. 5th ed. Prospect Heights, Ill.: Waveland Press, 2013. This excellent practical book shows how organizations should deal with the news media.

Lattimore, Dan, Otis Baskin, Suzette Heiman and Elizabeth Toth. *Public Relations: The Profession and the Practice*. New York: McGraw-Hill, 2011. This good survey is divided into four parts covering the profession, the process, the publics and the practice.

Newsom, Doug, and Jim Haynes. *Public Relations Writing: Form and Style*. 9th ed. Belmont, Calif.: Wadsworth, 2010. A truly thorough classic, this book even has a section on grammar, spelling and punctuation.

Novak, David. *Taking People with You*. Penguin: New York. 2011. Former CEO of YUM! Brands, Novak leadership lessons are rooted in principles of strategic communication. For aspiring leaders or PR people, a valuable read.

Ogilvy, David. *Ogilvy on Advertising*. Toronto: John Wiley, 1983. Get a copy, and read it. A must.

Phillips, David, and Philip Young. *Online Public Relations: A Practical Guide to Developing an Online Strategy in the World of Social Media*. 2nd ed. Philadelphia: Kogan Page, 2009. The authors discuss many new ways for creative people to reach large audiences.

Reis, Al, and Jack Trout. *Positioning: The Battle for Your Mind*. New York: McGraw-Hill, 2000. The simple advice that told industry that, to be successful, all it had to do was to find its niche. A classic that you will use and never forget.

Scott, David Meerman. *The New Rules of Marketing and PR: How to Use Social Media, Online Video, Mobile Applications, Blogs, News Releases and Viral Marketing to Reach Buyers Directly*. 6th ed. Wiley, 2017. Although the media landscape is dynamic, the advice in this book will remind PR professionals of the array of tools and strategies at their disposal.

Smith, Ronald. *Strategic Planning for Public Relations*. New York: Routledge, 2009. This book explains the shift from public relations to strategic communications.

Wilcox, Dennis L., Glen T. Cameron and Bryan H. Reber. *Public Relations: Strategies and Tactics*. 11th ed. Boston: Allyn & Bacon, 2014. These outstanding professors keep you up-to-date in the field.

SUGGESTED WEBSITES

LaunchPad Solo

launchpadworks.com

When you visit LaunchPad Solo for Journalism, you will find research links, exercises, and LearningCurve adaptive quizzing to help you improve your grammar and AP style usage. In addition, the site's video collection hosts the videos highlighted in this and other chapters as well as additional clips of leading professionals discussing important media trends.

www.freep.com/story/money/cars/general-motors/2018/07/03/onstar-number-service-emergency/735619002/

Here is the *Detroit Free Press* story on the coaching provided to the people who answer OnStar emergency calls. It is cited in the "On the Job" box on Dan Pierce in this chapter.

www.instituteforpr.org
This website offers information about public relations research, measurement, programs, seminars, publications, scholarship and so on from the Institute for Public Relations, which explores "the science beneath the art of public relations."

www.odwyerpr.com
On this website, you can also find *O'Dwyer's PR Report*, an excellent monthly publication that devotes each issue to a public relations specialty field. This independent publication (and its website) is often highly critical of the profession.

www.prsa.org
The website of the Public Relations Society of America has general information about the society, lists its chapters and sections, and offers information on publications, membership and accreditation, recognition and awards, conferences and seminars.

www.prwatch.org
This website, from the Center for Media and Democracy, investigates "public relations spin and propaganda." It sends out more than 1,000 news releases each day.

http://www.tbrandstudio.com
Promoted as "stories that influence the influencers," TBrand studio is the marketing arm of the *New York Times* and creates content likely to appeal to the publication's readers. Although its stories are intended to look like interesting feature stories, they are "branded content" that clients pay for. Each story leads with the notice that the story is "paid for and posted by [client]." Clients often expect that readers will share positive stories through their social networks.

EXERCISES

1. Imagine that a classmate is killed in a car accident. A small amount of money is donated to start a scholarship to honor his memory, but much more is needed to endow the scholarship. Several students who have been training to run in the Chicago Marathon decide to solicit money for each mile the runners complete. The proceeds will help support the scholarship. You decide to get involved. How would you advise them?
   a. Who is your target audience or audiences? How would you conduct research about them?
   b. Which medium would be most effective in reaching your audience?
   c. How will you make use of social media throughout your fundraising campaign?
   d. Write a detailed report of your plan.
2. **Your journalism blog.** On your blog, write a post explaining why you would like to work in public relations—or why you would not.
3. Visit with your college sports information director. Interview him about the most difficult aspects of his job. Write a report.
4. Interview a student from a small town. Then write a news release about his or her life and activities at the university, and email it to the town's newspaper.
5. Visit a local hospital. Interview the head of public relations there about their responsibilities. Write a story that includes anecdotes and stories that the person shared with you.

CHAPTER 19 MEDIA LAW

Photo credit: Guy Cali/Getty Images

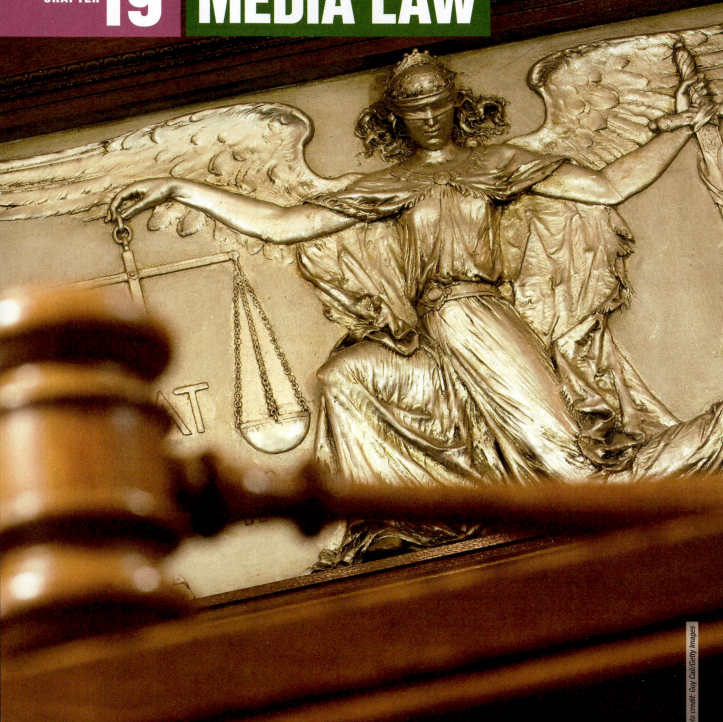

Thomas Jefferson famously wrote, "[W]ere it left to me to decide whether we should have a government without newspapers or newspapers without a government, I should not hesitate a moment to prefer the latter." Journalism is the lifeblood of democracy. The press seeks to hold the powerful accountable, inform citizens of the important news of the day, create forums for public debate and be a mirror for society to reflect on itself. To help the press realize these goals, the Founders drafted the First Amendment to the U.S. Constitution, which reads as follows:

> **Congress shall make no law respecting an establishment of religion, or prohibiting the free exercise thereof; or abridging the freedom of speech, or of the press; or the right of the people peaceably to assemble, and to petition the Government for a redress of grievances.**

But not all media law is rooted in the First Amendment. For example, as we will see later in this chapter, state and federal statutes govern access to government documents. Also, the U.S. Supreme Court did not interpret the First Amendment as affording broad freedoms to the press across the country until the 1930s. Upholding exceptional protection for freedom of the press against the weighty interests of national security, defamation of character and protection of privacy is an even more recent phenomenon.

In this chapter, we give you a brief overview of some of the major legal issues involving freedom of the press in the United States. We also point to the limits of First Amendment freedoms and offer important tips on how to avoid problems related to defamation, privacy and copyright. Our goal is to increase your awareness and appreciation for the laws that protect your valuable job and to give you a working knowledge of how to use these laws to your advantage as you set out in your journalism endeavors.

In this chapter, you will learn:

1. What rights you have as a journalist under the First Amendment and why you have them.
2. How to spot potentially libelous situations and what to do about them.
3. When you might be invading someone's privacy.
4. What kinds of problems you may face when protecting confidential sources.
5. What rights you have when obtaining access to courtrooms.
6. What rights you have to government documents and strategies for obtaining them.
7. What you should know about copyright and fair use.

First Amendment Theory: The "Why"

Before we address *how* the First Amendment protects (or doesn't protect) journalists, it is important to understand *why*, especially when more and more people say they don't trust journalists or they believe journalists are detrimental to society. Philosophers and legal scholars have given us several reasons for providing the press with exceptional legal protections for its work.

For instance, Alexander Meiklejohn (1872–1964), an American political philosopher, famously wrote in a 1948 book that the ultimate purpose of the First Amendment was that "everything worth saying shall be said" and that the most important site of First Amendment activity was not in the mouths of speakers but rather in the minds of hearers. According to Meiklejohn, the First Amendment protects freedom of speech and press so that citizens can make sound, rational and educated decisions when voting. That sounds easy enough.

What's the grammar error in this sentence?

Pakistani human rights activist Malala Yousafzai was almost killed by a Taliban assassin in October 2012; but she remains a dedicated advocate for girls' education.

See Appendix 1, Rule 9.

However, there is a lot of disagreement among journalists, scholars and judges about how law and policy should best facilitate a free and robust press. Is it constitutional for the government to implement policies that boost ownership of broadcast licenses among people of color, with the goal of ensuring that listeners get multiple perspectives about the news, even if it impinges on the rights of potential white owners? The Supreme Court said yes in *Metro Broadcasting v. FCC* (1990). Does the First Amendment allow "right of reply" laws that require newspapers to publish pieces written by political candidates in response to critical editorials, thereby ensuring voters receive multiple perspectives about a candidate? The Supreme Court said no in *Miami Herald v. Tornillo* (1974).

According to legal scholar Vincent Blasi, freedom of speech, freedom of the press and freedom of assembly share the common value of checking government power. His idea is known as the "checking value" theory of the First Amendment. Journalists know this phenomenon as their essential role of being a "watchdog" that holds government accountable. Blasi argues that journalism's ability to check power should become a (if not *the*) key piece in crafting First Amendment doctrine for all journalistic activities. For instance, according to Blasi's "checking value" theory, journalists would have a First Amendment right to refuse to reveal their anonymous sources before a grand jury. Under the theory, you would also have a *constitutional* right to access government information as opposed to less powerful rights set up by the federal Freedom of Information Act and state sunshine laws. So far, Blasi's theory has not been popular among judges. However, it remains a favorite theory among journalists because it holds journalism as playing an essential role in democracy.

The most common theory that judges rely on when deciding cases of press freedom is the "marketplace of ideas" theory. According to this theory, both freedom of speech and freedom of the press are instrumental in leading citizens to an understanding of truth. Marketplace theory sees individuals as rational beings who, when presented with a broad spectrum of ideas, can use reason to decide which ideas are valid and true. Restrictions by the government on which ideas can enter the marketplace violate that sense of reason, and so the First Amendment is needed to prevent government from imposing restrictions on ideas, both spoken and published.

Ultimately, no one theory can capture the complexity of the First Amendment. Courts often cite multiple (and sometimes contradicting) theories when crafting rulings. The theories discussed here are significant, but they are by no means exhaustive. Nevertheless, understanding theory is important for journalists. It is not enough to answer critics of the press with "Well, the First Amendment protects journalists." Journalists need to be armed with "the why."

Freedom from Prior Restraint

In 1931, the U.S. Supreme Court held for the first time in a narrow 5-4 decision that government attempts to censor the press are presumed unconstitutional under the First Amendment. The case, *Near v. Minnesota*, involved a rabble-rousing "journalist" named Jay Near and accusations he made in his weekly newspaper that officials in St. Paul were in cahoots with gangsters in trafficking bootlegged liquor through the Twin Cities. Claiming the accusations were false, the St. Paul officials tried to force Near to stop publishing. In holding city officials' censorship of Near unconstitutional, the Supreme Court redefined the law of prior restraint in the United States. Essentially, the court said that government attempts to stop the press from publishing, even if the press's stories were libelous or involved sensitive information, were forbidden under the First Amendment.

> **"The Government's power to censor the press was abolished so that the press would remain forever free to censure the Government."**
>
> ■ **Justice Hugo Black, concurring opinion in *New York Times Co. v. United States* (1971), the Pentagon Papers case**

In 1971, the Supreme Court decided another landmark case involving prior restraint: *New York Times v. United States* (also known as the Pentagon Papers case). On June 13, 1971, *The New York Times* published its first story involving classified documents that it had received from Daniel Ellsberg, a fellow at the RAND Corp. The documents dealt with U.S. political and military activity in Vietnam in the two decades leading up to the Vietnam War. The Nixon administration tried to prevent *The Times* (and later *The Washington Post*) from publishing any further stories involving the documents. It argued that the 1917 Espionage Act gave the government the power to restrain further publication because publication of the documents would threaten national security. The newspapers argued that this attempt to censor them was unconstitutional.

Relying on precedent from *Near* (**precedent** involves past decisions that courts rely on to decide cases currently before them), the court ruled 6-3 that the government's attempt to censor publication of the Pentagon Papers violated the First Amendment. It held that such prior restraints could be justified only if the government could prove publication would lead directly to "irreparable harm," such as loss of life, serious injury or serious, warlike destruction. That is a high—perhaps even impossible—bar for the government to reach. The Pentagon Papers case was a resounding victory for freedom of the press. As Justice Hugo Black put it in his concurring opinion:

> **In the First Amendment, the Founding Fathers gave the free press the protection it must have to fulfill its essential role in our democracy. The press was to serve the governed, not the governors. The Government's power to censor the press was abolished so that the press would remain forever free to censure the Government. The press was protected so that it could bare the secrets of government and inform the people. Only a free and unrestrained press can effectively expose deception in government.**

Defamation

Suing a person for a civil wrong like **defamation** (damage to one's reputation) or invasion of privacy (to be discussed later) is seen as a more appropriate solution than prior restraint for alleged harms caused by publication. In other words, let journalists publish, but let them also understand the legal risks of publishing a story. Fortunately, journalists enjoy strong protection under the First Amendment when faced with defamation lawsuits. This protection comes from another landmark U.S. Supreme Court case: *New York Times v. Sullivan* (1964).

At the height of the civil rights movement of the 1950s and 1960s, newspapers in large northern cities often published editorials and ran advertisements that denounced Jim Crow segregation laws in the South. They encouraged their readers to support the fight for racial equality by donating money and helping African-Americans register to vote in the South. In March 1960, *The New York Times* ran a full-page ad titled "Heed Their Rising Voices" to drum up this kind of support. The ad also accused police of locking African-American students inside a school cafeteria in Montgomery, Alabama, and stated that Martin Luther King Jr. had been arrested seven times on false charges. The ad was paid for by members of a committee helping King with his legal defense.

There were a few problems with the ad, however. The students had never been locked inside a cafeteria, although the Montgomery police had subjected them to other brutal treatment, and King had been arrested four times, not seven. Seizing on these factual inaccuracies, Montgomery's police commissioner, L.B. Sullivan, who was not directly named in the ad, sued *The Times* for defamation. At this time, defamation had a "strict liability" standard, meaning that to win a defamation case, a person had to show only that (1) the story was false and (2) it was published. That's it. Not surprisingly, Sullivan won easily. In fact, he won a $500,000 judgment—over $4 million in today's dollars—for damage to his reputation.

The New York Times appealed the verdict, and the case made its way to the U.S. Supreme Court. In a unanimous decision, the court threw out the lower court's verdict. The high court held that the strict liability standard that made it easy for Sullivan to win his defamation case was not consistent with the First Amendment. Freedom of the press required a much more rigorous standard of both fault and falsity. Writing for the court, Justice William Brennan held that to win a defamation case, public officials must prove what he called "actual malice." This meant that defamation would hold only if journalists knowingly published false information or published with reckless disregard for whether the information was true. Like the "irreparable harm" standard from the Pentagon Papers case, the actual malice standard is an incredibly high bar for government officials to prove. As for falsity, Brennan held that despite the inaccuracies in *The Times* ad, the accounts still carried a gist of the truth: African-Americans in the South were indeed being persecuted.

What does *Sullivan* mean for you as a journalist? It does *not* mean that you have a license to be lazy with verifying facts. However, even if your story is not 100 percent accurate, you have some protection from a libel suit.

In later cases, the court extended this same high level of protection (the actual malice test) to the press when faced with defamation suits from "public figures," such as celebrities or business moguls, because it is the press's job to hold these folks accountable, as well. Defining who is a public figure is not necessarily an easy task. A lot depends on context: Is the person a well-known figure in his or her community? Did the person thrust himself or herself into the limelight in relation to one specific issue?

Determining whether a defamation plaintiff is a public figure is an important factor in the outcome of defamation cases. In most states, everyday individuals—people who are not public officials or public figures—have to prove only that journalists acted negligently; that is, they didn't exercise a duty of care that any reasonable reporter would use in publishing false information. The negligence test makes it easier for ordinary citizens to win libel judgments against a careless press. Therefore, plaintiffs will try to make a strong case that they are average, everyday individuals, and lawyers for journalists will try to argue the opposite.

New York Times v. Sullivan did not make defamation lawsuits disappear. In 2016, an associate dean at the University of Virginia successfully proved that *Rolling Stone* magazine published defamatory statements falsely accusing her of acting with indifference toward a sexual assault victim.

Also, public figures and public officials still may threaten to sue journalists for defamation following damning coverage about them, even if the published information is true. They are unlikely to win these suits—as their lawyers no doubt advise them—but their goal is to win in the court of public opinion and to scare journalists away from reporting such stories. Another goal is to make the lawsuits costly and time-consuming for the press in an effort to discourage journalists from reporting on similar issues again. To prevent this tactic, some states have passed laws to limit strategic lawsuits against public participation. These anti-SLAPP laws seek to halt defamation suits early in the pretrial phase of the lawsuit to avoid costing the press time and money.

With the threat of defamation lawsuits still out there—whether serious ones from private individuals or frivolous ones from angry high-profile people—journalists need to know how to protect themselves. Journalists also need to be especially careful when reporting on certain issues that the law recognizes as libelous *per se*, meaning the harm done to the plaintiff's reputation by the accusation is obvious. Libel *per se* includes falsely reporting that someone has a "loathsome" disease, falsely accusing someone of serious immorality (such as sexual promiscuity or infidelity), or falsely accusing someone of committing a crime. For example, if the police say that Smith is arrested for robbery, you cannot report that Smith committed the robbery, only that he is *accused* of robbery.

As a journalist, you have three traditional defenses against libel: truth, privilege, and fair comment and criticism.These defenses also apply to material posted on social media.

Truth

First, verify claims made by your sources. Truth is the best defense against libel. Having physical documents that can verify sources' claims is especially helpful, as is having sources willing to talk on the record.

Privilege

Government officials have the *absolute privilege* to say whatever they like when they are acting in their official capacities. Why? In *New York Times v. Sullivan*, the Supreme Court said the United States should be a place full of wide-ranging, robust, uninhibited debates. As a country, we want officials to be able to have those debates.

And we also want journalists to report them. Therefore, journalists have a *qualified privilege* to report on what those officials say during official proceedings. The qualification is that the reports must be full, accurate and "neutral reporting." If an official source in your story makes a false and defamatory statement about someone, as long as you accurately report what you heard—and any rebuttal—you cannot be successfully sued.

Keep good notes, though. Proving actual malice requires proving that a journalist intentionally published false statements. Having good notes and documentation is the best way to keep plaintiffs from proving such intent.

Fair Comment and Criticism

Journalists also enjoy protection from defamation lawsuits when they express their opinions about public officials or public figures in a column or an editorial. For instance, a columnist could write, "Mayor Jones is a bad leader" or even "Mayor Jones is the worst mayor we have ever had." These statements are subjective and based purely on the columnist's own interpretation of facts about the mayor. They may be harmful to the mayor's reputation, but defamation requires falsity, and as the Supreme Court noted in the 1974 case *Gertz v. Robert Welch*, "There is no such thing as a false idea."

However, columnists need to be careful when they try to frame a factual statement as an opinion. Saying, "In my opinion, Mayor Jones committed tax fraud" is no different than saying, "Mayor Jones committed tax fraud." If that statement is false, the words "in my opinion" will not act as a magic talisman protecting you from a lawsuit from Mayor Jones. The fair comment and criticism protection also applies to movie and restaurant reviews. Again, you have to be offering opinions and can't misstate facts – for example, the number of health code violations at a restaurant.

Social Media and Other Cautions about Defamation

Generally, anything that journalists post on social media is subject to the same legal rules as something that a news organization might publish or broadcast. However, a 1996 law known as Section 230 of the Communications Decency Act grants platforms like Facebook and Twitter immunity from lawsuits sparked by **user-generated content**. In other words, the platforms are not held liable for what others post or tweet. Also, Facebook and Twitter are powerful platforms for public debate, but they are not the government. Therefore, if they remove UGC for being hateful, false or defamatory, individuals cannot sue them for violating the First Amendment as they could with government censorship.

One final note about defamation: The Supreme Court held in *Masson v. New Yorker* (1991) that it is not necessarily libel if a journalist alters his or her source's quotes in a story to make them sound clearer or more sensational. Journalists always should strive for accuracy, but they should not live in fear of being sued if they get a quote wrong. The court recognized that journalists need "breathing space" when doing their work. That said, the *Masson* decision does not give journalists a green light to make up stuff. Rather, it should give journalists comfort that as long as they practice a rigorous method of verifying information, they will be protected against a libel suit. The diagram in Figure 19.1 shows the various defenses to a libel suit.

FIGURE 19.1

An understanding of libel and related concepts is essential for journalism.

Data from: Dr. Sandra Davidson.

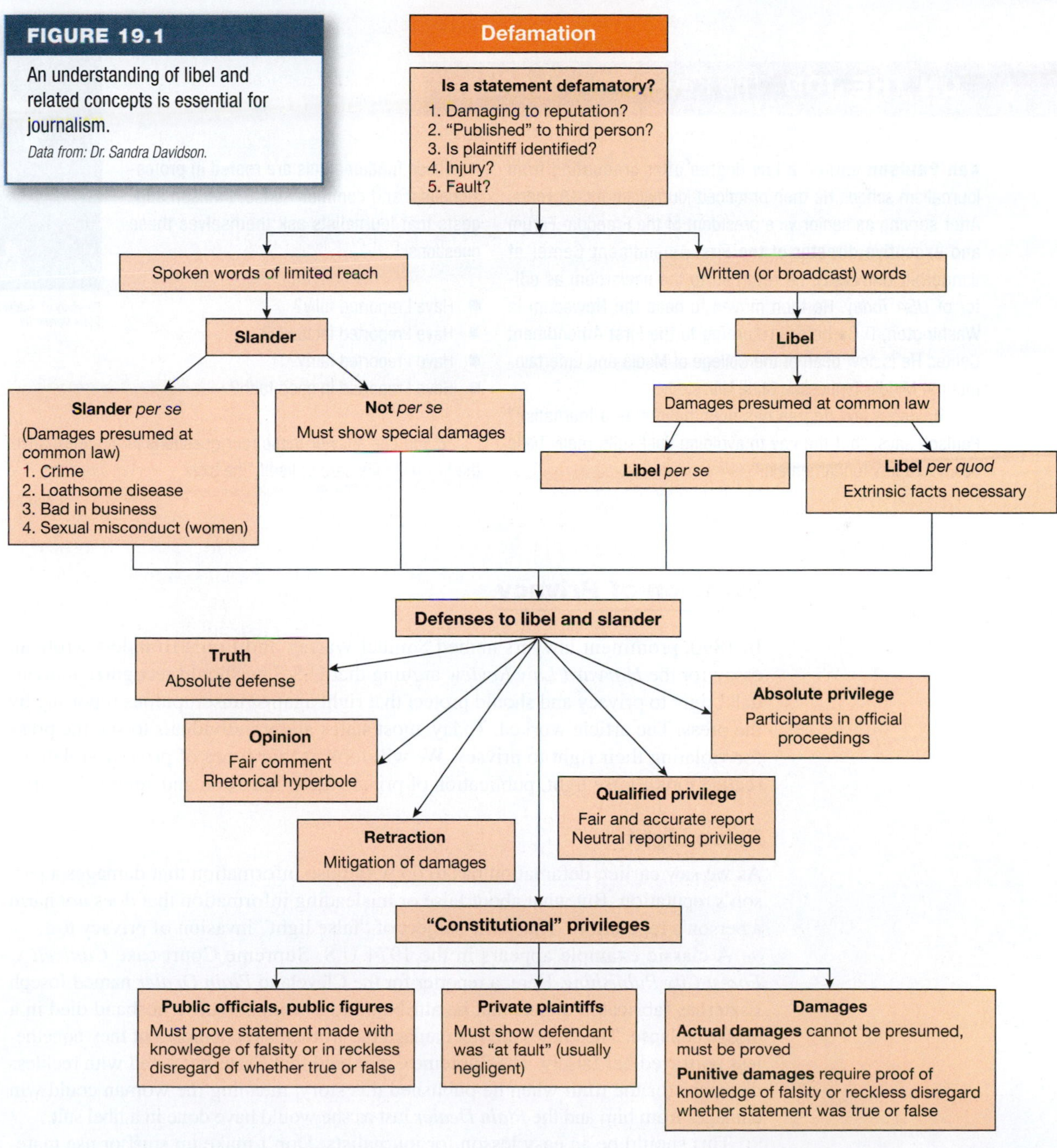
Defamation
Is a statement defamatory?
1. Damaging to reputation?
2. "Published" to third person?
3. Is plaintiff identified?
4. Injury?
5. Fault?
Spoken words of limited reach
Written (or broadcast) words
Slander
Libel
Slander per se
(Damages presumed at common law)
1. Crime
2. Loathsome disease
3. Bad in business
4. Sexual misconduct (women)
Not per se
Must show special damages
Damages presumed at common law
Libel per se
Libel per quod
Extrinsic facts necessary
Defenses to libel and slander
Truth
Absolute defense
Opinion
Fair comment
Rhetorical hyperbole
Retraction
Mitigation of damages
Absolute privilege
Participants in official proceedings
Qualified privilege
Fair and accurate report
Neutral reporting privilege
"Constitutional" privileges
Public officials, public figures
Must prove statement made with knowledge of falsity or in reckless disregard of whether true or false
Private plaintiffs
Must show defendant was "at fault" (usually negligent)
Damages
Actual damages cannot be presumed, must be proved
Punitive damages require proof of knowledge of falsity or reckless disregard whether statement was true or false

ON THE JOB The Keys to Avoiding Libel

Courtesy of Middle Tennessee State University

Ken Paulson earned a law degree after graduating from journalism school. He then practiced journalism for 18 years. After serving as senior vice president of the Freedom Forum and executive director of the First Amendment Center at Vanderbilt University, he returned to the newsroom as editor of *USA Today*. He then moved to head the Newseum in Washington, D.C., before returning to the First Amendment Center. He is now dean of the College of Media and Entertainment at Middle Tennessee State University.

"Having a law degree has been helpful as a journalist," Paulson says, "but the key to avoiding libel suits really boils down to a few fundamentals."

Those fundamentals are rooted in professionalism and common sense. Paulson suggests that journalists ask themselves these questions:

- Have I reported fully?
- Have I reported factually?
- Have I reported fairly?
- Have I reported in good faith?

"If you can answer those four questions in the affirmative, the law will take care of itself," he says.

Invasion of Privacy

In 1890, prominent lawyers named Samuel Warren and Louis Brandeis wrote an essay for the *Harvard Law Review* arguing that U.S. law should recognize individuals' right to privacy and should protect that right against unscrupulous reporting by the press. The article worked. Today, most states allow individuals to sue the press for violating their right to privacy. We will look at four types of privacy violations (called torts): false light, publication of private facts, intrusion and appropriation.

False Light

As we saw earlier, defamation has to do with false information that damages a person's reputation. But what about false or misleading information that does *not* harm a person's reputation? That's the subject of "false light" invasion of privacy tort.

A classic example appears in the 1974 U.S. Supreme Court case *Cantrell v. Forest City Publishing*. Here, a reporter for the Cleveland *Plain Dealer* named Joseph Eszterhas fabricated quotes that he attributed to a woman whose husband died in a bridge collapse. The quotes did not damage the woman's reputation, but they nonetheless portrayed her falsely. The Supreme Court held that Eszterhas acted with reckless disregard for the truth when he published this story, meaning the woman could win damages from him and the *Plain Dealer* just as she would have done in a libel suit.

This should be an easy lesson for journalists: Don't make up stuff or use material in the wrong context, and you won't get sued for false light. The same applies to visuals: Make sure the images and video you use accurately depict the people and organizations in your story.

Private Facts

One of the main concerns of Warren and Brandeis was that individuals would have no legal recourse to collect damages from the press if journalists published information that was purely private. The two were worried because such publications were not libelous given that the information was true.

So Warren and Brandeis suggested that if publication of (true) private facts was offensive to a reasonable person and not a matter of public concern, then individuals should be able to sue the press. According to Warren and Brandeis, this arrangement would balance the interests of protecting individuals' privacy with the interest of promoting a free and robust press.

Since this tort was created, courts have mixed records on its enforcement. The U.S. Court of Appeals for the Seventh Circuit held that an academic oral history that reported on the alcoholism and womanizing of one of its main characters without his consent did not violate the man's right to privacy. According to the court, the publication was not offensive, and the man's story was integral in discussing a matter of public concern: the human toll suffered by African-Americans following the Great Migration from Southern plantations to Northern industrial cities.

In 2016, however, a Florida jury found that the Gawker website had violated the right of privacy of Terry Bollea, whose stage name is Hulk Hogan, by posting portions of a sex tape depicting Bollea. The jury agreed with Bollea that the publication of the video was offensive to a reasonable person and did not involve a matter of public concern. After paying millions in damages to Bollea, Gawker went bankrupt.

In another case from Florida, the U.S. Supreme Court held that journalists could not be sued for publishing the name of a sexual assault victim if they received the name from a public record. In *Florida Star v. BJF* (1989), an intern at the *Florida Star* published a routine "police blotter" item with information from local police reports. The police mistakenly gave the intern the report containing the name and address of BJF, the victim of a sexual assault. The newspaper had a policy of not publishing the names of sexual assault victims, but an editor let this instance slip through the cracks. Although BJF won a settlement from the Jacksonville Police Department for negligently giving out her information, the Supreme Court held that journalists should not be subject to lawsuits for publishing information they got from a public record, regardless of how unethical it was to publish the information.

The bottom line for journalists is that if a salacious detail appears to be both offensive and not important to the public, it probably should not be published. Also, just because you *can* publish information contained in a public record doesn't mean you *should*. You may win in a court of law but be scrutinized in the court of public opinion.

Intrusion

As citizens, we can reasonably believe that no one is going to secretly record our conversations or film our actions in our homes, our cars or even our workplaces. Individuals have successfully sued journalists who have encroached on these sanctums in their reporting. In 1971, the U.S. Court of Appeals for the Ninth Circuit held that "the First Amendment is not a license to trespass, to steal, or to intrude by electronic means into the precincts of another's home or office."

In that case, *Dietemann v. Time*, journalists surreptitiously gained access to the home office of a "quack doctor" (Dietemann) to expose his questionable medical practices by secretly recording him at work. Even though the story involved an important matter of public concern, Dietemann had a reasonable expectation of privacy that he would not be the subject of an undercover report in his own home. In intrusion lawsuits, the public importance of the story is not a defense available to journalists.

The *Dietemann* case involved two issues related to intrusion: using deceit to gain entrance to his home (pretending to be patients seeking Dietemann's services) and using a hidden camera to film Dietemann's activities. Journalists should be concerned about each of these issues because they may decide some degree of deceit or use of hidden cameras is needed to get a story of public importance.

How can you stay on the right side of the law? Courts have offered some guidance. For example, the California Supreme Court held that use of deception to gain access to a person's home or office can amount to intrusion if it is "highly offensive to a reasonable person." What does that mean, exactly? Lying about having a connection to a person's close confidant would likely be considered intrusively deceitful, but pretending to be a member of the general public (such as being a secret shopper) likely would not be.

Not all uses of hidden cameras are unlawful. Journalists should check with how their state law defines reasonable expectation of privacy in the context of being secretly recorded. Some states, including New York, allow secret recordings in semipublic places, such as restaurants. Other states, including California, do not. Most courts have held that police officers do not have a reasonable expectation of privacy while performing their duties in public that would shield them from being recorded.

Bottom line: See what is allowed in your state. But even when the use of hidden cameras is *legally* permitted, journalists need to understand their news organization's *ethics* policies on using them. We discuss ethics in the next chapter.

> "There are only two occasions when Americans respect privacy. . . . Those are prayer and fishing."
>
> ■ Herbert Hoover, 31st U.S. president

Appropriation

You can also invade someone's privacy by using that person's name or likeness for commercial purposes, such as in an advertisement, without his or her consent. This tort rarely is applied to journalists, but advertisers and public relations professionals should be wary. Courts have interpreted broadly what a use of a person's likeness is.

For example, a Chicago-based grocery store chain published an advertisement to congratulate Michael Jordan for being inducted into the Basketball Hall of Fame. Because the ad used Jordan's number (23) and featured his shoes, Jordan successfully sued the grocery store for $8.9 million. Notice that the ad didn't say, "Michael Jordan shops at our store." The use of the likeness was more subtle, but it was a violation of Jordan's right to privacy nonetheless.

You May Be Committing Invasion of Privacy By . . .

- Trespassing on private property.
- Portraying someone in a "false light."
- Causing unwanted publicity that is offensive to a person of ordinary sensibilities.
- Using someone's image in an ad.

Other Newsgathering Issues

The First Amendment gives journalists strong protections against censorship before they publish and against lawsuits after they publish. Its record is more mixed when it comes to newsgathering—the process of collecting facts from people, places and documents.

Public Records

Government documents allow journalists to show the public hard evidence of government activities. They are vital to good reporting. However, the First Amendment does not grant journalists—or any member of the public, for that matter—the right to access such documents. Rather, statutes govern the extent of this right: The Freedom of Information Act, known as FOIA, covers records made by federal agencies, and each state has its own statute governing records made at the state, county or municipal level. These laws spell out what a public record is, what the process for getting these records is, which records are off limits, and how you can appeal if your request is denied.

At the federal level, the most common exemptions invoked to deny access to government documents are national security and privacy. The executive branch has the power to classify documents, making them off limits to the public because they contain information that could be damaging to national security if released. The national security exemption has been used to withhold all sorts of documents from the public—including photos of Osama bin Laden's dead body, information on the budget of the Guantánamo Bay prison, and even records on critical infrastructure such as bridges and dams—under the theory that disclosing such records could make them more vulnerable to terrorist attacks.

Examination of declassified documents has shown that sometimes the executive branch has been overzealous in classifying documents when there is minimal threat to national security. Such "overclassification," especially since the attacks of Sept. 11, 2001, has led journalists to be skeptical of the government's use of the national security exemption. That, in turn, has led journalists to rely more and more on government sources who leak classified documents, which has led to an increase in government crackdowns and prosecutions of leakers.

States have also cited national security to restrict access to government documents. For example, since the late 2000s, the New York Police Department has been using a controversial surveillance tool called a Z Backscatter Van, a vehicle that allows investigators to "see through" walls by using high-powered X-ray radiation. When journalists and civil liberties groups filed public records requests for basic information about the vans (How much do they cost to operate? Are they paid for with taxpayer dollars?), they were told the records were exempt because of national security concerns. The reason? If information about how these vans work became public, then terrorists could circumvent police efforts to surveil them. Meanwhile, the vans appear to expose people to harmful radiation and perhaps even violate their Fourth Amendment rights against unwarranted government searches. This case shows just how powerful and frustrating national security exemptions can be, even at a local level.

At the state and federal levels, privacy also has increasingly been invoked to withhold government documents from the public. Some privacy-related exemptions are reasonable. For instance, in Missouri, phone records of crisis hotlines are exempt to protect the privacy of victims of domestic abuse. However, some uses of privacy to justify withholding records may be excessive. For example, several states have passed laws exempting permits of gun owners, which had long been public record. In 2000, the Supreme Court held in *Reno v. Condon* that data held at state departments of motor vehicles should not be public record. Protecting privacy is something all people, even journalists, can support to some degree. However, when lawmakers and the public categorically place privacy concerns ahead of government transparency, journalists' ability to keep watch over government is hampered.

Aside from exemptions, there are other ways that public records laws can make it difficult for journalists to get documents. In some states, including Missouri and Kansas, government agencies have the ability to charge requesters—even journalists—high fees to pay for searches of documents. Sometimes, the fees are high enough to deter journalists (especially freelancers or citizen journalists).

Also, at both the federal and state levels, government agencies do not have deadlines by which to fulfill or deny your request. The FOIA does stipulate that federal agencies have 20 business days to *acknowledge* your request. But the only thing keeping agencies accountable for completing your request in a timely fashion is the large backlog of requests that the agencies are trying to whittle down. Sometimes a wait for records can be so long that the journalist's story goes stale, and the documents lose their importance.

Since 2013, Investigative Reporters and Editors, a nonprofit journalism training organization, has handed out its Golden Padlock Award for the most secretive publicly funded agency or individual.

Despite the hoops and hurdles of public records laws, all is not lost. To be successful in requesting public records, journalists should take the following advice to heart.

First, know open records laws (especially your own state's law) inside and out. Sometimes the best way to get access to records is to ask a public records officer for them, rather than filing a formal request. For this method to be successful, you will need to show the records custodian that you know the law entitles you to certain records. If this strategy fails, you always have the option of filing a formal request.

Also, knowing the law means knowing that you are entitled to records in a workable format. If you know that a public database exists as a Microsoft Excel

TIPS

How to Boost Your Odds of Getting Important Public Records

- Know the state and federal laws.
- Know what documents you want.
- Be polite and persistent.
- Show the public the importance of the documents.

file, for instance, you should ask for it in that format. If you don't, the agency could send you a PDF or a printout of physical pages that would be more difficult to analyze.

Second, know what you are looking for. Going on "fishing expeditions" by making a broad request for thousands of documents is in no one's best interest. It will take lots of time, it could potentially cost you and your news organization a lot of money, and it gums up the requesting process for other people (not to mention that it also draws the ire of records custodians, thereby jeopardizing a healthy working relationship with them).

Start by doing some detective work by talking to sources with knowledge of the existence of particular records. Those people often can help you narrow your search. Furthermore, know that agencies are not obligated to create a new document for you by using other publicly available information. They are required to give you only what they actually have, to the extent it isn't exempt. Save yourself a lot of hassle by asking for the pieces that you know exist. You can assemble them into a new document later.

Third, be resilient. As noted above, government agencies have dozens of ways to try to thwart your records requests. Persistently and professionally pushing back can lead those agencies to grant your requests. For example, if the agency says, "We'll get back to you," and you don't hear anything for a few weeks, follow up with emails, phone calls and in-person visits. If the agency says its policy is not to turn over certain records, ask how this internal policy is consistent with the law. If agency officials say they cannot make copies of certain records, then be willing to spend hours in their offices examining the records in person.

State laws and the federal FOIA give you the right to sue the agency if you believe it is improperly withholding documents. If you win, you often are entitled to have the government pay your attorney's fees. However, victory in court is not guaranteed, making this last-ditch effort a potentially expensive one. Still, at the federal level, litigation can lead agencies to create what is called a *Vaughn* index, named after a case from the 1970s called *Vaughn v. Rosen*. A *Vaughn* index is a detailed list of the records you have requested and the reasons the agency believes they should be exempt. Even if you lose the court battle, having the agency produce a *Vaughn* index can give you lots of information about what kinds of records an agency has, which can sometimes help you connect critical dots in an investigation.

Finally, journalists can help their own cause by being transparent about how they searched for and used government documents in their reporting. Unfortunately, government transparency is not typically a high priority for the public or lawmakers. Concerns for national security and privacy tend to have greater resonance with the public than government openness, leading the public to favor policies that further restrict access to would-be public documents. By showing the importance of public records laws to their reporting efforts (within the stories themselves), journalists can help put government openness on the radar of both the public and policymakers.

launchpadworks.com
WATCH: **"Bloggers and Legal Rights"**

- How do the legal protections and responsibilities of bloggers compare with those of print or television journalists?
- Should professional journalists have different rights and more protection than bloggers? Explain.

Newsgathering and Defining Who a Journalist Is

Although the First Amendment says Congress shall make no law restricting freedom of the press, it doesn't necessarily give the press more rights than other people. In two major cases from the 1970s, the U.S. Supreme Court declined to extend special rights to the press under the First Amendment. In *Branzburg v. Hayes*, the court held that the First Amendment did not give journalists a special right to refuse to reveal anonymous sources in grand jury testimonies. In *Houchins v. KQED*, the court held that the First Amendment did not grant the press special rights beyond those of the general public to access federal prisons: The press could go only where the public could go.

In both *Branzburg* and *Houchins*, the press made a pretty good argument that journalists are the eyes and ears of the people and thus should enjoy special rights to help get stories to the public. For example, the journalists in *Branzburg* argued that sometimes anonymous sources are necessary for reporting on illegal issues, such as drug trafficking or the activities of terrorist organizations. But the court saw the matter differently: Giving special rights to the press means defining who the press is according to constitutional doctrine. Otherwise, anyone could claim the right to interview prisoners inside their cells or refuse to testify before a grand jury.

Branzburg may have kept journalists from invoking a First Amendment right to refuse to name sources, but most states have statutes — often referred to as "shield laws" or "reporter's privilege statutes" — that journalists can rely on to keep sensitive sources anonymous. Journalists should find out if their state has such a law.

Next, journalists should read the law to understand who it covers and under what circumstances. These statutes recognize that reporters should be able to gather information without the fear that law enforcement will have a free pass to subpoena that information. Some statutes strictly and narrowly define who a journalist is. For example, Alabama's shield law protects only journalists who work for newspapers or broadcast stations, not magazines. Delaware's shield law requires journalists to earn their "principal livelihood by, or in each of the preceding 3 weeks or 4 of the preceding 8 weeks had spent at least 20 hours engaged in the practice of" journalism.

Other statutes, such as New York's, define journalism more broadly by focusing on basic functions of journalism: gathering and reporting information through a medium of mass communication. Therefore, bloggers receive protections under expansive laws like these. Some statutes, like Nebraska's, give journalists an absolute privilege not to have to testify about their sources in any court under any circumstances. Others, like Florida's, stipulate that journalists can keep their sources anonymous *unless* the journalist witnessed the source committing illegal activity. In Minnesota, journalists are forced to name their sources if law enforcement has exhausted every other option of finding out who the source is.

There is no federal shield law, meaning no law protects a journalist and his or her source if the FBI wants to determine the source's identity. However, a journalist based in one state and reporting in another state often has the choice of which state's shield law to rely on, if need be. For example, while reporting on a mass shooting in a movie theater in Aurora, Colorado, Fox News reporter Jana Winter obtained the diary of the shooter. The diary was not meant to be made public, but someone leaked it to Winter. Because she worked for a news outlet based in New York, Winter was able to rely on the stronger New York shield law to protect her source, even though Colorado law enforcement officials were the ones seeking to make her testify.

In the rare event you have a source with valuable information who you feel should remain anonymous, it is important to understand the protection and tools available to you. However, journalists should also know that the government has many other ways to find out who you're speaking with, such as by subpoenaing records of your call history from your phone provider. This insidious practice is legal because you don't own those records; the phone companies do. Therefore, journalists should communicate with sensitive sources through means that are less traceable, such as encrypted emails.

Journalists and the Judiciary

Reporting on the judicial system is essential to our democracy. We need to know how courts operate and ensure that justice gets meted out fairly. To help ensure that journalists engage in such reporting, the Supreme Court has held that journalists (indeed, all citizens) have a First Amendment right to attend criminal trials. In *Richmond Newspapers v. Virginia* (1980), the court held that criminal trials operated with an inherent "presumption of openness" to ensure that the accused receives due process.

However, journalists' First Amendment right to report on criminal trials can come into conflict with another constitutional right: individuals' Sixth Amendment right to a speedy trial by an impartial jury of their peers. The Supreme Court has decided two major cases dealing with these competing rights. In the 1966 case *Sheppard v. Maxwell*, the Supreme Court held that pretrial publicity (among other things) contributed to Dr. Sam Sheppard not receiving a fair trial after he was accused of murdering his wife. (Sam Sheppard's case led to the creation of the TV show and movie *The Fugitive*.) The court focused on the judge in Sheppard's trial, holding that he did not do enough to prevent harm being done to Sheppard's Sixth Amendment rights by mitigating the effects of pretrial publicity. (Sheppard was acquitted in a new trial.)

Following the guidance of *Sheppard v. Maxwell*, a Nebraska judge ordered news media not to report on the confession of an alleged murderer to avoid interfering with the accused's opportunity to receive a fair trial. However, in *Nebraska Press Association v. Stuart* (1976), the U.S. Supreme Court held that imposing such a prior restraint against the press should be the absolute last means judges should resort to when trying to protect the Sixth Amendment rights of a defendant. Other tools judges can and should rely on include changing the location of a trial, implementing strict policies for selecting jurors, and sequestering jurors (including forbidding them from using social media) after they are impaneled.

It is important for journalists to understand the awesome power that they have in reporting the news, particularly the power they have to shape the opinion of potential jurors toward someone accused of a crime.

Copyright

Journalists and strategic communicators also need to know when and how they can use material from other authors. Key elements of copyright law include the following:

- Copyrightable works are protected from the moment they are fixed in tangible form, whether published or unpublished.
- Copyright protection begins with a work's "creation and . . . endures for a term consisting of the life of the author and 70 years after the author's death."
- Works for hire and anonymous and pseudonymous works are protected for 95 years from publication or 120 years from creation, whichever is shorter.
- There is a "fair use" limitation on the exclusive rights of copyright owners. In other words, it may be permissible to quote excerpts from a copyrighted work without permission.

Fair Use

The elements of fair use were included in the 1976 Copyright Act:

- The nature of the new use.
- The nature of the original work.
- The amount or substantiality of the use of the original work.
- The effect of the use on the market of the original work.

At a time when user-generated content abounds online, journalists and those working in strategic communication need to be especially careful to avoid infringing the copyright of the authors of such content. Journalists can avoid such liability if they engage in a "fair use" of the original works.

The U.S. Supreme Court spelled out the application of fair use to journalism in the 1985 case *Harper & Row v. Nation Enterprises*. In that case, former President Gerald Ford was set to publish a 450-page memoir with the publishing company Harper & Row. Before the book's release, Harper & Row made a deal with *Time* magazine that allowed it to publish an excerpt from one of the book's most important parts: Ford's pardoning of Richard Nixon. However, *The Nation* magazine obtained a leaked copy of the memoir and published the account of Nixon's pardon before *Time* could publish its piece. The excerpt was no longer newsworthy to *Time*, so it voided its contract with Harper & Row, which sued *The Nation* for copyright infringement.

The Nation argued that its publication of the excerpt was journalistic in nature, so it should be considered a fair use. However, there's more to the fair-use test. The Supreme Court held that the first part of the fair-use test—the nature of the new work—should fall in favor of *The Nation*. Journalistic uses, the court said, generally can be viewed favorably as fair uses of copyrighted material, as opposed to commercial uses that simply seek a profit.

However, the court held that *The Nation* did not meet the three remaining prongs of the fair-use test. The original work was an unpublished manuscript, and the court held that U.S. copyright law recognizes the importance of allowing authors the right to determine how their works should be first published. As for the amount or substantiality of the work, even though *The Nation* only used a few pages of the 450-page book, the story that these pages told—the pardon—was deemed to be "the heart" of the book. Finally, by publishing this part of the book, *The Nation* damaged the market for Ford's book.

Exactly how the fair-use test may apply to journalists who take user-generated content without permission is up for speculation. In fall 2016, a San Francisco man filed a lawsuit against CBS for broadcasting, without his consent, a video that he recorded of his wife giving birth via Facebook Live. The plaintiff voluntarily withdrew the case. Nonetheless, the fact that this suit was even filed serves as a warning to journalists that taking UGC without permission is a potentially legally precipitous practice.

Before using UGC, journalists should know that little case law exists on whether or how UGC should receive protection as copyrighted work. Courts may view UGC as not having the same value as a book, song or film, which would give journalists an edge in the second and fourth prongs of the fair-use test. Or courts may not. For now, the best practice for journalists is to obtain permission before using something from the web or social media. Of course, keep in mind that Facebook and Twitter have also been accused of facilitating the spread of false and misleading stories. It is up to you to verify information.

> **"Journalists don't believe . . . the FOIA (Freedom of Information Act) was created to be turned on us as an excuse to hide information."**
>
> ■ **Sarah Overstreet, columnist**

Final Thoughts

Throughout your career, you may or may not have to deal with weighty legal issues such as defamation lawsuits or requests to name confidential sources in court. But being armed with a working knowledge of the law can empower you on the beat. If a public figure threatens to sue you for libel because he or she does not like a story you are planning to publish, you can proceed with confidence knowing that he or she will have a hard time suing you if you did your homework. If a public-records officer unduly denies your request for records, you can feel empowered to push back with threats of legal action.

Having a basic knowledge of media law also can help journalists stay on the right side of the law when situations arise. For instance, understanding that user-generated content is protected by copyright law will make journalists think twice before swiping individuals' videos and photos from the Internet.

Finally, knowing the limits of the law can help you become a more ethical journalist. Staying on the right side of the law is an important (though admittedly not a sufficient) way of ensuring ethical practice. The First Amendment does not afford exceptional protections to journalists so they can engage in the most fringe forms of journalism allowed. Rather, the purpose of these protections is to give journalists "breathing space"—space to do their jobs honorably and ethically for the public's benefit.

CHAPTER RESOURCES

SUGGESTED READINGS

Anderson, David A. "Freedom of the Press." *Texas Law Review* 80, no. 3 (2002): 429–530. Anderson's article reviews numerous court decisions that have helped give the press special status in American democracy.

Bollinger, Lee. *Uninhibited, Robust, and Wide Open: A Free Press for a New Century*. New York: Oxford University Press, 2010. Bollinger is one of the foremost scholars on matters of First Amendment jurisprudence. This book analyzes Supreme Court precedents on freedom of the press in great depth and then uses the analysis to chart a path for how the law can and must facilitate a free press in a technologically disruptive century.

Cuillier, David, and Charles N. Davis. *The Art of Access: Strategies for Acquiring Public Records*. Washington, D.C.: CQ Press, 2011. This book offers journalists dozens of strategies on where to look for public records, what kinds of stories can be written using public records, and how to be successful in acquiring those records.

Franklin, Marc, David Anderson, Lyrissa Barnett Lidsky and Amy Gajda. *Media Law: Cases and Materials*. 9th ed. New York: Foundation Press (University Casebook Series), 2016. This is a traditional casebook, ubiquitous in law schools. It includes a thoughtful selection of major media law cases, as well as insightful commentary on major issues facing media law today.

Middleton, Kent R., William E. Lee and Daxton R. Stewart. *The Law of Public Communication*. 9th ed. New York: Routledge, 2017. This book is one of the most thorough accounts of major cases and statutes that shape journalism and communication law.

SUGGESTED WEBSITES

LaunchPad Solo
launchpadworks.com
When you visit LaunchPad Solo for Journalism, you will find research links, exercises and LearningCurve adaptive quizzing to help you improve your grammar and AP style usage. In addition, the site's video collection hosts the videos highlighted in this and other chapters as well as additional clips of leading professionals discussing important media trends.

knightcolumbia.org
The Knight First Amendment Institute at Columbia University contains reports on current events involving media law, as well as essays from prominent scholars on major First Amendment issues.

www.rcfp.org
The website for the Reporters Committee for Freedom of the Press contains numerous guides on routine legal issues journalists face, such as the nature of state shield laws, privacy torts, and ways to navigate the federal Freedom of Information Act and state public record laws.

silha.umn.edu
The University of Minnesota's Silha Center for the Study of Media Ethics and Law produces its *Silha Bulletin* on current issues in media ethics and law three times a year. It is available for free on the center's website. The Silha Center also sponsors an annual lecture on an issue of media law featuring a prominent scholar, lawyer or media professional and posts the lecture videos on its website.

https://ssd.eff.org/en
The Electronic Frontier Foundation's Surveillance Self-Defense Guide explains electronic surveillance and suggests mechanisms for avoiding having your data, reporting notes and source information compromised.

EXERCISES

1. Do a search online for a news story on an issue of media law (such as defamation, invasion of privacy, access to records). As you read that story, ask yourself: How do the facts of the story relate to legal precedent discussed here? What questions do you still have after reading the story?
2. Major First Amendment cases deal with the conflict between freedom of the press and other important social interests: protecting reputation, honoring rights to privacy, ensuring national security. With a classmate, discuss and debate the pros and cons of protecting freedom of the press versus these and other important issues.
3. Visit the websites of some local, state and federal government agencies to see what kind of government records you can find directly on these sites. Consider the following questions: How valuable are these records? What kinds of stories could you create from them, if any? How easy are the records to find? If they are not easy to find, what could the agency do to make them more easily available?
4. Many people do not know much about First Amendment law in general or freedom of the press in particular. Try taking an informal poll of family and friends on whether they can name all five freedoms granted by the First Amendment (speech, press, religion, assembly, petition) or whether they can correctly identify the extent of protection that the press receives in a defamation case. Were their answers what you expected?

CHAPTER 20 ETHICS

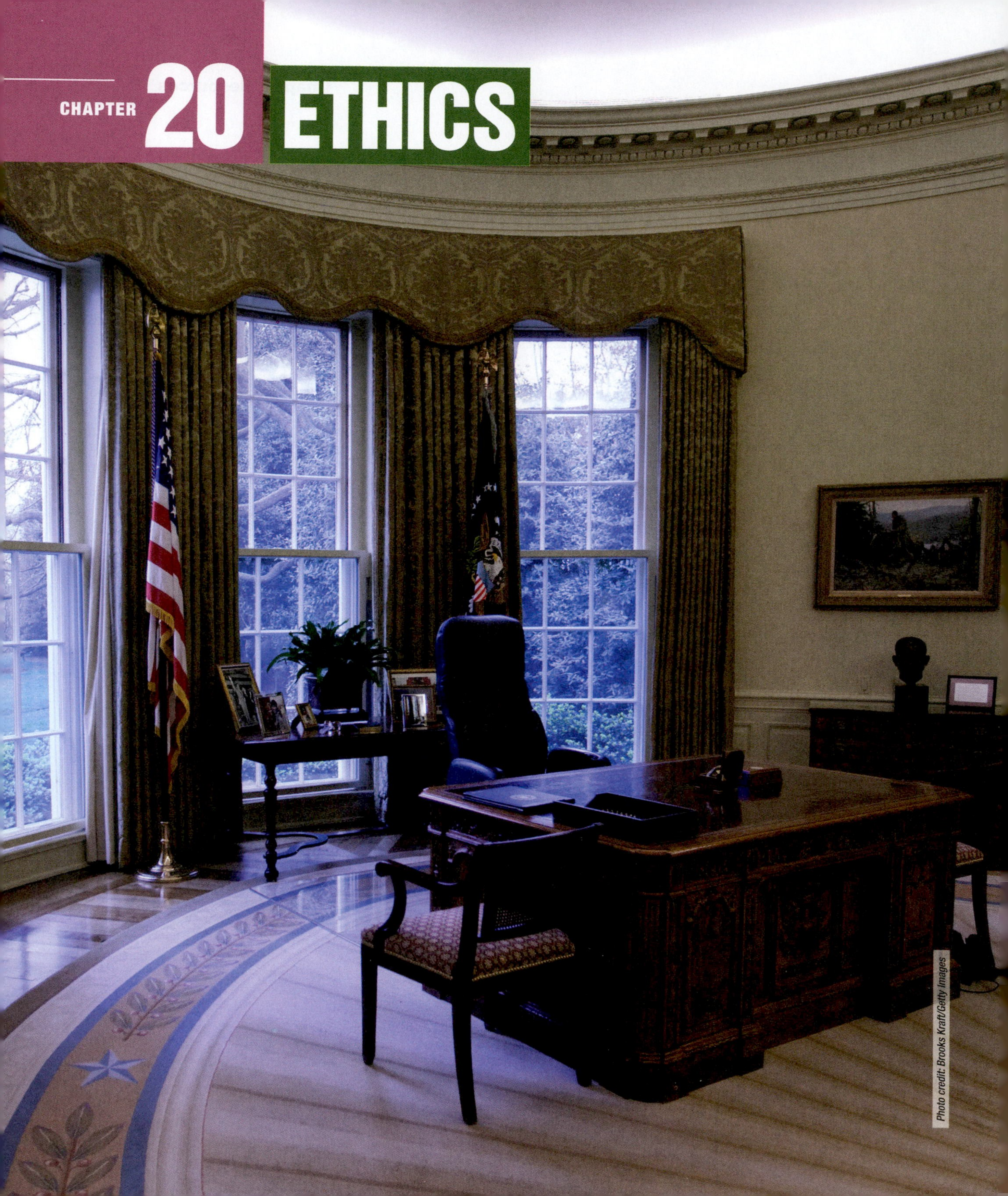
Photo credit: Brooks Kraft/Getty Images

In fall 2018, *The New York Times* stunned readers and the political establishment by publishing "I Am Part of the Resistance Inside the Trump Administration," an unsigned opinion essay. The author of the piece asserted that many senior officials were "working diligently from within to frustrate parts of his (President Donald Trump's) agenda and his worst inclinations." The writer ostensibly wanted to assure Americans that no matter how impetuous or ill-advised Trump's actions and statements might be, "there are adults in the room." The anonymous piece seemed to corroborate veteran journalist Bob Woodward's recently released book *Fear: Trump in the White House*, which also relied on anonymous sources to provide an inside look at the White House.

The president was not amused. He tweeted "TREASON" in all caps and suggested the U.S. Department of Justice should investigate who wrote the column. The White House press secretary, Sarah Huckabee Sanders, called on the article's author to resign.

Did readers have a right to know who wrote the column? Did the president have a right to know who his accuser/betrayer was? When is a news organization justified in using an anonymous source? When should it not? How should journalists decide?

How you answer those questions may depend on how you were raised and your values — in other words, your morals or principles. It might also depend on socialization — what you've seen your peers, including other journalists, do in similar situations. In any case, journalists at *The New York Times* faced an ethical dilemma. On the one hand, journalists want to be able to tell the whole truth — to name their important sources. On the other hand, journalists have accepted an important role in society — to be a watchdog for the people and a check on government power. If *The Times* didn't promise to keep the source anonymous, would the writer have agreed to publication? If *The Times* did promise to keep the source anonymous, should it break the promise?

Media ethics scholars Philip Patterson and Lee Wilkins say a true ethical dilemma is one in which your choice is not easy because you have competing values (for example, truth-telling and checking power) and you have multiple justifiable options. In many cases, you might be choosing the "least worst" option and explaining it to the public. Ethics is about what you do — the decisions you make and the ways you make them.

Can you trust the truth of a statement if you don't know who said it? Was *The Times* as "open and honest" with its readers as it could be when it ran the anonymous opinion essay? Whether people believe what media reports relates to the media's credibility. Unfortunately, less than half of Americans, 45 percent, trust the mass media to report news "fully, accurately and fairly," according to an October 2018 Gallup poll.

In this chapter, you will learn:

1. What the role of journalism codes of ethics is and why these codes are voluntary.
2. How the public perceives journalism ethics.
3. How several philosophical approaches can help you resolve ethical dilemmas.
4. How to apply a method of principled reasoning to ethical problems.
5. What ethical questions are of special importance to journalists.
6. How to recognize and avoid plagiarism.
7. How to apply ethics to social media.

launchpadworks.com
WATCH: **"Journalism Ethics: What News Is Fit to Print?"**

- Who decides what news is fit to publish, post or broadcast?
- Who decides issues such as whether to publish the names of sexual assault victims?
- Who should decide, and why?
- How might convergence make it harder for journalists to maintain long-held ethical standards?

The good news is this percentage is up from an all-time low of 32 percent in 2016. The bad news is the level of trust is down from a high of nearly 70 percent in 1976. Polling by both Gallup and the Pew Research Center also shows a growing divide in who trusts the press, with Democrats significantly more likely to trust the media in 2018 than did Republicans. In the case of the anonymous opinion essay published by *The Times*, odds are that a higher percentage of Democrats than Republicans would have agreed with *The Times*' decision.

Meanwhile, journalists are under more scrutiny than ever as bloggers and other commentators online and on social media call attention to every irregularity they see. Twitter users are quick to find errors, exaggerations and other problems with news coverage. As a result, journalists have responded by becoming much more transparent and by discussing their mistakes and failings.

They also try to explain themselves. For example, after *The New York Times* posted the anonymous opinion piece, the paper solicited and received more than 23,000 questions from readers. In response, on Sept. 8, 2018, op-ed editor James Dao answered several, including: Why did you publish this piece? How did you find this writer? Would you ever reveal your source? Did you consider the source's motives?

Readers were able to judge the responses for themselves: *The Times* argued that the piece "offered a significant first-person perspective we haven't presented to our readers before" and that the "public should have a chance to evaluate it for themselves." Dao said *The Times* trusted the source's identity because of "direct communication with the author, some background checking and testimony of the trusted intermediary." As for identifying the source only as a "senior White House official," Dao told readers: "we felt strongly that a broader categorization was necessary to protect the author from reprisal, and that concern has been borne out by the president's reaction to the essay."

The Q&A posted on *The Times*' Reader Center ran more than 1,200 words, about the same length as the opinion essay itself. Although *The Times* did not give up its source, it arguably worked to be transparent with its readers and demonstrated that it had spent time deliberating about the piece. Like many news organizations, *The Times* has posted professional guidelines for its staff—in essence, a code of ethics.

> **"You won't get the straight story from someone if you do it on the record. You will get a press release version of events."**
>
> **Bob Woodward in an interview with *The New York Times* about his book *Fear: Trump in the White House***

Journalism Codes of Ethics

Some professions, such as medicine and law, have the power to keep people from practicing unless they have membership in an association or a license to practice. These professions can also punish practitioners and even keep them from practicing if they violate the code of the profession.

Journalism is not a profession in that sense. Thanks to the First Amendment, the government can't issue licenses to journalists to allow them to work or prevent them from working. Although journalism has codes of ethics, those codes are largely voluntary. If a news organization has its own ethics code, supervisors expect journalists to understand and follow that code and might even suspend or fire a journalist who does not. However, there is no national code of ethics in the United States that each news organization *must* follow. In other words, whether journalists make ethical decisions is largely up to them and the news organizations for which they work.

Why can't someone force news organizations to "do the right thing"? Traditionally, news organizations and their owners have feared that such requirements might in some way infringe on freedom of the press or freedom of speech. Who should get to decide, for example, what "the right thing" is?

Rather than have the government step in, professional societies have written codes of ethics for practitioners that suggest best practices. Those associations include the American Business Media, the American Society of Business Press Editors, the American Society of Magazine Editors, the International Association of Business Communicators, the Public Relations Society of America and the Society of Professional Journalists. The SPJ Code of Ethics, for example, focuses on four major tenets: be truthful, minimize harm, be independent, and be accountable. (The full SPJ Code of Ethics appears in Appendix 3.)

Some critics condemn codes of ethics either for being hopelessly general and therefore ineffective or for being too restrictive. Others argue that strict codes help improve journalists' credibility, and some say they merely make journalists easy targets for libel suits. Nonetheless, many news organizations have established and enforced their own internal codes. Journalists who have plagiarized, for example, have been suspended or fired from their news organizations.

Still, journalists too often and too easily justify all of their actions by citing the First Amendment. Because of the relatively few legal restraints on journalism, journalists need to discuss ethical conduct. Although the law may allow you to do something, the more important question is whether you *should* do it. As the Commission on Freedom of the Press, also known as the Hutchins Commission, concluded in 1947, unless journalists set their own limits on what is acceptable and responsible, government will eventually and inevitably do it for them.

The 10 Absolutes of Reuters Journalism

Reuters journalists:

- Always hold accuracy sacrosanct.
- Always correct an error openly.
- Always strive for balance and freedom from bias.
- Always reveal a conflict of interest to a manager.
- Always respect privileged information.
- Always protect their sources from the authorities.
- Always guard against putting their opinion in a news story.
- Never fabricate or plagiarize.
- Never alter a still or moving image beyond the requirements of normal image enhancement.
- Never pay for a story and never accept a bribe.

■ Reuters, "Standards and Values," *Handbook of Journalism*

The Public Perception of Journalism Ethics

Even though many news organizations have their own codes of ethics, many U.S. citizens have never had much regard for journalists' ethics. In a Gallup poll published Dec. 19, 2016, less than a quarter of respondents (23 percent) rated the honesty and ethics of journalists as high or very high, and 41 percent rated them as low or very low. Those were the worst ratings journalists have received since 1976, when Gallup began asking Americans about the honesty and ethics of various professions.

However, people who accuse the news media of being unethical often have no clear notion of what journalism and journalism ethics are all about. They may confuse journalism with other forms of mass media. They may not understand that journalism ethics does not necessarily apply to shows featuring political satirists, activist TV commentators or celebrity watchers, for example. Such shows may have the veneer of journalism, but they use current events primarily for entertainment purposes or commentary.

To combat such distrust and increasing partisanship, journalists need to be on solid ground as they work to resolve ethical dilemmas and then explain their decision making to the public. Reviewing the work of ancient and more modern-day philosophers can help.

Ethics in the Blogosphere

Jay Rosen, journalism critic, author and scholar, who writes the blog PressLink, on ethics for bloggers:

- Good bloggers observe the ethic of the link. (That is, they make a point of inserting relevant links in their blogs so that readers can connect to one another and to other information about the blog's topic.)
- They correct themselves early, easily and often.
- They don't claim neutrality, but they do practice transparency.
- They aren't remote; they habitually converse.
- They give you their site but also other sites as a proper frame of reference.
- When they grab on to something, they don't let go; they "track" it.

Ethical Philosophies to Consider

When you encounter an ethical problem, you may find yourself drawing on your upbringing, your education and perhaps your religious training. As you work to make a reasoned decision, you should also consider the work of theorists who have studied ethical decision making, such as Immanuel Kant and John Stuart Mill. By applying their principles to journalism, you will increase the odds that you have carefully considered your options, made a well-reasoned decision and be able to explain your decision to the public.

Your personal ethics might derive from the way you answer one fundamental question: Does the end justify the means? In other words, should you ever do something that is not good in itself to achieve a goal that you think is good? Your answer to these questions can help guide you through ethical dilemmas and may differ in varying situations.

The Ethics of Duty

Some ethicists hold quite simply that we have a duty to do what is right. They believe that some actions are always right and some always wrong—that is, there exists in nature (or in divine revelation, for those with religious faith) a fixed set of principles or laws from which we should not deviate. For these people, the end *never* justifies the means.

Some refer to this ethical philosophy as **absolutism** or *legalism*. An absolutist sees one clear duty: to discover the rules and to follow them. For example:

- Suppose you believe that it's always wrong to lie. If you learn that a friend cheated on an exam and you are asked about your friend's actions by a college administrator, you would answer truthfully. You might be torn by loyalty to your friend, but you would not lie.
- Suppose you believe that it's wrong to keep someone else's property without permission. If you find a wallet with $500 inside, you would make every effort to return the wallet to its owner.

One such absolutist was Immanuel Kant (1724–1804). Kant proposed the "categorical imperative," a moral law that obliges you to do only those things that you would be willing to have everyone do as a matter of universal law. After you decide what the correct action is, you must regard your decision as unconditional and without exception, and you must do what you decide. For journalists, one such universal law might be "Tell the truth."

The journalist with this sense of duty might be concerned only with whether an event is newsworthy. If an event is interesting, timely, significant or important, it is to be reported, regardless of the consequences. The duty of the journalist is to report the news. Period. Newscaster Walter Cronkite once said that if journalists worried about all the possible consequences of reporting something, they would never report anything.

Journalists who believe they have a duty to tell the news dismiss criticism of the press for stories it delivers to the public. Stop blaming the messenger, they say. We don't make events happen; we just report them.

Although Kant suggested telling the truth was a worthy categorical imperative, he believed another universal law was not to treat human beings as a means to an end. In other words, an ethical journalist should treat a source as a human being, not just as a way to boost one's career. Even Kant's absolutism has nuance.

Another theorist, William David Ross (1877–1971), talks about duty in a different way. He argues that we humans all owe each other various duties, including the following:

- Fidelity—keeping our promises.
- Reparation—making things right if we've messed up.
- Gratitude—repaying someone who's helped you.
- Justice—giving more consideration or aid to those who deserve it.
- Beneficence—helping people when you can.
- Noninjury—not hurting someone when you can avoid doing so.

Read through the Society of Professional Journalists' Code of Ethics, and you'll see clear traces of Ross' work, particularly in the sections about minimizing harm and being accountable.

The Ethics of Final Ends or Consequences

Instead of stressing duties, many people believe that what makes an act ethical is not the act itself but the consequences of the act. In other words, they believe that the end can and often does justify the means. To them, it might be all right to lie on occasion or to break a promise. For example:

- Suppose your sister tells you that her husband is abusing her and she is moving to a shelter for battered women. If the husband asks you where your sister is, you would be justified in lying to protect her from him.
- Suppose a friend swears you to secrecy before telling you that he is feeling suicidal. If you believe the consequences of an action determine its ethics, you would be justified in breaking your promise and getting help for your friend.

TIPS

Ask These 10 Questions to Make Good Ethical Decisions

1. What do I know? What do I need to know?
2. What is my journalistic purpose?
3. What are my ethical concerns?
4. What organizational policies and professional guidelines should I consider?

(continued)

An important consideration is the intention of the person performing the act. What one person declares unethical, another person would do for a good purpose or a good reason. For example, police often work undercover, concealing their identity to apprehend criminals. They accept that they sometimes must lie or even become involved in criminal activities. Their purpose is to protect the public; their intention is to work for the good of society. The end justifies the means.

Some journalists would not hesitate to do the same. Some might require that certain conditions be in place before they would steal or use deceit, but then they would proceed. They believe their purpose is to be the watchdog of government, to protect the common good, to keep the public fully informed. Whatever they must do to accomplish these goals, they argue, is ethical.

The Greatest Good for the Greatest Number

Perhaps the clearest rationale for an "ends justifies the means" approach is utilitarianism, a philosophy first articulated by the English scholar Jeremy Bentham (1748–1832) and elaborated on by John Stuart Mill (1806–1873). Stated simply, utilitarianism calls for choosing the action that is most likely to yield the greatest good for the greatest number. One catch, however, is that it's sometimes extremely

ON THE JOB Develop Your Ability to Identify Ethical Situations

Jean McHale earned her bachelor's degree in journalism and began her career in editorial roles at employee newsletters and trade publications. She transitioned to public relations and media-relations roles in government, higher education and association management. McHale says she has faced ethical choices throughout her career, but few situations presented themselves as neatly packaged defining moments.

"I've learned to recognize when my internal caution light is flashing," she says. "It is often a time when I cannot muster the energy to start a simple task, or when I feel the urge to rush through an assignment to get it off my plate."

Throughout her career, McHale has been asked to demonstrate ethical reasoning skills — often even before landing the job: "In most every job interview I've had, I've been asked to describe an ethically challenging situation and how I handled it."

When responding to this question, McHale says, it isn't necessary to have a heroic watchdog story or to embellish your role in past situations. "Employers use this question to understand how you translate ethical principles into practice," she says. "It's fine to describe everyday situations and to explain why you chose to take action or why you elected not to take action. Being able to articulate your process for recognizing ethically challenging situations and working through them will show employers and colleagues that you strive to be transparent and are capable of critical thinking when evaluating a situation."

McHale offers this final advice: "I can't overemphasize the importance of trusting your unique values, education and experiences to guide the professional and ethical decisions you will encounter throughout your career."

© Denyce Weiler, Something Blue Photo

difficult to determine what's best for the greatest number of people in the short term compared to the long term.

Still, most journalists probably subscribe to this ethic. They know, for example, that publishing a story about the infidelities of a public official might destroy the person's reputation or hurt his or her family, but taking a view of seeking the greatest good for the greatest number, they decide that for the greater good, the public should have this information. The decision to publish will seem even more justifiable if the public official is involved in embezzlement or bribery or a possible threat to national security. Of course, even a duty-based approach to ethics might lead you to the same conclusion: You have a duty to tell the truth and a duty to be a watchdog over government.

Older Philosophies: The Golden Rule and the Golden Mean

Finally, before we move on to demonstrating how these philosophies can be used to inform your own decision making, let's consider two more: the golden rule and the golden mean.

The essence of the golden rule is "You shall love your neighbor as yourself." This ethic holds that all principles are relative to one absolute: love of neighbor. Many think of love of neighbor as an essential Judeo-Christian value, but the fact is that most religions, as well as secular humanism and other creeds, emphasize caring for others. To state it simply, this form of ethics always places people first. In every ethical dilemma, you must always do what is best for people. But sometimes you must choose between love for one person and love for a larger community of people.

Not to be confused with the golden rule is Aristotle's golden mean. For the ancient Greek philosopher, virtue was to be found somewhere between two extremes, if not the exact middle (or mean). For Aristotle, true courage would be found somewhere between cowardice and foolhardiness. If one thinks in terms of journalism, ethical reporting might lie somewhere between reporting everything you know and not reporting at all. In the case of the anonymous *New York Times* opinion essay, for example, the newspaper released some but not all the information about the author.

Resolving Ethical Issues

Having reviewed some ethical philosophies, you're now more prepared to engage in the process of ethical decision making. In other words, when faced with an ethical issue, you'll be more likely to recognize it and better equipped to make a reasoned, principled decision.

Principled reasoning assumes that you are not acting ethically if you do something simply because you have been told to do it or because that's what everyone else does. You also are not being ethical if you report a story just to beat the competition or just to attract clicks and page views.

(continued)

5. How can I include other people, with different perspectives and diverse ideas, in the decision-making process?
6. Who are the stakeholders — those affected by my decision? What are their motivations? Which are legitimate?
7. What if the roles were reversed? How would I feel if I were in the shoes of one of the stakeholders?
8. What are the possible consequences of my actions? Short-term? Long-term?
9. What are my alternatives to maximize my truth-telling responsibility and minimize harm?
10. Can I clearly and fully justify my thinking and my decision? To my colleagues? To the stakeholders? To the public?

■ Bob Steele, Nelson Poynter Scholar for Journalism Values

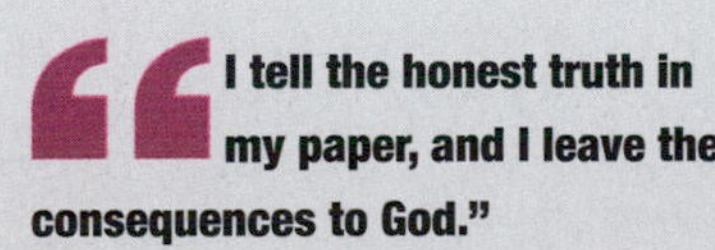

"I tell the honest truth in my paper, and I leave the consequences to God."

■ James Gordon Bennett, newspaper publisher, 1836

TIPS

Guidelines from the Society of Professional Journalists

The highest and primary obligation of ethical journalism is to serve the public. Journalists should do the following:

- Avoid conflicts of interest, real or perceived. Disclose unavoidable conflicts.
- Refuse gifts, favors, fees, free travel and special treatment, and avoid political and other outside activities that may compromise integrity or impartiality or may damage credibility.

To help journalists and others make ethical decisions, ethicists Clifford Christians, Kim Rotzoll and Mark Fackler adapted a model of moral reasoning devised by Ralph Potter of Harvard Divinity School. Called the Potter Box (Figure 20.1), the model has four elements:

- **Appraising the situation.** Making a good ethical decision begins with good reporting. You cannot make an ethical decision unless you know all the facts. Sometimes when you don't appraise a situation fully and get all of the facts, you end up being highly embarrassed.
- **Identifying values.** What are your personal values, your news organization's values, your community's values, the nation's values? For example, you might place high value on your personal credibility and on that of your news organization.

  When three-time Pulitzer Prize–winning *Washington Post* reporter Sari Horwitz was caught copying and pasting material from *The Arizona Republic* twice in six days, it wasn't just *The Post* that was harmed. As Dennis Wagner, the reporter who did most of the work on the original story, said, "It's bad because it undermines the credibility not just of *The Washington Post* but of journalists in general. People think we take shortcuts and cheat, and it's hurtful to all of us."

  Horwitz blamed deadline pressures for her actions and apologized. "It was wrong. It was inexcusable," she said. "And it is one of the cardinal sins in journalism. I apologize to *The Arizona Republic* and its reporters and editors."
- **Appealing to ethical principles.** Look at the various ethical principles discussed previously. Contrary to what many believe, it's not always sufficient to follow

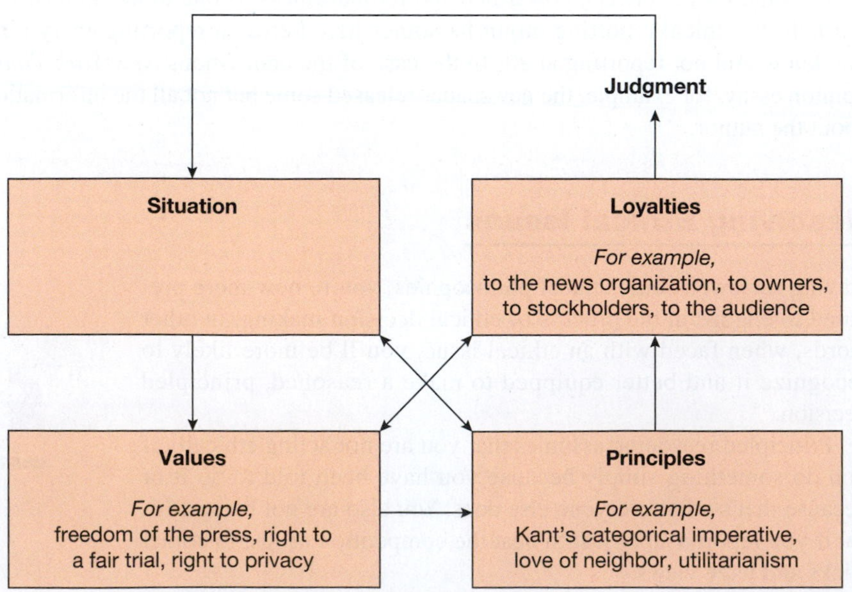

FIGURE 20.1

The Potter Box can help journalists analyze and resolve ethical problems.

your gut. If that were true, the world would have only ethical people in it. Nor are the principles meant to be a shopping list from which you choose items that serve your personal interest. The more principles you consider, the more alternatives you can consider. To be ethical, you might have to choose an alternative that is far from expedient.

It might be expedient to make up sources to fit a story you are reporting, but expedience is rarely if ever a good ethical principle. Madison Roberts, a freshman majoring in journalism at the University of Alabama, created names, years and majors for sources in her stories in *The Crimson White*, the university newspaper. She quoted nearly 30 students and a professor who did not exist and wrote a number of stories with only fabricated sources.

"I was overwhelmed and succumbed to a lot of pressure I'd been under," Roberts told the newspaper in an email. "I did it because *The Crimson White* had become so important to me that I didn't want to lose it."

- **Choosing loyalties.** As a journalist, Bill Kovach and Tom Rosenstiel argue, your first loyalty should be to citizens. In addition, you have loyalties to yourself. You must be able to look yourself in the mirror; you must be able to sleep at night. You also must weigh what you owe your employer and your sources.

  Sometimes being loyal to yourself and your own principles gets you thrown in jail or fired. Caitlin Curran believed that it was wrong for brokerage houses to sell worthless mortgage-backed securities. A photo of her carrying a sign of her belief went viral on the web, and she was fired from her part-time job as a web producer with a Public Radio International show on WNYC in New York. Curran knew the rules against activism, and she chose to do something she deemed more important.

- Be wary of sources offering information for favors or money; do not pay for access to news. Identify content provided by outside sources, whether paid or not.
- Deny favored treatment to advertisers, donors or any other special interests, and resist internal and external pressure to influence coverage.
- Distinguish news from advertising, and shun hybrids that blur the lines between the two. Prominently label sponsored content.

You need not consider the four elements in the Potter Box in any particular order. Also, don't stop reasoning after you have touched on the four elements. Principled reasoning should continue.

The main objection to the Potter Box is that using it takes too much time and is impractical in the deadline-driven business of journalism. However, as you become better acquainted with ethical principles and more practiced at principled reasoning, you will be able to make ethical decisions much more quickly and reasonably. You can develop ethical muscle memory.

> **"Boldly tell the story of the diversity and magnitude of the human experience. Seek sources whose voices we seldom hear."**
>
> ■ ***The Society of Professional Journalists, Code of Ethics***

> **"Reflexivity . . . includes not presuming that one has the monopoly on truth, allowing that one might be mistaken, and simply being able to see things from another's point of view."**
>
> ■ **Natalia Roudakova**

Ethical Problems for Journalists

As you work through ethical dilemmas and, as the Potter Box suggests, consider your loyalties and values, you should be aware of common issues journalists face. As we covered in Chapter 19, because of the First Amendment, American society has relatively few "rules" for journalists, but that does not excuse ethical lapses. If anything, journalists need to be more versed in applying ethical principles than ever before.

Deceit

When is it permissible to lie, misrepresent yourself or use a hidden audio recorder or camera? When may you steal documents? For those who value absolute rules, the answer is simple: Never! They would never want lying or concealing one's identity to become a universal law. For others, the answer is not easy.

Journalists and other writers have often concealed their identity in pursuit of a story. One reporter got a job in a grocery store to expose it for selling bad meat; an atheist became close to churchgoers to write a book about an evangelical church. Yet Fred Barnes, the executive editor at *The Weekly Standard*, says that if you're a journalist, it's dishonest to profess to be someone you're not.

> **"The media system is a significant source of political, cultural, and economic power and, as with all sources of power, is subject to calls for accountability—particularly in a democratic society. In advertising, the increasing trend of 'socially responsible' campaigns that link brands with social values or causes implicitly recognizes this reality."**
>
> ■ Patrick Lee Plaisance

When he worked for the *Los Angeles Times*, Ken Silverstein misrepresented his identity, "pretending to be the representative of a London-based energy company with business interests in Turkmenistan." He was reporting on Washington lobbyists who were selling their services to any client. In an essay in *Harper's*, Silverstein took the Washington press corps to task for being too timid about using deception as a reporting tool. (This Ken Silverstein is not to be confused with the Ken Silverstein who covers the energy industry and contributes columns to *Forbes*.)

A group of journalists in an ethical decision-making seminar at the Poynter Institute devised a list of criteria to justify the use of deceit. The box "Conditions Justifying the Use of Deceit by Journalists" below synthesizes their conclusions. The journalists agreed all the conditions listed must be present to justify deceit.

Conditions Justifying the Use of Deceit by Journalists

- An issue of profound public importance that is:
  - Of vital public interest, revealing system failure at high levels.
  - A preventive measure against profound harm to individuals.
- All other alternatives exhausted.
- Eventual full disclosure of the deception and the reason for it.
- Full commitment to the story by everyone involved.
- The harm prevented outweighs any harm caused.
- A meaningful, collaborative and deliberative decision-making process that takes into account:
  - Short- and long-term consequences of the deception.
  - The impact on credibility.
  - Motivations for actions.
  - The organization's editorial mission.
  - Legal implications.
  - Consistency of reasoning and action.

Conflicts of Interest

Conflicts of interest can crop up anywhere, especially in the area of politics. Journalists report on people in power; sometimes, they get too close to them.

In 2018, *New York Times* reporter Ali Watkins became a story herself when people learned that she had had an affair with James A. Wolfe, the married security director for the Senate Intelligence Committee. The information became public after the government indicted Wolfe on suspicion of lying to FBI agents during an investigation into suspected leaks of classified information. The Trump administration had secretly seized Watkins' email and phone records to try to determine the source of the leaks. According to the indictment, which *The New York Times* posted on its website, Watkins and Wolfe's affair started when Watkins was a college student reporting on the Senate committee as an intern. In the indictment, Watkins is identified as "Reporter #2." The indictment states that the affair ended in December 2017, the same month Watkins started work at *The Times*.

In a column for Poynter, veteran journalist Indira Lakshmanan noted that Watkins had reported several important stories related to the Senate Intelligence Committee during the time of her affair with Wolfe. Says Lakshmanan: "having a relationship on her beat made her vulnerable to attempted extortion, to having her personal life exposed in an indictment, to questions about her credibility."

Not all conflicts of interests are as extreme as Watkins', and such conflicts also can occur outside the political arena. The Public Relations Society of America's Member Code of Ethics states that a member shall "disclose financial interest (such as stock ownership) in a client's organization." Should business reporters be allowed to cover companies in which they own stocks? Should all reporters be required to list the companies in which they hold stocks? Should religion writers cover news and events of the religion to which they belong?

TIPS

Ethical Problems That Journalists Face

- Deceit.
- Conflicts of interest:
  - Friendship.
  - Freebies.
  - Checkbook journalism.
  - Participation in the news.
- Advertising pressure.
- Invasion of privacy.
- Withholding information.
- Incorrect and incomplete information.
- Plagiarism.

> **"Our careers should be longer than any one scoop or series. That means playing the long game—and not doing anything that could cost us our reputations."**
>
> **■ Indira Lakshmanan, executive editor at the Pulitzer Center on Crisis Reporting, in a column for Poynter.org**

Friendship

Friendship might be the greatest obstacle to the flow of information. No one knows whether friendship causes more stories to be reported or more stories to be killed. Either way, it sets up a powerful conflict of interest. If you are ever assigned to a story that involves a personal acquaintance, ask your supervisor to give the assignment to someone else.

Payola

Payola is a contraction of the words *pay* and *Victrola* (an early phonograph for playing LP records). Its etymology is a hint that payola began in the music industry in radio. It eventually became illegal in that industry and was never permitted in journalism. Journalists may not accept payment for a story other than from their employer. Also, news organizations discourage reporters from doing promotional work for people they cover.

But some news organizations have created sticky ethical situations for reporters. In an attempt to diversify their revenue streams, some — including *The Atlantic*, *The New York Times*, Politico and *The Washington Post* — hold events where members of the public can interact with journalists and industry experts. In May 2018, *The Atlantic* held a daylong conference on health care, and Bloomberg News reporter Cynthia Koons was offered a chance to interview the president and chief executive of the Pharmaceutical Research and Manufacturers of America lobbying group, known as PhRMA. The catch: PhRMA helped underwrite the conference, and Erik Wemple of *The Washington Post* reported that Koons' interview was listed as "sponsored content." Koons withdrew from doing the interview because of the perceived, if not real, conflict of interest. As Wemple writes about such events: "Who knows what punches the journalists may have pulled? When big money hangs over the proceedings, so does that very question."

Bloggers and online reviewers can also come under scrutiny for financial conflicts of interest. According to the Federal Trade Commission, the principle of truth in advertising applies. So if a blogger or influencer is receiving compensation for an endorsement, that business arrangement should be clearly disclosed to readers and viewers.

Some conflicts of interest may be less obvious. Should news agencies prohibit journalists from accepting speakers' fees? Should journalists give up their right to vote in elections or donate money or time to nonprofits?

Freebies

When journalists accept freebies from people they cover, the gifts always come with a price. They raise these questions:

- Will receiving the freebie influence the journalist's reporting? That is, can the journalist remain objective?
- Do gifts cause reporters to write stories they otherwise would not write?
- Does the public perceive the reporter who accepted or is suspected of accepting freebies as neutral?

As with other conflicts of interest, the perception is paramount. Some argue that the least reporters must do is disclose prominently in their stories any freebies they accepted. Reporters also should disclose how they were able to get the story and why accepting freebies was necessary.

Travel writers, for example, often are offered free trips, free cruises, free hotel accommodations and other freebies by companies that expect them to write about what they experience. Many small news outlets cannot afford to send their travel writers on expensive tours. Travel writers who accept freebies should mention doing so in their stories and allow readers to decide whether to trust the reporting.

After a lecture on this topic to travel writers, a participant approached the speaker and asked, "Are you saying that if a company gives you a free trip somewhere and you find some things to criticize, you're supposed to write about the negative aspects of the trip?" Yes.

Most news organizations have rules against accepting freebies. The Society of Professional Journalists says, "Nothing of value shall be accepted." Is a cup of coffee something of value? The Associated Press expects its staff members to return gifts of "nominal value." Is a baseball cap of nominal value?

> **"Conflict of interest is practically the only place in ethics where perceptions matter almost as much as what is the case."**
>
> ■ **Lee Wilkins, coauthor of *Media Ethics: Issues and Cases***

Checkbook journalism

Paying a source for information brings up a number of ethical questions:

- Must you always report that you paid a source for information?
- Should reporters be in the business of keeping other reporters from getting a story?
- Are paid sources more likely to have an ax to grind?
- Do paid sources come forward only for financial gain?
- Will the audience believe your story if you paid your source for it?
- If you pay some sources for information, will others start to demand pay for information?

In 2018, an Australian television station paid a deputy prime minister $150,000 (Australian dollars) for an interview with the official and his partner, a former staff member, after the birth of their child. "Watching the criticism that led him to take a leave of absence, I found myself wondering what was part of the negotiation," wrote Damien Cave, Sydney bureau chief for *The New York Times*. "Would the public be getting a less candid interview if the price for access had been $50,000? Would we get more if it was $200,000?" Cave said he appreciates the guidelines his news organization sets. Otherwise, he said, "the boundary between source (or interest group) and journalist can be shaped, if not erased, in ways that threaten to hamper candid reporting."

Although the U.S. television networks ABC and NBC announced in 2011 that they would no longer pay sources, *The New Yorker* reported in 2016 that the tabloid gossip news site TMZ regularly pays for news tips and videos. One video showed Baltimore Ravens star running back Ray Rice knocking out his then fiancée Janay Palmer in an elevator in an Atlantic City New Jersey hotel. The violence captured on video effectively ended Rice's NFL career. Whether TMZ produces journalism is arguable, but viewers may not know the difference.

Participation in the news

At times, journalists receive severe criticism for doing what seems to be right and humane. When network correspondents were seen on television performing medical treatment in Haiti, Carl Elliott of the University of Minnesota Center for Bioethics called it "a classic PR tactic using humanitarian aid as a public relations device, in order to drive up ratings for their network."

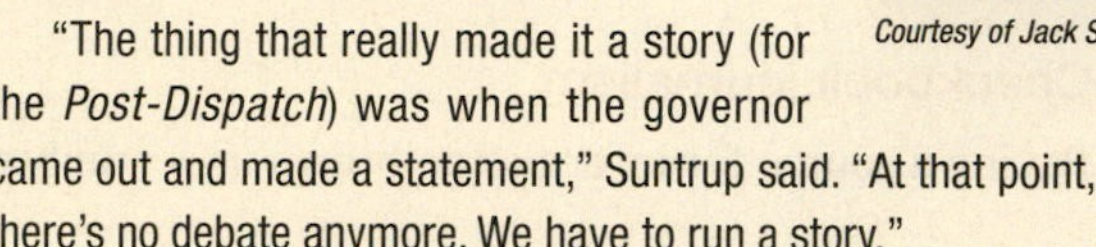

ON THE JOB What to Do When Rumors Keep Swirling

Courtesy of Jack Suntrup

Jack Suntrup covers politics and state government for the *St. Louis Post-Dispatch*. As an intern immediately after graduating from the University of Missouri, he helped the newspaper cover a legislative session, and he returned to the newspaper full time in July 2017. That fall, he started hearing rumors that the state's married governor, Eric Greitens, had had an extramarital affair with a married woman before his campaign for governor. The rumors were fairly detailed, including the woman's name and her current marital status (divorced).

Suntrup, who had taken investigative reporting at the Missouri School of Journalism, did some basic fact-checking. "I looked at the divorce filings, so I knew these were real people," he said. However, rumors of the affair had circulated in Missouri political circles before, and the newspaper proceeded with caution.

Post-Dispatch political editor Christopher Ave explained why in a podcast posted by the paper Jan. 12, 2018. "The rumor was so salacious, and it was so second- or third- or fourth-hand, that we're quite aware that as journalists, when we ask a source or sources about a rumor, we are in fact spreading the rumor," Ave said. "... Our job is to pursue the truth, but we don't pursue the truth at all costs. Part of our job as ethical journalists is understanding the consequences of our actions."

But as the rumors intensified, members of the investigating team decided they needed to learn everything they could about the story. The attorney for the woman's former husband contacted Suntrup, and the paper sent the ex-husband written questions through his attorney. On Jan. 4, Suntrup said, the newspaper received a copy of a tape the husband said he secretly made in which his then-wife discussed the alleged affair.

Because of the serious allegations the woman made in the tape, including blackmail, the team felt it was important to keep gathering information.

Suntrup said the paper was not ready to publish without directly receiving information from a firsthand participant. That changed on Jan. 10, the night of Greitens' state of the state address, when St. Louis TV station KMOV aired a report about the affair on its 10 p.m. newscast. KMOV published portions of the audio in which the woman admits to the affair. When KMOV confronted the governor, the governor released a statement confirming the affair.

"The thing that really made it a story (for the *Post-Dispatch*) was when the governor came out and made a statement," Suntrup said. "At that point, there's no debate anymore. We have to run a story."

The team published its story the night the KMOV report aired and told readers: "The *Post-Dispatch* also has possession of the audio and has interviewed the ex-husband. The newspaper had previously decided against writing a story based solely on the husband and the audio recording, because the woman in question has consistently declined to be interviewed. However, Greitens' public acknowledgment of an affair made it necessary to revisit that decision."

The newspaper later received permission from the ex-husband's attorney to release the pieces of the audio that KMOV used. (The tape ran more than one hour long, and the edited version the *Post-Dispatch* ran was about 2½ minutes.) The *Post-Dispatch* also alerted visitors to its website about the nature of the tape: "The recording, obtained by the *Post-Dispatch*, was made without the woman's consent, which is legal in Missouri. WARNING: Contains graphic details."

Over the next few months, lawmakers and law enforcement officials conducted numerous investigations into Greitens until he ultimately resigned in June 2018. Throughout that time, Suntrup and his colleagues respected the woman's privacy and did not identify her by name. "We didn't identify the husband either because that would have identified her," Suntrup said.

Suntrup says young reporters working on a similar story should keep knowledge of such stories within a close-knit group of colleagues. He said they should cautiously select sources to contact and should avoid repeating rumors when speaking to sources. He urges reporters to focus on gathering information from documents and people with direct knowledge of the event and to be skeptical of sources who offer second- or third-hand information.

Bob Steele, who taught journalism ethics at DePauw University, concurs. He told blogger Matea Gold of the *Los Angeles Times*: "If it's imperative that (a reporter) intervene and help medically, then take him out of his journalistic role and do that. But don't have him covering the same stories in which he's a participant. It muddles the journalist reporting. It clouds the lens in terms of the independent observation and reporting."

Must journalists be passive citizens? Must they give up all activity that advocates or shows a point of view? Must a religion reporter be an atheist? Richard Harwood, *Washington Post* ombudsman at the time, told a conference of journalists: "You have every right in the world to run for office, or participate in a political activity or lobbying activity. You don't have the 'right' to work for *The Washington Post*."

John Smalley, editor at the *Wisconsin State Journal*, told his staffers this:

> **People accept work-related policies and restrictions all the time. If you want to sell high-end clothing, you can't wear cut-off jeans to work. If you want to deliver Coca-Cola, you can't drink Pepsi in your truck.**
>
> **And if you want to be a journalist, you keep your politics to yourself. That's just the way it is, and it's a deal every journalist accepts when he or she joins the profession.**

In October 2017, *The New York Times* updated its guidelines to incorporate social media. The short answer: If you work for *The Times*, assume people know you work for *The Times*. Therefore, you cannot post anything on your social media accounts (private or official) on issues *The Times* might cover. "If our journalists are perceived as biased or if they engage in editorializing on social media, that can undercut the credibility of the entire newsroom," *The Time*s posted for its staff and the world to see.

> **"But I don't believe that paying sources is unethical, as long as it's disclosed to the reader; in some cases I think it makes for better journalism. It gives a fair share of the profits to sources who spend time and take risks."**
>
> ■ John Tierney, from "Newsworthy," reprinted from the New York Times Co.

Advertising pressure

It's likely you won't work long at a news organization before you realize some subjects are taboo to write about and others are highly encouraged. If you are lucky, you will work for a paper, station or magazine with a solid wall of separation between editorial and advertising, sometimes referred to as "the separation of church and state."

However, in some places, advertising salespeople are allowed to peek over that wall and see what stories the publication or station is planning to run. That information might help sell some advertising. Some say, "What could be wrong with that?"

The next step is for the advertising department to climb over the wall and suggest that the editorial department should do a story on some subject so that advertising can be sold. This could be justified as long as the stories are newsworthy and treat advertisers and non-advertisers equally.

But what if advertising salespeople begin to suggest or even to dictate what must and must not be covered?

> **"If you're not involved in the community at all and you're totally neutralized, you end up not knowing enough about the community, not being able to get enough leads and so on in order to do your job."**
>
> ■ Ethicist Louis W. Hodges, quoted by Tony Case in *Editor & Publisher*

Invasion of Privacy

In Chapter 19, we discussed what you legally *can* do as a journalist. What you *should* do is another question. Most journalists would cry out against an invasion of their own privacy. Yet many of them argue for a vague "right to know" when they report on others, especially if those others are public officials or public figures.

How much detail do readers or viewers need about the people in the news? Do they need to hear the angst of a woman who's been secretly recorded telling her husband about a sexual encounter with the state's married governor? That was the dilemma faced by television and newspaper reporters in St. Louis in January 2018. (For more on that story, see the "On the Job" box with Jack Suntrup.) Did citizens need to hear her voice to believe the accusations made against the governor? Work through the steps outlined in the Potter Box. Would you have made the same decisions? In journalism, the frequent head-on collisions between the right to know and the right to privacy are real.

Crime victims

The most obvious and talked-about issue related to the right to privacy is naming crime survivors, especially rape and sex-crime survivors. Although the U.S. Supreme Court has held that news agencies cannot be punished for publishing lawfully obtained information or information from a public record, should you publish that information?

Most journalists will not name a victim who does not want to be named because publishing the survivor's name may heap more suffering on that person. Still, Geneva Overholser, former editor of the *Des Moines Register*, has argued that running incomplete stories—articles that name suspects and not victims—perpetuates the stigma associated with sexual crimes. "When real people are credibly seen as having experienced something that we'd rather not acknowledge: That is when we believe at last in a problem's existence," Overholser wrote in 2014. Since then, she has applauded the women willing to go public to make accusations against once powerful men such as Bill Cosby, Larry Nassar and Harvey Weinstein.

Although Kelly McBride of the Poynter Institute does not advocate that journalists name victims who do not wish to be named, she does call for journalists to focus more on reporting sexual assault as a public health problem so "that the public might understand how it happens and how to prevent it." In a 2018 column, she wrote that newsrooms' ethics policies related to naming the victims of sexual assaults should include allowing victims the opportunity to tell their stories, as well as treating fairly those who have been accused.

Victims of child abuse and their families

In her column on anonymity policies, McBride also argued that journalists should hold schools, medical facilities and law enforcement accountable for protecting children. She applauded the work of the *Indianapolis Star*, which broke the first stories about Nassar, the official team doctor for USA Gymnastics who was later convicted of sexually assaulting hundreds of girls and young women.

Child abuse is news, and it should be, especially if it involves people in powerful roles or well-known celebrities such as former Subway pitchman Jared Fogle, whose foundation arranged for him to visit schools and urge children to adopt good eating habits and to exercise. The victims of Fogle's abuse, both those he abused physically and those in pornographic videos he viewed, apparently did not report his actions. Victims of child abuse are often ashamed to talk about it, even to their parents, and their parents are even more ashamed. But when one victim has the courage to speak, others often follow. That happened in the Nassar case, where ultimately 150 girls and women testified against the doctor in open court.

At what point should journalists include names in their reporting? And how graphically should the news media describe what victims were made to suffer? Should reporters visit the victims' parents? An ethical decision requires reflection. Is there a way to minimize harm to those who have already been harmed? What are your motives?

Juvenile offenders

Another ethical issue concerns publishing the names of juvenile offenders. News agencies traditionally have not published their names because they have held that juveniles are entitled to make juvenile mistakes, even if those mistakes are crimes. After all, juvenile court records are sealed. Again, the courts have upheld the right to publish juvenile offenders' names that are on the public record.

Some media critics have applauded the publication of the names of juvenile offenders. However, in addition to the stigma forever attached to the juvenile offender's name and the embarrassment to his or her parents and family, some worry that in some groups a youth's notoriety will encourage other young people to violate the law. Others argue that shame will stop other juveniles from committing crimes.

Sexual orientation

Another privacy concern is whether to reveal someone's sexual orientation if that person has not publicly done so. In its stylebook, The Associated Press recommends reporting on someone's sexual orientation only if it is pertinent to the story.

Public figures

These are just a few of the myriad privacy issues you will face. Journalists are still legally protected when writing about public officials and public figures, but how much detail should they include? What about the children of politicians or celebrities?

Websites exist that have files on nearly everyone. Some allow you to see what anyone has ever posted in a chat room. What should journalists use? What if a hacker leaks information to a news organization? What can be viewed as legitimate and trustworthy?

Photos and Video

The Associated Press Statement of News Values could not be clearer: "AP pictures must always tell the truth. We do not alter or digitally manipulate the content of a photograph in any way."

What's the grammar error in this sentence?

A candidate for the office of U.S. president must be a natural-born citizen of the U.S., and he must be at least 35 years old.

See Appendix 1, Rule 15.

The National Press Photographers Association Code of Ethics states: "Treat subjects with respect and dignity. Give special consideration to vulnerable subjects and compassion to victims of crime or tragedy. Intrude on private moments of grief only when the public has an overriding and justifiable need to see."

Those two rules are the primary ethical concerns for photojournalists of all media: telling the truth and minimizing harm.

To minimize harm, photographers and video journalists should respect people's dignity at crime and disaster scenes, and they need to be invited to a funeral unless it is for a public figure. With permission of the family, they may now photograph coffins containing deceased soldiers from U.S. military actions.

Judgments about using photos are often a matter of taste more than ethics. Here are some examples.

Perhaps you would not expect the New York *Daily News* to doctor a photograph to make it appear less gory, but that's what the paper did to its front-page picture in its coverage of the 2013 Boston marathon tragedy. The man on the back page of a wrap-around cover had a badly mangled, bloodied leg. You see a normal leg in the *Daily News* photo.

"The *Daily News* edited that photo out of sensitivity to the victims, the families and the survivors," *Daily News* spokesperson Ken Frydman said. "There were far more gory photos that the paper chose not to run, and frankly I think the rest of the media should have been as sensitive as the *Daily News*."

The New York *Daily News* did not show similar sensitivity telling the news about the slaying of WBDJ reporter Alison Parker and her cameraman Adam Ward in Roanoke, Virginia, in 2015. In three panels, the paper printed close-up images of the gunman's execution on its front page. A half dozen or more tabloids from around the world were equally insensitive with the photos and ran headlines emphasizing that the two victims were shot dead on "live TV." The (London) *Daily Mail*'s headline said a "gunman with a grudge shot news girl on live TV."

Some argued that there's a blurry line between showing and not showing the photos taken by the killer. How else would we witness the horror?

"The line is pretty clear to me. It is the moment when information becomes exploitation," former *USA Today* editor-in-chief Ken Paulson told Agence France Presse.

Freelance photographer R. Umar Abbasi was waiting for a train on the platform of the 49th Street subway station in Manhattan when he saw a man on a subway track about to be killed by an oncoming train. The photographer told the *New York Post*, "I just started running, running, hoping that the driver could see my flash." What his flashes did capture were pictures of a desperate man trying to save his life. The engineer saw the flashes but said he could not stop.

The New York Daily News *altered this photo of the aftermath of the Boston Marathon bombing to make the scene less disturbing to readers.*

SPORTS FINAL

DAILY NEWS

NEW YORK'S HOMETOWN NEWSPAPER

MARATHON MASSACRE

Terror bombs rock Boston

At least 3 dead and 140 injured

PAGES 2-11

NY Daily News via Getty Images

The *New York Post* could have stopped. It did not have to run the resulting photo—at least not on a full front page—but it did. It's one thing to ask whether the photographer should have dropped his camera and tried to save the man's life. There were others present who could have done so. Some people defended the photographer. But it is another question to ask whether the *Post* had any reason to run the photo on the front page.

Some people defended the newspaper's decision. But most people, including journalism professors and scholars, condemned the *Post* for being sensationalistic and insensitive. *USA Today* quoted Poynter's McBride as saying that printing the picture had no "journalistic purpose." She explained that it did "not bear witness to something people need to know about."

Withholding Information

A journalist's job is to report the news. The public expects it and even demands it. To deliberately withhold news from the public could pose an ethical dilemma.

Is it ever permissible to withhold information from the news organization for which you work? If you are a working journalist writing what you hope will be a best-selling book, may you save some "news" until after the book is published?

If you work as a journalist, are you ever off-duty? A doctor isn't. Doctors take an oath to treat the sick. If you witness something at a friend's house or at a party, do you tell your news director about it? One reporter was fired when his boss discovered that he had attended a rock band's postconcert party where lines of cocaine were openly available. The reporter did not include this information in his coverage of the band. His defense was that if he reported the illegal drug use, he would never get interviews with or access to other rock groups. His excuse didn't save his job.

When should you withhold information because the police ask you to or because it may jeopardize a case? In a column for Poynter, McBride wrote: "Cutting deals to withhold information is dangerous. It should be done with great caution, much forethought and only in rare circumstances." She also warns that "we too readily agree with police and keep information from the public."

However, sometimes withholding information is the ethical course. Few knew that Richard Engel, the chief foreign correspondent for NBC News, and his TV crew had spent five days in captivity in Syria. Their kidnapping was a secret because NBC, the other major television networks, and newspapers, such as *The New York Times*, agreed to keep the facts quiet until the safe return of the journalists.

Incorrect and Incomplete Information

When print publications get the news wrong, they typically inform readers of these mistakes in a corrections column, usually on the second page of the publication. Some online news sites, however, act as if they never make mistakes. They simply post new stories with updated information or act as if the first stories never appeared.

In its code of ethics, the Canadian Association of Journalists offers some tips for digital media. Relevant here: "When we correct errors online, we indicate that the content has been altered or updated, and what the original error was."

Online journalists often make up for incomplete information by using links to external sites. Are raw data journalism? How much and how often may you link to raw data and with what warnings or interpretations? There's little doubt that readers appreciate links to source data so they can make judgments for themselves. At the same time, good websites help readers navigate that information. Journalists are still trying to find the right balance between the two.

Plagiarism

No one wants you to use his or her work as your own. Everyone condemns **plagiarism**—journalism's capital offense. Plagiarism regularly raises its ugly head. Rookies and veterans in every area of journalism ruin their personal reputations and sully the reputations their news organizations.

BuzzFeed's political editor was fired after it was discovered that in 41 instances in his 500 stories there were "sentences or phrases copied word for word from other sites." In 2018, IGN, an online gaming publication, fired its editor for plagiarism.

CNN received no complaints about plagiarism, and yet one of its London bureau news editors had published about 50 stories containing 128 separate instances of plagiarism. Most of the material Marie-Louise Gumuchian had lifted came from "an extensive archive" of work she had done at Reuters. The plagiarism was discovered in a routine editing check by a single copy editor. CNN then ran it through plagiarism-flagging software that turned up "two or three things" that caused a deeper look at "all of her work."

A Reuters spokesperson said, "While employed by Reuters we were not aware of any concerns raised about Ms. Gamuchian's work. However in light of press reports we are reviewing her stories."

Perhaps the greatest temptation is to plagiarize material published online. But you also might be tempted to lift words from your own news organization's stories or from a wire report. Some reporters have felt justified taking quotes and verbatim sentences from news releases and inserting them into their stories. Make sure you're not plagiarizing when you think you're paraphrasing (Figure 20.2). And attribute, attribute, attribute. You always serve your readers best when you get your own quotations. Don't even reuse your own material or stories or columns without letting your readers know what you are doing. Remember, internet users are quite effective at spotting many of these practices. Bloggers and Twitter users will catch and expose you.

Beware of Plagiarism!

Roy Peter Clark of the Poynter Institute cautions against the following acts of plagiarism:

- Taking material verbatim (word for word) from the newspaper library.
- Using material verbatim from the wire services.
- Using material from other publications.
- Using news releases verbatim.
- Using the work of fellow reporters.
- Using old stories over again.

Plagiarism, Quotation and Paraphrase

Using an Attributed Quotation: Acceptable

The journalist fully identifies the source of the quotation and puts the source's exact words in quotation marks:

As William A. Henry III writes in *Time* magazine, reporters have a "First Amendment bond" with their readers. "Plagiarism," he writes, "imperils that bond, not because it involves theft of a wry phrase or piquant quote, but because it devalues meticulous, independent verification of fact—the bedrock of a press worth reading."

Paraphrasing a Quotation: Acceptable

The journalist identifies the source and restates the source's original idea in the journalist's own words:

William A. Henry III writes about the destructive effect on journalism that plagiarism can have, suggesting that it compromises the integrity of the reportorial research process.

Plagiarizing: Unacceptable

Even though the source is identified, the journalist errs by using the source's original words (in bold) without putting them in quotation marks. Simply using distinctive words and phrases without quotation marks can constitute plagiarism:

In writing about how plagiarism **imperils** a reporter's **bond** with readers, William A. Henry III says the practice goes beyond stealing **a wry phrase or piquant quote**. It **devalues the meticulous, independent verification of fact** that journalism depends on.

Plagiarizing: Unacceptable

The journalist has not identified the source and has not put the source's original words (in bold) in quotation marks. Changing the occasional word (for example, "striking" rather than "piquant") or the structure of a sentence is not sufficient to avoid plagiarism:

Plagiarism damages the reporter's **bond** with his or her readers. It goes beyond the **theft of a wry phrase or** striking **quote** and diminishes the foundation of journalism—**the meticulous, independent verification of facts.**

FIGURE 20.2

Writers sometimes misunderstand the nature of paraphrase. Simply altering a few words of a quotation, with or without attribution, often results in plagiarism rather than paraphrase.

Although it might seem impossible, some people believe writers can plagiarize and have absolutely no idea they are doing so. They say that sometimes something you have read becomes so familiar that you later consider it your own. Sometimes plagiarism results from sloppy note taking. Make sure you have a systematic way of taking notes that keeps track of the original source and allows you to distinguish between verbatim and paraphrased information.

You must question everything, check any doubts, avoid any hint of plagiarism and fight every impulse to use others' work. And just as certainly, you must resist temptations to make up people, to fabricate events and to invent quotations.

In November 2018, the *Houston Chronicle* retracted eight stories written by its bureau chief in Austin, Texas, because it could not verify the existence of dozens of his alleged sources. The journalist chose to resign.

Social Media Ethics

News appears not just on news organization websites but also on social media such as Facebook, Instagram and YouTube. Twitter has become an essential tool for obtaining tips and leads to stories. All the guidelines of journalism ethics apply to reporters' use of Twitter. When it updated its ethics guidelines in 2017, for example, NPR noted that many journalistic principles remained constant: "Treat those you encounter online with fairness, honesty and respect, just as you would offline. Verify information before passing it along. Be honest about your intent when reporting. Avoid actions that might discredit your professional impartiality."

CHAPTER RESOURCES

SUGGESTED READINGS

Christians, Clifford G., Mark Fackler, Kathy Richardson, Peggy Kreshel and Robert H. Woods Jr. *Media Ethics: Cases and Moral Reasoning*. 9th ed. Boston: Allyn Bacon, 2016. The authors apply the Potter Box method of principled reasoning to dozens of journalism, advertising and public relations cases.

Fletcher, Joseph. *Situation Ethics: The New Morality*. Louisville, Ky.: Westminster John Knox Press, 1997. First published in 1966, this classic work on Christian situation ethics is for some a breath of fresh air and for others heresy.

Kovach, Bill, and Tom Rosenstiel. *The Elements of Journalism: What Newspeople Should Know and the Public Should Expect*. 3rd ed. New York: Three Rivers Press, 2014. This book should be required reading for every journalism student and journalist.

Meyers, Christopher, ed. *Journalism Ethics: A Philosophical Approach*. New York: Oxford University Press, 2010. Even a quick look at this book's table of contents tells you it brings together the best journalism scholars writing about journalism's most vital topics.

Patterson, Philip, Lee Wilkins and Chad Painter. *Media Ethics: Issues and Cases*. 9th ed. Lanham, Md.: Rowman & Littlefield, 2019. This book offers an excellent discussion of journalism ethics with up-to-date cases.

Wilkins, Lee, and Clifford G. Christians, eds. *The Handbook of Mass Media Ethics*. New York: Routledge, 2009. In this handbook, scholars look at the intellectual history of mass media ethics over the past 25 years and summarize past and possible future research.

SUGGESTED WEBSITES

LaunchPad Solo
launchpadworks.com
When you visit LaunchPad Solo for Journalism, you will find research links, exercises and LearningCurve adaptive quizzing to help you improve your grammar and AP style usage. In addition, the site's video collection hosts the videos highlighted in this and other chapters, as well as additional clips of leading professionals discussing important media trends.

www.ijnet.org
This is the website of the International Journalists' Network. Here you can find the codes of ethics of nearly every country or press association that has one. It also reports on the state of the media around the world and contains media directories.

http://mediaschool.indiana.edu/research-2/ethics-case-studies
This site, from Indiana University's School of Journalism, contains a large set of cases to help you explore ethical issues in journalism. The initial cases were published in *FineLine*, a newsletter put out by Barry Bingham Jr.

Poynter.org
The Poynter Institute specializes in training journalists to do better on all fronts, including ethics. See, for example, Kelly McBride's column ("To tell the stories of sexual assault victims, it's time for a new look at anonymity policies"). In addition to thoughtful commentary on the latest ethical dilemmas journalists have faced, Poynter also offers a free online course on journalism ethics, as well as a free webinar.

www.spj.org
Click on "Resources & Missions" on the top of the screen. Then scroll down to "Ethics." The ethics site of the Society of Professional Journalists provides the SPJ Code of Ethics, ethics news, an ethics hotline, an SPJ ethics listserv, ethics case studies and other ethics resources.

EXERCISES

1. Search for at least two articles on whether to publish the names of one of the following:

   a. Juvenile criminal suspects and defendants.
   b. Victims of rape, molestation or other sex crimes.

   Write a brief essay about your findings.

2. Using what you have learned in this chapter, answer this question: Does the end ever justify the means? Give at least two examples.

3. You've learned that the daughter of a local bank president has been kidnapped. The kidnappers have not contacted the family, and police officials ask you to keep the matter secret for fear the abductors might panic and injure the child. Describe how a duty-based journalist or a utilitarian would make her decisions about how to handle the situation.

4. You're assigned to write a piece on a new bus service from your town to Chicago. Your editor tells you to ask the bus company for a free round-trip ticket. What will you do, and why?

5. For at least a year, reporters on your paper have heard rumors that a retirement home is negligent in its care of the elderly. Your editor asks you to get a job there as a janitor and to report what you find. How will you respond, and why?

6. You are a photographer. Your editor has told you to keep an eye out for any instances of police brutality. You happen to see a police officer knock down a homeless man and begin kicking him. Will you take photos, or will you attempt in some way to discourage the police officer from hurting the homeless man? Explain.

7. **Your journalism blog.** You are the theater critic for your news organization. A producer has offered you free tickets to an upcoming performance. Should you accept the tickets? Why or why not? Write a blog post explaining your conclusions, and invite others to comment on your blog.

20 Common Errors of Grammar and Punctuation

Grammar provides our language's rules of the road. When you have a green light, you proceed on faith that other drivers will not go through their red light. That's because drivers have a shared understanding of the rules of the road. Similarly, writers have a shared understanding of the grammar rules that ensure we understand what we are reading. Occasionally, as on the road, there is a wreck. We dangle participles, misplace modifiers and omit commas. If we write "Running down the street, his pants fell off," we are saying a pair of pants was running down a street. If we write "He hit Harry and John stopped him," the missing comma makes the meaning, on first reading, "He hit Harry and John."

To say what you mean—to avoid syntactic wrecks—you must know the rules of grammar. We have compiled a list of 20 common errors that we find in our students' stories and in the stories of many professionals. Avoid them, and you'll write safely.

To take quizzes based on this list of 20 common errors of grammar and punctuation, go to LearningCurve for AP Style on LaunchPad for Journalism at **launchpadworks.com**. There you will find advice and activities that go beyond grammar. LearningCurve offers exercises on Associated Press style—the style that makes news writing distinctly journalistic.

1. Incorrect comma in a series in Associated Press style

Use commas to separate the items in a series, but do not put a comma before *and* or *or* at the end of the series unless the meaning would be unclear without a comma.

Incorrect comma before *and* The film was fast-paced, sophisticated, and funny.

Clear without comma The film was fast-paced, sophisticated and funny.

A comma before *and* or *or* can prevent confusion.

Unclear without comma He demanded cheese, salsa with jalapeños and onions on his taco.

Adding a comma before *and* prevents readers from wondering if he demanded salsa containing both jalapeños and onions or if the salsa and the onions were two separate toppings.

Clear with comma He demanded cheese, salsa with jalapeños, and onions on his taco.

The sentence can be revised to mean salsa with both jalapeños and onions.

Clear revision without comma He demanded cheese and salsa with jalapeños and onions on his taco.

2. Run-on sentence

An independent clause contains a subject and a predicate and makes sense by itself. A run-on sentence—also known as a *comma splice*—occurs when two or more independent clauses are joined incorrectly with a comma.

Run-on John Rogers left the family law practice, he decided to become a teacher.

You can correct a run-on sentence in several ways. Join the clauses with a comma and one of the coordinating conjunctions (*and*, *but*, *for*, *nor*, *or*, *so* or *yet*), or join the clauses with a semicolon if they are closely related. Use a subordinating conjunction (such as *after*, *because*, *if* or *when*) to turn one of the clauses into a dependent clause. Or rewrite the run-on as two separate sentences.

Correcting a run-on with a comma and a coordinating conjunction

John Rogers left the family law practice, for he decided to become a teacher.

Correcting a run-on with a semicolon

John Rogers left the family law practice; he decided to become a teacher.

Correcting a run-on by making one independent clause a dependent clause

John Rogers left the family law practice when he decided to become a teacher.

Correcting a run-on by writing two separate sentences

John Rogers left the family law practice. He decided to become a teacher.

3. Fragment

A fragment is a word group that lacks a subject, a verb or both yet is punctuated as though it were a complete sentence. Another type of fragment is a word group that begins with a subordinating conjunction such as *because* or *when* yet is punctuated as though it were a complete sentence.

Fragments After she had placed her watch and an extra pencil on the table. Without feeling especially sorry about it.

Correct a fragment by joining it to the sentence before or after it or by adding the missing elements so that the fragment contains a subject and a verb and can stand alone.

Correcting a fragment by joining it to another sentence

After she had placed her watch and an extra pencil on the table, the student opened the exam booklet.

Correcting a fragment by turning it into a sentence

She apologized to her boss for the outburst without feeling especially sorry about it.

4. Missing comma(s) with a nonrestrictive element

A nonrestrictive element is a word, phrase or clause that gives information about the preceding part of the sentence but does not restrict or limit the meaning of that part. A nonrestrictive element is not essential to the meaning of the sentence; you can delete it and still understand clearly what the sentence is saying. Place commas before and (if necessary) after a nonrestrictive element.

Unclear The mayor asked to meet Alva Johnson a highly decorated police officer.

Clear The mayor asked to meet Alva Johnson, a highly decorated police officer.

Unclear His wife Mary was there.

Clear His wife, Mary, was there.

5. Confusion of *that* and *which*

The pronoun *that* always introduces restrictive information that is essential to the meaning of the sentence; do not set off a *that* clause with commas. The pronoun *which* introduces nonrestrictive, or nonessential, information; set off a nonrestrictive *which* clause with commas.

Incorrect The oldest store in town, Miller and Co., that has been on Main Street for almost a century, will close this summer.

Correct The oldest store in town, Miller and Co., which has been on Main Street for almost a century, will close this summer.

Incorrect The creature, which has been frightening residents of North First Street for the past week, has turned out to be a screech owl.

Correct The creature that has been frightening residents of North First Street for the past week has turned out to be a screech owl.

6. Missing comma after an introductory element

A sentence may begin with a dependent clause (a word group that contains a subject and a verb and begins with a subordinating conjunction such as *because* or *when*), a prepositional phrase (a word group that begins with a preposition such as *in* or *on* and ends with a noun or pronoun), an adverb such as *next* that modifies the whole sentence, or a participial phrase (a word group that contains a past or present participle, such as *determined* or *speaking*, that acts as an adjective). Use a comma to separate these introductory elements from the main clause of the sentence.

Dependent clause After the applause died down, the conductor raised his baton.

Prepositional phrase Without a second thought, the chicken crossed the road.

Adverb Furthermore, the unemployment rate continues to rise.

Participial phrases Waiting in the bar, José grew restless.

Saddened by the news from home, she stopped reading the letter.

Although it is always correct to use a comma after an introductory element, the comma may be omitted after some adverbs and short prepositional phrases if the meaning is clear.

> **Suddenly it's spring.**
>
> **In Chicago it rained yesterday.**

Always place a comma after two or more introductory prepositional phrases.

> **In May of last year in Toronto, Tom attended three conventions.**

Here are more examples:

Incorrect	Shaking her head at the latest budget information the library administrator wondered where to find the money for new books.
Correct	Shaking her head at the latest budget information, the library administrator wondered where to find the money for new books.
Incorrect	After a week of foggy, rainy mornings had passed he left Seattle.
Correct	After a week of foggy, rainy mornings had passed, he left Seattle.

7. Missing comma(s) between coordinate adjectives

Adjectives are coordinate if they make sense when you insert *and* between them or place them in reverse order.

> **The frightened, angry citizens protested the new policy.**
>
> **The frightened and angry citizens protested the new policy.**

The adjectives make sense with *and* between them, so they are coordinate.

> **The angry, frightened citizens protested the new policy.**

The adjectives make sense in reverse order, so they are coordinate. Separate coordinate adjectives with commas.

Incorrect	The gaunt lonely creature was also afraid.
Correct	The gaunt, lonely creature was also afraid.

8. Missing comma(s) in a compound sentence

Two or more independent clauses — word groups containing a subject and a verb and expressing a complete thought — joined with a coordinating conjunction (*and, but, for, nor, or, so* or *yet*) form a compound sentence. Place a comma before the conjunction in a compound sentence to avoid confusion.

Unclear	She works as a pharmacist now and later she plans to go to medical school.
Clear	She works as a pharmacist now, and later she plans to go to medical school.

9. Misused semicolon

In a compound sentence that has a coordinating conjunction joining the clauses, place a comma (not a semicolon) before the conjunction.

Incorrect The Chicago Cubs did not play in the World Series; but they did win their division.

Correct The Chicago Cubs did not play in the World Series, but they did win their division.

10. Misplaced or dangling modifier

Modifiers are words or phrases that change or clarify the meaning of another word or word group in a sentence. Place modifiers immediately before or directly after the word or words they modify. A *misplaced modifier* appears too far from the word or words it is supposed to modify in the sentence. A *dangling modifier* appears in a sentence that does not contain the word or words it is supposed to modify. A modifier at the beginning of a sentence should refer to the grammatical subject of the sentence.

Misplaced modifier Having predicted a sunny morning, the downpour (*subject*) surprised the meteorologist.

Correct Having predicted a sunny morning, the meteorologist (*subject*) did not expect the downpour.

Dangling modifier Working in the yard, the sun (*subject*) burned her badly.

Correct Working in the yard, she (*subject*) became badly sunburned.

11. Missing or misused hyphen(s) in a compound modifier

A compound modifier consists of two or more words used to modify a single noun. When a compound modifier precedes a noun, hyphenate the parts of the compound unless the compound consists of an adverb ending in *-ly* followed by an adjective.

Incorrect His over the top performance made the whole film unbelievable.

The freshly-printed counterfeit bills felt like genuine dollars.

The local chapter of Parents Without Partners will sponsor a come as you are party on Saturday.

Correct His over-the-top performance made the whole film unbelievable.

The freshly printed counterfeit bills felt like genuine dollars.

The local chapter of Parents Without Partners will sponsor a come-as-you-are party on Saturday.

12. Missing or misused apostrophe

Do not confuse the pronoun *its*, meaning "belonging to it," with the contraction *it's*, meaning "it is" or "it has." Although the possessive form of a noun uses an apostrophe (*Tom's*), possessive pronouns (*its, hers, his, ours, yours, theirs*) never take apostrophes.

Incorrect The car is lying on it's side in the ditch.

Its a blue 2009 Ford Taurus.

That new car of her's rides very smoothly.

Correct The car is lying on its side in the ditch.

It's a blue 2009 Ford Taurus.

That new car of hers rides very smoothly.

For clarity, avoid using the contraction ending in *-'s* to mean "has" instead of "is."

Unclear She's held many offices in student government.

Clear She has held many offices in student government.

13. Incorrect pronoun case

A pronoun that is the subject of a sentence or clause must be in the subjective case (*I, he, she, we, they*). A pronoun that is the direct object of a verb, the indirect object of a verb, or the object of a preposition must be in the objective case (*me, him, her, us, them*). To decide whether a pronoun in a compound construction—two or more nouns or pronouns joined with *and* or *or*—should be subjective or objective, omit everything in the compound except the pronoun, and see whether the subjective or objective case sounds correct.

Incorrect He took my wife and I to dinner.

Try that sentence without the first part of the compound, *my wife and*. It sounds incorrect.

Correct He took my wife and me to dinner.

Here's another example.

Incorrect Her and her family donated the prize money.

Try that sentence without the second part of the compound, *and her family*. It sounds incorrect.

Correct She and her family donated the prize money.

The pronouns *who* and *whom* often cause confusion. *Who* (or *whoever*) is subjective; *whom* (or *whomever*) is objective. If the pronoun appears in a question, answer the question using a pronoun (such as *I* or *me*) to determine whether to use the subjective or objective form.

Incorrect Who does Howard want to see?

Answering the question—*Howard wants to see me*—reveals that the pronoun should be objective.

Correct Whom does Howard want to see?

When *who* or *whom* is not part of a question, it introduces a dependent clause. Determine the case of the pronoun in the clause by removing the clause from the sentence and replacing *who* or *whom* with *I* and *me* to see which form is correct.

Incorrect She welcomed whomever knocked on her door.

The dependent clause is *whomever knocked on her door*. Replacing *whomever* with *I* and *me*—*I knocked on her door; me knocked on her door*—reveals that the subjective form, *whoever*, is correct.

Correct She welcomed whoever knocked on her door.

14. Lack of agreement between pronoun and antecedent

Pronouns must agree in number (singular or plural) and person (first, second or third) with their *antecedents*—the nouns or pronouns to which they refer. Do not shift, for example, from a singular antecedent to a plural pronoun or from a third-person antecedent to a first- or second-person pronoun.

Incorrect The class meets on Thursdays to check their work.

Correct The class meets on Thursdays to check its work.

Class members meet on Thursdays to check their work.

15. Biased language

Avoid stereotypes and biased language. Take special care to avoid gender-specific pronouns.

Biased A reporter must always check his work.

Acceptable Reporters must always check their work.

If you are a reporter, you must always check your work.

Biased Local politicians and their wives attended a dinner in honor of the visiting diplomat.

Acceptable Local politicians and their spouses attended a dinner in honor of the visiting diplomat.

Biased Dr. Jones, a deaf-mute, spoke about the challenges she faced in medical school.

Acceptable Dr. Jones, who cannot hear or speak, spoke about the challenges she faced in medical school.

16. Lack of agreement between subject and verb

Subject and verb must agree in number. Use the form of the verb that agrees with a singular or plural subject. Be especially careful to identify the subject correctly when words, such as a prepositional phrase, separate subject from verb.

Incorrect The bag with the green stripes belong to her.

Correct The bag with the green stripes belongs to her.

A compound subject with parts joined by *and* is always plural.

Incorrect A mystery writer and her daughter lives in the house by the river.

Correct A mystery writer and her daughter live in the house by the river.

When parts of a compound subject are joined by *or*, make the verb agree with the part of the compound closest to the verb.

Incorrect Either Mike or his sisters has the spare key.

Correct Either Mike or his sisters have the spare key.

17. Incorrect complement with linking verb

A linking verb such as *appear*, *be*, *become* or *feel* links a subject with a word or words that identify or describe the subject. When the identifying word—called a *subject complement*—is a pronoun, use the subjective case for the pronoun.

Incorrect That was him on the telephone five minutes ago.

Correct That was he on the telephone five minutes ago.

A word or words that describe the subject and follow a linking verb must be adjectives.

Incorrect She feels terribly about the things she said.

Correct She feels terrible about the things she said.

18. Incorrect use of subjunctive mood

Conditions contrary to fact require a verb to be in the subjunctive mood. Apply this rule in stories about all pending legislation at all levels of government. Use the subjunctive mood in "that" clauses after verbs of wishing, suggesting and requiring. In other words, use the subjunctive in dependent and independent clauses that do not state a fact.

Incorrect The bylaws require that he declares his candidacy by April 10.

Correct The bylaws require that he declare his candidacy by April 10.

Incorrect The bill will require everyone to register for the draft at age 18.

Correct The bill would require everyone to register for the draft at age 18.

19. Wrong word

Wrong-word errors include using a word that sounds similar to or the same as the word you need but means something different (such as writing *affect* when you mean *effect*) and using a word that has a shade of meaning that is not what you intend (such as writing *slender* when you want to suggest *scrawny*). Check the dictionary if you are not sure whether you are using a word correctly.

Incorrect Merchants who appear disinterested in their customers may lose business.

Correct Merchants who appear uninterested in their customers may lose business.

Incorrect The guests gasped and applauded when they saw the excessive display of food.

Correct The guests gasped and applauded when they saw the lavish display of food.

20. Incorrect verb form

Every verb has five forms: a base form (*talk*; *see*), a present-tense form (*talks*; *sees*), a past-tense form (*talked*; *saw*), a present-participle form used for forming the progressive tenses (*is talking*; *is seeing*), and a past-participle form used for forming the passive voice or one of the perfect tenses (*has talked*; *has seen*).

Dropping the ending from present-tense forms and regular past-tense forms is a common error.

Incorrect The police are suppose to protect the public.

Correct The police are supposed to protect the public.

Incorrect The city use to tax all clothing sales.

Correct The city used to tax all clothing sales.

Regular verbs end in *-ed* in the past tense and past participle, but irregular verbs do not follow a set pattern for forming the past tense and past participle (for example, *saw, seen*), so those forms of irregular verbs are frequently used incorrectly. Look up irregular verbs if you are uncertain of the correct form.

Incorrect The manager was not in the restaurant when it was robbed because he had went home early.

Correct The manager was not in the restaurant when it was robbed because he had gone home early.

Incorrect The thieves taked everything in the safe.

Correct The thieves took everything in the safe.

ANSWERS TO GRAMMAR CHECK ACTIVITIES

Chapter 1: The U.S., the U.K., Germany, China, Russia and France all agreed to the historic Iran nuclear deal.

Chapter 2: Scientists report that if greenhouse gas emissions continue at their current rates, many areas of the world will feel the effects by 2040.

Chapter 3: Donald Trump, the real estate magnate, says he hopes to become "the greatest jobs president that God ever created."

Chapter 4: South Korean President Park Geun-hye was impeached, and she was later sentenced to 24 years in prison for corruption.

Chapter 5: In May 2018, Prince Harry and Meghan Markle were married in St. George's Chapel, which King Edward IV began building at Windsor Castle in 1475.

Chapter 6: Ballot selfies, which may reveal whom a person voted for, could prompt the return of vote-buying, according to a prominent elections expert.

Chapter 7: The Alaskan peak known as Mount McKinley was officially restored to its original Koyukon name, Denali.

Chapter 8: The growth of gambling in New York, Pennsylvania, Maryland and Delaware has cut into casino revenue in Atlantic City, New Jersey.

Chapter 9: Formerly flying outside the State House in Charleston, S.C., the Confederate flag was taken down by state troopers after a vote in the state assembly.

Chapter 10: After Rowan County clerk Kim Davis refused to issue marriage licenses to same-sex couples, she spent five days in jail for contempt of court.

Chapter 11: In September 2015, Russia deployed half a dozen tanks and 35 armored carriers to Syria in a move to build up its military presence in the region.

Chapter 12: China's stock market crisis in August 2015 had a substantial effect on international markets.

Chapter 13: Since the U.S. Supreme Court's decision in *Obergefell v. Hodges,* federal law requires that every state issue marriage licenses to same-sex couples.

Chapter 14: It was Nikki Haley who became the first female governor of South Carolina in 2011, and it was she who resigned as the U.S. ambassador to the United Nations in 2018.

Chapter 15: With the melting glaciers around the world, some areas are dealing with the threat of decreased water supply.

Chapter 16: Relations between North and South Korea used to allow for occasional "reunion" meetings for families separated during the 1950-53 Korean War.

Chapter 17: Critics in Congress slammed the White House for what they say is its ineffective, disorganized attempt to train a Syrian rebel army against ISIS.

Chapter 18: New York hedge fund manager Martin Shkreli increased the price of his newly acquired drug, Daraprim, by 5,455 percent.

Chapter 19: Pakistani human rights activist Malala Yousafzai was almost killed by a Taliban assassin in October 2012, but she remains a dedicated advocate for girls' education.

Chapter 20: A candidate for the office of U.S. president must be a natural-born citizen of the U.S. and at least 35 years old.

Wire-Service Style Summary

Most publications adhere to rules of style to avoid annoying inconsistencies. Without a stylebook to provide guidance in such matters, writers would not know whether the word *president* should be capitalized when preceding or following a name, whether the correct spelling is *canceled* or *cancelled* (dictionaries list both), or whether *Twelfth Street* or *12th Street* is correct.

Newspapers use stylebooks to provide such guidance. For consistency, most newspapers follow rules in *The Associated Press Stylebook*. Many also list their own exceptions to AP style in a separate style sheet. There often are good reasons for local exceptions. For example, AP style calls for spelling out *First Street* through *Ninth Street* but using numerals for *10th Street* and above. But if a city has only 10 numbered streets, for consistency it might make sense to use *Tenth Street*.

This appendix is an abbreviated summary of the primary style rules. (See Chapter 12 for more on radio and television style.) This summary should be helpful even for those without a stylebook, but we provide it assuming that most users of this book have one. Why? Because this section includes only the rules used most frequently, arranged by topic to make them easier to learn. Only about 10 percent of the rules in a stylebook account for 90 percent of the style you will use regularly. You will use the rest of the rules about 10 percent of the time. It makes sense, therefore, to learn first the rules you will use most often.

Abbreviations and Acronyms

Punctuation of Abbreviations

- Generally speaking, abbreviations of two letters or fewer have periods:
  600 B.C., A.D. 1066
  8 a.m., 7 p.m.
  U.N., U.S., R.I., N.Y.
  8151 Yosemite St.
  EXCEPTIONS: *US* and *UN* in headlines only. *EU* for *European Union* on second reference in both text and headlines.
  EXCEPTIONS: *AM radio, FM radio, 35 mm camera, AP style, LA smog, D-Mass., R-Kan., IQ, TV, EU*
- Most abbreviations of three letters or more do not have periods:
  CIA, FBI, NATO
  mpg, mph
  EXCEPTION: *c.o.d.* for *cash on delivery* or *collect on delivery*

Symbols

- Always write out % as *percent* in a story, but you may use the symbol in a headline.
- Always write out & as *and* unless it is part of a company's formal name.
- Always write out ¢ as *cent* or *cents*.
- Always use the symbol $ rather than the word *dollar* with any actual figure, and put the symbol before the figure. Write out *dollar* only if you are speaking of, say, the value of the dollar on the world market.

Dates

- Never abbreviate days of the week except in a table.
- Don't abbreviate a month unless part of a specific date: *August 2016*; *Aug. 17*; *Aug. 17, 2016*.
- The five months spelled with five letters or fewer are never abbreviated: *March*; *April 20*; *May 13, 2016*; *June 1956*; *July of that year*.
- Never abbreviate *Christmas* as *Xmas*, even in a headline.
- *Fourth of July* is written out.
- *Sept. 11* and *9/11* are both acceptable.

People and Titles

- Some publications still use courtesy titles (*Mr.*, *Mrs.*, *Ms.*, *Miss*) on second reference in stories, although most seem to have moved away from them as sexist. Many publications use them only in quotations from sources. Others use them only in obituaries and editorials or in a second reference in stories mentioning a husband and wife. In the last case, some newspapers prefer to repeat the person's whole name or, especially in features, use the person's first name.
- Use the abbreviations *Dr.* (for a medical doctor, not someone with a Ph.D. degree), *Gov.*, *Lt. Gov.*, *Rep.*, *the Rev.*, and *Sen.* as well as abbreviations of military titles, on first reference; then drop the title on subsequent references. Some titles you might expect to see abbreviated before a name are not abbreviated in AP style: *Attorney General*, *District Attorney*, *President*, *Professor*, *Superintendent*.
- Use the abbreviations *Jr.* and *Sr.* after a name on first reference if appropriate, but do not set them off by commas.

Organizations

- Write out the first reference to most organizations in full rather than using an acronym: *National Organization for Women*. For *CIA* and *FBI*, however, the acronym may be used on the first reference. Do not use GOP on first reference to the Republican Party.
- You may use well-known abbreviations such as *FCC* and *NOW* in a headline even though they would not be acceptable on first reference in a story.
- Do not put the abbreviation of an organization in parentheses after the full name on first reference. If an abbreviation is confusing, don't use it at all. Instead, call the organization something like "the gay rights group" or "the bureau" on second reference.

- Use the abbreviations *Co., Cos., Corp., Inc.* and *Ltd.* at the end of a company's name even if the company spells out the word; do not abbreviate these words if followed by other words such as "of America." The abbreviations *Co., Cos.* and *Corp.* are used, however, if followed by *Inc.* or *Ltd.* (These latter two abbreviations are not set off by commas even if the company uses commas.)
- Abbreviate political affiliations after a name in the following way: *Sen. Josh Hawley, R-Mo., said....* Note the use of a single letter without a period for the party and the use of commas around the party and state abbreviations.
- Never abbreviate the word *association*, even as part of a name.

Places

- Abbreviate state names in lists, tables, credit lines, photo captions and political party affiliations. In the body of a story, don't abbreviate a state name that follows the name of a city in that state: *Brown City, Michigan.*
- Never abbreviate the six states spelled with five or fewer letters or the two noncontiguous states: *Alaska, Hawaii, Idaho, Iowa, Maine, Ohio, Texas, Utah.*
- Use the traditional state abbreviations, not the Postal Service's two-letter ones: *Miss.*, not *MS.* Here are the abbreviations used in some places, including in party affiliations (R-Ohio):

Ala.	Fla.	Md.	Neb.	N.D.	Tenn.
Ariz.	Ga.	Mass.	Nev.	Okla.	Vt.
Ark.	Ill.	Mich.	N.H.	Ore.	Va.
Calif.	Ind.	Minn.	N.J.	Pa.	Wash.
Colo.	Kan.	Miss.	N.M.	R.I.	W.Va.
Conn.	Ky.	Mo.	N.Y.	S.C.	Wis.
Del.	La.	Mont.	N.C.	S.D.	Wyo.

  EXCEPTION: Use the two-letter postal abbreviations when a full address is given that includes a ZIP code.
- Datelines on stories should contain a city name in capital letters followed by a comma and the name of the state (abbreviated if not one of the eight states that are never abbreviated). Use a nation's full name with foreign towns and cities unless they appear in the AP list of cities that stand alone in datelines.
- Don't abbreviate the names of thoroughfares if there is no street address with them: *Main Street, Century Boulevard West.*
- If the thoroughfare's name has the word *avenue, boulevard, street* or any of the directions on a map, such as *north* or *southeast*, abbreviate those words with a street address: *1044 W. Maple St., 1424 Lee Blvd. S., 999 Jackson Ave.*
- In a highway's name, always abbreviate *U.S.*, but never abbreviate a state's name. In the case of an interstate highway, the name is written in full on first reference, abbreviated on subsequent ones: *U.S. Highway 63, Massachusetts 2, Interstate 70* (first reference), *I-70* (second reference).
- Never abbreviate *Fort* or *Mount.*
- Always use the abbreviation *St.* for *Saint* in place names.
  EXCEPTIONS: *Saint John* in New Brunswick, *Sault Ste. Marie* in Michigan and Ontario
- Abbreviate *U.S., U.K.* and *U.N.* as both nouns and adjectives in text. No periods in headlines.

Miscellaneous

- Use the abbreviation *IQ* (no periods) in all references to *intelligence quotient.*
- Abbreviate and capitalize the word *number* when followed by a numeral: *No. 1.*
- Use the abbreviation *TV* (no periods) as an adjective or noun as an abbreviated form of *television.*
- Use the abbreviation *UFO* in all references to an *unidentified flying object.*
- Generally, spell out *versus,* but use the abbreviation *vs.,* not *v.,* for *versus* in short expressions: *guns vs. butter.* Use *v.* for court cases: *Marbury v. Madison.*

Capitalization

- Proper nouns are capitalized; common nouns are not. Unfortunately, this rule is not always easy to apply when the noun is the name of an animal, a food or a plant or when it is a trademark that has become so well-known that people mistakenly use it generically.
- Regions are capitalized; directions are not: *We drove east two miles to catch the interstate out West.*
- Adjectives and nouns pertaining to a region are capitalized: *Southern accent, Southerner, Western movie.*
- A region combined with a country's name is not capitalized unless the region is part of the name of a divided country: *eastern U.S., North Korea.*
- A region combined with a state name is capitalized only if it is famous: *Southern California, southern Colorado.*
- When two or more compound proper nouns are combined and have a word in common, the shared plural is lowercased: *Missouri and Mississippi rivers, Chrisman and Truman high schools.*
- Government and college terms are not always consistent.
  - *College departments* follow the animal, food and plant rule: Capitalize only words that are already proper nouns in themselves: *Spanish department, sociology department.* By contrast, always capitalize *a specific government department,* even without the city, state or federal designator and even if it's turned around with *of* deleted: *Police Department, Fire Department, Department of State, State Department.*
  - *College and government committees* are capitalized if the formal name is given rather than a shorter, descriptive designation: *Special Senate Select Committee to Investigate Improper Labor-Management Practices; rackets committee.*
  - *Academic degrees* are spelled out and lowercased: *bachelor of arts degree, master's degree.* Avoid abbreviations like *Ph.D., M.A.* and *B.A.,* except in lists.
  - Always capitalize (unless plural or generic) *City Council* and *County Commission* (but alone, *council* and *commission* are lowercased). *Cabinet* is capitalized when referring to advisers. *Legislature* is capitalized if the state's body is formally named that. *Capitol,* the building, is capitalized, but *capital,* the city, is not. Capitalize *City Hall* even without the city name but not *county courthouse* without the name of the county.
  - Never capitalize *board of directors* or *board of trustees* (but formal governing bodies, such as *Board of Curators* and *Board of Education,* are capitalized). *Federal, government* and *administration* are not capitalized. *President* and *vice president* are capitalized only before a name and only when not set off with a comma:

President Donald Trump and Vice President Mike Pence
the president, Donald Trump, said …

- *Military titles (Sgt., Maj., Gen.)* are capitalized before a name, as are *Air Force, Army, Marines* and *Navy* if referring to U.S. forces.
- *Political parties* are capitalized, including the word *party*: *Democratic Party, Socialist Party*. However, capitalize words such as *communist, democratic, fascist* and *socialist* only when they refer to a formal party rather than a philosophy.

■ Terms related to the internet are not always consistent.

- *Internet* is lowercase. Some other internet and technology terms are capitalized, and some are not: *BlackBerry(s), blog, cellphone, chat room, click-thru(s), crowdsourcing, home page, IP address, Listserv* (trademarked software), *retweet, smartphone, social media* (n., adj.), *tweet* (n., v.), *VoIP, Wi-Fi*.
- *World Wide Web* is capitalized. But *web, website, webcam, webcast* and *webmaster* are lowercased.
- *Email* (note lack of hyphen) and other similar terms (*e-book, e-commerce, e-business*) are lowercased.
- *IM* is acceptable for a second reference to *instant message*; also *IM*'ing, *IM*'d.
- The proper names *iPad, iPhone* and *iPod* should be capitalized at the start of a sentence or headline (*IPad, IPhone, IPod*).

■ Some religious terms (including holidays) are capitalized; most are not: *bar mitzvah, nirvana, Hanukkah, Ramadan*.

- *Pope* is lowercased except before a name: *the pope, Pope Francis*.
- *Mass* is always capitalized.
- Pronouns for *God* and *Jesus* are lowercased.
- Names of religious figures are capitalized: *Prophet Muhammad, Buddha*.
- Names of holy books are capitalized: *Talmud, Quran* (preferred to *Koran*). *Bible* is capitalized when meaning the Holy Scriptures and lowercased when referring to another book: *a hunter's bible*.
- Sacraments are capitalized if they commemorate events in the life of Jesus or signify his presence: *Holy Communion* but *baptism, communion*.

■ Proper names and adjectives for races, ethnicities, and nationalities and religions are capitalized, but color descriptions are not: *African-American, Arab, Asian* (preferred to *Oriental* for people), *black, Caucasian, Cherokee, Chinese* (singular and plural), *French Canadian, Muslim, Negro* (used only in names of organizations and quotations), *white*. (Note that *Arab*, which denotes ethnicity, and *Muslim*, which refers to religion, are not interchangeable. For example, many Arabs are Christian, and Muslims may be American, Indian, Indonesian or Turkish.)

■ *Illegal immigration* is an acceptable usage, but do not use *illegal immigrant, illegal alien* or *an illegal* as a noun to refer to a person: *he entered the country illegally*.

■ Formal titles of people are capitalized before a name, but occupational names are not: *President Donald Trump, Mayor Laura Miller, Coach Roy Williams, Dean Jaime Lopez, astronaut Ellen Ochoa, journalist Fred Francis, plumber Phil Sanders, pharmacist Roger Wheaton*. Some titles are not easy to recognize: *managing editor, chief executive officer*. When in doubt, put the title after the name, set it off with commas, and use lowercase.

■ Formal titles that are capitalized before a name are lowercased after a name: *Donald Trump, president of the U.S.*; *Mike Rawlings, mayor of Dallas*; *Roy Williams, coach of the North Carolina Tar Heels*; *Fred Wilson, dean of students*.

- Formal titles that are abbreviated before a name are written out and lowercased if they follow a name: *Gov. Andrew Cuomo*; *Andrew Cuomo, governor of New York; Sen. Lindsey Graham of South Carolina*; *Lindsey Graham, senator from South Carolina.*
- The first word in a direct quotation is capitalized only if the quote meets both of these criteria:
  - It is a complete sentence. Don't capitalize a partial quote.
  - It stands alone as a separate sentence or paragraph, or it is set off from its source by a comma or colon.
- A question within a sentence is capitalized: *My only question is, When do we start?*

Numbers

- Cardinal numbers (numerals) are used as follows:
  - Addresses: Always use numerals for street addresses: *1322 N. 17th St.*
  - Ages: Always use numerals, even for days or months: *3 days old*; *John Burnside, 56.*
  - Aircraft and spacecraft: *F-4, DC-10, Apollo 11.* Exception: *Air Force One.*
  - Clothes sizes: *size 6.*
  - Dates: Always use the numeral alone with no *st*, *nd*, *rd* or *th* after it: *March 20.*
  - Decades: *the 1980s*, *the '80s*, *the early 2000s* (or *first decade of the 21st century*).
  - Dimensions: *5-foot-6-inch guard* (but no hyphen when the word modified is one associated with size: *3 feet tall, 10 feet long*).
  - Highways: *U.S. 63.*
  - Millions, billions and trillions: *1.2 billion, 6 million.*
  - Money: Always use numerals, but starting with a million, write like this: *$1.4 million.*
  - Numbers: *No. 1, No. 2.*
  - Percentages: Always use numerals except at the beginning of a sentence: *4 percent.*
  - Recipes: Use numerals for all numbers for amounts: *2 teaspoons.*
  - Speeds: *55 mph*, *4 knots.*
  - Sports: Use numerals for just about everything: *8-6 score*, *2 yards*, *3-under-par*, *2 strokes.*
  - Temperatures: Use numerals for all except *zero*. Below zero, spell out *minus*: *minus 6*, not *–6* (except in tabular data).
  - Times: *4 a.m., 6:32 p.m., noon, midnight, five minutes, three hours.*
  - Weights: *7 pounds, 11 ounces.*
  - Years: Use numerals without commas. A year is the only numeral that can start a sentence: *1988 was a good year.*
- Numerals with the suffixes *st*, *nd*, *rd* and *th* are used as follows:
  - Political divisions (precincts, wards, districts): *3rd Congressional District.*
  - Military sequences: *1st Lt., 2nd Division, 7th Fleet.*
  - Courts: *2nd District Court, 10th Circuit Court of Appeals.*
  - Streets after *Ninth*: For *First* through *Ninth*, use words: *Fifth Avenue, 13th Street.*
  - Amendments to the Constitution after *Ninth*: For *First* through *Ninth*, use words: *First Amendment, 16th Amendment.*

- Words are used for numbers as follows:
  - Numbers less than 10, with the exceptions noted above: *five people*, *four rules*.
  - Any number at the start of a sentence except for a year: *Sixteen years ago. . . .*
  - Casual numbers: *about a hundred or so*.
  - Fractions less than one: *one-half*.
- Mixed numbers are used for fractions greater than one: *1 1/2*.
- Roman numerals are used for a man who is the third or later in his family to bear a name and for a king, queen, pope or world war: *John D. Rockefeller III*, *Queen Elizabeth II*, *Pope John Paul II*, *World War I*.

Suggested Website

www.apstylebook.com
The Associated Press provides its stylebook in several formats, including as a traditional printed book, an online subscription and a mobile device (smartphone or tablet) application.

Society of Professional Journalists' Code of Ethics

Preamble

Members of the Society of Professional Journalists believe that public enlightenment is the forerunner of justice and the foundation of democracy. Ethical journalism strives to ensure the free exchange of information that is accurate, fair and thorough. An ethical journalist acts with integrity.

The Society declares these four principles as the foundation of ethical journalism and encourages their use in its practice by all people in all media.

Seek Truth and Report It

Ethical journalism should be accurate and fair. Journalists should be honest and courageous in gathering, reporting and interpreting information.

Journalists should:

- Take responsibility for the accuracy of their work. Verify information before releasing it. Use original sources whenever possible.
- Remember that neither speed nor format excuses inaccuracy.
- Provide context. Take special care not to misrepresent or oversimplify in promoting, previewing or summarizing a story.
- Gather, update and correct information throughout the life of a news story.
- Be cautious when making promises, but keep the promises they make.
- Identify sources clearly. The public is entitled to as much information as possible to judge the reliability and motivations of sources.
- Consider sources' motives before promising anonymity. Reserve anonymity for sources who may face danger, retribution or other harm and have information that cannot be obtained elsewhere. Explain why anonymity was granted.
- Diligently seek subjects of news coverage to allow them to respond to criticism or allegations of wrongdoing.
- Avoid undercover or other surreptitious methods of gathering information unless traditional, open methods will not yield information vital to the public.
- Be vigilant and courageous about holding those with power accountable. Give voice to the voiceless.
- Support the open and civil exchange of views, even views they find repugnant.
- Recognize a special obligation to serve as watchdogs over public affairs and government. Seek to ensure that the public's business is conducted in the open and that public records are open to all.
- Provide access to source material when it is relevant and appropriate.

- Boldly tell the story of the diversity and magnitude of the human experience. Seek sources whose voices we seldom hear.
- Avoid stereotyping. Journalists should examine the ways their values and experiences may shape their reporting.
- Label advocacy and commentary.
- Never deliberately distort facts or context, including visual information. Clearly label illustrations and re-enactments.
- Never plagiarize. Always attribute.

Minimize Harm

Ethical journalism treats sources, subjects, colleagues and members of the public as human beings deserving of respect.

Journalists should:

- Balance the public's need for information against potential harm or discomfort. Pursuit of the news is not a license for arrogance or undue intrusiveness.
- Show compassion for those who may be affected by news coverage. Use heightened sensitivity when dealing with juveniles, victims of sex crimes, and sources or subjects who are inexperienced or unable to give consent. Consider cultural differences in approach and treatment.
- Recognize that legal access to information differs from an ethical justification to publish or broadcast.
- Realize that private people have a greater right to control information about themselves than public figures and others who seek power, influence or attention. Weigh the consequences of publishing or broadcasting personal information.
- Avoid pandering to lurid curiosity, even if others do.
- Balance a suspect's right to a fair trial with the public's right to know. Consider the implications of identifying criminal suspects before they face legal charges.
- Consider the long-term implications of the extended reach and permanence of publication. Provide updated and more complete information as appropriate.

Act Independently

The highest and primary obligation of ethical journalism is to serve the public.

Journalists should:

- Avoid conflicts of interest, real or perceived. Disclose unavoidable conflicts.
- Refuse gifts, favors, fees, free travel and special treatment, and avoid political and other outside activities that may compromise integrity or impartiality, or may damage credibility.
- Be wary of sources offering information for favors or money; do not pay for access to news. Identify content provided by outside sources, whether paid or not.
- Deny favored treatment to advertisers, donors or any other special interests, and resist internal and external pressure to influence coverage.
- Distinguish news from advertising and shun hybrids that blur the lines between the two. Prominently label sponsored content.

Be Accountable and Transparent

Ethical journalism means taking responsibility for one's work and explaining one's decisions to the public.

Journalists should:

- Explain ethical choices and processes to audiences. Encourage a civil dialogue with the public about journalistic practices, coverage and news content.
- Respond quickly to questions about accuracy, clarity and fairness.
- Acknowledge mistakes and correct them promptly and prominently. Explain corrections and clarifications carefully and clearly.
- Expose unethical conduct in journalism, including within their organizations.
- Abide by the same high standards they expect of others.

The SPJ Code of Ethics is a statement of abiding principles supported by additional explanations and position papers that address changing journalistic practices. It is not a set of rules, rather a guide that encourages all who engage in journalism to take responsibility for the information they provide, regardless of medium. The code should be read as a whole; individual principles should not be taken out of context. It is not, nor can it be under the First Amendment, legally enforceable.

Glossary

absolutism The ethical philosophy that holds that there is a fixed set of principles or laws from which there is no deviation. To the absolutist journalist, the end never justifies the means.

accuracy check A method of verifying the facts of a story.

advance A report covering the subjects and issues to be dealt with in an upcoming meeting or event.

anecdote An informative and entertaining story within a story.

annual percentage rate (APR) The annual cost of a loan expressed as a percentage. The basic method for computing APR is set forth in the Truth in Lending Act of 1968.

assessed value The amount that a government appraiser determines a property is worth.

attribution Identification of the source of the information or quotation.

average (1) A term used to describe typical or representative members of a group. (2) In mathematics, the result obtained when a set of numbers is added together and then divided by the number of items in the set.

beat A reporter's assigned area of responsibility. A beat may be an institution (such as a courthouse), a geographic area (such as a small town) or a subject (such as science). The term also refers to an exclusive story.

blotter An old-fashioned term for the arrest sheet that summarizes the bare facts of an arrest. Today this information is almost always stored on a computer.

change of venue The transfer of a court proceeding to another jurisdiction for prosecution. This often occurs when a party in a case claims that local media coverage has prejudiced prospective jurors.

chunking A method of displaying concepts in a news story in "chunks" to make it more readable and more quickly understandable.

citizen journalism A new form of media in which citizens actively participate in gathering and writing information, often in the form of news. Also called *participatory journalism* and *user-generated content*.

closed-ended question A direct question designed to draw a specific response (for example, "Will you be a candidate?").

commentary An essay, column or blog that comments on rather than just reports the news.

compound interest Interest paid on the total of the principal (the amount borrowed) and the interest that has already accrued.

content aggregator A company that collects and distributes news from traditional media sources but does little or no independent news gathering.

content words Words that can stand alone in their definitions (like nouns, verbs, and adjectives).

convergence A term defined in different ways by different people in the media industry but generally used to describe the coordination of print, broadcast and online reporting in a news operation.

crowdsourcing The practice of inviting unpaid readers and viewers to submit their own stories, photographs and video and sometimes to lend their expertise to help solve community problems.

defamation Damage done to a person's reputation.

delayed-identification lead The opening paragraph of a story in which the "who" is identified by occupation, city, office or any means other than by name.

dialogue A conversation between two or more people. The reporter normally is not part of the dialogue, except in interviews.

direct quote A quote inside quotation marks that captures the exact words of the speaker.

flat-file database A simple database program that allows users to keep track of almost any type of data. A simple address book is an example.

Freedom of Information Act A law passed in 1966 to make it easier to obtain information from federal agencies. The law was amended in 1974 to improve access to government records.

free press/fair trial controversy The conflict between a defendant's right to an impartial jury and a reporter's responsibility to inform the public.

function words Words that signal grammatical relationships rather than definitions (like prepositions, articles, and conjunctions).

hard lead A lead that reports a new development or newly discovered fact.

hard news Coverage of the actions of government or business or the reporting of an event, such as a crime, an accident or a speech. The time element often is important. See also *soft news*.

hashtag A phrase that consists of a number sign (#) and a word or words and is used to identify topics on social media, especially Twitter.

hypermedia Web links to audio, video and pictures.

hypertext A web document coded in HTML.

immediate-identification lead The opening paragraph of a story in which the "who" is reported by name.

indirect quotation A paraphrase of the speaker's words. Because it is a paraphrase, the words are not in quotation marks.

inflation The rising cost of living as time goes by. See also *Consumer Price Index*.

interviewing Having conversations with sources.

inverted pyramid The organization of a news story in which information is arranged in descending order of importance.

investigative journalism The pursuit of information that has been concealed, such as evidence of wrongdoing.

lead (1) The first paragraph or first several paragraphs of a newspaper story (sometimes spelled *lede*). (2) The story given the best display on page 1. (3) A tip.

lead-in An introduction to a filmed or recorded excerpt from a news source or from another reporter.

legacy media Traditional media outlets such as newspapers, magazines, broadcast television and the like.

libel Damage to a person's reputation caused by a false written statement that brings the person into hatred, contempt or ridicule or injures his or her business or occupational pursuit.

line-item budget A budget showing each expenditure on a separate line.

listicle An online article structured primarily as a numbered or bulleted list.

margin of error The difference between results from the entire population (all registered voters in your county, for example) and a random sample of the population. It is usually expressed as plus or minus *x* points. The *x* depends on the size of the sample. The larger the sample, the smaller the margin of error.

median The middle number in a series arranged in order of magnitude. It is often used when an average would be misleading. (If the series has an even number of items, the median is the average of the two "middle" numbers.) See also *average*.

millage rate The tax rate on property, determined by the government.

multiple-element lead The opening paragraph of a story that reports two or more newsworthy elements.

news hole The amount of space (in print) or time (in broadcast) available for news reporting.

news narrative A story that sums up the news in the first paragraph or two and then describes events chronologically rather than ranking them in descending order of importance.

page views The measurement of how many people open up a story online.

nut paragraph A paragraph that summarizes the key element or elements of a story. Nut paragraphs usually are found in stories not written in inverted pyramid form. Also called a *nut graf*.

objectivity A concept of journalism that holds journalists to rules that help them arrive at the best obtainable version of the truth—to report accurately, fairly and without bias.

one-party consent A law stating that only one party involved in a phone call has to consent to the recording of the call. This law varies from state to state.

online videoconferencing An internet-enabled, real-time communication where participants can both see and hear each other.

open-ended question A question that permits the respondent some latitude in the answer (for example, "How did you get involved in politics?").

open-records law A state or federal law guaranteeing public access to many—but not all—kinds of government records.

page views A measurement of how many people open a story online.

parallelism A technique of presenting ideas in similar grammatical forms.

paraphrase A technique that digests, condenses or clarifies a quotation to convey the meaning more precisely or succinctly than the speaker's words do; an indirect quotation. Quotation marks are not used with paraphrases.

PDF file A computerized document that preserves formatting.

percentage change A number that explains by how much something goes up or down.

percentage point A unit of measure used to express the difference between two percentages. For example, the difference between 25 percent and 40 percent is 15 percentage points.

plagiarism The act of using any part of another person's writing and passing it off as your own.

play A shortened form of *display*. A good story may be played at the top of page 1; a weak one may be played inside.

population In scientific language, the whole group being studied. Depending on the study, the population may be, for example, voters in St. Louis, physicians in California or all residents of the U.S.

precedent Past rulings that courts rely on to decide cases currently before them.

primary source A person who witnesses or participates in an event; an authentic document from an event.

principal The amount of money borrowed.

profile A story intended to reveal the personality or character of an institution or a person.

program budget A budget that clearly shows what each agency's activities cost.

proportion An explanation that relates one number to another or to the quantity or magnitude of a whole.

pull quote Quotations pulled from a passage of text.

question-and-answer A news story format that is a nearly verbatim transcript of an interview.

quote As a noun, a source's exact words (as in "I have a great quote here"). As a verb, to report a source's exact words inside quotation marks.

rate The amount or degree of something measured in relation to a unit of something else or to a specified scale. In statistics, rate often expresses the incidence of a condition per 100,000 people (such as a murder or suicide rate). Rate also can reflect the speed at which something is changing (such as inflation or the percentage increase in a budget each year).

relational database program A database program that permits users to determine relationships between two or more dissimilar databases. For example, a relational database program would enable a reporter to compare one database of people convicted of drunk driving with another database of school-bus drivers. The result would show how many bus drivers had drunk-driving convictions.

rundown A line-up of stories that are scheduled to appear in a newscast.

sample A portion of a group or population that is chosen for study as representative of the entire group.

search-engine optimization The process of making sure your story will be found when someone searches for its topic online.

secondary source A source who talked to a witness (such as a public safety official investigating a crime). The witness would be a *primary source*.

service journalism An aspect or a type of journalism that recognizes usefulness as one of the criteria of news. Taking into consideration content and presentation, service journalism presents useful information in a usable way (for instance, by placing key information in a list or graphic box).

setup In broadcasting, an introductory statement designed to pique the interest of listeners or viewers. In written accounts, the material between the opening of a narrative story and the body. It generally consists of the transition to the theme paragraph, the nut paragraph, and, when appropriate, the "so what" and "to be sure" statements and foreshadowing.

shovelware Stories posted on the web exactly as they appeared in print.

sidebar A secondary story intended to be run with a major story on the same topic. A story about a disaster, for example, may have a sidebar that tells what happened to a single victim.

simple interest Interest paid on the principal (the amount borrowed).

skeptical open-mindedness The process of fighting perceptions of bias to see the truth through an honest, impartial lens.

slug A word or words that identify a story as it is processed through the newsroom and newspaper plant or at a broadcast news station. A slug is usually placed in the upper left-hand corner of each take of a newspaper story.

sniff The preliminary phase of an investigation.

soft news Stories about trends, personalities or lifestyles. The time element usually is not important. See also *hard news*.

sound bite An audio recording that accompanies a story in radio or television news or, more recently, that is available even on newspaper websites as a supplement to the printed product.

spot news A timely report of an event that is unfolding in the moment.

stocks Ownership shares of a company.

strategic communication The use of research-based evidence to create strategies and tactics aimed at achieving a desired response from a given audience. Communicators coordinate the best combination of media, social, digital or interpersonal tactics to accomplish their organizational or marketing goals.

summary lead The first paragraph of a news story, in which the writer presents a synopsis of two or more events rather than focusing on any one of them.

teleprompter A mechanical or electronic device that projects broadcast copy next to the television camera lens so that a newscaster can read it while appearing to look straight into the lens.

tickler A file of upcoming events kept on paper or stored electronically at the assignment desks of most news organizations.

tie-back (1) The sentence or sentences relating a story to events covered in a previous story. Tie-backs are used in follow-up or continuing stories or in parts of a series. (2) The technique of referring to the opening of a story in the story's ending.

"to be sure" paragraph In stories focusing on one person or perspective, a statement reflecting the opinions of those who disagree with the person featured (as in "To be sure, not everyone agrees").

user-generated content See *citizen journalism*.

"you" lead The first paragraph of a story that is written using the informal, second-person pronoun "you."

Acknowledgments *(continued from page iv)*

Chapter 3

Susanne Rust Cary Spivak and Meg Kissinger, "Chemical Fallout: Bisphenol A Is in You," *Milwaukee Journal Sentinel*. © Milwaukee Journal Sentinel and reprinted with permission.

Stan Ketterer, "Evaluating Links." Reprinted by permission of the author.

Chapter 5

From *The Associated Press Stylebook, 2018*. Copyright © 2018 Associated Press. Reprinted by permission of Associated Press.

From C.J. Chivers, "Vows: Love's Long Road Home," *The New York Times*, November 10, 2017. Copyright © 2017 The New York Times. All rights reserved. Used under license.

Brian Conteras, "More details emerge about shark theft as San Antonio man makes bond," *San Antonio Express-News*, August 1, 2018. Copyright © Brian Conteras/San Antonio Express-News/ZUMA Press. Used with permission.

Posted by Philip B. Corbett, standards editor, on June 14, 2018, on The New York Times Reader Center. Copyright © 2018 The New York Times. All rights reserved. Used under license.

N'dea Yancey-Bragg, "Alabama college student walks almost 20 miles overnight to first day of work; CEO gives him his car" *USA Today*, July 17, 2018. Copyright © 2018 Gannett-USA Today. All rights reserved. Used under license.

Quoted in Pat Pratt, "Burton: Downtown is still safe," *Columbia Daily Tribune*, August 15, 2018. Reprinted by permission.

Chapter 6

"AG Hawley Files Lawsuit Against Branson Duck Vehicles and Ripley Entertainment" Press release, August 31, 2018. Reprinted by permission of the Missouri Attorney General's Office

Mayo Clinic News Release: "Celebrating Grand Opening Today for Mayo Clinic Square: Mayo Clinic, Minnesota timberwolves, Missesota Lynx" June 17, 2015. Reprinted by permission.

"ALERT: American Association of Poison Control Centers Warn About Potential Poison Exposure to Single-Load Laundry Packets," American Association of Poison Control Centers news release January 16, 2018. Reprinted by permission

"Humane Society of Missouri Confirms: Guilty Pleases Entered in Federal Court to Charges from Largest Dog Fighting Raid and Rescue in U.S. History" Humane Society of Missouri news release, September 14, 2017. Used with permission.

Chapter 8

Elizabeth Phillips, "Man Arrested in Attack Charged with Child Endangerment," *Columbia Missourian*, November 17, 2006. Copyright © 2006 by Columbia Missourian. Used with permission.

Asif Lakhani, "Parks and Recreation, City Council Discuss Plans for Parks Tax," *Columbia Missourian*, November 29, 2010. Copyright © 2010 by Columbia Missourian. Used with permission.

Chapter 9

Eli Saslow, "'It was my job, and I didn't find him': Stoneman Douglas resource officer remains haunted by massacre" *The Washington Post*, June 4, 2018. Copyright © 2018 The Washington Post. All rights reserved. Used under license.

Linda Keene, "San Diego didn't report earlier E. coli outbreak" *The Seattle Times*, March 11, 1993. Copyright © 1993 The Seattle Times. Reprinted with permission.

Jason Horowitz, "As Greek Wildfire Closed in, a Desperate Dash Ended in Death" *The New York Times*, July 24, 2018. Copyright © 2018 The New York Times. All rights reserved. Used under license.

Chapter 10

Lizzie Johnson, "Saving homes turns into searing regret," reprinted with permission from *San Francisco Chronicle*, July 16, 2018; permission conveyed through Copyright Clearance Center, Inc.

Jane Meinhardt, "Mother Accused of Being Criminal Ringleader," From the *Tampa Bay Times*, October 21, 1994. Copyright © 1994 Tampa Bay Times. All rights reserved. Used under license.

John Tully, "Horse Power," *Columbia Missourian*, November 27, 2004. Copyright © 2004 by Columbia Missourian. Used with permission.

Sean Morrison, "The Girl at the Edge of Everything," *Vox* magazine, May 21, 2015. Reprinted by permission.

Chapter 11

Eleanor Beaton, "How Sports Will Help Your Daughter Crack the Glass Ceiling" Huffington Post: Life blog, August 23, 2016. Reprinted by permission of the author.

Brett & Kate McKay, "The Eisenhower Decision Matrix: How to Distinguish Between urgent and important Tasks and Make Real Progress in Your Life," *The Art of Manliness*, October 23, 2013. Reprinted by permission.

Chapter 12

Copyright © Stacey Woelfel. Reprinted by permission of the author.

"Airplane Makes Emergency Landing, Clogs Interstate" Copyright © Stacey Woelfel. Reprinted by permission of the author.

GREENVILLE, SC (AP)Sheriffs in Five South Carolina Counties Are Offering People a Chance to Turn in Explosives, No Questions Asked, October 24, 2012. Copyright © 2012 Associated Press. Reprinted by permission.

Chapter 13

From Jim Yardley, "The Trials of Working With Prepared Remarks" in "Reporter's Notebook: My Travels With Pope Francis in Latin America," *The New York Times*, July 6, 2015. Copyright © 2015 The New York Times. All rights reserved. Used under license.

Chapter 14

Michael M. Grynbaum, "'Fake News' Goes Global as Trump, in Britain, Rips the Press," *The New York Times*, July 13, 2018. Copyright © 2018 The New York Times. All rights reserved. Used under license.

Michael M. Grynbaum, "Reporters, Facing a Hostile White House, Try a New Tactic: Solidarity," *The New York Times*, July 18, 2018. Copyright © 2018 The New York Times. All rights reserved. Used under license.

Excerpts from Michael C. Bender and Duston Volz, "Pence Calls on Google to Drop Mobile Search Project in China" Reprinted with permission from *The Wall Street Journal*, October 5, 2018. A18; permission conveyed through Copyright Clearance Center, Inc.

Chapter 15

Anna Brett, "When evidence goes untested, sex offenders go undetected, advocates say," *Columbia Missourian*, October 29, 2017. Reprinted by permission

Larry King, "Fleeing youth shot, dies after leading wild chase," *Columbian Missourian*, April 22, 1978. Reprinted by permission.

Chapter 17

Amy Julia Harris and Shoshana Walters, "They thought they were going to rehab. They ended up in chicken plants," *Reveal* from The Center for Investigative Reporting, October 2, 2017. https://www.revealnews.org/article/they-thought-they-were-going-to-rehab-they-ended-up-in-chicken-plants/. Reprinted by permission.

Chapter 20

Bob Steele, Nelson Poynter Scholar for Journalism Values, "Ask These 10 Questions to Make Good Ethical Decisions" Poynter Online, August 13, 2002 (updated August 30, 2015). Copyright © Bob Steele. Reprinted by permission of the author.

Index

Note: Page numbers in *italics* indicate boxed material; those in **boldface** indicate glossary terms; and those followed by f indicate figures.

Annotated Models

Copy Editing and Proofreading Symbols

Writing and editing for today's media are done almost exclusively on computers. Only in the book industry are some manuscripts still prepared on paper. Nevertheless, at some small newspapers and magazines, editors prefer to edit on paper. For that reason, failure to learn the copy editing symbols used in manuscript preparation is a mistake. There is a good chance you will need to use those symbols at some point in your career, if only to satisfy the occasional editor who prefers doing things the old-fashioned way.

You are even more likely to use proofreading symbols, which are used on galley proofs and page proofs to correct typeset copy. While there are some similarities in the two sets of symbols, there also are differences. The chart below illustrates the most common proofreading symbols (used to correct typeset copy), and the adjacent chart shows the most common copy editing symbols (used in manuscript preparation).

Proofreading Symbols

Symbol	Meaning	Symbol	Meaning
^	Insert at this point.	✓✓	Space evenly.
⊥	Push down space.	⁀	Close up entirely.
ℓ	Take out letter, letters or words.	[	Move to left.
ɘ	Turn inverted letter.	]	Move to right.
(lc)	Set lowercase.	⊔	Lower letter or word.
(wf)	Wrong font letter.	⊓	Raise letter or word.
(ital)	Reset in italic type.	(out see copy)	Words are left out.
(rom)	Reset in roman (regular) type.	//	Straighten lines.
(bf)	Reset in boldface type.	(¶)	Start new paragraph.
⊙	Insert period.	(no ¶)	No paragraph. Run together.
^,	Insert comma.	(tr)	Transpose letters or words.
^;	Insert semicolon.	(?)	Query; is copy right?
=|	Insert hyphen.	|—|	Insert dash.
˅'	Insert apostrophe.	□	Indent 1 em.
˅" ˅"	Enclose in quotation marks.	□□	Indent 2 ems.
≡	Replace with a capital letter.	□□□	Indent 3 ems.
#	Insert space.	(stet)	Let it stand.

Copy Editing Symbols

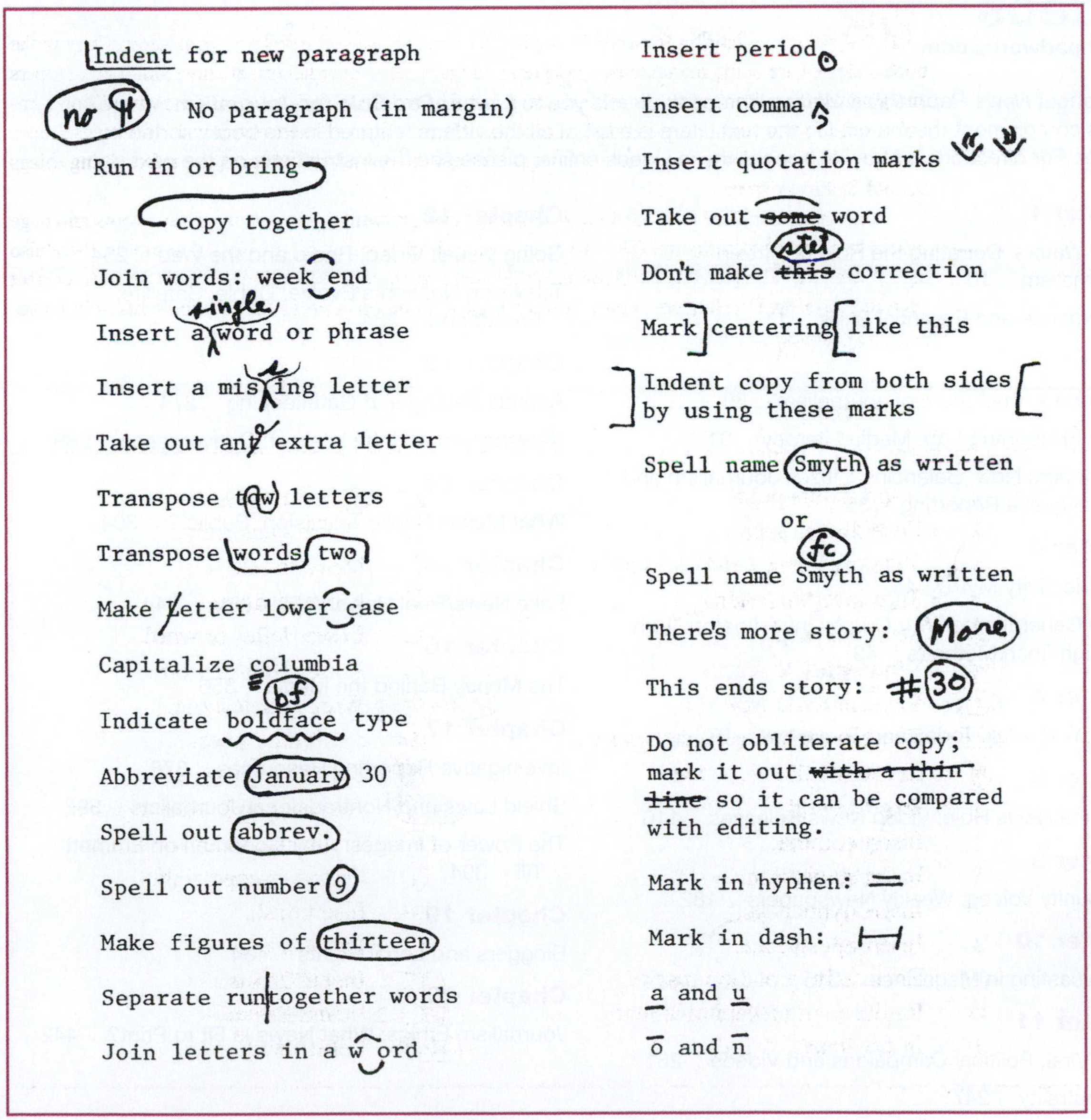

Indent for new paragraph

no ¶ No paragraph (in margin)

Run in or bring copy together

Join words: week end

Insert a word or phrase (single)

Insert a mis ing letter (s)

Take out any extra letter

Transpose tow letters

Transpose words two

Make Letter lower case

Capitalize columbia

Indicate boldface type (bf)

Abbreviate January 30

Spell out abbrev.

Spell out number 9

Make figures of thirteen

Separate runtogether words

Join letters in a w ord

Insert period ⊙

Insert comma

Insert quotation marks

Take out some word

Don't make this correction (stet)

Mark centering like this

Indent copy from both sides by using these marks

Spell name Smyth as written

or

Spell name Smyth as written (fc)

There's more story: More

This ends story: # 30

Do not obliterate copy; mark it out with a thin line so it can be compared with editing.

Mark in hyphen: =

Mark in dash: ⊢⊣

a and u

o and n

Videos

launchpadworks.com

Throughout *News Reporting & Writing*, the book directs you to ***LaunchPad Solo for Journalism***, where videos complement the material in the text. Here is a list of all the videos featured in the book, sorted by chapter. For directions on how to access these videos online, please see the instructions on the next page.